Lecture Notes in Computer Science 2968

Edited by G. Goos, J. Hartmanis, and J. van Leeuwen

T0180022

Springer
Berlin
Heidelberg
New York
Hong Kong
London
Milan
Paris
Tokyo

Jing Chen   Seongsoo Hong (Eds.)

Real-Time and Embedded Computing Systems and Applications

9th International Conference, RTCSA 2003
Tainan City, Taiwan, ROC, February 18-20, 2003
Revised Papers

 Springer

Series Editors

Gerhard Goos, Karlsruhe University, Germany
Juris Hartmanis, Cornell University, NY, USA
Jan van Leeuwen, Utrecht University, The Netherlands

Volume Editors

Jing Chen
National Cheng Kung University, Department of Electrical Engineering
1 University Road, Tainan City, 701, Taiwan, ROC
E-mail: jchen@mail.ncku.edu.tw

Seongsoo Hong
Seoul National University, School of Electrical Engineering and Computer Science
San 56-1 Sillim-dong, Gwanak-gu, Seoul 151-742, Korea
E-mail: sshong@redwood.snu.ac.kr

Library of Congress Control Number: 2004104587

CR Subject Classification (1998): C.3, D.4, C.2, D.2, H.4

ISSN 0302-9743
ISBN 3-540-21974-9 Springer-Verlag Berlin Heidelberg New York

Springer-Verlag is a part of Springer Science+Business Media

springeronline.com

© Springer-Verlag Berlin Heidelberg 2004
Printed in Germany

Typesetting: Camera-ready by author, data conversion by PTP-Berlin, Protago-TeX-Production GmbH
Printed on acid-free paper   SPIN: 11006497   06/3142   5 4 3 2 1 0

Preface

This volume contains the 37 papers presented at the 9th International Conference on Real-Time and Embedded Computing Systems and Applications (RTCSA 2003). RTCSA is an international conference organized for scientists and researchers from both academia and industry to hold intensive discussions on advancing technologies topics on real-time systems, embedded systems, ubiquitous/pervasive computing, and related topics. RTCSA 2003 was held at the Department of Electrical Engineering of National Cheng Kung University in Taiwan. Paper submissions were well distributed over the various aspects of real-time computing and embedded system technologies. There were more than 100 participants from all over the world.

The papers, including 28 regular papers and 9 short papers are grouped into the categories of scheduling, networking and communication, embedded systems, pervasive/ubiquitous computing, systems and architectures, resource management, file systems and databases, performance analysis, and tools and development. The grouping is basically in accordance with the conference program. Earlier versions of these papers were published in the conference proceedings. However, some papers in this volume have been modified or improved by the authors, in various aspects, based on comments and feedback received at the conference. It is our sincere hope that researchers and developers will benefit from these papers.

We would like to thank all the authors of the papers for their contribution. We thank the members of the program committee and the reviewers for their excellent work in evaluating the submissions. We are also very grateful to all the members of the organizing committees for their help, guidance and support. There are many other people who worked hard to make RTCSA 2003 a success. Without their efforts, the conference and this volume would not have been possible, and we would like to express our sincere gratitude to them. In addition, we would like to thank the National Science Council (NSC), the Ministry of Education (MOE), and the Institute of Information Science (IIS) of Academia Sinica of Taiwan, the Republic of China (ROC) for their generous financial support. We would also like to acknowledge the co-sponsorship by the Information Processing Society of Japan (IPSJ) and the Korea Information Science Society (KISS).

Last, but not least, we would like to thank Dr. Farn Wang who helped initiate contact with the editorial board of LNCS to publish this volume. We also appreciate the great work and the patience of the editors at Springer-Verlag. We are truly grateful.

Jing Chen and Seongsoo Hong

History and Future of RTCSA

The International Conference on Real-Time and Embedded Computing Systems and Applications (RTCSA) aims to be a forum on the trends as well as innovations in the growing areas of real-time and embedded systems, and to bring together researchers and developers from academia and industry for advancing the technology of real-time computing systems, embedded systems and their applications. The conference assumes the following goals:

- to investigate advances in real-time and embedded systems;
- to promote interactions among real-time systems, embedded systems and their applications;
- to evaluate the maturity and directions of real-time and embedded system technology;
- to bridge research and practising experience in the communities of real-time and embedded systems.

RTCSA started from 1994 with the International Workshop on Real-Time Computing Systems and Applications held in Korea. It evolved into the International Conference on Real-Time Computing Systems and Applications in 1998. As embedded systems is becoming one of the most vital areas of research and development in computer science and engineering, RTCSA changed into the International Conference on Real-Time and Embedded Computing Systems and Applications in 2003. In addition to embedded systems, RTCSA has expanded its scope to cover topics on pervasive and ubiquitous computing, home computing, and sensor networks. The proceedings of RTCSA from 1995 to 2000 are available from IEEE. A brief history of RTCSA is listed below. The next RTCSA is currently being organized and will take place in Sweden.

1994 to 1997: International Workshop on Real-Time Computing Systems and Applications

RTCSA 1994	Seoul, Korea
RTCSA 1995	Tokyo, Japan
RTCSA 1996	Seoul, Korea
RTCSA 1997	Taipei, Taiwan

1998 to 2002: International Conference on Real-Time Computing Systems and Applications

RTCSA 1998	Hiroshima, Japan
RTCSA 1999	Hong Kong, China
RTCSA 2000	Cheju Island, Korea
RTCSA 2002	Tokyo, Japan

From 2003: International Conference on Real-Time and Embedded Computing Systems and Applications

RTCSA 2003	Tainan, Taiwan

Organization of RTCSA 2003

The 9th International Conference on Real-Time and Embedded Computing Systems and Applications (RTCSA 2003) was organized, in cooperation with the Information Processing Society of Japan (IPSJ) and the Korea Information Science Society (KISS), by the Department of Electrical Engineering, National Cheng Kung University in Taiwan, Republic of China (ROC).

Honorary Chair

Chiang Kao	President of National Cheng Kung University

General Co-chairs

Ruei-Chuan Chang	National Chiao Tung University (Taiwan)
Tatsuo Nakajima	Waseda University (Japan)

Steering Committee

Tei-Wei Kuo	National Taiwan University (Taiwan)
Insup Lee	University of Pennsylvania (USA)
Jane Liu	Microsoft (USA)
Seung-Kyu Park	Ajou University (Korea)
Heonshik Shin	Seoul National University (Korea)
Kang Shin	University of Michigan at Ann Arbor (USA)
Sang H. Son	University of Virginia (USA)
Kenji Toda	ITRI., AIST (Japan)
Hideyuki Tokuda	Keio University (Japan)

Advisory Committee

Alan Burns	University of York (UK)
Jan-Ming Ho	IIS, Academia Sinica (Taiwan)
Aloysius K. Mok	University of Texas, Austin (USA)
Heonshik Shin	Seoul National University (Korea)
John A. Stankovic	University of Virginia (USA)
Hideyuki Tokuda	Keio University (Japan)
Jhing-Fa Wang	National Cheng Kung University (Taiwan)

Publicity Co-chairs

Lucia Lo Bello	University of Catania (Italy)
Victor C.S. Lee	City University of Hong Kong (Hong Kong)
Daeyoung Kim	Information and Communications University (Korea)
Sang H. Son	University of Virginia (USA)
Kazunori Takashio	Keio University (Japan)

Program Co-chairs

Jing Chen	National Cheng Kung University (Taiwan)
Seongsoo Hong	Seoul National University (Korea)

Program Committee

Giorgio C. Buttazzo	University of Pavia (Italy)
Jörgen Hansson	Linkoping University (Sweden)
Pao-Ann Hsiung	National Chung Cheng University (Taiwan)
Chih-Wen Hsueh	National Chung Cheng University (Taiwan)
Dong-In Kang	ISI East, USC (USA)
Daeyoung Kim	Information and Communications University (Korea)
Moon Hae Kim	Konkuk University (Korea)
Tae-Hyung Kim	Hanyang University (Korea)
Young-kuk Kim	Chungnam National University (Korea)
Lucia Lo Bello	University of Catania (Italy)
Kam-Yiu Lam	City University of Hong Kong (Hong Kong)
Chang-Gun Lee	Ohio State University (USA)
Victor C.S. Lee	City University of Hong Kong (Hong Kong)
Yann-Hang Lee	Arizona State University (USA)
Kwei-Jay Lin	University of California, Irvine (USA)
Sang Lyul Min	Seoul National University (Korea)
Tatsuo Nakajima	Waseda University (Japan)
Yukikazu Nakamoto	NEC, Japan (Japan)
Joseph Ng	Hong Kong Baptist University (Hong Kong)
Nimal Nissanke	South Bank University (UK)
Raj Rajkumar	Carnegie Mellon University (USA)
Krithi Ramamritham	India Institute of Technology, Bombay (India)
Ichiro Satoh	National Institute of Informatics (Japan)
Lui Sha	University of Illinois at Urbana-Champaign (USA)
Wei-Kuan Shih	National Tsing Hua University (Taiwan)
LihChyun Shu	National Cheng Kung University (Taiwan)
Sang H. Son	University of Virginia (USA)
Hiroaki Takada	Toyohashi University of Technology (Japan)
Yoshito Tobe	Tokyo Denki University (Japan)
Hans Toetenel	Delft University of Technology (Netherlands)
Farn Wang	National Taiwan University (Taiwan)
Andy Wellings	University of York (UK)
Wang Yi	Uppsala University (Sweden)

Reviewers

Lucia Lo Bello	Jörgen Hansson	Chih-Wen Hsueh
Giorgio C. Buttazzo	Seongsoo Hong	Dong-In Kang
Jing Chen	Pao-Ann Hsiung	Daeyoung Kim

Sponsoring Institutions

National Science Council (NSC), Taiwan, ROC
Ministry of Education (MOE), Taiwan, ROC
Institute of Information Science (IIS) of Academia Sinica, Taiwan, ROC
Information Processing Society of Japan (IPSJ), Japan
Korea Information Science Society (KISS), Korea

Table of Contents

Scheduling

Networking and Communication

Embedded Systems/Environments

Pervasive/Ubiquitous Computing

Systems and Architectures

Resource Management

File Systems and Databases

Performance Analysis

Tools and Development

Scheduling-Aware Real-Time Garbage Collection Using Dual Aperiodic Servers

Taehyoun Kim[1] and Heonshik Shin[2]

[1] SOC Division, GCT Research, Inc.,
Seoul 150-877, Korea
thkim@gctsemi.com
[2] School of Electrical Engineering and Computer Science, Seoul National University,
Seoul 151-742, Korea
shinhs@snu.ac.kr

Abstract. Garbage collection has not been widely used in embedded real-time applications since traditional real-time garbage collection algorithm can hardly bound its worst-case responsiveness. To overcome this limitation, we have proposed a scheduling-integrated real-time garbage collection algorithm based on the single aperiodic server in our previous work. This paper introduces a new scheduling-aware real-time garbage collection which employs two aperiodic servers for garbage collection work. Our study aims at achieving similar performance compared with the single server approach whilst relaxing the limitation of the single server approach. In our scheme, garbage collection requests are scheduled using the preset CPU bandwidth of aperiodic server such as the sporadic server and the deferrable server. In the dual server scheme, most garbage collection work is serviced by the secondary server at low priority level. The effectiveness of our approach is verified by analytic results and extensive simulation based on the trace-driven data. Performance analysis demonstrates that the dual server scheme shows similar performance compared with the single server approach while it allows flexible system design.

1 Introduction

As modern programs require more functionality and complex data structures, there is a growing need for dynamic memory management on heap to efficiently utilize the memory by recycling unused heap memory space. In doing so, dynamic memory may be managed explicitly by the programmer through the invocation of "malloc/free" procedures which is often error-prone and cumbersome.

For this reason, the system may be responsible for the dynamic memory reclamation to achieve better productivity, robustness, and program integrity. Central to this automatic memory reclamation is the garbage collection (GC) process. The garbage collector identifies the data items that will never be used again and then recycles their space for reuse at the system level.

In spite of its advantages, GC has not been widely used in embedded real-time applications. This is partly because GC may cause the response time of application to be unpredictable. To guarantee timely execution of a real-time application, all the

J. Chen and S. Hong (Eds.): RTCSA 2003, LNCS 2968, pp. 1–17, 2004.

components of the application must be *predictable*. A certain software component is *predictable* means that its worst-case behavior is bounded and known *a priori*.

This is because garbage collectors should also run in *real-time* mode for predictable execution of real-time applications. Thus, the requirements for real-time garbage collector are summarized and extended as follows [1]; First, a real-time garbage collector often interleaves its execution with the execution of an application in order to avoid intolerable pauses incurred by the stop-and-go reclamation. Second, a real-time collector must have mutators [1] report on any changes that they have made to the liveness of heap objects to preserve the consistency of a heap. Third, garbage collector must not interfere with the schedulability of hard real-time mutators. For this purpose, we need to keep the basic memory operations short and bounded. So is the synchronization overhead between garbage collector and mutators. Lastly, real-time systems with garbage collection must meet the deadlines of hard real-time mutators while preventing the application from running out of memory.

Considering the properties that are needed for real-time garbage collector, this paper presents a new scheduling-aware real-time garbage collection algorithm. We have already proposed a scheduling-aware real-time GC scheme based on the single server approach in [1]. Our GC scheme aims at guaranteeing the schedulability of hard real-time tasks while minimizing the system memory requirement. In the single server approach, an aperiodic server services GC requests at the highest priority level. It has been proved that, in terms of memory requirement, our approach shows the best performance compared with other aperiodic scheduling policies without missing hard deadlines [1].

However, the single server approach has a drawback. In terms of rate monotonic (RM) scheduling, the server must have the shortest period in order to be assigned for the highest priority. Usually, the safe server capacity for the shortest period may not be large enough to service a small part of GC work. For this reason, the single server approach may be sometimes impractical. To overcome this limitation, we propose a new scheduling-aware real-time GC scheme based on dual aperiodic servers. In the dual server approach, GC requests are serviced in two steps. The primary server atomically processes the initial steps such as flipping and memory initialization at the highest priority level. The secondary server scans and evacuates live objects. The effectiveness of the new approach is verified by simulation studies.

The rest of this paper is organized as follows. Sect. 2 presents a system model and formulates the problem addressed in this paper. The real-time GC technique based on the dual aperiodic servers is introduced in Sect. 3. Performance evaluation for the proposed schemes is presented in Sect. 4. This section proves the effectiveness of our algorithm by estimating various memory-related performance metrics. Sect. 5 concludes the paper.

2   Problem Statement

We now consider a real-time system with a set of n periodic priority-ordered mutator tasks, $\mathcal{M} = \{\mathcal{M}_1, \ldots, \mathcal{M}_n\}$ where $\mathcal{M}_n$ is the lowest-priority task and all the tasks follow rate monotonic scheduling [2]. The task model in this paper includes an additional

---

[1] Because tasks may *mutate* the reachability of heap data structure during the GC cycle, this paper uses the term "mutator" for the tasks that manipulate dynamically-allocated heap.

Table 1. Notations

Symbol	Description
$\mathcal{M}_i, \mathcal{M}_{i,j}$	Periodic mutator task i and its jth instance
C_i, T_i, D_i, R_i	Worst-case execution time, period, deadline, and response time of $\mathcal{M}_i$
A_i	Maximum amount of memory allocated by $\mathcal{M}_i$ during T_i
$\mathcal{G}_k$	k^{th} garbage collection request
C_{GC}, R_{GC}	Worst-case execution time of and response time of $\mathcal{G}$
L_k, L_k^*	Amount of live memory processed by $\mathcal{G}_k$ and its maximum value
M_{resv}	Memory reservation for hard real-time tasks
M	System Memory requirement
T_{s1}, T_{s2}	Periods of the primary server and the secondary server
C_{s1}, C_{s2}	Capacities of the primary server and the secondary server
$S_i(k), F_i(k)$	Start/Completion time of the kth instance of $\mathcal{M}_i$
$\delta_i(t)$	Idle time at priority level i at time t
$I_i(w)$	Interference of tasks with higher priority than that of $\mathcal{M}_i$ during the time interval $[0, w)$

property, memory allocation requirement of $\mathcal{M}_i$. $\mathcal{M}_i$ is characterized by a tuple $\mathcal{M}_i = (C_i, T_i, D_i, A_i)$ (see Table 1 for notations). Our discussion will be based on the following assumptions:

- *Assumption 1:* There are no aperiodic mutator tasks.
- *Assumption 2:* The context switching and task scheduling overhead are negligibly small.
- *Assumption 3:* There are no precedence relations among $\mathcal{M}_i$s. The precedence constraint placed by many real-time systems can be easily removed by partitioning tasks into sub-tasks or properly assigning the priorities of tasks.
- *Assumption 4:* Any task can be instantly preempted by a higher priority task, *i.e.*, there is no blocking factor.
- *Assumption 5:* C_i, T_i, D_i, and A_i are known *a priori*.

Although estimation of A_i is generally an application-specific problem, A_i can be specified by the programmer or can be given by a pre-runtime trace-driven analysis [3]. The target system is designed to adopt dynamic memory allocation with no virtual memory. In this paper, we consider a real-time copying collector proposed in [3], [4] for its simplicity and real-time property. This paper treats each GC request as a separate aperiodic task $\{\mathcal{G}_k(t_s^k, t_e^k), k \geq 1\}$ where t_s^k and t_e^k denote the release time and completion time of the kth GC request $\mathcal{G}_k$, respectively.

In our memory model, the cumulative memory consumption $m_c(\mathcal{M}_i, k, t)$ by a mutator task, defined for the interval $[t_s^k, t_s^{k+1})$, is a monotonic increasing function. Although the memory consumption function for each mutator can be various types of functions, we can easily derive the upper bound of memory consumption of $\mathcal{M}_i$ during t time units from the worst-case memory requirement of $\mathcal{M}_i$, which amounts to a product of A_i and the worst-case invocation number of $\mathcal{M}_i$ during t time units. Then, the cumulative memory consumption by all the mutator tasks at t' ($t_s^k \leq t' < t_s^{k+1}$) is bounded by the following equation.

$$m_c(k, t') \triangleq \sum_{i=1}^{n} m_c(\mathcal{M}_i, k, t') \leq \sum_{i=1}^{n} \left\{ \left(\left\lceil \frac{t'}{T_i} \right\rceil - \left\lfloor \frac{t_s^k}{T_i} \right\rfloor \right) A_i \right\} . \tag{1}$$

On the contrary, the amount of available memory depends on the reclamation rate of the garbage collector. For the copying collector, half of the total memory is reclaimed entirely at flip time. Actually, the amount of heap memory reproduced by $\mathcal{G}_k$ depends on M and the size of live objects L_k, and is bounded by $(\frac{M}{2} - L_k)$.

We now consider the property of real-time GC request $\mathcal{G}_k$. First, $\mathcal{G}_k$ is an aperiodic request because its release time is not known *a priori*. It is released when the cumulative memory consumption exceeds the amount of free (recycled) memory. Second, $\mathcal{G}_k$ is a hard real-time request. The kth GC request $\mathcal{G}_k(t_s^k, t_e^k)$ must be completed before $\mathcal{G}_{k+1}(t_s^{k+1}, t_e^{k+1})$ is released. In other words, the condition $t_e^k < t_s^{k+1}$ should always hold. Suppose that available memory becomes less than a certain threshold while previous GC request has not been completed yet. In this case, the heap memory is fully occupied by the evacuated objects and newly allocated objects. Thus, neither the garbage collector nor mutators can continue to execute any longer.

On the other hand, the system may also break down if there is no CPU bandwidth left for GC at t_s^{k+1} even though the condition $t_e^k < t_s^{k+1}$ holds. To solve this problem, we propose that the system should reserve a certain amount of memory spaces in order to prevent system break-down due to memory shortage. We also define a *reservation interval*, denoted by $\mathcal{R_G}$, to bound the memory reservation. The reservation interval represents the worst-case time interval $[t_s^k, t_\gamma)$, where $t_\gamma (\geq t_e^k)$ is the earliest time instant at which the CPU bandwidth for GC becomes available. Hence, the amount of memory reservation M_{resv} can be computed by the product of $\mathcal{R_G}$ and the memory requirement of all the mutator tasks during $\mathcal{R_G}$. There should also be memory spaces in which currently live objects are copied. As a result, for the copying collector addressed in this paper, the system memory requirement is given by:

$$M = 2(M_{resv} + L_k^*) = 2(\sum_{i=1}^{n} \left\lceil \frac{\mathcal{R_G}}{T_i} \right\rceil A_i + L_k^*) \tag{2}$$

where M_{resv} and L_k^* denote the worst-case memory reservation and the worst-case live memory, respectively. The reservation interval $\mathcal{R_G}$ is derived from the worst-case GC response time R_{GC} and the GC scheduling policy.

3   Dual Server Approach

3.1   Background

We have presented a scheduling-aware garbage collection scheme using single aperiodic server in [1], [3]. In the single server approach, GC work is serviced by an aperiodic server with a preset CPU bandwidth at the highest priority. The aperiodic server preserves its bandwidth waiting for the arrival of aperiodic GC requests. Once a GC request arrives in the meantime, the server performs GC as long as the server capacity permits; if it cannot finish within one server period, it will resume execution when the consumed execution time for the server is replenished. By assigning the highest priority, the garbage collector can start immediately on arriving $\mathcal{G}_k$ preempting the mutator task running.

However, the single server approach has a drawback. Under the aperiodic server scheme, the server capacity tends to be very small at the highest priority. Although the server capacity may be large enough to perform the initial parts of GC procedure such as flipping and memory initialization, it may not be large enough to perform single copying operation of a large memory block. Guaranteeing the atomicity of such operation may yield another unpredictable delay such as synchronization overhead. For this reason, this approach may be sometimes impractical.

3.2 Scheduling Algorithm

In this section, we present a new scheduling-aware real-time GC scheme based on dual aperiodic servers. In the dual server approach, GC is performed in two steps. The primary server performs flip operation and atomic memory initialization at the highest priority. The secondary server incrementally traverses and evacuates live objects. The major issue of dual server approach is to decide the priority of the secondary server and its safe capacity. We mean maximum server capacity which can guarantee the schedulability of given task set by *safe* capacity. The dual server approach can be applied to the sporadic server (SS) and the deferrable server (DS).

The first step is to find the safe capacity of the secondary server. This procedure is applied to each priority level of periodic tasks in given task set for simplicity. In doing so, we assume that the priority of the secondary server is assigned according to the RM policy. There is always a task of which period is identical to the period of the secondary server because we compute the capacity of the secondary server for the periods of periodic tasks. In this case, the priority of secondary server is always higher than that of such a task.

The maximum idle time at priority level i, denoted by $\delta(D_i)$, is set to the initial value of the capacity. For each possible capacity of the secondary server $C_{s2} \in [1, \delta(D_i)]$, we can find the maximum capacity at priority level i which can guarantee the schedulability of given task set using binary search. As a result, we have n alternatives for the parameters of the secondary server. The selection of the parameter is dependent on the primary consideration of system designer. In general, the primary goal is to achieve maximum server utilization. However, our goal is to minimize the memory requirement as long as there exists a feasible schedule for hard real-time mutators.

As mentioned in Sect. 2, the system memory requirement is derived from M_{resv} and L_k^*. The worst-case memory reservation is derived from R_{GC} under the scheduling policy used. Hence, we need a new algorithm to find R_{GC} under the dual server approach to derive the memory requirement.

For this purpose, we use the schedulability analysis which is originally presented by Bernat [5]. Let the pair of parameters (period, capacity) $= (T_s, C_s)$ of the primary server and the secondary server be (T_{s1}, C_{s1}) and (T_{s2}, C_{s2}), respectively. Then, we assign $T_{s1} = T_1$ and $C_{s1} = \sigma$ such that σ is the smallest time required for flipping and atomic

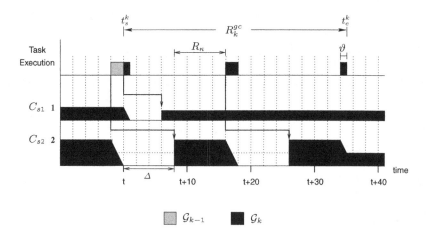

Fig. 1. Response time of $\mathcal{G}_k$ ($T_{s1} = 6, C_{s1} = 1, T_{s2} = 10, C_{s2} = 2, C_{GC} = 4$)

memory initialization. Traditional worst-case response time formulation can be used to compute R_{GC}.

In Theorem 1, we show the worst-case response time of GC under the SS policy.

Theorem 1. *Under the SS, for fixed C_{GC}, C_{s1}, T_{s1}, C_{s2}, and T_{s2}, the response time of the garbage collector R_{GC} of the dual server approach is bounded by the kth completion time of a virtual server task $\overline{SS_{s2}}$ with $T'_{s2} = T_{s2} + R_\kappa$ period, $C'_{s2} = \vartheta$ capacity, and $(T_{s2} - C_{s2})$ offset such that R_κ is the worst-case response time of a task $\mathcal{M}_\kappa$ which is the lowest priority task among the higher priority tasks than the secondary server,*
$$\vartheta = C_{GC} - C_{s1} - \left(\left\lceil \frac{C_{GC} - C_{s1}}{C_{s2}} \right\rceil - 1 \right) C_{s2} \text{ and } k = \left\lceil \frac{C_{GC} - C_{s1}}{C_{s2}} \right\rceil.$$

Proof. Let $\epsilon (> 0)$ be the available capacity of the secondary server when a new GC request is released. If the condition $C_{GC} - C_{s1} \leq \epsilon$ is satisfied, then the GC request $\mathcal{G}_k$ is completely serviced within one period of the secondary server. Otherwise, additional server periods are required to complete $\mathcal{G}_k$. The remaining GC work must be processed after the capacity of the secondary server is replenished. We assume that there is always C_{s1} capacity available when a new GC request arrives. This is because the replenishment period of the primary server will always be shorter than or equal to that of the secondary server. If this assumption is not valid, GC requests will always fail.

The interval, say Δ, between the beginning of $\mathcal{G}_k$ and the first replenishment of the secondary server is at most $(T_{s2} - C_{s2})$. In other words, the first period of the secondary server is released Δ time units after $\mathcal{G}_k$ was requested because the secondary server may not be released immediately due to interference caused by higher priority tasks. In the proof of Theorem 1, R_{GC} is computed by using the capacity of the sporadic server and the replenishment period.

Roughly, the worst-case response time of $\mathcal{G}_k$ coincides with the kth completion time of the secondary server with Δ offset such that $k = \left\lceil \frac{C_{GC} - C_{s1}}{C_{s2}} \right\rceil$. More correctly, it is the sum of Δ, any additional server periods required for replenishment, and the CPU demand remaining at the end of GC cycle. It results from the assumption that all the mutator tasks arrive exactly at which the first replenishment of the secondary server occurs. In this case, the second replenishment of the secondary server occurs at the time when all the higher priority tasks have been completed. Formally, in the worst-case, the longest replenishment period of the secondary server is equal to the worst-case response time of $\mathcal{M}_\kappa$ denoted by R_κ where $\mathcal{M}_\kappa$ is the lowest priority task among the higher priority tasks. Because the interference is always smaller than the worst-case interference at the critical instant, the following replenishment periods are always less than or equal to the first replenishment period. Hence, we can safely set the period of a virtual task $\overline{SS_2}$ to $(T_{s2} + R_\kappa)$. The CPU demand remaining at the end of GC cycle, say ϑ, is given by:

$$\vartheta = C_{GC} - C_{s1} - \left(\left\lceil \frac{C_{GC} - C_{s1}}{C_{s2}} \right\rceil - 1 \right) C_{s2} \, .$$

It follows that the sum of the server periods required and the CPU demand remaining at the end of GC cycle actually corresponds to the worst-case response time of the kth response time of a virtual server task $\overline{SS_{s2}}$ with T'_{s2} period and ϑ capacity. Because a task's response time is only affected by higher priority tasks, this conversion is safe without loss of generality. Fig. 1 illustrates the worst-case situation.
□

Since the DS has different server capacity replenishment policy, we have the following theorem.

Theorem 2. *Under the DS, for fixed C_{GC}, C_{s1}, T_{s1}, C_{s2}, and T_{s2}, the response time of the garbage collector R_{GC} of the dual server approach is bounded by the kth completion time of a virtual server task $\overline{SS_{s2}}$ with $T'_{s2} = T_{s2}$ period, $C'_{s2} = \vartheta$ capacity, and $(T_{s2} - C_{s2})$ offset such that $\vartheta = C_{GC} - C_{s1} - \left(\left\lceil \frac{C_{GC} - C_{s1}}{C_{s2}} \right\rceil - 1 \right) C_{s2}$ and $k = \left\lceil \frac{C_{GC} - C_{s1}}{C_{s2}} \right\rceil$.*

Proof. The server capacity for the DS is fully replenished at the beginning of server's period while the SS replenishes the server capacity exactly T_s time units after the aperiodic request was released. For this reason, the period of a virtual task T'_{s2} equals T_{s2}.
□

For the dual server approach, we do not need to consider the replenishment of server capacity in computing $\mathcal{M}_{resv}$. This is because there is always sufficiently large time interval to replenish the capacity of the primary server between two consecutive GC cycles. Finally we have:

$$M_{resv} = \sum_{i=1}^{n} \left\lceil \frac{R_{GC}}{T_i} \right\rceil A_i \, . \tag{3}$$

Let $F'_{s2}(k)$ denote the kth completion time of a virtual secondary server task $\overline{SS_{s2}}$. As shown above, $F'_{s2}(k)$ is equal to R_{GC}. To derive the memory requirement, we now present how we can find $F'_{s2}(k)$ with given parameters of the secondary server. We now apply Bernat's analysis to find $F'_{s2}(k)$. Bernat presents an extended formulation to compute the worst-case completion time of $\mathcal{M}_i$ at its kth invocation.

We explain briefly the extended worst-case response time formulation. Let us first consider the worst-case completion time of $\mathcal{M}_i$ at the second invocation. The completion time of the second invocation $F_i(2)$ includes its execution time and interference caused by higher priority tasks. The interference is always smaller than the worst-case interference at the critical instant. Formally, the idle time at priority level i at w, denoted by $\delta_i(w)$, is defined as the amount of CPU time can be used by tasks with lower priority than $\mathcal{M}_i$ during the period $[0, w)$ in [5]. Again, the amount of idle time at the start of each task invocation is written as:

$$\delta_i(k) = \delta_i(S_i(k)) .$$

Based on the above definitions, $F_i(2)$ includes the time required to complete two invocations of $\mathcal{M}_i$, the CPU time used by lower priority tasks (level-i idle time), and the interference due to higher priority tasks. Thus, it is given by the following recurrence relation:

$$\begin{cases} w^{(0)} & = S_i(2) + C_i \\ w^{(n+1)} = 2C_i + \delta_i(2) + I_i(w^{(n)}) \end{cases} \tag{4}$$

where $I_i(w^{(n)})$ denotes the interference caused by tasks with higher priority than task i. The correctness of Eq. (4) is proved in [5].

Similarly, the completion time of the kth invocation of $\mathcal{M}_i$, $F_i(k)$ is the sum of the time required to complete k invocations of $\mathcal{M}_i$, the CPU time used by lower priority tasks, and the interference due to higher priority tasks. Thus, we have $F_i(k)$ as the smallest w (≥ 0) such that:

$$w = kC_i + \delta_i(k) + I_i(w) . \tag{5}$$

More formally, $F_i(k)$ corresponds to the smallest solution to the following recurrence relation:

$$\begin{cases} w^{(0)} & = S_i(k) + C_i \\ w^{(n+1)} = kC_i + \delta_i(k) + I_i(w^{(n)}) . \end{cases} \tag{6}$$

As mentioned earlier, the worst-case response time of garbage collector equals $F'_{s2}(k)$. Following the definition of $F'_{s2}(k)$, it can be found by the worst-case response time analysis at the critical instant. For this reason, we can apply the Bernat's extended worst-case response time formulation to our approach without loss of generality. $F'_{s2}(k)$ is the smallest solution w (≥ 0) where $w^{(n+1)} = w^{(n)}$ to the following recurrence relation:

$$\begin{cases} w^{(0)} & = S_{s2}(k) + C'_{s2} \\ w^{(n+1)} = kC'_{s2} + \delta_{s2}(k) + I_{s2}(w^{(n)}), \end{cases} \tag{7}$$

where $S_{s2}(k) = (k-1)T'_{s2}$, $C'_{s2} = C_{GC} - C_{s1} - \left(\left\lceil \dfrac{C_{GC} - C_{s1}}{C_s2} \right\rceil - 1 \right) C_{s2}$,

$\delta_{s2}(k) = \delta_{s2}(S_{s2}(k))$, and $I_{s2}(w^{(n)}) = \displaystyle\sum_{M_j \in hp(\overline{SS}_{s2})} \left\lceil \dfrac{w^{(n)}}{T_j} \right\rceil C_j$. In Eq. (7), $S_{s2}(k)$

and $I_{s2}(w^{(n)})$ can be easily computed because T'_{s2} is known *a priori*. Hence, we need only to compute $\delta_{s2}(k)$ in order to compute $F'_{s2}(k)$.

To compute $\delta_{s2}(k)$, we assume another virtual task $\bar{\mathcal{M}}$ as follows:

$$\bar{\mathcal{M}} = (\bar{C}, \bar{T}, \bar{D}),$$
$$\text{where } \bar{T} = S_{s2}(k), \ \bar{D} = \bar{T}.$$

At the beginning of this section, we compute the safe capacity of the secondary server at priority level i by computing $\delta_i(D_i)$. Similarly, the amount of idle time between $[0, S_{s2}(k))$ which has been unused by the tasks with priorities higher than or equal to $\mathcal{M}_i$ corresponds to the upper bound for the execution time of the virtual task $\bar{\mathcal{M}}$. Then, $\delta_{s2}(k)$ is computed by obtaining the maximum $\bar{C}$ which can guarantee that the virtual task $\bar{\mathcal{M}}$ is schedulable. Formally, we have:

$$\delta_{s2}(S_{s2}(k)) = max\{\bar{C} \mid \bar{\mathcal{M}} \text{ is schedulable}\} . \tag{8}$$

The maximum $\bar{C}$ which satisfies the condition in Eq. (8) is the solution w where $w^{(n+1)} = w^{(n)}$ and $w^n \leq \bar{D}$ to the following equation:

$$w = \bar{C} + I'_i(w) \tag{9}$$

where $I'_i(w)$ denotes the interference caused by the tasks with higher than or equal priority to task i. A simple way of finding $\bar{C}$ is to perform binary search for the interval $[0, \bar{D})$ of which complexity is $O(log_2\bar{D})$. Actually, this approach may be somewhat expensive because, for each value $t \in [0, \bar{D})$, the worst-case response time formulation must be done for higher priority tasks. To avoid this complexity, Bernat also presents an effective way of computing $\delta_i(k)$ by finding more tighter bounds. However, his approach is not so cost-effective for our case which targets at finding a specific $F_i(k)$.

We present a simple approach to reduce the test space. It is possible by using the fact that $\bar{C}$ is actually the idle time unused by the tasks with higher than or equal to priorities than the secondary server. Using the definition of $I'_i(w)$, the interference of tasks with higher than or equal priority to $\mathcal{M}_i$, the upper bound for $\bar{C}$ is given by:

$$\bar{C} \leq S_{s2}(k) - I'_i(S_{s2}(k)) < S_{s2}(k) - \sum_{j \in hep(SS_2)} \left\lfloor \frac{S_{s2}(k)}{T_j} \right\rfloor C_j \tag{10}$$

where $hep(SS_2)$ denotes the set of tasks with higher than or equal priority to the secondary server.

The lower bound for $\bar{C}$ can also be tightened as follows. Given any time interval $w = [t_1, t_2)$, the worst-case number of instances of $\mathcal{M}_j$ within the interval can approximate $\left\lceil \dfrac{t_2 - t_1}{T_j} \right\rceil + 1$. We can optimize this trivial bound using the analysis in [3]. The analysis uses the worst-case response time of $\mathcal{M}_j$, R_j. It classifies the instances into three cases according to their invocation time. As a result of analysis, it follows that the number of instances of $\mathcal{M}_j$ within a given time interval w, denoted by ϕ_j is given by:

$$\phi_j = \left\lceil \frac{w}{T_j} \right\rceil + f(j), \text{ where}$$

$$f(j) = \begin{cases} 1 \text{ if } R_j \geq T_j - \left\{ w - (\left\lfloor \frac{w}{T_j} \right\rfloor T_j + 1) \right\} \\ 0 \text{ otherwise} . \end{cases} \tag{11}$$

For details, refer to [3].

The above formulation can be directly applied to finding the lower bound for $\delta_i(k)$ by substituting w for $S_{s2}(k)$. Finally, we have:

$$\bar{C} \geq S_{s2}(k) - \sum_{j \in hep(SS_2)} \left(\left\lceil \frac{S_{s2}(k)}{T_j} \right\rceil + f(j) \right) C_j . \tag{12}$$

3.3 Live Memory Analysis

We have proposed a three-step approach to find the worst-case live memory for the single server approach in [4]. According to the live memory analysis, the worst-case live memory L_k^* equals the sum of the worst-case global live memory $L_{k,glob}^*$ and the worst-case local live memory $L_{k,local}^*$. Usually, the amount of global live objects is relatively stable throughout the execution of application because global objects are significantly longer-lived than local objects. On the other hand, the amount of local live objects continues to vary until the time at which the garbage collector is triggered. For this reason, we concentrate on the analysis of the worst-case local live memory.

The amount of live objects for each task depends not on the heap size but on the state of each task. Although the amount of live memory is a function of A_i and varies during the execution of a task instance, it is stabilized at the end of the instance. Therefore, we find the worst-case live local memory by classifying the task instances into two classes: *active* and *inactive*[2]. Accordingly, we set the amount of live memory for an active task $\mathcal{M}_i$ to A_i in order to cover an arbitrary live memory distribution. By contrast, the amount of live memory for an inactive task $\mathcal{M}_j$ converges $\gamma_j A_j$ where γ_j denotes the stable live factor out of A_j. Consequently, the worst-case live local live memory is bounded by:

$$L_{k,local}^* = max(\sum_{\mathcal{M}_i \in active(t_s^k)} A_i + \sum_{\mathcal{M}_j \in inactive(t_s^k)} \gamma_j A_j) \tag{13}$$

where $active(t)$ and $inactive(t)$ denote the set of active tasks and the set of inactive tasks at time t, respectively. We also assume the amount of global live memory to be a constant $L_{k,glob}^*$ because it is known to be relatively stable throughout the execution of the application. Then, L_k^* equals the sum of $L_{k,local}^*$ and $L_{k,glob}^*$.

We now modify the live memory analysis slightly to cover the dual server approach. We first summarize the three-step approach as follows:

---

[2] We regard a task as *active* if the task is running or preempted by higher priority tasks at time instant t. Otherwise, the task is regarded as *inactive*.

- **Step 1. Find the active windows:** For each tasks, find the time intervals in which the task instances are running or preempted by higher priority tasks, *i.e.*, active. Those time intervals are referred as *active windows* and represented by $\mathcal{A}_{i,j} = [\mathcal{S}_{i,j}, \mathcal{F}_{i,j}]$ where $\mathcal{S}_{i,j}$ and $\mathcal{F}_{i,j}$ denote the earliest start time and the latest completion time of $\mathcal{M}_{i,j}$, respectively. First, we put a restriction on the periods of mutators; $\mathcal{M}_i$ is *harmonic* with respect to $\mathcal{M}_1$ [6]. This constraint helps to prune the search space. Second, the search space is limited to a hyperperiod H. We compute $\mathcal{S}_{i,j}$ from the worst-case completion time of a task instance $\mathcal{M}_{\kappa,l}$ where $\mathcal{M}_\kappa$ is the lowest priority task among the tasks such that their priorities are higher than that of $\mathcal{M}_i$ and $\exists l, (j-1)T_i = lT_k$ for $1 \leq l \leq \frac{H}{T_k}$. We also compute $\mathcal{F}_{i,j}$ under the assumption that the total capacity of aperiodic server is used for GC, *i.e.*, the garbage collector behaves like a periodic task. Then, $\mathcal{F}_{i,j}$ equals the sum of $(j-1)T_i$ and the worst-case response time of $\mathcal{M}_i$, denoted by R_i^s, including the interference caused by another periodic task with $(C_i, T_i, D_i, A_i) = (server\ capacity, T_1, T_1, 0)$.
- **Step 2. Find the transitive preemption windows:** Using the active windows found in Step 1, this step finds the preemption windows. The preemption window $\mathbf{P}_{\mathcal{M}_i \Rightarrow \ldots \Rightarrow \mathcal{M}_k}$ is the set of time intervals in which tasks $\mathcal{M}_i$, ..., $\mathcal{M}_k$ are all active. They are equivalent to the intervals overlapped among active windows for mutator tasks. Those tasks are active because one of them is running and the others are preempted by higher priority tasks.
- **Step 3. Compute the worst-case live memory:** This step computes the worst-case local live memory using Eq. (13).

As to the live memory, the worst-case scenario is that a GC request is issued when all the tasks are active. Generally, the possibility of a certain task being active [3] is proportional to CPU utilization of given task set. Hence, we try to find the worst-case local live memory under the highest utilization attainable. For this purpose, we assume the CPU bandwidth reserved for GC is fully utilized because the CPU utilization of periodic tasks for given task set is fixed.

And therefore, we need a simple modification on the computation of active windows in order that it may include the interference caused by the secondary server. In Step 1 of our live-memory analysis, $\mathcal{S}_{i,j}$ and $\mathcal{F}_{i,j}$ determine the active window of $\mathcal{M}_{i,j}$. Because the computation of $\mathcal{S}_{i,j}$ ignores the bandwidth reserved for GC, only the latest completion time $\mathcal{F}_{i,j}$ should be recomputed. Suppose that $R_i^{s'}$ denotes the worst-case response (completion) time of $\mathcal{M}_i$. Then, we can compute $R_i^{s'} = w$ using the following recurrence relation:

$$w = C_i + \sum_{l \in hp(i)} \left\lceil \frac{w}{T_l} \right\rceil C_l \qquad (14)$$

where $hp(i)$ is the set of tasks, including the aperiodic servers, whose priorities are higher than that of $\mathcal{M}_i$. The only difference from the single server approach is that $hp(i)$ does not always include the secondary server although it does include the primary server. This is because the secondary server may not have higher priority than that of $\mathcal{M}_i$ whilst

---

[3] In most cases, it means that the task is preempted by a higher priority task.

the primary server has the highest priority. Steps 2 and 3 are applied to the dual server approach without any modification. Example 1 clarifies the modified approach.

Example 1. Consider the task set whose parameters are as given in Table 2.

Table 2. Example task set: $T_{s1} = 10$, $C_{s1} = 1$, $T_{s2} = 30$, $C_{s2} = 6$

	C_i	T_i	D_i	A_i	γ_i	R_i^s
$\mathcal{M}_1$	2	10	10	988	0.43	3
$\mathcal{M}_2$	4	30	30	1028	0.36	16
$\mathcal{M}_3$	10	60	60	1200	0.38	29
$\mathcal{M}_4$	15	120	120	1696	0.27	108

- **Step 1.** The active windows of periodic tasks in the example are

$$\mathcal{A}_{1,j} = [10(j-1),\ 10(j-1)+3],$$
$$\mathcal{A}_{2,j} = [30(j-1)+2,\ 30(j-1)+16],$$
$$\mathcal{A}_{3,j} = [60(j-1)+6,\ 60(j-1)+29],$$
$$\mathcal{A}_{4,j} = [120(j-1)+18,\ 120(j-1)+108],\ \text{where } 1 \le j \le \frac{120}{T_i}.$$

- **Step 2.** Using the active windows found in Step 1, we can determine the preemption windows for the following combinations: $\mathcal{M}_1 \Rightarrow \mathcal{M}_2$, $\mathcal{M}_1 \Rightarrow \mathcal{M}_3$, $\mathcal{M}_1 \Rightarrow \mathcal{M}_4$, $\mathcal{M}_2 \Rightarrow \mathcal{M}_4$, $\mathcal{M}_3 \Rightarrow \mathcal{M}_4$, and $\mathcal{M}_1 \Rightarrow \mathcal{M}_3 \Rightarrow \mathcal{M}_4$.
- **Step 3.** As a result of Eq. (13), $\mathcal{M}_1 \Rightarrow \mathcal{M}_3 \Rightarrow \mathcal{M}_4$ is the combination that maximizes the amount of local live memory. In this case, $L_{k,local}^*$ is reduced by up to 13% compared with the trivial bound.

3.4   Worst-Case Memory Requirement

As mentioned in Sect. 3.2, the worst-case memory requirement is derived from the sum of the amount of memory reserved for hard real-time periodic mutators and the worst-case live memory. Because the reserved memory depends on the worst-case GC time C_{GC} and vice versa, we need to compute the amount of reserved memory, M_{resv}, iteratively. First, we set the amount of memory allocated by all the mutators during a hyperperiod to the initial value of M_{resv}. This is because, even in the worst-case, a GC cycle must be completed within a hyperperiod. Thereafter, the algorithm computes M_{resv} using C_{GC} and R_{GC} recursively until $M_{resv}^{(n+1)} = M_{resv}^{(n)}$. We can easily compute C_{GC} using L_k^* obtained from the off-line live memory analysis [4]. The worst-case response time for GC can also be computed using Theorem 1 and 2. In summary, M_{resv} is the smallest solution to the following recurrence relation:

$$
\begin{cases}
w^{(0)} &= \sum_{i=1}^{n} \dfrac{H}{T_i} A_i \\
w^{(n+1)} &= \sum_{i=1}^{n} \left\lceil \dfrac{R_{GC}(w^{(n)})}{T_i} \right\rceil A_i
\end{cases}
\tag{15}
$$

where $R_{GC}(w^{(n)})$ denotes the worst-case GC response time derived from the amount of memory reservation computed in the previous iteration. Finally, we can compute the system memory requirement using Eq. (15) in Sect. 2.

4   Performance Evaluation

This section presents the performance evaluation of our scheme. We show the efficiency of our approach by evaluating memory requirement through extensive analysis. Analytic results are verified by simulation based on trace-driven data. Experiments are performed on the trace-driven data acquired from five control applications written in Java and three sets of periodic tasks created out of the sample applications. The CPU utilization for those three task sets of TS1, TS2, and TS3 are 0.673, 0.738, and 0.792, respectively. The parameters used in the computation of the worst-case garbage collection work are

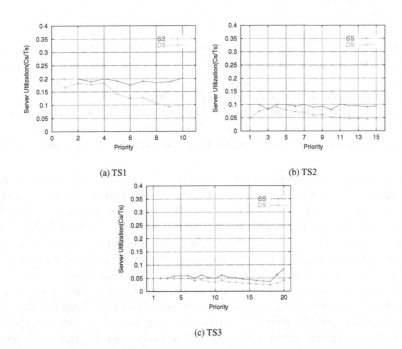

(a) TS1   (b) TS2

(c) TS3

Fig. 2. Capacity of the secondary server at each priority level.

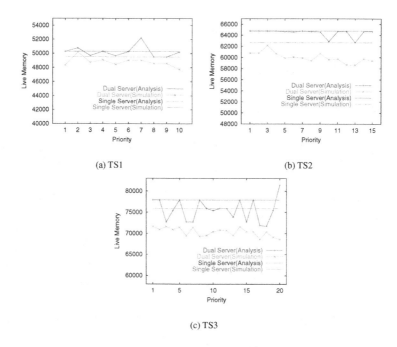

(a) TS1   (b) TS2

(c) TS3

Fig. 3. Live memory of each task sets for the dual server approach.

derived from a static measurement of the prototype garbage collector running on 50 MHz MPC860 with SGRAM. For details on the experiment environment, refer to [1]. Because the major goal of our approach is to reduce the worst-case memory requirement, our interest lies in the following three parameters. First, we compare the worst-case live memory of the dual server with that of the single server. Second, we analyze the worst-case memory reservation of both schemes. Third, we conduct a series of simulations to compare the feasible memory requirement. Figs. 3, 4, and 5 show performance evaluation results.

We first compute the capacity of the secondary server at each priority level using traditional worst-case response time formulation. For this purpose, the capacity of the primary server is set to $C_{s1} = 1$ for simplicity. The only job of the primary server is to flip two semispaces and to initialize the heap space. As shown in [3], efficient hardware support enables the memory initialization to be done within hundreds of microseconds. Hence, we make this assumption without loss of generality. Fig. 2 illustrates the capacity of the secondary server for the SS and the DS. The x axis is the priority level and the y axis is the maximum utilization that can be allocated to the secondary server. In all the graphs shown in this section, the lower the priority level in the graph the higher the actual priority is. And, the secondary server has higher priority than that of a periodic task which has identical period with it. The DS algorithm can also be directly applied to our approach. The graphs in Fig. 2 show that the capacity of the secondary server for the DS is generally smaller than that of the SS. As pointed out in [7], for the DS, the maximum server utilization occurs at low capacities; in other words, at high priorities under the RM policy. This is because the larger the capacity the larger the *double hit* effect, and therefore the lower the total utilization. However, as can be seen in Fig. 2, there is little difference in maximum server utilization of both schemes.

Fig. 3 illustrates the worst-case local live memory derived from the simulation and the analysis for the dual server approach. For comparison, the worst-case local live memory acquired from the simulation and the analysis for the single server approach is also presented. These results demonstrate that the analytic bound accords well with the simulation bound. The dual server approach also may reduce the worst-case local live memory by up to 8 % compared with the single server approach. It results from the fact that the dual server approach causes smaller interference over mutator tasks compared with the single server approach.

We also compare the memory reservation of the dual server approach with that of the single server approach. Fig. 4 illustrates the worst-case memory reservation for each task set. The graphs show that, at relatively high priority level, the dual server approach can provide comparable performance to the single server approach. The results also demonstrate that noticeable differences in memory reservation are observed from the priority levels 5 in TS1, 7 in TS2, and 7 in TS3, respectively. For the DS, we can find that at those priority levels the server utilization starts to decrease. Following Theorem 2 in Sect. 3.2, this server utilization has a great impact on the worst-case GC response time, and thus memory reservation. On the other hand, for the SS, the performance begins

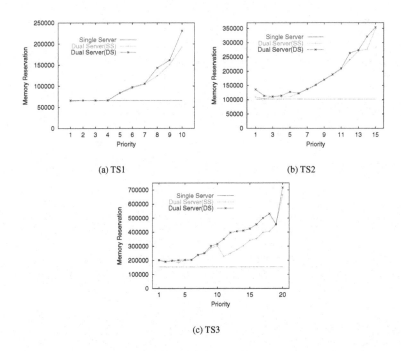

(a) TS1   (b) TS2

(c) TS3

Fig. 4. Memory reservation of given task sets.

to degrade at certain priority level though the server utilization has relatively uniform distribution. This is because the period of a virtual task representing the SS dual server is much longer than that of the DS server, which yields longer GC response time. For details, see Theorem 1 in Sect. 3.2.

Fig. 5 compares the feasible memory requirements of both schemes. We mean *feasible* memory requirement by the amount of heap memory to guarantee hard deadlines without memory shortage under a specific memory consumption behavior. In our study, the feasible memory requirement is found by iterative simulation runs. We regard a given memory requirement as feasible if no garbage collection errors and deadline misses are reported after 100 hyperperiods runs. In Fig. 5, the SS-based dual server approach provides feasible memory requirement comparable to the single server approach for all the task sets. For TS3, the single server approach remarkably outperforms the dual server approach. This is because the periodic utilization of TS3 is relatively high, and therefore the CPU utilization allocated for the secondary server is smaller than the cases for TS1 and TS2. A noticeable performance gap between the SS-based single server and the SS-based dual server is found in Fig. 5 (c). At the priority level 18, the performance gap between two approaches is maximized because the CPU utilization allocated for the secondary server is minimized at this priority level as shown in Fig. 2. It results in longer GC response time, and thus large heap memory is needed.

The results also report that the DS provides comparable performance to the SS at high priorities although, at low priorities, the SS generally outperforms the DS. For TS1,

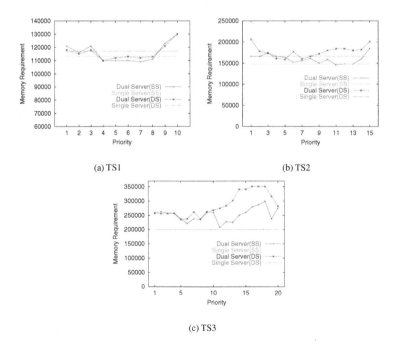

(a) TS1   (b) TS2

(c) TS3

Fig. 5. Feasible memory requirement of given task sets for the dual server.

the performance gap between two schemes is within 2.8 %. Although the capacities of the SS is much larger than those of the DS at low priority levels, the double hit effect offsets the difference. However, for TS3, a noticeable performance gap is observed at low priority levels. This is because the periodic utilization of TS3 is quite high, and therefore the double hit effect diminishes at low priorities. Although the DS may not provide stable performance compared with the SS, it can provide comparable performance to, even better than at some configuration, the SS. And, it has another advantage over the SS; its implementation and run-time overheads are quite low. In summary, the DS is still an attractive alternative to the SS in terms of scheduling-based garbage collection.

5 Conclusions

We have proposed a new scheduling-aware real-time garbage collection scheme. Our pre-vious work [1] employed single aperiodic server to service garbage collection requests. By integrating task scheduling with garbage collection algorithm, the scheme achieves small memory footprint while guaranteeing hard deadlines. However, this scheme is sometimes impractical because it may inevitably not reserve sufficiently large server capacity. A new scheduling-aware garbage collection scheme based on dual aperiodic servers is introduced to overcome the limitation of the single server approach while achieving similar performance compared with the single server approach. The results obtained in this paper are summarized as follows. In general, the dual server approach shows comparable performance to the single server whilst it enables more flexible system design. In addition, the DS can be an alternative solution to the scheduling-aware garbage collection scheme. Simulation results show that it can provide similar performance to the SS with smaller implementation and run-time overheads.

References

1. Kim, T., Chang, N., Shin, H.: Joint scheduling of garbage collector and hard real-time tasks for embedded applications. Journal of Systems and Software **58** (2001) 245–258
2. Liu, C.L., Layland, J.W.: Scheduling algorithms for multiprogramming in a hard real-time environment. Journal of the ACM **20** (1973) 46–61
3. Kim, T., Chang, N., Kim, N., Shin, H.: Scheduling garbage collector for embedded real-time systems. In: Proceedings of the ACM SIGPLAN 1999 Workshop on Languages, Compilers and Tools for Embedded Systems. (1999) 55–64
4. Kim, T., Chang, N., Shin, H.: Bounding worst case garbage collection time for embedded real-time systems. In: Proceedings of The 6th IEEE Real-Time Technology and Applications Symposium. (2000) 46–55
5. Bernat, G.: Specification and Analysis of Weakly Hard Real-Time Systems. Ph.D. Thesis, Universitat de les Illes Balears, Spain (1998)
6. Gerber, R., Hong, S., Saksena, M.: Guaranteeing end-to-end timing constraints by calibrating intermediate processes. In: Proceedings of Real-Time Systems Symposium. (1994) 192–203
7. Bernat, G., Burns, A.: New results on fixed priority aperiodic servers. In: Proceedings of Real-Time Systems Symposium. (1999) 68–78

On the Composition of Real-Time Schedulers*

Weirong Wang and Aloysius K. Mok

Department of Computer Sciences
University of Texas at Austin
Austin, Texas 78712-1188
{weirongw,mok}@cs.utexas.edu

Abstract. A complex real-time embedded system may consist of multiple application components each of which has its own timeliness requirements and is scheduled by component-specific schedulers. At run-time, the schedules of the components are integrated to produce a system-level schedule of jobs to be executed. We formalize the notions of schedule composition, task group composition and component composition. Two algorithms for performing composition are proposed. The first one is an extended Earliest Deadline First algorithm which can be used as a composability test for schedules. The second algorithm, the Harmonic Component Composition algorithm (HCC) provides an online admission test for components. HCC applies a rate monotonic classification of workloads and is a hard real-time solution because responsive supply of a shared resource is guaranteed for in-budget workloads. HCC is also efficient in terms of composability and requires low computation cost for both admission control and dispatch of resources.

1 Introduction

The integration of components in complex real-time and embedded systems has become an important topic of study in recent years. Such a system may be made up of independent application (functional) components each of which consists of a set of tasks with its own specific timeliness requirements. The timeliness requirements of the task group of a component is guaranteed by a scheduling policy specific to the component, and thus the scheduler of a complex embedded system may be composed of multiple schedulers. If these components share some common resource such as the CPU, then the schedules of the individual components are interleaved in some way. In extant work, a number of researchers have proposed algorithms to integrate real-time schedulers such that the timeliness requirements of all the application task groups can be simultaneously met. The most relevant work in this area includes work in "open systems" and "hierarchical schedulers" which we can only briefly review here. Deng and Liu proposed the open system environment, where application components may be admitted

---

* This work is supported in part by a grant from the US Office of Naval Research under grant number N00014-99-1-0402 and N00014-98-1-0704, and by a research contract from SRI International under a grant from the NEST program of DARPA

online and the scheduling of the component schedulers is performed by a kernel scheduler [2]. Mok and Feng exploited the idea of temporal partitioning [6], by which individual applications and schedulers work as if each one of them owns a dedicated "real-time virtual resource". Regehr and Stankovic investigated hierarchical schedulers [8]. Fohler addressed the issue of how to dynamically schedule event-triggered tasks together with an offline-produced schedule for time-triggered computation [3]. In [10] by Wang and Mok, two popular schedulers: the cyclic executive and fixed-priority schedulers form a hybrid scheduling system to accommodate a combination of periodic and sporadic tasks.

All of the works cited above address the issue of schedule/scheduler composition based on different assumptions. But what exactly are the conditions under which the composition of two components is correct? Intuitively, the minimum guarantee is that the composition preserves the timeliness of the tasks in all the task groups. But in the case an application scheduler may produce different schedules depending on the exact time instants at which scheduling decisions are made, must the composition of components also preserve the exact schedules that would be produced by the individual application schedulers if they were to run on dedicated CPUs? Such considerations may be important if an application programmer relies on the exact sequencing of jobs that is produced by the application scheduler and not only the semantics of the scheduler to guarantee the correct functioning of the application component. For example, an application programmer might manipulate the assignment of priorities such that a fixed priority scheduler produces a schedule that is the same as that produced by a cyclic executive for an application task group; this simulation of a cyclic executive by a fixed priority scheduler may create trouble if the fixed priority scheduler is later on composed with other schedulers and produces a different schedule which does not preserve the task ordering in the simulated cyclic executive. Hence, we need to pay attention to semantic issues in scheduler composition.

In this paper, we propose to formalize the notions of composition on three levels: schedule composition, task group composition and component composition. Based on the formalization, we consider the questions of whether two schedules are composable, and how components may be efficiently composed. Our formalization takes into account the execution order dependencies (explicit or implicit) between tasks in the same component. For example, in cyclic executive schedulers, a deterministic order is imposed on the execution of tasks so as to satisfy precedence, mutual exclusion and other relations. As is common practice to handle such dependencies, sophisticated search-based algorithms are used to produce the deterministic schedules offline, e.g., [9]. To integrate such components into a complex system, we consider composition with the view that: First, the correctness of composition should not depend on knowledge about how the component schedules are produced, i.e., compositionality is fundamentally a predicate on *schedules* and not *schedulers*. Second, the composition of schedules should be *order preserving* with respect to its components, i.e., if job x is scheduled before job y in a component schedule, then job x is still scheduled before

y in the integrated system schedule. Our notion of *schedule composition* is an interleaving of component schedules that allows preemptions between jobs from different components.

The contributions of this paper include: formal definitions of schedule composition, task group composition and component composition, an optimal schedule composition algorithm for static schedules and a harmonic component composition algorithm that has low computation cost and also provides a responsiveness guarantee. The rest of the paper is organized as follows. Section 2 defines basic concepts used in the rest of the paper. Section 3 addresses schedule composition. Section 4 defines and compares task group composition and component composition. Section 5 defines, illustrates and analyzes the Harmonic Component Composition approach. Section 6 compares HCC with related works. Section 7 concludes the paper by proposing future work.

2 Definitions

2.1 Task Models

Time is defined on the domain of non-negative real numbers, and the time interval between time b and time e is denoted by (b, e). We shall also refer to a time interval $(i, i+1)$ where i is a non-negative integer as a *time unit*. A *resource* is an object to be allocated to tasks. It can be a CPU, a bus, or a packet switch, etc. In this paper, we shall consider the case of a single resource which can be shared by the tasks and components, and preemption is allowed. We assume that context switching takes zero time; this assumption can be removed in practice by adding the appropriate overhead to the task execution time.

A *job* is defined by a tuple of three attributes (c, r, d) each of which is a non-negative real number:

- c is the *execution time* of a job, which defines the amount of time that must be allocated to the job;
- r is the *ready time* or *arrival time* of the job which is the earliest time at which the job can be scheduled;
- d is the *deadline* of the job which is the latest time by which the job must be completed.

A *task* is an infinite sequence of jobs. Each task is identified by a unique ID i. A task is either periodic or sporadic.

The set of periodic tasks in a system is represented by T_p. A *periodic task* is denoted by $(i, (c, p, d))$, where i identifies the task, and tuple (c, p, d) defines the attributes of its jobs. The jth job of i is denoted by job (i, j).

Suppose X identifies an object and Y is one of the attributes of the object. we shall use the notation $X.Y$ to denote the attribute Y of X. For instance, if (i, j) identifies a job, then $(i, j).d$ denotes the deadline of job (i, j).

The attributes in the definition of a periodic task, c, p and d, are non-negative real numbers:

- c is the *execution time* of a task, which defines the amount of time that must be allocated to each job of the task;
- p is the *period* of the task;
- d is the *relative deadline* of the task, which is the maximal length of time by which a job must be completed after its arrival. We assume that for every periodic task, $c \leq d \leq p$.

If a periodic task i is defined by (c, p, d), job (i, j) is defined by $(c, j \cdot p, j \cdot p + d)$.

A *sporadic task* is denoted by a tuple $(i, (c, p, d))$, where i identifies the task, and (c, p, d) defines the attributes of its jobs, as follows: The jth job of sporadic task i is identified as job (i, j), $j \geq 0$. The arrival times of jobs of a sporadic task are not known *a priori* and are determined at run time by an *arrival function A* that maps each job of a sporadic task to its arrival time for the particular run:

$A :: T_s \times \mathbf{N} \rightarrow \mathbf{R}$, where $\mathbf{N}$ is the set of natural numbers and $\mathbf{R}$ is the set of real numbers.
$A(i, j) = t$ if the job (i, j) arrives at time t.
$A(i, j) = \perp$ if the job (i, j) never arrivals.

The attributes c and d of a sporadic task are defined the same as those of a periodic task. However, attribute p of a sporadic task represents the *minimal* interval between the arrival times of any two consecutive jobs. In terms of the function A, $A(i, (j + 1)) - A(i, j) \geq p$ if $A(i, (j + 1))$ is defined.

For a sporadic task $(i, (c, p, d))$, job (i, j) is defined as $(c, A(i, j), A(i, j) + d)$.

A task group TG consists of a set of tasks (either periodic or sporadic). We shall use STG to denote a set of task groups. The term component denotes a task group and its scheduler. Sometimes we call a task group an application task group to emphasize its association with a component which is one of many applications in the system.

2.2   Schedule

A resource supply function Sup defines the maximal time that can be supplied to a component from time 0 to time t. Time supply function must be monotonically non-decreasing. In other words, if $t \leq t'$, then $Sup(t) \leq Sup(t')$.

The function S maps each job to a set of time intervals:

$S :: TG \times \mathbf{N} \rightarrow \{(\mathbf{R}, \mathbf{R})\}$ where TG is a task group, and $\mathbf{N}$ and $\mathbf{R}$ represent the set of natural numbers and the set of real numbers respectively.
$S(i, j) = \{(b_{i,j,k}, e_{i,j,k}) | 0 \leq k < h\}$ where k and h are natural numbers.

S is a *schedule* of TG under supply function Sup if and only if all of the following conditions are satisfied:

- **Constraint 1:** For every job (i, j), every time interval assigned to it in the schedule must be assigned in a time interval allowed by the supply function, i.e., for all $(b, e) \in S(i, j)$, $Sup(e) - Sup(b) = e - b$.

- **Constraint 2**: The resource is allocated to at most one job at a time, i.e.,
  time intervals do not overlap: For every $(b_{i,j,k}, e_{i,j,k}) \in S(i,j)$ and for every
  $(b_{i',j',k'}, e_{i',j',k'}) \in S(i', j')$, one of the following cases must be true:
  - $e_{i,j,k} \leq b_{i',j',k'}$; or
  - $e_{i',j',k'} \leq b_{i,j,k}$; or
  - $i = i'$, $j = j'$ and $k = k'$.
- **Constraint 3**: A job must be scheduled between its ready time and deadline:
  for every $(b, e) \in S(i,j)$,

$$(i,j).r \leq b < e \leq (i,j).d$$

- **Constraint 4**: For every job (i,j), the total length of all time intervals in
  $S(i,j)$ is sufficient for executing the job, i.e.,

$$\sum_{(b,e) \in S(i,j)} (e - b) \geq (i,j).c$$

Given a time t, if there exists a time interval (b, e) in $S(i,j)$ such that $b \leq t < e$, then job (i,j) is *scheduled at* time t, and task i is *scheduled at* time t.

An algorithm *Sch* is a *scheduler* if and only if it produces a schedule S for T under A and *Sup*.

A component C of a system is defined by a tuple (TG, Sch) which specifies the task group to be scheduled and the task group's scheduler. A set of components will be written as SC.

3   Schedule Composition

Suppose S_h is a schedule of a component task group TG_h. We say that the schedule S integrating the component schedules in $\bigcup TG_h$ is a composed schedule of all component schedules $\{S_h | 0 \leq h \leq n - 1\}$ if and only if there exists a function M which maps each scheduled time interval in S_h to a time window subject to the following conditions:

- For each time interval $(b, e) \in S_h(i,j)$, $M(h, (b, e)) = (b_h, e_h)$, and (b_h, e_h) is
  within the ready time and deadline of job (i,j);
- The time scheduled to job (i,j) by S between (b_h, e_h) is equal to $e - b$:

$$\sum_{(x,y) \in S(i,j) \text{ and } b_h \leq x \leq y \leq e_h} (y - x) = e - b$$

- $M(h, (b, e))$ is before $M(h, (b', e'))$ if and only if $(b, e) \in S_h(i,j)$ is before
  $(b', e') \in S_h(i', j')$.

The notion of schedule composition is illustrated in Figure 1 where the component schedule S_0 is interleaved with other component schedules into a composed

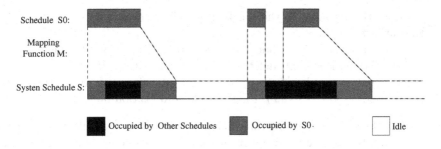

Fig. 1. Definition of Schedule Composition

schedule S. Notice that the time intervals occupied by S_0 can be mapped into S without changing the order of these time intervals.

To test whether a set of schedules can be integrated into a composed schedule, we now propose an extended Earliest Deadline First algorithm for schedule composition. From the definition of a schedule, the execution of a job (i, j) can be scheduled into a set of time intervals by a schedule S. We use the term $S(i, j)$ to denote the set of time intervals job (i, j) occupies. In the following, we shall refer to a time interval in $S(i, j)$ as a *job fragment* of the job (i, j). The schedule composition algorithm works as follows. A job fragment is created corresponding to the first time interval of the first job in each component schedule S_h that has not been integrated into S, and the job fragments from all schedules are scheduled together by EDF. After the job fragment, say for schedule S_h has completed, the job fragment is deleted and another job fragment is created corresponding to the next time interval in schedule S_h.

The schedule composition algorithm is defined below.

– Initially, all job fragments from all component schedules are unmarked.
– At any time t, *Ready* is a set that contains all the job fragments from all the component schedules that are ready to be composed. Initially, *Ready* is empty.
– At any time t, if there is no job fragment from component schedule S_h in *Ready*, construct one denoted as (h, c, r, d) by the following steps:
  • Let (b, e) be an unmarked time interval such that $(b, e) \in S_h(i, j)$ and for all unmarked time interval $(b', e') \in S_h(i', j')$, $b \le b'$;
  • Define the execution time of the job fragment as the length of the scheduled time interval: $c := e - b$;
  • Define ready time of the job fragment as the ready time of the job scheduled at (b, e): $r := (i, j).r$;
  • Define deadline of the job fragment as the earliest deadline among all jobs scheduled after time b by S_h:

  $$d := min(\{(i', j').d | (b', e') \in S_h(i', j') \text{ and } b \le b'\})$$

  • Mark interval (b, e).

- Allocate the resource to the job fragment in *Ready* that is ready and has the earliest deadline.
- If the accumulated time allocated to job fragment is equal to the execution time of the job fragment, delete the job fragment from *Ready*.
- If t is equal to the deadline of a job fragment before the completion of the corresponding job in *Ready*, the schedule composition fails.

In the above, the time intervals within a component schedule S_h are transformed into job fragments and put into *Ready* one by one in their original order in S_h. At any time t, just one job fragment from S_h is in *Ready*. Therefore, the order of time intervals in a component schedule is preserved in the composed schedule.

The extended EDF is optimal in terms of composability. In other words, if a composed schedule exists for a given set of component schedules, then the extended EDF produces one.

Theorem 1. *The extended EDF is an optimal schedule composition algorithm.*

Proof: If the extended EDF for composition fails at time f, then let s be the latest time that following conditions are all true: for any S_h, there exists $(b, e) \in S_h(i, j)$, $(i, j).r \geq s$, all time intervals before b in S_h are composed into S no later than time s, and for all (b', e') composed between s and f, the corresponding job fragment has deadline no later than f. Then for any time t between (s, f), there is a $(b', e') \in S(i', j')$ and $b' \leq t \leq e'$. The aggregate length of time intervals from component schedules that must be integrated between (s, f) is larger than $f - s$, therefore no schedule composition exists. ∎

Because of its optimality, the extended EDF is a composability test for any set of schedules. Although extend EDF is optimal, this approach, however, has a limitation: the input component schedules must be static. In other words, to generate system schedule at time t, the component schedules after time t need to be known. Otherwise, the deadline of the pseudo job in *Ready* cannot be decided optimally. Therefore, the extended EDF schedule composition approach cannot be applied optimally to dynamically produced schedules.

4   Task Group Composability and Component Composability

We say that a set of task groups $STG=\{TG_0, .., TG_{n-1}\}$ is *weakly* composable if and only if the following holds: Given any set of arrival functions $\{A_0, .., A_{n-1}\}$ for the task groups in STG, for any $0 \leq k \leq n - 1$, there exists a schedule S_k for TG_k under A_k, and $SS = \{S_0, .., S_{n-1}\}$ is composable. Obviously, weak composability is equivalent to the schedulability of task group $\bigcup_{STG} TG_k$. We say that a set of task groups STG is *strongly* composable if and only if the following holds: Given any schedule S_k of TG_k under any A_k, $SS = \{S_0, .., S_{n-1}\}$ is composable. The following is a simple example of strong composability.

Suppose there are two task groups. TG_0 consists of a periodic task $T_0 = (1, 5, 5)$, and TG_1 consists of a sporadic task $T_1 = (1, 5, 5)$. Then an arbitrary schedule S_0 for TG_0 and an arbitrary schedule S_1 of TG_1 can always be composed into a schedule S by the extended EDF no matter what the arrival function is. Therefore, this set of task groups are strongly composable.

Not all *weakly* composable sets of task groups are strongly composable. Suppose we change the above example of strongly composable set of task groups by adding another periodic task $T_2 = (4, 10, 10)$ to task group TG_0. Two schedules can be produced for TG_0 by a fixed priority schedulers: S_0 and S_0'. In S_0, suppose we give a higher priority to T_0, and therefore for all j, $S_0(0, j) = (5 \cdot j, 5 \cdot j + 1)$, and $S_0(2, j) = (10 \cdot j + 1, 10 \cdot j + 5)$. For S_0', suppose we give higher priority to T_2, and therefore for any number j, $S_0'(0, 2j) = (10 \cdot j + 4, 10 \cdot j + 5)$, $S_0'(0, 2j + 1) = (10 \cdot j + 5, 10 \cdot j + 6)$; $S_0'(2, j) = (10 \cdot j, 10 \cdot j + 4)$.

S_0 is composable with any schedule S_1 of TG_1, but S_0' is not. In S_0', for any j, the deadline of job $(0, 2 \cdot j)$ is at $10 \cdot j + 5$, and yet it is scheduled after job $(2, j)$ whose deadline is at $10 \cdot j + 10$. Because of the order-preserving property of schedule composition, it follows that every time interval $(10 \cdot j, 10 \cdot j + 5)$ must be assigned to S_0'. Thus, if a job of T_1 arrives at time $10 \cdot j$, schedule composition becomes impossible.

We say that a set of supply functions $SSup=\{Sup_0, .., Sup_{n-1}\}$ is *consistent* if and only if the aggregate time supply of all functions between any time interval (b, e) is less than or equal to the length:

$$\sum (Sup_k(e) - Sup_k(b)) \le e - b$$

Suppose $SC = \{(Sch_0, TG_0), .., (Sch_{n-1}, TG_{n-1})\}$ is a set of components. SC is composable if and only if given any set of arrival functions $SA = \{A_0, .., A_{n-1}\}$, there exists a set of consistent supply functions $SSup = \{Sup_0, .., Sup_{n-1}\}$ such that Sch_k produces schedule S_k of TG_k under arrival function A_k and supply function Sup_k, and $SS = \{S_0, .., S_{n-1}\}$ is composable.

Component composability lies between weak composability and strong composability of task groups in the following sense. A component has its own scheduler which may produce for a given arrival function, a schedule among a number of valid schedules under the arrival function. Therefore, given a set of components, if the corresponding set of task groups of these components are strongly composable, then the components are composable; if the task groups are not even weakly composable, the components are not composable. However, when the task groups are weakly but not strongly composable, component composability depends on the specifics of component schedulers.

To illustrate these concepts, we compare weak task group composability, strong task group composability and component composability in the following example which is depicted in Figure 2. Suppose there are two components $C_0 = (TG_0, Sch_0)$ and $C_1 = (TG_1, Sch_1)$. For any valid arrival function A for each of the task groups, there exists in general a set of schedules that may correspond to the execution of the task group under the arrival function set. In Figure 2, the circle marked as $SS_{0,0}$ represents the set for all possible schedules of TG_0 under A_0; and $SS_{0,1}$, $SS_{1,0}$, $SS_{1,1}$ are defined similarly. If TG_0 and TG_1 are strongly composable, then randomly pick a schedule S_0 from $SS_{0,x}$ and a schedule S_1 from $SS_{1,y}$ where x and y are variable and S_0 and S_1 are composable. If TG_0 and TG_1 are weakly composable, then for any x and y, there exists a schedule S_0 from $SS_{0,x}$ and there exists a schedule S_1 from $SS_{1,y}$ such that S_0 and S_1 are composable. The small circle marked as $SS_{0,0,s}$ is the set of all schedules that can be produced by the scheduler Sch_0 under A_0. Each point in $SS_{0,0,s}$ corresponds to one schedule, and one or multiple supply functions upon which Sch_0 produces $SS_{0,0,s}$. Circle $SS_{0,1,s}$, $SS_{1,0,s}$, $SS_{1,1,s}$ are defined similarly. If components C_0 and C_1 are composable, then for any pair of x and y, there exists a schedule S_0 in $SS_{0,x,s}$, and a schedule S_1 in $SS_{1,y,s}$, S_0 and S_1 are composable, and there exists a supply function Sup_0 corresponding to S_0 and a supply function Sup_1 corresponding to S_1, and Sup_0 and Sup_1 are consistent.

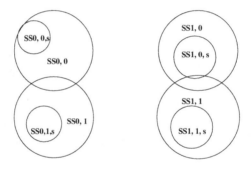

Fig. 2. Composability

In many scheduler composition paradigms, the resource supply functions can be determined only online for components that have unpredictable arrivals of jobs. Therefore it is often hard to define resource supply function *a priori*. However, we can introduce the notion of contracts to express the requirements imposed on the supply function by a component, as the interface between a component and the composition coordinator. In the next section, we shall discuss Harmonic Component Composition which makes use of explicit supply function contracts.

5   Harmonic Component Composition

We consider the tradeoff between composability and the simplicity in the design of the system-level scheduler to be a significant challenge in component composition. As an extreme case in pursuing simplicity, a coordinator may allocate resources among components based on a few coarse-grain parameters of each component, such as the worst case response time and bandwidth requirement. This type of solutions often does not achieve composability, i.e., admission of new components may be disallowed even when the aggregate resource utilization is low because of previous overly conservative capacity commitments. At the opposite extreme, the coordinator may depend on details about the components to perform complex analysis and may take on too many obligations from individual components, such that the system performance may eventually be degraded. We now propose a solution to meet the challenge by introducing class-based workloads. We call this approach Harmonic Component Composition (HCC).

5.1 Coordinator Algorithm

The system designer will select a constant K as the number of resource classes. A class k ($k \in [0, K)$) is defined by a class period $P_k = m^k$, where m is a designer-selected constant. We require a rate monotonic relation between the periods of classes: For any $0 \le l \le k \le K - 1$, $\frac{P_k}{P_l} = m^{l-k}$. Lower class has larger class number and longer class period.

When a component C is ready to run, it generates a supply contract and sends it to the coordinator. The supply contract is a list of workload defined as (k, l, w), where $k \le l$. The workload permits that up to w time units of resource supply can be on demand within any time interval of length m^l; and once a demand occurs, it must be met within m^k time units. Upon receiving a supply contract, the coordinator will admit a component if and only if it can satisfy the contract without compromising the contracts with previously admitted components.

When a demand is proposed to class k, it will be served within m^k time. To keep this guarantee, HCC maintains a straightforward invariant to make sure that supply needed online for class k or higher in any time interval with length m^k is less than or equal to m^k. To accomplish this, the aggregate workload admitted to class k or higher is constrained as if there is a *conceptual resource* associated with class k which is consumed by admitting any workload with class k or higher. Suppose that R_k represents the conceptual resource of class k. R_k is initiated as P_k. A workload (k, l, w) requires no conceptual resource from the classes higher than k, but requires that from every class lower than or equal to k. The value of the conceptual resource requirement of a workload (k, l, w) on class i is derived from the worst case occupation in a time interval of length P_i by the workload.

If a component C_h is admitted, the coordinator establishes a server identified with (h, k, l) for each workload (k, l, w) in the contract. The component to which the server belongs is identified by h, the class of the server is k, and (k, l) defines a subclass. All servers of class i are in a list L_i. The server is defined with a budget limit w and replenishment period of m^l. A server have four registers, *load, carry, budget* and *replenish*.

Initialization:

(1)	**foreach** $0 \le k \le K - 1$
(2)	$R_k := P_k$
(3)	L_k is set as an empty list

Contract Admission:

(1)	Upon component C_h proposes a contract V_h, which is a list of (k, l, w)
(2)	**foreach** $0 \le i \le K - 1$
(3)	$R'_i := R_i$
(4)	**foreach** $(k, l, w) \in V_h$
(5)	**foreach** $k \le i \le l$
(6)	$R'_i := R'_i - w$
(7)	**foreach** $l + 1 \le i \le K - 1$
(8)	$R'_i := R'_i - w \cdot (m^{i-l})$
(9)	**if** $\exists R'_i < 0$
(10)	reject component C_h and terminate this run of contract admission;
(11)	**foreach** $i \in [0, K - 1]$
(12)	$R_i := R'_i$
(13)	**foreach** $(k, l, w) \in V_h$
(14)	construct server (h, k, l) and add to the end of L_k, with the following initial values:
(15)	$budget = w$, $loaded = carry = 0$, $replenish$ as empty queue.

Referring to the algorithm specification above, a component C_h may *load* a server (h, k, l) by adding a value to its register *load* when the component C_h demands usage on the resource. If the value of the *load* register is positive, the server is *loaded*. If a loaded server has budget($budget > 0$), then the budget is consumed on the load and all or part of the loaded value becomes *carried* ($carry > 0$). At the start of a time unit $(t, t + 1)$ (which means t is a non-negative integer), if class k is the highest class with a carried server, then the first carried server in L_k supplies resource in the time unit $(t, t + 1)$.

The existing budget of a server is held in *budget*. When *load* and *budget* are both positive and $v = min(load, budget)$, both of them are reduced by v and *carry* is increased by v. Consumed budget will be replenished after m^l units of time. The queue *replenish* records the scheduled replenishments in the future.

Online Execution:

(1)	Upon the start of time unit $(t, t + 1)$:
(2)	**foreach** server (h, k, l)
(3)	Replenish budget:
(4)	**if** the head of queue in *replenish* is (t, val)
(5)	$budget := budget + val$
(6)	dequeue (t, val) from *repenish*
(7)	Carry work load:
(8)	**if** $load > 0$ and $budget > 0$
(9)	$v := min(load, budget)$
(10)	$carry := carry + v$
(11)	$budget := budget - v$
(12)	$load := load - v$
(13)	enqueue $(v, t + m^l)$ to *replenish*
(14)	Supply Resource:
(15)	Select server (h, k, l), such that k is the highest class with at least one carried server, and (h, k, l) is the first carried server in L_k.
(16)	$carry := carry - 1$
(17)	Supply resource to component C_h in time unit $(t, t + 1)$

When a component terminates, the coordinator reclaims the conceptual resources from the component.

Component termination:

(1)	Upon the termination of component C_h
(2)	**foreach** $(k, l, w) \in V_h$
(3)	delete server (h, k, l) from L_k
(4)	**foreach** $k \leq i \leq l$
(5)	$R_i := R_i + w$
(6)	**foreach** $l + 1 \leq i \leq K - 1$
(7)	$R_i := R_i + w \cdot (m^{i-l})$

5.2   Component Algorithm

In the HCC approach, a component generates a supply contract, and if admitted, it may demand supply from its servers. Different algorithms may be applied for different components in a composition. We describe one solution here as an example.

Assume that there is a component C_h, and its component scheduler is EDF. A task (c, p, d) is categorized to subclass $(\lfloor log_m d \rfloor, \lfloor log_m p \rfloor)$, and its execution time is added to the weight w of the workload with that subclass.

Supply Contract Generation:

(1)   **foreach** (k, l) such that $0 \le k \le l \le K - 1$
(2) $w_{k,l} := 0$
(3)   **foreach** $i \in T_h$
(4) $k := \lfloor \log_m i.d \rfloor$
(5) $l := \lfloor \log_m i.p \rfloor$
(6) $w_{k,l} := w_{k,l} + i.c$
(7)   **foreach** $w_{k,l} \ne 0$
(8)   add workload $(k, l, w_{k,l})$ into contract V_h

At run time, upon the arrival of a job (i, j), a demand for resource supply is added to the server corresponding to task i at the start of the next time unit.

Online execution:

(1)   Initialization:
(2)   **foreach** (k, l)
(3) $w_{k,l} := 0$;
(4)   Upon the arrival of job (i, j),
(5) $k := \lfloor \log_m i.d \rfloor$
(6) $l := \lfloor \log_m i.p \rfloor$
(7) $w_{k,l} := w_{k,l} + i.c$
(8)   Upon the start of time unit $(t, t + 1)$
(9)   **foreach** server (k, l) such that $w_{k,l} > 0$
(10) $load := load + w_{k,l}$;
(11) $w_{k,l} := 0$;

5.3   Example

Having described how HCC works, we illustrate the HCC approach by an example below.

In this example, we design a system with four components with the following specifications.

- Component C_0 consists of one task for emergency action and 2 periodic routine tasks. The emergency action takes little execution time and rarely happens, but when a malfunction occurs, the action must be performed immediately. We abstract this action by a sporadic task $T_0 = (1, \infty, 1)$, which means that the execution time and relative deadline are both 1, and the minimum interval between consecutive arrivals are infinite. The periodic routine tasks are given by $T_1 = (1, 80, 8)$, $T_2 = (1, 100, 10)$.

- Component C_1 is a group of periodic routine tasks defined as follows: $T_3 = (1, 3, 3)$, $T_4 = (1, 10, 10)$.
- Component C_2 is a bandwidth-intensive application, which needs 25 percent of the resource. It can be modeled as $T_5 = (16, 64, 64)$.
- Component C_3 has one periodic task $T_6 = (3, 30, 30)$.

The value of m and K are arbitrarily selected as 2 and 6 by the system designer, based on estimations of the potential workloads. Let us apply the contract generation as defined in this paper. Four contracts will be produced as follows. Recall that workload is defined as (k, l, w).

- $V_0 = \{(0, 6, 1), (3, 6, 2)\}$, where T_0 is mapped to workload $(0, 6, 1)$, T_1 and T_2 are mapped to $(3, 6, 2)$.
- $V_1 = \{(1, 1, 1), (3, 3, 1)\}$, where T_3 is mapped to $(1, 1, 1)$, and T_4 is mapped to $(3, 3, 1)$.
- $V_2 = \{(6, 6, 16)\}$.
- $V_3 = \{(4, 4, 3)\}$.

Suppose that all components become ready at time 0, and the admission decisions are made according to their index order. For all $0 \leq k \leq 6$, R_k remains non-negative when C_0, C_1, C_2 are admitted. However, during the admission of C_3, $R'_6 < 0$, therefore C_3 is not admitted. Table 1 shows the change of R_k during admission procedure, and Table 2 shows the established servers on all classes after that.

Assume that the first job of T_0 arrives at time 4 and the online executions of all components are defined as in this paper. We now show a step by step execution from time 0 to time 4.

At time 0, the budget registers of all servers have been initialized according to their weights, and the components add their current demands to the corresponding load registers, as shown in Table 3. Coordinator moves the in-budget loads into register *carry*, and the consumed budget are recorded for replenishments in

Table 1. Component Admission

	initial	Component 0 (0, 6, 1)	(3, 6, 2)	Component 1 (1, 1, 1)	(3, 3, 1)	Component 2 (6, 6, 16)		Component 3 (4, 4, 3)
R_0	1	0	0	0	0	0	R'_0	0
R_1	2	1	1	0	0	0	R'_1	0
R_2	4	3	3	1	1	1	R'_2	1
R_3	8	7	5	1	0	0	R'_3	0
R_4	16	15	13	5	3	3	R'_4	0
R_5	32	31	29	13	9	9	R'_5	3
R_6	64	63	61	29	21	5	R'_6	-7

Table 2. Servers on All Classes

L_0	$\{(0,0,6)\}$
L_1	$\{(1,1,1)\}$
L_2	
L_3	$\{(0,3,6),(1,3,3)\}$
L_4	
L_5	
L_6	$\{(2,6,6)\}$

Table 3. Register Image Right After Component Loading At Time 0

	budget	load	carry	replenish
(0, 0, 6)	1	0	0	
(1, 1, 1)	1	1	0	
(0, 3, 6)	2	2	0	
(1, 3, 3)	1	1	0	
(2, 6, 6)	16	16	0	

the future. The carried value of server $(1,1,1)$ becomes 1. Server $(0,0,6)$ is not carried, therefore server $(1,1,1)$ is selected to supply time between time $(0,1)$. Its *carry* is then decremented back to 0. Table 4 shows the register image after the execution of the coordinator.

Between time $(0,1)$, no load is added from any component. At time 1, server $(0,3,6)$ is selected to supply between $(1,2)$ so its *carry* is decremented, as shown in Table 5.

At time 2, server $(1,1,1)$ replenishes its budget, and server $(0,3,6)$ is selected as supplier and so its value of *carry* is decremented, as shown in Table 6.

At time 3, the second job of T_3 is ready, so C_1 loads server $(1,1,1)$ by 1, as shown in Table 7. On the coordinator side, budget is available for server $(1,1,1)$, therefore budget is consumed for the load and *carry* is incremented by 1. Budget is consumed, and therefore future replenishment is added to *replenish*. Then server $(1,1,1)$ is selected as supplier, and its *carry* is decremented by 1. Table 8 shows the register image after the coordinator execution.

At time 4, a job of task T_0 arrives. Therefore server $(0,0,6)$ is loaded by 1, as shown in Table 9. During the coordinator execution, budget is available for $(0,0,6)$ and consumed, future replenishment is stored, and the value of *carry* is incremented by 1. Then server $(0,0,6)$ is selected to supply, and its *carry* is decremented back to 0. Table 10 shows the register image after these executions.

It is noteworthy that a simple fixed-priority composition scheme cannot even compose C_0 and C_1 together for the following reason. Because of the short deadline of task T_0, C_0 must have the highest priority. Then there is a possibility that 3 continuous time units may be supplied to C_0, in which case task T_3 in C_1 may miss its deadline. The low composability is a result of not distinguish-

Table 4. Register Image Right After Coordinator Execution At Time 0

	budget	load	carry	replenish
$(0, 0, 6)$	1	0	0	
$(1, 1, 1)$	0	0	0	$\{(1, 2)\}$
$(0, 3, 6)$	0	0	2	$\{(2, 64)\}$
$(1, 3, 3)$	0	0	1	$\{(1, 8)\}$
$(2, 6, 6)$	0	0	16	$\{(16, 64)\}$

Table 5. Register Image Right After Coordinator Execution At Time 1

	budget	load	carry	replenish
$(0, 0, 6)$	1	0	0	
$(1, 1, 1)$	0	0	0	$\{(1, 2)\}$
$(0, 3, 6)$	0	0	1	$\{(2, 64)\}$
$(1, 3, 3)$	0	0	1	$\{(1, 8)\}$
$(2, 6, 6)$	0	0	16	$\{(16, 64)\}$

Table 6. Register Image Right After Coordinator Execution At Time 2

	budget	load	carry	replenish
$(0, 0, 6)$	1	0	0	
$(1, 1, 1)$	1	0	0	
$(0, 3, 6)$	0	0	0	$\{(2, 64)\}$
$(1, 3, 3)$	0	0	1	$\{(1, 8)\}$
$(2, 6, 6)$	0	0	16	$\{(16, 64)\}$

Table 7. Register Image Right After Component Loading At Time 3

	budget	load	carry	replenish
$(0, 0, 6)$	1	0	0	
$(1, 1, 1)$	1	1	0	
$(0, 3, 6)$	0	0	0	$\{(2, 64)\}$
$(1, 3, 3)$	0	0	1	$\{(1, 8)\}$
$(2, 6, 6)$	0	0	16	$\{(16, 64)\}$

ing the different types of workloads in C_0. In contrast, by Harmonic scheduler composition, C_0, C_1 and C_2 can be admitted one by one and served in the same time.

5.4   Analysis

If a component C_h is admitted by the coordinator, then the coordinator will supply resources to C_h according to the supply contract V_h. Assuming that

Table 8. Register Image Right After Coordinator Execution At Time 3

	budget	load	carry	replenish
$(0, 0, 6)$	1	0	0	
$(1, 1, 1)$	0	0	0	$\{(1, 5)\}$
$(0, 3, 6)$	0	0	0	$\{(2, 64)\}$
$(1, 3, 3)$	0	0	1	$\{(1, 8)\}$
$(2, 6, 6)$	0	0	16	$\{(16, 64)\}$

Table 9. Register Image Right After Component Loading At Time 4

	budget	load	carry	replenish
$(0, 0, 6)$	1	1	0	
$(1, 1, 1)$	0	0	0	$\{(1, 5)\}$
$(0, 3, 6)$	0	0	0	$\{(2, 64)\}$
$(1, 3, 3)$	0	0	1	$\{(1, 8)\}$
$(2, 6, 6)$	0	0	16	$\{(16, 64)\}$

Table 10. Register Image Right After Coordinator Execution At Time 4

	budget	load	carry	replenish
$(0, 0, 6)$	0	0	0	$\{(1, 68)\}$
$(1, 1, 1)$	0	0	0	$\{(1, 5)\}$
$(0, 3, 6)$	0	0	0	$\{(2, 64)\}$
$(1, 3, 3)$	0	0	1	$\{(1, 8)\}$
$(2, 6, 6)$	0	0	16	$\{(16, 64)\}$

there is a workload (k, l, w) in V_h, then a server (h, k, l) is established. Within any time interval of length m^l, up to w time units of supply may be loaded to the server, and every demand will obtain supply within m^k units of time since the demand is loaded. We call this the *responsiveness guarantee*. However, if the accumulated load exceeds w time units within a time interval of length m^l, the server is *overloaded* and the responsiveness guarantee will not be provided anymore. The rationale here is that if the component breaks the supply contract by overloading, the coordinator cannot guarantee prompt supply. On the other hand, A non-overloaded server always provides the responsiveness guarantee, even when other servers (including other servers of the same component) are overloaded. We shall prove the responsiveness guarantee.

First, we prove that in a non-overloaded server, load never waits for budget.

Lemma 1. *For a non-overloaded server* (h, k, l), *load* $\leq$ *budget at any non-negative integer time t after budget replenishment.*

Proof: Base Case: At time 0, Register *budget* is initialized to w, and a non-overloading component loads less than or equal to w at time 0. The lemma is true.

Induction case: Assume that for any non-negative integer $t \leq n$, the lemma is true. We now prove that the lemma is still true at time $n+1$ by contradiction.

Assume the contrary: The value of *load* and the value of *budget* at time $n+1$ after replenishment is x and y, and $x > y$.

Let $n' = max(0, (n+1-m^l))$. Assume that the budget consumed after time n' but before or at time n is z, then $y + z = w$;

Because the lemma is true at time n', all loads arrived before or equal to time n' are carried before or at time n', so budget consumed between (n', n) is for load arrived after n' and before or at time n. Because the lemma is true for time n, *load* is decreased to 0 after the execution of the coordinator at time n. Therefore, the aggregate load after time n' and before or at time n is equal to the budget consumption during the the same interval of time, which is z.

Also, the aggregate arrival of load after time n but before or at time $n+1$ is x. The aggregate arrival of load after time n' and before or at time $n+1$ is $x + z$. Thus $x + z > y + z = w$, and the server is overloaded, a contradiction. ∎

A non-negative integer time t is *class k un-carried* if all servers of class k or higher have zero value for *carry* before the coordinator execution at time t. At a class k un-carried time t, all previously loaded in-budget work for servers of class k or higher is completely supplied.

Lemma 2. *If t is a class k un-carried time, then there exists another class k un-carried time t' such that $t' \leq t + m^k$.*

Proof: According to the admission control algorithm, the aggregation of existing budget from all servers of class k or higher at time t before the coordinator execution and replenishment at or after time t and before $t + m^k$ will not exceed $P_k = m^k$. Therefore, the maximal aggregate value that can be added to *carry* of all servers of class k or higher will not exceed m^k. At any integer time t, if there exists a server of class k or higher with *carry* > 0, a supply is drawn from a server with class k or higher made and a *carry* is decreasing. If t' does not exist after time t and before time $t + m^k$, then *carry* is decreased by m^k at or after time t and before $t + m^k$, and time $t + m^k$ must be an class k un-carried time. Therefore the lemma holds. ∎

Theorem 2. *If server (h, k, l) is not overloaded at any time, it provides the responsiveness guarantee.*

Proof: Time 0 is a class k un-carried time. According to Lemma 2, at any time t, there exists another un-carried time t' for class k before or at time $t + m^k$. According to Lemma 1, if component C_h adds *load* at time t, the complete load is moved to *carry* at time t. Because *carry* $= 0$ at time t', the supply corresponding to the demand loaded at time t is made before time t'. Therefore responsiveness guarantee is maintained. ∎

The computational complexity of admission for a component C_h is bounded by $O(K \cdot |V_h|)$, where K is the maximal number of classes, and $|V_h|$ is the number of workloads in the contract which is bounded by K^2. The online coordinator overhead for each time unit is bounded by $O(n \cdot s)$, where n is the number of components and s is the maximal number of servers for a component which is bounded by K^2. Because the period of classes increases exponentially, K should be a small number.

6   Comparison with Related Work

There has been a significant amount of work on compositions in the last few years as has been pointed out in Section 1 of this paper. Instead of using EDF online for scheduling resource supply among components such as is in [2] and [5], our HCC approach distinguishes itself from these previous works by using a rate monotonic classification of workloads; the coordinator applies a fixed priority policy among workload classes. The urgency of workloads from components is expressed by their classes instead of explicit deadlines. The rate monotonic design of HCC makes admission control and budget management simple, yet maintains good composability. Many hard and/or soft real-time scheduling approaches depend on a server budget to control the resource supply to a component to maintain a fair share. Total Bandwidth Server [7] is one example of this approach. Like servers, HCC also makes use of the budget idea. Because HCC is not deadline-based and temporal workload control depends totally on budget control, HCC does not require as much communication (e.g., deadlines of newly arrived jobs) between the system-level scheduler and the component schedulers and is hence a less costly and easier to implement budget-enforcement strategy.

POSIX.4 [4] defines two fixed priority schedulers, which are $SCHD\_FIFO$ and $SCHD\_RR$. For both of them, there may exist multiple fixed priorities, and multiple tasks may be assigned to each priority. The tasks with the same priority are scheduled with First-In-First-Out by $SCHD\_FIFO$, and with Round Robin by $SCHD\_RR$. However, POSIX.4 defines neither priority assignment algorithm nor schedulability guarantee mechanism. Cayssials et al. propose an approach to minimize the number of priorities in a rate-monotonic fixed priority scheme, assuming that multiple tasks may be scheduled on the same priority [1]. HCC not only classifies tasks into priorities but also regulates tasks by servers.

7   Future Work

Whereas the Harmonic Component Composition is a dynamic approach in which the coordinator does not depend on internal knowledge of components, we are also investigating another approach to composition that improves composability and online resource supply efficiency by exploiting *a priori* knowledge of the components. Unlike the approach described in this paper, this alternative approach requires extensive offline computation. We believe that these two composition approaches span the two far ends of a wide spectrum of practical solutions for composing real-time schedulers. There is still much to be explored in the spectrum of solutions by a combination of the approaches. This is a subject for further investigation.

References

1. R.Cayssials, J. Orozco, J.Santos and R.Santos. Rate Monotonic Schedule of Real-Time Control Systems with the Minimum Number of Priority Levels, Euromicro Conference on Real Time Systems, pp. 54-59, 1999.
2. Z. Deng and J. Liu. Scheduling Real-Time Applications in an Open Environment. Real-Time Systems Symposium, pp. 308-319, December 1997.
3. G. Fohler. Joint Scheduling of Distributed Complex Periodic and Hard Aperiodic Tasks in Statically Scheduled Systems, Real-Time Systems Symposium, pp. 152-161, December 1995.
4. IEEE. Portable Operating System Interface(POSIX)—Part 1: Application Program Interface(API) [C Language] —Amendment: Realtime Extensions. IEEE 1-55937-375-X.
5. G. Lipari, J. Carpenter, S. Baruah. A Framework for Archieving Inter-Application Isolation in Multiprogrammed, Hard Real-Time Environment, Real-Time Systems Symposium, pp. 217-226, 2000.
6. A. K. Mok, X. Feng. Towards Compositionality in Real-Time Resource Partitioning Based on Regularity Bounds. Real-Time Systems Symposium, pp. 129-138, 2001.
7. M. Spuri, G. Buttazzo. Scheduling Aperiodic Tasks in Dynamic Priority Systems, Real-Time Systems Journal, Vol,10, pp.179-210, 1996.
8. J. Regehr, J. A. Stankovic. HLS: A Framework for Composing Soft Real-Time Schedulers. Real-Time Systems Symposium, pp. 3-14, 2001.
9. Duu-Chung Tsou. Execution Environment for Real-Time Rule-Based Decision Systems. PhD thesis, Department of Computer Sciences, The University of Texas at Austin, 1997.
10. W. Wang, A. K. Mok, Pre-Scheduling: Balancing Between Static and Dynamic Schedulers, UTCS Technical Report RTS-TR-02-01, 2002, http://www.cs.utexas.edu/users/mok/RTS/pubs.html.

An Approximation Algorithm for Broadcast Scheduling in Heterogeneous Clusters

Pangfeng Liu[1], Da-Wei Wang[2], and Yi-Heng Guo[3]

[1] Department of Computer Science and Information Engineering, National Taiwan University, Taipei, Taiwan
[2] Institute of Information Science, Academia Sinica
[3] Department of Computer Science and Information Engineering, National Chung Cheng University, Chiayi, Taiwan.

Abstract. Network of workstation (NOW) is a cost-effective alternative to massively parallel supercomputers. As commercially available off-the-shelf processors become cheaper and faster, it is now possible to build a PC or workstation cluster that provides high computing power within a limited budget. However, a cluster may consist of different types of processors and this heterogeneity within a cluster complicates the design of efficient collective communication protocols.

This paper shows that a simple heuristic called *fastest-node-first* (FNF) [2] is very effective in reducing broadcast time for heterogeneous cluster systems. Despite the fact that FNF heuristic does not guarantee an optimal broadcast time for general heterogeneous network of workstation, we prove that FNF always gives near optimal broadcast time in a special case of cluster, and this finding helps us show that FNF delivers guaranteed performance for general clusters. In a previous paper we showed a similar bound on the competitive ratio in a send-only communication model. This paper extends the result to a more realistic sender-receiver model. We show that FNF gives a total broadcast of $2T + \beta$, where T is the optimum time and β is a constant. This improves over the previous bound on $2\alpha T + \beta$ [17], where α is a theoretically unbounded ratio of the processor performance in the cluster.

1 Introduction

Network of workstation (NOW) is a cost-effective alternative to massively parallel supercomputers [1]. As commercially available off-the-shelf processors become cheaper and faster, it is now possible to build a PC or workstation cluster that provides high computing power within a limited budget. High performance parallelism is achieved by dividing the computation into manageable subtasks, and distributing these subtasks to the processors within the cluster. These off-the-shelf high-performance processors provide a much higher performance-to-cost ratio so that high performance clusters can be built inexpensively. In addition, the processors can be conveniently connected by industry standard network components. For example, Fast Ethernet technology provides up to 100 Mega bits per second of bandwidth with inexpensive Fast Ethernet adaptors and hubs.

J. Chen and S. Hong (Eds.): RTCSA 2003, LNCS 2968, pp. 38–52, 2004.

Parallel to the development of inexpensive and standardized hardware components for NOW, system software for programming on NOW is also advancing rapidly. For example, the *Message Passing Interface* (MPI) library has evolved into a standard for writing message-passing parallel codes [9,8,13]. An MPI programmer uses a standardized high-level programming interface to exchange information among processes, instead of native machine-specific communication libraries. An MPI programmer can write highly portable parallel codes and run them on any parallel machine (including network of workstation) that has MPI implementation.

Most of the literature on cluster computing emphasizes on *homogeneous* cluster – a cluster consisting of the same type of processors. However, we argue that heterogeneity is one of the key issues that must be addressed in improving parallel performance of NOW. Firstly, it is always the case that one wishes to connect as many processors as possible into a cluster to increase parallelism and reduce execution time. Despite the increased computing power, the scheduling management of such a *heterogeneous network of workstation* (HNOW) becomes complicated since these processors will have different performances in computation and communication. Secondly, since most of the processors that are used to build a cluster are commercially off-the-shelf products, they will very likely be outdated by faster successors before they become unusable. Very often a cluster consists of "leftovers" from the previous installation, and "new comers" that are recently purchased. The issue of heterogeneity is both scientific and economic.

Every workstation cluster, be it homogeneous or heterogeneous, requires efficient collective communication [2]. For example, a barrier synchronization is often placed between two successive phases of computation to make sure that all processors finish the first phase before any can go to the next phase. In addition, a scatter operation distributes input data from the source to all the other processors for parallel processing, then a global reduction operation combines the partial solutions obtained from individual processors into the final answer. The efficiency of these collective communications will affect the overall performance, sometimes dramatically.

Heterogeneity of a cluster complicates the design of efficient collective communication protocols. When the processors send and receive messages at different rates, it is difficult to synchronize them so that the message can arrive at the right processor at the right time for maximum communication throughput. On the other hand, in homogeneous NOW every processor requires the same amount of time to transmit a message. For example, it is straightforward to implement a broadcast operation as a series of sending and receiving messages, and in each phase we double the number of processors that have received the broadcast message. In a heterogeneous environment it is no longer clear how we should proceed to complete the same task.

This paper shows that a simple heuristic called *fastest-node-first* (FNF), introduced by Banikazemi et. al. [2], is very effective in designing broadcast protocols for heterogeneous cluster systems. The fastest-node-first technique schedules the processors to receive the broadcast in the order of their communication speed, that is, the faster node should be scheduled earlier. Despite the fact that the FNF heuristic does *not* guarantee optimal broadcast time for every heterogeneous network of workstations, we show that FNF does give near optimal broadcast time when the communication time of any slower processor in the cluster is a multiple of any faster processor. Based on this result, we show that FNF is actually an approximation algorithm that guarantees a broadcast time within $2T + \beta$, where T is the optimal broadcast time and β is the maximum difference between two processors. This improves over the previous bound $2\alpha T + \beta$ [17] where α is the maximum ratio between receiving and sending costs, and can be arbitrarily large theoretically. In a previous paper [19] we show a similar result for a communication model where the communication cost is determined by the sender only. This paper shows that FNF can still achieve guaranteed performance when the model determines the communication costs based on both the sender and the receiver.

We also conduct experiments on the performance of the fastest-node-first technique. The cluster we construct in our simulation consists of three types of processors, and the number of nodes is 100. We construct the schedules from a random selection and FNF, and apply them on the heterogeneous cluster model. Experimental results indicate that FNF gives superior performance over random selection, for up to 2 times of throughput.

The rest of the paper is organized as follows: Section 2 describes the communication model in our treatment of broadcast problem in HNOW. Section 3 describes the fastest-node-first heuristic for broadcast in HNOW. Section 4 gives the theoretical results for broadcast. Section 5 describe the experimental results that we compare the completion time of our heuristics(FNF) with the random-select algorithms, and Section 6 concludes.

2   Communication Model

There have been two classes of models for collective communication in homogeneous cluster environments. The first group of models assumes that all the processors are fully connected. As a result it takes the same amount of time for a processor to send a message to any other processor. For example, both the Postal model [5] and LogP model [15] use a set of parameters to capture the communication costs. In addition the Postal and LogP model assume that the sender can engage in other activities after a fixed startup cost, during which the sender injects the message into the network and is ready for the next message. Optimal broadcast scheduling for these homogeneous models can be found in [5,15]. The second group of models assume that the processors are connected by an arbitrary network. It has been shown that even when every edge has a unit communication cost (denoted as the Telephone model), finding an optimal broadcast schedule remains NP-hard [10]. Efficient algorithms and network topologies for other similar problems related to broadcast, including multiple broadcast, gossiping and reduction, can be found in [7,11,12,14,18,21,22,23].

Various models for heterogeneous environments have also been proposed in the literature. Bar-Nod et al. introduced a heterogeneous postal model [4] in which the communication costs among links are not uniform. In addition, the sender may engage another communication before the current one is finished, just like homogeneous postal and LogP model. An approximation algorithm for multicast is given, with a competitive ratio $log k$ where k is the number of destination of the multicast [4]. Banikazemi et al. [2] proposed a simple model in which the heterogeneity among processors is characterized by the speed of sending processors, and show that a broadcast technique called *fastest-node-first* works well in practice. We will refer to this model as the *sender-only model*. Based on the sender-only model, an approximation algorithm for reduction with competitive ratio 2 is reported in [20], and the fastest- node-first technique is shown to be also 2-competitive [19]. Despite the fact that the sender-only model is simple and has a high level abstraction of network topology, the speed of the receiving processor is not accounted for. In a refined model proposed by Banikazemi et al. [3], communication overheads consists of both sending and receiving time, which we will refer to as the *sender-receiver* model. For the sender-receiver model the same fastest- node-first is proven (Libeskind-Hadas and Hartline [17]) to have a total time of no more than $2\alpha T + \beta$, where α is the maximum ratio between receiving and sending time, β is the maximum difference between two receiving time, and T is the optimal time. We adopt the sender- receiver model in this paper and improve this bound to $2T + \beta$. Other models for heterogeneous clusters include [6,16].

2.1   Model Definition

The model is defined as follows: A heterogeneous cluster is defined as a collection of processors $p_0, p_1, ..., p_{n-1}$, each capable of point-to-point communication with any other processor in the cluster. Each processor is characterized by its speed of sending and receiving messages, and the network is characterized by the speed to route a message from the source to the destination. Formally, we define the *sending time* of a processor p, denoted by $s(p)$, to be the time it needs for p to send a unit of message into the network. The network is characterized by its latency L, which is the time for the message to go from its source to its destination. Finally we define the *receiving time* of a processor p, denoted by $r(p)$, to be the time it takes for p to retrieve the message from the network interface. We further assume that the processor speed is *consistent*, that is, if a processor p can send messages faster than another processor q, it can also receive the messages faster. Formally we assume that for two processors p and q, $s(p) \leq s(q)$ if and only if $r(p) \leq r(q)$.

The communication model dictates that the sender and receiver processors cannot engage in multiple message transmissions simultaneously. That is, a sender processor must complete its data transmission to the network before sending the next message, that is, a processor can only inject messages into the network at an interval specified by its sending time. This restriction is due to the fact that processor and communication networks have limited bandwidth, therefore we would like to exclude from our model the unrealistic algorithm that a processor simply sends the broadcast message to all the other processors simultaneously. Similarly, the model prohibits the simultaneous receiving of multiple messages by any processor.

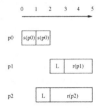

Fig. 1. A broadcast send-receive communication model.

2.2   Broadcast Problem Description

We consider an example with two fast processors p_0, and p_1, and one slow processor p_2. The fast processors have sending time 1 and receiving time 2, the slow processor has sending time 2 and receiving time 3, and the network latency L is 1. We assume that p_0 is the source and that it sends a message to p_2 at time 0. The message enters the network at time 1 since $s(p_0)$ is 1, and leaves the network at time $1 + L = 2$, and is received by p_2 at time $2 + r(p_2) = 5$. After sending a message into the network at time 1, p_0 can immediately send another message to p_1 and inject it into the network at time $1 + s(p_0) = 2$. The message is finally received by p_1 at time $2 + L + r(p_1) = 5$. See Figure 1 for an illustration.

2.3   Simplified Model Description

We can simplify the model as follows: Since a receiving node p always has to wait for $L + r(p)$ time steps before it actually receives the message, we can add the network latency L into the receiving time. The processor p_2 therefore receives its message at time $s(p_0) + r(p_2) = 1 + 4 = 5$, and p_1 receives its message from p_0 at time $2s(p_0) + r(p_1) = 5$. See Figure 2 for an illustration.

Assume that a processor q sends a message to the other processor p at time t, then p becomes *ready to receive* at time $t + s(q)$, since p now can start receiving the message, and we denote the ready to receive time of p by $R(p)$. At time $t + s(q) + r(p)$ p becomes *ready to send* because it can start sending its own message now, and we use $S(p)$ to denote the ready to send time of p. That is, a processor p can finish sending messages into the network at time $S(p) + s(p), S(p) + 2s(p), ..., S(p) + i * s(p)$, where i is a positive integer, until the broadcast is finished.

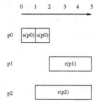

Fig. 2. A simplified send-receive communication model.

3   Fastest-Node-First Technique

It is difficult to find the optimal broadcast tree that minimizes the total broadcast time in a heterogeneous cluster, therefore a simple heuristic called *fastest-node-first* (FNF) is proposed in [2] to find a reasonably good broadcast schedule for the original sender-only heterogeneous model [2].

3.1   Fastest-Node-First Scheduling for Broadcast

The FNF heuristic works as follows: In each iteration the algorithm chooses a sender from the set of processors that have received the broadcast message (denoted by A), and a receiver from the set that have not (denoted by B). The algorithm picks the sender s from A because, as the chosen one, it can inject the message into the network as early as possible. The algorithm then chooses the fastest processor in B as the destination of s. After the assignment, r is moved from B to A and the algorithm iterates to find the next sender/receiver pair. Note that this same technique can be applied to both models – the sender only and the sender-receiver heterogeneous models – since we assume that the sending and receiving times are consistent among processors. The intuition behind this heuristic is that, by sending the message to those fast processors first, it is likely that the messages will propagate more rapidly.

The fastest-node-first technique is very effective in reducing broadcast time [2,17,19]. The FNF has been shown in simulation to have a high probability to find the optimal broadcast time when the transmission time is randomly chosen from a given table [2]. The FNF technique also delivers good communication efficiency in actual experiments. In addition, FNF is simple to implement and easy to compute.

3.2   FNF Not Guarantee Optimal Broadcast Time

Despite its efficiency in scheduling broadcast in heterogeneous systems, the FNF heuristic does not guarantee optimal broadcast time [2,6] in sender-only model. Since the sender-only model is a special case of the sender-receiver model, FNF is not optimal in the sender-receiver model either. For example, in the situation of Figure 1 FNF will not achieve optimal time, as Figure 3 indicates.

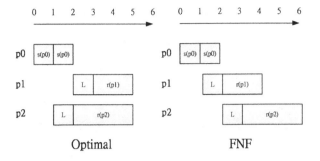

Fig. 3. A counterexample that FNF always produces the optimal broadcast time since the fast processor p_0 sends message to the faster p_1 first, instead of the slower p_2.

4   Theoretical Results

Despite the fact that FNF cannot guarantee optimal broadcast time, we show that FNF is optimal in some special cases of heterogeneous clusters. Based on the results of these special cases, we show that the fastest-node-first algorithm produces a schedule with guaranteed performance.

Theorem 1. [2]

There exists an optimal schedule in which all processors sends messages without delay. That is, for all processor p in T, starting from its ready to send time, p repeatedly sends a message with a period of its sending time until the broadcast ends.

With Theorem 1, we can simply discard those schedules that will delay messages, and still find the optimal one. Since there is no delay, we can characterize a schedule as a sequence of processors sorted in their *ready to receive time*. Since no delay is allowed, any scheduling method must schedule s, the processor in A that could have completed the sending at the earliest time, to send a message immediately. Formally we define $P = (p_0, ..., p_{n-1})$ to be a sequence of n processors sorted in their ready to receive time and the processors appear in P in non-decreasing sending speed, except for the source s_0. The total broadcast time of P (denoted by $T(P)$) is by definition $\max_{i=1}^{n-1} S(p_i)$, the latest *ready to send* time among all the processors[1]. A broadcast sequence P is *optimal* if and only if for any other permutation of P (denoted by P'), $T(P) \leq T(P')$.

Let p be a processor and $NS_P(p, t)$ be the *number* of messages successfully *sent* at and before time t by p in the sequence P. Formally, $NS_P(p, t) = \lfloor \frac{t - S(p)}{s(p)} \rfloor$, for $t \geq S(p)$. We can define ready to receive time $R(p_i)$ and ready to send time $S(p_i)$ recursively (Eqn. 1). that is, the ready to receive time of the i-th processor in P is the earliest time when the total number of messages sent by the first $i - 1$ processors reaches i.

---

[1] Note that the processor that has the latest ready to receive time may not have the latest ready to send time.

$$R(p_0) = 0 \quad \text{and} \quad S(p_0) = 0$$

$$R(p_i) = \min\{t| \sum_{j=0}^{i-1} NS_P(p_j, t) \geq i\}, \quad 1 \leq i \leq n-1$$

$$S(p_i) = R(p_i) + r(p_i), \quad 1 \leq i \leq n-1 \tag{1}$$

4.1   Power 2 Clusters

In this section we consider a special case of heterogeneous clusters in which all the sending and receiving costs are power of 2, and we refer to such clusters as power 2 clusters [19]. Similar notation is also used in [17]. We show that FNF technique does guarantee minimum ready to receive time for the last processor receiving the broadcast message in a power 2 cluster, and this is the foundation of our competitive ratio analysis.

Henceforth we will focus on minimizing the ready to receive time of the last processor in a sequence $P = (p_0, ..., p_{n-1})$, which is denoted as $TR(P) = R(p_{n-1})$. We will later relate our finding with the latest ready to send time among all the processors, denoted by $TS(P) = \max_{i=0}^{n-1} S(p_i)$, which is the time the broadcast actually takes. We choose this approach since $TR(P)$ is much easier to handle in our mathematical analysis than $TS(P)$.

We first establish a lemma that it is always possible to switch a processor p with a slower processor q that became ready to receive right ahead of p (with the exception that q is the source) so that p and q will contribute more on the NS function after the switch. We then use an induction to show that this modification will not increase the ready to receive time of the processors thereafter, including the last one in the sequence. This leads to the optimality of FNF for the last ready to receive time in a power 2 cluster.

Lemma 1. *Let p be a first faster processor that became ready to receive right after a slower processor q in a sequence P, that is, $R(p) = t_1 > R(q) = t_0$, and $s(p) < s(q)$. By switching p with q in P we obtain a new sequence P'. Then, in this new sequence P', $R(p)$ is moved forward from t_1 to t_0, and $R(q)$ is delayed from t_0 to no later than t_1, and $NS_{P'}(p, t) + NS_{P'}(q, t) \geq NS_P(p, t) + NS_P(q, t)$, for $t \geq t_0$.*

Proof. Let's consider the time interval from t_0 to t_1. Since p is the first faster processor that becomes ready to receive *right after* a slower processor q, no processor becomes ready to receive between t_0 and t_1. Since, in P', p is moved to q's position in P, p has $R(p) = t_0$. As p is faster in sending *and* receiving, q becomes ready at or before t_1 from Equation 1. For our purpose we will assume that q becomes ready to receive at time t_1 since if the time is earlier, it is more likely that $NS_{P'}(p, t) + NS_{P'}(q, t) \geq NS_P(p, t) + NS_P(q, t)$, for $t \geq t_0$.

Let $d = t_1 - t_0$. Since all the ready to receive time is integer, d is at least 1. It is easy to see that when d is larger, $NS_{P'}(p, t) + NS_{P'}(q, t)$ is more likely to be larger than $NS_S(p, t) + NS_S(q, t)$, when $t > t_0$. In fact, from p's point of view, when the sequence changes from P to P', the $NS(p)$ increases between

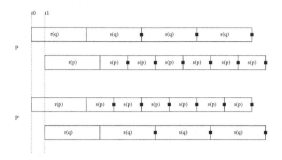

Fig. 4. An illustration that the NS function in P and P'. The black squares indicate where the NS function increases by 1. Note that the NS function in P' is no less than in P for all time later than t_0. In this example $r(p) = r(q) = 4$, $s(p) = 2$, $s(q) = 4$, and $d = 1$.

$\lfloor \frac{d}{s(p)} \rfloor$ and $\lceil \frac{d}{s(p)} \rceil$, but the decrease in $NS(q)$ is only between $\lfloor \frac{d}{s(q)} \rfloor$ and $\lceil \frac{d}{s(q)} \rceil$. The increase in $NS(p)$ is larger than the decrease in $NS(q)$ when d is sufficiently large, since $s(q)$ is at least twice as large as $s(p)$. In addition, $r(p)$ is no larger than $r(q)$, and that means $NS(p)$ increases earlier than the decrease of $NS(q)$. Therefore, by moving p further ahead in time, it becomes easier for the increase of the NS function from p to compensate the decrease of the NS function from q, when the sequence changes from P to P'. Therefore it suffices to consider the worst case when $d = 1$.

Let us consider the change of NS function from q's point of view. q is delayed by only one time step, so $NS_S(q)$ is at most greater than $NS_{S'}(q)$ by 1, which only happens at time interval $[t_0 + r(q) + ks(q), t_0 + r(q) + ks(q) + 1)$, where k is a positive integer, $r(q)$ is the receiving time of q, and $s(q)$ is the sending time of q. See Figure 4 for an illustration. However, during this interval $NS_{P'}(p)$ will be larger than $NS_P(p)$ by one since $s(q)$ is a multiple of $s(p)$, and $r(q)$ is a multiple of $r(p)$ due to speed consistency. This increase compensates the decrease due to q and the Lemma follows.

After establishing the effects of exchanging the two processors on the NS function, we argue that the ready to receive time of the processors after p and q will not be delayed from P to P'. We prove this statement by an induction and the following lemma serves as the induction base:

Lemma 2. *Let p and q be the $(j-1)^{th}$ and j^{th} processor in P, then the ready to receive time of p_{j+1} in P' is no later than in P.*

Proof. The lemma follows from Lemma 1 and the fact that the ready to receive time of the first $j+1$ processors in the sequence is not changed, except for p and q. Here we use the subscript to indicate whether the NS function is defined on P or P', and for ease of notation we remove the same second parameter t from all occurrences of NS functions.

$$R_{P'}(p_{j+1}) = \min\{t| \sum_{l=0}^{j} NS_{P'}(p_l) \geq j+1\}$$

$$= \min\{t|(\sum_{l=0}^{j-2} NS_{P'}(p_l)) + NS_{P'}(p) + NS_{P'}(q) \geq j+1\}$$

$$= \min\{t|(\sum_{l=0}^{j-2} NS_{P}(p_l)) + NS_{P'}(p) + NS_{P'}(q) \geq j+1\}$$

$$\leq \min\{t|(\sum_{l=0}^{j-2} NS_{P}(p_l)) + NS_{P}(p) + NS_{P}(q) \geq j+1\}$$

$$= R_P(p_{j+1})$$

Lemma 3. *The ready to receive time of p_l in P' is no later than in P, for $j+1 \leq l \leq n-1$.*

Proof. We complete the proof by the induction step. Assume that the ready to receive time of p_{j+m} in P' is no later than in P, for $1 \leq m \leq n-j-1$. Again for ease of notation, we remove the same second parameter t from all occurrences of NS functions.

$$R_{P'}(p_{j+m+1})$$

$$= \min\{t| \sum_{l=0}^{j+m} NS_{P'}(p_l) \geq j+m+1\}$$

$$= \min\{t|((\sum_{l=0}^{j-2} NS_{P'}(p_l)) + NS_{P'}(p) + NS_{P'}(q) + \sum_{l=j+1}^{j+m} NS_{P'}(p_l)) \geq j+m+1\}$$

$$\leq \min\{t|((\sum_{l=0}^{j-2} NS_{P}(p_l)) + NS_{P}(p) + NS_{P}(q) + \sum_{l=j+1}^{j+m} NS_{P'}(p_l)) \geq j+m+1\}$$

$$\leq \min\{t|((\sum_{l=0}^{j-2} NS_{P}(p_l)) + NS_{P}(p) + NS_{P}(q) + \sum_{l=j+1}^{j+m} NS_{P}(p_l)) \geq j+m+1\}$$

$$= R_P(p_{j+m+1})$$

The second-to-the-last inequality follows from Lemma 1, and the last inequality follows from the induction hypothesis that all the processors from p_{j+1} to p_{j+m} have earlier ready to receive time (hence earlier ready to send time) in P' than in P, so they will have larger NS function, and a smaller t to satisfy Equation 1. One immediate result from Lemma 2 and 3 is that for any processor sequence of a power 2 cluster, including the optimal ones, the final ready to receive time will never be increased by making the faster processors ready to receive earlier than slower ones. Now we have the following theorem:

Theorem 2. *The fastest-node-first algorithm gives optimal final ready to receive time for a power 2 cluster.*

4.2   An Approximation Algorithm

We can use Theorem 2 to show that FNF is actually an approximation algorithm of competitive ratio 2 for the final ready to receive time. By increasing the transmission time of processors, we can transform any heterogeneous cluster into a power 2 cluster. We increase the sending and receiving time of each processor p to be $2^{\lceil \log s(p) \rceil}$ and $2^{\lceil \log r(p) \rceil}$ respectively. We will show that FNF, optimal for the transformed cluster, also gives a schedule at most twice that of the optimal final ready to receive time for the original cluster.

Theorem 3. *The fastest-node-first scheduling has a final ready to receive time no greater than twice that of the optimal final ready to receive time.*

Proof. Let P be a sequence that gives optimal final ready to receive time for a heterogeneous cluster C, and C' be the power 2 cluster transformed from C. We apply the same sequence P on C and C' and let T and T' be the final ready to receive time TR respectively, that is, before and after the power 2 cluster transformation. We argue that this increase in transmission time will at most double the TR, that is, $T' \le 2T$. This is achieved by an induction on the processor index i. We argue that p_i, which is ready to receive at time $R(p_i)$ for C, becomes ready to receive no later then $2R(p_i)$ for C'. The induction step follows from the fact that all the previous p_j for $j < i$, become ready no later than $2R(p_j)$ for C', and that both the sending time of the previous p_j, $j < i$, and the receiving time of p_i are, at most doubled from C to C'.

Now we apply FNF scheduling on C' and let T'' be the resulting final ready to receive time. Since C' is a power 2 cluster, it follows from Theorem 2 that T'' is no more than T'. Finally, we apply the same FNF scheduling on C and let T^* be the resulting final ready to receive time. T^* should be no more than T'' since the sending and receiving times of each corresponding processor are higher in C' than in C. As a result T^* is no greater than T'', which in turn is no greater than T', which in turn is no more than $2T$.

Theorem 4. *The total broadcast time from fast-node-first technique is at most $2T + \beta$, where T is the optimal total broadcast time, and β is $\max\{r(p_i)\} - 2\min\{r(p_i)\}$.*

Proof. Let P be an optimal schedule in total broadcast time. Let p be the last processor that became ready to receive in P. As a result the optimal total broadcast time T is at least $R_P(p) + r(p)$. Let p' be the last processor that became ready to receive according to FNF. From Theorem 3 we have $R_{P'}(p') < 2R_P(p)$. Note that this inequality holds when P is any schedule, and not necessarily the optimal schedule for the final ready to receive time. The total broadcast time using FNF is $R_{P'}(p') + r(p')$, which is at most $2R_P(p) + r(p') = 2R_P(p) + 2r(p) + r(p') - 2r(p) \le 2T + \beta$.

5 Experimental Results

This section describes the experimental results and compare the completion times of our heuristics (FNF) with those of a random-selection algorithm and a trivial lower bound. The experimental results indicate that FNF outperforms the random-selection algorithm by a factor of 2 in average, and is not very far away from the lower bound.

5.1 Experimental Environment

The input cluster configurations for our experiments are generated as follow: We assume that the number of classes in a cluster is 3. We vary the cluster size from 6 to 100, and set one third of the nodes to be fast processors, one third to be normal processors, and the others to be slow processors. For each processor in the same class, we assign the same sending time and receiving cost to it, that is, each node in the fast processor group has sending time 1 and receiving time 2, the sending and receiving time for normal processors are 5 and 6 respectively, finally the time for slow processors are 10 and 11.

We compare the results from FNF and random selection. We repeat the experiments for random-selection algorithm for 200 times and compute the average broadcast time. On the other hand since FNF is a deterministic algorithm, for each cluster size we test the FNF algorithm for only once.

5.2 FNF Heuristics and Random-Select Algorithm

We describe our implementation of FNF as follows: The program uses an array to represent the set of processors that have not yet received broadcast message (denoted by R-set), and a priority queue for the set of processors that have received the broadcast message (denoted by S-set). The elements in the R-set array are sorted according to their communication speed, and the elements in the S-set are ordered so that the processor that could send out the next message fastest has the highest priority. In other words, the processors in the S-set are sorted according to their availability in time. Initially the S-set has the broadcast source and the R-set is empty, and the simulation time is set to zero. The priority queue design simplifies and speeds up the simulation, since the simulator can be driven by events, not by time.

In each iteration we check if all nodes have received the broadcast message. If this is not the case then we will schedule the next message. We pick the next sender (with the highest priority) from the S-set priority queue, and the receiver that has the minimum receiving time from the R-set. After choosing the sender and the receiver, we calculate the updated available time for the sender and new available time for the receiver, and place them into the S-Set (the chosen receiver is therefore removed from the R-set). At the end the R-set will be empty and the ready-to-send time of the last receiver is the total broadcast time. Figure 5 gives an example of a broadcast scheduling among 6 node.

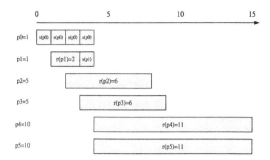

Fig. 5. The example of FNF algorithm under 6 node case.

We now describe the random-selection algorithm. Due to the random nature of this algorithm, we will not need to maintain any priority queue or sorted array. We randomly choose a sender from the S-set and a receiver from the R-set for the next message. We repeatedly schedule the transmission until all processors receive the message. The average time for the last receiver to receive its messages is the time that we are interested in.

5.3   Timing Comparison

Figure 6 shows the experimental results. The completion time of FNF is about half of the average time of random-selection algorithm.

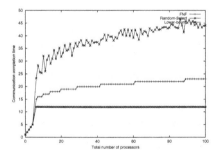

Fig. 6. The comparison of two scheduling algorithms.

We also give a lower bound on the optimal communication time for our experimental cluster. No matter how the processors are scheduled, the broadcast source must spend at least one unit of time to send the message, and a slow destination processor must at least spend eleven units of time to receive the message. As a result, the lower bound is at least 12 Figure 6 shows that the total time of FNF is no more than twice that of the lower bound in our experiments.

From our experiments, we observed that it is almost impossible to find a single case from 200 times of random-selection that gives a better broadcast time than the FNF algorithm. In addition, the broadcast time of the FNF algorithm might be very close to optimal since our lower bound estimate is very rough. These timing results also indicate that the completion time grows very slowly when the size of the cluster increases, even when the cluster has up to 100 processors. Our experimental results are consistent with those obtained by previous theoretical sections. In addition, the FNF schedule is very easy to compute and efficient to use.

6   Conclusion

FNF is a very useful technique in reducing broadcast time. In a previous paper we show that FNF gives a broadcast schedule at most twice that of the optimal time for the sender-only communication model[19]. For a more realistic sender-receiver model adapted by this paper, we show that FNF gives a broadcast schedule at most twice that of the optimal time plus a constant. This improves over the previous bound by a performance ratio factor. In practice this factor is bounded by 1.85 [17], but could be unbounded theoretically.

We also describe the experimental results in which we compare the completion time of our heuristics (FNF) with a random-selection algorithm. The experimental results indicate that FNF outperforms the random-selection algorithm by a factor of 2 in average. In addition, we also compare the timing results of FNF with a very roughly estimated lower bound, and FNF always gives a total broadcast time within twice of the lower bound.

There are many research issues open for investigation. For example, it will be interesting to extend this technique to other communication protocols, including reduction and all-to-all communication. For example, we showed that for reduction there is a technique called "slowest-node-first" [20] that also guarantees 2-competitiveness in sender-only model. It would be interesting to extend the result to the sender-receiver model, as we did for broadcasting in this paper. In addition, it will be worthwhile to investigate the possibility to extend the analysis to similar protocols like parallel prefix, all-to-all reduction, or all-to-all broadcasting. These questions are very fundamental in designing collective communication protocols in heterogeneous clusters, and will certainly be the focus of further investigations in this area.

References

1. T. Anderson, D. Culler, and D. Patterson. A case for networks of workstations (now). In *IEEE Micro*, Feb 1995.
2. M. Banikazemi, V. Moorthy, and D.K. Panda. Efficient collective communication on heterogeneous networks of workstations. In *Proceedings of International Parallel Processing Conference*, 1998.
3. M. Banikazemi, J. Sampathkumar, S. Prabhu, D. Panda, and P. Sadayappan. Communication modeling of heterogenous networks of workstations for performance characterization of collective operations. In *Proceedings of International Workshop on Heterogeneous Computing*, 1999.

4. A. Bar-Noy, S. Guha, J. Naor, and Schieber B. Multicast in heterogeneous networks. In *Proceedings of the 13th Annual ACM Symposium on theory of computing*, 1998.
5. A. Bar-Noy and S. Kipnis. Designing broadcast algorithms in the postal model for message-passing systems. *Mathematical Systems Theory*, 27(5), 1994.
6. P.B. Bhat, C.S. Raghavendra, and V.K. Prasanna. Efficient collective communication in distributed heterogeneous systems. In *Proceedings of the International Conference on Distributed Computing Systems*, 1999.
7. M. Dinneen, M. Fellows, and V. Faber. Algebraic construction of efficient networks. *Applied Algebra, Algebraic Algorithms, and Error Correcting codes*, 9(LNCS 539), 1991.
8. J. Bruck et al. Efficient message passing interface(mpi) for parallel computing on clusters of workstations. *Journal of Parallel and Distributed Computing*, Jan 1997.
9. Message Passing Interface Forum. MPI: A message-passing interface standard. Technical Report UT-CS-94-230, 1994.
10. M. R. Garey and D. S. Johnson. *Computer and Intractability: A guide to the theory of NP-Completeness*. W. H. Freeman, 1979.
11. L. Gargang and U. Vaccaro. On the construction of minimal broadcast networks. *Network*, 19, 1989.
12. M. Grigni and D. Peleg. Tight bounds on minimum broadcast networks. *SIAM J. Discrete Math.*, 4, 1991.
13. W. Gropp, E. Lusk, N. Doss, and A. Skjellum. High-performance, portable implementation of the MPI Message Passing Interface Standard. *Parallel Computing*, 22(6):789–828, 1996.
14. S. M. Hedetniemi, S. T. Hedetniem, and A. L. Liestman. A survey of gossiping and broadcasting in communication networks. *Networks.*, 18, 1991.
15. R. Karp, A. Sahay, E. Santos, and K. E. Schauser. Optimal broadcast and summation in the logp model. In *Proceedings of 5th Ann. Symposium on Parallel Algorithms and Architectures*, 1993.
16. R. Kesavan, K. Bondalapati, and D. Panda. Multicast on irregular switch-based networks with wormhole routing. In *Proceedings of International Symposium on high performance computer architecture*, 1997.
17. R. Libeskind-Hadas and J. Hartline. Efficient multicast in heterogeneous networks of wrokstations. In *Proceedings of 2000 International Workshop on Parallel Processing*, 2000.
18. A. L. Liestman and J. G. Peters. Broadcast networks of bounded degree. *SIAM J. Discrete Math.*, 1, 1988.
19. P. Liu. Broadcast scheduling optimization for heterogeneous cluster systems. *Journal of Algorithms*, 42, 2002.
20. P. Liu and D. Wang. Reduction optimization in heterogeneous cluster environments. In *Proceedings of the International Parallel and Distributed Processing Symposium*, 2000.
21. D. Richards and A. L. Liestman. Generalization of broadcast and gossiping. *Networks*, 18, 1988.
22. J.A. Ventura and X. Weng. A new method for constructing minimal broadcast networks. *Networks*, 23, 1993.
23. D. B. West. A class of solutions to the gossip problem. *Discrete Math.*, 39, 1992.

Scheduling Jobs with Multiple Feasible Intervals

Chi-sheng Shih[1], Jane W.S. Liu[2], and Infan Kuok Cheong[3]

[1] University of Illinois, Urbana IL 61801, USA
cshih@uiuc.edu
[2] Microsoft Corporation, Redmond, WA 98052, USA
janeliu@microsoft.com
[3] BMC Software, Inc., Austin, Texas 78759, USA
Infan_Cheong@bmc.com

Abstract. This paper addresses the problem of scheduling real-time jobs that have multiple feasible intervals. The problem is NP-hard. We present an optimal branch-and-bound algorithm. When there is time to compute the schedule, this algorithm can be used. Otherwise, the simple heuristics presented here can be used. In addition, a priority-boosting EDF algorithm is designed to enhance the timeliness of jobs. Simulation results show that the combined use of the heuristics and the priority boosting EDF algorithm performs nearly as well as the optimal algorithm.

1 Introduction

In some real-time applications, a job may have more than one feasible interval. Such a job can be scheduled to begin its execution in any of its feasible intervals. It is said to complete in time if the job completes by the end of the interval. If the job remains incomplete at the end of the interval, the scheduler terminates the job, and the partial work done by the job is lost. The scheduler then schedules the job to execute from the start in a later feasible interval. The job misses its deadline if it remains incomplete by the end of its latest feasible interval.

An example of such an application is missile jamming. A missile jamming system tries to intercept each cruise missile before it hits its target by jamming the missile's guidance system. In general, a cruise missile flies for a long distance and may pass several jamming-prohibited areas, such as metropolitan areas, before reaching its target. Destroying the missile's guidance system close to such an area may cause unacceptably large collateral damages. Hence, the missile can be jammed only before or after it flies over these areas. The time intervals when the missile is not over or close to any jamming-prohibited area are the feasible intervals of the job. The starts and ends of the intervals are either known a prior or can be estimated from past information. The jamming job only needs to be executed to completion once in one of its feasible intervals.

The optional jobs in the error-cumulative imprecise computation model studied by Choeng[1] are also examples of jobs with multiple feasible intervals. In the imprecise computation model, a job consists of two parts: mandatory and optional part. The mandatory part must complete by its deadline and the optional

J. Chen and S. Hong (Eds.): RTCSA 2003, LNCS 2968, pp. 53–71, 2004.

part can be skipped if there are not enough resources. Skipping the optional part introduces error into the result produced by the job. In some real-time applications like radar tracking, the error from the incomplete optional parts of jobs in a periodic task accumulates. The error-cumulative model introduces a threshold for the cumulative error of the task. When the cumulative error becomes greater than the threshold, the task fails. (In a radar tracking system, the system may lost the tracked target if the cumulative error becomes greater than a given threshold.) To confine the error within the threshold, the optional part must execute completely at least once in every predetermined number N of periods. We can view the optional part of one job in N periods as a job with N feasible intervals, which are intervals left over after the mandatory parts of the jobs complete. As long as the job with N feasible intervals completes in time, the error of the periodic task is under the allowed threshold.

Our model resembles real-time workload models that allow some jobs to be skipped. Examples of these models are the skip-over model [2], reward-based model [3], (error-cumulative) imprecise computation model [1,4], and (m,k)-firm guarantee model [5]. However, these models are concerned with periodic tasks. The relative deadlines of (optional) jobs in all periods of a task are the same. Optional jobs are not required to complete in some of these models: These jobs can be terminated at any time or discarded entirely and produce results with different levels of precision. In contrast, our model assumes that the length of feasible intervals (i.e., the relative deadlines) are arbitrary. This factor introduces another dimension of complexity. In addition, jobs are not optional: Each job must execute from start to completion in one of its feasible intervals, and the job fails to meet its timing requirement if it does not complete by the end of its latest feasible interval.

This paper presents an exponential optimal algorithm and several simple heuristics for finding a feasible schedule for jobs with multiple feasible intervals. The optimal algorithm uses the branch and bound approach to reduce the time required for finding a feasible schedule for a given job set. This algorithm is optimal in the sense that there is no feasible schedule if the algorithm cannot find one. These heuristics are extensions of traditional bin-packing heuristics: First Fit Decreasing (FFD), Last Fit Decreasing (LFD), Best Fit Decreasing (BFD), and Worst Fit Decreasing (WFD).

The paper also presents a priority-boosting EDF algorithm that is designed to enhance the timeliness of jobs. The algorithm makes use of the result produced by the optimal algorithm or a heuristic algorithm, which is the selection of a feasible interval for each job that is schedulable. According to the priority-boosting EDF algorithm, jobs are prioritized based on (1) the feasible interval selected for each job and (2) job deadlines: The closer the selected feasible interval of a job is to the scheduling time, the higher priority of the job. The heuristics and the priority-boosting algorithm are evaluated by extensive simulations. The performances are compared against that of the optimal algorithm.

Following this introduction, Section 2 describes the task model and defines the terms used here. The section also states the problems of scheduling jobs with multiple feasible intervals. Section 3 presents an exponential optimal algorithm, several polynomial-time heuristics, and the priority-boosting EDF algorithm. Section 4 evaluates the heuristics and the combined use of the heuristics and the priority-boosting EDF algorithm. Finally, Section 5 summarizes the paper.

2 Formal Models and Problem Statements

Thus far, and in our subsequent discussion, we use the term job as it is commonly used in real-time systems literature [6,7,8]: A *job* is an instance of computation, or the transmission of a data packet, or the retrieval of a file, and so on. We focus here on scheduling jobs and call the jobs J_1, J_2, and so on.

Multiple Feasible Interval Jobs. Each multiple feasible interval job is characterized by its temporal parameters including its execution time, release time, and a set of feasible intervals. The *execution time*, denoted by e, is the amount of time required to complete the execution of the job when it executes alone and has all the resources it requires. Throughout our discussion, we assume that for the purpose of determining whether each job can complete by its deadline, knowing its worst case execution time (WCET) is sufficient. By the execution time of a job, we mean its WCET.

The *release time* of a job, denoted by r, is the instant of time at which the job becomes known to the scheduler. A job is said to be *eligible* in the time interval from its release time to the instant when the job completes.

Associated with each job is a set of disjoint time intervals, called *feasible intervals*. The earliest feasible interval of a job begins at or after its release time. The job can be scheduled and executed only in its feasible intervals. Once a job begins to execute in a feasible interval, it must complete by the end of the interval in order to produce a correct result. The scheduler may terminate the job (and the partial work done by the job is lost) if the job remains incomplete at the end of the interval. In that case, the scheduler will reschedule the job to execute from the start in a later feasible interval of the job if such an interval exists. In this paper, we assume that the scheduler always terminates the job at the end of its feasible interval if it remains incomplete at the time, regardless whether it has a later feasible interval or not.

We denote each feasible interval by $FI = (L, R]$ where L and R represents the start time and end time of the interval, respectively. We use $FI_{i,j}$ to denote the j-th feasible interval of job J_i. The set of feasible intervals of job J_i is denoted by $\mathbf{FI}_i = \{FI_{i,1}, FI_{i,2}, \ldots, F_{i,n(i)}\}$ where $n(i)$ is the number of feasible intervals of job J_i and intervals in the set are indexed in ascending order of their start times. We represent a multiple feasible interval job J_i by $J_i = (r_i, e_i, \mathbf{FI}_i)$. We focus on this kind of jobs. Hereafter, we omit "multiple feasible interval" as long as there is no ambiguity.

Figure 1 shows an example. Each box above a time line represents a feasible interval. In this example, job J_1 has only one feasible interval; job J_2 has two feasible intervals; and job J_3 and J_4 have three feasible intervals. Traditional

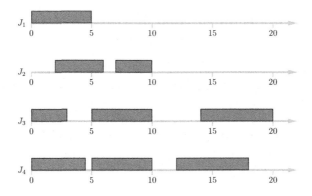

$$\mathbf{J} = \{J_1, J_2, J_3, J_4\}$$
$$J_1 = (0, 1.5, \{(0, 5]\})$$
$$J_2 = (2, 2, \{(2, 6], (7, 10]\})$$
$$J_3 = (0, 2, \{(0, 3.5], (5, 10], (14, 20]\})$$
$$J_4 = (0, 3, \{(0, 4.5], (5, 10], (12, 18]\})$$

Fig. 1. Example of multiple feasible interval jobs

real-time workload models consider only jobs exemplified by job J_1. At any time t, the term current feasible interval of a job refers to the interval which begins before t and ends after or at t. Clearly, a job may not have a current feasible interval at t.

The *absolute deadline* of a job is the instant of time by which its execution is required to be completed. For a multiple feasible interval job, we can consider the end time of each feasible interval as an absolute deadline of that job. In other words, a job with $n(i)$ feasible intervals has $n(i)$ absolute deadlines. By the absolute deadline of a job at time t, we mean the end time of the current feasible interval of the job if the job has current feasible interval at time t. The deadline of a job at t is infinite if the job does not have current feasible interval at t. Hereafter, we use the term deadline to mean absolute deadline and denote it by d.

System workload, denoted by $u(t)$, is the total instantaneous utilization of eligible jobs in the system at time t. The instantaneous utilization of a multiple feasible interval job at time t is equal to its execution time divided by the length of its current feasible interval if it has current feasible interval at time t. The instantaneous utilization of the job is zero if it does not have a current feasible interval.

We call a failed attempt to complete the execution of a job in one of its feasible intervals a *deadline miss*. More precisely, a deadline miss occurs at the end of a feasible interval if a job executes in the feasible interval and remains incomplete at that time. The following definition states the timing constraint of a job with multiple feasible intervals.

Definition 1 (In-Time Completion).

An execution of a job J completes in time if and only if there is no deadline miss between the time when it starts and the time when it completes. A job J meets its timing constraint, or simply that it completes in time, if and only if one of its execution completes in time.

When every job only has one feasible interval, Definition 2.1 is same as the traditional definition of in-time completion.

Problem Formulation. The problem of scheduling jobs with multiple feasible intervals can be divided into two problems: feasible interval selection and job scheduling. Since each job must be executed entirely in one of its feasible intervals, the scheduler may first choose for the job an interval among all the feasible intervals of the job. The feasible interval selection problem is concerned with how to make this selection. At any time in a system containing jobs with multiple feasible intervals, eligible jobs may or may not be in their selected feasible intervals and all eligible jobs compete for the same resources. The job scheduling problem is concerned with how to schedule these jobs if the scheduler aims to achieve other performance goals in addition to ensuring the in-time completion of every job.

These problems are stated more formally below.

1. Feasible Interval Selection: Given a set of multiple feasible interval jobs, $\mathbf{J} = \{J_1, J_2, ..., J_M\}$, we want to find a feasible interval $FI_i \in \mathbf{FI}_i$ for each job J_i such that all jobs can meet their real-time requirements defined by Definition 2.1 when every job executes only in its selected feasible interval. We refer to such a set of selected intervals collectively as a feasible (interval) selection.

2. Multiple Feasible Interval Job Scheduling: Given a set of multiple-feasible interval jobs, $\mathbf{J} = \{J_1, J_2, ..., J_M\}$, and the selected feasible interval FI_i for each job J_i, we want to schedule these jobs so that they all complete in-time and their response times are small.

If scheduling is done off-line or the release times of all jobs are identical, the timing parameters of all jobs are known when the scheduler selects feasible intervals for them. For this case, we seek a branch-and-bound optimal algorithm for use when there is time to search for a feasible selection and simple heuristics for use when there is little time to do search for a selection. In general, the jobs are not released at the same time or the timing parameters are not available until the jobs are released. In this case, the branch-and-bound feasible interval selection algorithm is not suitable. The heuristics are simple enough for use repeatedly when jobs are released.

In our subsequent discussion, we assume that the jobs are to be executed on a single processor. Since the preemptive EDF algorithm is known to be optimal for uniprocessor scheduling, we assume that the scheduler uses this algorithm. This simplifying assumption can be easily removed by including a schedulability analysis algorithm that is appropriate for the scheduling scheme used by the system.

3 Algorithms

In this section, we first show that the problem of selecting a feasible interval for every job in a set of multiple feasible interval jobs so that all jobs complete in time is NP-hard. We then present an exponential optimal algorithm that chooses a feasible intervals for each job in the job set whenever the job set is schedulable and a set of heuristics that attempt to find feasible intervals in polynomial time. Finally, we present an EDF-based algorithm for scheduling the jobs after feasible intervals have been selected for them.

3.1 NP-Hardness

The following theorem states that finding a feasible schedule for a set of multiple feasible interval jobs is NP-hard.

Theorem 3.1. Finding a feasible schedule for a set of multiple feasible interval jobs when timing parameters of the jobs are all known is NP-hard.

Proof. We prove the theorem by showing that a restricted version of this problem is as hard as the bin-packing problem [9], a NP-complete problem. To do so, consider a set of multiple feasible interval jobs $\mathbf{J} = \{J_1, J_2, ..., J_M\}$. The sets of feasible intervals for all jobs are identical, i.e., $\mathbf{FI}_1 = \mathbf{FI}_2 = ... = \mathbf{FI}_M$. Moreover, the lengths of all feasible intervals are identical.

Each feasible interval can be considered as a bin in the bin-packing problem. The length of each feasible interval is the bin capacity. Each job is an object to be packed into a bin; the size of the object is the execution time of the job. To complete all jobs selected to complete in an interval without any deadline miss, the sum of execution times of the jobs in the interval must be no greater than the length of the feasible interval. Clearly, the problem of finding a feasible interval for each job such that every job can complete within its selected feasible interval is as same as finding a bin for each object such that all objects can be packed into the bins.

Since the restricted version of the problem of finding a feasible schedule of multiple feasible interval jobs is a bin-packing problem, we can conclude that the problem is as hard as a NP-complete problem. Hence, the problem is NP-hard.   □

3.2 Branch and Bound Algorithm

We now describe a branch-and-bound (BB) algorithm. It selects a feasible interval for every job in the given set of jobs when all the jobs are schedulable or declares the job set infeasible when some jobs in the set are not schedulable.

Pruning Condition. The condition of pruning the search space is the schedulability condition[1]. When analyzing the schedulability of a subset of jobs, the BB algorithm checks whether the jobs in the subset are schedulable (i.e., they have no deadline miss) when they are scheduled to execute in the EDF order in their selected feasible intervals. A subset of jobs is said to be feasible if all the jobs in the subset are schedulable and infeasible if otherwise. When a subset of jobs is infeasible, the BB algorithm can eliminate all subsets containing the infeasible subset. This obvious fact allows the BB algorithm to disregard parts of the search tree.

Branch and Bound Strategy. Figure 2 shows the search tree for a job set **J** of M jobs. Each node u in the tree is labeled with a M-tuple vector X. The vector represents feasible interval selections for a subset of jobs. Specifically, the i-th element of a vector X is either $FI_{i,*}$ or $FI_{i,j}$ for some $j = 1, 2, \ldots, n(i)$. The element being $FI_{i,*}$ means that a feasible interval has not yet been selected for job J_i. The element being $FI_{i,j}$ means that the j-th feasible interval of J_i is selected. The vector $\langle FI_{1,*}, FI_{2,*}, \ldots, FI_{M,*} \rangle$ labeling the root represents that no feasible interval has been selected.

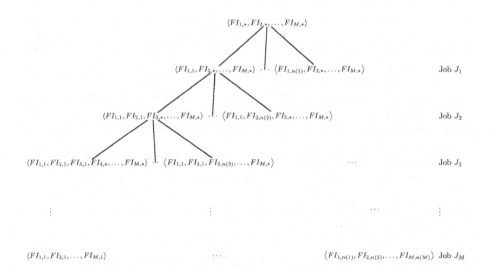

Fig. 2. Search Tree

On the first level of the tree, there are $n(1)$ nodes. Each node represents a different feasible interval selection for job J_1. For a set **J** of M jobs, the length

---

[1] This condition can be considered as the lower bound in a branch-and-bound algorithm: A solution is disregarded when its bound is greater than the lower bound.

of the longest path from the root to a leaf node is M. The leaf nodes enumerate all possible combinations of selected feasible intervals for jobs in the set **J**. (For example, the vector labeling the leftmost leaf node indicates that the earliest feasible interval of every job is selected for that job in the combination.)

The BB algorithm visits the search tree in the depth-first manner starting from the root. When visiting node u, the algorithm checks if the schedule corresponding to X_u (i.e., the schedule of jobs in the selected feasible intervals represented by X_u) is feasible. While conducting schedulability analysis, the algorithm ignores the jobs whose feasible intervals are not yet selected. If the schedule corresponding to X_u is not feasible, the children of node u are not visited because none of the schedules corresponding to these nodes can be feasible. Hence, the algorithm returns to the parent of node u. If the schedule corresponding to X_u is feasible, the algorithm continues visiting the children of node u if there exists any. If node u is a leaf node, the algorithm stops and returns X_u as a feasible interval selection for the job set **J**. If none of the children of node u has a feasible schedule and its parent is not the root, the algorithm returns to its parent to consider other sibling nodes. If its parent is the root, the algorithm has exhausted the search space; the algorithm stops and reports a failure of finding a feasible schedule for the job set **J**.

Figure 3 shows the pseudo code of the branch-and-bound algorithm. Function DFSCHECK performs a depth-first search starting from job J_k when given a combination of feasible intervals that have been selected for $J_1, J_2, ..., J_{k-1}$. Function DFSCHECK selects one feasible interval at each iteration for job J_k. It selects j-th feasible interval $FI_{k,j}$ where $1 \leq j \leq n(k)$ for job J_k on line 3 and analyzes the schedulability of the job set $\{J_1, ..., J_k\}$ on line 4. If the job set is infeasible, it continues the next iteration. Otherwise, it continues to visits a child node. If feasible intervals have been selected for all jobs, the function stops and returns the selection on line 8. If not, it calls Function DFSCHECK to select a feasible interval for job J_{k+1}.

Function BRANCH_AND_BOUND_FISELECTION initializes the array of selected feasible intervals and calls Function DFSCHECK to visit the search tree starting from job J_1. The function completes and returns the array of selected feasible intervals produced by Function DFSCHECK if the array exists or declares the given job set infeasible if the array does not exist.

3.3   Fewer Feasible Interval First (FFIF) Based Algorithm

We present in this section several heuristics that are extensions of traditional bin-packing heuristics such as First Fit Decreasing (FFD), Last Fit Decreasing (LFD), Best Fit Decreasing (BFD), and Worst Fit Decreasing (WFD) [9]. While the feasible interval selection problem and the bin-packing problem are similar, they are differ in many fundamental ways: Feasible intervals are not identical in length. The feasible interval selected for each job must be from the feasible interval set of the job. Different jobs may have different feasible intervals. These factors make it necessary for us to extend the traditional bin-packing heuristics so they can be used for feasible interval selection.

DFSCHECK(SelectedFI, k)

Input. SelectedFI: the array of the indexes of selected feasible intervals.

      k: select one feasible interval for job J_k.

Output. SelectedFI: the array of selected feasible intervals.

1 for each feasible interval $FI_{k,j}$ of job J_k

2   do

3   Select feasible interval $FI_{k,j}$ for job J_k;

4   if $\{J_1, ..., J_k\}$ is schedulable in their selected feasible intervals

5   then

6   if feasible intervals for all jobs are selected

7   then

8   Return SelectedFI;

9   else

10   Call DFSCHECK to select one feasible interval for J_{k+1};

11   Return SelectedFI if the array exists;

12 end

13 Return NULL as no feasible schedule is founded;

BRANCH_AND_BOUND_FISELECTION($FI[M]$)

Input. FI: the array of feasible intervals for M jobs

Output. SelectedFI: the array of selected feasible intervals if exists.

1 Initialize the selection array;

2 Call DFSCHECK(SelectedFI, 1) to select the feasible interval for job J_1;

3 return SelectedFI or the declaration that the job set is not feasible;

Fig. 3. Optimal algorithm for selecting feasible intervals

Fewer Feasible Interval First (FFIF) Based Algorithms process the jobs in non-descending order according to the number of feasible intervals. Intuitively, the algorithms may have a better chance to find a feasible schedule of all jobs by processing jobs having fewer feasible intervals first. This is the rationale behind the FFIF-based algorithms. All FFIF-based algorithms sort all the eligible jobs according to the numbers of their feasible intervals and process them in non-descending order. Similar to the optimal algorithm, when checking whether a job is schedulable in a feasible interval, the algorithms consider only the job being processed and jobs for which feasible intervals have already been selected.

As stated earlier, the scheduler uses EDF algorithm. It is well known that all jobs can be scheduled to complete by their deadlines if at any time t, the total instantaneous utilization of all eligible jobs that are ready for execution is no greater than 1 [10] (also Theorem 7.4 in [11]). To reduce the time complexity of the heuristic algorithms, the scheduler uses this sufficient condition for schedulability analysis. In other words, the scheduler checks the system workload $u(t)$ for $t \geq 0$ to determine whether this condition is met when deciding whether a job is schedulable in a feasible interval. (More precisely, the scheduler checks whether $u(t) \leq 1$ whenever the system workload changes.)

The individual algorithms among the FFIF-based algorithms differ in their selections of a feasible interval for each job. When selecting a feasible interval for a job, *FFIF-First Fit* algorithm selects the first feasible interval of the job in which the job is schedulable. In contrast, *FFIF-Last Fit* algorithm selects the last feasible interval in which the job is schedulable. FFIF-First Fit algorithm should work well when the system is lightly loaded and the release times of jobs are generally fall apart. Choosing the first schedulable feasible interval allows eligible jobs to complete before new jobs are released. However, when the system is heavily loaded, FFIF-First Fit algorithm may not be able to find a feasible schedule for jobs with fewer feasible intervals. FFIF-Last Fit algorithm generally delays the executions of jobs if possible. In this case, a job that is released later and has few feasible intervals is more likely to be schedulable when the system is heavily loaded.

FFIF-First Fit and FFIF-Last Fit algorithm should work well when feasible intervals of a job are similar in length. However, these two algorithms may not work well when the job's feasible intervals have dramatically different lengths. *FFIF-Best Fit* and *FFIF-Worst Fit* algorithm take into account of this factor. FFIF-Best Fit algorithm selects the feasible interval which has the largest maximal system workload. Specifically, the algorithm computes the maximal system workload for each feasible interval of the job being processed, assuming that the job is scheduled in the interval. Then, the algorithm selects the feasible interval which produces the largest maximal system workload among all intervals in which the job is schedulable. In contrast, FFIF-Worst Fit algorithm selects the feasible interval during which the maximal system workload is the smallest and in which the job is schedulable. Hence, FFIF-Worst Fit algorithm distributes the system workload over the time line.

The time complexity of these four heuristics is $O(nM^2)$ where n is the maximum number of feasible intervals of a job and M is the number of jobs in the job set: The complexity of sorting the jobs is $O(M \log M)$. For each job, the scheduler checks if the system workload $u(t)$ is greater than 1 for $t \geq 0$. In the worst case, the scheduler has to check the system workload for $M-1$ time instants. Hence, the time complexity of conducting the schedulability analysis for one job is $O(nM)$. The decision of selecting the feasible interval takes constant time. Therefore, the time required to find a feasible interval for all jobs is $O(nM^2)$. The complexity can be reduced to $O(nM \log M)$ when a range tree is used to speed up schedulability analysis.

Figure 4 gives an illustrative example. The given job set is the same as the one given in Figure 1. Feasible intervals $(0, 5]$, $(7, 10]$, and $(14, 20]$ have already been selected for job J_1, J_2, and J_3, respectively. The system workload $u(t)$ of this schedule is shown as the solid line in Figure 4(a) and (b). Job J_4 is the next job to be processed. The dash line in Figure 4(b) shows the system workload if job J_4 executes in one of these three intervals. FFIF-First Fit and FFIF-Last Fit algorithm selects the first interval $(0, 4.5]$ and the last interval $(12, 18]$ for job J_4, respectively. FFIF-Best Fit algorithm selects the first interval $(0, 4.5]$ because its maximal system workload is less than 1 and is the largest. FFIF-Worst Fit

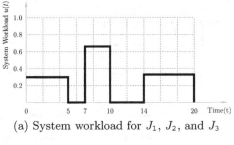

(a) System workload for J_1, J_2, and J_3

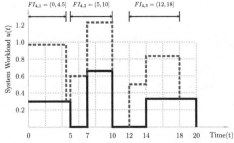

(b) System workload assuming J_4 executes in one of its feasible intervals

Fig. 4. FFIF-based algorithms

algorithm selects the last interval because its maximum system workload is the smallest.

The optimal algorithm and four FFIF-based heuristics are better suited when the release times of all jobs are identical or when scheduling is off-line. For on-line scheduling, the scheduler may repeatedly apply such an algorithm as each job is released on the new job and all the eligible jobs if the number of jobs is small. Alternatively, it may process jobs in First-Come-First-Serve (FCFS) order. Depending on the rule used to select a feasible interval for each job, we have FCFS-First Fit, FCFS-Last fit, FCFS-Best Fit, and FCFS-Worst Fit.

3.4 Priority Boost EDF Algorithm

We now describe an algorithm, called *Priority-Boosting EDF* algorithm, that makes use of the information on selected feasible intervals produced in the selection step to ensure the in-time completion of every job and to reduce the response time of the job. One may question why not simply extend the EDF algorithm a natural way: The scheduler considers each eligible job ready for execution in each of the job's feasible intervals and schedules all ready jobs on the EDF basis based on the current deadlines of the jobs. In other words, the scheduler skips the feasible interval selection step and schedules jobs solely on the basis of their feasible intervals and deadlines.

The example in Figure 5 illustrates why this approach may fail, while a scheduler that first selects a feasible interval for each job and makes use of this

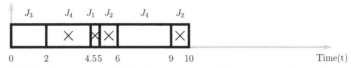

(a) Schedule by the EDF algorithm solely based on job deadlines.

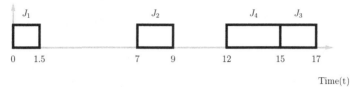

(b) Schedule by the EDF algorithm based on job deadlines and selected feasible intervals.

Fig. 5. Schedule by the EDF algorithm

information in its scheduling decision may success. Suppose that the system has the jobs J_1, J_2, J_3, and J_4 given in Figure 1. Each box in Figure 5 represents an execution of a job and a cross symbol in a box represents an incomplete execution. Figure 5(a) shows the schedule when ready jobs are scheduled by the EDF algorithm according to their current deadlines. In this example, job J_3 has the earliest deadline; it executes first and completes at time 2. Job J_4 completes in time in its second attempt at time 9. However, job J_1 and J_2 cannot complete in time before the ends of their latest feasible intervals. Figure 5(b) shows the schedule when jobs are scheduled by the EDF algorithm only when they are in their selected feasible intervals. In this example, the selected feasible intervals of job J_1, J_2, J_3, and J_4 are $(0, 5]$, $(7, 10]$, $(14, 20]$, and $(12, 18]$, respectively. All jobs complete in time.

The *Priority-Boosting EDF* algorithm is designed to take advantage of the information on selected feasible intervals. It views the selected feasible interval of each job as a reserved time interval for the job. In this interval, the job executes in the foreground. Outside of this interval, the job executes in the background. Specifically, the algorithm considers an eligible job ready for execution only in its feasible intervals. The algorithm assigns priorities to ready jobs based on two properties: selected feasible intervals and job deadlines. Each ready job is assigned a priority within $(0, 1]$. Suppose that the Q-th feasible interval is selected for job J_i. In the q-th feasible interval of the job for $q = 1, 2, \ldots, Q$, the priority of the job is $\frac{q}{Q}$. The larger the number, the higher the priority. In short, the priority of a job monotonically increases as long as it remains incomplete. Whenever the priorities tie, job deadlines are used to break the tie as the traditional EDF algorithm does.

By assigning a priority within the range $(0, 1]$, Priority-Boosting EDF algorithm simulates the behavior of queuing jobs in multi-level foreground and background queues by one queue. Jobs in their selected feasible intervals have

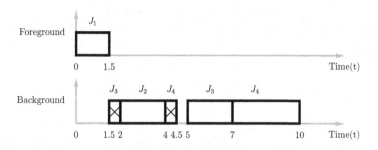

Fig. 6. Schedule by Priority-Boosting EDF algorithm

priority 1 and always execute before jobs that are not in their selected feasible intervals. Hence, Priority-Boosting EDF algorithm guarantees that every job completes in time in its selected feasible interval or sooner if the schedulability condition holds. When all jobs are not in their selected feasible intervals, the algorithm gives the highest priority to the job having the least number of feasible intervals before its selected feasible interval. As a result, the job has a better chance to complete in time before its selected feasible interval and leaves the system. The reserved time for the job is released to accommodate new arrivals.

Figure 6 shows the schedule for the jobs in Figure 5 when they are scheduled by Priority-Boosting EDF algorithm. Jobs scheduled in their selected feasible intervals execute in the foreground; otherwise, jobs execute in the background. Job J_1 starts at time 0 and completes at time 1.5 because it is the only job whose priority is 1 in that time interval. At time 1.5, the priorities of job J_3 and J_4 are both $\frac{1}{3}$. Job J_3 starts because its deadline is earlier. Then, at time 2, job J_2 preempts jobs J_3 because its priority $\frac{1}{2}$ is higher than the priority $\frac{1}{3}$ of job J_3. Job J_4 follows at time 4 in the background but is not able to complete in time. At time 5, job J_3 and J_4 are ready again and have the identical priority and deadline. Job J_3 is selected arbitrarily and completes at time 7. Finally, job J_4 continues to finish.

When jobs are scheduled only in their selected feasible intervals, each job executes once and always in the foreground as illustrated in Figure 5(b). Priority-Boosting EDF algorithm uses the information on the selected feasible intervals to allow some jobs to execute in the background. Although jobs may execute more than once, most of them complete earlier. For instance, job J_3 completes at time 7 in this example but completes at 17 in Figure 5(b).

4   Performance Evaluation

We compared the performance of the heuristics through extensive simulations. Simulation parameters are chosen to ensure broad coverage. The performance of the heuristics are compared against the performance of the branch-and-bound algorithm.

Table 1. Simulation Parameters

Parameters	Value
Workload parameters	
Number of jobs	10, 15, 20, 25, 30, 35, 40
Average arrival rate	$\lambda = 20, 2, .2$ job releases per second(Poisson)
Job Parameters	
WECT	100 ms
Number of feasible intervals	Uniform(1, 5), Uniform(1, 10)
Interval Length	Uniform(200ms, 500ms), Uniform(200ms, 1000ms)
Distance between intervals	Uniform(100ms, 300ms)

We evaluate the heuristics when jobs are processed in the first-come-first-serve (FCFS) order and in the fewer-feasible-interval-first (FFIF) order. As stated earlier, the heuristics use the sufficient condition $u(t) \leq 1$ for schedulability test. To make the performance comparison fair, the branch-and-bound algorithm also uses this sufficient condition rather than the exact test of constructing an EDF schedule and checking for in-time completion. Moreover, a job is rejected if the scheduler cannot find a feasible interval for the job.

We evaluated the priority-boosting EDF algorithm as well as the (2-level) foreground-background (F/B) EDF algorithm. The F/B EDF algorithm gives each ready job priority 1 when the job is in its selected feasible interval and priority 0 when the job is not in its selected feasible interval. Priority ties are broken on the EDF basis.

Because of space limitation, we present only representative results. Results for other cases are similar to the ones presented in Figures 7 to 10.

4.1   Workload Generation and Performance Metrics

We generate workloads based on two parameters: the number of jobs and average arrival rate. The former is the number of jobs in the job set; the latter is the average number of jobs released within each second on the average. Each job is characterized by four parameters. They are execution time, number of feasible intervals, length of each feasible interval, and temporal distance between two consecutive feasible intervals. By temporal distance, we mean the difference in time between the start of a feasible interval of the job and the end of an earlier feasible interval of the job if there is an earlier feasible interval. Before each run of the simulation starts, timing parameters of jobs in the job set are generated. For all of the cases simulated, the execution times of all jobs are identical. The lengths of feasible intervals and the temporal distances between two consecutive feasible intervals are uniformly distributed. The specific values of the parameters used in the simulations are listed in Table 1.

We use two metrics to measure the performance of the algorithms. They are the mean completion rate and the mean last response time. *Completion rate* is the fraction of jobs in the job set completing in time as defined in Definition 1. While computing the mean value, we only count the job sets that are schedulable. Hence, the mean completion rate for the branch-and-bound algorithm is always

1. However, the heuristics may not be able to complete all jobs in time. The higher the completion rate of an algorithm, the better the algorithm..

The *last response time* is the largest response time of all jobs in a given job set. When every job in the job set has only one feasible interval, all work-conservating scheduling algorithms (i.e., priority-driven algorithms) achieve the same last response time. However, this is not true when jobs have multiple feasible intervals. Figure 5 and 6 illustrates this fact. The last response times for different scheduling algorithms differ. The last response time measures the efficiency of an algorithm in scheduling jobs to complete in time. If an algorithm is inefficient in the sense that it frequently schedules jobs to produce void results, jobs will likely to complete in time late if they complete in time at all. In general, an efficient algorithm is able to achieve a smaller last response time. Mean last response time is the mean value of the last response times collected from sample job sets. For the sake of fairness, we only count the job sets in which every algorithm schedules all jobs to complete in time. Otherwise, a smaller last response time can be achieved by not completing all jobs in time.

4.2   Results and Discussions

The 90% confidence interval for each data point plotted below is no more than 0.1% of data value.

Mean Completion Rate. We simulated a heavy workload in which all jobs arrive at time 0 and the number of feasible intervals for each job is uniformly distributed from 1 to 5.

Figure 7 shows the mean completion rates for the algorithms.

We see that the mean completion rates are always lower when jobs are processed in the FCFS order (plotted as dashed lines) than when jobs are processed in the FFIF order (plotted as dotted lines). Specifically, processing jobs in the FFIF order increases the mean completion rates by about 10% to 15% for the First-Fit and Best-Fit algorithm. These results suggest that the First-Fit and Best-Fit should not be used when the scheduler cannot process jobs in the FFIF order, for instance, when scheduling is done on-line. These two algorithms often select the first or second feasible interval for each job. When the system is heavily loaded, the feasible intervals often overlap. When processing jobs in the FCFS order, First-Fit and Best-Fit algorithm often cannot find feasible schedules for jobs that are release late and have only one or two feasible intervals.

The FFIF-based heuristic algorithms achieve mean completion rates that are within 10% of the BB algorithm. In particular, the Worst-Fit algorithm consistently outperforms other algorithms when jobs are processed in the FFIF order. Note that the complexities of the Worst-Fit and Best-Fit algorithm are generally larger because they repeat the schedulability test for every feasible interval of every job.

When the job arrival rate decreases, the mean completion rates of FFIF-based algorithms become closer to that of the BB algorithm. The difference between performances of different heuristics also become smaller.

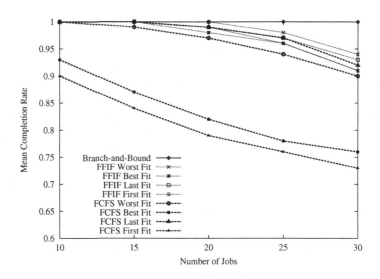

Fig. 7. Mean Completion Rates(Number of FIs=1∼5)

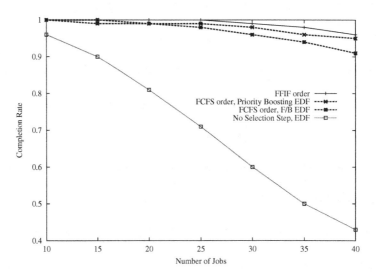

Fig. 8. Mean Completion Rates for Worst Fit algorithm(Number of FIs=1∼10)

Figure 8 shows the mean completion rates when feasible intervals are selected by the Worst Fit algorithm and jobs are scheduled according to the priority-boosting EDF and the F/B EDF algorithms.

When jobs are processed in the FFIF order, these scheduling algorithms have the same performance. Hence only one plot is included here. By giving each job a monotonically increasing priority as time becomes closer to the selected

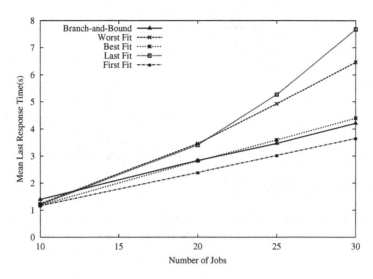

Fig. 9. Mean Last Response Time with F/B EDF algorithm(Number of FIs=1∼20)

feasible interval of the job, the priority-boosting EDF algorithm can improve the mean completion rate when jobs are processed in FCFS order. In particular, the combined use of the FCFS-Worst Fit algorithm and Priority-Boosting EDF algorithm performs nearly as well as the FFIF-Worst Fit algorithm. We also show in this figure the mean completion rates when there is no selection step and jobs are scheduled solely by EDF algorithm as exemplified by Figure 5(a). As we can see, when jobs are thus scheduled, the mean completion rate drops dramatically as the number of jobs in the job set increases.

Mean Last Response Time. Figure 9 shows the mean last response times for the BB algorithm and the heuristics. Ready jobs are scheduled according to the F/B EDF algorithm. In this simulation, when feasible intervals are selected by the branch-and-bound algorithm, jobs are scheduled only in their selected feasible intervals. As a result, the mean last response times for the branch-and-bound algorithm may not be the minimal. Not surprisingly, the mean last response time is the smallest and largest when feasible intervals are selected by the First-Fit and Last-Fit algorithm, respectively. Moreover, when the feasible intervals are selected by the Worst Fit algorithm, the mean last response time is large in general because the Worst Fit algorithm distributes the workload over the time line.

Figure 10 shows the mean last response time when the Priority-Boosting EDF algorithm is used. As we can see, jobs complete earlier in general when compared with the F/B EDF algorithm. The mean last response times achieved by all four hueristics are close. The result shows that Priority-Boosting EDF algorithm not only completes jobs earlier but also increases the completion rate.

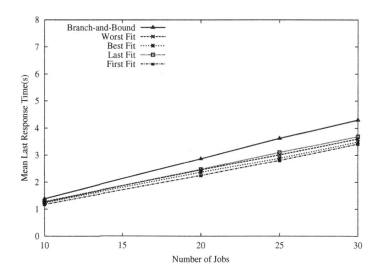

Fig. 10. Mean Last Response Time with Priority-Boosting EDF algorithm(Number of FIs=1∼20)

In summary, our simulation results show that the FFIF-Worst Fit algorithm can select feasible intervals such that the completion rate is close to that by the branch-and-bound algorithm. When the system is heavily loaded, the difference of mean completion rates is always less than 10%. When jobs are processed in the FCFS order, the combination of the Worst-Fit algorithm and Priority-Boosting EDF algorithm performs as well as the FFIF-Worst Fit algorithm.

5   Summary

We presented here the multiple feasible interval job model which characterizes real-time applications in which a job is constrained to execute in disjoint time intervals. These intervals are called feasible intervals. We developed an exponential-time branch-and-bound algorithm and several polynomial-time heuristics for selecting a feasible interval for each job so that all jobs can complete in time. After feasible intervals have been selected for all jobs that are schedulable, the Priority-Boosting EDF algorithm presented here improves the timeliness of jobs.

We evaluated the proposed heuristics by extensive simulations and compared their performance against that of the branch-and-bound algorithm. The result shows that FFIF-Worst Fit algorithm performs as well as the branch-and-bound algorithm. Whenever it is not possible to sort the jobs based on the number of feasible intervals of jobs, the combined use of the FCFS Worst-Fit algorithm and Priority-Boosting algorithm achieves the similar performance of the FFIF-Worst Fit algorithm.

Acknowledgment. This work is supported in part by a grant from the MURI program N00014-01-0576, in part by ONR N0004-02-0102, and in part by Lockheed Martin Corporation 1-5-36137.

References

[1] I. K. Cheong. *Scheduling Imprecise Hard Real-Time Jobs with Cumulative Error.* PhD thesis, University of Illinois at Urbana-Champaign, 1992.

[2] G. Koren and D. Shasha. Skip-over: Algorithms and complexity for overloaded systems that allow skips. In *Proceedings of the IEEE Real-Time Systems Symposium*, pages 110–117, 1995.

[3] H. Aydin, P. Mejia-Alvarez, R. G. Melhem, and D. Mossè. Optimal reward-based scheduling of periodic real-time tasks. In *Proceedings of the IEEE Real-Time Systems Symposium*, pages 79–89, 1999.

[4] J.-Y. Chung, J. W.-S. Liu, and K.-J. Lin. Scheduling periodic jobs that allow imprecise results. *IEEE Transaction on Computers*, 39(9):1156 – 1175, September 1990.

[5] M. Hamdaoui and P. Ramanathan. A dynamic priority assignment technique for streams with (m, k)-firm deadlines. *IEEE Transaction on Computers*, 44(12):1443 – 1451, December 1995.

[6] C. L. Liu and J. Layland. Scheduling algorithms for multiprogramming in a hard real-time environment. *Journal of the ACM*, 20(1):46–61, 1973.

[7] C.-C. Han and K.-J. Lin. Scheduling distance-constrained real-time tasks. In *Proceedings of the IEEE Real-Time Systems Symposium*, pages 300 – 308, Dec. 1992.

[8] B. Sprunt, L. Sha, and J. Lehoczky. Aperiodic task scheduling for hard-real-time systems. *Real-time Systems Journal*, July 1989.

[9] M. R. Garey and D. S. Johnson. *Computers and intractability: a guide to the theory of NP-completeness.* W. H. Freeman, 1979.

[10] Z. Deng, J. W.-S. Liu, and J. Sun. A scheme for scheduling hard real-time application in open system environment. In *Proceedings of the 9th Euromicro Conference on Real-Time Systems*, pages 191–199, Toledo, Spain, June 1997. IEEE.

[11] J. W.-S. Liu. *Real-Time Systems.* Prentice Hall Inc., 2000.

Deterministic and Statistical Deadline Guarantees for a Mixed Set of Periodic and Aperiodic Tasks*

Minsoo Ryu[1] and Seongsoo Hong[2]

[1] College of Information and Communications,
Hanyang University, Haengdang-Dong 17,
Seongdong-Gu, Seoul 133-791, Korea
msryu@redwood.snu.ac.kr
[2] School of Electrical Engineering and Computer Science,
Seoul National University, San 56-1,
Shillim-Dong, Gwanak-Gu, Seoul 151-742, Korea
sshong@redwood.snu.ac.kr

Abstract. Current hard real-time technologies are unable to support a new class of applications that have real-time constraints but with dynamic request arrivals and unpredictable resource requirements. We propose two new admission control approaches to address this problem. First, we present an efficient schedulability test, called utilization demand analysis, to handle periodic and aperiodic tasks with deterministic execution times. The utilization demand is defined as the processor utilization required for a mixed task set to meet deadlines with certainty, thus for deterministic deadline guarantees. We show that the utilization demand analysis eliminates the need for complicated schedulability analysis and enables on-line admission control. Second, we present a statistical admission control scheme using effective execution times to handle stochastic execution times. Effective execution times are determined from the deadline miss probability demanded by the application and stochastic properties of task execution times. Every task is associated with an effective execution time and is restricted to using processor time not exceeding its effective execution time. This scheme allows every task to meet its deadline with a specified probability without being interfered with, and greatly simplifies the admission control when combined with the utilization demand analysis.

1 Introduction

The emergence of distributed multimedia applications with demanding QoS requirements is setting forth new challenges for real-time systems. Such new ap-

---

* The work reported in this paper was supported in part by the Korea Research Foundation Grant (KRF-2003-003-D00340), by the research fund of Hanyang University (HY-2003-T), by the National Research Laboratory (NRL) Grant M1-9911-00-0120, by the Institute of Computer Technology (ICT), and by the Automation and Systems Research Institute (ASRI).

J. Chen and S. Hong (Eds.): RTCSA 2003, LNCS 2968, pp. 72–87, 2004.

plications including video conferencing and interactive distance learning require real-time performance guarantees for the delivery and processing of continuous media data. However, despite recent developments in real-time computing, current hard real-time solutions cannot be directly applied to these applications. While most real-time research has put an emphasis on the periodic task model [15,2,12,3,14] in which task arrivals and execution times are deterministic, multimedia applications have two distinguishing characteristics. First, processor usage patterns include both periodic and aperiodic tasks. For example, a query for continuous media requires periodic tasks for delivery and processing of continuous data, and a query on a database of static data types requires aperiodic tasks. Second, task execution times are either deterministic or stochastic, such as CBR (constant bit rate) video data versus VBR (variable bit rate) data. In this paper, we attempt to provide deadline guarantees via admission control for real-time tasks while allowing randomness in arrivals and execution times. Such deadline guarantees can be either deterministic or statistical depending on the characteristics of task execution times. When task execution times are upper bounded and their bounds are known, deterministic deadline guarantees can be provided so that all tasks meet deadlines at run-time. The deterministic guarantee provides the highest level of deadline guarantees, however, it may be an overly conservative approach for some multimedia applications which are not greatly impacted by infrequent deadline misses. This necessitates statistical deadline guarantees. When task execution times are not bounded or exhibit great variability, a statistical approach provides probabilistic deadline guarantees with a specified probability.

We present new admission control approaches for both types of deadline guarantees. First, we propose an efficient schedulability test, called *utilization demand analysis*, to handle periodic and aperiodic tasks with deterministic execution times. The utilization demand is defined as the processor utilization required for a mixed task set to meet all deadlines. We use the utilization demand to develop a schedulability test for deterministic deadline guarantees under EDF. We show that the utilization demand analysis eliminates the need for complicated schedulability analysis and enables on-line admission control. Also, as we will see later, the utilization demand provides a useful means for statistical deadline guarantees.

Second, we present two admission control schemes to provide statistical deadline guarantees by bounding the probability that tasks miss deadlines. In general, priority driven scheduling algorithms like EDF, unlike WFQ (weighted fair queueing), inherently lack the "isolation" mechanism to protect tasks from one another. If a task runs arbitrarily long, bounding deadline miss probabilities of its subsequent tasks is significantly problematic. To overcome this problem, we propose to discard tasks that match specific criteria. Our first approach is to discard tasks missing deadlines, and this allows us to compute deadline miss probabilities under the worst case. The shortcoming of this approach, however, is that it leads to computationally complex algorithms since computing probabilities generally requires expensive convolution operations. Our second approach improves upon the first one by aggressively discarding tasks. We use *effective execution times* which are determined from the deadline miss probability demanded by the application and stochastic properties of execution times. Every task is associated with an effective execution time and is restricted to using processor time not exceeding its effective execution time. If a task consumes processor time more than its effective execution time, it is immediately discarded. This scheme allows every task to meet its deadline with a specified probability without being interfered with, and greatly simplifies the admission control when combined with the utilization demand analysis.

1.1   Related Work

A number of techniques have been proposed to handle mixes of periodic and aperiodic tasks [13,16,6,17,7,8]. The algorithms in [13,16,6,17] assume that aperiodic tasks are soft real-time and give preferential treatment to periodic tasks. In these aproaches, aperiodic tasks are handled at a lower priority level in the background, or at a some fixed priority level by a special periodic task which serves aperiodic requests with its limited capacity. The algorithms proposed in [11,5] handle aperiodic tasks with explicit deadlines. Also, they are known to be optimal with regard to specific criteria, for example, of the response time or processor utilization. However, they not only require complete knowledge of the periodic tasks, but also have high computational complexities when used on-line. In our model, all aperiodic tasks have explicit deadlines and are scheduled by the same scheduling policy as periodic tasks. Moreover, our utilization demand method eliminates the need for complicated schedulability analysis, requiring low run-time overhead.

In the meantime, several researchers have worked on non-deterministic solutions to real-time scheduling problems with stochastic execution times. The statistical rate monotonic scheduling (SRMS) in [1] is a non-deterministic version of the classical rate monotonic scheduling. Under the assumption that the accurate execution time of a task is known when the task arrives, SRMS allows one to compute the percentage of deadline misses. Tia *et al.* [18] proposed two methods to handle stochastic task execution times, *probabilistic time-demand analysis* and *transform-task method*. The probabilistic time-demand analysis attempts to provide a lower bound on the probability that a periodic task meets its deadline under fixed priority scheduling. The probabilistic time-demand analysis is based on the notion of critical instant at which the first instances in all periodic tasks are released simultaneously. The critical instant leads to the worst case when all tasks complete before their deadlines, i.e., when no backlog exists. However, it has not been proven for unbounded execution times that the critical instant is the worst case. Another method, called transform-task method, divides each task into a periodic task and a sporadic task. The periodic task has the same period as the original task and has a fixed execution time that should be chosen such that all the periodic tasks in the system are schedulable. If the actual execution time of a periodic task is larger than the fixed execution time at run-time, the excessive portion of the task is modeled as a sporadic task that can be scheduled by either a sporadic server or a slack stealing algorithm.

The key idea of our effective execution time method is similar to that of the transform-task method in that each task is associated with a fixed amount of execution time and its processor usage is enforced accordingly. Our contribution is to give a formal definition of effective execution times based on the notion of statistical schedulability and to combine effective execution times with the utilization demand analysis in order to provide an efficient, statistical version of admission control scheme. In fact, the use of effective execution times allows us to easily extend existing deterministic scheduling algorithms and analysis techniques to handle stochastic execution times.

The remainder of this paper is organized as follows. In Section 2, we discuss our models and assumptions. Section 3 describes the utilization demand method for schedulability analysis of aperiodic tasks with known worst case execution times. This method is then applied to a mixed set of periodic and aperiodic tasks. Section 4 introduces two techniques for statistical deadline guarantees. The first technique bounds deadline miss probabilities by discarding tasks missing deadlines. The second technique uses effective execution times as its discard criterion. We will combine effective execution times with utilization demands to provide an efficient admission test. We then conclude in Section 5.

2   Models and Assumptions

Consider a set of aperiodic tasks $Q = \{\tau_1, \tau_2, \ldots, \tau_i, \ldots\}$ where tasks are in arrival order, i.e., τ_i arrives earlier than τ_{i+1}. We use $Q(t) \subset Q$ to denote the set of tasks that have arrived before t and have not completed by t. Every aperiodic task $\tau_i \in Q$ has an arrival time A_i, an execution time requirement e_i, and a relative deadline d_i from its arrival time. The absolute deadline D_i of τ_i is computed by $D_i = A_i + d_i$. If the execution time e_i is bounded from above, then its least upper bound is denoted by e_i^{max}. Otherwise, we assume that e_i is an independent random variable and is distributed according to probability density function (pdf) $g_{e_i}(e)$.

We use similar notation for periodic tasks. Periodic task $\tilde{\tau}_i$ with period $\tilde{T}_i$ can be considered as a finite or infinite sequence of aperiodic requests. Such aperiodic requests are referred to as *periodic task instances* which are denoted by $\tilde{\tau}_{i,j}$. Each periodic task instance $\tilde{\tau}_{i,j}$ has an execution time requirement $\tilde{e}_{i,j}$ and a common relative deadline $\tilde{d}_i$. Note that we use the periodic task model [15] where the relative deadline of a task is equal to its period, i.e., $\tilde{d}_i = \tilde{T}_i$. If $\tilde{e}_{i,j}$ is upper bounded for all j, then the least upper bound is denoted by $\tilde{e}_i^{max}$. Otherwise, we assume that all $\tilde{e}_{i,j}$ are independent random variables that are identically distributed according to the same probability density function $g_{\tilde{e}_i}(e)$. Unlike aperiodic tasks, we use $\tilde{A}_i$ to denote the release time of the first instance $\tilde{\tau}_{i,1}$. Using this, the absolute deadline $\tilde{D}_{i,j}$ of $\tilde{\tau}_{i,j}$ is computed by $\tilde{D}_{i,j} = \tilde{A}_i + (j - 1)\tilde{T}_i + \tilde{d}_i$.

In our discussions, we assume a simple system architecture consisting of two components, an admission controller and a processor scheduler, as in Figure 1. The admission controller, through admit or reject, is responsible for ensuring that the system can provide promised deadline guarantees for all tasks accepted. The processor scheduler in turn allocates processor time to tasks according a particular scheduling algorithm. This simple architecture allows us to consider a wide variety of models for end system operation and configuration. Note that in the case of deterministic deadline guarantees, a periodic task is said to be schedulable if all instances meet their deadlines. To do so, the admission controller is responsible for admission of all future instances of accepted periodic tasks.

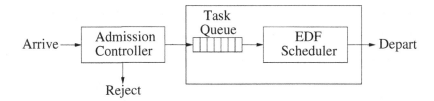

Fig. 1. End system architecture

The scheduling algorithm considered here is earliest deadline first (EDF)[15]. EDF was selected for two reasons. First, EDF is known to be optimal for deterministic deadline guarantees in the sense that it can schedule any task set which is schedulable by any other algorithm. Even though optimality of EDF has not been proven in a statistical environment, it still serves as a benchmark for other scheduling algorithms. Second, EDF algorithm allows for utilization-based schedulability tests which incur little run-time overhead. Under EDF, if the utilization of a task set does not exceed one, then the set is schedulable. We will show that, in the next section, the utilization-based test and our utilization demand analysis can be combined successfully into an integrated schedulability test. Note that though we choose EDF for task scheduling, most of our techniques are applicable to a variety of priority driven scheduling algorithms.

3   Utilization Demand Analysis and Deterministic Deadline Guarantees

In this section we introduce the utilization demand analysis which provides a schedulability test for a mixed task set. We first define utilization demands for aperiodic tasks, and derive a necessary and sufficient schedulability condition. We then develop an integrated schedulability test for a mixed set. The schedulability tests developed in this section are used for deterministic deadline guarantees.

Table 1. Summary of notation

Notation	Meaning
Q	Set of aperiodic tasks
$Q(t)$	Set of aperiodic tasks that have arrived before t and have not completed by t
$Q(t, hp(\tau))$	Set of aperiodic tasks that have higher priorities than τ_i in $Q(t)$
$\tau_i, \tilde{\tau}_i, \tilde{\tau}_{i,j}$	Aperiodic task, periodic task, periodic task instance
A_i, e_i, d_i, D_i	Arrival time, execution time, relative deadline, and absolute deadline of τ_i
f_i	Finish time of τ_i
e_i^{max}	Worst case execution time of τ_i
$e_{i,t}^{past}$	Allocated processor time for τ_i by t
$e_{i,t}^{res}$	Maximum residual execution time of τ_i at t ($e_{i,t}^{res} = e_i^{max} - e_{i,t}^{past}$)
$d_{i,t}^{res}$	Lead time of τ_i at t ($D_i - t$)
$\tilde{A}_i, \tilde{e}_{i,j}, \tilde{d}_i, \tilde{D}_{i,j}$	Release time, execution time, relative deadline, and absolute deadline of $\tilde{\tau}_{i,j}$
$\tilde{T}_i$	Period of $\tilde{\tau}_i$
$\tilde{e}^{max}$	Worst case execution time of $\tilde{\tau}_i$
$g_{e_i}(e), g_{e_{i,t}^{res}}(e)$	pdf of e_i, pdf of $e_{i,t}^{res}$
$u_{Q(t)}(\tau_i)$	Utilization demand of $\tau_i \in Q(t)$
$U_{Q(t)}$	Maximum utilization demand of $Q(t)$

3.1   Utilization Demands for Aperiodic Tasks

Consider a set of aperiodic tasks $Q = \{\tau_1, \tau_2, \ldots, \tau_i, \ldots\}$ under priority driven scheduling policy. In order to determine $Q(t)$ is schedulable at t, we need to consider two dynamic variables for each task $\tau_i \in Q(t)$, maximum residual execution time $e_{i,t}^{res}$ and lead time $d_{i,t}^{res}$. At time t, the maximum residual execution time $e_{i,t}^{res}$ of τ_i is the maximum of remaining processor time to complete τ_i. The lead time $d_{i,t}^{res}$ of τ_i is the difference between its absolute deadline D_i and the current time t [10], i.e., $D_i - t$. Keeping these two dynamic variables provides sufficient information for the schedulability test of $Q(t)$. Table 1 summarizes the notation used throughout this paper.

We are now ready to define utilization demands for aperiodic tasks. Roughly, a utilization demand of $\tau_i \in Q(t)$ is defined as the processor time required to meet its deadline divided by its lead time. Since τ_i can start only after its higher-priority tasks complete, we need to consider the sum of residual execution times of itself and its higher-priority tasks. Let $Q(t, hp(\tau_i)) \subset Q(t)$ be the set of tasks that have higher priorities than τ_i. The utilization demand of τ_i is defined by

$$u_{Q(t)}(\tau_i) \overset{\text{def}}{=} \frac{\sum_{\tau_j \in Q(t, hp(\tau_i))} e_{j,t}^{res} + e_{i,t}^{res}}{d_{i,t}^{res}}. \tag{1}$$

The maximum utilization demand $U_Q(t)$ is defined for the set $Q(t)$ as below.

$$U_{Q(t)} \stackrel{\text{def}}{=} \max_i [u_{Q(t)}(\tau_i)]. \tag{2}$$

The following theorem shows a necessary and sufficient schedulability condition for an aperiodic task set.

Theorem 3.1. *Aperiodic task set* $Q(t) = \{\tau_m, \tau_{m+1}, \dots, \tau_n\}$ *is schedulable if and only if*

$$U_{Q(t)} \leq 1. \tag{3}$$

Proof. We consider the "if" part first. Let f_i be the worst case finish time of $\tau_i \in Q(t)$. The finish time f_i will be current time plus the sum of residual execution times of higher priority tasks including τ_i's execution time. By the definition of utilization demand in Eq.(1), we have

$$f_i = t + \sum_{\tau_j \in Q(t, hp(\tau_i))} e_{j,t}^{res} + e_{i,t}^{res}$$
$$= t + d_{i,t}^{res} \cdot u_{Q(t)}(\tau_i)$$
$$= t + (D_i - t) \cdot u_{Q(t)}(\tau_i).$$

Since $u_{Q(\tau_i, t_i)} \leq U_{Q(t)} \leq 1$,

$$t + (D_i - t) \cdot u_{Q(t)}(\tau_i) \leq t + (D_i - t)$$
$$\leq D_i.$$

Next, we consider the "only if" part. The proof is by contradiction. If we assume that $Q(t) = \{\tau_1, \tau_2, \dots, \tau_n\}$ is schedulable and $U_Q(t_i) > 1$, then there exists τ_i such that $u_Q(\tau_i, t) > 1$. Hence,

$$f_i = t + \sum_{\tau_j \in Q(t, hp(\tau_i))} e_{j,t}^{res} + e_{i,t}^{res}$$
$$= t + (D_i - t) \cdot u_{Q(t)}(\tau_i)$$
$$> t + (D_i - t) = D_i.$$

This contradicts the assumption that $Q(t)$ is schedulable.   □

Obviously, a new task arrival affects the schedulability of $Q(t)$ while task departures do not. Therefore, the above schedulability test is valid only until the next arrival time of a new task. This necessitates testing of schedulability at every task arrival. Figure 2 illustrates the maximum utilization demand $U_{Q(t)}$ with several task arrivals and departures. At t_3, the utilization demand jumps to above one. It is easy to show that if $U_{Q(t)}$ is less than one at t, $U_{Q(t)}$ is a decreasing function of time until the next arrival time.

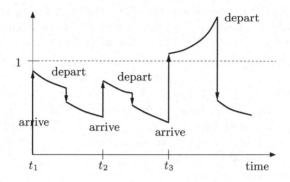

Fig. 2. Utilization demand for a dynamic task set with arrivals and departures

Our second theorem shows the *subadditivity* property of the utilization demand function. This property is essential in devising an integrated shedulability condition for a mixed set of periodic and aperiodic tasks.

Theorem 3.2. *For any two aperiodic task sets,*

$$U_{Q_1(t) \cup Q_2(t)} \le U_{Q_1(t)} + U_{Q_2(t)}. \tag{4}$$

Proof. See Appendix A.

3.2   Schedulabiltiy Condition for a Mixed Task Set

We now generalize the utilization demand analysis for a mixed set of periodic and aperiodic tasks. Basically, all instances of periodic tasks can be considered as aperiodic tasks. This gives a possibility to apply the utilization demand method to periodic tasks. Suppose that $P = \{\tilde{\tau}_1, \tilde{\tau}_2, \ldots, \tilde{\tau}_N\}$ is a set of periodic tasks. This periodic task set can be associated with an equivalent aperiodic task set Q_P which consists of all task instances generated by P. Thus, P is schedulable if and only if all tasks in Q_P are schedulable.

In the following theorem, we show an important relationship between the utilization demand and the utilization of a periodic task set. The following theorem states that the utilization of P is equal to or greater than the maximum utilization demand of Q_P.

Theorem 3.3. *Let* $U_P = \sum_{i=1}^{N} \frac{\tilde{e}_i^{max}}{\tilde{T}_i}$ *be the utilization of periodic task set* $P = \{\tilde{\tau}_1, \tilde{\tau}_2, \ldots, \tilde{\tau}_N\}$. *If* P *is schedulable by EDF, then*

$$U_{Q_P(t)} \le U_P \tag{5}$$

for all $t \ge 0$.

Proof. For an arbitrary t, suppose that $Q_P(t) = \{\tau_m, \ldots, \tau_i, \ldots, \tau_n\}$. Without loss of generality, assume that the maximum utilization demand is $U_{Q_P(t)} = u_{Q_P(t)}(\tau_i)$. At this moment t, we inject a new periodic task into P such that P is still schedulable. Consider a new periodic task $\tilde{\tau}_*$ whose period is $\tilde{T}_* = D_i - A_i$. We set $\tilde{e}_* = \tilde{T}_* \cdot (1 - U_P)$ so that $U_P + \frac{\tilde{e}_*}{\tilde{T}_*} = 1$, then $P \cup \{\tilde{\tau}_*\}$ will be schedulable by EDF. If we release the first instance $\tilde{\tau}_{*,1}$ immediately before A_i, then $\tilde{\tau}_{*,1}$ has an absolute deadline earlier than τ_i. According to EDF policy, the priority of $\tilde{\tau}_{*,1}$ is higher than that of τ_i. Hence, τ_i would be preempted and delayed by the amount of $\tilde{e}_*$, but τ_i still meets its deadline D_i. Let f_i^{new} be the finish time of delayed τ_i, then we have

$$f_i^{new} = f_i + \tilde{e}_*$$
$$= t + (D_i - t) \cdot u_{Q_P(t)}(\tau_i) + \tilde{e}_* \leq D_i. \tag{6}$$

By subtracting $(t_i + \tilde{e}_*)$ from both sides of Ineq.(6) and deviding both sides by $(D_i - t)$, we have

$$u_{Q_P(t)}(\tau_i) \leq \frac{D_i - \tilde{e}_* - t}{D_i - t} \tag{7}$$

$$= 1 - \frac{\tilde{e}_*}{D_i - t} \tag{8}$$

$$= 1 - (1 - U_P) = U_P. \tag{9}$$

Eq.(9) follows from $\tilde{e}_* = \tilde{T}_*(1 - U_P) = (D_i - t)(1 - U_P)$. This completes the proof. $\qquad \square$

We are now able to derive a schedulability condition for a mixed task set. Let P be the set of periodic tasks and its utilization be U_P. The following theorem gives a sufficient condition.

Theorem 3.4. *Given periodic task set P and aperiodic task set $Q(t)$, if $U_P + U_{Q(t)} \leq 1$, then $P \cup Q(t)$ is schedulable by an EDF scheduler.*
Proof. Let Q_P be the equivalent aperiodic task set of P. It suffices to show that $Q_P(t) \cup Q(t)$ is schedulable for any t. We show that $U_{Q_P(t) \cup Q(t)} \leq 1$.

$$U_{Q_P(t) \cup Q(t)} \leq U_{Q_P(t)} + U_{Q(t)} \tag{10}$$
$$\leq U_P + U_{Q(t)} \leq 1. \tag{11}$$

Ineq.(11) follows from Theorem 3.2 and Ineq.(11) follows from Theorem 3.3. This completes the proof. $\qquad \square$

Using Theorem 3.4 one can easily determine the schedulability for a mixed task set in a similar fashion as with the utilization-based test for periodic task sets. Note that all periodic tasks can meet deadlines under EDF algorithm if the sum of their utilization factors does not exceed one. It is easy to see that the algorithm for the utilization demand analysis has a run time of $O(n)$ where n is the number of aperiodic tasks in the system. Computing utilization demands requires maintaining small data structure for residual execution times and lead times. Also, this requires low run-time overhead, since these variables need to be computed only when new tasks arrive.

4   Effective Execution Times and Statistical Deadline Guarantees

In this section, we present two statistical approaches to handling stochastic execution times. We use two *task discard* policies to bound deadline miss probabilities. The first approach is based on deadline miss handling. It discards tasks missing deadlines, and this allows us to bound deadline miss probabilities of tasks. The second approach associates each task with a fixed amount of processor time, *effective execution time*, that is allocated to the task. It discards any task whose processor usage exceeds its allocated processor time. Combined with the utilization demand analysis, effective execution times enable an efficient admission control with a surprising simplicity.

4.1   Statistical Deadline Guarantees with Deadline Miss Handling

A statistical approach allows for a small deadline miss probability. Specifically, the probabilistic deadline guarantee is provided in the form of

$$Pr(f_i > D_i) \le \epsilon \tag{12}$$

where ϵ is generally small, e.g., $\epsilon = 0.01$. Using this condition, we can formally define the statistical version of schedulability.

Definition 1. If the probability that a task τ_i misses its deadline is equal to or less than ϵ, τ_i is said to be *statistically schedulable with probability* $1 - \epsilon$

Consider a task τ_i and a task set Q. We will use the execution time e_i and residual execution $e_{i,t}^{res}$ as random variables throughout this section. The deadline miss probability of τ_i can be stated as

$$Pr(f_i > D_i) = Pr(\sum_{\tau_j \in Q(A_i, hp(\tau_i))} e_{j,A_i}^{res} + \sum_{\tau_k \in Q((A_i, f_i], hp(\tau_i))} e_k + e_i > d_i) \tag{13}$$

where $Q((A_i, f_i], hp(\tau_i))$ contains τ_i's higher priority tasks that will be admitted between the arrival and completion of τ_i. Thus, to provide the statistical guarantee for τ_i, an admission policy must always ensure $Pr(f_i > D_i) \le \epsilon$ by appropriately maintaining the future task set $Q((A_i, f_i], hp(\tau_i))$. Whenever a new task τ_k arrives, the system needs to ensure $Pr(f_i > D_i) \le \epsilon$ for every τ_i as well as $Pr(f_k > D_k) \le \epsilon$ for τ_k.

We now apply Eq.(13) to periodic tasks. As mentioned above, we assume that tasks missing deadlines are immediately discarded. Without this assumption, a periodic task instance $\tilde{\tau}_{i,j}$ may not complete by the release of a subsequent instance $\tilde{\tau}_{i,j+1}$. Since such a backlog $\tilde{\tau}_{i,j}$ can be arbitrarily long, all the subsequent task instances may miss deadlines. This is called the *domino effect* [4]. Discarding tasks that miss deadlines avoids such domino effects and keeps the system predictable. The following theorem provides a statistical schedulability condition for a periodic task set. The intuition that motivates the theorem is that we can find the worst case since future arrivals are known due to the periodicity.

Theorem 4.1. *Suppose tasks missing deadlines are immediately discarded for a given periodic task set $P = \{\tilde{\tau}_1, \tilde{\tau}_2, \ldots, \tilde{\tau}_N\}$. Task $\tau_i \in P$ is statistically schedulable with probability $1 - \epsilon$ if the following holds.*

$$Pr(\tilde{f}_{i,j} > \tilde{D}_{i,j}) \leq Pr(\sum_{k=1}^{N} \tilde{e}_k \cdot (\lfloor \frac{\tilde{T}_i}{\tilde{T}_k} \rfloor + 1) \geq \tilde{T}_i). \tag{14}$$

Proof. Consider the equivalent aperiodic task set Q_P of P. At time $\tilde{A}_{i,j}$, we have $Q_P(\tilde{A}_{i,j}) = \{\tau_m, \ldots, \tau_n\}$ where τ_n is $\tilde{\tau}_{i,j}$. Since $d_n = \tilde{d}_i = \tilde{T}_i$ for τ_n, we can write Ineq.(13)

$$Pr(f_n > D_n)$$
$$= Pr(\sum_{\tau_k \in Q_P(A_n, hp(\tau_n))} e_{k,A_n}^{res} + \sum_{\tau_k \in Q_P((A_n, f_n], hp(\tau_n))} e_k + e_n > \tilde{T}_i).$$

We can see that $Q_P(A_n, hp(\tau_n))$ can include no more than one instance per each periodic task $\tilde{\tau}_k \in P$, since all the previous instances are finished or discarded before their deadlines. Thus, we have

$$\sum_{\tau_k \in Q_P(A_n, hp(\tau_n))} e_{k,A_n}^{res} \leq \sum_{\tilde{\tau}_k \in P} \tilde{e}_k. \tag{15}$$

We then find the worst-case workload of $\sum_{\tau_k \in Q_P((A_n, f_n], hp(\tau_n))} e_k + e_n$. For each periodic task $\tilde{\tau}_k \in P$, there are at most $\lfloor \frac{\tilde{T}_i}{\tilde{T}_k} \rfloor$ new arrivals at Q_P in the interval $(A_n, f_n]$ where $\tilde{T}_i = \tilde{d}_i \geq f_n - A_n$. Thus,

$$\sum_{\tau_k \in Q_P(A_n, hp(\tau_n))} e_k + e_n \leq \sum_{\tilde{\tau}_k \in P} \lfloor \frac{\tilde{T}_i}{\tilde{T}_k} \rfloor \tilde{e}_k. \tag{16}$$

It immediately follows from Eq.(15) and Eq.(16)

$$\sum_{\tau_k \in Q_P(A_n, hp(\tau_n))} e_{k,A_n}^{res} + \sum_{\tau_k \in Q_P(A_n, hp(\tau_n))} e_k + e_n$$
$$\leq \sum_{\tilde{\tau}_k \in P} \tilde{e}_k + \sum_{\tilde{\tau}_k \in P} \lfloor \frac{\tilde{T}_i}{\tilde{T}_k} \rfloor \tilde{e}_k. \tag{17}$$

This leads to Ineq.(14).   □

By combining Eq.(13) and Eq.(14), we can obtain the following admission condition for a mixture of a periodic task set $P = \{\tilde{\tau}_1, \tilde{\tau}_2, \ldots, \tilde{\tau}_i, \ldots, \tilde{\tau}_N\}$ and an aperiodic task set $Q(t) = \{\tau_m, \ldots, \tau_j, \ldots, \tau_n\}$. Aperiodic task $\tau_i \in Q(t)$ can be admitted if the following can be satisfied.

$$Pr(f_i > D_i) = Pr\Big(\sum_{\tau_j \in Q(A_i, hp(\tau_i)) \cup Q_P(A_i, hp(\tau_i))} e_{j,A_i}^{res} + \sum_{\tilde{\tau}_j \in P} \lfloor \frac{d_i}{\tilde{T}_j} \rfloor \tilde{e}_j$$

$$+ \sum_{\tau_k \in Q(A_i, f_i], hp(\tau_i))} e_k + e_i > d_i \Big) \leq \epsilon \qquad (18)$$

where $\sum_{\tilde{\tau}_i \in P} \lfloor \frac{d_i}{\tilde{T}_i} \rfloor \tilde{e}_i$ represents the sum of execution times of periodic task instances that arrive with higher priorities than τ_i during the execution of τ_i.

Applying the above condition to admission control requires computing deadline miss probabilities at run-time. If task execution times are statistically independent, we can compute deadline miss probabilities by convolving sum of random variables. For instance, the probability given in Eq.(13) can be written as below.

$$Pr(f_i > D_i)$$

$$= Pr\Big(\sum_{\tau_j \in Q(A_i, hp(\tau_i))} e_{j,A_i}^{res} + \sum_{\tau_k \in Q((A_i, f_i], hp(\tau_i))} e_k + e_i > d_i \Big) \qquad (19)$$

$$= 1 - \int_{Q(A_i, hp(\tau_i)) \cup Q_{[A_i, f_i]} \cup \{\tau_i\}} g_{e_{j,t}^{res}}(e) * \ldots g_{e_k}(e) * \ldots g_{e_{i,t}}(e) de \qquad (20)$$

where $g_{e_{j,t}^{res}}(e)$ is the pdf of $e_{j,t}^{res}$ for $\tau_j \in Q(A_i, hp(\tau_i))$, $g_{e_k}(e)$ is the pdf of e_k for $\tau_k \in Q((A_i, f_i], hp(\tau_i))$, and $g_{e_{i,t}}(e)$ is the pdf of e_i. Let $e_{j,t}^{past}$ be the processor time consumed by τ_j from its arrival time to current time t. Given the probability density function $g_{e_j}(e)$, we have

$$g_{e_{j,t}}(e) = \begin{cases} 0 & \text{if } e < 0 \\ \frac{g_{e_j}(e + e_{j,t}^{past})}{1 - G_{e_j}(e_{j,t}^{past})} & \text{otherwise} \end{cases} \qquad (21)$$

where $G_{e_j}(e_{j,t}^{past}) = \int_0^{e_{j,t}^{past}} g_{e_j}(e) de$.

In fact, the admission control using Eq.(18) leads to computationally complex algorithms since it involves expensive convolution operations. Note that convolution operations are very expensive. For instance, the computational complexity of convolution $g * h$ is known to be $O(n^2)$ where n is the number of points in discretized functions of g and h. Although the run-time overhead can be reduced if we use FFT (Fast Fourier Transform) [9], the algorithm still requires $O(n \log_2 n)$ for $g * h$. Our next approach eliminates the need for convolutions by taking advantage of effective execution times, thus enabling efficient on-line admission control.

4.2   Effective Execution Times and Overrun Handling

The approach in the previous section is based on the assumption that tasks missing deadlines are discarded. This allows us to bound deadline miss probabilities but leads to computationally complex algorithms. Our second approach improves upon this by aggressively discarding tasks. Every task is associated with a particular amount of processor time, called effective execution time, and the admission control is performed using effective execution times. If any task overruns its effective execution time, it is immediately discarded. By overrun, we mean that a task consumes processor time more than its effective execution time.

The objective of preventing task overruns is to isolate tasks from one another. Under this scheme, every task can independently receive processor time up to the amount of its effective execution time. Thus, the deadline miss probability of a task is not adversely affected by other tasks. If we choose appropriate values for effective execution times for a given bound ϵ, tasks can be statistically schedulable with probability $1 - \epsilon$. To choose the minimal processor time required for a given bound, we can define the effective execution time e_i^ϵ of τ_i as a function of the required deadline miss probability ϵ and probability density function $g_{e_i}(e)$.

$$\int_0^{e^\epsilon} g_{e_i}(x)dx = 1 - \epsilon. \tag{22}$$

Clearly, discarding overrun tasks has the implication that execution times are bounded. The great benefit of this is that it allows us to integrate effective execution times and the deterministic techniques we developed in section 3. Using effective execution times, we can define statistical versions of utilization demand and maximum utilization demand as below.

$$u_{Q(t)}^\epsilon(\tau_i) \stackrel{def}{=} \frac{\sum_{\tau_j \in Q(t,hp(\tau_i))} e_{j,t}^{res,\epsilon} + e_i^\epsilon}{d_{i,t}^{res}} \quad and \quad U_{Q(t)}^\epsilon \stackrel{def}{=} \max_i [u_{Q(t)}^\epsilon(\tau_i)] \tag{23}$$

where $e_{j,t}^{res,\epsilon} = e_{j,t}^\epsilon - e_{j,t}^{past}$.

Using the above definitions, the following theorem provides a statistical version of schedulability condition for a mixed set.

Theorem 4.2. *Given a periodic task set P and aperiodic task set $Q(t)$, $Q_P \cup Q(t)$ is statistically schedulable with probability $1 - \epsilon$ if the following holds.*

$$U_{Q(t)}^\epsilon + U_P^\epsilon \leq 1 \tag{24}$$

where $U_P^\epsilon = \sum_{\tau_i \in P} \frac{\tilde{e}_i^\epsilon}{T_i}$.

Proof. Let $S(t)$ be $Q(t) \cup Q_P$. Thus, it suffices to show that any aperiodic task τ_i in $S = \{\tau_1, \ldots, \tau_i, \ldots\}$ is statistically schedulable if $U_{S(t)}^\epsilon \leq 1$. Consider the deadline miss probability of $\tau_i \in S$.

$$Pr(f_i > D_i) = Pr(\sum_{\tau_j \in S(A_i, hp(\tau_i))} e_{j,A_i}^{res} + \sum_{\tau_j \in S((A_i, f_i], hp(\tau_i))} e_j + e_i > D_i). \tag{25}$$

Since $e_j^{res} \leq e_j^{res,\epsilon}$ and $e_j \leq e_j^\epsilon$ for any τ_j, we have

$$Pr(f_i > D_i) = Pr(\sum_{\tau_j \in S(A_i, hp(\tau_i))} e_{j,A_i}^{res} + \sum_{\tau_j \in S((A_i, f_i], hp(\tau_i))} e_j + e_i > D_i) \tag{26}$$

$$\geq Pr(\sum_{\tau_j \in S(A_i, hp(\tau_i))} e_{j,A_i}^{res,\epsilon} + \sum_{\tau_j \in S((A_i, f_i], hp(\tau_i))} e_j^\epsilon + e_i > D_i). \tag{27}$$

$U^{\epsilon}_{S(t)} \le 1$ implies $\sum_{\tau_j \in S(A_i, hp(\tau_i))} e^{res,\epsilon}_{j,A_i} + \sum_{\tau_j \in S((A_i, f_i], hp(\tau_i))} e^{\epsilon}_j + e^{\epsilon}_i \le D_i$, thus we have

$$
Pr(f_i > D_i) \ge Pr\Big(\sum_{\tau_j \in S(A_i, hp(\tau_i))} e^{res,\epsilon}_{j,A_i} + \sum_{\tau_j \in S((A_i, f_i], hp(\tau_i))} e^{\epsilon}_j + e_i >
$$

$$
\sum_{\tau_j \in S(A_i, hp(\tau_i))} e^{res,\epsilon}_{j,A_i} + \sum_{\tau_j \in S((A_i, f_i], hp(\tau_i))} e^{\epsilon}_j + e^{\epsilon}_i \Big)
$$

$$
= Pr(e_i > e^{\epsilon}_i). \tag{28}
$$

This completes the proof.   □

In many applications, it may be unnecessarily stringent to discard overrun tasks. If the system is not overloaded, it is often advantageous to allow overruns as long as its further execution does not interfere with other admitted tasks. There are two other possibilities for handling overruns without affecting statistical guarantees for other admitted tasks. The first one is to give second chances to overrun tasks. Under this, the overrun task, whether it is periodic or aperiodic, is treated as a new aperiodic task. This task can receive processor time if it passes new admission test. The other one is to provide utilization slack. The use of utilization slack is similar to the idea of slack stealing [6, 11]. By Theorem 3.4, we can determine utilization slack and estimate available processor time for an overrun task. The following theorem shows how to estimate available processor time.

Theorem 4.3. *Suppose that $\tau_i \in Q(t) \cup Q_P$ under EDF overruns at time t, where Q_P is an equivalent aperiodic task set of P. Let e^{slack}_i be the available processor time for τ_i such that every task τ_j in $Q(t) \cup Q_P$ is statistically schedulable with probability $1 - \epsilon$. The available processor time $e^{slack}_i(t)$ satisfies the following*

$$
e^{slack}_i(t) \le d^{res}_{i,t} \cdot (1 - U^{\epsilon}_P - U^{\epsilon}_{Q(t)}) \tag{29}
$$

where U_P is the utilization of P.
Proof. Let $S(t)$ be $Q(t) \cup Q_P$. Clearly, τ_i has the highest priority in $S(t)$ at t, since τ_i is executing at t. Thus, if we increase the execution time of τ_i to $e_i + e^{slack}_i$, this affects utilization demands of all the remaining tasks in $S(t)$. Let $\hat{u}_{S(t)}(\tau_j)$ be a new utilization demand for any $\tau_j \in S(t)$, then we can write

$$
\hat{u}_{S(t)}(\tau_j) = \frac{\sum_{\tau_k \in S(t, hp(\tau_j))} e^{res,\epsilon}_{k,t} + e^{res,\epsilon}_{j,t} + e^{slack}_i}{d^{res}_{j,t}} \tag{30}
$$

$$
= \frac{\sum_{\tau_k \in S(t, hp(\tau_j))} e^{res,\epsilon}_{k,t} + e^{res,\epsilon}_{j,t}}{d^{res}_{j,t}} + \frac{d^{res}_{i,t} \cdot (1 - U^{\epsilon}_P - U^{\epsilon}_{Q(t)})}{d^{res}_{j,t}}. \tag{31}
$$

Since $d^{res}_{i,j} \le d^{res}_{j,t}$,

$$
\hat{u}_{S(t)}(\tau_j) \le \frac{\sum_{\tau_k \in S(t, hp(\tau_j))} e^{res,\epsilon}_{k,t} + e^{res,\epsilon}_{j,t}}{d^{res}_{j,t}} + (1 - U^{\epsilon}_P - U^{\epsilon}_{Q(t)}) \tag{32}
$$

$$
\le U_P + U^{\epsilon}_{Q(t)} + (1 - U^{\epsilon}_P - U^{\epsilon}_{Q(t)}) = 1. \tag{33}
$$

5   Conclusion

We have proposed three approaches to deadline guarantees for a mixed set of periodic and aperiodic tasks. First, we have presented a new schedulability analysis, called utilization demand analysis, which can be applied to periodic and aperiodic tasks with deterministic execution times. We have shown that the algorithm for this analysis has a run time of $O(n)$, and thus it enables an efficient on-line admission control. Second, we have presented a statistical admission control scheme based on deadline miss handling. By discarding tasks missing deadlines, this scheme allows us to bound deadline miss probabilities of tasks. Third, we have presented an improved statistical scheme using effective execution times. By handling overruns, effective execution times allow tasks to meet deadlines with a specified probability without being interfered with. Combined with the utilization demand analysis, effective execution times greatly simplify the admission control.

There are several future research directions. First, we could extend the untilization demand analysis for fixed priority scheduling algorithms such as rate monotonic (RM) algorithm. Second, we could evaluate a tradeoff between deadline miss probability and throughput of the system. Although we have not considered this problem in this paper, the results presented here will be useful in such evaluation.

References

1. Atlas, A. K., Bestavros, A.: Statistical Rate Monotonic Scheduling. IEEE Real-Time Systems Symposium, IEEE Computer Society Press (1998), 123–132
2. Audsley, N., Burns, A., Richardson, M., Wellings, A.: Hard Real-Time Scheduling: The Deadline-Monotonic Approach. IEEE Workshop on Real-Time Operating Systems and Software (1991), 133–137
3. Baker, T. and Shaw, A.: The Cyclic Executive Model and Ada. The Journal of Real-Time Systems (1989), 1(1):7–25
4. Buttazzo, G.: Value vs. Deadline Scheduling in Overload Conditions. IEEE Real-Time Systems Symposium, IEEE Computer Society Press (1995), 90–99
5. Chetto, H., Chetto, M.: Some Results of the Earliest Deadline First Scheduling Algorithm. IEEE Transactions on Software Engineering, IEEE Computer Society Press (1989), 15(10):1261–1268
6. Davis, R., Tindell, K., Burns, A.: Scheduling Slack Time in Fixed Priority Preemptive Systems. IEEE Real-Time Systems Symposium, IEEE Computer Society Press (1993), 222–231
7. Fohler, G.: Joint Scheduling of Distributed Complex Periodic and Hard Aperiodic Tasks in Statically Scheduled Systems. IEEE Real-Time Systems Symposium, IEEE Computer Society Press (1995), 22–33
8. Isovic, D., Fohler, G.: Online Handling of Hard Aperiodic Tasks in Time Triggered Systems. The 11th Euromicro Conference on Real-Time Systems (1999)
9. Johnson, J. R., Johnson, R. W.: Challenges of Computing the Fast Fourier Transform. Optimized Portable Application Libraries Workshop (1997)
10. Lehoczky, J. P.: Real-Time Queueing Theory. IEEE Real-Time Systems Symposium, IEEE Computer Society Press (1996), 186–195

11. Lehoczky, J. P., Ramos-Thuel, S.: An Optimal Algorithm for Scheduling Soft-Aperiodic Tasks in Fixed-Priority Preemptive Systems. IEEE Real-Time Systems Symposium, IEEE Computer Society Press (1992), 110–123
12. Lehoczky, J. P., Sha, L., Ding, Y.: The Rate Monotonic Scheduling Algorithm: Exact Characterization and Average Case Behavior. IEEE Real-Time Systems Symposium, IEEE Computer Society Press (1989), 166–171
13. Lehoczky, J. P., Sha, L., Strosnider, J.: Enhanced Aperiodic Responsiveness in Hard Real-Time Environments. IEEE Real-Time Systems Symposium, IEEE Computer Society Press (1987), 261–270
14. Leung, J., Merill, M.: A Note on the Preemptive Scheduling of Periodic, Real-Time Tasks. Information Processing Letters (1980), 11(3):115–118
15. Liu, C., Layland, J.: Scheduling Algorithm for Multiprogramming in a Hard Real-Time Environment. Journal of the ACM (1973), 20(1):46–61
16. Sprunt, B., Sha, L., Lehoczky, J. P.: Aperiodic Task Scheduling for Hard-Real-Time Systems. The Journal of Real-Time Systems (1989), 1(1):27–60
17. Spuri, M., Buttazzo, G.: Scheduling Aperiodic Tasks in Dynamic Priority Systems. Journal of Real-Time Systems (1996), 10(2):1979–2012
18. Tia, T.-S., Deng, Z., Shankar, M., Storch, M., Sun, J., Liu, L.-C.: Probabilistic Performance Guarantee for Real-Time Tasks with Varying Computation Times. IEEE Real-Time Technology and Applications Symposium (1995) 164–173

Appendix: Proof of Theorem 3.2.

Let $Q_1(t) \cup Q_2(t) = \{\tau_m, \ldots, \tau_p, \ldots, \tau_n\}$. Using Eq.(1) and Eq.(2), we have

$$U_{Q_1(t)\cup Q_2(t)} = max\{\frac{e^{res}_{m,t}}{d^{res}_{m,t}}, \ldots, \frac{e^{res}_{m,t}+, \ldots, +e^{res}_{p,t}}{d^{res}_{p,t}}, \frac{e^{res}_{m,t}+, \ldots, +e^{res}_{n,t}}{d^{res}_{n,t}}\} \quad (34)$$

Suppose that the maximum utilization demand is $U_{Q_1(t)\cup Q_2(t)} = \frac{e^{res}_{m,t}+, \ldots, +e^{res}_{p,t}}{d^{res}_{p,t}}$. Without loss of generality, suppose $\tau_p \in Q_1(t)$. Let $Q_1^*(t) \subset Q_1(t)$ be the set of tasks whose residual execution times $e^{res}_{i,t}$ appear in $\frac{e^{res}_{m,t}+, \ldots, +e^{res}_{p,t}}{d^{res}_{p,t}}$, and let $Q_2^*(t) \subset Q_2(t)$ be the set of tasks whose residual execution times $e^{res}_{j,t}$ appear in $\frac{e^{res}_{m,t}+, \ldots, +e^{res}_{p,t}}{d^{res}_{p,t}}$. Then, we can write

$$\frac{e^{res}_{m,t} + \ldots + e^{res}_{p,t}}{d^{res}_{p,t}} = \frac{\sum_{\tau_i \in Q_1^*(t)} e^{res}_{i,t} + \sum_{\tau_j \in Q_2^*(t)} e^{res}_{j,t}}{d^{res}_{p,t}} \quad (35)$$

Since priorities are assigned according to EDF, $d^{res}_{p,t}$ is the maximum of $\{d^{res}_{i,t} : \tau_i \in Q_1^*(t) \cup Q_2^*(t)\}$. Let $d^{res}_{q,t}$ be the maximum of $\{d^{res}_{i,t} : \tau_i \in Q_2^*(t)\}$, then we have $d^{res}_{q,t} \leq d^{res}_{p,t}$. Hence,

$$\frac{\sum_{\tau_i \in Q_1^*(t)} e^{res}_{i,t} + \sum_{\tau_j \in Q_2^*(t)} e^{res}_{j,t}}{d^{res}_{p,t}} \leq \frac{\sum_{\tau_i \in Q_1^*(t)} e^{res}_{i,t}}{d^{res}_{p,t}} + \frac{\sum_{\tau_j \in Q_2^*(t)} e^{res}_{j,t}}{d^{res}_{q,t}} \quad (36)$$

$$\leq U_{Q_1(t)} + U_{Q_2(t)} \quad (37)$$

Real-Time Disk Scheduling with On-Disk Cache Conscious

Hsung-Pin Chang[1], Ray-I Chang[2], Wei-Kuan Shih [3], and Ruei-Chuan Chang [4]

[1] Department of Electronic Engineering, National Changhua University of Education,
Changhua, Taiwan, R.O.C.
hpchang@cc.ncue.edu.tw
[2] Institute of Information Management, National Central University,
Chungli, Taiwan, R.O.C.
rchang@mgt.ncu.edu.tw
[3] Department of Computer Science, National Tsing Hau University,
Hsinchu, Taiwan, R.O.C.
wshih@cs.nthu.edu.tw
[4] Department of Computer & Information Science, National Chiao Tung University,
Hsinchu, Taiwan, R.O.C
rc@cc.nctu.edu.tw

Abstract. Previous real-time disk scheduling algorithms assume that each disk request incurs a disk mechanical operation and only consider how to move the disk head under real-time constraints. However, with the increased capacity of on-disk cache, modern disk drives read-ahead data aggressively. Thus, the on-disk cache may service lots of requests without incurring physical disk access. By exploring the design methodology of on-disk cache, in this paper, we propose CARDS: a cache-aware real-time disk scheduling algorithm that takes the on-disk cache into consideration during scheduling. Therefore, the scheduling algorithm can help to minimize the cache miss ratio. Besides, the service timing estimation is more accurate in schedulability analysis since the cache effect is considered. A simulation-based evaluation shows CARDS to be highly successful as compared to the classical real-time disk scheduling algorithms. For example, under sequential workload with 10 sequential streams, the data throughput of CARDS is 1.1 times of DM-SCAN.

1 Introduction

In a computer system, after disk scheduling, disk requests are sent to and served by the disk drive [14]. However, because the excess delay caused by the disk mechanical operation, a random access memory, i.e., on-disk cache, is equipped in disk drives to bridge the speed gap between the main memory and disk and acts as a speed-matching buffer [8-9, 15]. Nevertheless, in the last couple of years, the drastically improvement of hardware technology has driven an increased capacity of on-disk cache. Since caches work on the premise that the issued tasks have spatial and tempo-

J. Chen and S. Hong (Eds.): RTCSA 2003, LNCS 2968, pp. 88–102, 2004.
© Springer-Verlag Berlin Heidelberg 2004

ral locality, with the hope of repeated or sequential access patterns, the on-disk cache can service most requested data without incurring physical disk accesses. If the majority of the accesses to disk are serviced by the on-disk cache, the I/O delay will be significant reduced.

Cache design methodology gives cache designers a competitive edge in the market. Therefore, manufacturers either patent them or consider their implementation a trade secret. However, if the parameters of on-disk cache are disclosed, the caching effect would be taken into consideration during the disk scheduling. Consequently, the scheduling algorithm can help to, not just by cache replacement scheme, preserve the principles of spatial and temporal locality, which in turn results in a higher hit ratio. Furthermore, the service timing estimation is more accurate in schedulability analysis since the caching effect is considered during scheduling. Otherwise, a task's execution time must assume in the worst case that a mechanical disk access is incurred. This results in an over estimation of system resource usage and decreases system performance.

The idea of taking the on-disk cache into account in disk scheduling is also seen in [18]. They mentioned that requests that can be satisfied by the cache should be given higher priority to be accessed from disk cache. However, they only simulate the caching effect for the performance evaluations of conventional disk scheduling algorithms, which have no timing requirements.

On the basis of an existing real-time disk scheduling algorithm, DM-SCAN [1], we propose the CARDS (cache-aware real-time disk scheduling) algorithm that considers the on-disk cache effect during the scheduling of real-time disk tasks. After the completion of DM-SCAN algorithm, CARDS algorithm reorders the tasks that can be served by on-disk cache. That is, disk requests whose accesses have the spatial locality are made closer to meet their temporal locality, and thus increase the cache hit probability. Experimental results shows that, under sequential accesses, our proposed cache-aware algorithms obtains larger data throughput than DM-SCAN since the increased cache hit ratio. For example, under sequential workload with 10 sequential streams, the data throughput of CARDS is 1.1 times of DM-SCAN.

In the rest of this paper, we shall first introduce the disk service model in a real-time environment, including on-disk cache design methodology, the timing characteristics of real-time tasks, and the objective of real-time disk scheduling algorithm in Section 2. Section 3 reviews the related works. In Section 4, we introduce the terms used for the proposed algorithm. Section 5 presents the proposed CARDS algorithms. The experimental results are shown in Section 6. Finally, Section 7 summarizes this paper.

2   Background

2.1 Design Methodology of On-Disk Cache

The on-disk cache is often organized as a number of segments. A segment is a sequence of data blocks managed as a unit; that is, each segment contains data that is disjoint from all other segments. Some disk drives dynamically resize the number (and size) of cache segment based on recent access characteristics to ensure greater utilization.

With the incorporation of on-disk cache, the data path to the disk will be interposed by the on-disk cache. In addition to retrieve the requested data blocks, most disks, based on analyzing access and usage pattern of the requests, also perform read-ahead. It is because that many applications process data sequentially that the next request will be for data following the current request. By read-ahead, the requested data of subsequent accesses will have been resided in the cache and shorten the service time.

Compared with the capacity of a disk drive, the on-disk cache size is smaller. Consequently, segment replacement occurs when the cache is full of data and a new data block is requested. Note that, the replacement algorithm has a profound impact on the cache performance. A good replacement scheme should evict the segment that has no immediate access and retain the data more likely to be accessed soon. For example, random replacement (RR), least recently used (LRU), and least frequently used (LFU) are some of the well-known cache replacement algorithms [10, 17].

2.2   Real-Time System

Assume that the *start-time* and *finish-time* denote the actual times at which a task is started and completed, respectively. To characterize the timing characteristics of a real-time task, two parameters are associated with it to determine the proper start-time and finish-time.

- *Ready time* : the earliest time at which a task can start
- *Deadline*   : the latest time at which a task must be completed

To satisfy the real-time requirements, the start-time of a task should not be earlier than its ready time. Additionally, its finish-time should not be later than the related deadline [16]. Depending on the consequence of a missed deadline, real-time tasks are further classified into *hard* and *soft*. A real-time task is said to be *hard* if missing its timing constraints will cause serious damage and system will misbehave. In contrast, a real-time task is said to be *soft* if meeting its timing constraints is desirable for performance, but a missed deadline does not influence the correctness of system behavior. A schedule of real-time tasks is said to be *feasible* if all tasks can be sequentially served according to the specified real-time requirements. In this paper, we address the hard real-time system.

2.3   Real-Time Disk Scheduling Problem

As stated above, disk tasks in a real-time system must be associated with timing characteristics to describe their timing constraints. Accordingly, a real-time disk task T_i is denoted by five parameters $(t_i, l_i, b_i, r_i, d_i)$ where t_i is the track location, l_i is the sector number, b_i is the data size, r_i is the ready time and d_i is its deadline. Assume that the schedule sequence is T_jT_i. Because disk tasks are non-preemptive, the start-time s_i and finish-time f_i of a real-time task T_i with schedule T_jT_i are thus computed by $s_i = \max\{r_i, f_j\}$ and $f_i = s_i + c_{j,i}$, respectively. Note that, $c_{j,i}$ denotes the service time of task T_i with schedule sequence T_jT_i. If T_i is a cache hit, $c_{j,i}$ is the value of cache access time. Otherwise, $c_{j,i}$ represents the time spent to access the physical disk.

Given a set of real-time disk tasks $T = \{T_1, T_2, ..., T_n\}$ where n is the number of input disk tasks and the i-th disk task T_i is denoted by $(r_i, d_i, t_i, l_i, b_i)$. The objective of a real-time disk scheduling algorithm is to find a *feasible* schedule $T_z = T_{z(1)}T_{z(2)}...T_{z(n)}$ with *maximal throughput*. The index function $Z(i)$, for $i = 1$ to n, is a permutation of $\{1, 2, ..., n\}$. Define *schedule finish-time* as the finish time it takes to serve all input tasks according to their respective timing constraints. Clearly, this is the finish-time of the latest task $f_{z(n)}$. Therefore, the disk throughput is calculated as follows.

$$\text{Throughput} = \sum_{i=1}^{n} b_{z(i)} \bigg/ f_{z(n)} \; \Box \; (f_{z(n)})^{\Box 1}. \tag{1}$$

The obtained disk throughput is related to the inverse of schedule finish-time. If the input schedule is completed earlier, more data throughput is obtained. The data throughput improvement of scheduler Z compared with scheduler X can be computed as

$$\text{Throughput improvement} = (1 - f_{z(n)}/f_{x(n)}) * 100\% . \tag{2}$$

Therefore, the problem objective defined to maximize throughput can be achieved by minimizing the schedule finish-time. We formally formulate the real-time disk scheduling problem as follows.

Definition 1: Real-Time Disk Scheduling

Given a set of n real-time disk tasks $T = \{T_1, T_2, ..., T_n\}$ where the i-th task $T_i = (r_i, d_i, t_i, l_i, b_i)$, find a feasible schedule $T_z = T_{z(1)}T_{z(2)}...T_{z(n)}$ that resolves $\min_{\Box z}\{f_{z(n)}\}$ under $r_{z(i)} \Box s_{z(i)}$ and $f_{z(i)} \Box d_{z(i)}$ for $1 \Box z(i) \Box n$. $\Box$

3   Related Work

The SCAN algorithm was first proposed by Denning for scheduling conventional disk tasks [5] and has been shown as an optimal algorithm under amortized analysis and probability model [4]. However, due to the lack of timing consideration, the SCAN algorithm is not suitable for scheduling real-time disk tasks. To address a task's real-time characteristic, EDF (Earliest Deadline First) was proposed and shown to be optimal if tasks are independent [11]. Nevertheless, in terms of disk scheduling, the service time of a disk task depends on its previous task's track location. The assumption that tasks are independent is not held. Actually, taking only deadlines into account without considering the cost of service time, EDF incurs excessive seek-time costs and results in poor disk throughput [13].

Consequently, various approaches have been dedicated to combine the features of SCAN type of seek optimizing algorithms with EDF type of real-time scheduling algorithms [2-3]. For these algorithms, they start from an EDF schedule and then reschedule tasks to minimize seek and/or rotational latency under real-time constraints. For example, the well-known SCAN-EDF scheme was proposed that first schedules tasks with the earliest deadlines [13]. If two or more tasks have the same deadline, these tasks are serviced according to their relative track locations, *i.e.*, by SCAN algorithm. Since only tasks with the same deadline are seek-optimized, the obtained data throughput improvement is limited.

To increase the probability of applying SCAN algorithm to reschedule input tasks, DM-SCAN (<u>D</u>eadline <u>M</u>odification-<u>SCAN</u>) proposed the concept of maximum-scannable-group (MSG) [1]. An MSG is a set of continuous tasks that can be rescheduled by SCAN without missing their respective timing constraints. Given an EDF schedule $T = T_1T_2...T_n$, MSG G_i started from task T_i is defined as the sequent tasks $G_i = T_iT_{i+1}T_{i+2}...T_{i+m}$ where task T_j satisfies following criteria

$$f_j \sqcap d_i \text{ and } r_j \sqcap s_i \text{ for } j = i \text{ to } i+m . \tag{3}$$

A simple example to demonstrate the identification of MSGs is shown in Fig. 1. Given an EDF schedule $T=T_1T_2T_3T_4T_5$. To calculate MSG G_2, we have $f_2 \sqcap d_2$, $r_2 \sqcap s_2$ and $f_3 \sqcap d_2$, $r_3 \sqcap s_2$, but $f_4 > d_2$ although $r_4 \sqcap s_2$. Thus, $G_2=T_2T_3$. Following the same approach, other MSGs can be obtained as $G_1=T_1$, $G_3=T_3T_4$, $G_4=T_4T_5$ and $G_5=T_5$, respectively.

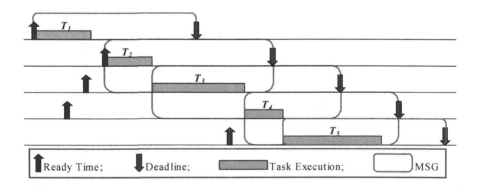

Fig. 1. An example to demonstrate the identification of MSGs.

After the identification of MSGs, DM-SCAN reschedules tasks in each MSG by seek-optimizing SCAN scheme to minimize total service time. Note that the rescheduled result destroys the EDF sequence. Because DM-SCAN requires the input tasks based on EDF order, a deadline modification scheme is proposed to modify tasks' deadlines and transfers the rescheduled non-EDF sequence into a pseudo EDF order.

Here, "pseudo" means that the tasks are ordered by the modified deadlines. For example, given the schedule sequence T_iT_j, a pseudo deadline $d_{s(i)}$ is derived as $d_{s(i)} =$ **min**$\{d_i, d_{s(j)}\}$. By the deadline modification scheme, DM-SCAN iteratively reschedules tasks from the derived pseudo EDF schedule to obtain more data throughput.

4 CARDS: Cache-Aware Real-Time Disk Scheduling Algorithm

4.1 Preliminaries

In this section, we describe the terms used in this paper. Given a set of n real-time disk tasks, assume that for each disk access T_i, $1 \Box i \Box n$, if a cache miss occurs, the cache logic will bring a data size of   into the on-disk cache and the content of data blocks brought into cache is denoted by E_i. Thus, **size**$(E_i) =$. Note that, the value of depends on the cache segment size, and if read-ahead is performed, also on the read-ahead size. To distinguish a set of tasks whose accesses having the principles of spatial locality, we define the concept of *principal task* and *cached task*.

Definition 2: Principal Task and Cached Task
Given a set of real-time disk tasks $T_1T_2..T_n$, if T_j's requested data block b_j is included in E_i, where $1 \Box i < j \Box n$. Then, T_i is called the *principal task* of T_j and denoted as $P(T_j)=T_i$. In addition, T_j is called the *cached task* of T_i and denoted as $C(T_i)=T_j$.

Definition 3: Immediate Principal Task and Immediate Cached Task
Given a set of real-time disk tasks $T_1T_2..T_n$, assume that $P(j)=T_i$ (i.e., $C(i)=T_j$), where $1 \Box i < j \Box n$. If there exists no T_j's principal tasks (or T_i's cached tasks) between T_i and T_j, then task T_i is called the *immediate principal task* of T_j and denoted as $G(T_j) = T_i$. In addition, task T_j is called the *immediate cached task* of T_i and denoted as $H(T_i) = T_j$.

Therefore, T_j is cache hit if $E_{G(T_j)}$ is resident in the on-disk cache when T_j is issued. In other words, a cache hit occurs for T_j if the cached data of $G(T_j)$ remains in the cache, that is, has not yet been replaced when T_j is issued. Consequently, if T_j and $G(T_j)$ would be scheduled close enough such that the cached data of $G(T_j)$ have not yet been flushed when T_j is issued, then T_j can be serviced by the on-disk cache and shorten its access time.

However, in a real-time system, a derived schedule must be feasible. Therefore, scheduling T_j and $G(T_j)$ to be closer must not violate both T_j and $G(T_j)$'s timing constraints. In addition, since other tasks may be influenced as this *cache-aware* scheduling, the deadlines of the influenced tasks should not be violated to guarantee a feasible schedule. Therefore, when and how to perform such cache-aware scheduling scheme under real-time constraints posed a challenge in the design of our scheduling algorithm.

4.2 CARDS Algorithm

On the basis of the DM-SCAN, in this section, we propose the CARDS algorithm. As described in Section 4, to increase cache hit ratio, $G(T_i)$ and T_i must be close enough to prevent $E_{G(Ti)}$ from being replaced when T_i is executed. Thus, after the running of DM-SCAN algorithm, the CARDS reschedules tasks to make $G(T_i)$ and T_i closer while meeting tasks' timing constraints.

Suppose that the number of cache segments is m and LRU is used as the cache replacement algorithm. Before describing the CARDS algorithm, for task T_k, we first introduce the *miss function* $f(k)$ as:

$$f(k) = \begin{cases} 1 & \text{if } T_k \text{ introduces a cache miss} \\ 0 & \text{if } T_k \text{ introduces a cache hit} \end{cases}. \tag{4}$$

By the miss function, the concept of *flush point* of T_i, $P(i)$, is introduced such that

$$\sum_{l=i}^{P(i)} f(l) = m + 1 \quad \text{or } P(i) = n \text{ if } n \text{ is reached}. \tag{5}$$

As shown in Fig. 2, $P(i)$ represents the position that E_i is flushed to the disk. Therefore, T_j should be executed before $T_{P(i)}$, if possible, to be cache hit. Therefore, CARDS schedules T_j just immediately before the flush point of T_i, $P(i)$, if the rescheduling result does not violate tasks' timing constraints.

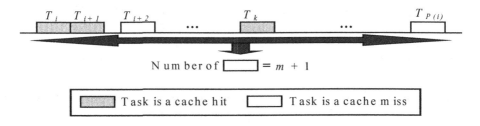

Fig. 2. The identification of a flush point.

Assume that after the running of DM-SCAN, the derived schedule $S = T_1 T_2 ... T_n$. Then, the CARDS identifies pairs of cached tasks and their immediate principal tasks. For each pair of cached task T_j, $j \in [1, n]$, and its immediate principal task T_i ($= G(T_j)$), CARDS must decide whether T_j should be scheduled to be closer to T_i and, if yes, which position is suitable for T_j to be scheduled. The steps that are performed by the CARDS for each pair of cached task T_j and its immediate principal task T_i are shown in the following.

1. Calculate the value of $P(i)$ by Equation (4) and (5).
2. If T_j is in front of $T_{P(i)}$, as shown in Fig. 3a, T_j can be serviced by the on-disk cache by the cached data of T_i. Therefore, no rescheduling is needed for T_j.

3. However, if T_j is after or equal to $T_{P(i)}$, i.e., $P(i) \square j$, then cache miss will occur when T_j is issued. Consequently, CARDS tries to schedule T_j to execute before $T_{P(i)}$. Depending on the values of r_j, ready time of T_j, and $s_{P(i)}$, start time of $T_{p(i)}$, two different cases may exist:

    (a)   If $s_{P(i)} \square r_j$, as shown in Fig. 3b, then T_j can not be advanced to execute before $T_{P(i)}$ since its ready time falls behind the start time of $T_{P(i)}$. Consequently, no reordering is performed for T_j.

    (b)   If $s_{P(i)} > r_j$, as shown in Fig. 3c, then T_j can be advanced to execute before $T_{P(i)}$. Although the time at which T_j could be started is between $\mathbf{max}(d_j, r_j)$ and $s_{P(i)}$, CARDS reschedules T_j into the $(P(i)-1)^{th}$ position, i.e., immediate before $T_{P(i)}$. Note that, the rescheduling of T_j may result in an infeasible schedule. Therefore, a feasibility checking must be performed for each rescheduling operation by the techniques described in Section 5.2.

From above algorithm, the increase of cache hit probability thus realized with the CARDS by rescheduling tasks that have the opportunity to be cache hit after the DM-SCAN scheme.

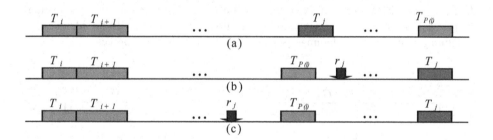

Fig. 3. Three cases for CARDS algorithm. (a) Tj is guaranteed to be cache hit and thus no movement is needed as it is scheduled before the $T_{P(i)}$. (b) No movement is needed for Tj because its ready time is after the start time of $T_{P(i)}$. (c) By moving Tj in front of $T_{P(i)}$, Tj thus can be cache hit.

4.3 Feasibility Checking

As shown in Fig. 4, when task T_i is rescheduled, some tasks are influenced by an increased or decreased delay of finish time. Therefore, feasibility checking must be performed when rescheduling a task and, if an infeasible schedule is produced, this rescheduling operation cannot be activated. The checking for feasibility involves computing start-time and finish time for each request in a schedule and thus a naive computation algorithm has $O(n)$ complexity. To accelerate the checking process, the concept of a *conjunction group* is introduced.

Fig. 4. The condition when a task T is moved from α to β. Tasks in region A are not influenced. However, tasks in the region B may be delayed. Besides, tasks within the region C may be delayed or advanced for execution depends on whether T's access results in a cache hit or miss at location β.

Definition 4: Conjunction Group

Given a set of real-time disk tasks $T = T_1T_2...T_n$, a conjunction group G_i is defined as a number of continuous tasks $G_i = T_iT_{i+1}...T_{i+m}$ with each task T_k for $k = i +1$ to $i+m$ satisfies $r_k \square f_{k-1}$. $\square$

Therefore, tasks in a conjunction group will be executed one by one without any free time slice between them. Note that, as shown in Fig. 5, conjunction groups may be merged or split when a rescheduling operation is taken place. By the idea of conjunction group, following lemmas assist to simplify the checking process.

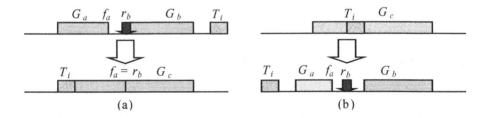

(a)   (b)

Fig. 5. Conjunction groups may be merged or split when a rescheduling operation is occurred. (a) Ti is rescheduled to the front of Ga. As a result, conjunction group Ga and Gb are merged into Gc since rb $\square$ fa. (b) Ti is rescheduled out from Gc. As a result, conjunction group Gc is split into Ga and Gb since fa < rb.

Lemma 1. Assume that a conjunction group $G_k = T_kT_{k+1}...T_l$ and task T_m is rescheduled from position α to β. If T_i, $i\square$ [k, l-1], is influenced by a delayed execution of ε, then for all tasks T_j, $j\square$ [i + 1, l], their execution are also delayed by ε.
   Proof. For a real-time task T_{i+1}, $s_{i+1} = \max\{r_{i+1}, f_i\}$ and $f_{i+1} = s_{i+1} + e_{i+1}$, where e_{i+1} denotes T_{i+1}'s execution time. Since $T_{i+1}\square G_k$, from the definition of conjunction group,

$$s_{i+1} = f_i \text{ and } f_{i+1} = s_{i+1} + e_{i+1} = f_i + e_i .$$ (6)

Because T_i is delayed by ε, i.e., f_i is increased by ε, thus from Equation (6), s_{i+1} and f_{i+1} are also delayed by ε. Following the same arguments, task T_j, T_j, $j\square$ [i + 2, 1], is also influenced by an delayed execution of ε $\square$.

Lemma 2. Assume that a conjunction group $G_k = T_k T_{k+1}...T_l$ and a task T_m is rescheduled from position α to β. If T_i, $i\square$ [k, 1 - 1], i.e., T_i is within G_k, is thus influenced by an advanced execution of ε, then for all tasks T_j, $j\square$ [i + 1, 1], their execution are also advanced by ε, if G_k is not split.

Proof. The proof can be derived as the proof of Lemma 2. $\square$

Given the set of tasks in a schedule, we define the slack l_i of task T_i as follows.

$$l_i = d_i - f_i .$$ (7)

That is, the slack l_i represents the duration for which T_i can be delayed without violating its deadline. As lemma 1 and 2 show, the increase/decrease of finish time is the same for all tasks in a collaboration group. Accordingly, we only maintain the smallest value of slack for each collaboration group rather than maintaining it for individual requests. As a result, when a movement operation is done, we only have to check the task with the smallest value of slack to see whether its deadline is missed, if a delayed execution is occurred. Besides, the checking process is stopped when a free time slice, i.e., no task is executed, is encountered. Note that, conjunction groups may be merged or split as a delayed or advanced execution, and thus the slack value should be updated correspondingly. From above, the overhead of feasibility checking is significantly reduced by the introduction of slack and conjunction group. Therefore, CARDS can quickly verify whether a movement of a task results in an infeasible schedule or not.

5 Experimental Results

In this section, the performance of the CARDS is evaluated. Section 4.1 shows the platform used for our experiments and the characteristics of input workload. In Section 4.2, the experimental results of the CARDS are presented to compare their performance.

5.1 Experiment Platform

As stated above, the characteristics of on-disk cache must be explored so that cacheaware scheduling scheme can then be applied. Because disk manufactures consider their on-disk cache implementation scheme a technical secret, thus we use the disk drive parameters derived from [7], which uses the techniques of on-line extraction [6, 19]. Table 1 shows some important parameters of Quantum Altas 10K MAG 3091, which is used as the target disk in our experiments [7, 12]. The seek time cost is calculated by the extracted data from [7]. The rotational latency is assumed half of the time of a full track revolution. The on-disk cache parameters of Quantum Altas 10K MAG 309, which is based on the extracted data of [7], are shown in Table 2.

Table 1. Quantum Atlas 10K: MAG3091 disk parameters

Year	1999
Capacity	9.1 GB
No. of cylinders	10,042
No. of surface	6
No. of sectors per track	334
Sector size	512 bytes
Revolution speed	10,000 RPM

Table 2. Quantum Atlas 10K: MAG3091 disk cache parameters

Size	2 MB
No. of buffer segments	10
Segment size	374 sectors
Transfer time	0.184 ms

There are two kinds of workloads in our experiments, one is random and the other is sequential. The workload of random tasks is uniformly distributed over the disk surface. For sequential workload, it consists of a number of sequential streams and random requests. Each sequential stream in our simulations emulates the sequential access pattern and consists of five sequential requests; the accessed block of first request is also randomly distributed over the disk surface. Then, the following requests access the block immediate after their previous tasks. In addition, the number of random requests in a sequential workload is selected as one third of the total requests. The accessed blocks of these random tasks are also uniformly distributed over the disk surface. The size of data accessed by each request, either sequential or random, is normally distributed with a mean of 36 KB. For random workload, if there are n random tasks, the ready times of tasks are randomly generated from 0 to $6*n$ ms. After a random time interval, $0\sim5*n$ ms, the related deadlines are uniform distributed within $0\sim10*n$ ms. For sequential workload, if there are m sequential streams, the total number of input tasks $n = 1.5 * (5*m)$. Since there are five sequential tasks in a stream, the ready time of each sequential task in a stream is randomly generated between 0 and $2*n/5$ ms after its previous task and its deadline is uniform distributed within $0\sim20*n/5$ ms after a random time interval, $0\sim10*n/5$ ms. For the random tasks in the sequential workload, their ready times are random generated between 0 and $2*n$ ms. After a random time interval, $0\sim10*n$ ms, their related deadlines are uniformly distributed within $0\sim20*n$ ms. The cache replacement scheme is assumed LRU. If a cache miss occurs, the cache logic will read ahead a data size of 354 sectors (177KB), including the requested one, into a least-recently-used cache segment. In all following experiments, fifty experiments are conducted with different seed for random number generation and the average value is measured.

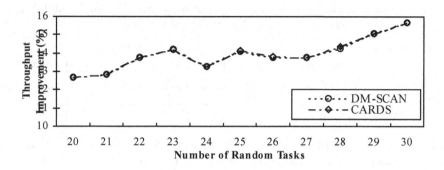

Fig. 6. Throughput improvement of CARDS under different number of random tasks. The throughput improvement is compared to EDF.

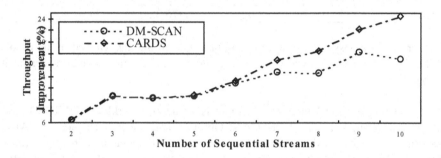

Fig. 7. Throughput improvement of CARDS for sequential workload with different number of sequential streams. The throughput improvement is compared to EDF.

5.2 Experimental Results

If the same number of real-time tasks is given, a well-behaved scheduling algorithm must maximize data throughput under guaranteed real-time constraints. Given random access workload, the data throughput improvements of DM-SCAN and CARDS under different number of input tasks are shown in Fig. 6. The derived throughput improvement is compared with EDF. Fig. 7 presents the same experiment for different sequential workloads. Besides, the minimum, maximum, and average schedule fulfill time of two approaches with a sequence of twenty-five random tasks are also presented in Table 3. Table 4 presents the same performance metrics but under sequential workload with ten streams.

On-disk cache works on the premise that the input workload follows the principles of temporal and spatial locality. Thus, given random tasks, the throughput improvements presented in Fig. 6 shows little differences between CARDS and DM-SCAN.

Table 3. Given 26 random tasks, the minimum, maximum, average schedule fulfill-time, and throughput improvement compared with EDF for different schemes.

Algorithms	Schedule Fulfill-Time (msec)			
	minimum	maximum	average	improvement
EDF	262.10	355.86	309.74	0.0 %
DM-SCAN	230.48	314.60	267.05	15.66%
CARDS	230.48	314.60	267.05	15.68%

Table 4. Under sequential workload with 10 sequential streams, the minimum, maximum, average schedule fulfill-time, and throughput improvement compared with EDF for different schemes.

Algorithms	Schedule Fulfill-Time (msec)			
	minimum	maximum	average	improvement
EDF	453.31	543.15	498.51	0%
DM-SCAN	376.99	473.61	413.24	17.11%
CARDS	327.04	442.02	376.32	24.51%

There is little possibility that a random task will hit the data cached in the on-disk cache. Therefore, cache-aware scheduling has no means to increase the cache hit probability.

In contrast, as shown in Fig. 7, if input is sequential workload, CARDS obtains larger data throughput than DM-SCAN. Observe that, the performance of CARDS performs better than DM-SCAN with the increase of number of sequential streams. Since the number of cache segment is ten, when the number of cache segments is considerably larger than that of sequential streams, the on-disk cache capacity is thus larger enough to sustain a great deal of blocks accessed by each sequential task. Thus, the derived throughput difference between DM-SCAN and CARDS is not significant. However, when the number of sequential streams is increased, CARDS increases the on-disk cache utilization and obtains further data throughput than DM-SCAN.

6   Conclusions

To be in competitive edge in the market, disk manufactures consider their disk implementation as a technical secret. However, if the information of on-disk cache is explored, the disk scheduling algorithm can exploit this information to derive a schedule minimizing the cache miss probability. In this paper, we thus propose the CARDS algorithm that considers the caching effect during the scheduling. As a result, the disk scheduling scheme can also be actively involved in reducing the cache miss ratio. In addition, the timing analysis is more accurate since the on-disk cache is considered during scheduling and thus, if a cache hit occurs, cache transfer time is used as the task's execution time for schedulability analysis without assuming the worst case that each disk task incurs a physical disk mechanical operation. The experiments demonstrate that the proposed schemes indeed obtain larger data through-put than DM-SCAN. For example, under sequential workload with 10 sequential streams, the data throughput of CARDS is 1.1 times of DM-SCAN.

The CARDS is based on the *static* manner of an on-disk cache; that is, the scheduling scheme is aligned to the on-disk cache's behavior. However, in recent design of on-disk cache, the number (and hence size) of cache segment is configurable. In addition, read-ahead can be enable/disable dynamically. As a result, our future work would propose an aggressive cache-aware real-time disk scheduling scheme that changes the behavior of on-disk cache dynamically during the scheduling.

References

1. Chang, R.I., Shih, W.K., and Chang, R.C., Deadline-Modification-SCAN with Maximum Scannable-Groups for Multimedia Real-Time Disk Scheduling, *Proc. Real-Time Systems Symp.*, pp. 40-49, 1998.
2. Chang, H.P., Chang, R.I., Shih, W.K., and Chang, R.C., Enlarged-Maximum-Scannable-Groups for Real-Time Disk Scheduling in a Multimedia System," *Proc. Computer Software and Applications Conf. (COMPSAC)*, IEEE Comput. Soc., pp. 383-388, 2000.
3. Chang, H. P., Chang, R. I., Shih, W. K., and Chang, R. C., "Reschedulable-Group-SCAN Scheme for Mixed Real-Time/Non-Real-Time Disk Scheduling in a Multimedia System," *Journal of Systems and Software*, Vol. 59, No. 2, pp.143-152, Nov. 2001.
4. Chen, T. S., Yang, W. P., and Lee, R.C.T., "Amortized Analysis of Some Disk-Scheduling Algorithms: SSTF, SCAN, and N-Step SCAN," *BIT*, Vol. 32, No. 4, pp. 546-558, 1992.
5. Denning, P.L., "Effects of Scheduling on File Memory Operations," *Proc. of AFIPS SJCC*, pp. 9-21, 1967.
6. Ganger, G., "System-Oriented Evaluation of Storage Subsystem Performance," Ph.D. Dissertation, CSE-TR243-95, University of Michigan, Ann Arbor, June 1995.
7. Ganger, G. and Schindler, J., "Database for Validated Disk Parameters for DiskSim," http://www.ece.cmu.edu/~ganger/disksim/diskspecs.html.
8. Hospodor, Andy, "Hit Ratio of Caching Disk Buffers," *Proc. IEEE Computer Society International Conf.*, pp. 427-432, 1992.
9. IBM Corporation, "Larger Disk Cache Improves Performance of Data-Intensive Applications," White Paper, October, 1998.
10. Karedla, R., Love, J. S., and Wherry, B. G., "Caching Strategies to Improve Disk System Performance," *IEEE computer*, Vol. 27, No. 3, pp. 38-46, March 1994.
11. Liu, C. L and Layland, J. W., "Scheduling Algorithms for Multiprogramming in a Hard Real-Time Environment," *Journal of ACM*, Vol. 20, No. 1, pp. 46-61, 1973.
12. Quantum Corporation, Quantum Atlas 10K, http://www.quantum.com/products/hdd/atlas_10k/atlas_10k_specs.htm
13. Reddy, A. L. N. and Wyllie, J. C., "Disk Scheduling in a Multimedia I/O System," *Proc. ACM International Conf. on Multimedia*, pp. 225-233, 1993.
14. Ruemmler, C. and Wyllie, J. C., "An Introduction to Disk Drive Modeling," *IEEE Computer*, Vol. 27, No. 3, pp. 17-28, 1994.

15. Shriver, E., Merchant, A., and Wilkes, J., "An Analytic Behavior Model for Disk Drives with Readahead Caches and Requests Reordering," *Proc. ACM SIGMETRICS*, pp. 182-191, 1998.
16. Stankovic, J. A. and Buttazzo, G. C., "Implications of Classical Scheduling Results for Real-Time Systems," *IEEE Computer*, Vol. 28, No. 6, pp. 16-25, June 1995.
17. Thiebaut, D., Stone. S. H, and Wolf, J. L., "Improving Disk Cache Hit-Ratios Through Cache Partitioning," *IEEE Transaction on Computers*, Vol. 41, No. 6, pp. 665-676, 1992.
18. Worthington, B. L., Ganger, G. R., and Patt, Y. N., "Scheduling Algorithms for Modern Disk Drives," *Proc. ACM SIGMETRICS*, pp. 241-151, 1994.
19. Worthington, B. L., Ganger, G. R., Patt, Y. N., and Wilkes, J., "On-Line Extraction of SCSI Disk Drive Parameters," *Proc. ACM SIGMETRICS*, pp. 136-145, 1995.

Probabilistic Analysis of Multi-processor Scheduling of Tasks with Uncertain Parameters

Amare Leulseged and Nimal Nissanke

School of Computing, Information Systems and Mathematics
South Bank University, 103 Borough Road, London SE1 0AA, UK

Abstract. A new approach is proposed for the probabilistic assessment of schedulability of periodic tasks with uncertain characteristics in dynamic multi–processor scheduling. It is aimed at non–critical real–time applications such as multimedia, which allow some leeway with respect to compliance with timing requirements, provided that certain minimum Quality of Service (QoS) requirements are met. Uncertainties are taken into account through random variables at the task arrival times and by characterising subsequent task characteristics in probabilistic terms. By examining each pair of possible computation time and deadline of a given task at each time unit in relation to the same of other tasks, an execution pattern is derived. This forms the basis for computing various QoS attributes such as probability of successful execution, latency in response time, jitter, etc. Illustrative examples address, amongst others, the performance of two particular algorithms, EDF and LLF, in the presence of uncertainties in task characteristics.

1 Introduction

It is a common practice in real–time scheduling algorithms to assume that task characteristics such as computation time and deadline are known precisely, sometimes in advance, and remain constant throughout the life time of the task. However, this is rarely the case in practice and the lack of precise prior knowledge about task characteristics remains a major concern in scheduling. This applies especially to non–critical real–time applications such as multimedia systems, computer vision, real–time tracking based on radar or sonar. Computational tasks in them tend to vary widely in execution times depending on the complexity of the specific task instance being handled. In addition, tasks may or may not arrive at fixed periodic intervals. Experiments in [12] show deviations of actual periods from the nominal ones and a tendency for them to alternate between short and long periods in consecutive instances. In the face of such unpredictabilities, task deadlines too are subject to change in order to indirectly account for uncertainties in task execution times and request times.

A common approach to dealing with uncertainties so arising is to adopt a worst–case strategy and to assign an extreme value to the computation time, regardless of its frequency relative to its other possible values and its representativeness. This is an acceptable solution in critical applications but is an overly

J. Chen and S. Hong (Eds.): RTCSA 2003, LNCS 2968, pp. 103–122, 2004.
© Springer-Verlag Berlin Heidelberg 2004

demanding one in non–critical applications. In applications such as multimedia user perception is not affected often by such variation to the same degree, while in other applications there are more tolerant alternative ways to dealing with occasional failures. Under such circumstances under–utilisation of computing resources resulting from worst–case considerations could seriously undermine the cost–effectiveness of such applications. This underlines the importance of arriving at an acceptable balance between the Quality of Service (QoS) and the overall system performance, such as throughput and resource utilisation in terms of processor workloads. However, uncertainties in task characteristics must still be dealt with, because missing deadlines result in both QoS violations and wastage of computing resources, to the detriment of the balance between both factors mentioned above.

For tasks with uncertain parameters, on–line and off–line scheduling algorithms and schedulability analysis have been proposed in the literature. Zhou et. al [12] propose a modified rate–monotonic schedulability analysis, incorporating two new experimentally determined parameters to account for uncertainties in operating system overheads, namely, a constant representing the CPU utilisation of operating system activities and a worst–case timer delay factor. A Statistical Rate-Monotonic Scheduling approach [1], with an implementation described in [2], allows scheduling of periodic tasks with highly variable execution times expressed through a probability density function. It also allows the consideration of statistical QoS requirements defined in terms of the probability of a random instance of the task chosen from an arbitrarily long execution history meeting its deadline. Recently, Manolache et al [9] have presented an approach to performance analysis of periodic task sets with their execution times specified as a continuous probability distribution. Although it is a non preemptable and is confined to single processor environments, the approach is elegant and shares the same objective as this paper. Dealing with the so–called monotone processes, i.e., those where the quality of the result keep improving after surpassing a minimum threshold computation time, Chung et. al [3] propose an imprecise computational model that involves a mandatory initial part and an optional follow–on part. Mandatory parts of all tasks are to be executed within the deadline of each task, while the optional part is left free to execute longer, if it can be accommodated, thus refining and improving the result. Hamann et. al [7] extends the imprecise computational model by incorporating an additional minimum reservation time for each task that assures a certain probability of successfully completing a given percentage of its optional parts. In assessing computational times of real–time tasks, there have been several attempts such as [11] based on deterministic code analysis. Recognition of their inappropriateness is evident from works such as [8] devoted to an estimation of execution times statistically from past observations. As is demonstrated in [6] using Gumbel distribution for estimating the worst–case execution time (WCET), statistical models are likely to result in a more realistic assessment of execution times.

The works devoted to uncertainties in task characteristics are extensive. The above are a small selection illustrating a range of approaches addressing, in different ways, how to improve the quality of computations, or the QoS as understood in modern computer applications, while maintaining a high resource utilisation level.

In this context, our previous work [10] dealt with a probabilistic analysis of dynamic multi–processor scheduling with emphasis on the overall performance of the scheduling environment as a whole. In contrast, this paper shifts the focus to the scheduling of individual tasks, addressing at the same time the overall performance of the scheduling environment. The paper shows how an appropriate balance between the QoS or system performance and resource utilisation could be achieved purely from a scheduling perspective. The tasks are periodic but otherwise can be of any general form with respect to uncertainties in computation times and deadlines. As in [10], the framework is tied to a sufficiently general scheduling environment, namely, a multi–processor dynamic environment. It is based on a completely probabilistic characterisation of the problem that can be achieved within a discrete model. The paper examines, in particular, the performance of two well–known scheduling algorithms: Least Laxity First (LLF) and Earliest Deadline First (EDF). Using examples, it also illustrates how the QoS parameters are affected by various factors, among them, the number of available processors, the scheduling strategy, as well as the effect of computational requirements of the tasks on one another.

Organisation of this paper is as follows. Section 2 presents the core ideas of the proposed framework. Following on, Section 3 examines practically useful performance and QoS indicators. Section 4 presents a detailed illustration of the potential uses of the proposed framework, with respect to QoS and algorithmic superiority. Section 5 concludes the paper with a summary of achievements.

2 Analytical Framework

2.1 Representation of Tasks

In this work, computation times and deadlines of tasks are assumed to vary over time in an unpredictable manner, while their arrival times are left fixed at periodic intervals. Whatever the sources of uncertainties are, such uncertain parameters may be expressed in the form of probabilistic distributions. Alternatively, such uncertain parameters may originate from the problem specification, possibly, in a probabilistic form as Quality of Service targets to be achieved.

As a result, the chosen variable task parameters can be described, in general, in the form of distribution functions over a given sampling space. Supposing that there are n tasks in the system, computation time of each of the tasks τ_i, for $i = 1, 2, \cdots, n$, at its arrival time is denoted by C_i and its laxity (urgency, measured as the length of time from current time to the deadline minus the computation time) by L_i. Each task τ_i is requested periodically with a fixed period of T_i starting from time zero. It is important to note that C_i and L_i are two random variables because at the time of τ_i's arrival their values are totally unpredictable, except in a probabilistic sense. Let the sampling spaces of C_i and

L_i be the sets $1 .. c_{max}$ and $0 .. l_{max}$ respectively, where the notation $x .. y$ denotes the set of numbers from x to y inclusively. Subsequent to τ_i's arrival, its computation time and laxity are still described probabilistically over the same spaces, though no longer as random variables. Let us refer to the area enclosed within $-1 \leqslant l \leqslant l_{max}$ and $0 \leqslant c \leqslant c_{max}$ in a two–dimensional coordinate system with axes l and c as the *task domain* and denote it by $\bar{S}$. Note that the laxity value -1 is intended solely for keeping track of tasks that have failed so that the line $l = -1$ contains only those tasks that may have already failed. Mathematically, $\bar{S}$ is the Cartesian product $-1 .. l_{max} \times 0 .. c_{max}$, but excluding the point (-1, 0). $\bar{S}$ can be partitioned into a *scheduling domain*, denoted by S, and an *exit domain*, denoted by E. The former is defined as $S = 0 .. l_{max} \times 1 .. c_{max}$, while the latter as $E = \bar{S} - S$.

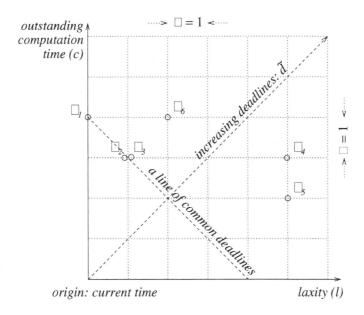

Fig. 1. Task representation in the scheduling domain

For the purpose of visualisation, Figure 1 illustrates the above in a deterministic setting, with 'tokens' showing the location of tasks at a particular instant in time and the coordinates l and c indicating, respectively, the laxity and the computation time of each task. As time progresses, each token moves either downward, signifying its execution, or leftward, signifying its non–execution. In a multi–processor environment with m identical processors, the scheduler's task at each clock tick is to move at most m tokens one division downwards. An underlying assumption of this execution model is that tasks are not bound to particular processors and that the migration cost of tasks between processors is negligibly small. A token reaching the l-axis at such an instant signifies the successful completion of the relevant task, whereas a token crossing the c-axis its failure to meet the deadline. All tasks currently under execution are thus located within the bounds of the scheduling domain S and the tasks which have already gone through the system are in the exit domain E. Tasks in E comprise the tasks which have failed to meet their deadlines (remaining on $l = -1$ after reaching it) and the tasks which have been successfully executed by their deadlines (remaining on $c = 0$ after reaching it), both with certain non–zero probabilities in the probabilistic setting. The tasks in both S and E are the only ones in the task domain.

Following the usual convention, the joint probability mass function (PMF) of the two random variables L_i and C_i is denoted by $p_{L_i,C_i}(l,c)$ or, for brevity, by $p_i(l,c)$. As a function of two random variables, it describes the probability of τ_i arriving at a point (l,c), i.e., the probability of τ_i having a laxity l and computation time c at the time of τ_i's arrival. Thus

$$p_i(l,c) = p_{L_i,C_i}(l,c) = P(L_i = l, C_i = c)$$
$$= P_{L_i,C_i}[\{(l',c') : l' = l, c' = c\}]. \tag{1}$$

The jointly distributed random variables L_i and C_i are jointly discrete, for it is a requirement that the sum of the joint probability mass function over the points (l,c) where $p_i(l,c) > 0$ is equal to one. Though the latter PMF is defined over the whole task domain, our interest is only in those points where $p_{L_i,C_i}(l,c) > 0$.

At the time of arrival, every task has, as described by (1), a totally random value for its PMF. However, as the tasks are executed, the values of their PMFs change with time. In this respect, let us adopt an extended notation for dealing with their evolution over time. First, let us refer to the probability of τ_i having the value (l,c) in its PMF at time t as $p_i^t(l,c)$. At times t when $t \bmod T_i$ is equal to zero, that is, when τ_i is freshly requested, $p_i^t(l,c)$ is to have a random value described in accordance with (1). At other times, $p_i^t(l,c)$ is not random and is determined by $p_i^{t-1}(l,c)$ and the manner in which τ_i has been executed at time $(t-1)$. This can be expressed as

$$p_i^t(l,c) = p_i^{init}(l,c) \qquad\qquad \text{if } t \bmod T_i = 0\,,$$
$$= next_i^t(p_i^{t-1}(l,c)) \qquad \text{otherwise}\,. \tag{2}$$

where $p_i^{init}(l,c)$ is an initialisation PMF (1) to be used at request times of τ_i, while $next_i$ is a function updating the PMF that existed at time $(t-1)$ taking into account whether τ_i has been executed at $(t-1)$ or not. For any task τ_i at a point (l,c) in E, the following holds: $p_i^t(l,c) \neq 0 \Rightarrow p_i^{t+1}(l,c) \geqslant p_i^t(l,c)$ for all t, with the exception of time values just prior to fresh requests, and either $l = -1$ or $c = 0$. In other words, failures and successes are irreversible, despite the fact that in a probabilistic paradigm their occurrence is not necessarily definite. The purpose of this study is, essentially, to characterise the functions $next_i$s in (2) for each and every task in the system and, thereby, to establish execution patterns of tasks and other execution metrics of practical interest.

2.2   Scheduling Algorithms and Selection of Tasks for Execution

A task τ_i, which is at a point (l, c) at time t with some non–zero probability, at time $(t + 1)$ would be either at the point $(l, c - 1)$ with some probability, say, $v_i^t(l, c)$, if τ_i has been executed (moved vertically downward) at t, or at the point $(l - 1, c)$ with a probability of $h_i^t(l, c) = (1 - v_i^t(l, c))$, if it has not been executed (moved horizontally leftward) at t. Thus, $v_i^t(l, c)$ denotes the execution probability of τ_i while at (l, c) at time t. This would depend on several factors, including the scheduling algorithm being used to schedule the tasks in the system and, hence, the level of priority the task has been assigned.

For generality, let the scheduling algorithm be expressed using a (linear) function $f(l, c)$ of l and c defined on natural numbers. Let the scheduler assign task priorities depending on the value of f at each point. To be specific, for example, let this function be of the form $f(l, c) = a\, l + b\, c$, with a and b being constants and let us assume the scheduler to work in such a manner that tasks with smaller values of $f(l, c)$ are assigned higher priorities. As particular cases, with $a = 1$ and $b = 1$, constant value of $f(l, c)$ corresponds to EDF while with $a = 1$ and $b = 0$, it corresponds to LLF.

The generality of the function f calls for some clarifications. Firstly, it is to be noted that the range of f should occupy a contiguous stretch of natural numbers starting from 0 or 1, depending on the scheduling algorithm. Any non–arbitrary priority assignment should aim at ensuring that lines of constant values of $f(l, c)$ result in a regular pattern of contours, each one unit apart, over the scheduling domain. Using appropriate forms for f, a variety of scheduling algorithms is conceivable within the chosen representation. Despite their theoretical and, possibly, practical interest, this avenue is not pursued here any further.

For a task τ_i at (l, c) at time t with a non-zero probability, this would result in a certain (non–negative) value K for $f(l, c)$. At each point (mass value) (l', c') in S where $p_i^t(l', c')$ is greater than zero, τ_i will thus generally have a different value of f. At this point in time, the tasks in the system can be classified into three sets: Ω_1^t representing the set of all tasks each having a value of $f(l', c') < K$, Ω_2^t representing the set of all tasks, including $\tau_i(l, c)$, each having a value of $f(l', c') = K$ and, finally, Ω_3^t representing the set of all tasks each having $f(l', c') > K$ or has been already either executed successfully or has failed.

Letting Ω be the set of all tasks in the system, we note that $\Omega = \bigcup_{k=1}^{3} \Omega_k^t$. Provided that $p_i^t(l, c) > 0$, the sets Ω_k^t, which are also dependent on (l, c), can be defined as

$$\Omega_1^t(l, c) = \{\tau_k \mid k \in 1 .. n \wedge \exists (x, y) \in S \bullet (p_k^t(x, y) > 0 \wedge f(x, y) < f(l, c))\}. \quad (3)$$
$$\Omega_2^t(l, c) = \{\tau_k \mid k \in 1 .. n \wedge \exists (x, y) \in S \bullet (p_k^t(x, y) > 0 \wedge f(x, y) = f(l, c))\}. \quad (4)$$
$$\Omega_3^t(l, c) = \{\tau_k \mid k \in 1 .. n \wedge \exists (x, y) \in S \bullet (p_k^t(x, y) > 0 \wedge f(x, y) > f(l, c))\} \cup$$
$$\{\tau_m \mid m \in 1 .. n \wedge \exists (x, y) \in E \bullet p_m^t(x, y) > 0\}. \quad (5)$$

For better readability, let us simply write from now on Ω_k^t instead $\Omega_k^t(l, c)$ defined above, for $k = 1, 2, 3$, unless the omission of (l, c) causes an ambiguity otherwise. Let us also write $p_{\tau_j}^t(\Omega_k^t)$ for the probability of τ_j being in the set Ω_k^t at time t.

It is important to note that the sets in (3)–(5) are not necessarily pairwise disjoint since a task can belong to more than one set at the same time. In other words, for $j = 1, 2, \ldots, n$, τ_j can be in one, two or all three sets of Ω_k^t, for $k = 1, 2, 3$, simultaneously, in each case with a probability of $p_{\tau_j}^t(\Omega_k^t)$. Obviously,

$$0 \leqslant p_{\tau_j}^t(\Omega_k^t) \leqslant 1 \text{ but } \sum_{k=1}^{3} p_{\tau_j}^t(\Omega_k^t) = 1.$$ As our concern here is to calculate

probability of $\tau_i(l, c)$ being executed at time t, let us introduce the notation $\bar{\Omega}_k^t = \Omega_k^t \backslash \{\tau_i\}$, for $k = 1, 2, 3$, so that as a result τ_i is excluded from the set $\bar{\Omega}_k^t$.

Letting τ_i continue to be the task under consideration for scheduling, let us now select the sets ω_k^t, for $k = 1, 2, 3$, such that

a) $\omega_k^t \subseteq \bar{\Omega}_k^t$ (i.e., each is a subset of the corresponding set in (3)–(5))
b) $\omega_1^t \cup \omega_2^t \cup \omega_3^t = \Omega \backslash \{\tau_i\}$ (i.e., together they account for all the tasks in the system, except for τ_i)
c) $\omega_j^t \cap \omega_k^t = \emptyset$ for $j, k = 1, 2, 3$ and $j \neq k$ (i.e., they are pairwise mutually disjoint)

Let p_k, a non–negative integer, represents the number of tasks in each of the sets ω_k^t, for $k = 1, 2, 3$, in such a way that $p_1 + p_2 + p_3 = n - 1$. As an implication, task distribution in the scheduling domain is such that at the given point in time, among the tasks other than τ_i, at least p_1 tasks will be in $\bar{\Omega}_1^t$, at least p_2 tasks in $\bar{\Omega}_2^t$ and at least p_3 tasks in $\bar{\Omega}_3^t$. This is one of the possible scenarios. Since $0 \leqslant p_k \leqslant |\bar{\Omega}_k^t|$, the number of such possible scenarios can be determined mathematically. For the time being, let $R_i^{t, \omega}(l, c)$ denote the set of all such possible scenarios, i.e., the set of 3-tuples of the form $(\omega_1^t, \omega_2^t, \omega_3^t)$.

2.3   Task Execution Probability

When τ_i is under consideration for execution at a particular point (l, c) in any of the scenarios $r \in R_i^{t, \omega}(l, c)$ described above, it will be executed with some probability $v_{i,r}^t(l, c)$, obviously with $0 \leqslant v_{i,r}^t(l, c) \leqslant 1$. The value of $v_{i,r}^t(l, c)$ depends on three factors: a) the probability of realisation of the scenario r, b) the number of processors available for executing the tasks in r, and c) the number of other tasks in r competing with τ_i, if any, at the same priority level as defined by $f(l, c)$. The probability $v_{i,r}^t(l, c)$ is a conditional probability because, in effect, we are considering external factors affecting τ_i's execution, assuming that τ_i is at (l, c).

Dealing with (a) first, let $P_{\omega_k^t}$, $k = 1, 2, 3$, represents the product of the probabilities of tasks in ω_k^t being in that set. That is

$$P_{\omega_k^t} = \begin{cases} \displaystyle\prod_{\tau_j \in \omega_k^t} p_{\tau_j}(\omega_k^t) & \text{if } \omega_k^t \neq \emptyset, \\ 1 & \text{if } \omega_k^t = \emptyset. \end{cases} \tag{6}$$

Then, the probability of realisation of the particular scenario r is the product of $P_{\omega_k^t}$ values defined above for $k = 1, 2$ and 3. Turning to (b) and (c), suppose that there are m processors. Letting ρ be the probability of τ_i being executed by any one of the m processors in the face of any competition offered by other tasks operating at the same priority level, ρ can be determined as

$$\rho = \begin{cases} 1 & \text{if } p_1 + p_2 \leqslant m - 1, \\ \frac{m - p_1}{p_2 + 1} & \text{if } p_1 \leqslant m - 1 \wedge p_1 + p_2 > m - 1, \\ 0 & \text{otherwise}. \end{cases} \tag{7}$$

The above constrains the manner in which the tasks can be chosen for execution and, thus, limits the number of scenarios eligible for execution.

The probability of τ_i being executed as described above in the scenario r may now be given as

$$v_{i,r}^t(l, c) = P_{\omega_1^t} \times P_{\omega_2^t} \times P_{\omega_3^t} \times \rho. \tag{8}$$

In computing τ_is overall probability of execution at (l, c) at time t, that is $v_i^t(l, c)$, all possible scenarios in $R_i^{t,\omega}(l, c)$ must be taken into consideration. That is

$$v_i^t(l, c) = \sum_{r \in R_i^{t,\omega}(l,c)} v_{i,r}^t(l, c). \tag{9}$$

Having obtained the conditional probability $v_i^t(l, c)$ of τ_i at (l, c) at time t, it is now possible to derive the actual execution probability of τ_i as the joint probability of the event captured in (9) in conjunction with the event that τ_i is actually at (l, c). An analogous reasoning applies to the corresponding probability of τ_i missing execution (non-execution) at (l, c) at time t. Let $ex_i^t(l, c)$ denote the probability of τ_i being executed at (l, c) at time t and, likewise, $ms_i^t(l, c)$ the probability of τ_i missing execution. These can be defined as

$$ex_i^t(l, c) = p_i^t(l, c) \times v_i^t(l, c). \tag{10}$$
$$ms_i^t(l, c) = p_i^t(l, c) \times h_i^t(l, c) = p_i^t(l, c) - ex_i^t(l, c). \tag{11}$$

Consequently, the probability of τ_i being at (l, c) at the next time unit $(t + 1)$ depends on the probability of τ_i having been executed at $(l, c+1)$ at time t and the probability of τ_i having missed execution at $(l+1, c)$ at time t. This results in

$$p_i^{t+1}(l, c) = ex_i^t(l, c + 1) + ms_i^t(l + 1, c). \tag{12}$$

With the derivation of (12), it is time to revisit the function $next_i^t$, introduced in (2). In fact, our discussion from Section 2.2 onward, and the derivations made since then, constitute the definition of $next_i^t$, albeit implicitly. The above reasoning applies to all the time values over the period of a given instance of every task. This process of computation can be continued over any desired interval time.

Let us outline the computations involved in *next* in the form of an abstract algorithm. It is defined here as a recursive algorithm $next^t$ with respect to time t covering all tasks (and not just for τ_i as indicated by the notation $next_i^t$). It is to be executed for each time value in the simulation period – typically the Least Common Multiple (LCM) of the task periods. It performs the necessary calculations for all tasks and, as appropriate, for all points in the task domain. As its result, $next^t$ returns a three-dimensional matrix. If this matrix is referred to as p^t so that its elements can be referred to as $p^t(i, l, c)$, it is clear that $p^t(i, l, c)$ is essentially an interchangeable notation for $p_i^t(l, c)$.

```
1.   algorithm next^t
2.   begin
3.      if t > 0 then p^t := next^{t-1}
4.      for i ∈ 1 .. n do
5.         if t mod T_i = 0 then p^t(i, l, c) := p^{init}(i, l, c) for (l, c) ∈ S̄
6.      end for
7.      if t = 0 return p^t
8.      for i ∈ 1 .. n do
9.         for K from K_{min} to K_{max} do
10.           calculate Ω_{j,K} for j from 1 to 3
11.           if i ∈ Ω_{2,K} then calculate ex_i^t(l, c) and ms_i^t(l, c)
12.        end for
13.     end for
14.     for i ∈ 1 .. n do
15.        for (l, c) ∈ S̄ do
16.           result(i, l, c) := ex_i^t(l, c + 1) + ms_i^t(l + 1, c) if (l, c) ∈ S
17.           result(i, l, c) := p_i^t(l, c) + ms_i^t(l + 1, c)      if (l = -1) and (c > 0)
18.           result(i, l, c) := p_i^t(l, c) + ex_i^t(l, c + 1)      if (l ⩾ 0) and (c = 0)
19.        end for
20.     end for
21.     return result
22.  end algorithm next^t
```

In Lines from 3 to 6, the algorithm computes the $p_i^t(l, c)$ for each task τ_i at time unit t. In effect, this is achieved using either the function $next^{t-1}$ (computed in the previous time step) if t is greater than zero and is not a renewal time of τ_i, or the specified initial value of $p_i^{init}(l, c)$ if t is a renewal time of τ_i. The latter applies also to the case when $t = 0$. In the case of a renewal, a distinction is to made depending on whether the point (l, c) concerned is in the scheduling domain or in the exit domain. For this reason, $p^t(i, l, c)$ in Line 5 is to be defined as

$$p^{init}(i, l, c) = \begin{cases} p_i^{init}(l, c) & \text{if } (l, c) \in S, \\ 0 & \text{if } (l, c) \in E. \end{cases} \tag{13}$$

According to Line 7, for $t = 0$ the algorithm terminates by returning the matrix p^t as its *result*. The rest of the algorithm applies therefore only for $t > 0$. The loop within Lines 9 and 11 is executed for the range values, say, from some

K_{min} to some K_{max}, of the priority assignment function f. Within this loop, $\Omega_{j,K}$s are computed for $j = 1, 2, 3$ (Line 10). Then for all tasks sharing the priority level K, the functions ex and ms are computed (loop within Lines 8–13). Then in Lines from 14 to 20 the result to be returned as the value of the function $next^t$ is computed. As noted above, it is a three-dimensional matrix of probabilities covering the points in the whole of the task domain for each of the n tasks. At each of the points in the scheduling domain, these probabilities are computed as the sum of ex and ms functions applied, as appropriate, to the point above it and to the point on its right (Line 16). If a task misses its execution while on the l axis, then the associated probability is added to the probability of it having already failed, i.e. the probability of it already lying on the line $l = -1$ (Line 17). Likewise, if a task is executed while on the line $c = 1$, then the associated probability is added to the probability of it having already successfully computed, i.e. the probability of it already lying on the line $c = 0$ (Line 18).

3   Performance and Quality of Service Issues

Once the relevant quantities are computed using the concepts introduced in Section 2, they may be used to compute other practically more meaningful indicators. Among them are the probability of successful execution, or failure, of a given task instance within its period and other Quality of Service measures such as jitter (irregularity in successful termination time between successive task instances), the number of processors required to guarantee a pre-specified QoS performance measure and so on.

First, let us introduce several common assumptions and notations. Let L denote the LCM of the periods of the n tasks under consideration. All tasks are assumed to arrive for the first time simultaneously at time zero and thereafter each task τ_i repeats itself within L every T_i time units. $S_{i,j}^k$ denotes the probability of successful execution of $\tau_{i,j}$, i.e. jth instance of τ_i, at the kth time unit in its period, where $j = 1, 2, \cdots, L/T_i$ and $k = 1, 2, \cdots, T_i$. Analogously, $F_{i,j}^k$ denotes the probability of failure of $\tau_{i,j}$ at the kth time unit. It is assumed that the request time for the $\tau_{i,j}$ coincides with the end of the period of $(j-1)$th instance. Note that $\tau_{i,j}$ can terminate only from next time unit onward since it must last at least one unit of time.

Expressions (10) and (11) are of immediate use in the computation of the probabilities $S_{i,j}^k$ and $F_{i,j}^k$. Letting $S_{i,j}$ and $F_{i,j}$ denote the sum of these two respective probabilities over $\tau_{i,j}$'s period, they can be defined as

$$S_{i,j} = \sum_{k=(j-1)T_i+1}^{jT_i} \left(\sum_{l=0}^{l_{max}} ex_i^k(l, 1) \right). \tag{14}$$

$$F_{i,j} = \sum_{k=(j-1)T_i+1}^{jT_i} \left(\sum_{c=1}^{c_{max}} ms_i^k(0, c) \right). \tag{15}$$

Letting $R_{i,j}$ be a variable representing the response time of $\tau_{i,j}$ the probability of it successfully terminating within the first d_i time units of its period, $0 < d_i \leqslant T_i$, can be defined as

$$Pr(R_{i,j} \leqslant d_i) = \sum_{k=1}^{d_i} S_{i,j}^{(j-1)T_i+k} . \tag{16}$$

and the mean of $R_{i,j}$ within $\tau_{i,j}$'s period is

$$\sum_{k=1}^{T_i} k \, S_{i,j}^{(j-1)T_i+k} . \tag{17}$$

If desired, the above may be further averaged over the whole LCM. The measures (14) and (15) could also be used in assessing the value of partial computations in monotone processes, mentioned in Section 1, and acceptable limits of loss rates in applications such as multimedia transmissions.

Turning to jitter control, suppose that the jth instance of task τ_i successfully terminates at the kth time unit in its period and the $(j+1)$th instance at the lth time unit in its own period. The irregularity in the response times of consecutive instances of τ_i can then be defined as $g = \mid k - l \mid$; see [4]. Let J_i be a variable denoting the mean regularity *success jitter* of τ_i, i.e., the mean regularity jitter between consecutive instances of a given task terminating with some probability of success in their respective periods. The probability of τ_i experiencing a mean regularity success jitter g, $0 \leqslant g \leqslant T_i$, can be defined as

$$Pr(J_i = g) = \sum_{j=1}^{L_i} \left(\sum_{k=(j-1)T_i+1}^{jT_i} S_{i,j}^k (S_{i,j+1}^{k+T_i+g} + S_{i,j+1}^{k+T_i-g}) \right) . \tag{18}$$

where $L_i = LCM/T_i$. The probability of mean regularity success jitter J_i not exceeding a value g is

$$Pr(J_i \leqslant g) = \sum_{x=0}^{g} \sum_{j=1}^{L_i} \left(\sum_{k=(j-1)T_i+1}^{jT_i} S_{i,j}^k (S_{i,j+1}^{k+T_i+x} + S_{i,j+1}^{k+T_i-x}) \right) . \tag{19}$$

Probability of successful execution of a task, or a set of tasks, is an important measure in guaranteeing a required level of any QoS attribute. If $S_i(m, n)$ denotes the probability of successful execution of task τ_i in an environment with m processors and a total of n tasks, then an increase in m is generally expected to raise $S_i(m, n)$ while an increase in n to lower it. However, these effects are not necessarily linear or simple. This is because the task parameters also play a role in affecting one another's execution. Though the interplay of these factors has not been a subject addressed in this work, an example later (see Section 4 and Figure 9) illustrates the effect of the number of processors on successful task executions.

4   An Illustrative Example

In order to illustrate the capabilities of the proposed framework, this section considers three examples. These share certain tasks in common and comprise five tasks altogether. In order to distinguish them, let us refer to these examples through the set of tasks used in each, namely, as Task Set 1, 2 and 3 respectively. Task Set 1 consists of the tasks in $\{\tau_1, \tau_2, \tau_3\}$, Set 2 the tasks in $\{\tau_1, \tau_2, \tau_3, \tau_4\}$ and, finally, Set 3 the tasks in $\{\tau_1, \tau_2, \tau_3, \tau_4, \tau_5\}$. Task Sets 2 and 3 are intended to illustrate the effect of the increased workload due to competition offered by τ_4, and τ_4 and τ_5, respectively on the execution of tasks in Set 1, i.e., τ_1, τ_2 and τ_3. Characteristics of tasks are partly shown in Figure 2. For example, according to

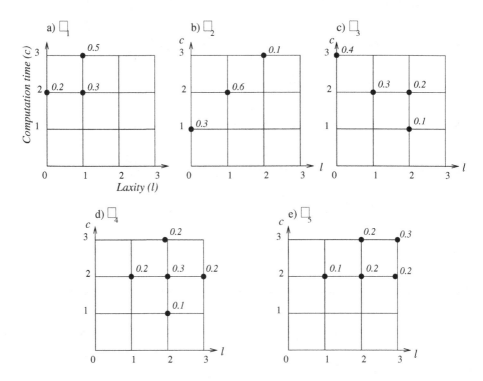

Fig. 2. Characteristics L_i and C_i of tasks τ_i, $i = 1, \cdots, 5$, at request times

Figure 2(a), the probability of task τ_1 arriving with a laxity 1 and a computation time 2 is 0.3, whereas it can arrive with the same laxity but a computation time 3 with a probability of 0.5. The periods of the five tasks, τ_i, $i = 1, 2, \cdots, 5$ are 4, 6, 5, 5 and 6 respectively. Unless otherwise stated, the number of processors used are 2.

Turning to the results, Figure 3 shows the 'patterns' of successful execution of tasks τ_i, $i = 1, 2$ and 3, in Task Set 1. This covers an interval of time spanning over 30 units of time, that is, half the LCM of the task periods. Each point on a curve gives the probability of successful execution of the task concerned at the corresponding unit of time t, i.e. $S_{i,j}^t$ for $\tau_{i,j}$, introduced in Section 3. Obviously, there should have been a companion figure accompanying this, not shown for reasons of space, giving the probabilities of task failures at each time unit and for each task. Figure 3, which is essentially the PMFs of successful execution of successive task instances adjoined together, is intended primarily at giving an initial insight into the computations involved. What counts in subsequent computations of QoS indicators is the cumulative probability of successful execution of each task instance, that is, $S_{i,j}$ for $\tau_{i,j}$ introduced in (14).

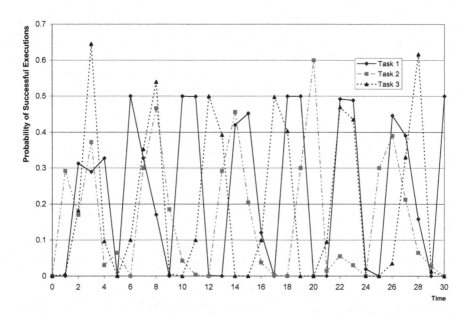

Fig. 3. Patterns of successful execution of τ_1, τ_2 and τ_3 in LLF in Task Set 1

Figure 4 shows the cumulative probabilities of successful execution of tasks τ_1, τ_2 and τ_3 only in the EDF regime over their respective periods in all three Task Sets over the the LCM of task periods. It illustrates the adverse effect of the increased workload due to τ_4 in Task Set 2, and τ_4 and τ_5 in Task Set 3 on the execution of τ_1, τ_2 and τ_3. Figure 5 gives the same for execution in the LLF regime, showing a noticeable improvement in the performance of tasks τ_1 and τ_3 compared to that in the EDF regime, though τ_2 is worse off under LLF. Direct comparisons are made in Figures 6 and 7 to expose the nature of this effect; in Figure 6 with respect to τ_1, τ_2 and τ_3 in Task Set 3 and in Figure 7 with respect to τ_1 in all three Task sets. Despite their inadequacy for drawing any general conclusions, these examples tend to suggest a link between the algorithms and the more dominant task characteristic on the probability of successful execution.

Based on (18), the probability of tasks τ_i, $i = 1, 2, 3, 4$, experiencing mean regularity success jitter ranging from 0 to their respective periods, T_i, has been

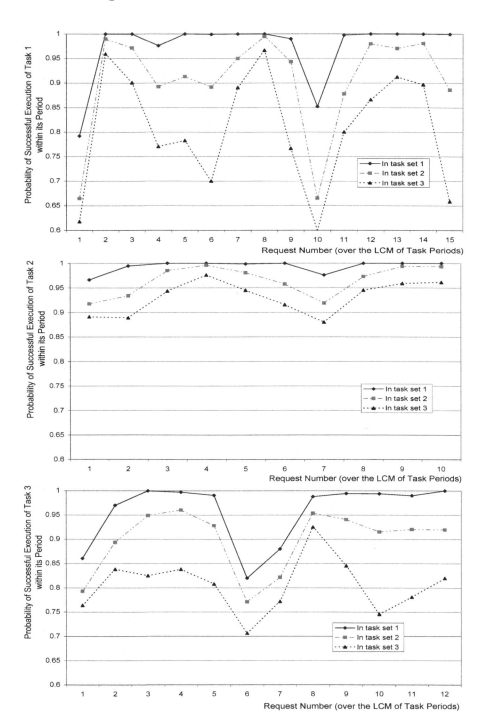

Fig. 4. τ_1, τ_2 and τ_3 in EDF in Task Sets 1, 2 and 3

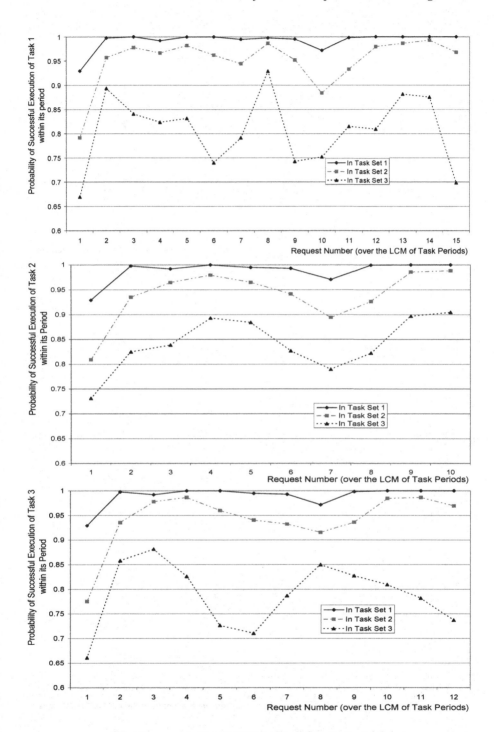

Fig. 5. τ_1, τ_2 and τ_3 in LLF in Task Sets 1, 2 and 3

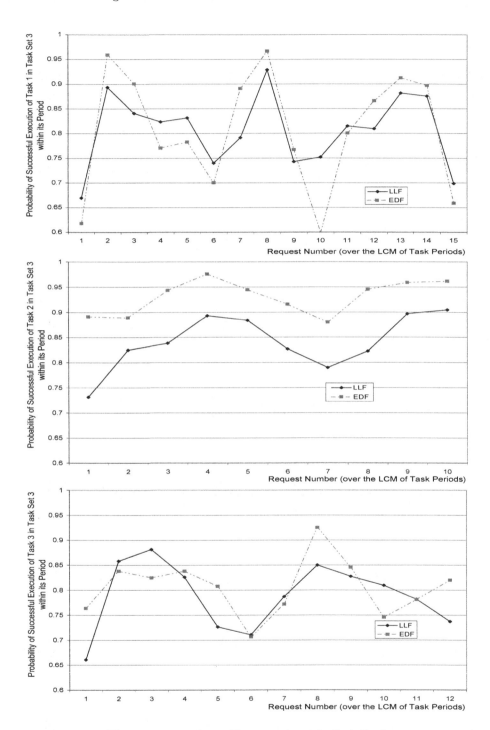

Fig. 6. τ_1, τ_2 and τ_3 with LLF and EDF in Task Set 3

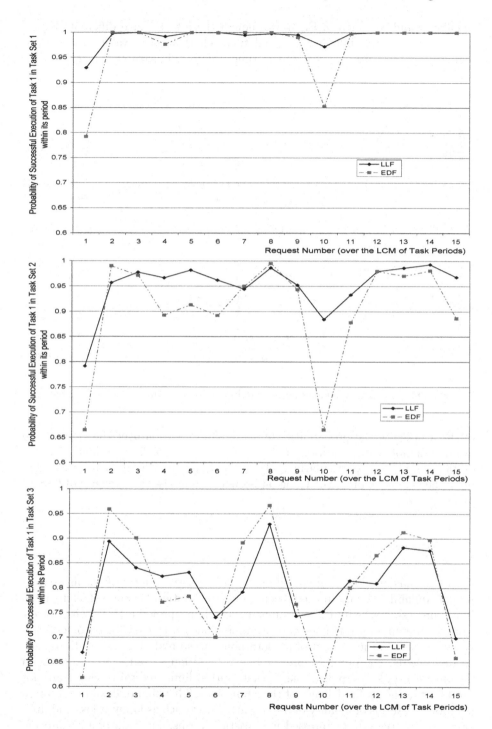

Fig. 7. τ_1 with LLF and EDF in Task Sets 1, 2 and 3

calculated and is shown in Figure 8.Though these tasks have different characteristics, these probabilities are found to reach their peak values for a mean
regularity success jitter of one unit of time. Figure 9 illustrates the dependence

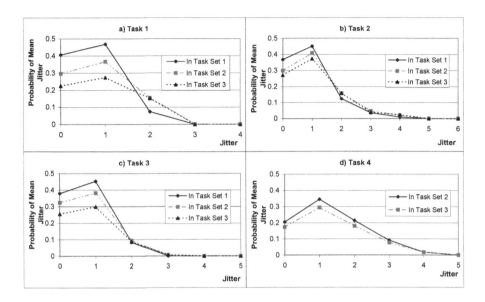

Fig. 8. Effects of workload on probability of mean regularity success jitter

of the average of the probabilities of successful execution over the LCM on the
available number of processors as it is varied from 1 to 5. This kind of information could be a particularly useful as a design tool as it enables a direct
quantified comparison of the trade-off between resources and the level of QoS to
be achieved.

5   Conclusions

This work has developed an entirely new probabilistic framework for investigating schedulability issues in the presence of uncertainties. It is aimed at dynamic
multi–processor scheduling environments involving periodic tasks with uncertainties in computation times and deadlines. Such a framework becomes especially relevant in the context of modern non-critical real–time applications such
as multimedia, computer vision, on–line recognition systems, etc. A common
denominator of such applications is that, within limits, certain failures are not
fatal for the successful delivery of their functions. This kind of flexibility is often
expressed in terms of Quality of Service attributes such as latency, loss and drop
rates, jitter, etc., often expressed in statistical terms. The task of guaranteeing
QoS measures is often compounded by uncertainties in the parameters of various

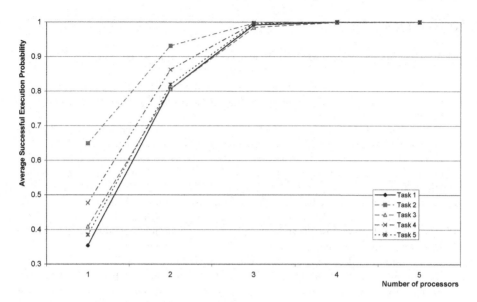

Fig. 9. Dependence of the average successful execution probability over the LCM on the available number of processors

computational tasks. Both these factors are suggestive of the appropriateness of probabilistic paradigm in the study of such issues.

Each task is represented by a fixed period and a set of non–zero probabilities characterising the task having certain random pairs (points) of computation times and laxities at its arrival time. In between arrival times, computation times and the laxities are continued to be described probabilistically, though not in a random manner. Then considering each such point separately, the probability of the task concerned being executed is examined in different scenarios involving other tasks. Knowing the probability of realisation of each scenario, any competition due to tasks operating at the same priority level for the available number of processors as well as the probability of the task concerned being there, the probability of it being executed is computed. This enables the computation of execution patterns of all tasks over a desired interval of time. This forms the basis for calculating several important QoS measures, such as those mentioned above. A range of examples demonstrate the capabilities of the framework as well as unique benefits of probabilistic analysis.

Novelty of the proposed approach has raised several important issues requiring further research in relation to its practical applicability. This includes, amongst others, an assessment of complexity of the approach as proposed, an exploration into heuristic techniques for managing this complexity in relation to problem sizes encountered in practice, and a verification of the approach using stochastic simulations.

References

1. A. Atlas and A. Bestavros. Statistical rate monotonic scheduling. In *19th IEEE Real-Time Systems Symposium*. 1998. pages 123–132,
2. A. Atlas and A. Bestavros. Design and Implementation of Statistical Rate Monotonic Scheduling in KURT Linux. In *Proceeding of IEEE Real-Time Systems Symposium*. 1999. pages 272–276.
3. J.-Y. Chung, J.W.S. Liu, and K.-J. Lin. Scheduling periodic jobs that allow imprecise results *IEEE Transactions on Computers*, 39(9), 1990. pages 1156–1174.
4. L. David, F. Cottet and N. Nissanke. Jitter Control in On-line Scheduling of Dependent Real-time Tasks. In *22nd IEEE Real-Time Systems Symposium*, London, UK, 2001.
5. M. L. Dertouzos and A.K. Mok. Multi-processor on-line scheduling of hard real-time systems. *IEEE Trans. on Software Engineering*, 15(12), December 1989.
6. S. Edgar and A. Burns Statistical Analysis of WCET for Scheduling. *22nd IEEE Real-Time Systems Symposium*. London, UK. 2001. pages 215–224.
7. C. -J. Hamann, J. Löser, L. Reuther, S. Schönberg, J. Wolter, and H. Härtig. Quality-Assuring Scheduling Using Stochastic Behaviour to Improve Resource Utilisation. In *22nd IEEE Real-Time Systems Symposium*, London, UK, 2001. pages 119–128.
8. M. A. Inverson, F. Ozguner, and L. Potter. Statistical prediction of Task Execution Times through Analytic Benchmarking for Scheduling in a Heterogeneous Environment. *IEEE Transactions on Computers*. 48(12), 1999.
9. S. Manolache, P. Eles and Z. Peng Menory and Time-efficient Schedulability Analysis of Task Sets with Stochastic Execution Time. *13th Euromicro Conference on Real–Time Systems, 2001, Pages 19–26*
10. N. Nissanke, A. Leulseged and S. Chillara. Probabilistic Performance Analysis in Multiprocessor Scheduling. *Conputing and Control Engineering Jounal. 13(4), August 2002, Pages 171–179.*
11. A. C. Shaw. Reasoning about Time in Higher-Level Language Software *IEEE Trans. on Software Engineering*. 15(7), 1989.
12. L. Zhou, K. G. Shin and E. A. Rundensteiner. Rate-monotonic scheduling in the presence of timing unpredictability. *IEEE Real-Time Technology and Applications Symposium*. 1998. pages 22–27.

Real-Time Virtual Machines for Avionics Software Porting and Development

Lui Sha

CS, UIUC
lrs@cs.uiuc.edu

Abstract. Generalized rate monotonic scheduling (GRMS) theory has now been widely adopted in practice and supported by open standards. This creates strong incentives for the avionics industry to migrate from traditional cyclical executive based system to a GRMS based systems. This paper presents some of the important considerations in the migration of a cyclical executive based system to a GRMS based system.

1 Introduction

In the past, avionics software systems used a federated architecture, where each subsystem had its own processor, with cyclical executives. As processors become faster, and the analytic hard real-time scheduling method □ *Rate Monotonic Analysis (RMA)* □ is supported by open standards, industry would like to:

• Port and integrate old software subsystems to a modern processor with minimal re-certification needs,
• Incrementally develop new software using *RMA*.

From the perspective of software porting, integration and recertification, the most important property to preserve is the *Isolation property:* under the federated architecture, each subsystem has its own physical processor; the execution of tasks on one processor cannot interfere with the execution of tasks on other processors. We must ensure this logically in the system architecture of fast modern processors.

A software architecture on a processor, where its partitions satisfy the *isolation property,* is called a Logical

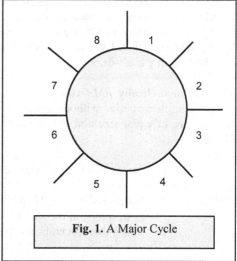

Fig. 1. A Major Cycle

J. Chen and S. Hong (Eds.): RTCSA 2003, LNCS 2968, pp. 123–135, 2004.

Federated Architecture (LFA). Each partition in LFA is called a Real-Time Virtual Machine (*RTVM*), which is a virtual machine with protected timing properties.

From a scheduling perspective, LFA can be realized easily by using a simple TDM scheduler. From a scheduling perspective, this is a special form of two level schedulers [5] and is not the most efficient one in terms of realizable schedulability for *RTVMs*. However, it has the best backward compatibility to legacy avionic software written with cyclical executives. Those legacy software was typically written in a way that assumes a deterministic usage of time slots in its task dispatching table. TDM provides fixed slots and thus preserves the structure of the dispatching table, resulting in easy porting and recertification. In avionics, the cost of recertification dwarfs hardware costs.

As illustrated in Figure 1, a *RTVM* is simply a sequence of time slots in the major cycle. For example, $RTVM_1$ uses {*1, 3, 4*}, $RTVM_2$ uses {*2, 5, 7*} and slots {*6, 8*} are reserved for future use. The major cycle should be no longer than the shortest period of all the tasks, unless we use equally spaced *RTVMs* with a temporal distance between adjacent *RTVMs* less the period of the shortest period. Experience shows that letting major cycle to be shorter than the shortest period of all tasks tends to make *RTVM* reconfiguration easier during system evolution. In the rest of this paper, we assume that the major cycle is shorter than all the periods. The results can be easily generalized if we wish to remove this assumption.

From an application perspective, each *RTVM* can have its own scheduling policy, thus facilitating porting and integration of legacy applications. When the software in a legacy *RTVM* needs to be modified significantly, it is time to convert it to an *RMA* based *RTVM* and take advantage of *RMA's* optimality, flexibility and schedulability analysis. Independent of scheduling policies, subsystems with different criticality can be assigned to different *RTVMs* to facilitate certification. New subsystems should use *RMA* based *RTVM*. The objective of this study is to extend the results of *RMA* in the context of *RTVM*. *RMA* based *RTVM* can add/subtract integer numbers of time slots and then apply schedulability analysis.

Although theoretically *RMA* can have slots with fractional sizes, this creates complexity in implementation without significant practical value. Thus, we assume that all the slots are of equal size and only an integer number of slots are allocated to any *RTVM*.

☐ *RMA* presumes that the processor can be taken away from a task at arbitrary instances of time.
   o   When a slot of a *RTVM* becomes active, the highest priority ready task, if any, in the *RTVM* is executed.
   o   When this slot ends, the executing task, if any, will be suspended.

☐ Cyclical executive assumes that it owns the processor for each of the assigned time slot.

Legacy subsystems using cyclical executives should first pick the slots of their *RTVMs*. *RMA* based *RTVMs* are more flexible, and they can use any leftover slots.

Finally, it is important to remember that *RTVM* is a simulation of the federated architecture on a shared physical processor. And the key property we want to ensure is the isolation property. To ensure the validity of the isolation property, the software engineering process shall enforce the following rules:

1. Each *RTVM* should have its own address space, simulating the memory protection offered by separated physical processors.
2. Data sharing between applications in different *RTVMs* should use message passing, simulating how applications communicate under the federated architecture. The strong coupling caused by the use of global shared variables among subsystems in different *RTVMs* violates the isolation property.
3. All the computing resources, e.g., memory, CPU cycles (time slots) and communication ports, should be pre-allocated, simulating different processors with their private resources. Dynamic physical and logical resource allocation would lead to interactions between *RTVMs*, violating the isolation property.
4. Device I/O should be initiated and completed within a single slot, simulating private I/O in separated physical processors.
5. The worst-case kernel service time across a *slot boundary*, denoted as K_{slot}, should be kept small and deterministic. An application task may initiate a kernel service, e.g., lock or unlock a semaphore, at or near the end of a slot. Nevertheless, a kernel service, once started, should continue until it is completed, even if the execution runs across the nominal boundary of a slot. Under this policy, K_{slot} is simply part of the overhead time when we switch from one slot to another.

Remark: Kernel services are shared by all the *RTVMs*. A sufficient condition to prevent the creation of dependency between *RTVMs* via the use of kernel services is the following rule: when crossing any slot boundary, the kernel must finish its existing services before passing the control to the applications in the next slot. Theoretically, we only need to cut off kernel service dependency across the boundaries of *RTVMs*. But cutting off the dependency at each slot boundary keeps the kernel code simple, independent of how slots are assigned at the application level. This allows for the flexible reassignment of slots to *RTVMs*.

Remark: An application task can, of course, hold a lock on semaphore across the boundary of slots. This would only block other application tasks in the same *RTVM*, since we do not permit shared variables across *RTVMs*. What is important is that system calls, e.g., lock a semaphore, must be finished before next slot starts. This has to be verified at the application level.

2 Schedulability Bounds

The schedulability bounds of *RMA* depend on the availability of information about the size of the *RTVM* and the application task parameters. Up to a limit, the more we know about the parameters, the larger will be the bound. Different parameters will become available at different stages of system development and have different degrees of volatility. For example, we usually know the number of tasks and their frequencies before knowing their execution times. Task frequencies are also much less likely to change than execution times. We will know the task set parameters more accurately as design and implementation processes. From an application perspective, there are different types of schedulability bounds based on application needs.

1) RTVM Bound: the scheduling bound when only the size of the *RTVM* is known. A set of tasks is schedulable as long as its total utilization is less than the *RTVM Bound*. This bound is conservative because it assumes the worst possible combination of parameters. However, it is useful for initial sizing of RTVM and hardware sizes where conservatism is a virtual.

2) RMA Exact Schedulability Check: In the late stage of system development, we know *RTVM* size, task frequencies and their worst-case execution times and would like to have a higher degree of schedulability.

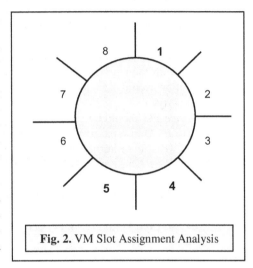

Fig. 2. VM Slot Assignment Analysis

In order not to clutter the exposition, we shall first derive the fundamental results under the following assumptions:

- ☐ All tasks are independent, that is, they do not synchronize with one another.
- ☐ Context switching time of application tasks is zero.
- ☐ The slot switching overhead time is zero.
- ☐ Task frequencies are constants. They do not drift.

All these assumptions will be removed once the key result is obtained.

2.1 Modeling the Effect of Slot Assignments

From the perspective of a task in a given real-time virtual machine, $RTVM_i$, the processor will be taken away for two reasons: 1) a high priority task becomes ready, and 2) the current slot of $RTVM_i$ is ended, and a slot in another *RTVM* has started.

In the schedulability analysis of a given Task $\square_i$, the effect of a higher priority periodic Task $\square_h = (C_h, T_h)$ is that Task $\square_h$ will take away the processor C_h units of time every

T_h units of time when Task ⊡ is active[1]. The effect of an unassigned slot in the major cycle T_1 is that the processor will be taken away from Task ⊡ one slot time every T_1 units of time when Task ⊡ is active. Thus, we can model the effect of an unassigned slot as a high priority periodic task, called a *Slot Task*, with execution time that is equal to the slot time, and period that is equal to the major cycle.

Example 1: As illustrated in Figure 2, from the perspective of a task in $RTVM_1 = \{1, 4, 5\}$, we can account for the effect of the five slots not assigned to $RTVM_1$, Slots 2, 3, 6, 7, 8, by five Slot Tasks: {(Slot_2_time, T_1), (Slot_3_time, T_1), (Slot_6_time, T_1), (Slot_7_time, T_1) and (Slot_8_time, T_1)}.

When we model a *RTVM*, we must keep in mind that the slots used by a virtual machine should be kept flexible to allow for reassignments. That is, we should be able to replace $RTVM_1$'s slots $\{1, 5, 4\}$ with another three slots, e.g., $\{6, 7, 8\}$, without redoing the schedulability analysis.

Theorem 1: For tasks in a given $RTVM_i$, the effect of slots not assigned to $RTVM_i$ can be represented by a single periodic task, called the *VM Periodic Task*, whose period is that of the major cycle, T_1, and whose computation time is equal to the sum of the length of all the slots not assigned to $RTVM_i$.

Proof: First, each slot not assigned to $RTVM_i$ is modeled by a Slot Task whose period equals to T_1, and whose computation time equals to the slot time. Next, we assign each Slot Task a priority P that is higher than the priorities of all the application tasks in $RTVM_i$, since a Slot Task will always take away the processor from an application task. By Liu and Layland's critical instance theorem[1], we know that the maximal preemption from these Slot Tasks occurs when all of the tasks start at time $t = 0$, the starting of the first slot assigned to $RTVM_i$. Under the critical instance arrangement, all the Slot Tasks will have the same period, T_1, the same starting time $t = 0$, and the same priority P. Hence their combined preemption can be modeled by a single periodic task, the *VM Periodic Task*, with period, T_1, and execution time C_1 equal to the sum of the length of all the slots not assigned to $RTVM_i$. QED.

Remark: Slot Tasks, by the physical nature of the major cycle, cannot all start at the same time. Having all the tasks starting at the same time, however, is an accurate logical model of the situation: we would like our application tasks to start at the origin of the major cycle, but the slots assigned to the *RTVM* for our application tasks are those at the end of the major cycle.

Example 2: In Example 1, the *VM Periodic Task* is the combination of the five Slot Tasks represented by (*Sum_of_5_slot_Times*, T_1). In the rest of the paper, we shall denote the *VM Periodic Task* as ⊡ = (C_1, T_1).

In summary, we model the effects of the slots <u>not</u> assigned to a *RTVM* by a single high priority periodic task, the *VM Periodic Task*, whose computation time is the sum

---

[1] That is, Task ⊡ is executing or ready to execute.

of all the unavailable slots and whose period is that of the major cycle. This worst-case modeling method allows for flexible reassignment of time slots without redoing the schedulability analysis. We shall use this method throughout this report.

Notation: When we have n application periodic tasks in a *RTVM*, the schedulability model for these n tasks will have $n+1$ tasks, $\{\tau_1...\tau_{n+1}\}$. In this paper, Task τ_1 models the *VM Periodic Task*. Tasks $\{\tau_2...\tau_{n+1}\}$ are the n application tasks in the *RTVM*.

Definition: The size of a *RTVM*, U_{vm}, is defined as the percentage of CPU cycles assigned to a *RTVM*.

Remark: U_{vm} is just the sum of the duration of all the assigned slots divided by the period of the major cycle.

Notation: The total utilization of tasks $\{\tau_1...\tau_{n+1}\}$ is denoted as $U(1..n+1)$, and the total utilization of application tasks $\{\tau_2...\tau_{n+1}\}$ is denoted as $U(2..n+1)$.

Definition: A utilization bound for n application tasks in a *RTVM*, $U_B(2..n+1)$, is said to be sufficient, if the n application tasks will always meet their deadlines as long as $U(2..n+1) \leq U_B(2..n+1)$.

Remark: There are infinitely many sufficient bounds, since any bound that is less than a known sufficient bound is also a sufficient bound.

Notation: The scheduling bound for n application tasks in a *RTVM* plus the corresponding *VM Periodic Task* is denoted as $U_B(1..n+1)$.

Notation: The maximal sufficient bound for n tasks in a *RTVM*, $U_{Bmax}(2..n+1)$, is defined as the largest one in the set of all the sufficient bounds. The bound $U_{Bmax}(1..n+1)$ denotes the largest sufficient bound of the n application tasks plus the *VM Periodic Task*.

Remark: If the bound is independent of the number of application tasks, we will drop the parameter (1 (or 2)..$n+1$) in the notation of utilization, e.g., $U(1$ (or $2)..n+1)$, and in the notation of a scheduling bound, e.g., $U_{Bmax}(1$ (or $2)..n+1)$,. That is, we will use U and U_{Bmax}, when the bound is independent of the number of application tasks.

2.2 Real-Time Virtual Machine Bound with only Utilization Information

This bound gives the maximal flexibility, for it assumes that we only know the percentage of the CPU available for the *RTVM* and nothing else. The price to pay for this flexibility and robustness is a low schedulability bound, since we must assume the worst possible combination of all the parameters.

Let U_1 denote the utilization of the *VM Periodic Task* and let U_{vm} represent the utilization of the *RTVM*. We have $U_{vm} = (1 - U_1)$.

Theorem 2: Given an arbitrary number of independent periodic application tasks with deadlines at the ends of their periods, total utilization U, and a *RTVM* with capacity U_{vm}, these tasks are schedulable on the *RTVM* using the rate monotonic scheduling algorithm, if:

$$U \leq U_{Bmax} = ln(2/(2 - U_{vm}))$$

Proof: Given n tasks executing within a *RTVM* with capacity U_{vm}, by Theorem 1, the effect of all the unassigned slots is modeled by the *VM Periodic Task*. Thus, we have the task set $\{\tau_1 ... \tau_{n+1}\} = \{(C_1, T_1), (C_2, T_2), ..(C_{n+1}, T_{n+1})\}$. We assume $T_1 \leq T_2 ... \leq T_{n+1}$.

For independent periodic tasks, Liu and Layland[1] proved that the worst case for Task τ_i occurs when: 1) all the higher priority tasks and Task τ_i start at the same instant, and 2) the ratio between any two tasks is less than 2, i.e., $T_{n+1}/T_1 < 2$, and 3) the computation time, C_i, of each task is the difference between T_{i+1} and T_i. That is, $C_1 = T_2 - T_1, ..,C_i = T_{i+1} - T_i$ and $C_{n+1} = T_{n+1} - 2(C_1 + .. + C_n) = 2T_1 - T_{n+1}$.

The maximal sufficient bound is found by identifying the schedulable task set with the minimal utilization under the worst-case condition [1]. To minimize the task set utilization under the worst-case condition defined above:

Let $r_i = T_{i+1}/T_i, 1 \leq i \leq n$. Note that $T_{n+1}/T_1 = r_1 r_2 . r .._n$, and that $U_1 = C_1/T_1 = r_1 - 1$.

The total processor utilization including that of the *VM Periodic Task* for unassigned slots is:

$$U(1..n+1) = (T_2 - T_1) / T_1 + ..+ (2T_1 - T_{n+1})/T_{n+1}$$
$$= r_1 + r_2 + ..+ r_n + 2/(r_1 r_2 . r .._n) - (n+1)$$

Since U_1 is a given constant, it follows that r_1 is a constant. Let $k = r_1$ for notational clarity, since we use r to denote a variable. We have:

$$U(1..n+1) = k + r_2 + ..+ r_n + 2/(k r_2 . r .._n) - (n+1)$$

Let $\partial U(1..n+1)/\partial r_i = 0, 2 \leq i \leq n$, we have:
$$k r_2^2 r_3 \cdots r_n = 2$$
$$k r_2 r_3^2 \cdots r_n = 2$$
$$...$$
$$k r_2 r_3 \cdots r_n^2 = 2$$

Taking a ratio between two successive equations, we have $r_2 = r_3, r_3 = r_4, .., r_{n-1} = r_n$. Let $r = r_i, 2 \leq i \leq n$ and solve for r, we have $r = (2/k)^{1/n}$. It follows that

$$U(1..n+1) = k + r_2 + ..+ r_n + 2/(k r_2 . r .._n) - (n+1)$$

$$= k + (n\text{-}1)r + 2/(k\,r^{(n\text{-}1)}) - (n+1)$$

Substituting the solution of r into the equation above, we obtained the minimal task utilization and thus the maximal sufficient bound. Recalling that $k = r_1 = U_1+1$, we have:

$$U_{B\max}(1..n+1) = k + (n\square 1)(\frac{2}{k})^{\frac{1}{n}} + (\frac{2}{k})\frac{1}{\left(\left(\frac{2}{k}\right)^{\frac{1}{n}}\right)^{\frac{1}{(n\square 1)}}} \square (n+1)$$

$$= k + (n\square 1)(\frac{2}{k})^{\frac{1}{n}} + (\frac{2}{k})(\frac{2}{k})^{\frac{1\square n}{n}} \square (n+1)$$

$$= k + n(\frac{2}{k})^{\frac{1}{n}} \square (n+1)$$

$$= U_1 + 1 + n(\frac{2}{U_1+1})^{\frac{1}{n}} \square n \square 1$$

$$= U_1 + n(\frac{2}{U_1+1})^{\frac{1}{n}} \square n$$

$$= U_1 + n((\frac{2}{U_1+1})^{\frac{1}{n}} \square 1)$$

Recalling that $U_1 = 1 \square U_{vm}$, the maximal utilization bound for the n application tasks alone is:

$$U_{B\max}(2..n+1) = n((\frac{2}{U_1+1})^{\frac{1}{n}} \square 1) = n((\frac{2}{2\square U_{vm}})^{\frac{1}{n}} \square 1)$$

$$U_{B\max} = \ln\left(\frac{2}{2\square U_{vm}}\right) \quad \text{as } n\square\square. \quad \text{QED.}$$

Remark: If the *RTVM* gets 100% of the processor, *RTVM* bound becomes the well-known result of $\ln(2)$.

2.3 Exact Bounds

The objective of our *RTVM* formulation is to keep things simple: simple to implement, simple to integrate, simple to analyze and simple to re-certify. Indeed, by Theorem 1, the schedulability analysis of a set of n application tasks in a *RTVM* is equivalent to the schedulability analysis of a set of $n+1$ tasks that includes the *VM Periodic Task*. Hence the exact test can be used without modification. The exact schedulability test developed in [3] is described here for completeness. For each Task $\square$:

$$t_{k+1} = C_i + \sum_{j=1}^{i\square 1} \left\lceil \frac{t_k}{T_j} \right\rceil C_j \text{ where } t_0 = \sum_{j=1}^{i} C_j$$

Test terminates when $t_{k+1} > T_i$ (not schedulable)

or when $t_{k+1} = t_k \square T_i$ (schedulable)

Furthermore, we note that the exact schedulability analysis is in fact an efficient simulation of fixed priority scheduling. Thus, it is equally applicable to *RMA* or any other fixed priority assignment method.

2.4 Relaxation of Assumptions

Again by Theorem 1, the schedulability analysis of a set of n application tasks in a *RTVM* is equivalent to the schedulability analysis of a set of $n+1$ tasks that includes the *VM Periodic Task*. As a result, methods for context switching and blocking that were described in [2] are directly applicable. We first examine the context switching, the blocking, and the frequency drift in isolation. We will then integrate them with the use of the scheduling bounds developed in this report.

2.4.1 Application Task Context Switching Time and Slot Switching Time

Each job (or instance) of a periodic task could generate at most two context switches $\square$ the starting context switching and the completion context switching.

Example 3: As illustrated in Figure 3, low priority Task $\square_3$ starts and preempts the system idle task at $t = 0$ with its starting context switching. Context switching times are colored in white. At time t_1, Task $\square_2$ starts and preempts this low priority Task $\square_3$ with its starting context switching. At t_2, high priority Task $\square_1$ starts and preempts Task $\square_2$ with its starting context switching. Task $\square_1$ executes to completion at t_3 with its completion context switching, and the processor is given to Task $\square_2$. At t_4, Task $\square_2$

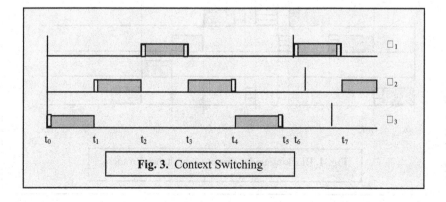

Fig. 3. Context Switching

finishes with its completion context switching and the processor is given to Task $\square_3$. Finally, at t_5, Task $\square_3$ completes and ends with its completion context switching, and the processor is passed to the system idle task, which does not terminate.

Nevertheless, to account for the worst- case context switching, we need to add two worst-case context switching times to the execution time of each application task.

Finally, as illustrated in Figure 1, whenever we switch from one slot to the next, there is one context switching for task executions. In addition, there is the worst-case kernel service time across a slot boundary, K_{slot}. Hence, the computation time of the *VM Periodic Task* with *n* slots should be: $C_1 = n*(Slot\_time + S + K_{slot})$, where *S* is the worst case slot switching time.

2.4.2   Blocking

Although there are better real time synchronization protocols available, only the priority inheritance protocol is currently available in most commercially available real time operating systems. Thus, we review the blocking under this protocol. Under the Priority Inheritance Protocol [4], a task can be blocked multiple times or even deadlocked. However, we shall assume that deadlock is avoided by not using nested locks or by totally ordering the sequence of locking. We assume that a real-time task will not suspend itself inside a critical section so that the duration of each critical section can be measured and that a job (an instance) of a periodic task will not unlock and then lock the same semaphore again. These assumptions imply that proper real-time software architecture is followed to handle the interface with external activities such as screen and disk I/O so that large and varying delays from such activities will not negatively impact the real-time loops.

Example 4: Figure 4 illustrates the direct blocking and indirect blocking that can be experienced by a task. At time t_0, Task $\square_4$ starts and it locks semaphore SEM_1 at t_1. At t_2, both Task $\square_3$ and Task $\square_2$ become ready. Since Task $\square_2$ has higher priority, it exe-

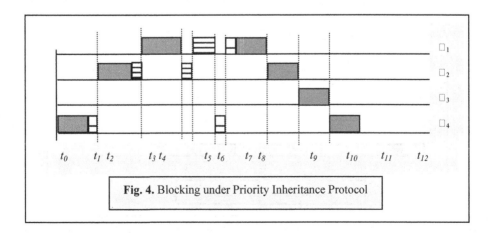

Fig. 4. Blocking under Priority Inheritance Protocol

cutes. At t_3, Task $\square_2$ locks semaphore SEM_2. At time t_4, Task $\square_1$ preempts $\square_2$ and starts to execute. At t_5, Task $\square_1$ tries to lock Semaphore SEM_2. Since SEM_2 is locked by Task $\square_2$, Task $\square_1$ is blocked by Task $\square_2$ via SEM_2. So Task $\square_2$ resumes its execution and inherits $\square_1$'s priority. At t_6, Task $\square_2$ unlocks SEM_2 and returns to its assigned priority. Task $\square_1$ locks SEM_2, preempts Task $\square_2$, and executes. At t_7, Task $\square_1$ unlocks SEM_2 and tries to lock SEM_1. However, SEM_1's lock is held by Task $\square_4$. So Task $\square_4$ inherits Task $\square_1$'s priority and resumes its execution of its critical section. Note that at this point, Task $\square_3$ is blocked by Task $\square_4$. At t_8, Task $\square_4$ unlocks SEM_1 and returns to its assigned priority. Task $\square_1$ locks SEM_1 and resumes its execution. At t_9, Task $\square_1$ finishes its execution. Task $\square_2$ resumes and finally finishes at t_{10}. Task $\square_3$ begins its execution and finishes at t_{11}. Task $\square_4$ resumes then finishes at t_{12}.

In this example, there are two forms of blocking going on. First, direct blocking due to conflicts on semaphores. Task $\square_1$ shares two semaphores with lower priority tasks and thus experiences direct blocking. The worst case of direct blocking for a task is one blocking per semaphore shared with lower priority tasks under the assumptions listed in the beginning of this section. Task $\square_1$ shares two semaphores with lower priority tasks, and it encounters two blockings in this example. Second, there is also the indirect blocking experienced by Task $\square_3$, which does not use locks. However, it has still to wait for the execution of Task $\square_4$'s critical section in interval $[t_7, t_8]$. This is an example of indirect blocking. A task will experience an indirect blocking whenever a higher priority task and a lower priority task share a lock. The worst-case blocking of a task is, therefore, the sum of its direct blocking time plus the sum of its indirect blocking time.

In summary, the worst-case number of direct blockings is once per semaphore. The worst-case number of indirect blocking is once per semaphore shared by a higher and a lower priority task. The worst-case blocking time associated with a semaphore is the longest critical section used by a lower priority task plus two context switching times associated with the execution of a critical section.

In new software development, the blocking time is best tracked by a tool, although a simple spreadsheet program is often adequate. However, it is very time consuming to find out all the blocking time details in legacy software. Fortunately, there is an easy way out at the expense of CPU cycles. One can write a program to scan the source code and to count the number of semaphores. Suppose there are n semaphores. The worst-case is that every task experiences n blockings, directly or indirectly. This is because the same semaphore cannot cause both direct and indirect blockings to the same task. So the worst-case blocking time for any task, except the lowest priority task which always has zero blocking time, is the total number of locks times the sum of the longest critical section and two context switching time. This method looks very inefficient and it is. But in the big picture of system development, it is often justifiable. Real-time software, except real-time database applications, tends to use a smaller number of locks and the critical sections tend to be short. Second, when old software is ported, the new hardware is usually many times faster, and there often are some CPU cycles to burn. And it is often cheaper to waste a little hardware than to reverse-engineer all the details.

2.5 Integration

We now put everything together. First, we shall use the highest frequencies to guard against frequency drifts. Second, we need to measure the worst-case context switching time and let it be S. Finally, we need to compute the worst-case blocking time for each task. Let the blocking time of Task i be B_i.

$$U_{vm} = n(slot\_time \square 2S)/T_1, \text{ where } T_1 \text{ is the period of the major cycle.}$$

Using the most general *RTVM* bound, the task set is schedulable if

$$\frac{C_2 + 2S + B_2}{T_2} + ... + \frac{C_n + 2S + B_n}{T_n} + \frac{C_{n+1} + 2S}{T_{n+1}} \square \ln(\frac{2}{2 \square U_{vm}})$$

Finally, to use the exact schedulability analysis, the steps are:

1. Construct the *VM Periodic Task* whose period is that of the major cycle and whose computation time $C_1 = k*(slot\_time+2S)$, where k is the number of slots unavailable to the *RTVM*.

2. Replace the computation time of each task C_i with C_i+2S, $2 \square i \square n+1$.

3. Replace the deadline T_i with $(T_i - B_i)$

4. Perform the exact schedulability analysis for the task set $\{\square_1 ... \square_{n+1}\}$.

3 Summary and Conclusion

In this paper, we have carefully specified a model of *RTVM* that is easy to implement and preserves the vital isolation property of federated architecture that use multiple physical processors. We call this architecture the Logical Federated Architecture (LFA). LFA makes software easier to port and integrate. It also allows us to isolate software with different criticality levels. We have developed a comprehensive set of bounds with different information requirements. From an application perspective, there are five bounds:

1) RTVM Bound: the scheduling bound when only the size (utilization) of the *RTVM* is known. A set of task is schedulable as long as its total utilization is less than the *RTVM* Bound.

2) RMA Exact Schedulability Check: This gives the largest bound, but we need to know *RTVM* size, task frequencies and their worst-case execution times.

Acknowledgement. I want to thank Richard Bradford, Joel Crosmer, Greg Shelton, and Joseph (Perry) Smith for helpful discussions and comments. In particular, I want to thank Greg Shelton for the discussion on *RTVM* implementation rules and Richard Bradford for his careful review of the drafts and for his many insightful comments and valuable suggestions.

References

[1] Liu, C. L., and J. W. Layland, "Scheduling Algorithms for Multiprogramming in a Hard Real-Time Environment," *Journal of the Association for Computing Machinery*, Vol.20, No.1, January 1973.

[2] Sha, L., and Goodenough, J. B., 'Real-Time Scheduling Theory and Ada", *IEEE Computer*, Vol. 23, No.4, April 1990, pp. 53-62.

[3] Lehoczky, J. P., Sha, L., Ding, D. Y., 'The Rate Monotonic Scheduling Algorithm: Exact Characterization and Average Case Behavior", *Proceedings of the IEEE Real-Time System Symposium*, 1989, pp. 166-171.

[4] Sha, L., Rajkumar, R., Lehoczky, J. P., 'Priority Inheritance Protocols: An Approach to Real-Time Synchronization", *IEEE Transactions on Computers*, Vol. 39, No. 9, September 1990, pp. 1175-1185.

[5] Liu, J., 'Real Time Systems", Prentice Hall, 2000

Algorithms for Managing QoS for Real-Time Data Services Using Imprecise Computation[*]

Mehdi Amirijoo[1], Jörgen Hansson[1], and Sang H. Son[2]

[1] Department of Computer Science, Linköping University, Sweden
{meham,jorha}@ida.liu.se
[2] Department of Computer Science, University of Virginia, Virginia, USA
son@cs.virginia.edu

Abstract. Lately the demand for real-time data services has increased in applications where it is desirable to process user requests within their deadlines using fresh data. The real-time data services are usually provided by a real-time database (RTDB). Here, since the workload of the RTDBs cannot be precisely predicted, RTDBs can become overloaded. As a result, deadline misses and freshness violations may occur. To address this problem we propose a QoS-sensitive approach to guarantee a set of requirements on the behavior of RTDBs. Our approach is based on imprecise computation, applied on both data and transactions. We propose two algorithms to dynamically balance the workload and the quality of the data and transactions. Performance evaluations show that our algorithms give a robust and controlled behavior of RTDBs, in terms of transaction and data quality, even for transient overloads and with inaccurate run-time estimates of the transactions.

1 Introduction

Lately the demand for real-time data services has increased and applications used in manufacturing, web-servers, e-commerce etc. are becoming increasingly sophisticated in their data needs. The data used span from low-level control data, typically acquired from sensors, to high-level management and business data. In these applications it is desirable to process user requests within their deadlines using fresh data. In dynamic systems, such as web servers and sensor networks with non-uniform access patterns, the workload of the databases cannot be precisely predicted and, hence, the databases can become overloaded. As a result, deadline misses and freshness violations may occur during transient overloads. To address this problem we propose a quality of service (QoS) sensitive approach to guarantee a set of requirements on the behavior of the database, even in the presence of unpredictable workloads. Our scheme is important to applications where timely execution of transactions is emphasized, but where it is not possible to have accurate analysis of arrival patterns and execution times.

---

[*] This work was funded, in part by CUGS (the National Graduate School in Computer Science, Sweden), CENIIT (Center for Industrial Information Technology) under contract 01.07, and NSF grant IIS-0208758. ©RTCSA 2003.

J. Chen and S. Hong (Eds.): RTCSA 2003, LNCS 2968, pp. 136–157, 2004.
© Springer-Verlag Berlin Heidelberg 2004

Our approach is based on imprecise computation [9], where it is possible to trade off resource needs for quality of requested service. This has successfully been applied to applications where timeliness is emphasized, e.g., avionics, engine control, image processing [4,11], networking [12], and approximation algorithms for NP-complete problems [18]. In our work, the notion of impreciseness is applied on both data and transactions, and the goal is to satisfy a QoS specification, in terms of data and transaction impreciseness, giving the desired quality of the provided service. We propose two dynamic balancing algorithms, FCS-IC-1 and FCS-IC-2, to balance the quality of the data and the transactions. Main challenges include unpredictability of workload, in terms of unknown arrival patters and inaccurate execution time estimates, but also effective balancing between transaction and data quality. To solve this issue, we apply feedback control scheduling [10] to provide robustness under these conditions.

The suggested algorithms, FCS-IC-1 and FCS-IC-2, are designed such that the behavior of a RTDB can be controlled, even in the presence of load variation and inaccurate execution time estimates. We have carried out a set of experiments to evaluate the performance of the algorithms. In the simulation studies we have applied a wide range of workload and run-time estimates to model potential unpredictabilities. The studies show that FCS-IC-1 and FCS-IC-2 give a robust and controlled behavior of RTDBs, in terms of transaction and data quality, even for transient overloads and when we have inaccurate run-time estimates of the transactions. This has been shown by comparing the performance against selected baseline algorithms.

The rest of this paper is organized as follows. A problem formulation is given in Section 2. In Section 3, the assumed database model is given. In Section 4, we present our approach and in Section 5, the results of performance evaluations are presented. In Section 6, we give an overview on related work, followed by Section 7, where conclusions and future work are discussed.

2   Problem Formulation

In our model, data objects in a RTDB are updated by update transactions, e.g. sensor values, while user transactions represent user requests, e.g. complex read-write operations. The notion of imprecision is applied at data object and user transaction level. The data quality increases as the imprecision of the data objects decreases. Similarly, the quality of user transactions increases as the imprecision of the results produced by user transactions decreases. Note that quality of user transactions is related to quality of data. Since user transactions access and read data objects, decreasing the quality of data may lead to a decrease in the quality of user transactions. However, in this work we model user transaction quality and data quality as orthogonal entities and, hence, quality of data and quality of user transactions are considered to be independent. In the future, we will extend our model to capture more advanced relations between user transaction quality and data quality.

In practice, a database administrator (DBA) specifies a desired QoS level in terms of steady-state and transient-state behavior of data and user transaction quality. The goal is to adapt the behavior of the RTDB such that the given QoS specification is satisfied. This is achieved by balancing the workload among update and user transactions. In general, lowering the user transaction workload leads to increased resources available for update transactions, resulting in an increase in data quality. Similarly, lowering the update transaction workload results in an increase in user transaction quality.

Starting with data impreciseness, for a data object stored in the RTDB and representing a real-world variable, we can allow a certain degree of deviation compared to the real-world value and if such deviation can be tolerated, arriving updates may be discarded. In order to measure data quality we introduce the notion of *data error*. Let d_i denote an arbitrary data object and T_j a transaction updating d_i. The data error, denoted DE_i, of a data object d_i is defined as a function of the current value (denoted $CurrentValue_i$) of d_i and the update value (denoted $UpdateValue_j$) of the latest arrived update transaction, T_j, i.e. $DE_i = \Phi(CurrentValue_i, UpdateValue_j)$. The data error of a data object gives an indication of how much the value stored in the RTDB deviates from the corresponding value in the real-world, given by the latest arrived update transaction.

The workload of updates is adjusted by manipulating the data error, which is done by considering an upper bound for the deviation between the values of the data objects stored in the RTDB and the corresponding values in the real-world. The upper bound is given by the *maximum data error* (denoted MDE) and is set based on a set of performance variables giving the current state of the RTDB (e.g. quality of user transactions). The data error is adjusted by the following criteria. An update transaction (T_j) is discarded if the data error of the data object (d_i) that is to be updated by T_j is less or equal to MDE (i.e. $DE_i \leq MDE$). In contrast, an update transaction is executed and committed if the corresponding DE_i is greater than MDE.

If MDE increases, more update transactions are discarded as we tolerate greater data error, hence, lower data quality. Similarly, if MDE decreases, fewer update transactions are rejected, resulting in a lower data error, and consequently, greater data quality. The goal of our work is to derive algorithms for adjusting data error, such that the data and the user transaction quality satisfy a given QoS specification. A major issue is how to compute MDE, depending on the user transaction quality.

3   Data and Transaction Model

3.1   Database Model

We consider a firm RTDB model, in which tardy transactions, i.e., transactions that have missed their deadlines, add no value to the system and therefore are aborted. We consider a main memory database model, where there is one CPU as the main processing element.

3.2 Data Model and Data Management

In our data model, data objects can be classified into two classes, temporal and non-temporal [14]. For temporal data, we only consider base data, i.e., data that hold the view of the real-world and are updated by sensors. A base data object d_i is considered temporally inconsistent or stale if the current time is later than the timestamp of d_i followed by the absolute validity interval of d_i (denoted AVI_i), i.e. $CurrentTime > TimeStamp_i + AVI_i$.

Define the the data error of a data object d_i as,

$$DE_i = 100 \times \frac{|CurrentValue_i - UpdateValue_j|}{|CurrentValue_i|}(\%)$$

where $UpdateValue_j$ is the value of the latest arrived transaction updating d_i.

3.3 Transaction Model

Transactions are classified either as update transactions or user transactions. Update transactions arrive periodically and may only write to temporal data objects (i.e. base data objects). User transactions arrive aperiodically and may read temporal and read/write non-temporal data. The inter-arrival time of user transactions is exponentially distributed.

User and update transactions (T_i) are assumed to be composed of one *mandatory subtransaction* (M_i) and #O_i optional subtransactions (denoted $O_{i,j}$, where $1 \leq j \leq \#O_i$). For the remainder of the paper, let,

$$t_i \in \{M_i, O_{i,1}, \ldots, O_{i,\#O_i}\}$$

denote a subtransaction of T_i.

We use the milestone approach [9] to transaction impreciseness. Thus, we have divided transactions into subtransactions according to milestones. A mandatory subtransaction is completed when it is completed in a traditional sense. The mandatory subtransaction gives an acceptable result and it is desired to complete the mandatory subtransaction before the transaction deadline. The optional subtransactions depend on the mandatory subtransaction and may be processed if there is enough time or resources available. While it is assumed that all subtransactions (t_i) arrive at the same time as the parent transaction (T_i), the first optional subtransaction (i.e. $O_{i,1}$) becomes ready for execution when the mandatory subtransaction completes. In general, an optional subtransaction, $O_{i,j}$, becomes ready for execution when $O_{i,j-1}$ (where $2 \leq j \leq \#O_i$) completes. Hence, there is a precedence relation given by,

$$M_i \prec O_{i,1} \prec O_{i,2} \prec \ldots \prec O_{i,\#O_i}.$$

A transaction is completed once its mandatory subtransaction is completed. We set the deadline of all subtransactions to the deadline of the parent transaction. A subtransaction is terminated if it is completed or has missed its deadline. A transaction (T_i) is terminated when its last optional subtransaction (i.e.

$O_{i,\#O_i}$) is completed or one of its subtransactions has missed its deadline. In the latter case, all subtransactions that are not completed are terminated as well.

For update transactions we assume that there are no optional subtransactions (i.e. $\#O_i = 0$). Hence, each update transaction consists only of a single mandatory subtransaction. This assumption is based on the fact that updates do not use complex logical or numerical operations and, hence, have a lower execution time than user transactions.

In our transaction model, the estimated average utilization of the transactions is known. However, the average or the actual utilization is not known. Hence, a feature in our model is that it models systems in unpredictable environments where the actual CPU utilization of transactions is time-varying and unknown to the scheduler.

4   Approach

Below we describe our approach for managing the performance of a RTDB in terms of transaction and data quality. First, we start by defining QoS and how it can be specified. An overview of a feedback control scheduling architecture is given, followed by issues related to modeling of the architecture and design of controllers. Finally, we present the algorithms FCS-IC-1 and FCS-IC-2.

4.1   Performance Metrics and QoS Specification

In our approach, the DBA can explicitly specify the required database QoS, defining the desired behavior of the database. In this work we adapt both steady-state and transient-state performance metrics. The metrics are as follows:

– *Deadline Miss Percentage of Mandatory User Subtransactions* (M^M). In a QoS specification the DBA can specify the deadline miss percentage of mandatory subtransactions given by,

$$M^M = 100 \times \frac{\#DeadlineMiss^M}{\#Terminated^M}(\%)$$

where $\#DeadlineMiss^M$ denotes the number of mandatory subtransactions that have missed their deadline, and $\#Terminated^M$ is the number of terminated mandatory subtransactions. We exclusively consider user transactions admitted to the system.

– *Deadline Miss Percentage of Optional User Subtransactions* (M^O). M^O is the percentage of optional subtransactions that have missed their deadline. M^O is defined by,

$$M^O = 100 \times \frac{\#DeadlineMiss^O}{\#Terminated^O}(\%)$$

where $\#DeadlineMiss^O$ denotes the number of optional subtransactions that have missed their deadline, and $\#Terminated^O$ is the number of terminated optional subtransactions. We exclusively consider user transactions admitted to the system.

- *Maximum Data Error* (*MDE*). This metric gives the maximum data error tolerated for the data objects, as described in Section 2.
- *Overshoot* (M_p) is the worst-case system performance in the transient-state (see Figure 1) and it is given as a percentage. The overshoot is applied to M^O, M^M, and MDE.
- *Settling time* (T_s) is the time for the transient overshoot to decay and reach the steady-state performance (see Figure 1).
- *Utilization* (U). In a QoS specification the DBA can specify a lower bound for the utilization of the system.

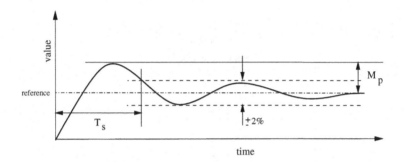

Fig. 1. Definition of settling time (T_s) and overshoot (M_p)

We define *Quality of Data* (QoD) in terms of MDE. An increase in QoD refers to a decrease in MDE. In contrast a decrease in QoD refers to an increase in MDE. We measure user transaction quality in terms of deadline miss percentage of optional subtransactions, i.e. M^O. This is feasible in the case when optional subtransactions contribute equally to the final result.

The DBA can specify a set of target levels or references for M^M, M^O, and MDE. A QoS requirement can be specified as the following: $M_r^M = 1\%$ (i.e. reference M^M), $M_r^O = 10\%$ (i.e. reference M^O), $MDE_r = 2\%$ (i.e. reference MDE), $U \geq 80\%$, $T_s \leq 60s$, and $M_p \leq 30\%$. This gives the following transient performance specifications: $M^M \leq M_r^M \times (M_p + 100) = 1.3\%$, $M^O \leq 13\%$, and $MDE \leq 2.6\%$.

4.2   Feedback Control Scheduling Architecture

In this section we give an overview of the feedback control scheduling architecture. Further, we identify a set of control related variables, i.e., performance references, manipulated variables, and controlled variables.

The general outline of the feedback control scheduling architecture is given in Figure 2. Admitted transactions are placed in the ready queue. The transaction handler manages the execution of the transactions. At each sampling instant, the

controlled variables, miss percentages and utilization, are monitored and fed into
the miss percentage and utilization controllers, which compare the performance
references, M_r^M, M_r^O, and U_r, with the corresponding controlled variables to
get the current performance errors. Based on these the controllers compute a
change, denoted ΔU, to the total estimated requested utilization. We refer to
ΔU as the manipulated variable. Based on ΔU, the QoD manager changes the
total estimated requested utilization by adapting the QoD (i.e. adjusting MDE).
The precision controller then schedules the update transactions based on MDE.
The portion of ΔU not accommodated by the QoD manager, denoted ΔU_{new},
is returned to the admission control, which enforces the remaining utilization
adjustment.

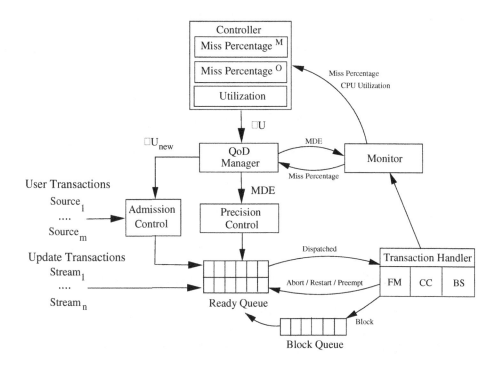

Fig. 2. Feedback control scheduling architecture

The streams ($Stream_i$) generate update transactions, whereas user transactions are generated and submitted by sources ($Source_i$).

The transaction handler provides a platform for managing transactions. It
consists of a freshness manager (FM), a unit managing the concurrency control
(CC), and a basic scheduler (BS). The FM checks the freshness before accessing
a data object, using the timestamp and the absolute validity interval of the
data. If a user transaction is accessing a stale data object and the transaction

deadline is later than the next update arrival, the transaction is blocked. It is then made ready when the corresponding update commits. However, if the transaction deadline is earlier than next update arrival, the stale data object is used. We use earliest deadline fist (EDF) as a basic scheduler to schedule user transactions. Conceptually, transactions are scheduled in a multi-level queue system. Update transactions and mandatory user subtransactions are placed in the highest priority queue, whereas optional user subtransactions are placed in a lower priority queue. We employ two-phase locking with highest priority (2PL-HP) [1] for concurrency control, where a conflict is resolved by allowing the transaction with the highest priority to lock the data object. 2PL-HP is chosen since it is free from priority inversion and has well-known behavior.

Admission control is applied to control the flow of transactions into the database. When a new transaction is submitted to the database, the admission controller (AC) decides whether or not it can be admitted to the system.

Precision controller discards an update transaction writing to a data object (d_i) having an error less or equal to the maximum data error allowed, i.e. $DE_i \leq MDE$. However, the update transaction is executed if the data error of d_i is greater than MDE. In both cases the time-stamp of d_i is updated.

4.3   System Modeling and Controller Design

We have modeled the controlled system, i.e. RTDB, according to the analytical approach proposed in [10]. The approach has been adapted such that it supports mandatory and optional subtransactions. For derivation and tuning of the model we refer to [2].

We employ two feedback control scheduling policies, called FC-M and FC-UM [10], to control user transaction quality in the presence of unpredictable workload and inaccurate execution time estimates. Depending on the algorithm used, we apply different feedback control scheduling policies. FCS-IC-1 uses the FC-UM policy, while FCS-IC-2 employs FC-M.

FC-M uses a miss percentage control loop to control the system miss percentage with regards to a reference. Here, separate control loops are used for mandatory and optional subtransactions. Miss percentages of mandatory and optional subtransactions, M^M and M^O, are monitored and controlled with regards to the specified references, i.e. M_r^M and M_r^O.

FC-UM, on the other hand, employs utilization and miss percentage controllers. This has the advantage that the DBA can simply set the utilization reference to a value that causes the desired deadline miss percentage in the nominal case (e.g. based on profiling), and set the miss percentage references (M_r^M and M_r^O) according to the application requirements. For all controllers, the control signal ΔU is computed to achieve the target miss percentage given by the references.

We have extended FC-UM in a way that the reference utilization, denoted U_r, is constantly updated online. The utilization reference is dynamically updated according to a linear increase and exponential decrease scheme. Initially, U_r is set to an initial value. As long as the utilization controller has the control (i.e. the miss percentages are below their references), the utilization reference is increased by a certain step. As soon as one of the miss percentage controllers takes over (i.e. miss percentage above the reference), U_r is reduced exponentially. This is to prevent a potential deadline miss percentage overshoot due to an too optimistic utilization reference. Note that this approach is self-adapting and does not require any knowledge about the underlying workload model.

We have adapted and tuned the feedback controllers, but we do not include these details in this paper due to space limitations. The interested reader is referred to [2].

4.4   Algorithm Specification

We present two algorithms for managing data and user transaction impreciseness. Both are based on adjusting the utilization and the miss percentages using feedback control. The utilization adjustment is enforced partially by adjusting the QoD, which requires setting MDE according to the utilization adjustment (ΔU), as described in Section 4.2. We adapt the following notation of describing discrete variables in the time-domain; $A(k)$ refers to the value of the variable A during the time window $[(k-1)W, kW]$, where W is the sampling period and k is the sampling instant.

Given a certain $\Delta U(k)$, we need to set $MDE(k+1)$ such that the utilization (or resources) gained when discarding update transactions correspond to $\Delta U(k)$. Remember that setting $MDE(k+1)$ greater than $MDE(k)$ results in more discarded update transactions and, hence, an increase in gained utilization. Similarly, setting $MDE(k+1)$ less than $MDE(k)$ results in fewer discarded update transactions and, hence, a decrease in gained utilization. In order to compute $MDE(k+1)$ given a certain $\Delta U(k)$, we use a function $f(\Delta U(k))$ that returns, based on $\Delta U(k)$, the corresponding $MDE(k+1)$. The function f holds the following property. If $\Delta U(k)$ is less than zero, then $MDE(k+1)$ is set such that $MDE(k+1)$ is greater than $MDE(k)$ (i.e. QoD is degraded). Similarly, if $\Delta U(k)$ is greater than zero, then $MDE(k+1)$ is set such that $MDE(k+1)$ is less than $MDE(k)$ (i.e. QoD is upgraded). We will return to the concepts around f in section 4.5.

FCS-IC-1. FCS-IC-1 (Feedback Control Scheduling Imprecise Computation 1) is based on the extended FC-UM policy (as described in Section 4.3). By using an adaptive scheme where the utilization reference is constantly updated, the utilization yielding the target miss percentage can be approximated. The exponential utilization reduction used with FC-UM decreases the risk for a potential miss percentage overshoot. In addition to this, FCS-IC-1 performs the following.

The system monitors the deadline miss percentages and the CPU utilization. At each sampling period, the CPU utilization adjustment, $\Delta U(k)$, is derived. Based on $\Delta U(k)$ we perform one of the following. If $\Delta U(k)$ is greater than zero, upgrade QoD as much as $\Delta U(k)$ allows. However, when $\Delta U(k)$ is less than zero, degrade the data according to ΔU, but not beyond the highest allowed MDE

(i.e. $MDE_r \times (M_p + 100)$). Degrading the data further would violate the upper limit of MDE, given by the QoS specification. In the case when $\Delta U(k)$ is less than zero and MDE equal to $MDE_r \times (M_p + 100)$, no QoD adjustment can be issued and, hence, the system has to wait until some of the currently running transactions terminate. An outline of FCS-IC-1 is given in Figure 3.

Monitor $M^M(k)$, $M^O(k)$, and $U(k)$
Compute $\Delta U(k)$
if $(\Delta U(k) > 0$ and $MDE(k) > 0)$ then
    Upgrade QoD according to $MDE(k+1) := f(\Delta U(k))$
    Inform AC about the portion of $\Delta U(k)$ not accommodated by QoD upgrade
else if $(\Delta U(k) < 0$ and $MDE(k) < MDE_r \times (M_p + 100))$ then
    Downgrade QoD according to $MDE(k+1) := f(\Delta U(k))$
    Inform AC about the portion of $\Delta U(k)$ not accommodated by QoD downgrade
else if $(\Delta U(k) < 0$ and $MDE(k) = MDE_r \times (M_p + 100))$ then
    Reject any incoming transaction
else
    Inform the AC of $\Delta U(k)$
end if

Fig. 3. FCS-IC-1

FCS-IC-2. In FCS-IC-2, the FC-M policy is used (as opposed to FCS-IC-1, where FC-UM is applied). In the case of FCS-IC-1, the miss percentages may stay lower than their references, since the utilization is exponentially decreased every time one of the miss percentages overshoots its reference. Consequently, the specified miss percentage references (i.e. M_r^M and M_r^O) may not be satisfied. In FCS-IC-2, the utilization controller is removed to keep the miss percentages at the specified references.

One of the characteristics of the miss percentage controllers is that as long as the miss percentages are below their references (i.e. $M^M \leq M_r^M$ and $M^O \leq M_r^O$), the controller output ΔU will be positive.[1] Due to the characteristics of f (i.e. $\Delta U(k) < 0 \Rightarrow MDE(k+1) > MDE(k)$ and $\Delta U(k) > 0 \Rightarrow MDE(k+1) < MDE(k)$), a positive ΔU is interpreted as a QoD upgrade. Consequently, even if the miss percentages are just below their references, QoD remains high. We would rather that the miss percentage of optional subtransactions (M^O), which corresponds to user transaction quality, increases and decreases together with data quality (MDE). For this reason, in FCS-IC-2, the QoD manager is extended such that MDE is set not only by considering ΔU, but also according to the current transaction quality given by M^O. When ΔU is less than zero (miss

---

[1] If we have transient oscillations, ΔU, may temporally stay positive (negative) even though the ATE has changed from being below (above) the reference to be above (below) the reference value. This is due to the integral operation, i.e., due to earlier summation of errors, which represents the history and therefore cause a delay before a change to the utilization is requested and has effect.

percentage overshoot), MDE is set according to f. However, when ΔU is greater or equal to zero, MDE is set according to the moving average of M^O. The moving average of M^O is computed by,

$$M_{MA}^O(k) = \alpha M^O(k) + (1 - \alpha)M_{MA}^O(k - 1)$$

where α $(0 \leq \alpha \leq 1)$ is the forgetting factor [16]. Setting α close to 1 results in a fast adaptation, but will also capture the high-frequency changes of M^O, whereas setting α close to 0, results in a slow but smooth adaptation. The latter results in the data quality varying with the transaction quality. When M_{MA}^O is relatively low compared to M_r^O, MDE is set to a low value relative to MDE_r. As M_{MA}^O increases, MDE increases but to a maximum value of $MDE_r \times (M_p + 100)$. A further increase violates the QoS specification. The algorithm outline is given in Figure 4.

Monitor $M^M(k)$ and $M^O(k)$
Compute $\Delta U(k)$
if $(\Delta U(k) \geq 0)$ **then**
   Adjust $MDE(k + 1)$ according to
        $MDE(k + 1) := \min(\frac{M_{MA}^O(k)}{M_r^O}MDE_r, MDE_r \times (M_p + 100))$
   if $(MDE(k) < MDE(k + 1))$ **then**
      Add the utilization gained after QoD degrade to $\Delta U(k)$
   else
      Subtract the utilization lost after QoD upgrade from $\Delta U(k)$
   end if
   Inform AC of the new $\Delta U(k)$
else if $(\Delta U(k) < 0$ and $MDE(k) < MDE_r \times (M_p + 100))$ **then**
   Downgrade QoD according to $MDE(k + 1) := f(\Delta U(k))$
   Inform AC about the portion of $\Delta U(k)$ not accommodated by QoD downgrade
else
   {i.e. $\Delta U(k) < 0$ and $MDE(k) = MDE_r \times (M_p + 100)$}
   Reject any incoming transaction
end if

Fig. 4. FCS-IC-2

4.5   QoD Management

The preciseness of the data is controlled by the QoD manager which sets $MDE(k)$ depending on the system behavior. When f is used to compute $MDE(k + 1)$ based on $\Delta U(k)$ (as in FCS-IC-1 and some cases in FCS-IC-2) the following scheme is used.

Rejecting an update results in a decrease in CPU utilization. We define *gained utilization*, $GU(k)$, as the utilization gained due to the result of rejecting one or more updates during period k. $GU(k)$ is defined as,

$$GU(k) = \sum_i \frac{\#RU_i(k)}{\#AU_i(k)} \times EU_i$$

where $\#RU_i(k)$ is the number of rejected update transactions T_i generated by $Stream_i$, $\#AU_i(k)$ the number of arrived update transactions T_i, and EU_i is the estimated utilization of the update transactions T_i.

An important issue is how to set $MDE(k+1)$ given a certain $\Delta U(k)$. Basically, we want to set $MDE(k+1)$ such that,

$$GU(k+1) = \begin{cases} GU(k) - \Delta U(k), & \Delta U(k) < GU(k), \\ 0, & \Delta U(k) \geq GU(k). \end{cases}$$

This requires that we can predict $GU(k+1)$ induced by $MDE(k+1)$. Note that given $MDE(k+1)$ we can only estimate the corresponding $GU(k+1)$ since our problem is of probabilistic nature. For this mentioned reason, we introduce the notion of *predicted gained utilization*,

$$PGU = g(MDE)$$

where given an MDE, the corresponding GU can be predicted. We derive g based on system profiling, where we measure GU for different MDEs. The function g is then derived by linearizing the relationship between GU and MDE. By taking the inverse of g,

$$MDE = g^{-1}(PGU) = \mu \times PGU \tag{1}$$

we can compute a $MDE(k+1)$ based on a $PGU(k+1)$ where,

$$PGU(k+1) = \begin{cases} GU(k) - \Delta U(k), & \Delta U(k) < GU(k), \\ 0, & \Delta U(k) \geq GU(k). \end{cases} \tag{2}$$

Since RTDBs are dynamic systems in that the behavior of the system and environment is changing, the relation between GU and MDE is adjusted on-line. This is done by measuring $GU(k)$ for a given $MDE(k)$ during each sampling period and updating μ. Note that on-line profiling also has the advantage of requiring less accurate parameters computed from off-line analysis.

By applying Equation (1) and (2), we compute $MDE(k+1)$ according to the following,

$$MDE(k+1) = f(\Delta U(k)) =$$
$$= \min(\mu \times PGU(k+1), MDE_r \times (M_p + 100)).$$

Since MDE is not allowed to overshoot more than $MDE_r \times (M_p + 100)$, we use a *min* operator to guarantee this.

5   Performance Evaluation

In this section a detailed description of the performed experiments is given. The goal and the background of the experiments are discussed, and finally the results are presented.

5.1   Experimental Goals

The main objective of the experiments is to show whether the presented algorithms can provide guarantees based on a QoS specification. We have for this reason studied and evaluated the behavior of the algorithms according to a set of performance metrics. The performance evaluation is undertaken by a set of simulation experiments, where a set of parameters have been varied. These are:

- Load (*Load*). Computational systems may show different behaviors for different loads, especially when the system is overloaded. For this reason, we measure the performance when applying different loads to the system.
- Execution Time Estimation Error (*EstErr*). Often exact execution time estimates of transactions are not known. To study how runtime error affects the algorithms, we measure the performance considering different execution time estimation errors.

5.2   Simulation Setup

The simulated workload consists of update and user transactions, which access data and perform virtual arithmetic/logical operations on the data. Update transactions occupy approximately 50% of the workload. Note that the load applied to the database is based on submitted user and update transactions and the tested approaches may reduce the applied load by applying admission control.

In our experiments, one simulation run lasts for 10 minutes of simulated time. For all the performance data, we have taken the average of 10 simulation runs and derived 95% confidence interval, denoted as vertical lines in the figures. The following QoS specification is used: $M_r^M = 1\%$, $M_r^O = 10\%$, $MDE_r = 2\%$, $U \geq 80\%$, $T_s \leq 60s$, and $M_p \leq 30\%$.

We use the following notation where the metric X_i refers to the transaction T_i, while $X_i[t_i]$ is associated with the subtransaction t_i (where $t_i \in \{M_i, O_{i,1}, \ldots, O_{i,\#O_i}\}$).

Data and Update Transactions. The simulated DB holds 1000 temporal data objects (d_i) where each data object is updated by a stream ($Stream_i$, $1 \leq i \leq 1000$). The period (P_i) is uniformly distributed in the range (100ms,50s) (i.e. $U : (100ms, 50s)$) and estimated execution time (EET_i) is given by $U : (1ms, 8ms)$. The average update value (AV_i) of each $Stream_i$ is given by $U : (0, 100)$. Upon a periodic generation of an update, $Stream_i$ gives the update an actual execution time (AET_i) given by the normal distribution $N : (EET_i, \sqrt{EET_i})$ and a value ($UpdateValue_i$) according to $N : (AV_i, AV_i \times VarFactor)$, where $VarFactor$ is uniformly distributed in (0,1). The deadline is set according to $D_i = ArrivalTime_i + P_i$.

User Transactions. Each $Source_i$ generates a transaction T_i, consisting of one mandatory subtransaction and $\#O_i$ ($1 \leq \#O_i \leq 3$) optional subtransaction(s) ($1 \leq j \leq \#O_i$). $\#O_i$ is uniformly distributed between 1 and 3.

The estimated (average) execution time of the subtransactions $(EET_i[t_i])$ is given by $U : (10ms, 20ms)$. The estimation error $EstErr$ is used to introduce execution time estimation error in the average execution time given by $AET_i[t_i] = (1 + EstErr) \times EET_i[t_i]$. Further, upon generation of a transaction, $Source_i$ associates an actual execution time to each subtransaction, which is given by $N : (AET_i[t_i], \sqrt{AET_i[t_i]})$. The deadline is set according to $D_i = ArrivalTime_i + EET_i \times SlackFactor$. The slack factor is uniformly distributed according to $U : (20, 40)$.

It is assumed that the number of data accesses $(\#DA_i[t_i])$ for each subtransaction is proportional to $EET_i[t_i]$. Hence, longer subtransactions access more data. Upon a transaction generation, $Source_i$ associates an actual number of data accesses given by $N : (\#DA_i[t_i], \sqrt{\#DA_i[t_i]})$ to each subtransaction of T_i. The data set accessed by a transaction is partitioned among the subtransactions such that the partitions are mutually disjoint. However, the data sets accessed by transactions may overlap.

5.3   Baselines

To the best of our knowledge, there has been no earlier work on techniques for managing data impreciseness and transaction impreciseness, satisfying QoS or QoD requirements. Previous work within imprecise computing applied to tasks focus on maximizing or minimizing a performance metric (e.g. total error). The latter cannot be applied to our problem since in our case we want to control a set of performance metrics such that they converge towards a set of references given by a QoS specification. For this reason, we have developed two baseline algorithms, Baseline-1 and Baseline-2. We use the baselines to study the impact of the workload on the system. Here, we can establish the efficiency of FCS-IC-1 and FCS-IC-2 by comparing the operational envelope of the algorithms, i.e., we can compare the resistance to failure of the algorithms with regard to applied load and/or run-time estimation errors. The baselines are given below.

Baseline-1. The preciseness of the data is adjusted based on the relative miss percentage of optional subtransactions. Conceptually, MDE increases as M^O increases. MDE is set according to $MDE(k+1) = \min(\frac{M^O(k)}{M_r^O} MDE_r, MDE_r \times (M_p + 100))$. A simple AC is applied, where a transaction (T_i) is admitted if the estimated utilization of admitted transactions and T_i is less or equal to 80%.

Baseline-2. In Baseline-1, a significant change in MDE may introduce oscillations in miss percentages. Baseline-2 is similar to Baseline-1, but here MDE is increased and decreased stepwise. The outline of the algorithm is as follows. If $M^O(k)$ is greater than zero, increase $MDE(k)$ by a step (MDE_{step}) until $MDE_r \times (M_p + 100)$ is reached (i.e. $MDE(k + 1) = \min(MDE(k) + MDE_{step}, MDE_r \times (M_p + 100)))$. If $M^O(k)$ is equal to zero, decrease $MDE(k)$ by a step (MDE_{step}) until zero is reached (i.e. $MDE(k+1) = \max(MDE(k) - MDE_{step}, 0))$. The same AC as in Baseline-1 is used here.

5.4   Results of Varying Load

The setup of the experiment is given below, followed by the presentation of the results. Figure 5 shows the average M^O and MDE.

Experimental setup. We measure M^M, M^O, MDE, and U. The experiment setup is as follows. We apply loads from 50% to 200%. The execution time estimation error is set to zero (i.e. $EstErr = 0$).

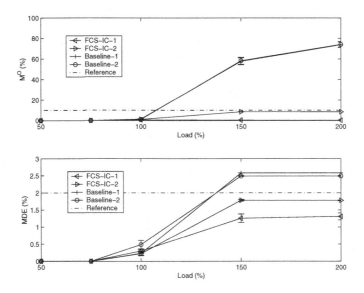

Fig. 5. Average performance for $Load = 50, 75, 100, 150,$ and 200%, $EstErr = 0$

Average Miss Percentage of Mandatory Subtransactions. Miss percentage of mandatory subtransactions (M^M) has been observed to be zero[2] for all four algorithms and, therefore, this has not been included in Figure 5. The specified miss percentage reference (M_r^M), have been set to 1% and this is not satisfied. This is due to higher priority of mandatory subtransactions compared to optional subtransactions. According to our investigations, the miss percentage of mandatory subtransactions start increasing when the miss percentage of optional subtransactions is over 90% [2]. Consequently, since the miss percentage of optional subtransactions does not reach 90%, the miss percentage of mandatory subtransactions remains at zero.

Average Miss Percentage of Optional Subtransactions. For Baseline-1 and Baseline-2, the miss percentage of optional subtransactions (M^O) increases as the load increases, violating the reference miss percentage, M_r^O, at loads exceeding 150%. In the case of FCS-IC-1, M^O is near zero at loads 150% and

---

[2] We have not observed any deadline misses.

200%. Even though the miss percentage is low, it does not fully satisfy the QoS specification. This is in line with our earlier discussions regarding the behavior of FCS-IC-1. The low miss percentage is due to the utilization controller since it attempts to reduce potential overshoots by reducing the utilization, which in turn decreases the miss percentage. FCS-IC-2 on the other hand shows a better performance. The average M^O at 150% and 200% is $8.5 \pm 0.1\%$, which is fairly close to M_r^O. In our model tuning of the controlled system, we have assumed worst-case setups and set $EstErr$ to one. In this experiment we have set $EstErr$ to zero, resulting in a certain model error[3]. If $EstErr$ is set to one, we can see that that the average M^O is close to M_r^O. This is shown in Section 5.5.

Average MDE. The average MDE for Baseline-1 and Baseline-2 violates the reference MDE set to 2%. In contrast, in the case of FCS-IC-1, MDE is significantly lower than MDE_r. Since the miss percentages are kept low at all times, they are not likely to overshoot. Consequently, the control signal from the miss percentage controllers is likely to be positive, which is interpreted by the QoD manager as an QoD upgrade and, hence, MDE will not reach the level of MDE_r. This is further explained in Section 5.6, where the transient performance of the algorithms is discussed. FCS-IC-2 provides an average MDE closer to MDE_r, given by $1.78 \pm 0.024\%$ at loads 150% and 200%. However, MDE does not reach MDE_r since MDE is set according to the relative M^O (which does not reach M_r^O).

Average Utilization. For all approaches, the utilization satisfies the QoS specification as it is above the specified 80% for loads between 100-200%, reaching almost 100% at 200% applied load.

5.5 Results of Varying EstErr

The setup of the experiment is given below, followed by the presentation of the results. Figure 6 shows the average M^O and MDE.

Experimental setup. We measure M^M, M^O, MDE, and U. The experiment setup is as follows. We apply 200% load. The execution time estimation error is varied according to $EstErr = 0.00, 0.25, 0.50, 0.75,$ and 1.00.

Average Miss Percentage of Mandatory Subtransactions. As in the previous experiment (see Section 5.4), M^M is zero for all approaches and $EstErr$. The discussion regarding average miss percentage of mandatory subtransactions given in Section 5.4 also apply here and are not further discussed.

Average Miss Percentage of Optional Subtransactions. As expected, Baseline-1 and Baseline-2 do not satisfy the QoS specification. In fact, M^O increases as $EstErr$ increases, reaching a value close to 90% for both algorithms. As we can see, FCS-IC-1 and FCS-IC-2 are insensitive against varying $EstErr$. Note that when analyzing FCS-IC-2, we can see that M^O grows towards M_r^O as $EstErr$ increases in value. M^O for $EstErr$ set to zero and $EstErr$ set to one is $8.47 \pm 0.036\%$ and $9.23 \pm 0.17\%$, respectively. This is the result of the

---

[3] By model error we mean the deviation of the model used compared with the actual system being controlled.

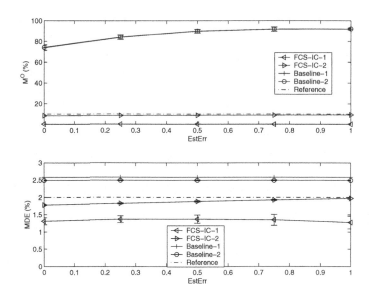

Fig. 6. Average performance for $EstErr = 0$, 0.25, 0.50, 0.75, and 1.0, $Load = 200\%$

discussions given in Section 2. As $EstErr$ increases, the model error decreases and, hence, the controlled system becomes closer to the actual model. This gives a more accurate picture of the system and the controllers are therefore able to control the system in a more correct way.

Average MDE. Baseline-1 and Baseline-2 violate the specified MDE reference. For FCS-IC-1 average MDE does not change considerably for different $EstErr$. In the case of FCS-IC-2, average MDE grows towards MDE_r, with increasing $EstErr$. The adjustment of MDE depends on the relative M^O and, hence, the average MDE grows as the average M^O grows, reaching a value of $1.97 \pm 0.03\%$.

5.6   Transient Performance

Studying the average performance is often not enough when dealing with dynamic systems. Therefore we study the transient performance of FCS-IC-1 and FCS-IC-2 when $Load$ is set to 200% and $EstErr$ set to one. Figures 7 and 8 show the transient behavior of FCS-IC-1 and FCS-IC-2. The dash-dotted line indicates maximum overshoot.

Starting with FCS-IC-1, we can note that M^O is kept low at all times. This is expected since the average M^O was shown to be low. The reader may have noticed that MDE is greater than zero in the interval 20-150 where M^O is zero. Since MDE is greater than zero, it is clear that ΔU may become negative during that period. This is due to the behavior of the utilization controller. Initially, the utilization is below the reference (U_r). As the utilization increases and no miss percentage overshoots are observed, U_r increases linearly until a miss percentage

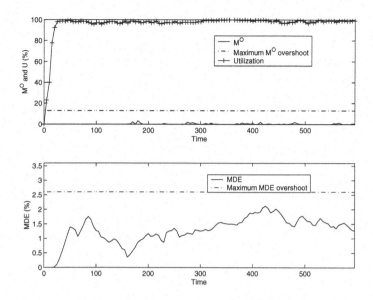

Fig. 7. Transient performance for FCS-IC-1. $EstErr = 1.0$, $Load = 200\%$

is observed (one of the miss percentage controllers takes over) in which case U_r is reduced exponentially. In FCS-IC-1, U_r is only increased if the utilization controller has taken over. Our investigations show that the utilization controller takes over once the utilization overshoots U_r, resulting in a negative ΔU and, hence, U_r being increased too late. Consequently, the negative ΔU leads to an increase in MDE.

FCS-IC-2 shows a more satisfying result as both M^O and MDE increase and decrease together. Both M^O and MDE are kept around M_r^O and MDE_r, respectively. Although the average M^O is close to M_r^O, we can see that M^O often overshoots its reference. The highest M^O has been noted to 25.7%. This is higher than the specified maximum miss percentage of 13% (i.e. $M^O \leq 13\%$). One cause to such overshoot is the various disturbances like data conflicts, resulting in restarts or aborts of transactions. Further, we have set $EstErr$ to one, which yields a higher overshoot than in the case when $EstErr$ is set to zero (i.e. no execution time estimation error). The results of setting $EstErr$ to zero is shown is Figure 9. Here we can see that the variance of miss percentage is much smaller than in the case when $EstErr$ is set to one.

5.7   Summary of Results and Discussions

It has been shown that FCS-IC-1 and FCS-IC-2 are insensitive against load variations and inaccurate execution time estimations. FCS-IC-1 can manage to provide near zero miss percentage for optional subtransactions. We have also seen that FCS-IC-1 can efficiently suppress miss percentage overshoots. However, the performance of FCS-IC-1 does not fully comply with the given QoS specification.

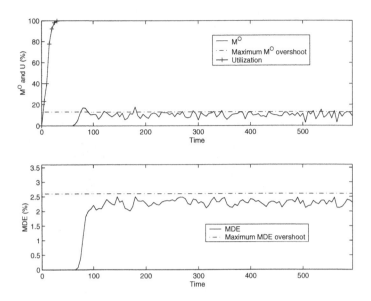

Fig. 8. Transient performance for FCS-IC-2. $EstErr = 1.0$, $Load = 200\%$

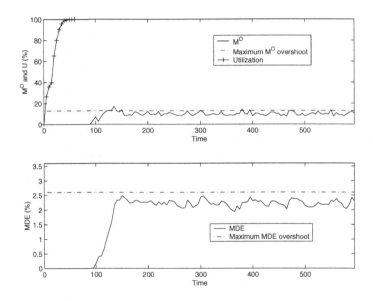

Fig. 9. Transient performance for FCS-IC-2. $EstErr = 0.0$, $Load = 200\%$

Miss percentages and MDE are kept significantly lower than the references, violating the given QoS specifications. This is due to the exponential decrease in utilization every time M^O overshoots its reference.

In FCS-IC-2, M^O and MDE are consistent with their specified references. In addition, we have seen that the data and user transaction quality increase and decrease together. FCS-IC-2, however, produces overshoots higher than the maximum allowed overshoot, as given by the QoS specification.

We conclude that FCS-IC-1 should be applied to RTDBs where overshoots cannot be tolerated, but where consistency between the controlled variables and their references is relaxed, i.e., we do not require the system to produce the desired miss percentages and MDE. The experiments show that FCS-IC-2 is particularly useful when consistency between the controlled variables and their references are emphasized, but some overshoots higher than the maximum allowed can be accepted.

6   Related Work

In the past few years, feedback control scheduling has been receiving special attention [10,13,3]. Lu et al. have presented a feedback control scheduling framework, where they propose three algorithms for managing the miss percentage and/or utilization [10]. In the work by Parekh et al., the length of a queue of remote procedure calls (RPCs) arriving at a server is controlled [13]. Changing the periodicity of a set of tasks in response to load variations has been suggested in [3]. If the estimated load is found to be greater than a threshold, task periods are enlarged to find the desired load. In contrast to FCS-IC-1 and FCS-IC-2, aperiodic tasks are not considered in their model.

Labrinidis et al. introduced the notion of QoD [8]. Here, web pages are cached at the server and the back-end database continuously updates them. Their proposed update scheduling policy can significantly improve data freshness compared to FIFO scheduling. Kang et al., presented a feedback control scheduling architecture used to control the transaction miss percentage and utilization of a real-time database by dynamically balancing update policies (immediate or on-demand) of a set of data [7].

Liu et al. proposed an imprecise computation model [9]. They presented a set of imprecise scheduling problems associated with imprecise computing and also gave an algorithm for minimizing the total error of a set of tasks. Shih et al. presenting two algorithms for minimizing the maximum error for a schedule that minimizes the total error [15]. Hansson et al. proposed an algorithm, OR-ULD, for minimizing total error and total weighted error [5]. The approaches presented by Liu, Shih, and Hansson require the knowledge of accurate processing times of the tasks, which is often not available in RTDBs. Further, they focus on maximizing or minimizing a performance metric (e.g. total error). The latter cannot be applied to our problem, since in our case we want to control a set of performance metrics such that they converge towards a set of references given by a QoS specification.

The correctness of answers to databases queries can be traded off to enhance timeliness. Query processors, APPROXIMATE [17] and CASE-DB [6] are examples of such databases where approximate answers to queries can be produced within certain deadlines. However, in both approaches, impreciseness has been applied to only transactions and, hence, data impreciseness has not been addressed. Further, they have not addressed the notion of QoS. In our work, we have introduced impreciseness at data object level and considered QoS in terms of transactions and data impreciseness.

7 Conclusions and Future Work

The need for real-time data services has increased during the last years. As the run-time environment of such applications tends to be dynamic, it is imperative to handle transient overloads efficiently. It has been shown that feedback control scheduling is quite robust to errors in run-time estimates (e.g. changes in workload and estimated execution time). Further, imprecise computation techniques have shown to be useful in many areas where timely processing of tasks or services is emphasized. In this work, we combine the advantages from feedback control scheduling and imprecise computation techniques, forming a framework where a database administrator can specify a set of requirements on the database performance and service quality. We present two algorithms, FCS-IC-1 and FCS-IC-2, for managing steady state and transient state performance in terms of data and transaction impreciseness. FCS-IC-1 and FCS-IC-2 give a robust and controlled behavior of RTDBs, in terms of transaction and data quality, even during transient overloads and when we have inaccurate run-time estimates of the transactions.

For our future work, we are establishing techniques for managing data and user transaction impreciseness in a distributed environment and we develop policies for handling derived data. Different approaches to modeling the controlled system will be considered.

Acknowledgment. The authors wish to thank Kyoung-Don Kang at the University of Virginia, Charlottesville, for providing and helping us with the simulator used to perform the experiments.

References

1. R. Abbott and H. Garcia-Molina. Scheduling real-time transactions: A performance evaluation. *ACM Transactions on Database System*, 17:513–560, 1992.
2. M. Amirijoo. Algorithms for managing QoS for real-time data services using imprecise computation, 2002. Master's Thesis Report LiTH-IDA-Ex-02/90, www.ida.liu.se/~rtslab/master/past.
3. G. C. Buttazzo and L. Abeni. Adaptive workload managment through elastic scheduling. *Journal of Real-time Systems*, 23(1/2), July/September 2002. Special Issue on Control-Theoretical Approaches to Real-Time Computing.
4. X. Chen and A. M. K. Cheng. An imprecise algorithm for real-time compressed image and video transmission. In *Proceedings of the Sixth International Conference on Computer Communications and Networks*, pages 390–397, 1997.

5. J. Hansson, M. Thuresson, and S. H. Son. Imprecise task scheduling and overload managment using OR-ULD. In *Proceedings of the 7th Conference in Real-Time Computing Systems and Applications*, pages 307–314. IEEE Computer Press, 2000.

6. W. Hou, G. Ozsoyoglu, and B. K. Taneja. Processing aggregate relational queries with hard time constraints. In *Proceedings of the 1989 ACM SIGMOD International Conference on Management of Data*, pages 68–77. ACM Press, 1989.

7. K. Kang, S. H. Son, and J. A. Stankovic. Service differentiation in real-time main memory databases. In *Proceedings of 5th IEEE International Symposium on Object-oriented Real-time Distributed Computing*, April 2002.

8. A. Labrinidis and N. Roussopoulos. Update propagation strategies for improving the quality of data on the web. *The VLDB Journal*, pages 391–400, 2001.

9. J. W. S. Liu, K. Lin, W. Shin, and A. C.-S. Yu. Algorithms for scheduling imprecise computations. *IEEE Computer*, 24(5), May 1991.

10. C. Lu, J. A. Stankovic, G. Tao, and S. H. Son. Feedback control real-time scheduling: Framework, modeling and algorithms. *Journal of Real-time Systems*, 23(1/2), July/September 2002. Special Issue on Control-Theoretical Approaches to Real-Time Computing.

11. P. Malinski, S. Sandri, and C. Reitas. An imprecision-based image classifier. In *The 10th IEEE International Conference on Fuzzy Systems*, pages 825–828, 2001.

12. V. Millan-Lopez, W. Feng, and J. W. S. Liu. Using the imprecise-computation technique for congestion control on a real-time traffic switching element. In *International Conference on Parallel and Distributed Systems*, pages 202–208, 1994.

13. S. Parekh, N. Gandhi, J. Hellerstein, D. Tilbury, T. Jayram, and J. Bigus. Using control theory to achieve service level objectives in performance managment. *Journal of Real-time Systems*, 23(1/2), July/September 2002. Special Issue on Control-Theoretical Approaches to Real-Time Computing.

14. K. Ramamritham. Real-time databases. *International Journal of Distributed and Parallel Databases*, (1), 1993.

15. W. K. Shih and J. W. S. Liu. Algorithms for scheduling imprecise computations with timing constraints to minimize maximum error. *IEEE Transactions on Computers*, 44(3):466–471, 1995.

16. K. J. Åström and B. Wittenmark. *Adaptive Control*. Addion-Wesley, second edition, 1995.

17. S. V. Vrbsky and J. W. S. Liu. APPROXIMATE - a query processor that produces monotonically improving approximate answers. *IEEE Transactions on Knowledge and Data Engineering*, 5(6):1056–1068, December 1993.

18. S. Zilberstein and S. J. Russell. Optimal composition of real-time systems. *Artificial Intelligence*, 82(1–2):181–213, 1996.

On Soft Real-Time Guarantees on Ethernet*

Min-gyu Cho and Kang G. Shin

Real-Time Computing Laboratory
Department of Electrical Engineering and Computer Science
The University of Michigan
Ann Arbor, MI 48109-2122, U.S.A.
{mgcho,kgshin}@eecs.umich.edu

Abstract. The medium access protocol of Ethernet, CSMA/CD, has an inherent limitation in providing real-time guarantees. Since Ethernet is the most commonly-used local area network (LAN) technology due to its low cost, high bandwidth and robustness, it is very important to overcome this problem so that Ethernet can be used as a network for soft real-time applications like multimedia. An *adaptive traffic smoother* (ATS) was proposed as a kernel-level software solution that provides soft real-time guarantees on Ethernet.

This paper addresses the reconfigurability, scalability and portability of ATS. First, a mechanism to read and adjust several user-specific parameters of ATS is discussed, and metrics or parameters to indicate the achievement of the user-required Quality-of-Service (QoS) are developed since these parameters are indirectly related to the user-specific QoS. Our experimental evaluation validates the feasibility of enhancing the reconfigurability and portability of ATS. Second, ATS is extended to a switched Ethernet which is commonly used for scalability. Our solution employs an ATS for each port of the switch for real-time packet delivery guarantees. Finally, a prototype of the user-level ATS is implemented and evaluated to enhance the portability of ATS. The performance of this user-level ATS is shown to be comparable to that of the kernel-level implementation, while enhancing both the reconfigurability and portability of real-time Ethernet solutions.

Keywords: Ethernet, CSMA/CD, adaptive traffic smoother (ATS), real-time communication, reconfigurability, scalability, portability

1   Introduction

Ethernet [3] is the most popular local area network (LAN) technology connecting end-hosts due to its low cost, high bandwidth and robustness. Ethernet adopts the carrier sense multiple access with collision detection (CSMA/CD) protocol for its medium access control (MAC) protocol. In the CSMA/CD protocol, upon detection of a collision, each host takes a random amount of time before making a retransmission attempt according to the binary exponential backoff algorithm, to resolve the contention. Since the backoff time is decided randomly by each host, the packet may collide again with other

---

* This work reported in this paper was supported in part by DARPA under the US AFRL contracts F30602-01-02-0527.

packets during its retransmission. Thus, it is difficult to provide real-time guarantees on Ethernet. However, predictable delay guarantees are important for many time-sensitive applications, and the demand for such applications is growing.

The timely delivery of control messages between programmable logic controllers (PLCs) is required in factory automation systems. Traditionally, the proprietary networks such as Allen-Bradley's Universal Remote I/O Link [4] or CAN Bus [5] are commonly used in such a system to provide real-time guarantees for control messages. But these proprietary networks are expensive while their bandwidth is generally low. Thus, the manufacturing automation industry has been pursuing use of commercial off-the-shelf network products to replace or back up the proprietary networks. The low price and proven robustness of Ethernet make it an attractive candidate if it can provide real-time guarantees.

Real-time guarantees are also crucial to multimedia applications. The increase of network bandwidth along with the processor's computing power has enabled the real-time transmission of multimedia data such as voice over IP (VoIP), video conferencing, streaming audio/video and home entertainment systems. These applications require the real-time delivery guarantees of multimedia data. Most of the research on providing the Quality of Service (QoS) for these applications focused on wide area networks (WANs) instead of LANs, as there is more unpredictability in a WAN than in a LAN due to its complex topology. However, it is not possible to provide end-to-end delay guarantees without providing such guarantees on end-hosts' LAN. Since Ethernet is the dominant LAN technology, we will focus on how to provide real-time guarantees on Ethernet.

Numerous approaches have been taken to overcome the inherent limitations of Ethernet. A typical approach is to modify the Ethernet MAC layer to provide timeliness guarantees [6,7,8,9,10,11]. Even though real-time guarantees can be achieved with these approaches, changing already-installed network interface cards (NICs) is very expensive and difficult, if not impossible.

Switches such as IEEE802.1p or IEEE802.12 [14] can be used, instead of a hub, to support real-time guarantees. With a full-duplex switch, a collision domain is separated, and thus, the transmission delay of real-time packets can be bounded. However, the most commonly-deployed topology for Ethernet is the segmented Ethernet since the cost of a switch is much higher than that of a hub. Thus, the real-time guarantee on Ethernet is still important to provide the end-to-end real-time guarantees.

Also proposed are software solutions without modifying the hardware. Rether [12] is a virtual token ring implementation on top of the Ethernet without modifying the Ethernet MAC layer. RTCC [13] is another example of this approach. It uses a centralized node to gather state-related information such as real-time packet arrival time, and determine when and how to send a packet for each participating node. The existing NICs can be used for this approach, but both of these examples require a significant modification to operating systems to handle token management or to elect the central node. Thus, the implementation or the porting of such a solution is very expensive.

Kweon and Shin [2] proposed an *adaptive traffic smoother* (ATS) to provide soft real-time guarantees on an Ethernet, which also takes a purely kernel-level software approach. They installed an ATS on each host between the Ethernet MAC layer and the IP layer. The ATS regulates the generation rate of non-RT traffic on each host, and the traffic generation rate is adapted to the underlying network load condition. Since there is no explicit method to measure the network load on Ethernet, packet collisions on the medium are used as an indirect indicator of the network load. Under the ATS, the traffic generation rate is increased slowly in the absence of collision, while it is reduced to a half when the outgoing packet experiences a collision. This simple scheme is shown to be very effective in reducing the deadline miss ratio of RT messages while maintaining an acceptable level of non-RT traffic throughput. However, there are three important limitations in this approach. First, there are several parameters that control the behavior of ATS. However, these parameters cannot be adjusted in the original implementation of ATS, and are not directly related to the QoS that the end-user may require. Second, the original ATS focused only on a single Ethernet while the use of switched-Ethernets is very common for the scalability of the LAN. Finally, the portability of the original ATS is poor since it is implemented inside the kernel.

In this paper, we improve the ATS in [2] to solve the above problems as follows. First, a reconfiguration mechanism is provided to adjust the user-specific parameters of ATS, and a performance monitoring mechanism is developed and added. Second, the adaptive traffic smoothing scheme in ATS is adopted for each port of a switch for its extension to the switched-Ethernet. A prototype of such switch is implemented on a Linux box and its performance is compared to other setups. Finally, a user-level ATS is proposed to increase the portability.

The rest of the paper is organized as follows. Section 2 describes the adaptive traffic smoother. The problem statement and approaches are described in Section 3. The implementation details are given in Section 4, and the performance evaluation is presented in Section 5. The paper concludes with Section 6.

2   Adaptive Traffic Smoother

The detail of an ATS is given in [2], but it is described briefly here for completeness. The main idea of a traffic smoother is to reduce the probability that a real-time packet collides with other packets by regulating a host's traffic injection into the Ethernet. A traffic smoother is inserted between the Ethernet MAC layer and the IP layer, and smoothes non-RT traffic. A *fixed-rate traffic smoother* [1] is the original traffic smoother, in which the network load is regulated under a certain limit, named a *network-wide input limit*. Each host has a portion of the network-wide input limit, called a *station input limit*, and a host's outgoing traffic is kept under its station input limit. This traffic smoother is effective in providing real-time guarantees on Ethernet, but it is inflexible and inefficient in transmitting non-RT traffic since (i) each node is assigned a constant bandwidth regardless of the network load condition, and (ii) the station input limit is decreased as the number of hosts increases. When all hosts do not synchronously generate non-RT traffic, which is usually the case, the bandwidth reserved for those hosts not generating non-RT traffic is left unused, thus seriously degrading the throughput of non-RT traffic.

The adaptive traffic smoother, on the other hand, changes adaptively its station input limit according to the current network load. Since the direct information on the current network load is unavailable to the local node on Ethernet, the collision status report provided by NIC is used to estimate the load. In the absence of collision, the station input limit is increased while it is decreased in the presence of collision. More specifically, the ATS uses the *Harmonic-Increase and Multiplicative-Decrease Adaptation* (HIMD) mechanism. HIMD provides traffic control similar to that of TCP, which increases the traffic generation rate additively in the absence of congestion detection, but decreases it multiplicatively upon detection of congestion or packet loss.

The ATS works similarly to a leaky-bucket filter, maintaining two parameters, credit bucket depth (CBD) and refresh period (RP). A credit of CBD bytes is replenished every RP seconds, so the station input limit can be given as CBD/RP. The CBD is fixed at the maximum transmission unit (MTU) of Ethernet to reduce the burstiness and the RP is changed according to HIMD. RP is decreased by Δ every τ seconds in the absence of collision, thus increasing the station input limit harmonically. On the other hand, it is checked if there has been a collision within α seconds after the previous change of RP. Upon detection of a collision, RP is doubled, thus decreasing the station input limit multiplicatively, and the current credit is vacated. Also the value of RP is bounded by RP_{min} and RP_{max}, i.e., RP is no less than RP_{min} and no greater than RP_{max}. Here α, Δ, τ, RP_{min}, and RP_{max} are user-specific parameters. The ATS will show different characteristics when these parameters are altered.

3   Problem Statement and Solution Approach

3.1   Support of Reconfigurability

The original implementation of ATS did not provide any means of altering the user-specific parameters; these parameters are hard-coded in the kernel, and cannot be adjusted without recompiling the kernel. However, different applications may have different QoS requirements. For example, RT control messages may be required to be delivered within 50 ms of their generation with 99% probability in an automated manufacturing system, while voice packets may be required to be delivered within 100 ms with 95% probability.

We designed and developed a reconfiguration mechanism to dynamically adjust the user-specific parameters without recompiling or rebooting. With this mechanism, ATS parameters can be easily adjusted for different application requirement. By adjusting ATS parameters, one can make a tradeoff between the non-RT throughput and the deadline miss ratio of RT messages, i.e., one can get higher bandwidth at the expense of increasing RT message deadline misses. This can be analyzed qualitatively as follows. If Δ is increased, RP decreases faster, i.e., more traffic is generated. Thus, the non-RT throughput will increase while the deadline miss ratio increases. Similarly, the larger RP_{min}, the lower the maximum bandwidth consumed by a node. Thus, as RP_{min} is increased, the maximum non-RT traffic decreases, thus improving RT performance. However, it should be noted that a large RP_{min} costs non-RT throughput even though only one host is generating the traffic.

We also developed metrics to monitor and characterize the performance at run-time. Since the quantitative change of performance is difficult to predict *a priori*, the user can exploit these metrics when s/he adjusts the ATS parameters. The metrics we used are the number of transmitted packets, n_{total}, and the number of packets that miss the deadline, n_{miss}. If the desired delay bound is set by the user, both the number of the transmitted

RT packets and the number of the packets taken longer than the specified bound will be identified and counted. The deadline miss ratio can be inferred from these numbers by a simple calculation: $deadline\ miss\ ratio = n_{miss}/n_{total}$.

The delay measured here is the transmission delay, i.e., the interval from the time when a packet is passed to the device, and to the time when a packet is successfully transmitted. This delay excludes the protocol processing time on both the sender and the receiver sides plus the propagation delay on the medium. This interval may vary due to collisions and backoffs, which are the source of Ethernet's unpredictability and the main focus of this paper.

3.2 Switched-Ethernet Extension

The original ATS was designed for a single Ethernet, while switches are commonly used in today's LANs as the number of hosts increases. Use of switches can dramatically improve the overall throughput and delay of a LAN, as they separate the collision domain and forward packets from one collision domain to another only when necessary. Thus, one can improve scalability by using ATS in a switched-Ethernet.

However, the performance of ATS can be degraded significantly when applied to the switched-Ethernet, because bursty traffic on an Ethernet can be generated by the switch. Each port of a switch generates traffic following the CSMA/CD protocol like a host on a single Ethernet. Since it does not observe the HIMD policy, it can generate bursty traffic, which may collide with RT packets and delays their transmission. We, therefore, propose to enforce the HIMD policy at each port of the switch. Each switch port as well as hosts on the Ethernet will then follow the HIMD policy, thus guaranteeing the timely delivery of packets. Since it is the current trend to add flexible configuration and programming features to a switch, this approach will soon be feasible. In such a case, each port should maintain the traffic smoother parameters, such as the current credit and the last collision time, to reflect the fact that a different ATS shows a different traffic-generation behavior.

3.3 User-Level Implementation

The implementation of ATS depends heavily on the underlying operating system, since the interface between the IP layer and the device driver differs from one operating system to another. Thus, implementing the ATS on one operating system requires OS-dependent code, which is typically difficult and time-consuming to develop and debug. The original ATS in [2] requires kernel modification including the device driver for Linux and building a new network driver interface specification (NDIS) [15] driver for Windows NT.

The portability of ATS will be enhanced if it is built in the application level and requires a minimum change to the underlying operating system, while there are a few potential problems in this approach. When the ATS is implemented in the user-level, the most significant change is its position in the protocol stack as shown in Fig. 1. A user-level ATS sits on top of the UDP or TCP/IP layer while a kernel-level ATS lies between the Ethernet MAC layer and the IP layer. The potential problem of this approach is that there may be some packets being processed in the TCP/IP (or UDP/IP) protocol stack when a collision occurs. Since such packets are beyond the control of a user-level ATS, they will be transmitted by the host and they may result in more collisions with RT

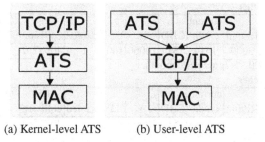

(a) Kernel-level ATS   (b) User-level ATS

Fig. 1. Comparison between the kernel-level adaptive traffic smoother and the user-level adaptive traffic smoother. The kernel-level adaptive traffic smoother resides between the IP layer and the MAC layer, while the user-level adaptive traffic smoother resides on top of transport layer.

packets from other hosts, thus causing the RT packets to miss their deadlines. Another potential problem is that one application is ignorant of the traffic generated by another application since each application has its own ATS, i.e., each application smoothes its own traffic independently of others'. However, each traffic smoother will reduce its traffic-generation rate upon detection of a collision. Therefore, the overall behavior of a user-level ATS will be more sensitive to collisions when more than one application inject non-RT traffic at the same time.

4   Implementation

4.1   Enhanced Reconfigurability and Scalability

The ATS is re-implemented on Linux 2.2.19 to enhance its reconfigurability. The new implementation improved the reconfigurability by enabling the end-user to alter the user-specific parameters and observe the resultant QoS changes. The ATS is also modified to work independently as a per-Ethernet device so that a Linux box may emulate a switch.

The ATS uses two queues to prioritize RT packets over non-RT packets. RT packets can be differentiated from non-RT packets by the type-of-service (ToS) field in the IP header, which can be set by *setsockopt()* system call in Linux. When the device is ready, the high-priority queue is checked, and the packet at the head of the queue, if any, is sent to the device. A packet in the low-priority queue can be dequeued and sent to the device only when a positive credit is available.

The ATS needs to know when the most recent collision has occurred. Ethernet devices have status reporting features that can be used for this purpose. The device driver for the NIC should be modified such that the time of the most recent collision is recorded. The Ethernet device generates, or can be set to generate, an interrupt when a packet is successfully transmitted or a packet is discarded after experiencing a pre-specified number of collisions. In the interrupt handling routine, a small size of code is inserted to record the time when the last transmitted packet experienced a collision. The time unit

cat /proc/net/tsmoother

Inter-face	RP	RPmax	RPmin	current credit	CBD	α	Δ	enabled	last collision	QoS bound	# trans-mitted	# missed
eth0	3000	100000	3000	1514	1514	10000	100	1	4065717	2	8611	1192

echo "eth0 min 1000" > /proc/net/tsmoother

cat /proc/net/tsmoother

Inter-face	RP	RPmax	RPmin	current credit	CBD	α	Δ	enabled	last collision	QoS bound	# trans-mitted	# missed
eth0	1000	100000	1000	1514	1514	10000	100	1	4076586	2	8611	1192

Fig. 2. Example of getting/setting parameters through the proc file system. The output is formatted in the table for better readability. The real output is similar to the above table.

used here is *jiffies*.[1] Every device driver needs to be modified, but this modification was very minor: in most cases, less than 10 lines of code.

The proc file system of Linux is exploited to facilitate the reading and setting of the ATS parameters. The proc file system is a pseudo file system which resides in main memory. Various types of system information can be conveniently retrieved and/or set through the proc file system. One entry (*/proc/net/tsmoother*) is added for ATS. When this file is read, it prints out the parameters of the traffic smoothers in all the active devices. Also, it can be written with appropriate data to change the ATS parameters, including enabling/disabling it.

Fig. 2 shows the use of the proc file system to get and set the parameters of ATS. As shown in this example, the current value of the ATS parameters can be read from */proc/net/tsmoother*. Also some parameters can be changed by writing the appropriate data to the file. To write data to the proc file, we use *"device param value"*, where *device* indicates the network device name used in Linux such as *eth0*; *param* is the appropriate parameter name; and *value* is the new value for the specified parameter. In the above example, the value of RP_{min} is changed to 1000, which means 1 ms. Table 1 summarizes the information reported by reading the proc file and the corresponding parameter names used to alter their values. Here τ cannot be altered since it depends on the system time resolution and is fixed to 1 ms in the current implementation. The unit of the parameters is μs except for *goal* whose unit is ms.

The required upper bound of a delay of real-time packet transmission, which can be considered as a deadline, can be set. Once the deadline is set, the number of real-time packets transmitted and the number of real-time packets that missed the deadline are recorded. It is straightforward to calculate the deadline miss ratio with these two numbers. The delay measured here is the transmission delay as mentioned earlier.

In order to emulate a switch that follows the HIMD policy, a Linux box with multiple NICs is used. Each NIC on the Linux box emulates a port of the switch. For each NIC, the ATS parameters can be set independently, thus yielding independent and different behaviors of the ATS.

---

[1] *jiffies* is the time unit maintained in the Linux kernel. It is incremented by 1 every time interrupt, which is 10 ms by default. But the time resolution is changed at 1 ms for finer granularity measurements in the implementation.

Table 1. The field reported by the proc file system and its meaning, and the parameter names used to change their values.

Field Name When Read	Parameter Name	Description
RP		the current RP
RPmax	max_rp	RP_{max}
RPmin	min_rp	RP_{min}
netshare		the current credit
cbd	cbd	CBD
alpha	alpha	α
delta	delta	Δ
en	enabled	enabled(1)/disabled(0)
last coll		the jiffies when the most recent collision occur
goal	qos	the required delay
xmit		the number of RT packets transmitted
missed		the number of RT packets delayed longer than specified bound

Table 2. The functions provided by a prototype of the user-level adaptive traffic smoother library.

Function Name	Description
ts_init(struct ts_params *tsp)	initialize an adaptive traffic smoother
ts_set(struct ts_params *tsp)	set the parameters to a new value
ts_get(struct ts_params *tsp)	get the current parameters
ts_send(int fd, const void *msg, size_t len, int flags)	a wrapper function to the existing socket function
ts_thread()	a background thread for *refresh*

4.2   User-Level Adaptive Traffic Smoother

A user-level traffic smoother is designed as a user-level library so that it can be linked with other application programs that require ATS. The functions provided by this library are summarized in Table 2.

A user-level program can initialize the user-level adaptive traffic smoother by invoking *ts_init()* function. It initializes the ATS with the given parameters and generates a background thread using the POSIX thread library. The background thread executes the *ts_thread()* function, which decreases the refresh period periodically and replenishes the credits once every refresh period. Since this procedure is implemented at user-level, the interval between two successive invocations of this procedure may not be uniform. Thus, the refresh period is decreased proportionally to the time elapsed since the last invocation.

The *ts_send()* function can be used as a wrapper of the socket function to transmit a data such as *send()*. All the parameters of this function are identical to those of *send()* provided in the UNIX environment. When this procedure is invoked, the *send()* function is invoked only when the current credit is positive.

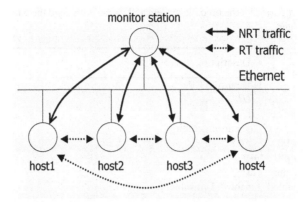

Fig. 3. Testbed setup used to measure the performance. Hosts exchange RT messages with each other, and non-RT messages with the monitor station.

The parameters of user-level traffic smoother can be easily queried and adjusted with *ts_get()* and *ts_set()*, respectively. The argument taken by these functions is a pointer to *struct ts_param*, which is defined as follows.

```
struct ts_param {
    unsigned long rp;      /* RP */
    unsigned long rp_max;  /* RPmax */
    unsigned long rp_min;  /* RPmin */
    unsigned long alpha;   /* alpha */
    unsigned long delta;   /* delta */
    unsigned long tau;     /* tau */
    int cbd;               /* cbd */
    volatile int ns;       /* the current credit */
    int enabled;           /* whether enabled */
    int congested;         /* to indicate the recent collision */
};
```

The names of the most fields are self-explanatory and correspond to the ATS parameters. The *enabled* field indicates if the smoothing is enabled, and the *congested* field is set by the background thread to indicate whether there is a collision recently.

A user-level ATS still requires a very small (less than 10 lines of code) kernel modification to get the information of the most recent collision: a device driver should be modified to record the time when the collision occurred.

5   Performance Evaluation

5.1   Experimental Setup

To validate our solutions, we performed experiments on a testbed that mimics a factory automation system. In a typical automated factory system, PLCs exchange RT messages

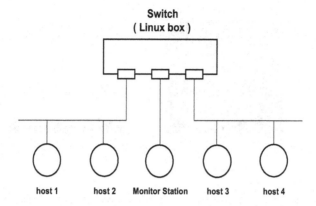

Fig. 4. Testbed setup used to measure the performance of ATS in the switched-Ethernet. Linux box with multiple NICs emulates a switch, and separates the collision domains. As in single Ethernet environment, hosts exchange RT messages with each other, and non-RT messages with the monitor station.

with each other, and non-RT messages with a monitoring system. Our testbed is shown in Fig. 3. Four Pentium 75 MHz laptops with 24M RAM are used as hosts to emulate PLCs, and one Pentium 133 MHz laptop with 32M RAM is used as the monitor station.

Each host generates a 1-Kbyte-long RT message every 100 ms. At the same time, each host sends non-RT traffic to the monitor station continuously to saturate the network. The roundtrip delay is measured for RT messages since it is very difficult to measure the one-way delay without precise time synchronization. The delay is measured at the application layer, i.e., the delay will include the protocol processing time as well as the packet transmission time. In addition to the RT roundtrip delay, the overall non-RT throughput is measured.

Fig. 4 shows the testbed setup used to measure the performance of the ATS extended to the switched-Ethernet. Four hosts and a monitor station exchange the same traffic. But the collision domain is separated into 3 domains by the switch. Two collision domains contain two hosts each, and the third collision domain is used for the monitor station. Since the monitor station consumes more bandwidth than the hosts, it is natural to allocate one separate collision domain (i.e., a port in the switch), to the monitor station.

The parameters throughout the performance evaluation are, unless specified otherwise, set as: $RP_{min} = 3\ ms$, $RP_{max} = 50\ ms$, $\alpha = 10\ ms$, $\Delta = 100\ \mu s$. For most of the experiments, we adjusted the Δ value since the performance is sensitive to this parameter, and the non-RT throughput is not sacrificed significantly.

5.2 Validation of Reconfigurability Enhancement

The usability is enhanced in the new implementation of the ATS as shown in the previous sections. To verify its usability enhancement, the sensitivity of the ATS parameters is plotted in Fig. 5. Also the metrics to show the QoS achievement are evaluated.

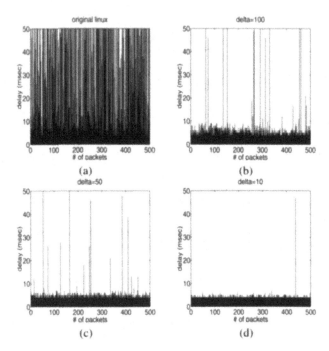

Fig. 5. The roundtrip delay of RT messages with (a) original Linux, (b) $\Delta = 100$, (c) $\Delta = 50$, and (d) $\Delta = 10$.

Fig. 5 shows the roundtrip delay of the RT packets with different parameters. Fig. 5(a) shows the roundtrip delay measured without the ATS, while Fig. 5(b)-(d) show the roundtrip delay with different Δ values. With the ATS, the roundtrip delay is significantly reduced and well-bounded. Also it can be observed that the delay characteristics vary with different Δ values.

Fig. 6 and 7 present more quantitative analyses of the performance. Fig. 6 shows the deadline miss ratio for different Δ values. The x-axis of the graphs is the deadline in terms of *ms* and the y-axis is the deadline miss ratio. Obviously, the deadline miss ratio decreases as the deadline increases. Fig. 7 shows the throughput of non-RT traffic for different Δ values. As Δ gets larger, the RP decreases faster, i.e., the traffic generation is increased faster. Thus, as Δ increases, the non-RT throughput will increase while the deadline miss ratio will increase.

The above graphs have shown that the behavior of the ATS is affected by the Δ value. The parameters other than Δ also affect the performance of ATS. Generally, the deadline miss ratio is higher when the overall throughput is high, but it may be possible that one set of parameters gives a lower deadline miss ratio and a higher throughput than another set of parameters. The parameters can be changed easily to observe their effects on the performance of ATS.

Fig. 8 shows the deadline miss ratio inferred from the new metrics measured. Here the delay is measured as an interval from the time when a packet is copied to the device to the time when the packet is successfully transmitted by the device. This delay will

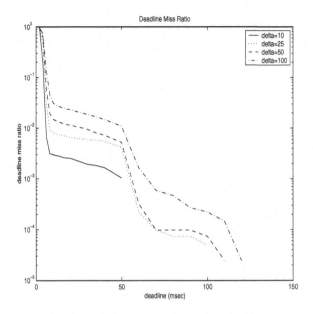

Fig. 6. The deadline miss ratio (of roundtrip delay) with different Δ values. Δ is adjusted to 10, 25, 50, and 100 μsec. The performance varies significantly depending on Δ value.

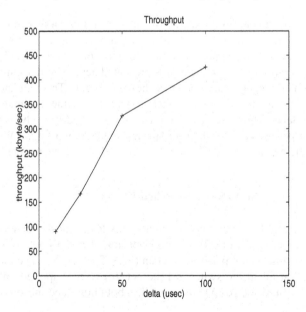

Fig. 7. The throughput of non-RT traffic with different Δ values. The throughput as well as the deadline miss ratio varies depending on the Δ value. There is a tradeoff between the throughput and the deadline miss ratio.

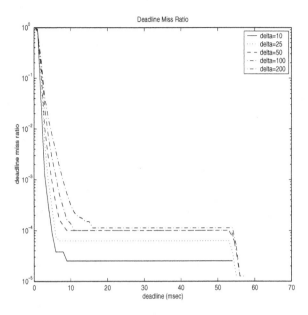

Fig. 8. The deadline miss ratio inferred from the metrics of the enhanced adaptive traffic smoother.

be affected most by the current network utilization, i.e., the number of collisions that a packet has experienced with other packets. Note that the delay is the roundtrip delay of a RT packet measured at the application layer for most of the other graphs representing the deadline miss ratio. However, the delays presented here exhibit a similar trend to the delays measured at the application layer as shown in Fig. 6. This validates the fact that the transmission delay reported by the enhanced traffic smoother is a major factor of the variance in the delay. Thus, the deadline miss ratio inferred from the new metrics can be used as a proper indicator of the user-specified QoS achievement. With the help of these metrics, the parameters of ATS may be adjusted to achieve the desired QoS.

5.3   Performance of the ATS in a Switched Ethernet

The performance of ATS when it is applied not only to end-hosts but also to the switch is compared to other cases, to validate the extension of ATS to the switched-Ethernet. Four sets of experiments are performed when (a) ATS is used on a single Ethernet, (b) ATS is not used at all in the switched-Ethernet, (c) ATS is applied only to hosts on the switched-Ethernet, and (d) ATS is applied to both hosts and the switch ports in the switched-Ethernet.

Fig. 9 and 10 show the roundtrip delays and the deadline miss ratio, respectively. The performance of the switched-Ethernet without the ATS is poorer than that of a single Ethernet with the ATS. When the traffic smoother is applied only to hosts on the switched network, the performance is no better than that of the traffic smoother on the single Ethernet. Only when the ATS is applied to both hosts and the switch, the

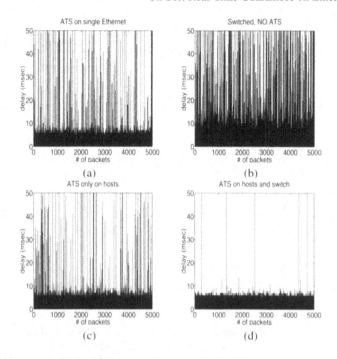

Fig. 9. Real-time message delay in different situations: (a) ATS is used on a single Ethernet, (b) ATS is not used at all in the switched-Ethernet, (c) ATS is applied only to hosts on the switched-Ethernet, and (d) ATS is applied to both hosts and the switch in the switched-Ethernet.

performance is improved significantly as compared to that of the single Ethernet with the ATS.

5.4   Performance of User-Level ATS

To validate the feasibility of the user-level ATS, the same set of experiments is performed with both the user-level and the kernel-level traffic smoothers in the testbed described in Section 5.1. Fig. 11 plots the deadline miss ratio of the user-level traffic smoother vs. that of the kernel-level traffic smoother when Δ is adjusted to 25 μs and 100 μs, respectively. Two observations can be made from these graphs. First, it is observed that the performance curve of the user-level ATS shows a similar trend to that of kernel-level ATS. This implies that we can change the characteristics of the user-level ATS by adjusting the parameters. Second, the performance of the user-level ATS can be adjusted similarly to that of the kernel-level ATS by adjusting the parameters. As shown in the graph, the performance of the user-level ATS is poorer than that of the kernel-level ATS when the same parameters are used. This is because the packets in the TCP/IP stack which are beyond the control of the user-level ATS may be transmitted even right after a collision, and may collide with other packets. However, the performance of user-level ATS can be improved by adjusting the parameters such that the performance obtained

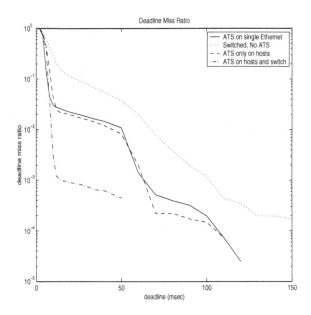

Fig. 10. The comparison of the deadline miss ratio when (i) ATS is used on a single Ethernet, (ii) ATS is not used at all in the switched-Ethernet, (iii) ATS is applied only to hosts on the switched-Ethernet, and (iv) ATS is applied to both hosts and the switch in the switched-Ethernet.

from the user-level ATS is comparable to or better than the performance of the kernel-level ATS with the different parameter.

The potential problem of the user-level ATS is that the performance may become worse if more than one application generate non-RT traffic on a given host since each application adapts its traffic generation. To address this issue, experiments are performed by changing the number of applications generating non-RT traffic on one host. A continuous stream of non-RT traffic is generated by each application, and the number of applications (i.e., the number of non-RT streams) is changed from 1 to 3 while keeping the RT traffic intact.

Fig. 12 shows the deadline miss ratio when the number of non-RT streams is changed. While the number of non-RT streams ranges from 1 to 3, the performance of the kernel-level ATS remains almost unchanged since it smoothes traffic at the Ethernet MAC layer which all the packets go through. One interesting result is that the deadline miss ratio of the user-level ATS is affected little when the number of non-RT streams on one host is changed. Also, the overall throughput of the user-level ATS is only $2 \sim 7\%$ lower than that of the kernel-level ATS, and the overall throughput remains stable regardless of the number of non-RT streams. Throughout these experiments, we were able to verify the feasibility of the user-level ATS. Even though its performance is somewhat poorer than the kernel-level ATS, the user-level ATS can be used for soft real-time guarantees with the minimum modification on the underlying operating system.

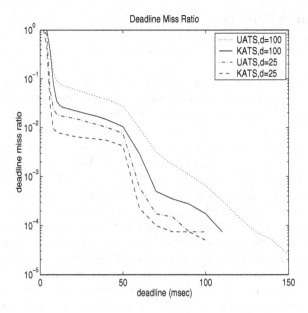

Fig. 11. The deadline miss ratio: kernel-level implementation vs. user-level implementation when $\Delta = 25\mu sec$ and when $\Delta = 100\mu sec$.

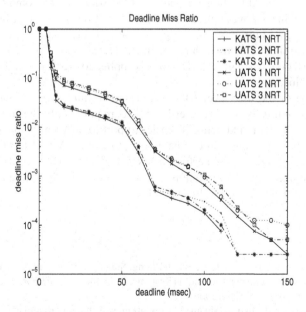

Fig. 12. The comparison between the kernel-level adaptive traffic smoother and the user-level traffic smoother when there are multiple stream of non-RT traffic.

6 Concluding Remarks

ATS is a software solution to provide soft real-time guarantees on Ethernet by regulating each host's traffic generation rate according to the network utilization. Even though it is shown to be effective in providing real-time guarantees in a heavily-loaded network without degrading the throughput unacceptably, it has some limitations. First, it provides no means of adjusting its several user-specific parameters for different QoS requirements and to monitor its performance at run-time. Second, it is designed only for a single Ethernet while switches are commonly used for scalability. Third, it has relatively poor portability since it is designed and implemented in the kernel. This paper addressed all of these problems.

To enhance the reconfigurability, a mechanism to retrieve and modify the ATS parameters at run-time is developed using the proc file system on a Linux machine. Also, the metrics to represent the QoS achievement with the given parameters are made available, when the delay bound of transfer delay is specified. We applied these enhanced reconfigurability mechanisms and evaluated the ATS performance for different parameter values. With the help of these mechanisms, user-specific parameters can be adjusted to meet the QoS requirement. It will be convenient to the user if these parameters are adjusted automatically when the desired QoS is specified. This is left as future work, but its difficulty lies in the fact that those parameters are dependent on each other, thus making it difficult to modify them.

The ATS is extended to the switched-Ethernet, which is the common topology of LANs. More specifically, we applied the HIMD policy to every port of a switch. A switch is emulated using a Linux box, and the performance is evaluated and compared to the performance on a single Ethernet. Our experimental results have shown that performance can be improved only when the HIMD policy is applied to every port of the switch under heavy network loads.

A prototype of the user-level ATS was designed, implemented, and evaluated to address the portability issue. The user-level ATS requires only the minimum change on the operating system, and hence, is easier to port to different platforms. Its performance is slightly worse than, but comparable to, that of the kernel-level ATS. Also the user-level ATS shows the stable performance even when the number of non-RT stream changes whose traffic-generation rate is adjusted independently. These results validate the feasibility of the user-level traffic smoother.

References

1. Seok-Kyu Kweon, Kang G. Shin and Qin Zheng, Statistical Real-Time Communication over Ethernet for Manufacturing Automation Systems, *Proceedings of IEEE Real-Time Technology and Applications Symposium*, June 1999.
2. Seok-Kyu Kweon, Kang G. Shin and Gary Workman, Achieving Real-Time Communication over Ethernet with Adaptive Traffic Smoothing, *in Proceedings of IEEE Real-Time Technology and Applications Symposium*, pages 90-100, June 2000.
3. IEEE Standard 802.3-1985. Carrier-Sensed Multiple Access with Collision Detection CSMA/CD, 1985.
4. Universal Remote I/O Link, http://www.ab.com/catalogs/b113/comm/urio.html

5. Robert Bosch GmbH, "CAN Specification Version 2.0," September 1991.
6. N. F. Maxemchuk, A Variation on CSMA/CD That Yields Movable TDM Slots in Integrated Voice/Data Local Networks, *The Bell System Technical Journal*, 61, (7), pages 1527-1550, September 1982.
7. Y. Shimokawa and Y. Shiobara, Real-time Ethernet for industrial applications, *Proceedings of IECON*, pages 829-834, 1985.
8. W. Zhao and K. Ramamritham, Virtual Time CSMA Protocols for Hard Real-time Communication, *IEEE Transactions on Software Engineering*, pages 938-952, August 1987.
9. R. Court, Real-time Ethernet, *Computer Communications*, vol. 15, pages 193-201, April 1992.
10. D. W. Pritty, J. R. Malone, S. K. Banerjee, and N.L. Lawrie, A real-time upgrade for Ethernet based factory networking, *Proceedings of IECON*, pages 1631-1637, 1995.
11. J. Sobrinho, A. S. Krishnakumar, EQuB - Ethernet Quality of Service Using Black Bursts, *Proceeding of the 23rd Conference on Local Computer Networks*, pages 286-296, Boston, Massachusetts, October 1998.
12. C. Venkatramani, and T. Chiueh. Design, Design, Implementation, and Evaluation of a Software-based Real-Time Ethernet Protocol, *ACM SIGCOMM 95*, pages 27-37. 1995.
13. Z. Wang, G. Xiong, L. Luo, M. Lai, and W. Zhou. A Hard, Real-Time Communication Control Protocol Based on the Ethernet, *Proceedings of the 7th Australian Conference on Parallel and Real-Time Systems (PART00)*, pages 161-170, November, 2000.
14. M. Molle, 100Base-T/IEEE802.12/Packet Switching, *IEEE Communication Magazine*, pages 64-73, August 1996.
15. The Network Driver Interface Specification (NIDS) Interface, http://www.microsoft.com/

BondingPlus: Real-Time Message Channel in Linux Ethernet Environment Using Regular Switching Hub *

Hsin-hung Lin, Chih-wen Hsueh, and Guo-Chiuan Huang

Real-Time Systems Laboratory
Department of Computer Science and Information Engineering
National Chung Cheng University
Chiayi, Taiwan 621, R.O.C.
{lsh,chsueh,hgc89}@cs.ccu.edu.tw

Abstract. Bandwidth management is very important to quality of service of network applications. Communications and data transmissions between hosts in a LAN environment may be large in many systems, such as clustering systems and parallel systems. If the network bandwidth is not enough, real-time packets may be delayed and miss their timing constraints. There are many technologies developed to increase host bandwidth in a LAN environment, but most of them need switching hubs with special support such as IEEE Link Aggregation Standard and are very expensive. In this paper, we propose a real-time message channel, BondingPlus, in Linux Ethernet environment which can make use of multiple Ethernet adapters simultaneously between hosts connected with regular switching hubs. When receiving packets from upper network layer, BondingPlus schedules packets in data link layer. Real-time packets can be dispatched into a higher-priority queue so that the packets can be transmitted through the physical Ethernet interface right away. Furthermore, real-time applications can transmit real-time packets via one or several dedicated network adapters which create real-time message channels between hosts and thus reduce transmission delay and jitter dramatically, especially suitable for applications that have high bandwidth and real-time requirements. This approach is implemented in two Linux kernel modules and is backward compatible, flexible and transparent to users. BondingPlus pseudo Ethernet device driver module receives packets from upper network layer and dispatches the packets to multiple physical network adapters with a single IP address. ARP+ protocol module is responsible for maintaining a table of the mapping between an IP address and its corresponding MAC addresses of multiple physical network adapters.

Keyword: IEEE Link Aggregation Standard, channel bonding, packet scheduling, network scheduling

---

* Supported in part by a research grant from the ROC National Science Council under Grants NSC-89-2213-E-194-056

J. Chen and S. Hong (Eds.): RTCSA 2003, LNCS 2968, pp. 176–193, 2004.

1   Introduction

Bandwidth plays an important role in quality of service of network applications. For example, clustering systems and parallel systems in a LAN environment, communications and data transmissions between hosts are large. If the network bandwidth is not enough, real-time packets may be delayed and miss their timing constraints [3,11]. Therefore, bandwidth management is very important. Furthermore, in many server applications, transactions with real-time constraints or priorities need to be processed and send results back as soon as possible. Although we can use several network adapters at a host to obtain higher bandwidth, but one IP address is needed for each network adapter and thus is not practical in large-scale systems.

In IEEE 802.3 network specification [17], Link Aggregation Standard is proposed to merge bandwidth and specify many other features. As shown in Figure 1, it comprises an optional sublayer between MAC Client and MAC Control sublayers. This standard is mainly targeted at routers and there are products of many manufacturers which support Link Aggregation Standard using hardware or software approaches, such as CISCO EtherChannel [19], Intel Link Aggregation [5], Sun Trunking [14], and Linux Bonding [9]. Although bandwidth can be increased, these approaches need special switching hubs with Link Aggregation Standard support, which means extra costs are needed.

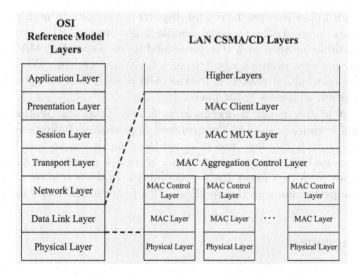

Fig. 1. IEEE802.3 Link Aggregation Layer

In [20], Srinidhi Varadarajan and Tzi-cker Chiueh proposed the design and implementation of a real-time Fast Ethernet switch , EtheReal, which provides bandwidth guarantees to real-time applications running on Ethernet using a personal computer. When a real-time application attempts to set up a real-time connection, it sends a reservation request to a user-level process (RTCD) on the same host, which sends the reservation request to the EtheReal switch to which the sending host is directly connected. The connected switch forwards this request to the next switch, and so on, until it reaches the destination node. If the real-time connection request is admitted, resources, including bandwidth, CPU cycle and data buffer, on EtheReal switches are reserved and dedicated to the service of the real-time connection.

Nowadays, switching hubs which support 100BASE-TX and Full-Duplex are very inexpensive and still have very high packet filtering/forwarding rate. We would like to make use of these inexpensive devices and make use of several network adapters simultaneously with only one IP address to increase bandwidth between hosts connected with regular inexpensive switching hubs. By scheduling packets in data link layer, real-time packets can be dispatched into a higher-priority queue so that the packets can be transmitted through the physical Ethernet interface right away [13,16]. Furthermore, real-time applications can transmit real-time packets via one or several dedicated network adapters which create real-time message channels between hosts and thus reduces the transmission delay and the jitter of real-time packets massively [8,12] without modification to the hardware on both host machines and connected switching hubs.

The proposed approach comprises two Linux kernel drivers [1,4,7,15]. BondingPlus driver module is a pseudo Ethernet device driver responsible for receiving packets from upper network layer and dispatching packets to multiple physical Ethernet interfaces. ARP+ protocol module maintains an ARP+ table, which is a mapping table between each IP address and its corresponding MAC addresses of multiple physical network adapters in a LAN environment. When BondingPlus driver transmits a packet, it queries ARP+ table and changes the source and destination addresses of the packet.

The rest of this paper is organized as follows. The next section describes background knowledge used in the proposed approach, including switching hub operations, Linux packet flow, and Ethernet Bonding Driver. Section 3 details the design issues and the solutions we propose. Section 4 shows the implementation details of our work in a Linux LAN environment. In Section 5, we measure and analyze the performance of BondingPlus. This paper is concluded in Section 6.

2   Background

In this section, we introduce how packets are handled in a switching hub and Linux network traffic control which can give us a good view of how to manipulate a packet before it is sent to the buffer of a network adapter. We also introduce Linux Ethernet Bonding Driver, which is a software implementation of Link Aggregation standard in Linux.

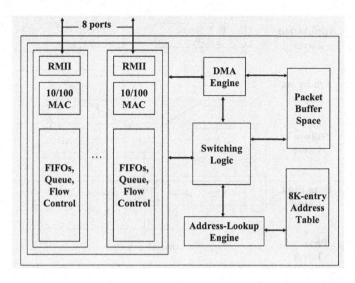

Fig. 2. Brief Architecture of Switching Hub(RealTek RTL8308B)

2.1   Packet Handling in Switching Hub

In a switching hub, there is a controller that controls the flow of input packets. For example, Figure 2 shows the brief architecture of RealTek RTL8308B, an 8-port 10/100Mbps Ethernet switch controller [6]. It can operate in full-duplex mode and supports non-blocking 148800 packets/second wire speed forwarding rate and flow control. RealTek RTL8308B has a 2M-bit packet buffer. When packets come into the FIFO queue, they will be copied into the packet buffer and manipulated by the switching logic. There is an 8K-entry address hashing table which contains the mappings between ports and destination MAC addresses. When a packet is received from a port, the switching logic records the source MAC address of this packet and creates a mapping in the address hashing table. Then it hashes the destination MAC address of the packet to get a location index of the address hashing table. If a valid location index is found, the packet is forwarded to the corresponding destination port. Otherwise, the incoming packet is broadcasted to all ports.

2.2   Packet Flow in Linux Protocol Stack

As shown in Figure 3, Linux protocol stack is based on TCP/IP and is normally considered as a 4-layer system [18]. Linux uses a common packet data structure (called socket buffer structure) to represent a packet throughout all protocol layers. Parameters and payloads would not need to be copied between different protocol layers. Figure 4 is the abstraction of the Linux traffic path. When an application generates a packet, the packet is sent to transport layer (TCP or UDP layer) through a socket. After the packet is handled in transport layer,

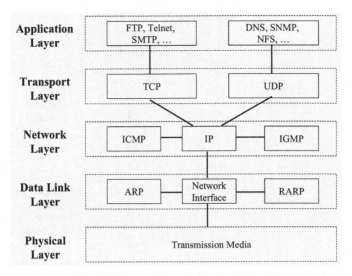

Fig. 3. Linux Network Protocol Stack

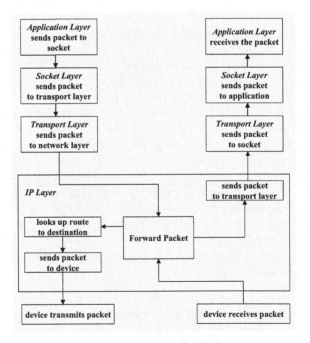

Fig. 4. Linux Traffic Path

it is then sent to network layer (IP layer). The network layer is responsible for determining the route of packets. If the packet is for another computer, the network layer sends it to data link layer. The data link layer sends packets via an available output device, such as Ethernet adapter, serial port, printer port, etc.

When a packet is arrived, the input interface checks whether the packet is for this computer, for example, an Ethernet adapter checks the destination MAC address field when receiving a packet. If so, the network interface driver sends the packet to the network layer. The network layer checks the destination of the packet. If the packet is for this computer, the network layer sends it to transport layer and finally to the application. Otherwise, the packet is sent back to an output device.

2.3   Linux Generic Packet Scheduler

Linux provides a rich set of traffic control functions [2]. For an Ethernet device, the default queuing discipline is Linux Generic Packet Scheduler. When Linux Generic Packet Scheduler is being initialized, the initial function creates three queues (called 3-band FIFO queue, the first, the second, and the third queue respectively) for socket buffers. Linux Generic Packet Scheduler provides a set of functions to access the 3-band FIFO queue, such as to enqueue a packet, to return the next packet in queue eligible for sending, to put a packet back into the queue after dequeuing, etc. When a packet is needed for sending, Linux Generic Packet Scheduler searches the first queue to find one. If there are packets in the first queue, it returns the first packet. Otherwise, Linux Generic Packet Scheduler searches the second queue and then the third queue. Packets in the second and the third queue will not be processed while there are still packets waiting for transmitting in the first queue. Therefore, packets in the first queue have the highest priority when sending and should be processed as soon as possible.

Linux Generic Packet Scheduler also creates a mapping table between the priority of a socket buffer and the 3-band FIFO queue. The mapping table is illustrated in Figure 5. The priority value is extracted from a packet and used as an index to look up the corresponding queue number in the mapping table when enqueuing. For example, if the priority of a packet is 1 and the number in the mapping table is 2, this packet should be queued in the third queue.

2.4   Linux Ethernet Bonding Driver

Linux Ethernet Bonding Driver is a kernel driver that can aggregate traffic over several ports [9]. It has two main features: high availability and load balancing. In this section, we will focus on the implementation of load balancing. Figure 6 is the architecture of Linux Ethernet Bonding Driver.

When Linux Ethernet Bonding Driver is initialized, it creates a pseudo Ethernet device and registers itself in Linux Kernel. The Linux kernel then initializes the pseudo Ethernet device and creates a link list which is responsible to contain physical Ethernet devices (called slaves) which can be used by the pseudo Ethernet device. To make the pseudo Ethernet device work, we have to assign an IP address and add routing setting to it. The pseudo Ethernet device is set as a master device of the slaves and adds them into its link list. The MAC address of the pseudo Ethernet device is set as the same as the first physical Ethernet device of its slave list. All the MAC addresses of the subsequent physical Ethernet devices are set as the same as the pseudo Ethernet device.

When a packet from upper network layer (usually is IP layer) is needed to be transmitted by the Bonding driver, the kernel passes the socket buffer to it. The Bonding driver selects an active physical Ethernet device from its slave list, changes the output device of the socket buffer to the selected device and then enqueues the packet into the queue of the selected physical Ethernet device driver. The physical Ethernet device is responsible for sending the packet when the NET_TX_SOFTIRQ softirq of Linux kernel is activated.

When a packet is received by one of the slaves, the driver of this slave device creates a new socket buffer and copies the data of the received packet into the socket buffer. Then the driver stores the socket buffer into an appropriate queue for latter handling. When NET_RX_SOFIRQ softirq is activated, the Linux kernel processes the packet queue. The Bonding driver changes the input device of the socket buffer to the pseudo Ethernet device. Thus when a packet received from any of the slave devices, the kernel will regard that the packet as received from the pseudo Ethernet device. Furthermore, the Bonding mechanism operates under TCP/IP layer, so it is fully compatible with upper layers.

3   Design Issues

We intend to use regular switching hubs to dispatch network packets between connected computers with multiple Ethernet adapters in a LAN environment without modification to the hardware on both host machines and connected

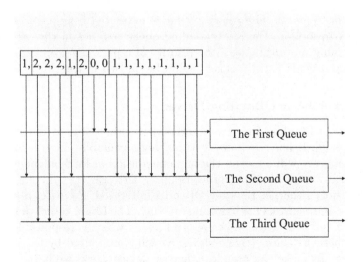

Fig. 5. Mapping Between Socket Buffer Priority and 3-band FIFO Queue

switching hubs. Packets are scheduled in data link layer so that real-time packets are sent via one or several dedicated network adapters which create real-time message channels. Real-time packets need not to compete for the network bandwidth against non-real-time packets. Moreover, non-real-time packets can be sent simultaneously via other network adapters.

We design the BondingPlus pseudo network driver to dispatch packets from upper network layer to physical Ethernet adapters. The BondingPlus driver is responding for receiving socket buffer from upper network layer and changing the output device of the socket buffer and then sends it to the corresponding queue of the physical Ethernet adapter. When the socket buffer is to be sent on the BondingPlus driver, the Linux kernel fills the MAC address of one of the physical Ethernet interface in the source address field and uses ARP protocol to query the destination MAC address while building the Ethernet header of this packet. But ARP protocol is a one to one mapping between IP address and MAC address, which means although we can send packets through multiple network adapters, but always receives packets from one of the network adapters. Real-time input packets would have to compete with lower priority packets. In order to solve this problem, we design a new protocol, ARP+ protocol, to keep the mapping between an IP address and all of the MAC addresses of the host.

3.1 BondingPlus Architecture

As shown in Figure 7, in the proposed approach, there is a pseudo Ethernet driver, BondingPlus, which resides between IP layer and physical Ethernet interface driver. BondingPlus is responsible for changing the attributes of socket buffer, including source MAC address, destination MAC address and output

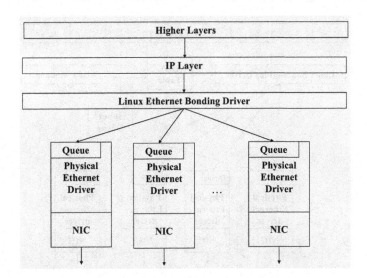

Fig. 6. Linux Ethernet Bonding Driver Architecture

device. After the attributes are changed, BondingPlus finds an active physical Ethernet interface to send the socket buffer. The ARP+ protocol also resides between IP layer and physical Ethernet interface driver. When an ARP+ packet is received, the kernel calls the ARP+ protocol handling routine and passes the ARP+ packets to it. The ARP+ protocol handing routine then parses the ARP+ packet and updates the corresponding ARP+ table.

3.2   BondingPlus Driver

When the BondingPlus pseudo Ethernet driver is installed into Linux kernel, it creates a pseudo Ethernet master device and registers it to kernel. Bonding-Plus also creates a physical Ethernet interface pool (slave list) and an ARP+ table. After IP address initialization has been done, IP address, MAC address and the suffix of the IP address of the BondingPlus driver are copied into the corresponding entry of the ARP+ table. The MAC address of the BondingPlus driver is obtained by the first slave device of its slave list.

BondingPlus diver sets a SLAVE flag and a NOARP flag to all its slave devices. Packets received from a slave device with SLAVE flag set are considered as received from its master device. NOARP flag forbids slave devices from replying an ARP query. Only the master device should reply a ARP query so that it would not cause other hosts to update their ARP table frequently. After setting all slave devices, BondingPlus broadcast the MAC addresses of all its slave devices using ARP+ protocol.

3.3   ARP+ Protocol

Traditional ARP protocol is a one to one mapping between IP address and MAC address which can not meet our requirement in using regular switching

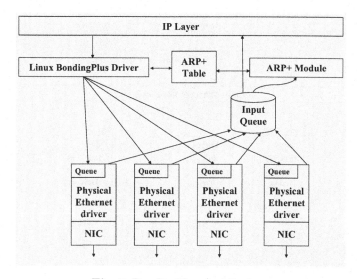

Fig. 7. BondingPlus Architecture

hubs because only the MAC address of one of the physical network adapters of the destination host can be obtained and thus real-time input packets may have to compete with other lower priority packets. In order to achieve a one to many mapping between an IP address and multiple MAC addresses, we design a proprietary packet which can only be understood and interpreted by the ARP+ protocol without interfering existing protocols. Figure 8 shows our proprietary ARP+ protocol packet. There are four types of ARP+ packet:

- ARPP_BROADCAST: When a host is loaded with BondingPlus driver and ARP+ protocol module, it broadcasts an ARPP_BROADCAST packet containing all the MAC addresses of its physical network adapters, so that hosts can obtain the MAC address list of every newly joined host.
- ARPP_REPLY: When a host receives an ARPP_BROADCAST packet, it unicasts an ARPP_REPLY packet to notify the newly joined host with its MAC addresses. It ensures newly joined hosts can obtained the latest MAC address list of other hosts.
- ARPP_CHANGE: When a host changes its MAC address list, such as adding or removing one or more physical network adapters, it broadcasts an ARPP _CHANGE packet. Hosts receiving an ARPP_CHANGE packet update the corresponding entry in their ARP+ tables.
- ARPP_CLEAR: When a host is going to unload or ready to shut down, it broadcasts an ARPP_CLEAR packet to notify other hosts. Hosts receiving an ARPP_CLEAR packet clear the corresponding entry in their ARP+ tables.

After the ARP+ header are the IP address and MAC addresses of the sender. Currently, we limit an ARP+ packet to contain at most 8 MAC address entries. It is practical because most personal computers have no more than 8 PCI and ISA slots to accommodate 8 Ethernet adapters.

The ARP+ protocol module is to maintain the ARP+ table passed from BondingPlus driver. Every ARP+ table contains a pointer array of 256 entries which point to a dynamic allocated array containing MAC addresses. The suffix of an IP address is used as an index of the ARP+ table for finding the corresponding MAC addresses.

3.4 Backward Compatible

The BondingPlus driver parses every received socket buffer and gets information from it. If an outgoing socket buffer is not an IP protocol packet, the BondingPlus driver only changes the output device of the socket buffer and then puts it into the queue of the output device. If the socket buffer is a valid IP protocol packet, the BondingPlus driver extracts the suffix of the IP address and uses it as an index to query the ARP+ table to get the destination MAC addresses. If the destination MAC address is not found, which means the destination host is not loaded with BondingPlus driver, the BondingPlus driver of the sending host chooses an active physical Ethernet device, assigns it to the output device of the

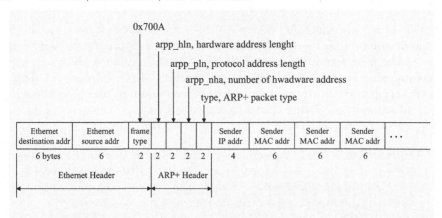

Fig. 8. ARP+ Protocol Packet Type

socket buffer, and then puts the socket buffer into the queue of the output device. If the destination MAC addresses is found in ARP+ table, the BondingPlus driver selects one of the available MAC addresses of the destination host, copies it to the destination MAC address field of the socket buffer, and then selects an active physical Ethernet device to send the packet.

There are several scenarios between two hosts. If host A is loaded with BondingPlus driver but other host B is not. When host A wishes to connect to host B, it issues an ARP request and host B replies host A with an ARP reply. Host A and host B can obtain the MAC address from the other host by ARP protocol. When host A is going to send a packet to host B and can not find the MAC addresses of host B in the ARP+ table. Host A selects an active physical Ethernet device and simply sends the packet without modifying the destination MAC address which is obtained by ARP protocol. It is similar as above when host B wishes to connect to host A. Although there is packet scheduling of outgoing traffic of Host A, but there is no real-time traffic control between two hosts.

If both hosts are loaded with BondingPlus driver, but only host A has multiple physical Ethernet interfaces. When host A wishes to connect to host B, host A and host B can obtain all MAC addresses from each other by ARP+ protocol. When host A is going to send a packet to host B, it selects an active physical Ethernet device to send the packet. When host B is going to send a packet to host A, it can select a MAC address of host A from its ARP+ table and modifies the destination MAC address of the packet. In this scenario, although there is packet scheduling of both output and input network traffic of Host A, but there is still no real-time traffic control between two hosts.

If two hosts are both loaded with BondingPlus driver and both the hosts have multiple physical Ethernet adapters. Both hosts can obtain all the MAC addresses from each other by ARP+ protocol. By similar steps described above, there is packet scheduling of both output and input network traffic in both hosts. Moreover, real-time channels can be established between two hosts.

Table 1. Test Bed

System Parameters	Settings
CPU	Intel Celeron 1.2GHz
Memory	256MB
Operating System	Mandrake 8.1
Kernel Version	2.4.18
Network Adapter	Intel 21143
Switching Hub	DLink DES-1024R+

Table 2. Bandwidth Overhead Test

	Without BondingPlus	With BondingPlus
Bandwidth	94.05Mb/s	94.01Mb/s

Table 3. System Utilization Overhead Test

	Without BondingPlus	With BondingPlus
Minimum User Time	0s	0s
Maximum User Time	0s	0s
Minimum System Time	2.11s	2.33s
Maximum System Time	2.32s	2.49s
Average System Time	2.25s	2.40s

4   Performance Evaluation

In order to evaluate the performance of our work, we design the following experiments. Section 4.1 measures the overhead of the proposed approach. Section 4.2 and Section 4.3 show the results of reducing the delay when transmitting higher priority packets using TCP and UDP respectively. We use two Intel machines to perform the experiments and the system parameters are listed in Table 1. There are four network adapters on each machine which are directly connected to the switching hub.

We use Netperf [10], a networking performance benchmark, to measure the performance. Netperf is design in client/server architecture. One machine executes its client, netperf, and the other executes its server, netserver. The client generates packets and sends them to the server. In order to reduce the impact of I/O operations, we use 32KB as sending and receiving buffer size.

4.1   Overhead Evaluation

In order to measure the effect on system by the proposed approach, we perform the following experiments. The first experiment is to measure the overhead on network bandwidth. We use one adapter on each machine with the default kernel driver as a comparison and then execute Netperf to measure the performance. We perform the same experiment but use BondingPlus driver for instead. The results are shown in Table 2. Our approach only decreases network bandwidth for less than 0.05%.

The second experiment is to measure the overhead on CPU utilization. We execute Netperf to send and receive packets for 60 second and measure the user time and system time consumed by Netperf. As the results show in Table 3, our approach only increase 6.6% of CPU time.

4.2   Real-Time Packet Transmission over TCP

When Linux kernel allocates a new socket buffer, the priority of the buffer will be set to the default value, 0. Every packet is put in the same queue of the Linux generic packet scheduler. If the load of a network adapter is high, real-time packets may be delayed by other packets. In order to reduce the delay when transmitting real-time packets, we put real-time packets in the first queue of the

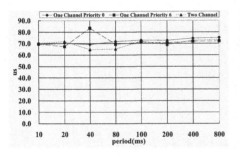

(a) *Maximum TCP Transmission Time*

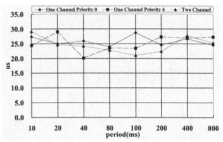
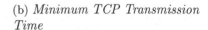

(b) *Minimum TCP Transmission Time*

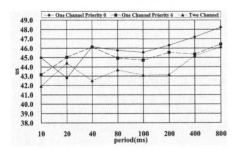

(c) *Average TCP Transmission Time*

(d) *StdDev TCP Transmission Time*

Fig. 9. TCP Transmission Time from Application to BondingPlus

Linux generic packet scheduler. Furthermore, we can send real-time packets and other packets using different physical network adapters.

One of the testing programs generates 1400 bytes real-time packets (can be regarded as higher priority packets) periodically and the other is taken to be an interference source which continuously generates a large buffer of lower priority packets. Three different scenarios are tested:

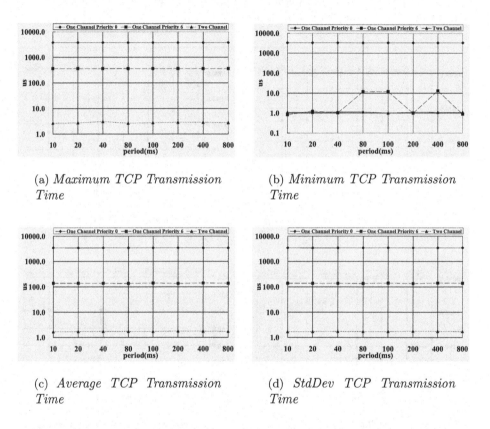

(a) *Maximum TCP Transmission Time*

(b) *Minimum TCP Transmission Time*

(c) *Average TCP Transmission Time*

(d) *StdDev TCP Transmission Time*

Fig. 10. TCP Transmission Time from BondingPlus to Physical Ethernet Driver

- One Channel Priority 0: In this scenario, real-time packets and the interference packets have the same priority, 0. They are put in the second queue of the Linux Generic Packet Scheduler and are processed by the physical Ethernet driver.
- One Channel Priority 6: The priority of real-time packets are set to higher priority, 6, using setsockopt() system call and the priority of the interference packets are set to 0. Real-time packets are put in the first queue of the Linux Generic Packet Scheduler and are processed first.

– Two Channel: This scenario sends and receives the real-time packets via a
  dedicated physical network adapter in each machine and so do the lower
  priority packets.

Figure 9 shows the maximum, minimum, average and the standard deviation
of TCP transmission time from application to BondingPlus driver. The time is
mainly spent in TCP and IP layer which are not controlled by the proposed
approach. The average transmission time is between 42us to 49us and there are
almost no different between 3 scenarios.

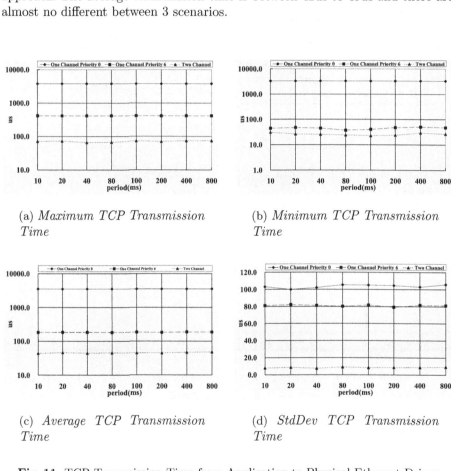

(a) *Maximum TCP Transmission Time*

(b) *Minimum TCP Transmission Time*

(c) *Average TCP Transmission Time*

(d) *StdDev TCP Transmission Time*

Fig. 11. TCP Transmission Time from Application to Physical Ethernet Driver

Figure 10 shows the maximum, minimum, average and the standard deviation
of TCP transmission time from BondingPlus driver to physical Ethernet driver.
The results show that when all packets are transmitted in the same queue of a
network adapter, the transmission time of real-time packets from BondingPlus
driver to physical Ethernet driver is very long because they must compete with
lower priority packets. The transmission time can be reduced dramatically if we

put real-time packets in the first queue, but it is still interfered by the lower priority packets because the standard deviation is still large. Only transmitting the real-time packets and the lower priority packets using different physical network adapters can obtain the lowest transmission overhead and jitter.

Figure 11 are the maximum, minimum, average and the standard deviation of TCP transmission time from application to physical Ethernet driver. The time from application to BondingPlus driver is almost constant time and thus the time from BondingPlus driver to physical Ethernet adapter is the main factor of packet transmission time. Although One Channel Priority 6 transmissions highly reduce the packet transmission time of real-time packets, Two Channel transmissions obtain the best improvement.

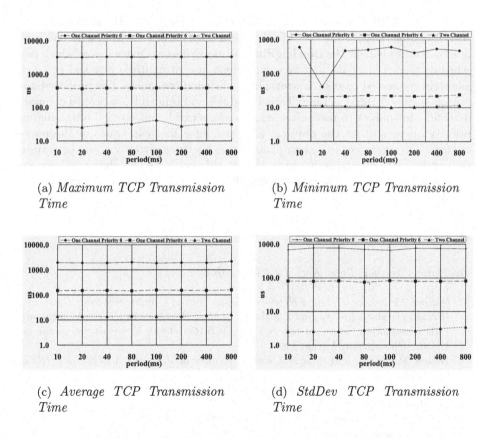

(a) *Maximum TCP Transmission Time*

(b) *Minimum TCP Transmission Time*

(c) *Average TCP Transmission Time*

(d) *StdDev TCP Transmission Time*

Fig. 12. UDP Transmission Time from Application to Physical Ethernet Driver

4.3   Real-Time Packet Transmission over UDP

We perform the same experiments on real-time packet transmissions over UDP. The results are similar to the transmission over TCP, but UDP packet transmission time is shorter than TCP packet transmission time. Still, the time from application to BondingPlus driver is almost constant time and thus the time from BondingPlus driver to physical Ethernet adapter is the main factor of packet transmission time. As shown in Figure 12, although One Channel Priority 6 transmissions highly reduce the packet transmission time of real-time packets, Two Channel transmissions obtain the best improvement.

5   Conclusion

We propose ARP+ protocol to maintain the mapping of an IP address and its corresponding MAC addresses of hosts in a Linux LAN environment. We also design and implement the BondingPlus pseudo Ethernet device driver which can schedule packets in data link layer and make use of multiple physical network adapters connected to regular switching hubs simultaneously. The proposed approach is implemented as Linux kernel modules and is flexible, backward compatible and transparent to users. Real-time packets can be dispatched into a higher priority queue so that the physical Ethernet interfaces can transmit the packets first. Furthermore, real-time packets can be transmitted via one or several dedicated network adapters which create real-time message channels between hosts and thus reduces the transmission delay and the jitter of real-time packets dramatically.

References

1. Tigran Aivazian. *Linux Kernel 2.4 Internals.* http://www.tldp.org/LDP/lki/index.html.
2. Werner Almesberger. *Linux Network Traffic Control - Implementation Overview.*
3. Riccardo Bettati. *End-to-End Scheduling to Meet Deadlines in Distributed Systems.* PhD dissertation, technical report UIUCDCS-R-94-1840, University of Illinois at Urbana-Champaign, August 1994.
4. Daniel P. Bovet and Marco Cesati.   *Understanding the LINUX KERNEL.* O'REILLY, 2001.
5. Intel Corporation. *Intel Link Aggregation.* http://www.intel.com/support/express/switches/53x/31460.htm.
6. REALTEK CORPORATION. *The RTL8308B DATASHEETS.* http://www.realtek.com.tw.
7. Jon Crowcroft and Iain Phillips. *TCP/IP and Linux Protocol Implementation.* WILEY, 2002.
8. Marco D and John A. Stankovic. Scheduling distributed real-time tasks with minimum jitter". *IEEE TRANSACTIONS ON COMPUTERS*, 49(4):303 316, 2000.
9. Thomas Davis. http://sourceforge.net/projects/bonding/.
10. Rick Jones. http://www.netperf.org/.

11. D.W. Leinbaugh. Guaranteed response time in a hard real-time environment. *IEEE Trans. Software Eng.*, January 1980.
12. Kwei-Jay Lin and Ansgar Herkert. Jitter control in time-triggered systems. In *Proc. 29th Hawaii Conference on System Sciences*, Maui, Hawaii, January 1996.
13. Masahiko Nakahara Masaaki Iwasaki, Tadashi Takeuchi and Takahiro Nakano. Isochronous scheduling and its application to traffic control. *IEEE 19th Real-Time Systems Symposium*, December 1998.
14. Sun Microsystems. *Sun Trunking.*
   http://wwws.sun.com/products-n-solutions/hw/networking/
   connectivity/suntrunking.
15. Alessandro Rubini and Jonathan Corbet. *LINUX DEVICE DRIVERS: Second Edition.* O'REILLY, 2001.
16. L. Sha and S.S. Sathaye. A systematic approach to designing distributed real-time systems. *IEEE Computer*, 26(9):68–78, September 1993.
17. IEEE 802.3 Std. *IEEE 802.3 CSMA/CD Access Method.* IEEE, 2000.
18. Richard Stevens. *TCP/IP Illustrated Volume 1.* Addison Wesley, 1994.
19. CISCI SYSTEMS. *ETHERCHANNEL.* http://www.cisco.com/en/US/tech.
20. Srinidhi Varadarajan and Tzi cker Chiueh. Ethereal: A host-transparent real-time fast ethernet switch. In *International Conference on Network Protocols (ICNP)*, October 1998.

An Efficient Switch Design for Scheduling Real-Time Multicast Traffic[*]

Deming Liu and Yann-Hang Lee

Department of Computer Science and Engineering
Arizona State University
Tempe, AZ 85287
{dmliu, yhlee}@asu.edu

Abstract. In this paper we put forth a switch design in terms of architecture and service discipline for real-time multicast traffic in packet switching networks. A parallel switching architecture called POQ (parallel output-queued) is employed, which take the advantages of both OQ (output-queued) and IQ (input-queued) switch architectures, i.e., non-blocking and low speedup of switch buffer. Basing on the POQ architecture we propose a hierarchical service discipline called H-EDF-RR (hierarchical earliest-deadline-first round-robin), which intends to simultaneously schedule both unicast and multicast traffic composed of fixed-length cells with guaranteed performances. Analyses show that this design can provide tight delay bounds and buffer requirements, and has computational complexity of O(1). These properties make the proposed switch design well suitable in real-time distributed systems.

Keywords: Packet Switching Network, Quality of Service, Real-Time Communications, Multicasting, Earliest Deadline First Round Robin

1 Introduction

Along with the tremendous development in computer and communication network, the wide use of optical fiber, packet switching and etc. enables many new distributed applications such as digital audio, digital video and teleconference. These applications are often characterized by quality of service (QoS) in terms of bandwidth, delay, jitter and loss rate. Similarly in many industrial automation and transportation systems, networking presents the opportunity for system optimization as subsystems can be integrated and operated cooperatively.

One example is the aircraft databus, which is aimed to support various traffic types coming from cabin entertainment systems, passage intranet, and avionics instruments. Under many application scenarios in aircraft communication networks, real-time data acquisition systems need to send acquired data to multiple destinations with stringent delay requirements. Usually we can use some traffic models to represent this kind of multicast traffic. The delay requirement of the multicast traffic can also be stated as deadlines. It is more important that we build deterministic communication networks,

---

[*] This work was sponsored in part by the Federal Aviation Administration (FAA) via grant DTFA03-01-C-00042. Findings contained herein are not necessarily those of the FAA.

J. Chen and S. Hong (Eds.): RTCSA 2003, LNCS 2968, pp. 194–207, 2004.

which can efficiently transport both unicast and multicast traffic subject to deadline constraints. In packet switching networks, switches are developed intending to provide statistical multiplexing and QoS-guaranteed transmission services. Unicasting, also known as point-to-point, is common in most QoS-guaranteed applications. However many applications such as video-on-demand, distance learning, and data acquisition in avionics systems produce multicast traffic, requiring that the same piece of data (a packet or a cell) from a source is transmitted to multiple destinations. For transferring multicast traffic efficiently in switching networks, there must be a thorough consideration in terms of architecture and scheduling in switch design.

Multicasting in a packet switch means that a packet arriving at an input port is forwarded to more than one output ports in the switch. Even though the effect of multicasting can be achieved by transferring the same packet from the source to multiple destinations in multiple times as unicast does, special switches supporting multicast traffic are preferred because doing multicasting with point-to-point communication may result in significant load increase to the network. Presented in [1], a survey of multicast switches indicates that multicast switches should include a packet-replicating function in order to efficiently convey multicast traffic. Among different multicast switch fabrics, crossbar network is attractive since it is based on simple mesh network and thus has no internal blocking inherently. According to different buffer positions, there are two types of crossbar networks, i.e., OQ (output-queued) and IQ (input-queued).

In an OQ switch, all packets that arrive from different input ports and are destined to the same output port are buffered into a queue located at the output port. The service scheduler repeatedly selects a packet from the output queue for transmission. Because of absence of input contention points OQ switches are non-blocking inherently. As far as QoS is concerned, there are numerous service disciplines that support guaranteed performances with OQ switches [7]. Since all packets are buffered in their own destination queues as they arrive, the copies of a multicast packet can be delivered to their destination queues as well. However OQ switches are subject to a fatal drawback that the *speedup factor*, defined as the ratio of buffer memory rate to line rate, is as high as N for an $N \times N$ OQ switch since the number of packets that want to enter a given output buffer in a packet slot can be as large as the number of input ports. The demand of high buffer rate constrains OQ switches in broadband networks. To avoid this limitation, designers proposed to limit the number of packets that can be transferred into an output buffer in one packet slot. Nevertheless packet drop is inevitable in this case, which is not allowed in most real-time applications.

In an IQ switch, packets arriving on each input port are placed into smoothing buffers, prior to the placement in the destination output ports. During each scheduling slot, the head packets in all the buffers are candidates for being transferred to their output ports. If several head packets contend for the same output port, only one of them is selected according to contention resolution scheme, while the rest remain in the buffers and contend again in the next packet slot. In contrast with OQ switches that require high switch fabric speed, the switch fabric speed of IQ switches is the same as that of input or output lines. The ease of speedup factor leads to a wide use of IQ switches.

Unfortunately IQ switches suffer from a phenomenon known as *head of line (HOL) blocking*. The effect occurs when a packet in any given buffer is denied to access to its output port, even though there are no other packets requiring the same output port, simply because the packet in the head of that buffer was blocked in a contention for a totally different output port. In fact, the delay for a given packet may grow unbounded even for an offered load less than 100%. Therefore it is very difficult, if not impossible, to guarantee the required QoS for each individual traffic flow. Hence most scheduling disciplines in IQ switches are best-effort instead of hard real-time [11] [12] [13].

The non-deterministic delay caused by HOL blocking can be resolved by a VOQ (virtual output-queued) structure [4], in which there are N buffers for each input port, one for each output port in an $N \times N$ switch. However we cannot avoid the matching problem involving high computational complexity in order to find the maximal flow between input and output ports during each scheduling slot. Also IQ switches have to face a difficult issue in supporting packets intended for more than one output ports, i.e., multicasting. If a head packet is of this kind, it has to contend simultaneously for all the outputs it is intended for. HOL blocking can be aggravated if the contention resolution schemes are applied independently during each scheduling slot.

Whereas IQ switches require a lower fabric speedup, OQ switches provide higher throughput. To take both advantages of the two architectures, a new switch structure, combined input and output queuing (CIOQ) switch, was proposed such that a compromise is made between these two aspects. In the CIOQ structure, there exist buffers in both input and output sides. Researchers have proved that CIOQ switches can achieve 100% throughput for unicast traffic with a speedup factor of 2 [5]. Contrary to the case of unicast traffic, for which IQ switches can yield the same throughput as OQ switches, it has been shown in experiments and analytical modeling that a throughput limitation exists in IQ switches (including CIOQ switches since CIOQ switches have IQ architecture essentially) loaded with multicast traffic [4].

As for scheduling disciplines of multicast switches, there are two basic strategies, non-fanout splitting and fanout splitting [4]. The *fanout* is defined as the number of different destinations that a multicast packet has. During each scheduling slot, the decision about which backlogged packets can be transferred is made according to a scheduling discipline. The fact that multicast packets have multiple destinations implies that some scheduling disciplines, called *non-fanout splitting,* may elect to transfer in just one scheduling slot the multicast packet to all destinations, while others, called *fanout splitting*, may elect to transfer the packet in several scheduling slots, reaching non-overlapping and exhaustive subsets of destinations.

In discussion of scheduling disciplines, *work-conserving* policies are significant in the sense that they transmit as many packets as possible in each scheduling slot [6]. Obviously when scheduling multicast traffic, non-fanout splitting is non-work conversing policy, while fanout splitting may be work conserving. With the assumption that the scheduler has no knowledge of the multicast copies of HOL packets, it has been shown that work-conserving policy provides more throughput than non-work conserving policy [6]. Thus, in terms of throughput, a fanout splitting discipline could be better off than a non-fanout splitting discipline. On the other hand, it might introduce a side effect of variant jitters as multiple copies are scheduled for transmission at different slots. We have known that in addition to imitate a unicast OQ switch with a speedup factor of 2, a CIOQ can attain an equivalent performance as an OQ switch for multicast traffic by making copies of each multicast packet in each input buffer with a speedup factor of $F+1$ where F is the maximum fanout [5]. We should note that there is a constraint that the copies of a multicast packet cannot be transferred to output ports simultaneously. To get extra performance, an intrinsic multicast CIOQ switch is of our interest, which can transfer copies of a multicast packet simultaneously. The intrinsic performance loss of IQ architecture with respect to OQ architecture loading with multicast traffic is shown in [4]. The speedup requirement of IQ switch that offers 100% throughput for multicast traffic depends upon the cardinality of input or output ports. There is no result about the exact relationship of the two parameters.

QoS-based scheduling for multicast traffic has been investigated recently. Results in [2] show that HOL FCFS (first come first served) discipline has a performance superior to that of the non-FCFS disciplines and assigning priority according to packet age in queue is a worthwhile feature for multicast packet switches. In fact, the core of a multicast traffic scheduler is basically a contention resolution algorithm. Chen and Hayes [3] suggested a priority-based scheme called cyclic priority scheme to schedule multicast traffic from the point of view of electronic circuit implementation, using the revision scheduling, a sequential combination of a non-fanout splitting discipline and a fanout splitting discipline. The revision scheduling performs well in the terms of delay-throughput performance. In general, most research results on switching of multicast traffic are based on the perspective of statistical analysis rather than determinism investigation [9].

The complication of multicast scheduling may come from the traffic imbalance between input and output sides of a switch. Since a multicast packet coming from an input port is destined to multiple output ports, the traffic injected to the output ports from multicast traffic could be much larger than that from unicast traffic. Moreover, given that multiple copies are created at same time, the traffic pattern is quite bursty. The most multicast disciplines we introduced above cannot be used in hard real-time communications in that they either assume a statistical model or allow packets to be dropped.

Integrating unicasting and multicasting scheduling with QoS guarantees is a challenge for IQ switches. However, recognizing that a multicast packet can be considered as multiple unicast packets in parallel, we can employ switches with parallel structure to achieve the advantages of both OQ and IQ switches, i.e., no-blocking and low speedup factor. In the rest of this paper we will introduce a parallel switching architecture equipped with a hierarchical service discipline that can transfer both unicast and multicast traffic with guaranteed performances. Detailed analyses of delay bounds and buffer requirements suggest that the proposed approach is appropriate for distributed real-time systems loading with multicast traffic.

The rest of this paper is organized as follows. In Section 2 we describe the proposed switching architecture, called POQ (parallel output-queued), and how it supports multicast traffic. Section 3 introduces the H-EDF-RR (hierarchical earliest-deadline round-robin) scheduling discipline designed for this parallel architecture. Section 4 presents the delay bound and buffer requirement analyses for H-EDF-RR discipline under POQ architecture. Finally the conclusions are given in Section 5.

2   A Parallel Switch Architecture – POQ (Parallel Output-Queued)

Subject to HOL blocking, a pure IQ switch has a limited throughput of 58.6% with FIFO input buffers in the worst case [15]. To avoid HOL blocking, the VOQ switch architecture can be constructed as shown in Fig. 1 where separate queues for all output ports are added at each input port. Thus a buffered packet cannot be blocked by the packets destined to different output ports. If the fabric speedup factor of VOQ switches is greater than 1, buffers are required on the output side. Although the VOQ architecture removes HOL blocking, they still suffer from the problem of input and output matching because VOQ switches only permit one head packet of all queues in each input port to be transmitted during each scheduling slot. To increase output throughput we have to find an optimal match, e.g. maximum, maximal or stable matching [16]. Almost any optimal matching can involve high computational complexity that is not acceptable in implementing high-speed switching networks. In fact, for multicast traffic, simulation results and analytical modeling in [4] suggest that IQ switches cannot yield the same throughput as OQ switches. In other words, 100% throughput may be attained for any multicast traffic pattern in IQ switches, however, in the cost of too high speedup factor preventing from physical implementation for high-speed networks. The computational complexity of matching algorithm and the high-speedup requirement restrained VOQ switches from applications in transferring hard real-time multicast traffic.

Due to the difficulties of VOQ switches in supporting real-time traffic, especially QoS guarantees for multicast traffic, in this paper we bring in a parallel output-queued (POQ) switch architecture shown in Fig. 2. The architecture of POQ can be regarded as a derivative of VOQ. The most obvious difference between VOQ and POQ is that multiple head packets in the queues of an input port in POQ can be transmitted to their destinations in the same scheduling slot whereas only one can be done under VOQ. This modification in structure results in a substantial performance improvement. In addition, output buffers are not necessary in POQ architecture. A similar POQ architecture is discussed in [8] where the authors numerated more drawbacks than advantages. We will probe the merits of POQ switches under real-time multicast traffic. Basing on the architecture of POQ switches, we can easily observe its attractive characteristics as follows.

    ☐   Buffer speed is only required to be the same as the line speed for both reading and writing operations. In other words, a speedup factor of 1 is enough

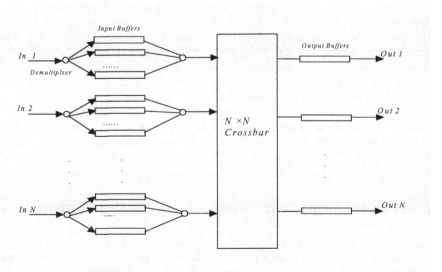

Fig. 1. VOQ switch architecture

for POQ switches for any traffic patterns. When a unicast packet arrives it is routed to a buffer according to its destination. Similarly when a multicast packet arrives all its copies are demultiplexed to the corresponding buffers in a parallel way. During each scheduling slot any output port can take one packet as long as there are some buffered packets destined to it.

☐ The throughput of a POQ switch can reach 100%. An $N{\times}N$ POQ switch can be thought as N $N{\times}1$ OQ switches that work in parallel, one for each output port. In contrast to VOQ switches, there is no need to find any optimal matching.

☐ Since a POQ switch is essentially OQ switch, all service disciplines developed so far for OQ switches can be applied to POQ switches. There are a number of service disciplines for OQ switches that support performance-guaranteed services [7]. Instead of using a centralized scheduler, a distributed approach can be adopted such that a scheduler is located at each output port.

☐ It is possible to integrate the scheduling of unicast and multicast traffic with guaranteed performance in a POQ switch. This originates from the fact that POQ switches, belonging to OQ switches in essence, have the ability of transmitting multicast traffic inherently. Unicast traffic can just be thought as a special case of multicast traffic that the fanout of any packet is one.

For expressly describing multicasting service discipline, we shall clarify several terms used in the following text. A *session* is a connection in a packet switching network from one source node to one destination node. For unicast traffic, a *unicast session* can be establish with QoS parameters and will be used to transmit packets between applications at the source and destination nodes. On the contrary, a *multicast session*, consisting of multiple overlapping sessions with a unique source and multiple destinations, is used for multicast traffic. The *path* of a session is defined as the consecutive switch sessions along the session and each switch session is a pair of input and output ports of a switch. Under the POQ architecture, a *switch session* is uniquely identified by a packet buffer connecting the same pair of input and output ports. When

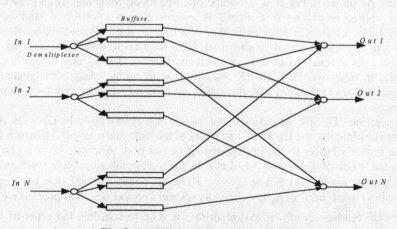

Fig. 2. A parallel switch structure - POQ

a packet of a unicast session arrives at an input port, it will be queued in the buffer on its session path. On the other hand, for an arriving packet of a multicast session, multiple copies will be inserted to the corresponding multiple buffers. As each buffer is shared by multiple sessions, we must take into account the issues of fairness and bandwidth reservation for each switch session. In the next section, we will apply a hierarchical service discipline to POQ architecture such that the performances of both unicast and multicast sessions are guaranteed.

3   Hierarchical Earliest Deadline First Round Robin Scheduling

In a network constructed with POQ switches, we can think a session as a connection that traverses a sequence of switch buffers from a source node to a destination node. The buffers are allocated in the switches along the session path and may be shared by multiple sessions. If we are not concerned about how packets of multiple sessions are multiplexed inside a buffer, N distributed schedulers, one at each output port, can be deployed to select a buffer from which the head packet is transmitted to the output port. We call a scheduler in this level *output scheduler*. On the other hand, arriving packets of multiple sessions may join a buffer according to a FIFO order or an order based on deadline and QoS requirements. We need a scheduler at this level called *input scheduler*. Thus, an input scheduler institutes a service discipline among the sessions sharing a switch session and an output scheduler determines the order in which the switch sessions traversing the same output port are served. Apparently, both schedulers must address the issues of fairness and QoS requirements. As we reveal the necessity of two levels of schedulers in routing packets in POQ architecture for both unicast and multicast traffic, we introduce an efficient performance-guaranteed discipline, H-EDF-RR (hierarchical earliest-deadline-first round-robin), in which EDF-RR (earliest deadline first round robin) schedulers are used in both the two levels.

EDF-RR proposed in [10] is an *O(1)* algorithm based on fixed-length cells for OQ switches. As shown in Fig. 3, it is a frame-oriented round-robin algorithm in nature. A frame is composed of a number of cells. A session reserves a portion of bandwidth by holding some cell slots in a frame. Instead of arranging the cells reserved by all active sessions in any arbitrary or dynamic order, EDF-RR tries to transfer them in an order such that cells attached to an active session are distributed in a frame as uniformly as possible. In other words, EDR-RR does its best to mimic ideal GPS (generalized processor sharing) scheduler with the constraint of non-preempted fixed-length traffic unit, cells.

To describe EDF-RR, we define that a frame consists of n fixed-length cells. A cell has, for convenience, the length of 1 in terms of the time that it takes to transmit a cell from a switch's buffer to the corresponding output port. Alternatively we just normalize the length of a cell slot to 1. Let K be the total number of active sessions associated with an output port and m_i ($1 \leq i \leq K$) be the number of cell slots occupied by the session i in a frame. n/m_i is defined as *session i period*. The non-preemptive non-idling EDF (earliest-deadline-first) algorithm is used to schedule the order of transmitting cells in a frame. If a session is idle, it will be skipped during the transmission and the cell slots it occupies can be reclaimed for backlogged sessions. The EDF-RR discipline is given as follows.

EDF-RR Discipline

(a) An n-cell frame is partitioned among K active sessions (all unused band-

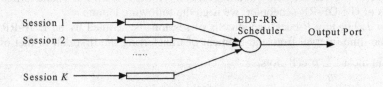

Fig. 3. An EDF-RR scheduler for multiple sessions

width can be considered as one idle active session) such that session i ($1 \leq i \leq K$) transfers m_i cells in the frame. Session i is assumed to have cells arrived at time jp_i (suppose a frame starts from time 0) with corresponding deadlines at $(j+1)p_i$, where $p_i = n/m_i$ and $j = 0, 1, 2, \ldots m_i-1$.

(b) If all K sessions are backlogged, the frame described in (a) is transferred repeatedly such that in every frame the cells are transmitted in a non-preemptive non-idling EDF order. Determining transmission order is needed only when there are sessions established, cancelled or updated, which happen infrequently. The associated overhead can be ignored since a new transmission order can be computed in parallel to the current transmission, and is swapped at the next frame boundary.

(c) If there is not backlog any more for a session during the current frame, their cell slots in a frame are skipped. The remaining backlogged sessions are transferred in the same order as in (b). In this case the size of a frame is reduced.

Table 1 shows the scheduling order of an example frame with the size of 10, in which sessions 1, 2 and 3 shares 5, 3 and 2 cell slots respectively (the numbers in Table 1. denote the relevant sessions).

Table 1. The example of scheduling order in a frame

1	2	1	3	1	2	1	2	1	3

According to [10] we have the following two theorems for EDF-RR discipline on delay bound and buffer requirement.

Theorem 1. If session i traffic flow that consists of a sequence of cells is constrained by traffic model $\sigma_i + \dfrac{m_i}{n}t$ (in cells), the delay a cell experiences passing through an

EDF-RR scheduler is not more than $(\sigma_i + 2)\dfrac{n}{m_i}$ cell slots.

Theorem 2. If session i traffic flow that consists of sequence of cells and is constrained by traffic model $\Box_i + \dfrac{m_i}{n} t$ (in cells) passes through an EDF-RR scheduler without buffer overflow, the buffer size the scheduler needs is no more than $\Box_i + 2$ cells.

Theorem 1 gives the delay bound of a cell with EDF-RR. For characterizing delay bounds of H-EDF-RR scheduler, we need the following lemma.

Lemma 1. For any P backlogged cells of session i scheduled by an EDF-RR scheduler, the time interval from the moment of transferring the first cell to that of the Pth cell is at most $\dfrac{n}{m_i} P$ cell slots.

This property is trivially true by considering that there is one cell transferred every $\dfrac{n}{m_i}$ cell slot in any busy interval after the first cell is scheduled [10].

H-EDF-RR service discipline is divided into two levels each of which is an EDF-RR discipline. In the high level, an output scheduler is located at every output port guaranteeing fairness among the switch sessions to the port. In the low level, an input scheduler is located at each buffer to guarantee the fairness among sessions that share the same switch session. In other words, an input scheduler decides which cell in the current queue is available for the scheduling of the corresponding output scheduler.

H-EDF-RR Discipline

(A) *Output Scheduling*

An n-cell high-level frame for an output port is partitioned among K active switch sessions destined to the output port such that m_i cell slots in a frame can be used to transmit the cells from switch session i ($1 \Box i \Box K$). EDF-RR is applied to schedule these K switch sessions.

(B) *Input Scheduling*

A n_i-cell low-level frame for switch session i is partitioned among K_i active sessions associated with switch session i such that m_{ih} cell slots in the frame can be used to transmit the cells from session h ($1 \Box h \Box K_i$). EDF-RR is applied to schedule these K_i sessions.

Since the first step of EDF-RR for both output scheduling and input scheduling needs to do only if bandwidth sharings of uincast or multicast sessions are updated, which we suppose to be infrequent events, H-EDF-RR has the computational complexity of $O(1)$ resulting from the fact that it is frame-oriented round-robin. Because the idle cell slots in any high-level or low-level frame are skipped, H-EDF-RR is a work-conserving policy.

4 Analysis of Delay Bounds and Buffer Requirements

For analyzing delay bounds and buffer requirements of the H-EDF-RR discipline under a POQ switch, we assume ($\Box$, $\Box$) traffic model for all active sessions. Denote a session S_{ih} the hth session in switch session i. Then for S_{ih} that is constrained by ($\Box_{ih}$,

$\square_{ih}$), there are at most $\square_{ih}+\square_{ih}t$ units of traffic during any time interval t. At an output port of a POQ switch armed with a H-EDF-RR scheduler, the output scheduler is in charge of K active switch sessions. A n-cell high-level frame is partitioned among the K switch sessions such that m_i cell slots are allocated to switch session i. Similarly an n_i-cell low-level frame is partitioned among K_i sessions that share switch session i such that m_{ih} cell slots are allocated to session S_{ih}. Therefore we have Theorem 3 giving the delay bound for a POQ switch with a H-EDF-RR scheduler.

Theorem 3. If the traffic flow of S_{ih} is constrained by traffic model $\square_{ih}+\dfrac{m_{ih}}{n_i}\dfrac{m_i}{n}t$, the delay that a cell of S_{ih} experiences in a POQ switch with a H-EDF-RR scheduler is not more than $[(\square_{ih}+2)\dfrac{n_i}{m_{ih}}+2]\dfrac{n}{m_i}$.

Proof. A H-EDF-RR scheduler can be considered as two EDF-RR schedulers in serial. Thus the delay that a cell in S_{ih} experiences is composed of three parts. One is the delay that comes from the source flow's burstiness. The other two result from input and output EDF-RR schedulers respectively.

The burstiness delay can be bounded by the expression as follows, which can be regarded as the delay of a cell in S_{ih} when passing through a GPS scheduler with rate $\dfrac{m_{ih}}{n_i}\dfrac{m_i}{n}$ reserved for S_{ih}.

$$\square_{ih}\frac{n_i}{m_{ih}}\frac{n}{m_i} \tag{1}$$

The input scheduler delay can be understood as the delay experienced by a cell of a uniform traffic flow of rate $\dfrac{m_{ih}}{n_i}\dfrac{m_i}{n}$ passing through the input scheduler, an EDF-RR scheduler of output rate $\dfrac{m_i}{n}$. By Theorem 1 (note that in Theorem 1 we assume the output rate of a EDF-RR scheduler is 1 cell per cell slot), this part of delay is bounded by $2n_i/m_{ih}$ time units, where one time unit is n/m_i cell slots. Thus the input scheduler delay is bounded by

$$2\frac{n_i}{m_{ih}}\frac{n}{m_i} \tag{2}$$

Similarly the output scheduler delay can be understood as the delay experienced by a cell of a uniform traffic flow of rate $\dfrac{m_i}{n}$ passing through the output scheduler with output rate of 1 cell per cell slot. By Theorem 1, the output scheduler delay is bounded by

$$2\frac{n}{m_i} \tag{3}$$

Making a summation of the three parts of delay bounds gives the total delay bound.

$$[(\square_{ih} + 2)\frac{n_i}{m_{ih}} + 2]\frac{n}{m_i} \qquad (4)$$

■

The portion of the delay of a session S_{ih} cell as shown in (2) results from the blocking of cells of other sessions in switch session i. The portion of delay shown in (3) comes from the blocking of cells of other switch sessions traversing the same output port. Since (3) is relatively the small term of (4), it may be ignored in some applications. In the proof of Theorem 3, we just individually get the worst-case delays of uniform traffic for both input and output schedulers. In fact the two worst cases cannot happen simultaneously and thus the delay bound in Theorem 3 can be as tight as

$$(\square_{ih} + 2)\frac{n_i}{m_{ih}}\frac{n}{m_i} \qquad (5)$$

Instead of using formal proof, we give an explanation of (5) below. For simplifying the explanation, we assume that S_{ih} has uniform traffic model of rate $\frac{m_{ih}}{n_i}\frac{m_i}{n}$ originally, accordingly ignoring its burstiness as we considered the delays of input and output schedulers in the proof of Theorem 3. A cell c of S_{ih} may experience the worst-case total delay caused by the H-EDF-RR scheduler when it is the first transferred cell of a busy interval of S_{ih}. We consider the following three cases. (i) There are no other cells except c backlogged in switch session i buffer from c's arrival to departure. But in this case, we can simplify the total delay of c caused by the H-EDF-RR scheduler to $\frac{2n}{m_i}$ ($\square 2\frac{n_i}{m_{ih}}\frac{n}{m_i}$) by Theorem 1. (ii) In addition to c, there are some cells backlogged in switch session i buffer from c's arrival to departure whereas none of these cells was being transferred when c arrived. Then according to EDF-RR service discipline the worst-case delay of c caused by the H-EDF-RR scheduler cannot exceed $2\frac{n}{m_i} + \frac{n_i}{m_{ih}}\frac{n}{m_i}$, where $\frac{2n}{m_i}$ and $\frac{n_i}{m_{ih}}\frac{n}{m_i}$ result from output and input schedulers respectively. If $\frac{n_i}{m_{ih}} < 2$, c will get chance to transfer in the next cell slot available for switch session i according to EDF-RR scheduling, and thus the delay of c caused by the H-EDF-RR scheduler will be at most $\frac{2n}{m_i}$ ($\square 2\frac{n_i}{m_{ih}}\frac{n}{m_i}$). If $\frac{n_i}{m_{ih}} \square 2$ instead, the delay will be at most $2\frac{n}{m_i} + \frac{n_i}{m_{ih}}\frac{n}{m_i}$ ($\square 2\frac{n_i}{m_{ih}}\frac{n}{m_i}$). (iii) In addition to c, there are some cells backlogged in switch session i buffer from c's arrival to departure and one of these cells was being transferred when c arrived. Then there are at most $\frac{2n_i}{m_{ih}}$ cells that need to be transferred before c since the input EDF-RR scheduler can have at most $\frac{2n_i}{m_{ih}}$ cells from other sessions that block c's transfer. According to Lemma 1, the

$\frac{2n_i}{m_{ih}}$ cells can be scheduled by the output scheduler in $2\frac{n_i}{m_{ih}}\frac{n}{m_i}$ cell slots because the

output rate of switch session i buffer is $\frac{m_i}{n}$ cells per cell slot according to bandwidth

reservation scheme of the output EDF-RR scheduler. In other words, the delay caused

by the H-EDF-RR scheduler to c is not more than $2\frac{n_i}{m_{ih}}\frac{n}{m_i}$ in this case. Following

the above analysis and also considering the delay from the original burstiness of S_{ih},
we have (5). In the particular scenario that n_i is equal to m_i, we may think an EDF-RR
scheduler at the output port that switch session i passes through schedules all sessions
passing this output port such that session S_{ih} shares m_{ih} cell slots in a n-cell frame.

Thus (5) is simplified to $(\square_{ih}+2)\frac{n}{m_{ih}}$, which is consistent with Theorem 1.

   The delay bound can be easily extended to the multiple-node case. We suppose that
session S_{ih} traffic flow traversing k nodes is constrained by $\square+\square$, where $\square$ is the
minimum bandwidth reservation for S_{ih} on all the k nodes. The upper delay bound of a
cell in S_{ih} as the cell passes through the k nodes is given by $\square+2k$.
$\hfill\square$

   In order to use memory efficiently for POQ switches, we assume that a buffer may
be shared by multiple sessions. Therefore cells from any session can be buffered to
the corresponding switch session buffer as long as the buffer is not full. The detailed
buffer sharing mechanism [14] is beyond the scope of this paper. Basing on this assumption, we have Theorem 4 giving the buffer requirement for a POQ switch armed
with a H-EDF-RR scheduler.

Theorem 4. If the traffic flow of session S_{ih} ($h = 1, 2 \ldots K_i$, where K_i is the number of
active sessions in switch session i) in switch session i, which consists of a sequence of

cells and is constrained by traffic model $\square_{ih}+\frac{m_{ih}}{n_i}\frac{m_i}{n}t$, passes through a H-EDF-RR

scheduler without buffer overflow, the buffer size that switch session i requires is not

more than $\sum\limits_{h=1}^{K_i}\square_{ih}+2$ cells.

Proof. Denote $R_{ih}(t_1, t_2)$ the traffic coming in $[t_1, t_2]$ for S_{ih} and $R_i(t_1, t_2)$ the amount of
traffic arriving in $[t_1, t_2]$ for switch session i. Then we have

$$R_{ih}(t_1,t_2) \square \square_{ih} + \frac{m_{ih}}{n_i}\frac{m_i}{n}(t_2 \square t_1), h = 1, 2, \ldots, K_i$$

Therefore,

$$R_i(t_1,t_2) = \sum_{h=1}^{K_i} R_{ih}(t_1,t_2) \square \sum_{h=1}^{K_i}\square_{ih} + (\sum_{h=1}^{K_i}\frac{m_{ih}}{n_i})\frac{m_i}{n}(t_2 \square t_1)$$

According to bandwidth allocation for switch session i, $\sum\limits_{h=1}^{K_i}\frac{m_{ih}}{n_i}\square 1$. Hence

$$R_i(t_1,t_2) \square \sum_{h=1}^{K_i}\square_{ih} + \frac{m_i}{n}(t_2 \square t_1)$$

This means that switch session i traffic satisfies model $(\sum_{h=1}^{K_i} \square_{ih}, \frac{m_i}{n})$. Since the switch session i flow passes through the output EDF-RR scheduler, by Theorem 2 we have the buffer requirement as follows.

$$\sum_{h=1}^{K_i} \square_{ih} + 2$$

∎

The H-EDF-RR discipline can guarantee performance of sessions. However it requires N^2 input schedulers and N output schedulers for an $N \times N$ POQ switch. This cost may not be acceptable in terms of electronic implementation. For simplifying the scheduling, we can remove input schedulers and leave output schedulers only. Theorem 5 shows that even not as good as original H-EDF-RR, this simplification still can guarantee multicasting delay bound as long as multicast traffic rate is constrained.

Theorem 5. If the traffic flow of session S_{ih} ($i = 1, 2, \dots K$, $h = 1, 2 \dots K_i$, where K is the number of active switch sessions of an output port and K_i the number of active sessions in switch session i) in switch session i, which consists of a sequence of cells and is constrained by traffic model $\square_{ih} + \frac{m_i}{n}\square_{ih}t$ and the condition $\sum_{h=1}^{K_i} \square_{ih} \square 1$, passes through only an output EDF-RR scheduler, the delay a cell in S_{ih} experiences is not more than $(\sum_{h=1}^{K_i}\square_{ih} + 2)\frac{n}{m_i}$.

Proof. Refer to the proof of Theorem 4, we know that switch session i traffic satisfies model $(\sum_{h=1}^{k_i}\square_{ih}, \frac{m_i}{n})$. Since switch session i flow passes through only the output EDF-RR scheduler, by Theorem 1 we have the upper delay bound as follows.

$$(\sum_{h=1}^{K_i}\square_{ih} + 2)\frac{n}{m_i}$$

∎

In the analysis above, we do not assume any difference between unicasting and multicasting in that unicasting is looked as the special case of multicasting. Normally switching networks offer connection-oriented services for real-time traffic. In a networks composed of POQ switches and served by H-EDF-RR disciplines, the process of setting up a multicast session involves two levels of bandwidth reservation along multiple paths since a multicast session is established from one node to multiple nodes. This increases the time of establishing multicast sessions. We need to design efficient connection-establishing algorithms to fully employ the advantages of POQ and H-EDF-RR. Also we have to face some application-dependent problems, for instances, how to determine and optimize frame size for both input and output schedulers and how to determine cell length. These subjects are beyond the discussion of this paper.

5 Conclusions

In this paper, we propose a solution to integrate unicast and multicast traffic scheduling in packet switching networks with guaranteed performances. A parallel switching architecture, POQ, is introduced that takes the advantages of both OQ and IQ switching architectures, i.e., non-blocking and the low rate of switch buffer up to line speed. Therefore POQ architecture is endowed the attractive capability of supporting multicast traffic. For efficiently scheduling multicast traffic for POQ architecture, a hierarchical service discipline working on fixed-length cells, H-EDF-RR, is employed based on EDF-RR discipline that serves OQ switches. Guaranteed performances for a POQ switch armed with H-EDF-RR disciplines is analyzed in terms of delay bounds and buffer requirements while loading with multicast traffic. Analytical results show that guaranteeing performance of multicast traffic is possible in this solution in terms of both architecture and service discipline.

References

[1]   Ming-Huang Guo and Ruay-Shiung Chang, "Multicast ATM Switches: Survey and Performance Evaluation," *SIGCOMM Computer Communication Review*, Vol. 28, No. 2, April 1998.

[2]   Joseph Y. Hui and Thomas Renner, "Queueing strategies for multicast packet switching," in *Proc. IEEE Globecom*, San Diego, CA, 1990, pp. 1431-1437.

[3]   Xing Chen and Jeremiah F. Hayes, "Access control in multicast packet switching," *IEEE/ACM Trans. Networking*, Vol. 1, Dec. 1993, pp. 638-649.

[4]   M. Ajmone Marsan, A. Bianco, et al, "On the throughput of input-queued cell-based switches with multicast traffic," *INFOCOM 2001, IEEE Proceedings*, Vol. 3, 2001, pp. 1664-1672.

[5]   Shang-Tse Chuang, Ashish Goel, et al, "Matching output queueing with a combined input/output-queued switch," *IEEE Journal on Selected Areas in Communications*, Vol. 17, No. 6, June 1999, pp. 1030-1039.

[6]   Zhen Liu and Rhonda Righter, "Scheduling multicast input-queued switches," *Journal of Scheduling*, Vol. 2, 1999, pp. 99-114.

[7]   Hui Zhang, "Service disciplines for guaranteed performance service in packet-switching networks," *Proceeding of the IEEE*, Vol. 83, No. 10, Oct. 1995, pp. 1374-1396.

[8]   Yuval Tamir and Gregory L. Frazier, "Dynamically-allocated multi-queue buffers for VLSI communication switches," *IEEE Transactions on Computers*, Vol. 41, No. 6, June 1992, pp. 725-737.

[9]   Jeremiah F. Hayes, Richard Breault, et al, "Performance analysis of a multicast switch," *IEEE Transactions on Communications*, Vol. 39, No. 4, April 1991, pp. 581-587.

[10]   Deming Liu, Yann-Hang Lee, "An efficient scheduling discipline for packet switching networks using earliest deadline first round robin," preparing for submission.

[11]   Nick McKeown, "The iSLIP scheduling algorithm for input-queued switches," *IEEE/ACM Transactions on Networking*, Vol. 7, No. 2, April, 1999, pp. 188-201.

[12]   C. Minkenberg, "Integrating uincast and multicast traffic scheduling in a combined input- and output queued packet-switching system," *Computer Communications and Networks 2000, Proceedings, Ninth International Conference*, pp. 127-134.

[13]   Balaji Prabhakar, Nick McKeown, et al, "Multicast scheduling for input-queued switches," *IEEE Journal on Selected Areas in Communications*, Vol. 15, No. 5, June 1997, pp. 855-866.

[14]   Rajeev Sivaram, Craig B. Stunkel, et al, "HIPIQS: a high-performance switch architecture using input queuing," *IEEE Transactions on Parallel and Distributed systems*, Vol. 13, No. 3, March 2002, pp. 275-289.

[15]   M. J. Karol, M.Hluchyj, and S. Morgan, "Input versus output queuing on a space-division packet switch," *IEEE Transactions on Communications*, Vol. COM-35, 12, December 1987, pp. 1347-1356.

[16]   Ge Nong and Mounir Hamdi, "On the provision of quality-of-service guarantees for input queued switches," *IEEE Communications Magazine*, December 2000, pp. 62-69.

XRTJ: An Extensible Distributed High-Integrity Real-Time Java Environment

Erik Yu-Shing Hu*, Andy Wellings, and Guillem Bernat

Real-Time Systems Research Group
Department of Computer Science
University of York, York, YO105DD, UK
{erik,andy,bernat}@cs.york.ac.uk

Abstract. Despite Java's initial promise of providing a reliable and cost-effective platform-independent environment, the language appears to be unfavourable in the area of high-integrity systems and real-time systems. To encourage the use of Java in the development of distributed high-integrity real-time systems, the language environment must provide not only a well-defined specification or subset, but also a complete environment with appropriate analysis tools. We propose an extensible distributed high-integrity real-time Java environment, called XRTJ, that supports three attributes, i.e., predictable programming model, dependable static analysis environment, and reliable distributed run-time environment. The goal of this paper is to present an overview of our on-going project and report on its current status. We also raise some important issues in the area of distributed high-integrity systems, and present how we can deal with them by defining two distributed run-time models where safe and timely operations will be supported.

Keywords: Real-Time Java (RTJ), High-Integrity Systems, Distributed RTJ, Static Analysis Environment, Distributed Run-Time Environment

1   Introduction

There is a trend towards using object-oriented programming languages, such as Java and C++, to develop high-integrity real-time systems because the use of such languages has several advantages, for instance reusability, data accessibility and maintainability. Typically, high-integrity systems, where failure can cause loss of life, environmental harm, or significant financial penalties, have high development and maintenance costs due to the customised nature of their components. Therefore, the use of object-oriented programming in such systems may offer a number of benefits including increased flexibility in design and implementation, reduced production cost, and enhanced management of complexity in application areas.

---

* This work has been funded by the EPSRC under award number GR/M94113.

J. Chen and S. Hong (Eds.): RTCSA 2003, LNCS 2968, pp. 208–228, 2004.
© Springer-Verlag Berlin Heidelberg 2004

The Java technology with its significant characteristics, including cost-effective platform-independent environment, relatively familiar linguistic semantics, and support for concurrency, has many features for developing real-time and embedded systems. It also provides well-defined *Remote Method Invocation* (RMI) features which support distributed applications on the Java architecture.

However, despite Java's initial promise, the language appears to be unfavourable in the area of high-integrity systems [22] and real-time systems [7]. Its combination of object-oriented programming features, its automatic garbage collection, and its poor support for real-time multi-threading are all seen as particular impediments.

The success of high-integrity real-time systems undoubtedly relies upon their capability of producing functionally correct results within defined timing constraints. In order to support a predictable and expressive real-time Java environment, two major international efforts have attempted to provide real-time extensions to Java: the Real-Time Specification for Java (RTSJ) [5] and the Real-Time Core extensions to Java [9]. These specifications have addressed the issues related to using Java in a real-time context, including scheduling support, memory management issues, interaction between non-real-time and real-time Java programs, and device handling, among others.

However, the expressive power of all these features, along with the regular Java semantics, means that very complex programming models can be created, necessitating complexity in the supporting real-time virtual machine and tools. Consequently, Java, with the real-time extensions as they stand, seems too complex for confident use in high-integrity systems. Furthermore, in addition to the difficulties with analysing applications developed in these frameworks with all the complex features, there is no satisfactory static analysis approach that can evaluate whether the system will produce both functionally and temporally correct results in line with the design at run-time.

For the above reasons, to encourage the use of Java in the development of high-integrity real-time systems, the language environment must provide not only a well-defined specification or subset, but also a complete environment with appropriate analysis tools. Hence, we propose an extensible distributed high-integrity real-time Java environment, called XRTJ, that supports the following attributes:

- Predictable programming model
- Dependable static analysis environment
- Reliable distributed run-time environment

The XRTJ environment has been developed with the whole software development process in mind: from the design phase to run-time phase. The XRTJ environment includes: the Ravenscar-Java profile [23], a high-integrity subset of RTSJ; a novel Extensible Annotations Class (XAC) format that stores additional information that cannot be expressed in Java class files [18]; a static analysis environment that evaluates functional and temporal correctness of applications, called XRTJ-Analyser [18]; an annotation-aware compiler, called XRTJ-

Compiler; a modified real-time Java virtual machine, called XRTJ-Virtual Machine that supports a highly reliable run-time environment.

The aim of the paper is to present an overview of our on-going project and report on its current status. The rest of the paper is organised as follows. Section 2 presents an overview of the XRTJ environment. Further details of the static analysis environment and distributed run-time environment are provided in Section 3 and 4 respectively. Section 5 shows a simple example that demonstrates how our approach can be used in a practical application. Section 6 gives a brief review of related work while Section 7 presents the current status of the project. Finally, conclusions and future work are presented in Section 8.

2   XRTJ Environment Overview

The major goal of our project is to provide a predictable and portable programming environment to develop distributed high-integrity real-time systems. The XRTJ environment is targeted at cluster-based distributed high-integrity real-time Java systems, such as consumer electronics and embedded devices, industrial automation, space shuttles, nuclear power plants and medical instruments.

To encourage the use of real-time Java in high-integrity systems, we have introduced the Ravenscar-Java profile [23]. The profile or restricted programming model excludes language features with high overheads and complex semantics, on which it is hard to perform temporal and functional analyses. Further details of the profile are given in Section 2.1.

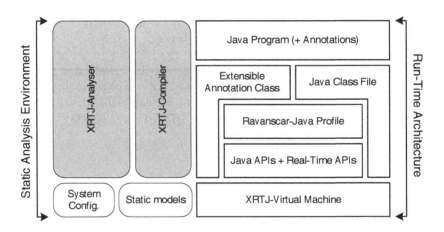

Fig. 1. A basic block model of the XRTJ environment

Based on the Ravenscar-Java profile, we propose a highly dependable and predictable programming environment to develop distributed high-integrity real-time applications. As shown in Figure 1, the XRTJ environment can be divided into two main parts: a *Static Analysis Environment*, which offers a number of tools that conduct various static analyses including program safety and timing analysis; a *Distributed Run-Time Environment*, in which highly predictable and dependable distributed capabilities are provided.

Before a detailed discussion of each environment, two major components of the XRTJ environment will be introduced. In our environment, to facilitate the various static analysis approaches and provide information that cannot be expressed in either Java source programs or Java bytecode, an extensible and portable annotation[1] class format called Extensible Annotations Class (XAC) file is proposed [18]. To generate XAC files, an annotation-aware compiler, named XRTJ-Compiler, which can derive additional information from either manual annotations or source programs, or both, is also introduced. Taking advantage of the knowledge accumulated with the compiler, different analysis tools may be integrated into the XRTJ-Compiler to carry out various verifications or validations either on source programs or Java bytecode.

Essentially, the *static analysis environment* supports various analysis techniques by means of the XRTJ-Analyser where program safety analysis and timing analysis can be statically carried out. In the XRTJ environment, Java programs extended with specific annotations, such as timing annotations or model checking annotations[2], are compiled into Java class files and XAC files by either a simple XAC translator and a traditional Java compiler or the XRTJ-Compiler. A conformance test that verifies whether the applications obey the rules defined in the Ravenscar-Java profile or whether the manual annotations are correct can also be conducted during the compilation. The XAC files, together with the Java class files, are used by the XRTJ-Analyser to perform various static analyses. As shown in Figure 1, various *static models*, such as a *Virtual Machine Timing Model* (VMTM)[3], can be provided to perform different static analysis approaches on the XRTJ-Analyser. Further aspects of the static analysis environment are discussed in Section 3.

The *distributed run-time environment* provides mechanisms for underlying systems to facilitate both functionally and temporally correct execution of applications. This infrastructure is targeted at cluster-based distributed infrastructure where remote objects are statically allocated during the design phase. In order to accommodate a diverse set of the implementations on the underlying platforms or virtual machines, two run-time environments with different levels of distribution are supported in the XRTJ run-time environment. This will be explored further in Section 4.

---

[1] The term *annotations*, in this paper, means both manual annotations and annotations generated by the XRTJ-Compiler automatically.

[2] Model-checkers, such as JPF2[6], which requires special annotations, may be employed in our architecture to facilitate safety checks of concurrent programs.

[3] VMTM is a timing model for the target virtual machine including a list of the worst-case execution time of native methods and Java bytecode instructions.

2.1   Ravenscar-Java Profile

We have presented a Java profile for the development of software-intensive high-integrity real-time systems in [23]. The restricted programming model removes language features with high overheads and complex semantics, on which it is hard to perform timing and functional analyses. The profile fits within the J2ME framework [31], fullfils the NIST Real-Time Java profile requirements [7] and is consistent with well-known guidelines for high-integrity software development, such as those defined by the U.S. Nuclear Regulatory Commission [16].

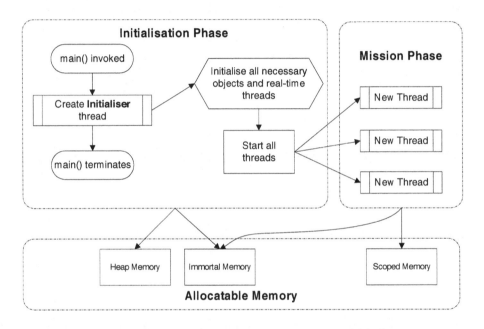

Fig. 2. Two execution phases of Ravenscar Virtual Machine

Its computational model defines two execution phases, i.e. initialisation and mission, as shown in Figure 2. In the initialisation phase of an application, all necessary threads and memory objects are created by an `Initializer` thread, whereas in the mission phase the application is executed and multithreading is allowed based on the imposed scheduling policy. There are several new classes that should ultimately enable safer construction of Java programs (for example, `Initializer, PeriodicThread,` and `SporadicEventHandler`), and the use of some existing classes is restricted or simplified due to their problematic features in static analysis. For instance, the use of any class loader is not permitted in the mission phase, and the size of a scoped memory area, once set, cannot be changed.

Further restrictions include (see [23] for a full list)

– No nested scoped memory areas are allowed,

- Priority Ceiling Emulation must be used for all shared objects between real-time threads,
- Processing groups, overrun and deadline-miss handlers are not supported,
- Asynchronous Transfer of Control is not allowed, and
- Object queues are not allowed (i.e. no `wait, notify,` and `notifyAll` operations).

Restrictions are also imposed on the use of the Java language itself, for example

- `continue` and `break` statements in loops are not permitted, and
- Expressions with possible side effects must be eliminated.

Most subsets of Java or the RTSJ (e.g. [3,28]) overlook some important elements of the language, for example, multithreading and the object-oriented programming model. Thus many of the advantages of Java are lost. However, the Ravenscar-Java profile attempts to cover the whole language issues, as well as the run-time model. The profile is expressive enough to accommodate today's demanding requirements for a powerful programming model, yet concise enough to facilitate the implementation of underlying platforms of virtual machines.

3   Static Analysis Environment

The static analysis environment consists of two components: program safety analysis and timing analysis. The former highlights program safety in terms of functional correctness and concurrency issues, such as safety and liveness, whereas the latter emphasises the analysis of timing issues in terms of temporal correctness. For the most part, these static analysis approaches may be carried out individually or combinatorially. A block diagram of the XRTJ architecture for the static analysis environment is given in Figure 3 and further details of each major component are discussed in subsequent sections.

3.1   XAC (Extensible Annotation Class) File

One of the key components in the XRTJ architecture is the XAC format that provides information for the various analysis tools that cannot be stored in Java class files without making them incompatible with the traditional Java architecture [18]. The XAC format has been designed with two main goals in mind: *portability*, to support both platform independence and language independence, and *extensibility*, to hold extra information needed for other analysis tools. Therefore, the XAC files are easy to extend for various purposes or apply in annotation-aware tools or JVMs.

Each XAC file is generated for a specific Java class file, and so the relationship between a Java class file and an XAC file is one to one. Essentially, the offset numbers of bytecode in a method are stored with the associated annotations in the XAC file. Therefore, the corresponding bytecode and annotation may easily

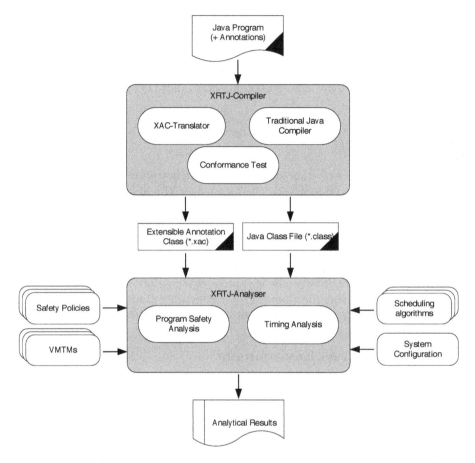

Fig. 3. A block diagram of the XRTJ architecture for static analysis environment

be reconstructed in analysis tools. A checksum is also provided in XAC files to facilitate analysis tools or JVMs to verify the consistency between the Java class file and the XAC file. Further details of the XAC file are discussed in [18].

In addition, using XAC files has benefits for distributed systems as XAC files do not increase the size of traditional Java class files. Therefore, if the XAC files are not required at run-time, they do not need to be either loaded into the target JVM or transferred among distributed machines.

3.2   XRTJ-Compiler

Compiler techniques have been applied to analysis approaches, such as worst-case execution time analysis and program safety analysis, in order to achieve more accurate results. For example, Vrchoticky [35] has suggested compilation support for fine-grained execution time analysis, and Engblom et al. [13] have proposed a WCET tool called *Co-transformation*, integrated with compilation support, to achieve safer and tighter estimation of timing analysis approaches. These approaches show that compilation support can not only address the optimisation issues introduced by compilers, but also provide additional information that may accumulate from the source code level for particular analysis tools.

In the XRTJ environment, an annotation-aware compiler (XRTJ-Compiler) is introduced in order to both manipulate annotations and validate that the contexts of source program code obey those rules defined in the Ravenscar-Java profile. On the whole, the XRTJ-Compiler extracts both manual annotations introduced for timing analysis and specific annotations that can be derived from source code level for particular purposes. For instance, the XRTJ-compiler derives *Abstract Syntax Trees*(AST) and *Worst-Case Execution Frequency* (WCEF)[4] vectors of specific applications to facilitate the WCET analysis (Section 3.4). Furthermore, the requirements of other static analysis tools, such as information needed for model checkers and other safety analysis tools, may also be produced by the XRTJ-Compiler and can be stored in associated XAC files.

It can be observed that the XRTJ-Compiler may provide valuable information not only to achieve more precise and reliable results from analysis tools, but also to facilitate the implementation of various static analysis tools on the XRTJ infrastructure.

3.3   Program Safety Analysis

The inherent complexity in the verification of non-trivial software means that unsafe programs could be produced and used under critical situations. This is increasingly the case as today's programming models become more complex. Our Ravenscar-Java profile [23] has been developed with such concerns in mind, so that programs become easier to analyse, and the run-time platform will also be simpler to implement.

By program safety, we mean that a program will behave according to its functional (and temporal) specification, and not exhibit any erroneous actions throughout its lifetime. Erroneous actions include data races, deadlocks, and memory overflows. Also, in the context of real-time Java and the Ravenscar profile, we also need to ensure that the rules defined in the profile and RTSJ are observed. These rules are checked when programs are compiled and tested for conformance to the profile. This conformance test alone will remove many possible errors in the program. For example, deadlocks, and side effects in expressions can be prevented. The following subsections address some issues that are not directly addressed by the profile, but which are still important in validating the safety of a Java program.

---

[4] WCEF vectors represent execution-frequency information about basic blocks and more complex code structures that have been collapsed during the first part of the portable WCET analysis.

Verification of the Java Memory Model's effect. As reported in [26,29], the Java memory model (JMM) in [14] is a weaker model of execution than those supporting *sequential consistency*. It allows more behaviours than simple inter-leaving of the operations of the individual threads. Therefore, verification tools that simply examine Java source code or even bytecode are prone to producing false results [29]. Because the semantics of the JMM can lead to different im-plementations, some virtual machines may support sequential consistency, while others may not for performance reasons. This does not match the Java's *write once, run anywhere*[5] philosophy.

However, we can develop restricted fragments of Java programs for which the JMM guarantees sequential consistency (as opposed to the approach in [29]), given that there is a means to efficiently analyse Java bytecode to locate only necessary synchronizations. Libraries will still be considered because such an analysis tool will operate at the bytecode level. The point-to and escape analysis [8,30] can be used to trace escaping and possibly shared objects, as well as improving overall performance by allocating non-escaping objects in the stack of a method. This approach, in fact, is how our analysis algorithm has been designed to uncover data races.

The underlying assumption of our algorithm is that any reads and writes on a shared object in a method must be enclosed within the same synchronized block (or method) in order not to have any data races. In other words, any syntactical gap between a read and write that are not covered by a single synchronized block will cause possible data races in a multithreaded environment because either a read or write action can be lost. This is true even when a shared object is indirectly read and updated using a local object. For example, an interleaving of another thread that may update the shared object can occur in between the indirect read and a (synchronized) write in the method, resulting in a lost write. Thus, any indirect reads and writes should also be treated in a similar manner to direct ones on a shared object.

Another similar case is the following: even when both a read and write are synchronized, there can still be data races if the two blocks are guarded by two different synchronized blocks and can be interleaved by other threads in between. Our algorithm is capable of analysing all such conditions, thus detecting problematic data races by tracing all shared objects and checking whether they are properly guarded by synchronized blocks or methods [21].

Memory Usage Analysis. Shortage of memory space at run-time can be devastating in high integrity systems, but at the same time, oversupply of it will be costly. Considering the new memory areas introduced in the RTSJ, we may need a different means of estimating the worst-case memory space that a program requires at run-time, so that only the required amount of memory for each area will be allocated. For this purpose the RTSJ defines the `SizeEstimator` class, but the `getEstimate()` method does not return the actual amount of memory that an object of a class and its methods dynamically use, but simply the total

---

[5] Programs may still run anywhere, but possibly with different or unsafe behaviours.

size of the class's static fields. In this sense, the class is not readily usable in estimating the required memory size for an RTSJ application.

However, the Ravenscar-Java profile places some restrictions on the use of RTSJ's memory areas; for example, access to scoped memory areas must not be nested and such memory areas cannot be shared between `Schedulable` objects [23]. These restrictions greatly ease the development of an algorithm that will inspect each thread's logic to discover all classes it instantiates. After that, by making use of control and data flow information extracted from the code and the XAC file (such as loop bounds), the algorithm will be able to tell how many instances of each class are created by a thread. This information can then be used to produce a tight upper bound of the amount of memory that a thread utilises at run-time by applying `reserve()` and `getEstimate()` methods of the `SizeEstimator` class at the target platform before system despatching. This thread-oriented memory usage analysis algorithm is currently being developed.

Other Pre-runtime Analyses. In addition to the ones introduced above, our static analyser (XRTJ-Analyser) is also intended to do the following analyses:

- Exception propagation analysis, and
- Dynamic memory access check analysis.

The first analysis stems from the fear that the propagation of any unchecked exceptions at run-time can be hazardous, while the latter is concerned with eliminating unpredictable runtime overheads caused by dynamic checks of the virtual machine. Memory access checks can be prevented by means of the point-to and escape analysis [8,30], which will be integrated in our XRTJ analyser together with an efficient exception propagation analysis technique.

3.4   Timing Analysis

Timing analysis is crucial in real-time systems to guarantee that all hard real-time threads will meet their deadlines in line with the design. In order to ensure this, appropriate scheduling algorithms and schedulability analysis are required. Typically, most scheduling algorithms assume that the *Worst-Case Execution Time* (WCET) estimation of each thread has to be known prior to conducting the schedulability analysis. Therefore, estimating WCET bounds of real-time threads is of vital importance. In addition, having accurate timing estimations enables the developer to allocate resources more precisely to the system during the design phase.

On the whole, most WCET approaches [13,35,27] are tied to either a particular language or target architecture. Moreover, RTSJ has kept silent on how the WCET estimations can be carried out on the highly portable Java architecture. Consequently, it is unlikely to achieve Java's promise of "write once, run anywhere" or perhaps more appropriately for real-time "write once carefully, run anywhere conditionally" [5].

Hence, in order to offer a predictable and reliable environment for high-integrity real-time applications, a number of timing analysis issues need to be addressed, for example:

- How the WCET analysis can be carried out on a highly portable real-time Java architecture,
- How the run-time characteristics of Java, such as high frequency of method invoking and dynamic dispatching, can be addressed,
- How schedulability analysis can be conducted statically, and
- What techniques need to be provided to take account of the supporting distributed run-time environment.

The subsequent sections explore how these issues can be addressed in the static analysis environment of the XRTJ infrastructure to be able to ensure that real-time threads will meet their time constraints.

Portable WCET Analysis. A portable WCET analysis approach based on the Java architecture has been proposed by Bernat et al. [4], and extended by Bate et al. [2] to address low-level analysis issues. This section presents how the portable WCET analysis can be adapted for our environment to be able to perform the WCET analysis statically [18].

The portable WCET analysis uses a three-step approach: high-level analysis (i.e. analysing the annotated Java class files and computing the portable WCET information in the form of Worst-Case Execution Frequency (WCEF) vectors [2, 4]), low-level analysis (i.e. producing a Virtual Machine Time Mode (VMTM) for the target platform by performing platform-dependent analysis on Java byte code instructions implemented for the particular platform), and conducting the combination of the high-level analysis with the low-level analysis to compute the actual WCET bound of the analysed code sections.

In our environment, the XRTJ-Compiler analyses the annotated Java programs and extracts the WCEF vectors during the compilation. The WCET vectors and WCET annotations are stored in the XAC file by the XRTJ-Compiler automatically. Therefore, after compilation, the class files and XAC files are ready for WCET analysis tools. To be able to build VMTMs of various platforms for real-time and embedded Java-based systems in an efficient way, we are developing a timing analysis benchmark that can build a VMTM of a target platform automatically simply by providing a native method that can access the machine cycle of the target platform. A WCET analysis tool in the XRTJ-Analyser, then, performs the combination of the high-level analysis with the low level VMTM to compute the actual WCET bound of the analysed code sections.

WCET Annotations. Dynamic dispatching issues have been considered in compiler techniques for a number of years [1,11,12]. Unfortunately, these approaches cannot be directly applied to WCET analysis since they are solely optimising dynamic binding and do not guarantee that all dynamic binding will be resolved before run-time. However, in WCET analysis for hard real-time systems, the execution time of every single method has to be known prior to executing it. Therefore, most approaches in the WCET analysis field have simply assumed that dynamic dispatching features should be prohibited. It is possible that these restrictions could make applications very limited and unrealistic because they might eliminate the major advantages of object-oriented programming [17].

In [17], we have explored the ways in which dynamic dispatching can be addressed in object-oriented hard real-time systems with the use of appropriate annotations. Our approach shows that allowing the use of dynamic dispatching can not only provide a more flexible way to develop object-oriented hard real-time applications, but it also does not necessarily result in unpredictable timing analysis. Moreover, it demonstrates how to achieve tighter and safer WCET estimations.

It is an open question for most annotation-based approaches as to how to verify if the provided annotations are correct. Combining optimisation techniques, such as Class Hierarchy Analysis (CHA) [11] or Rapid Type Analysis (RTA) [1], with our approach allows the annotations to be verified, if there is no dynamic linking at run-time. For example, applying the CHA approach, we can easily get the maximum bound of the class hierarchies information from the Java bytecode.

Schedulability Analysis. This section demonstrates how schedulability can be carried out for our real-time Java architecture in line with the portable WCET analysis. In [18], we have illustrated how real-time parameters, including priority and dispatching parameters, for the set of threads and WCET estimates can be produced from the Java class files and XAC files. Given the WCET estimates and real-time parameters, the schedulability analysis can be conducted easily. In the XRTJ-Analyser, only the system configuration information is needed. Following the system configuration, the XRTJ-Analyser loads the scheduling algorithm and carries out the schedulability analysis. Scheduling algorithms must provide scheduling characteristics, algorithms which can calculate other scheduling parameters, such as release-jitter, blocking time, response-time, and resource access protocols which are provided to manage the priority inversion problems. The XRTJ-Analyser produces the result of the analysis of the system. The output file provides not only the result of the analysis, but also includes timing and scheduling information, such as response time, release-jitter, and blocking time.

Support for Distributed Features. It should be noted that analysing the WCET bound of real-time threads in a distributed run-time environment differs from a standalone run-time environment. In particular, there are a number of issues that need to be clarified to achieve safe and tight WCET estimation and schedulability analysis of real-time threads containing remote method invocations. In the XRTJ infrastructure, we assume that one compatible virtual machine resides on each node in the cluster network and no recursive remote method invocations are allowed. In accordance with these assumptions, the WCET estimation and schedulability can be carried out as follows.

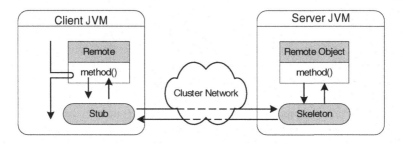

Fig. 4. The Java's RMI architecture [19]

Based on Java's RMI architecture shown in Figure 4, a *stub*[6] needs to be provided on the local virtual machine, whereas a *skeleton*[7] resides on the remote virtual machine [19]. In line with this architecture, holistic schedulability analysis can be performed [33,25]; the response time estimations of all remote methods and the skeleton on the server node have to be analysed as sporadic threads during the schedulability analysis.

As to the client node, the WCET estimation of a real-time thread that holds remote method invocations differs from those that only comprise local method invocations. One should note that the WCET estimation of a remote method on the client node should not take into account the execution time of the remote method because a remote method is translated by the stub that resides on the local virtual machine and is executed on remote virtual machines. The WCET bound of a remote method invocation, therefore, should only take account of the execution time of the stub.

4   Distributed Run-Time Environment

This section is mainly concerned with the distributed run-time environment of the XRTJ infrastructure, which is targeted at cluster-based distributed high-integrity real-time systems. Moving from a centralised environment to a distributed environment requires the following issues to be addressed:

– How objects are allocated to nodes in the cluster,
– What form of communication is supported between distributed objects,
– How the model of communication can be integrated into Ravenscar-Java, and
– What impact the model has on the XRTJ environment.

For high-integrity environments, objects should be statically allocated to each node in the cluster. Therefore, the term *distributed* in this paper means

---

[6] A *stub* is a class that automatically translates remote method calls into network communication setup and parameter passing.

[7] A *skeleton* is a corresponding class that accepts these network connections and translates them into actual method calls on the actual object.

statically distributed whereby remote objects are allocated to nodes during the design phase. Although there have been many different communication models proposed for distributed Java programs (tuplespaces, distributed events, etc) most are based on top of the Java's RMI mechanism. XRTJ assumes the existence of a real-time RMI facility [36], such as that proposed by Miguel [10].

To accommodate existing practice, which is a stated goal of the project, two static distributed run-time environments are introduced, including *Initialisation Distributed Environment*, in which RMI is only allowed for use in the initialisation phase of an application, and *Mission Distributed Environment*, where a restricted real-time RMI model [36] can be used during the mission phase. The following subsections give further details on each of these and show how those issues mentioned previously can be addressed.

4.1   Initialisation Distributed Environment

The Ravenscar-Java profile does not support any remote interfaces on its main classes. Neither are they serialisable. Consequently, no remote operation can be applied to periodic threads or sporadic event handlers. This implies that they cannot be passed over the network during the mission phase of the RVM.

However, in order to provide not only high predictability and reliability, but also some degrees of support for distributed applications, which may reduce the development and maintenance costs of overall systems, the *initialisation distributed environment* is introduced. The motivation of providing this environment can be observed by a simple example given in Section 5. In such systems, communications between a server and each node, including loading data and reporting status, is essential and this can be achieved easily if the run-time environment provides distributed features in the initialisation phase.

In line with the framework proposed for integrating the RTSJ and Java's RMI [36], the standard RTSJ may offer a distributed environment with a minimal distribution level, defined as Level 0 integration by Wellings et. al. [36]. Following this approach, the initialisation distributed environment can be applied to either a standard Real-Time Java Virtual Machine (RTJVM) or a Ravenscar Virtual Machine (RVM). In such a run-time environment, both RTJVMs and RVMs can support a distributed environment defined as Level 0 distribution in [36] before all real-time threads are started (i.e. the initialisation phase of Ravenscar-Java).

In the mission phase of the RVM or after executing the real-time threads in a standard RTJVM, no remote method invocation is allowed. However, if the Ravenscar-Java profile supports aperiodic or non real-time threads, it is possible to use RMI in such threads with lower priority than real-time threads. Obviously, there is no modification required for standard RTJVMs or RVMs to support distributed high-integrity real-time Java-based applications in this environment.

4.2   Mission Distributed Environment

Supporting distributed features in the mission phase makes it necessary to address more issues, such as how to guarantee statically that all hard real-time threads will meet their deadlines, when distributed virtual machines can enter the mission phase and when real-time RMI can be used without rendering hard real-time tasks unsafe.

To offer a more flexible way to develop distributed high-integrity applications in the XRTJ environment without loss of predicability and dependability, the *mission distributed environment* is introduced. To support this distributed environment, three execution phases are proposed in the XRTJ-Virtual Machine (XRTJ-VM), including *initialisation* phase, *pre-mission* phase and *mission* phase.

In the mission distributed environment, all remote objects are allocated during the design phase and the XRTJ-VM supports Level 1 (i.e. real-time RMI) distribution defined by Wellings et. al. [36]. The program safety and timing analysis can be carried out with static analysis tools as mentioned in Section 3.4 during the static analysis phase. Note that the response time of all remote objects and threads, and the skeleton on the server node can be analysed as sporadic threads during the schedulability analysis, since they are allocated during the design phase.

The initialisation phase of the XRTJ-VM can be assumed to be the same as the initialisation the RVM mentioned previously. However, it should be noted that allocations, registrations, reference collections of all remote objects that are allowed for use in the mission phase have to be done during the initialisation phase.

Since the invocations of real-time RMI [36] are allowed in the mission phase of the XRTJ-VM, one should note that a virtual machine executing in its mission phase must not attempt to invoke a remote method on another virtual machine that is not running under the mission phase. The use of such invocations may result in unpredictable and unanalysable real-time threads running in the mission phase. To address this issue, synchronisation needs to be provided to decide when distributed virtual machines can enter into the mission phase at the same time. In line with the synchronization, all XRTJ-VMs in the same cluster network can be in the waiting stage after initialising. This phase is named the *pre-mission* phase of the XRTJ-VM.

The only difference between the mission phase of the RVM and the mission phase of the XRTJ-VM is that the invocations of pre-instantiated remote objects are allowed during the mission phase of XRTJ-VM. Furthermore, the XRTJ-VM supports the notion of real-time remote objects, real-time RMI, and simple distributed real-time threads [36] to enable the development of high-integrity real-time systems with greater flexibility.

5   Example

In this section, we present a simple example, which we hope is realistic enough to illustrate the application of our approach. Assume that there is an automated industrial production line where a number of multi-purpose robots and their controllers are employed. Each robot station (i.e. a robot and its controller) is linked over a network to the main server that will provide them with tailor-made instructions or tasks, depending on the models of products[8]. Once robot stations are set up with particular tasks, they will remain unchanged until new tasks are required to manufacture different products.

Our first distribution model, the Initialisation Distributed Environment described in Section 4.1, can be utilized in this situation, minimizing complexity in program analysis and in the implementation of underlying systems. In this manner, dependable software can be developed using our restricted programming model (i.e. the Ravenscar-Java profile), and static program safety and timing analysis techniques integrated in the XRTJ-Analyser. In the initialisation phase of all the robot stations, they will be given specific tasks by the main server by means of RMI. Having passed the initial phase, all the robots can begin their assigned operations, but are not allowed to invoke remote methods any more. A brief list of pseudo code for the robot controller is shown in Figure 5.

However, there are many other situations where robot controllers need to communicate with the server while in operation. For instance, a robot may inspect products using an overhead camera, send images to the server and require real-time feedback, assuming that the server has more powerful processors and resources to process images and distinguish faulty goods. In such cases, our second distribution model, the Mission Distributed Environment (see Section 4.2) is a valid approach. As with the code given in Figure 5, robot stations may invoke remote methods in the initialisation phase, as well as in the mission phase to cooperate with the server in a real-time manner as explained in Section 4.2. The pre-mission phase may be required to synchronize operations of the robots. However, in this more tolerant model of system distribution, static timing and schedulability analysis become more challenging, thus as we discussed briefly in Section 3.4 a holistic schedulability analysis should be performed to obtain response times of real-time threads communicating across a network.

6   Related Work

A consortium of European companies and research institutes have been working on a high-integrity distributed deterministic Java environment called HIDOORS [34]. The targeted applications of HIDOORS are similar to ours, but the project is mainly based on the Real-Time Core Extension specification [9], whereas our project is in line with the Real-Time Specification for Java [5]. However, there is a limited amount of information available on the HIDOORS project, and it is

---

[8] Robots need to be able to handle different models or versions of products manufactured in volume.

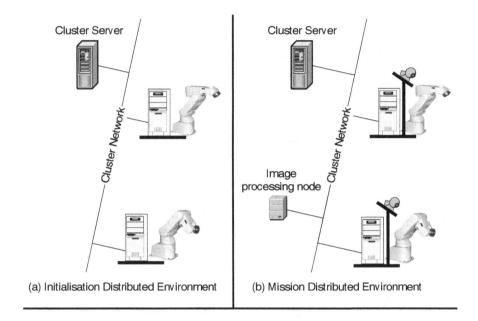

(a) Initialisation Distributed Environment   (b) Mission Distributed Environment

```
import ravenscar.*;
...
public class RobotController extends Initializer {
  public void run() {                    // Initialisation routine
    // Get Server's instructions/tasks via RMI
    ...
    // Set up real-time threads and sporadic event handlers
    // with appropriate parameters. For example,
    PeriodicThread robotRoutine1 = new PeriodicThread (
      new PriorityParameters(10),    // Priority:10
      new PeriodicParameters(
        new AbsoluteTime(0, 0),        // Start time
        new RelativeTime(5333, 0)     // Period
      ),
      new Runnable() {                    // Application logic
        public void run() {
          // Logic for the robot controller
          // Here, real-time RMI may be used
              in the mission distributed environment
          ...
          // Events may be fired
        };
      }
    );
    robotRoutine1.start();              // Start of Mission Phase!
  }

  public static void main (String [] args) {
    RobotController init = new RobotController();
    init.start();
  }
}
...
```

Fig. 5. An industrial automation environment

not clear how program safety analysis and timing analysis can be carried out in their preliminary report [34]. It should be noted that the HIDOORS project has attempted to provide a predictable implementation of the full Java langauge, whereas our project relies on the Ravenscar-Java profile.

Moreover, there has been considerable work in the area of formal verification of Java programs and bytecode, and Hartel and Moreau [15] systematically review most of this. Of particular interest to us are the verification techniques for Java Card applications based on the J2ME architecture [31], and Leroy [24], who recently developed an efficient on-card bytecode verifier. Leroy's approach is superior to other existing work in that it requires much less memory at run-time, and it handles additional features of the Java language (e.g. subroutines). Although our work does not directly deal with formal verification techniques at the moment, we feel encouraged by such developments, and may be able to incorporate them into our XRTJ-Analyser in the future.

7 Current Status

Currently we are modifying the Kopi Java compiler [20] to facilitate development of the XRTJ-Compiler. Our prototype XRTJ-Compiler can extract annotations from the source code and produces XAC files during compilation. The implementation of our prototype involved modifications to abstract syntax trees in order to map the annotation to the associated Java bytecodes. The prototype shows the feasibility of providing extra information that cannot be expressed in both Java programs and Java bytecode for static analysis tools. We are also working on the XRTJ-Compiler in order to provide a virtual machine timing model of a particular virtual machine automatically for the portable WCET analysis.

In addition, program safety and timing analysis tools are under development and will be integrated into the XRTJ-Analyser. The goal of the XRTJ-Analyser is to provide a user friendly graphic interface for the static analysis environment in future. We are also working on the reference implementation of RTSJ (RTSJ-RI), which is released by TimeSys [32], on Linux platform. A number of modifications will be conducted on the RTSJ-RI to be able to support mechanisms enforced both functionally and temporally correct results of applications in the distributed run-time system.

We have also created a website (http://www.xrtj.org) on which the most up-to-date information on this project can be found.

8 Conclusion and Future Work

In this paper, we have presented an overview of the XRTJ environment that is expected to facilitate the development of distributed high-integrity real-time systems based on Java technology. The three main aims of the XRTJ are to develop a predictable programming model, a sophisticated static analysis environment, and a reliable distributed run-time architecture.

Bearing these aims in mind, we have addressed several of the problematical features of the Java language, its run-time architecture, and the Real-Time Specification for Java. Our novel approaches include the Ravenscar-Java profile, program-safety and timing analysis techniques, and a distributed run-time environment. However, the profile may be supported by different architectures, and the analysis techniques are versatile enough to apply to other programming models. We have also raised some important issues in the area of distributed high-integrity systems, and presented how we can deal with them by defining two distributed run-time models, i.e. Initialisation Distributed Environment and Mission Distributed Environment, where safe and timely operations will be supported.

There are also some open issues, including design methodologies and tools; these should facilitate formal verification of systems at design stage. We intend to work towards these issues in the course of our implementation. We consequently feel confident that the XRTJ environment will provide a logical and practical base for future high-integrity real-time systems.

Acknowledgements. The authors would like to thank Dr. Guillem Bernat and Dr. Steve King for their contribution to many of the ideas expressed in this paper.

References

1. D. Bacon and P. Sweeney. Fast Static Analysis of C++ Virtual Function Calls. *Proceedings of the ACM Conference on Obejct-oriented Programming Systems, Languages, and Applications (OOPSLA'96)*, October 1996. San Jose, California.
2. I. Bate, G. Bernat, G. Murphy, and P. Puschner. Low-Level Analysis of a Portable Java Byte Code WCET Analysis Framework. *In 6th IEEE Real-Time Computing Systems and Applications RTCSA-2000*, pages 39–48, December 2000.
3. S. Bentley. The Utilisation of the Java Language in Safety Critical System Development. MSc dissertation, Department of Computer Science, University of York, 1999.
4. G. Bernat, A. Burns, and A. Wellings. Portable Worst-Case Execution Time Analysis Using Java Byte Code. *In proc. 6th Euromicro conference on Real-Time Systems*, pages 81–88, June 2000.
5. G. Bollella, J. Gosling, B. M. Brosgol, P. Dibble, S. Furr, D. Hardin, and M. Turnbull. *Real-Time Specification for Java*. Addison Wesley, 2000.
6. G. Brat, K. Havelund, S. Park, and W. Visser. Java PathFinder- Second generation of a Java model checker. *In Proc. of Post-CAV Workshop on Advances in Verification*, 2000.
7. L. Carnahan and M. Ruark, (eds.). Requriements for Real-Time Extensions for the Java Platform. NIST Special publications 500-243, National Institute of Standard and Technology, http://www.nist.gov/rt-java, September 1999.
8. J.-D. Choi, M. Gupta, M. J. Serrano, V. C. Sreedhar, and S. P. Midkiff. Escape Analysis for Java. *Proceedings of the Conference on Object-Oriented Programming Systems, Languages, and Applications - OOPSLA*, pages 1–19, 1999.

9. J. Consortium. Real-Time Core Extensions for Java platform. *International J Consortium Specification*, Revision 1.0.14, September 2000. http://www.j-consortium.org/rtjwg/.

10. M. de Miguel. Solutions to Make Java-RMI Time Predictable. *Proceedings of the 4th IEEE International Symposium on Object-Oriented Real-Time Distributed Computing ISORC-2001*, pages 379–386, 2001.

11. J. Dean, D. Grove, and C. Chambers. Optimisation of Object-Oriented programs using Static Class Hierarchy Analysis. *ECOOP' 95 Conference Proceedings*, Springer Verlag LNCS 952:77–101, 1995.

12. D. Detlefs and O. Agesen. Inlining of Virtual Methods. *ECOOP' 99 Conference Proceedings*, Springer Verlag LNCS 1628:258–277, 1999.

13. J. Engblom, A. Ermedahl, and P. Altenbernd. Facilitating Worst-Case Execution Times Analysis for Optimized Code. *In Proc. of the 10th Euromicro Real-Time Systems Workshop*, June 1998.

14. J. Gosling, B. Joy, G. Steele, and G. Bracha. *Java Language Specification*. Addison-Wesley, 2nd. edition, 2000.

15. P. H. Hartel and L. Moreau. Formalizing the Safety of Java, the Java Virtual Machine, and Java Card. *ACM Computing Surveys*, 33(4):517–588, 2001.

16. H. Hetcht, M. Hecht, and S. Graff. Review Guidelines for Software Languages for Use in Nuclear Power Plant Systems. NUREG/CR- 6463, U.S. Nuclear Regulatory Commission, http://fermi.sohar.com/J1030/index.htm, 1997.

17. E. Y.-S. Hu, G. Bernat, and A. J. Wellings. Addressing Dynamic Dispatching Issues in WCET Analysis for Object-Oriented Hard Real-Time Systems. *Proceedings of the 5th IEEE International Symposium on Object-Oriented Real-Time Distributed Computing ISORC-2002*, pages 109–116, April 2002.

18. E. Y.-S. Hu, G. Bernat, and A. J. Wellings. A Static Timing Analysis Environment Using Java Architecture for Safety Critical Real-Time Systems. *Proceedings of the 7th IEEE International Workshop on Object-Oriented Real-Time Dependable Systems WORDS-2002*, pages 77–84, January 2002.

19. M. Hughes, M. Shoffner, and D. Hamner. *Java Network Programming*. Manning, 2nd. edition, October 1999.

20. Kopi. The Kopi Project. DMS Decision Management Systems Gmb. Hhttp://www.dms.at/kopi/.

21. J. Kwon, A. Wellings, and S. King. A Safe Mobile Code Representation and Runtime Architecture for High-Integrity Real-Time Java Programs. *Work-in-Progress proceedings of the 22nd IEEE Real-Time Systems Symposium*, pages 37–40, 2001.

22. J. Kwon, A. Wellings, and S. King. Assessment of the Java Programming Language for Use in High Integrity Systems. Technical Report YCS 341, Department of Computer Science, University of York, http://www.cs.york.ac.uk/ftpdir/reports/YCS-2002-341.pdf, 2002.

23. J. Kwon, A. Wellings, and S. King. Ravenscar-Java: A High Integrity Profile for Real-Time Java. *Proceedings of Java Grande-ISCOPE 2002*, pages 131–140, November 2002.

24. X. Leroy. On-Card Bytecode Verification for Java Card. *Springer-Verlag LNCS*, 2140:150–164, 2001.

25. J. C. Palencia and M. G. Harbour. Exploiting precedence relations in the schedulability analysis of distributed real-time systems. *In Proc. of the 20st IEEE Real-Time Systems symposium (RTSS)*, pages 328–339, 1999.

26. W. Pugh. Fixing the Java Memory Model. *Proceedings of Java Grande Conference 1999*, pages 89–98, 1999.

27. P. Puschner and A. Burns. A Review of Worst-Case Execution-Time Analysis. *Real-Time Systems*, 18(2/3):115–128, 2000.

28. P. Puschner and A. Wellings. A Profile for High-Integrity Real-Time Java Programs. *Proceedings of the 4th IEEE International Symposium on Object-Oriented Real-Time Distributed Computing ISORC-2001*, pages 15–22, 2001.

29. A. Roychoudhury and T. Mitra. Specifying Multithreaded Java Semantics for Program Verification. *Proceedings of the International Conference on Software Engineering - ICSE*, pages 489–499, 2002.

30. A. Salcianu and M. Rinard. Pointer and escape analysis for multithreaded programs. *ACM SIGPLAN Notices*, 36(7):12–23, 2001.

31. Sun Microsystems. Java 2 Platform Micro Edition (J2ME) Technology for Creating Mobile Devices. White paper, Sun Microsystems, http://java.sun.com/j2me/docs/, 2002.

32. TimeSys. Real-Time Java. TimeSys. http://www.timesys.com/prodserv/java/.

33. K. Tindell and J. Clark. Holistic Schedulability Analysis for Distributed Hard Real-Time Systems. *Microprocessing and Microprogramming - Euromicro Journal (Special Issue on Parallel Embedded Real-Time Systems)*, 40:117–134, 1994.

34. J. Ventura, F. Siebert, A. Walter, and J. Hunt. HIDOORS - A high integrity distributed deterministic Java environment. *Proceedings of the 7th IEEE International Workshop on Object-Oriented Real-Time Dependable Systems WORDS-2002*, pages 113–118, January 2002.

35. A. Vrchoticky. Compilation Support for Fine-Grained Execution Time Analysis. *In Proc. of the ACM SIGPLAN Wrokshop on Language, Compiler and Tool Support for Real-Time Systems*, 1994.

36. A. Wellings, R. Clark, D. Jensen, and D. Wells. A Framework for Integrating the Real-Time Specification for Java and Java's Remote Method Invocation. *Proceedings of the 5th IEEE International Symposium on Object-Oriented Real-Time Distributed Computing ISORC-2002*, pages 13–22, April 2002.

Quasi-Dynamic Scheduling for the Synthesis of Real-Time Embedded Software with Local and Global Deadlines

Pao-Ann Hsiung[1], Cheng-Yi Lin[1], and Trong-Yen Lee[2]

[1] Department of Computer Science and Information Engineering
National Chung Cheng University, Chiayi, Taiwan
hpa@computer.org
[2] Department of Electronic Engineering
National Taipei University of Technology, Taipei, Taiwan

Abstract. Often real-time embedded software is specified as a set of interacting tasks that have local deadlines on subtasks and global deadlines on each task. Currently available scheduling algorithms guarantee only a single level of deadlines, either all local or all global, but not both. We propose a *quasi-dynamic scheduling* algorithm for simultaneously guaranteeing both types of deadlines, while satisfying all precedence constraints among subtasks and among tasks. Through this scheduling procedure, we are able to formally synthesize real-time embedded software from a network of Periodic Time Petri Nets specification. Application examples, including a driver for the Master/Slave role switch in Bluetooth wireless communication devices, are given to illustrate the feasibility of the scheduling algorithm.

Keywords: Real-time embedded software, Periodic Time Petri Nets, quasi-dynamic scheduling, software synthesis, local and global deadlines

1 Introduction

Often a real-time embedded system task is composed of some constituent subtasks, each of which has its own *local deadline*, while the task itself has a *global deadline*. Current scheduling algorithms do not explicitly consider such multilevel deadlines leading to the necessity for work-around efforts. We propose a scheduling algorithm to resolve this issue and show how it can be used for synthesizing real-time embedded software specifications into actual program code.

As a motivating example depicted in Fig. 1, consider the *Modular Mobile Dispatching System* (MMDS) [19], which consists of a GPS receiver, a GIS database, a GSM communication module, and other I/O peripherals for dispatching of vehicles through a call center. Besides the local deadlines on each GPS, GIS, and GSM task, there is also a global deadline on each scenario which is composed of several tasks with precedence

---

[1] This work was supported in part by a project grant NSC91-2213-E-194-008 from the National Science Council, Taiwan.

J. Chen and S. Hong (Eds.): RTCSA 2003, LNCS 2968, pp. 229–243, 2004.

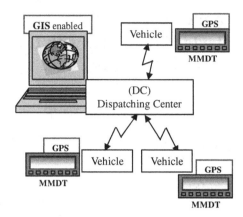

Fig. 1. Modular Mobile Dispatching System

and concurrency relationships. A typical scenario would be that of a vehicle driver encountering an emergency situation, in which the driver uses MMDS and expects to get help within 4 minutes from the time a call is made from the vehicle to the call center. Within this time span, MMDS must get GPS location information, transmit it to the call center through GSM communication, the call center must plot the driver's location on a digital map using GIS, locate the nearest help on the map, dispatch help (such as an ambulance) to the location by notifying the target help through GSM, while providing navigation guidelines through an active GIS database.

There are several issues involved in such a typical real-time scenario, as detailed in the following.

– How to determine which subtasks are concurrently enabled at any point of execution?
– How to check if each subtask completes execution within its local deadline, while satisfying all precedence constraints among the subtasks?
– How to check if each task completes execution within its global deadline?
– How to obtain an optimal schedule of all system tasks such that shortest execution time is guaranteed, if one exists?
– How to estimate the amount of memory space required for the execution of a real-time embedded software system?

Corresponding to each of the above issues, we propose a set of solutions in the form of a scheduling method called *Quasi-Dynamic Scheduling* (QDS), which incorporates the respective solutions as briefly described in the following. Details will be given when the algorithm is described in Section 4.

– *Concurrently Enabled Group*: We maintain a group of concurrently enabled subtasks, while the system's behavior is statically simulated to satisfy all precedence relationships.
– *Tentative Schedulability Check*: Since the group of concurrently enabled subtasks changes dynamically with system execution, its schedulability can be checked only tentatively for the current group.

- *Global System Timer*: A global system timer is maintained that keeps count of the current total amount of processor time taken by the execution of all tasks.
- *Pruned Reachability Tree*: Because schedulability checks are only tentative for a group of subtasks, a reachability tree is created so that an optimal schedule can be found. Heuristics are applied to prune the tree on-the-fly while it is being created.
- *Maximum Memory Estimation*: Using various memory estimation techniques, both static and dynamic memory space allocations are statically counted, including memory spaces for both local and global variables.

Basically, quasi-dynamic scheduling is a combination of quasi-static scheduling and dynamic scheduling. Data dependent branch executions are statically decomposed into different behavior configurations and quasi-statically scheduled [20]. For each quasi-statically decomposed behavior configuration, dynamic scheduling is employed to satisfy all local deadlines of each subtask, all precedence constraints among subtasks, and all global deadlines of each task.

To illustrate the importance of this research result, consider how existing scheduling approaches must be applied to a system with both local and global deadlines. In this case, there is a need for work-around methods such as making global deadline the sum of all local deadlines in a critical path of the task. The user is burdened with the responsibility of analyzing a task and finding the critical path, a non-trivial task in some cases, apriori to scheduling. Further, this work-around method only works if the global deadline is not smaller than the sum of all local deadlines in a critical path of a task, because otherwise it would amount to restraining each local deadline, thus making an otherwise schedulable system unschedulable. In summary, the work presented here is not only a flexibility enhancement to current scheduling methods, but also a necessary effort in checking schedulability for real systems.

This article is organized as follows. In Section 2, we delve on some previous work in quasi-static scheduling and real-time scheduling related to the synthesis of real-time embedded software. In Section 3, we formulate our target problem to be solved, our system model, and give an illustrative example. In Section 4, we present our quasi-dynamic scheduling algorithm and how it is applied to the running example. Section 6 concludes the article giving some future work.

2   Previous Work

Since our target is formally synthesizing real-time embedded software, we will only discuss scheduling algorithms that have been used for this purpose.

Due to the importance of ensuring the correctness of embedded software, *formal synthesis* has emerged as a precise and efficient method for designing software in control-dominated and real-time embedded systems [6,11,20,21]. Partial software synthesis was mainly carried out for communication protocols [18], plant controllers [17], and real-time schedulers [1] because they generally exhibited regular behaviors. Only recently has there been some work on automatically generating software code for embedded systems [2,16,20], including commercial tools such as MetaH from Honeywell. In the following, we will briefly survey the existing works on the synthesis of real-time embedded software, on which our work is based.

Previous methods for the automatic synthesis of embedded software mostly do not consider temporal constraints [15,16,20,21], which results in temporally infeasible schedules and thus incorrect systems. Some recently proposed methods [11,14] explicitly take time into consideration while scheduling, but have not solved the multilevel deadlines issue. Details of each method are given in the rest of this section.

Lin [15,16] proposed an algorithm that generates a software program from a concurrent process specification through intermediate Petri-Net representation. This approach is based on the assumption that the Petri-Nets are safe, *i.e.*, buffers can store at most one data unit, which implies that it is always schedulable. The proposed method applies *quasi-static scheduling* to a set of safe Petri-Nets to produce a set of corresponding state machines, which are then mapped syntactically to the final software code.

A software synthesis method was proposed for a more general Petri-Net framework by Sgroi et al. [20]. A quasi-static scheduling (QSS) algorithm was proposed for *Free-Choice Petri Nets* (FCPN) [20]. A necessary and sufficient condition was given for a FCPN to be schedulable. Schedulability was first tested for a FCPN and then a valid schedule generated by decomposing a FCPN into a set of *Conflict-Free* (CF) components which were then individually and statically scheduled. Code was finally generated from the valid schedule.

Later, Hsiung integrated quasi-static scheduling with real-time scheduling to synthesize real-time embedded software [11]. A synthesis method for soft real-time systems was also proposed by Hsiung [12]. The free-choice restriction was first removed by Su and Hsiung in their work [21] on extended quasi-static scheduling (EQSS). Recently, Gau and Hsiung proposed a more integrated approach called time-memory scheduling [6,13] based on reachability trees.

A recently proposed *timed quasi-static scheduling* (TQSS) method [14] extends two previous works: (1) the QSS [20] method by handling non-free choices (or complex choices) that appear in system models, and (2) the EQSS [21] by adding time constraints in the system model. Further, TQSS also ensures that limited embedded memory constraints and time constraints are also satisfied. For feasible schedules, real-time embedded software code is generated as a set of communicating POSIX threads, which may then be deployed for execution by a *real-time operating system*.

Balarin et al. [2] proposed a software synthesis procedure for reactive embedded systems in the *Codesign Finite State Machine* (CFSM) [3] framework with the POLIS hardware-software codesign tool [3]. This work cannot be easily extended to other more general frameworks.

Besides synthesis of software, there are also some recent work on the verification of software in an embedded system such as the *Schedule-Verify-Map* method [8], the linear hybrid automata techniques [7,9], and the mapping strategy [5]. Recently, system parameters have also been taken into consideration for real-time software synthesis [10].

3   Real-Time Embedded Software Synthesis

Our target is the formal synthesis of real-time embedded software, with local and global deadlines, using scheduling techniques. A system is specified as a set of concurrent tasks, where each task is composed of a set of subtasks, with precedence relationships. Time constraints are classified into two categories: *local* deadlines and *global* deadlines. A local deadline is imposed on the execution of a subtask, whereas a global deadline is imposed on the execution of a task in a system model [6,13].

Previous work on software synthesis were mainly based on a subclass of the Petri net model (introduced later in Section 3.1). We also adopt the Petri net model for software requirements specification, but we associate explicit semantics to the firing time intervals, which will explained when our system model *Periodic Time Petri Net* (PTPN) is defined. Just like *Time Complex-Choice Petri Nets* (TCCPN) used in [14], PTPN places no free-choice restriction on the model expressivity and adds timing constraints on each transition, which represents a subtask. Thus, a wider domain of applications can be precisely modeled by PTPN. Details on the PTPN system model, our target problem, and an illustrative example will be described in Sections 3.1, 3.2, and 3.3, respectively.

3.1 System Model

We define PTPN as follows, where $\mathcal{N}$ is the set of positive integers.

Definition 1. *Periodic Time Petri Nets (PTPN)*
A Periodic Time Petri Net is a 5-tuple (P, T, F, M_0, τ), *where:*

- *P is a finite set of places,*
- *T is a finite set of transitions,* $P \cup T \neq \emptyset$, $P \cap T = \emptyset$, *and some of the transitions are* source *transitions, which fire periodically,*
- $F : (P \times T) \cup (T \times P) \rightarrow \mathcal{N}$ *is a weighted flow relation between places and transitions, represented by arcs. The flow relation has the following characteristics:*
    - *Synchronization at a transition is allowed between a branch arc of a choice place and another independent concurrent arc.*
    - *Synchronization at a transition is not allowed between two or more branch arcs of the same choice place.*
    - *A self-loop from a place back to itself is allowed only if there is an initial token in one of the places in the loop.*
- $M_0 : P \rightarrow N$ *is the initial marking (assignment of tokens to places), and*
- $\tau : T \rightarrow N \times (N \cup \infty)$, *i.e.,* $\tau(t) = (\alpha, \beta)$, *where* $t \in T$, α *is the* transition execution time, *and* β *is transition local deadline. We will use the abbreviations* $\tau_\alpha(t)$ *and* $\tau_\beta(t)$ *to denote the transition execution time and deadline, respectively.*   □

Graphically, a PTPN can be depicted as shown in Fig. 2, where circles represent places, vertical bars represent transitions, arrows represent arcs, black dots represent tokens, and integers labeled over arcs represent the weights as defined by F. A place with more than one outgoing transition is called a *choice* place and the transitions are said to be *conflicting*. For example, p_0 is a choice place and t_1 and t_2 are conflicting transitions in Fig. 2.

3.2 Problem Formulation

A user specifies the requirements for a real-time embedded software by a set of PTPNs. The problem we are trying to solve here is to find a construction method by which a set

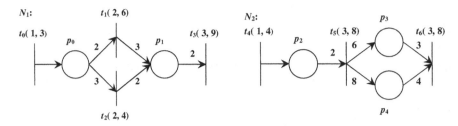

Fig. 2. Illustration Example

of PTPNs can be made feasible to execute on a single processor as a piece of software code, running under given finite memory space and time constraints. The following is a formal definition of the real-time embedded software synthesis problem.

Definition 2. *Real-Time Embedded Software Synthesis*
Given a set of PTPNs, an upper-bound on available memory space, and a set of real-time constraints such as periods and deadlines for each PTPN, a piece of real-time embedded software code is to be generated such that:

- *it can be executed on a single processor,*
- *it satisfies all the PTPN requirements, including precedence constraints and local deadlines,*
- *it satisfies all global real-time constraints, including PTPN (task) periods and deadlines, and*
- *it uses memory no more than the user-given upper-bound.*   □

As described in Section 1, there are five issues involved in solving this problem and the solutions to these issues are integrated into a quasi-dynamic scheduling method, which will be presented in Section 4. Due to page-limit, we leave out the code generation part of software synthesis [21].

3.3   Illustration Example

This is a simple toy example to illustrate how our proposed scheduling method works. The PTPN model for this example is shown in Fig. 2, which consists of two nets $N_1 = (P_1, T_1, F_1, M_{01}, \tau_1)$ and $N_2 = (P_2, T_2, F_2, M_{02}, \tau_2)$, where $P_1 = \{p_0, p_1\}$, $P_2\{p_2, p_3, p_4\}$, $T_1 = \{t_0, t_1, t_2, t_3\}$, $T_2 = \{t_4, t_5, t_6\}$, the flow relations F_1, F_2, and the firing intervals τ_1, τ_2 are obvious from the numbers on the arcs and transitions, respectively. The initial markings M_{01}, M_{02} are all empty.

4   Quasi-Dynamic Scheduling

To solve the several issues raised in Section 1 for synthesizing real-time embedded software, a *Quasi-Dynamic Scheduling* (QDS) method is proposed. QDS employs both quasi-static and dynamic scheduling techniques. Details of the QDS algorithm are presented in Tables 1, 2, 3. Rather than going into the details of each step of the algorithms, we present the main ideas as follows.

- Data dependent branch executions are statically decomposed into different behavior configurations and quasi-statically scheduled using EQSS [20,21]. (Step 1 of Table 1)
- For each quasi-statically decomposed behavior configuration, dynamic scheduling is employed to satisfy the local deadline of each subtask, all precedence constraints among subtasks, and the global deadline of each task as follows.
  - A global system clock is maintained for each schedule to record the elapse of time on the execution (firing) of each transition. Similarly, a global memory usage record is kept for each schedule.
  - To find a feasible schedule, a reachability tree is constructed in a depth-first search manner (Step 15 of Table 2), where each node represents a marking that is associated with a group of enabled transitions and each edge represents the firing of a selected transition. Exhaustive construction of the tree is avoided by pruning it under appropriate conditions (heuristics), which are described as follows.
    * *Negative Laxity*: There is not enough time left for at least one of the enabled transitions to execute until completion. (Steps 4, 5 of Table 3)
    * *Local Deadline Violation Forecast*: After a simulation-based analysis of the group of enabled transitions, if it is found that none of the transitions can be executed last in the group, then that group of transitions is not schedulable. (Steps 6–10 of Table 3)
    * *Global Deadline Violation*: The system clock has exceeded the global deadline of at least one of the PTPN. (Steps 4, 5 of Table 2)
    * *Memory Bound Violation*: The memory usage has exceeded a user-given upper bound. (Steps 6, 7 of Table 2)
  - For each node in the tree, not all successor nodes are generated. Some nodes are not generated under various conditions as described in the following. (Steps 11–25 of Table 3)
    * If there is at most only one *urgent* transition, with execution time $(\tau_\alpha(t))$ same as its remaining time $(\rho(t))$ (i.e., $\tau_\alpha(t) = \rho(t) \rightarrow$ zero laxity), then only one successor node is generated.
    * All transitions whose execution can be deferred such that even if they are the last ones to execute among the currently enabled transitions, they will still satisfy their respective deadlines, then their corresponding nodes are not generated. This heuristic is applied provided some successor node can be generated.

Some advantageous features of QDS are as follows.

- *No need of WCET analysis*: After quasi-dynamic scheduling, we have total execution time for each system schedule, which is smaller than the total worst-case execution time (WCET) of all the transitions in that schedule.

Table 1. Quasi Dynamic Scheduling

$\mathbf{QDS}(S, \mu, \psi)$
$S = \{A_i \mid A_i = (P_i, T_i, F_i, M_{i0}, \tau_i), i = 1, 2, \ldots, n\};$
μ: integer;   // maximum memory
ψ: global real-time constraints; // periods, deadlines, etc.
{
$\quad m = \mathbf{EQSS}(S, \mu, H);$ // $m = |H|$, H: EQSS schedules [21]   (1)
$\quad \text{for}(j = 0; j < m; j + +)$ {   (2)
$\quad\quad G = \mathbf{initial\_group}(H, j);$ (3)
$\quad\quad \text{if}(\mathbf{schedule\_tree}(H, G, S, \psi, \mu))\ \text{output}(H, j);$ // refer to Table 2   (4)
$\quad\quad \text{else return Unschedulable\_Error};$ (5)
$\quad$}
}

Table 2. Schedule Tree Traversal in Quasi Dynamic Scheduling

$\mathbf{schedule\_tree}(H, G, S, \psi, \mu)$
H: set of EQSS schedules;
G: group of concurrently enabled transitions;
S: set of PTPN;
ψ: global real-time constraints; // periods, deadlines, etc.
μ: integer;   // maximum memory
{
$\quad \text{if}(\mathbf{choose\_schedulable}(G, G') == \text{False}) \text{ return False};$ (1)
$\quad \text{for each transition } t \in G'$ {   (3)
$\quad\quad STime = t \to exec + G \to STime;$ (4)
$\quad\quad \text{if } (STime > deadline(\psi)) \text{ continue};$ // Global Deadline Violation   (5)
$\quad\quad SMem = t \to mem + G \to SMem;$ (6)
$\quad\quad \text{if } (SMem > \mu) \text{ continue};$ // Memory Bound Violation   (7)
$\quad\quad G'' = \mathbf{copy}(G);$ (8)
$\quad\quad G'' \to STime = STime; G'' \to SMem = SMem;$ (9)
$\quad\quad \mathbf{fire\_trans}(t);$ (10)
$\quad\quad \text{if } (\mathbf{last\_firing}(t))\ G'' = G'' \backslash \{t\};$ (11)
$\quad\quad \text{for each transition } t' \in \mathbf{successor}(t, S)$ (12)
$\quad\quad\quad G'' = G'' \cup \{t'\};$ // add newly enabled transitions   (13)
$\quad\quad \text{if}(G'' == NULL) \text{ return True};$ // end of schedule   (14)
$\quad\quad \text{if}(\mathbf{schedule\_tree}(H, G'', S, \psi, \mu)) \text{ return True};$ // DFS traversal   (15)
$\quad$}
$\quad \text{return False};$ (16)
}

- *Optimal schedules*: QDS always generates a set of optimal schedules because all feasible schedules are explored using the reachability tree.
- *Efficient scheduling*: QDS uses several different heuristics to avoid searching exhaustively in the solution space and these heuristics are proven to be helpful, but harmless, that is, they do not eliminate any optimal schedule.

Table 3. Selection of Schedulable Transitions in Quasi Dynamic Scheduling

```
choose_schedulable(G, G′)
G: group of concurrently enabled transitions, G′: group pointer
{
    G3 = G; G4 = NULL;    // G1, G2, G3, G4 : pointers to group of transitions    (1)
    while(True) {                                                                  (2)
        G1 = G2 = NULL;                                                            (3)
        for each transition t ∈ G3 {    // check remain time > execution time      (4)
            if(t → remain < t → exec) return False;                               (5)
            Gtime += t → exec;                                                     (6)
        } // end of for
        for each transition t ∈ G3 {    // divide G3 into two subgroups: G3 = G1 ∪ G2    (7)
            if(t → remain >= Gtime) G1 = G1 ∪ {t};                                (8)
            else G2 = G2 ∪ {t};    } // end of for                                (9)
        if (G1 == NULL) return False;    // no last one to fire, so stop building node    (10)
        else if (comp_group(G1, G3)) {    // G1 == G3?                            (11)
            G′ = G3;                                                              (12)
            return True; }                                                        (13)
        else {    // choose the transitions which will fire next time             (14)
            G3 = NULL;                                                            (15)
            Gtime = 0;                                                            (16)
            for each transition t ∈ G2    Gtime += t → exec;                      (17)
            for each transition t ∈ G1 {                                          (18)
                Gtime′ = Gtime + t → exec;                                        (19)
                for each transition t′ ∈ G2 {                                     (20)
                    if (t′ → remain >= Gtime′) { G3 = G3 ∪ {t}; break; } } }      (21)
            G3 = G2 ∪ G3;                                                         (22)
            if (comp_group(G3, G4)) {                                             (23)
                G′ = G3; return True; }                                           (24)
            G4 = G3;    } // end else                                             (25)
    } // end of while
}
```

- *Multi-objective optimizations*: Since both time and memory constraints are considered during scheduling, QDS allows a user to easily optimize the resulting schedules in terms of either shortest schedule time or smallest memory usage. Trade-offs are inevitable between these two objectives, and QDS leaves such trade-off analysis to the user.
- *All issues solved*: All the issues presented in Section 1 are solved by QDS.

Limitations of QDS are as follows.

- *Predefined transition parameters*: Execution time and local deadlines must be user given or derived from some analysis of the software code represented by a transition.
- *Interrupt handling*: QDS must be extended to handle interrupts. This part of the work is still ongoing and the basic idea is to include the set of allowable interrupts to the parameters of each transition and to consider the worst-case of interrupts arriving

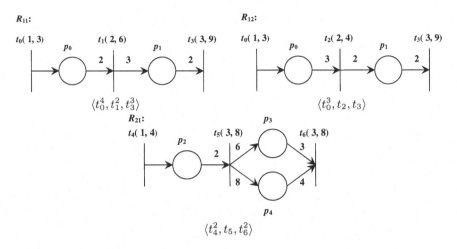

Fig. 3. EQSS schedules for Illustration Example

during the execution of each transition. Some heuristics can be applied here to avoid obtaining too large an estimate.

- *Different periods and deadlines*: Currently, in QDS it is assumed that all PTPN have the same periods and deadlines. This restriction can be easily removed by scheduling a time slot that spans the least common multiple of all periods.
- *Different phases (arrival times)*: QDS cannot handle different phases or arrival times of PTPN. Currently, it is assumed that they all arrive at the same time.

To illustrate how QDS works, we use the running illustrative example given in Fig. 2. First of all, EQSS is applied to the two PTPN. The resulting conflict-free components and corresponding schedule for each of those components are given in Fig. 3. There are totally three such components: R_{11} and R_{12} for N_1 and R_{21} for N_2. But, the EQSS schedule for each component has some degree of choices in the repeated firings, for example in the schedule for R_{11}, $\langle t_0^4, t_1^2, t_3^3 \rangle$, it can also be scheduled as $\langle t_0^2, t_1, t_3, t_0^2, t_1, t_3 \rangle$. QDS explores this degree of choices for satisfying the local deadlines and global deadlines of each system configuration, where a system configuration is a combination of one conflict-free component from each PTPN. Thus, there are totally two system configurations for this example, namely $\{R_{11}, R_{21}\}$ and $\{R_{12}, R_{21}\}$.

On applying QDS to this example, we found that it is indeed schedulable and satisfies all local and global deadlines. Though there are two reachability trees for the two system configurations, we present only one of them for illustration. The reachability tree for $\{R_{12}, R_{21}\}$ is presented in a tabular form in Table 4. The first column is the index of the nodes in the tree and the last column gives the child nodes of the corresponding node from the first column. G is the group of concurrently enabled transitions in the marking represented by that node. α is the execution time (earliest-firing time) of each transition. ρ is the time left before a transition deadline is reached. $STime$ and $SMem$ are the current global records of system time and memory, respectively. $G' \subseteq G$ is the subset transitions that are chosen for possible scheduling in the generation of successor

Table 4. QDS scheduling for R_{12} and R_{21}

node	G	α	$\rho = \beta - now$	STime	SMem	fireable?	fired!	next node
0	t_0	1	3	0	0	Yes	t_0	1
	t_4	1	4			Yes		
1	t_0	1	3	1	1	Yes	t_0	2
	t_4	1	3			Yes		
2	t_0	1	3	2	2	Yes	t_0	3
	t_4	1	2			Yes		
3	t_2	2	4	3	3	No		
	t_4	1	1			Yes	t_4	4
4	t_2	2	3	4	4	Yes	t_2	5
	t_4	1	4			Yes		
5	t_3	3	9	6	3	No		
	t_4	1	2			Yes	t_4	6
6	t_3	3	8	7	4	Yes	t_3	7
	t_5	3	8			Yes		
7	t_5	3	5	10	2	Yes	t_5	8
8	t_6	3	8	13	14	Yes	t_6	9
9	t_6	3	8	16	7	Yes	t_6	Schedule Found!
Schedule Time & Memory				19	14			

Table 5. EQSS Schedules for Bluetooth M/S Role Switch

PTPN	$|T|$	$|P|$	d_i	π_i	$|Q|$	EQSS Schedules	Time
Host A	7	5	45	45	4	$A_{11} = \langle t_0, t_1, t_2, t_4, t_5, t_6 \rangle$,	$[20, 41]$
						$A_{12} = \langle t_0, t_1, t_2, t_4, t_7 \rangle$	$[8, 40]$
						$A_{13} = \langle t_0, t_1, t_3, t_5, t_6 \rangle$	$[18, 34]$
						$A_{14} = \langle t_0, t_1, t_3, t_7 \rangle$	$[6, 33]$
HC/LM A	21	15	45	45	6	$A_{21} = \langle t_0, t_1, t_2, t_4, t_6, t_7, t_{10}, t_{11}, t_{12}, t_{14} \rangle$	$[17, 35]$
						$A_{22} = \langle t_0, t_1, t_3, t_5, t_6, t_8, t_{10}, t_{14} \rangle$	$[15, 29]$
						$A_{23} = \langle t_0, t_1, t_2, t_4, t_6, t_7, t_{10}, t_{11}, t_{13}, t_{15}, t_{16}, t_{18} \rangle$	$[20, 40]$
						$A_{24} = \langle t_0, t_1, t_2, t_4, t_7, t_{11}, t_{13}, t_{15}, t_{16}, t_{18} \rangle$	$[18, 37]$
						$A_{25} = \langle t_0, t_1, t_2, t_4, t_6, t_7, t_{10}, t_{11}, t_{13}, t_{15}, t_{17}, t_{19}, t_{20} \rangle$	$[21, 42]$
						$A_{26} = \langle t_0, t_1, t_3, t_5, t_6, t_9, t_{15}, t_{17}, t_{19}, t_{20} \rangle$	$[18, 35]$
Host B	7	5	45	45	4	Same as for Host A	
HC/LM B	21	15	45	45	6	Same as for HC/LM A	

$|T|$: number of transitions, $|P|$: number of places, d_i: PTPN deadline,
π_i: PTPN period, $|Q|$: number of EQSS schedules.

nodes. The 8th column consists of the actual transitions that are fired and thus also gives the schedule that is generated by QDS. At the end of Table 4, it is found that the system configuration is schedulable. The total time and memory used are 19 time units and 14 memory units, respectively. Similarly, when QDS is applied to the other system configuration $\{R_{11}, R_{21}\}$, it is schedulable and the total time and memory used are 28 time units and 18 memory units, respectively.

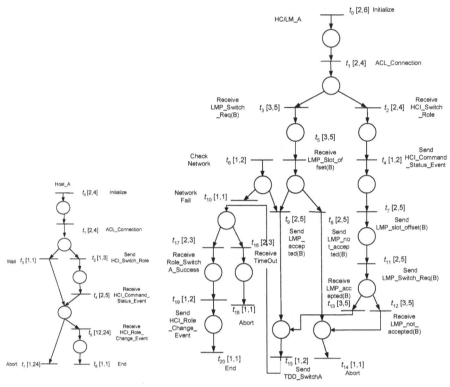

Fig. 4. PTPN model of Host A
in Bluetooth M/S switch

Fig. 5. PTPN model of HC/LM A in Bluetooth M/S switch

5   Application Example

The QDS method for software synthesis was applied to several real-world applications such as ATM virtual private network scheduling, Bluetooth wireless communication protocol, motor speed control system, and medic-care system. For purpose of illustration, we describe one of the examples, which is a real-time embedded software driver for the master-slave role switch between two wireless Bluetooth devices. In the Bluetooth wireless communication protocol [4], a *piconet* is formed of one master device and seven active slave devices.

In our PTPN model of an M/S switch between two devices A and B, there are totally four Petri nets as follows. Host of device A as shown in Figure 4, Host Control / Link Manager (HC/LM) of device A as shown in Figure 5, host of device B similar to that for A, and HC/LM of device B similar to that for A. Timings for the transitions are allocated as follows. A Bluetooth device times out after 32 slots of $625\mu s$ each, which is totally 0.02 second. Thus in our model, we take 0.01 second as one unit of time.

The proposed QDS algorithm (Table 1), was applied to the given system of four PTPN. First, EQSS is applied. The results of EQSS scheduling are given in Table 5.

Table 6. QDS scheduling for A_{11} and A_{25}

node	G	α	$\rho = \beta - now$	STime	SMem	fireable?	fired!	next node
0	$t_{1,0}$	2	4	0	0	No		
	$t_{2,0}$	2	6			No		
	$t_{2,6}$	1	2			Yes	$t_{2,6}$	1
1	$t_{1,0}$	2	3	1	1	No		
	$t_{2,0}$	2	5			No		
	$t_{2,10}$	1	1			Yes	$t_{2,10}$	2
2	$t_{1,0}$	2	2	2	0	Yes	$t_{1,0}$	3
	$t_{2,0}$	2	4			No		
3	$t_{1,1}$	2	4	4	1	No		
	$t_{2,0}$	2	2			Yes	$t_{2,0}$	4
4	$t_{1,1}$	2	2	6	2	Yes	$t_{1,1}$	5
	$t_{2,1}$	2	4			No		
5	$t_{1,2}$	1	3	8	2	No		
	$t_{2,1}$	2	2			Yes	$t_{2,1}$	6
6	$t_{1,2}$	1	1	10	2	Yes	$t_{1,2}$	7
	$t_{2,2}$	2	4			No		
7	$t_{2,2}$	2	3	11	2	Yes	$t_{2,2}$	8
	$t_{1,4}$	2	5			No		
8	$t_{2,4}$	1	2	13	2	Yes	$t_{2,4}$	9
	$t_{1,4}$	2	3			No		
9	$t_{1,4}$	2	2	14	2	Yes	$t_{1,4}$	10
	$t_{2,7}$	2	5			No		
10	$t_{2,7}$	2	3	16	2	Yes	$t_{2,7}$	11
	$t_{1,5}$	12	24			No		
11	$t_{2,11}$	2	5	18	2	Yes	$t_{2,11}$	12
	$t_{1,5}$	12	22			No		
12	$t_{2,13}$	3	5	20	2	Yes	$t_{2,13}$	13
	$t_{1,5}$	12	20			No		
13	$t_{2,15}$	1	2	23	2	Yes	$t_{2,15}$	14
	$t_{1,5}$	12	17			No		
14	$t_{2,17}$	2	3	24	2	Yes	$t_{2,17}$	15
	$t_{1,5}$	12	16			No		
15	$t_{2,19}$	1	2	26	2	Yes	$t_{2,19}$	16
	$t_{1,5}$	12	14			No		
16	$t_{1,5}$	12	13	27	2	No		
	$t_{2,20}$	1	1			Yes	$t_{2,20}$	17
17	$t_{1,5}$	12	12	28	1	Yes	$t_{1,5}$	18
18	$t_{1,6}$	1	1	40	1	Yes	$t_{1,6}$	Schedule Found!
	Schedule Time & Memory			41	2			

The last column in Table 5 gives the best-case and worst-case execution times of each net EQSS schedule. Further, reachability trees were constructed for all the 24 different configurations. All deadlines and periods are given as 45 time units. For illustration purpose, the application QDS to one of the configurations $\{A_{11}, A_{25}\}$ is given in Table 6, which has a schedule time of 41 time units and memory usage of 2 memory units. It is finally derived that the system is schedulable.

6   Conclusion

No more workarounds are needed when both local and global deadlines are to be satisfied because quasi-dynamic scheduling (QDS) has solved this problem in the context of real-time embedded software synthesis. QDS has integrated static and dynamic scheduling to efficiently derive an optimal schedule time or memory based on some simple heuristics.

Application examples show that we can avoid the worst case analysis when QDS can used for scheduling. Through a real-world example on the master/slave role switch between two wireless Bluetooth devices, we have shown the feasibility of our approach. In the future, we plan to extend QDS in several ways: to handle dissimilar periods and deadlines, to handle interrupts during scheduling, and to estimate transition parameters such as execution time.

References

1. K. Altisen, G. Gössler, A. Pneuli, J. Sifakis, S. Tripakis, and S. Yovine. A framework for scheduler synthesis. In *Real-Time System Symposium (RTSS'99)*. IEEE Computer Society Press, 1999.
2. F. Balarin and M. Chiodo. Software synthesis for complex reactive embedded systems. In *Proc. of International Conference on Computer Design (ICCD'99)*, pages 634 – 639. IEEE CS Press, October 1999.
3. F. Balarin and et al. *Hardware-software Co-design of Embedded Systems: the POLIS approach*. Kluwer Academic Publishers, 1997.
4. J. Bray and C. F. Sturman. *Bluetooth: Connect Without Cables*. Prentice Hall, 2001.
5. J.-M. Fu, T.-Y. Lee, P.-A. Hsiung, and S.-J. Chen. Hardware-software timing coverification of distributed embedded systems. *IEICE Trans. on Information and Systems*, E83-D(9):1731–1740, September 2000.
6. C.-H. Gau and P.-A. Hsiung. Time-memory scheduling and code generation of real-time embedded software. In *Proc. of the 8th International Conference on Real-Time Computing Systems and Applications (RTCSA'02, Tokyo, Japan)*, pages 19–27, March 2002.
7. P.-A. Hsiung. Timing coverification of concurrent embedded real-time systems. In *Proc. of the 7th IEEE/ACM International Workshop on Hardware Software Codesign (CODES'99)*, pages 110 – 114. ACM Press, May 1999.
8. P.-A. Hsiung. Embedded software verification in hardware-software codesign. *Journal of Systems Architecture — the Euromicro Journal*, 46(15):1435–1450, December 2000.
9. P.-A. Hsiung. Hardware-software timing coverification of concurrent embedded real-time systems. *IEE Proceedings — Computers and Digital Techniques*, 147(2):81–90, March 2000.
10. P.-A. Hsiung. Synthesis of parametric embedded real-time systems. In *Proc. of the International Computer Symposium (ICS'00), Workshop on Computer Architecture (ISBN 957-02-7308-9)*, pages 144–151, December 2000.
11. P.-A. Hsiung. Formal synthesis and code generation of embedded real-time software. In *Proc. of the 9th ACM/IEEE International Symposium on Hardware Software Codesign (CODES'01, Copenhagen, Denmark)*, pages 208 – 213. ACM Press, April 2001.
12. P.-A. Hsiung. Formal synthesis and control of soft embedded real-time systems. In *Proc. of IFIP International Conference on Formal Techniques for Networked and Distributed Systems (FORTE'01)*, pages 35–50. Kluwer Academic Publishers, August 2001.
13. P.-A. Hsiung and C.-H. Gau. Formal synthesis of real-time embedded software by time-memory scheduling of colored time Petri nets. In *Proc. of the Workshop on Theory and Practice of Timed Systems (TPTS'2002, Grenoble, France), Electronic Notes in Theoretical Computer Science (ENTCS)*, April 2002.
14. P.-A. Hsiung, T.-Y. Lee, and F.-S. Su. Formal synthesis and code generation of real-time embedded software using timed quasi-static scheduling. In *Proc. of the 9th Asia-Pacific Software Engineering Conference (APSEC)*, pages 395–404. IEEE CS Press, December 2002.
15. B. Lin. Efficient compilation of process-based concurrent programs without run-time scheduling. In *Proc. of Design Automation and Test Europe (DATE'98)*, pages 211 – 217. ACM Press, February 1997.

16. B. Lin. Software synthesis of process-based concurrent programs. In *Proc. of Design Automation Conference (DAC'98)*, pages 502 – 505. ACM Press, June 1998.

17. O. Maler, A. Pnueli, and J. Sifakis. On the synthesis of discrete controllers for timed systems. In *22th Annual Symposium on Theoretical Aspects of Computer Scoence (STACS'95)*, volume 980, pages 229 – 242. Lecture Notes in Computer Science, Springer Verlag, March 1995.

18. P. Merlin and G.V. Bochman. On the construction of submodule specifications and communication protocols. *ACM Trans. on Programming Languages and Systems*, 5(1):1 – 75, January 1983.

19. W.-B. See, P.-A. Hsiung, T.-Y. Lee, and S.-J. Chen. Modular mobile dispatching system (MMDS) and logistics. In *Proc. of the 2002 Annual Conference on National Defense Integrated Logistics Support (ILS)*, pages 365–371, August 2002.

20. M. Sgroi, L. Lavagno, Y. Watanabe, and A. Sangiovanni-Vincentelli. Synthesis of embedded software using free-choice Petri nets. In *Proc. Design Automation Conference (DAC'99)*. ACM Press, June 1999.

21. F.-S. Su and P.-A. Hsiung. Extended quasi-static scheduling for formal synthesis and code generation of embedded software. In *Proc. of the 10th IEEE/ACM International Symposium on Hardware/Software Codesign (CODES'02, Colorado, USA)*, pages 211–216. ACM Press, May 2002.

Framework-Based Development of Embedded Real-Time Systems

Hui-Ming Su and Jing Chen

Department of Electrical Engineering
National Cheng Kung University, Tainan city, Taiwan, R.O.C.
ken@rtpc06.ee.ncku.edu.tw, jchen@mail.ncku.edu.tw

Abstract. This paper presents a framework-oriented approach to efficient development of embedded real-time systems. A framework is an architectural pattern in development approaches that, based on object-oriented techniques, provides a reusable template to extend applications. The creation of framework is quite difficult although a well-defined framework is powerful in significantly improving the productivity of developers. The basic concept underlying this approach is that applications can be developed effectively through integrating domain-specific design patterns. The presented framework is developed with three mature design patterns, namely task scheduling pattern, ceiling priority pattern and static allocation pattern, as a basis to address the common issues such as task scheduling and resource management in the development of embedded real-time systems. The task scheduling pattern provides a priority-based scheduling mechanism. The ceiling priority pattern implements the ceiling priority protocol to resolve the problems of unbounded blocking while the static allocation pattern provides a mechanism on memory optimization for objects and message queues used by tasks. Developers using this framework simply need to add required application-specific classes and customize some component classes according to the design specifications.

1 Introduction

While applications based on embedded real-time system products are being widely used today, successful deployment of embedded real-time systems and applications depends on reduced development cost and time-to-market in which the degree of reuse and tailorability are important factors. The main issues in developing embedded real-time systems arise from the complexity of managing data resources and scheduling of tasks with interaction. Scheduling tasks with timing constraints has been the most important issue. Although cyclic executive is one popular approach to address both the issues of scheduling and resource contention at the same time, priority-based scheduling has been a widely accepted approach, especially when concerns such as flexibility, reusability and reconfigurability are taken into account [1]. Priority-based task scheduling relies on proper priority assignment. The priority of a task can be fixed and remains unchanged during its execution such as Rate Monotonic Schedul

J. Chen and S. Hong (Eds.): RTCSA 2003, LNCS 2968, pp. 244–253, 2004.
© Springer-Verlag Berlin Heidelberg 2004

ing (RMS) [2]. In dynamic priority systems, a task is assigned its priority at run-time based on some strategy such as Earliest Deadline First (EDF) [2].

When there are interactions among tasks, more complicated issues arise. For example, priority inversion occurs when sharing resources in multitasking environment [19]. If a low priority task locks a resource and then is preempted by a high priority task that needs the locked resource, the high priority task it is blocked from executing by the low priority task. Worse, tasks with intermediate priority may preempt the low priority task thereby lengthens the blocking time experienced by the blocked high priority task. This blocking, if not bounded can cause missing deadline. The famous priority-inheritance protocol is developed to solve this problem [3]. As another example, heap fragmentation is one problem in managing data resources. Fragmentation can arise when different sized blocks are allocated and released asynchronously from a heap. Overtime, the free space on the heap might fragment into small blocks. It might lead to allocation failures when a request is made which exceeds the size of the largest available block even though more than enough memory is available.

Task scheduling, unbounded blocking and memory fragmentation are just some of the common issues in developing embedded real-time systems. There have been solutions proposed to individually address these problems. In this paper, a framework-based approach is presented as an integrated resolution. A framework [4] is an architectural pattern that provides an extensible template for applications within a domain. The basic concept underlying this framework-based approach is that applications can be developed effectively through integrating domain-specific design patterns. Within the OO arena, an object-oriented application framework (OOAF) is a reusable, "semi-complete" application that can be specialized to produce customized applications [5]. OOAFs are application-domain-specific reuse methods proposed for general-purpose systems. However there are relatively few works on applying framework to the design of an embedded real-time system.

This paper is organized into the following sections. Section 2 discusses some related works. The concept of our framework construct is presented in Section 3 by elaborating the framework-based design approach with pattern views and class views. Section 4 describes briefly how to apply the framework construct. Finally, Section 5 gives a summary of this work.

2   Related Works

Framework is not a new idea. There have been quite a few literatures on various aspects of framework. However, there appears relatively few works on applying framework to the development of embedded real-time systems. In the following, three frameworks proposed for real-time systems are discussed.

The Object-Oriented Real-Time System Framework (OORTSF) presented by Kuan, See and Chen [6] is a relatively simple framework-based developing environment. Their framework construct was built upon the classes used in real-time application development without notions of design patterns. Since no design patterns specific to developing real-time system application were proposed, it might result in difficult comprehension of the collaboration among the classes. In addition, applying OORTSF in developing a system might introduce complication when the design patterns are unclear. The flexibility of specifying real-time objects, the ease of using OORTSF, the benefits of applying OORTSF, and other issues related to OOAFs appeared unclear from the work.

RTFrame is an application framework solution developed especially for real-time system design by Hsiung [7]. It consists of five components, namely Specifier, Extractor, Scheduler, Allocator, and Generator. Together with RTFrame, several design patterns for developing real-time systems were presented. It therefore has a clear process for designing an embedded real-time system. However, the dependency relationship between those components needs to be clearly identified. The circumstance emerges easily when using RTFrame to design a new application and developers must be careful in coping this issue.

Hsiung *et al* presented VERTAF through integration of three technologies, namely, object-oriented technology, software component technology and formal verification technology [8]. It uses formal verification technology for model check in design phase to guarantee the system correctness. VERTAF is an improvement of RTFrame. However, the same issue exists as in RTFrame.

3 Framework-Based Design

A framework is rendered as a stereotypically package in UML [4]. A framework is composed of a set of elements, including, but certainly not limited to, classes, interfaces, use cases, components, nodes, collaborations, and even other frameworks. Frameworks have been in many cases target technology for developing embedded real-time systems. However, based on the fact that embedded systems are application-specific, it is not easy, if not impossible, to develop a general framework that can be applied to all kinds of embedded real-time systems. The framework proposed in this paper is designed for the environment of single processor running a multitasking preemptive kernel and employing priority-based scheduling. It is presented in the following from two structural aspects: the pattern view and the class view.

3.1 Pattern View

A pattern is defined as a solution to a problem that is common to a variety of contexts in software development [4]. The pattern view presents the framework that encompasses a collection of patterns that work together to solve the problems in designing embedded real-time systems. Three patterns are developed in the framework proposed here: task scheduling pattern, ceiling priority pattern and static allocation pattern. The task scheduling pattern is designed for priority-based task scheduling. It is able to process non-periodic tasks and tasks with dynamic priority assignment. The ceiling priority pattern addresses unbounded blocking with the ceiling priority protocol [9]. The static allocation pattern provides a memory optimization mechanism.

Certainly, there are many kinds of patterns for designing a system. What we proposed here is developed specifically for developing embedded real-time systems.

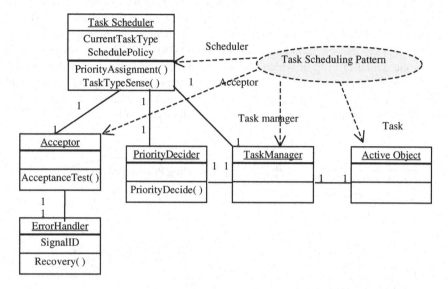

Fig.1. Task Scheduling Pattern

3.1.1 Task Scheduling Pattern

The task scheduling pattern (Fig.1) assumes a priority-based scheduling policy of either static priority assignment or dynamic priority assignment is employed. The priority decider class is designed for decide dynamic priority at run time. The ready task with the highest priority will then be selected and dispatched. Developer can implement his particular scheduling policy by overriding the method of this class.

As shown in Fig. 1, there is another auxiliary class, namely *acceptor* class in this pattern. The acceptor class is designed for scheduling non-periodic tasks with a task acceptance test which can be overridden by developer supplied method. The basic task acceptance test checks whether or not a task can be scheduled to meet its deadline by simply comparing the available system slack time based on current system workload to the worst-case execution time of that task [1]. The task will be admitted if the system has enough remaining capacity, otherwise the task is denied and an error handler will be invoked.

3.1.2 Ceiling Priority Pattern

The ceiling priority pattern (Fig. 2) in fact implements the ceiling priority protocol which is one member of the well-known priority inheritance protocol family developed to address the issue of unbounded blocking due to resource sharing among

tasks. Its basic idea is that each resource is associated with an attribute called its priority ceiling and the task allocated this resource executes at the priority of its priority
ceiling [1]. A task thus has two related attributes: nominal priority and current priority. The nominal priority of a task is its normal executing priority which is assigned
according to a certain static priority assignment rule such as rate monotonic scheduling (RMS) [2] or deadline monotonic scheduling (DMS) [10]. The current priority of
a task is the actual priority at which the task is executing. The value of the priority
ceiling attribute of a resource is the highest nominal priority of any task that would
use that particular resource. The current priority of a task is changed to the priority
ceiling of a resource the task has locked as long as the latter is higher.

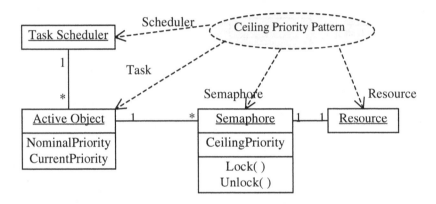

Fig. 2. Ceiling Priority Pattern

When a task wants to enter a critical section, it needs to request locking a resource
semaphore to protect its critical section. The locking service of resource management
module sets the current priority of this task to the priority ceiling before task execution proceeds. Since the priority ceiling is the highest nominal priority of all tasks that
use the same resource, the scenario is that once a task is granted locking a semaphore
it will not be blocked by lower priority tasks. In addition, tasks with priority higher
than the running task's but no higher than the priority ceiling will be blocked. When
the task exits from a critical section and unlocks the semaphore, its current priority
resumes to the previous value (if there is one). The ceiling priority pattern identifies
interacting objects and implements the ceiling priority protocol to realize the above
scenario. The pattern can be extended when the priority of task is dynamically assigned and the concept of dynamic priority ceiling is applied [11].

3.1.3 Static Allocation Pattern

The underlying concept of static allocation pattern (Fig.3) is to pre-allocate all objects
and create the maximum number of message objects when the system starts up. If a

sending object needs to communicate with another object, it must send a request to the message manager to get a free message object. The receiving object returns the message object to the message manager after it is consumed. No other memory object is allocated after the system is initialized to run and no object is deleted before the system is shutdown. Because memory is never released, heap fragmentation will not occur. In addition, system overhead is minimized during run-time because there is no need to invoke object constructors.

If a task wants to request a message, it must acquire a free message object from the message queue object. The message queue class is designed for messages management. This service accepting message request of a task will check whether any free message object is available or not. The state of the first free message object will be set to a flag marking it has being assigned and its pointer will be returned if the first free message is available. Otherwise, NULL will be returned. If a message is consumed, a service of the message queue object will be requested to release this message object.

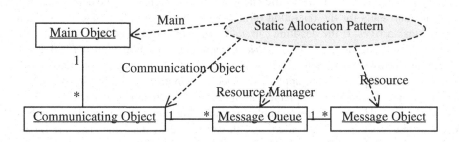

Fig. 3. Static Allocation Pattern

3.2 Class View

The framework provides classes such as timers, threads, semaphores, state machines, states, events, and a set of operating system abstractions. These classes have well-defined structural and stable relationships. Designer can reuse these classes of the framework by inheriting or associating. The classes implementing the above patterns and others are described below. The names are prefixed by *FW* which stands for *FrameWork*.

In embedded real-time systems, a task is a thread which reacts to events. It is implemented via instantiating an active class [12], which is associated with a message queue. The supper class of an active class is called *FWTask*. An active class inherits this class will has a thread and a private message queue. Attributes associated with an active class of a task are nominal priority, current priority, relative deadline, period, worst-case execution time and task type. The nominal priority is the task's assigned priority when it is released. The current priority is the task's priority at a particular time instant of interest. The relative deadline, worst execution time and period specify the basic timing properties of the task. The type of a task can be periodic or non-periodic. The scheduler will carry out an acceptance test for a non-periodic task. Operations of an active class include *suspend, resume, destroy, start, stop, sendEvent, receiveEvent* and *dispatchEvent*. The first five operations are the operations for suspending, resuming, destroying, starting and stopping a thread. The last three operate on events for a thread.

An embedded real-time system is usually event-driven. Each task maintains a private message queue. It receives messages by the message queue and dispatches messages to another object. The *FWEventQueue* class is responsible for the management of a message queue. Its operations are *add, delete, isEmpty, front* and *rear*. The *FWEvent* class is the base class for the message. In the context of statecharts, messages can trigger transitions between states.

Semaphores are used to control access to a shared resource, signal the occurrence of an event and allow tasks to synchronize their activities. The class *FWSemaphor* implements this mechanism. It has an attribute, ceiling priority, which has been described earlier. The associated operations are lock and unlock.

The *FWAcceptor* class is a specific class, which is designed for the acceptance test. The scheduler calls for the operation of acceptance test *acceptTest* first when a non-periodic task arrives. If the deadline can not be met, the error event is asserted and an error handler is dispatched. The *FWPriorityDescider* class is designed for dynamic scheduling policy such as EDF. The operation, *priorityDecide* is a virtual function for the designer to implement the application-specific dynamic scheduling policy. These two classes are designed for implementation of the task scheduling pattern.

The *FWTimerManager* is responsible for managing the central timer in an embedded real-time system. It is an additional thread that provides timer support for the application. The application therefore contains at least two threads, one thread for the application and the other for the timer management. The *FWTimerManager* class manages timeout requests and issues timeout events to the application objects. It is a singleton object in the execution framework. Singleton means only one instance can be created [12]. The *FWTimerManager* has a timer that notifies it periodically whenever a fixed time interval has passed. At any given moment, the *FWTimerManager* holds a collection of timeouts that should be posted to the thread when their time is up.

Another singleton class is *FWMain* which stands for the entry point to launch the application, similar to the *main()* function for C/C++ language. The *FWMain* class is a special case of *FWTask*. The operations associated with *FWMain* are *initHardware, initOS, createThread* and *start*. These operations must be invoked in that sequence. The *initHardware* and *initOS* operations are virtual functions for the designer to implement respectively the properties dependent of the selected hardware platform and operating system. Application tasks are created by the *createThread* operation. The *start* operation set the system into running after constructing the thread of time ticker.

4 Applying Framework

Developers using this framework simply need to add required application-specific classes and customize some component classes according to the design specifications. Classes of new objects can be defined using the classes of this framework by inheritance. In some special cases, developer may need to extend the framework. It is not difficult to do so because new design patterns can be added without impact on the three basic patterns.

In general, there are three steps in using this framework-oriented development process. The first step is defining the tasks and the values of their attributes. The task scheduling policy is chosen in this step. The second step is designing application classes and mapping them into active classes. Classes of new objects are added to the framework during this step. Third, setting the information related quality of service and task interaction such as resource sharing. Information provided in this step will be used to derive attribute values of the active classes.

The three patterns and the component classes mentioned previously have been implemented using C++ programming language to construct the framework. An application wizard is currently being implemented. It can guide the developer in the process of constructing a prototype of the application and producing skeleton source code including the framework service classes and the application classes. The developer can then modify the generated code to finish the application development.

5 Summary

A framework-oriented approach to efficient developing embedded real-time systems is presented in this paper. Using framework for system development has demonstrated the benefit in significantly improving the productivity of developers. The issue concerned by developers is how to build a good framework construct as it is difficult to devise a single framework adaptable to all kinds of systems. This is the same in developing embedded real-time systems. The presented framework is composed of three well-defined patterns as a basis specifically for developing embedded real-time systems. The patterns implement mechanisms of priority-based task scheduling, ceiling priority protocol, and memory optimization. In this framework, since attributes of classes representing abstraction of the system are fixed, the operations of classes will bind the behavior of developed system to a predicable state. Developers using this framework simply need to add required application-specific classes and customize some component classes according to the design specifications.

References

1. Jane W. S. Liu: Real-Time Systems, Prentice-Hall Inc., 2000, ISBN 0-13-099651-3.
2. C. L. Liu, J. W. Layland: Scheduling algorithms for multiprogramming in a hard-real time environment. Journal of the Association for Computing Machinery, 20(1): 46–61, January 1973.
3. L. Sha, R. Rajkumar, and J. P. Lehoczky: priority Inheritance Protocols, An Approach to Real-Time Synchronization, IEEE Transactions on Computers, Vol. 39, NO.9, September 1990, pp.1175-1185.
4. G. Booch, J. Rumbaugh, I. Jacobson: The Unified Modeling Language User Guide, Addison-Wesley Longman, 1999, ISBN 0-201-57168-4.
5. R. Johnson and B. Foote: Designing reusable classes, Journal of Object-Oriented Programming, 1(5): 22–35, June 1988.
6. T. Y. Kuan, W. B. See, S. J. Chen: An object-oriented real-time framework and development environment, In Proc. OOPSLA'95 Workshop #18, 1995.
7. P.A. Hsiung: RTFrame: An Object-Oriented Application Framework for Real-time Application, Proceedings of the 1998 IEEE, Technology of Object-Oriented Languages, pp. 138-147, 1998.
8. P. A. Hsiung, T. Y. Lee, W. B. See, J. M. Fu, and S. J. Chen, VERTAF: An Object-Oriented Application Framework for Embedded Real-Time Systems, Proc. of the 5th IEEE International Symposium on Object-Oriented Real-Time Distributed Computing, pp. 322-329, IEEE Computer Society Press, April 29-May 1, 2002.
9. L. Sha and J. B. Goodenough: Real-Time Scheduling Theory and Ada, IEEE Computer, Vol.23, No.4, April 1990, pp 53-63.
10. N. Audsley, A. Burns, A. Wellings: Hard Real-Time Scheduling: the Deadline Monotonic Approach, Proc. of the 8th IEEE Workshop on Real-Time Operating Systems and Software, may 1991.
11. M. I. Chen and K. J. Lin: Dynamic Priority Ceiling: A concurrency Control Protocol for Real-Time Systems, Real-Time System Journal, Vol. 2, No. 4, Nov. 1990, pp.325-346.
12. I-Logix: Code Generation Guide. http://www.ilogix.com. July 2002.
13. B. P. Douglas: Designing real-time systems with UML, parts 1, 2 and 3, Embedded Systems programming, March-May 1998.
14. B. P. Douglass: Doing hard-time: developing real-time systems with UML, objects, frameworks, and patterns, Addison-Wesley, 1999, ISBN 0-201-49837-5.
15. B. P. Douglass: REAL-TIME UML: Developing Efficient Objects For Embedded Systems Secondary Edition, Addison-Wesley Longman, 1999, ISBN 0-201-65784-8.
16. M. Fayad and D.C. Schmidt: Object-oriented application frameworks, Communications of the ACM, Special Issue on Object-Oriented Application Frameworks, 40(10), October 1997.
17. F. Kon and R.H. Campbell: Dependence Management in Component-Based Distributed Systems, IEEE Concurrency, January/March 2000(Vol. 8, No. 1), pp 26-36.
18. M. Fowler: UML Distilled: Applying the Standard Object Modeling Language, Addison-Wesley Longman, 1997, ISBN 0-201-32563-2.
19. M. Gergeleit, J. Kaiser and H. Streich: Checking timing constraints in distributed object-oriented programs, ACM OOPS Messenger, 7(1):51–58, January 1996.
20. I. Jacobson, G. Booch, J. Rumbaugh: The unified software development process, Addison-Wesley, 1999, ISBN 0-201-57169-2.
21. Jean J. Labrosse: MicroC/OS-II THE REAL-TIME KERNEL, Miller Freeman, Inc, 1999 ISBN: 0-87930-543-6.

22. Martin Fowler, Kendall Scott: UML Distilled, Second Edition, Addison-Wesley ISBN: 0-201-65783-X 1999.
23. J. Michael and A. McLaughlin: Real-Time Extension to UML, Dr. Dobb's Journal December 1998.
24. R. Martin, D. Richle and F. Buschmanu: Pattern Languages of Program Design 3, Addison-Wesley Longman, 1999.
25. B. P. Douglass: Real-Time Design Patterns, White Paper, I-Logix. http://www.ilogix.com. July 2002.

OVL Assertion-Checking of Embedded Software with Dense-Time Semantics*

Farn Wang[1] and Fang Yu[2]

[1] Dept. of Electrical Engineering, National Taiwan University
farn@cc.ee.ntu.edu.tw
[2] Institute of Information Science, Academia Sinica, Taiwan
{view,yuf}@iis.sinica.edu.tw

Abstract. OVL (Open Verification Library) is designed to become a standard assertion language of the EDA (Electronic Design Automation) industry and has been adopted by many companies. With OVL, verification process can blended seamlessly into the development cycles of complex systems. We investigate how to use OVL assertions for the verification of dense-time concurrent systems. We have designed a C-like language, called TC (timed C), for the description of real-time system with OVL assertions between code lines. We explain how to translate TC programs into optimized timed automata, how to translate OVL assertions into TCTL (Timed Computation-Tree Logic) formulae, and how to analyze assertions when not satisfied. The idea is realized in our translator RG (RED Generator).

In addition, we have developed several new verification techniques to take advantage of the information coming with OVL assertions for better verification performance. The new techniques have been incorporated in our high-performance TCTL model-checker RED 4.0. To demonstrate how our techniques can be used in industry projects, we report our experiments with the L2CAP (Logical Link Control and Adaptation Layer Protocol) of Bluetooth specification.

Keywords: Assertions, specification, state-based, event-driven, model-checking, verification

1   Introduction

In the last decade, many formal verification tools with proprietary (i.e., commercial or tool-specific) assertion languages have emerged in the industry [4, 12, 16, 20, 21, 27]. However, as Forster discussed, the lack of standards in assertion languages not only can frustrate engineers but also can create significant chaos and damage to the healthy progress of verification technology [7]. But what

---

* The work is partially supported by NSC, Taiwan, ROC under grants NSC 90-2213-E-001-006, NSC 90-2213-E-001-035, and the by the Broadband network protocol verification project of Institute of Applied Science & Engineering Research, Academia Sinica, 2001.

J. Chen and S. Hong (Eds.): RTCSA 2003, LNCS 2968, pp. 254–278, 2004.

should a standard assertion language look like ? A good assertion language must blend seamlessly into the development cycles of system designs. In real-world projects, engineers naturally describe their systems in programming languages and insert comment lines to assert some intuitive properties between codes, such as preconditions or post conditions. If a verification tool asks engineers to rewrite their C-codes in automata descriptions or Petri net descriptions and to make up some assertions offline of the programming cycle, then the engineers will more likely be reluctant to accept the tool in fear of extra workload and deadline misses. Thus, providing a natural method to bridge this gap in the verification of real-time concurrent systems is one main goal in this paper.

OVL (Open Verification Library) [7, 23] is a new initiative in VLSI industry for unifying the many commercial EDA (Electronic Design Automation) tools, by providing a set of predefined specification modules instantiated as assertion monitors. It is supported by EDA industry companies and donated to Accellera (an electronic industry standards organization) in anticipation to make OVL an industry standard. With OVL, engineers can write assertions as comment lines in their HDL (Hardware Description Language [6, 26]) programs.

OVL was originally designed for the assertions of VLSI circuits, which are highly synchronous discrete-time systems. In the cycle-based environment, they have no notion of time within a clock cycle and evaluate the logic between state elements and/or ports in the single slot. Since each logic element is evaluated only once per cycle ,with the coming of multi-multimillion-gate SOC (System-on-a-Chip) [25] in the new century, we believe that clock skews may eventually invalidate the synchrony assumptions. In the event-based environment, opposite to the cycle-based environment, a design element may be evaluated several times in a cycle because the different arrival time of inputs and the feedback of signals from downstream design elements and this provides a highly accurate enviroment [25]. However, today's industry projects usually only use static timing analysis [22, 24] to guarantee real-time properties Thus it will be of great interest if we can extend OVL assertions to dense-time model in formal verification.

Such an extension will also allow embedded system engineers to take advantage of verification technology with minimum effort in their development cycles. And that is also the motivation of this research. To blend seamlessly into the development cycles, it is important that system designs can be described in a format close to programming languages. In section 5, we define a new language, called *Timed C (TC)*, with C-like syntax and OVL assertions as comment lines. TC is designed for efficient mechanical translation from C-programs into input languages of our TCTL model-checker RED 4.0 for formal verification. The input to RED 4.0 consists of a *timed automata* [3] (with synchronization channels [18]) and a *TCTL (Timed Computation-Tree Logic)* [1] specification. In section 5, we discuss how to mechanically translate TC programs to optimized (for verification performance) timed automata with synchronizers.

In section 7, we present four types of OVL assertions and demonstrate how to translate these OVL assertions, with dense-time semantics, to TCTL formulae. In some cases, we have to create auxiliary processes and state-variables to monitor the satisfaction of OVL assertions. We have realized all these ideas in a translator, *RG (RED Generator)*, which translates TC programs into input format to RED [28, 29, 30, 31, 32, 33], a high-performance TCTL model-checker for timed automata.

The positions of OVL assertions in a program may also shed light on the possibility of verification performance enhancement. If an assertion is declared specifically in a process' program, usually it means that the assurance of the assertion is strongly linked to the behavior of this process. Then by carefully abstracting out state information of other processes, state-space representation can be significantly simplified and performance improvement in verification can be obtained. This intuition has led us to the design of several *localized abstraction* functions, which are explained in section 8. Unlike the previous work on approximate model-checking [35], our new abstraction technique is specially tailored to take advantage of the information hidden in OVL assertions. And our experiment with this new technique of localized abstract reduction indeed shows that performance improvement can be gained in verification with the information hidden in OVL assertions.

To demonstrate the usefulness of our techniques for real-world projects, in section 9, we have experimented to model and verify the *L2CAP (Logical Link Control and Adaptation Layer Protocol)* of Bluetooth specification [10]. Bluetooth, a wireless communication standard, has been widely adopted in industry. We model two devices, communicating with the L2CAP of Bluetooth, in TC and carry out experiments to verify various properties between the two devices. The experiments are by themselves important because of the wide acceptance and application of the protocol.

Moreover, since OVL assertions are written in between code lines, their dissatisfaction may provide valuable feedback for code debugging and direction to system refinement. When there are more than one assertions in a TC program and some of them are not satisfied, RED is capable of identifying which assertions are not satisfied. It is also possible to use the counter-example generation capability of RED to better understand the system behavior and diagnose the design bugs.

The remainder of this paper is organized as follows. Section 2 discusses the verification tool framework. Section 3 and 4 introduce the input language to RED 4.0, i.e., *synchronized concurrent timed automata (SCTA)* and TCTL. Section 5 discusses the language of TC(Timed C) and algorithms for translating TC constructs into optimized SCTA subgraphs. Section 6 describes OVL assertions. Section 7 discusses how to translate OVL assertions into TCTL formulae. Section 8 introduces our localized abstraction technique specially tailored for performance verification of OVL assertions. Section 9 reports our verification experiments with L2CAP. Section 10 concludes the paper with remarks on future plan of the work.

Formal semantics of SCTA and TCTL can be found in appendices A and B respectively. An example of TC program with OVL assertion and its corresponding optimized SCTA can be found in appendices ?? and ?? respectively.

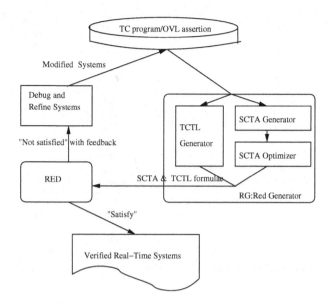

Fig. 1. Software architecture

2   Verification Tool Framework

The software architecture of our verification framework is shown in figure 1. On the top, users describe the system designs in our C-like language, TC, with OVL assertions as comments between code lines. After parsing and analyzing a TC program, our translator RG generates a file, in the format of input language to our TCTL model-checker RED, with an SCTA and a TCTL formulus. An SCTA includes a set of *process automata* communicating with each other with binary *synchronizers* [18] and global variables. The global automaton for the whole system is the Cartesian product of the process automata. Some process automata describe the system behaviors while others monitor the satisfaction of the OVL assertions.

The TCTL formulus is derived from the OVL assertions. If there are more than one assertions, then their corresponding TCTL formulae conjunct together to construct the final TCTL formulus.

We use two phases in the generation of SCTAs. The first phase generates an SCTA, which is further optimized in the second phase. The optimization program used in the second phase can also be used independently to help users of RED in optimizing their system descriptions.

After the SCTA and TCTL-formulus are generated, users may feed them to RED [28, 29, 30, 31, 32], our TCTL model-checker. Our RED is implemented with the new BDD-like data-structure of CRD (Clock-Restriction Diagram) [30, 31, 32, 33]. If RED says that the SCTA does not satisfy the TCTL formulus, RED can identify among the many OVL assertions which ones are not satisfied

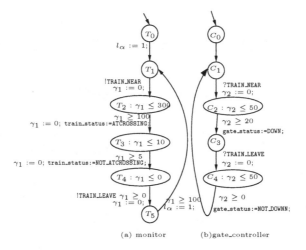

Fig. 2. Process automata of the railroad crossing system

and may generate counter-example traces in some situations. Users can use this information as feedback to fix bugs and re-execute this verification cycle. On the other hand, if RED says the SCTA satisfies the TCTL formulus, the correctness of the system design is formally confirmed.

3   Synchronized Concurrent Timed Automata (SCTA)

We use the widely accepted model of *timed automata* [3] with synchronizers [18]. A *timed automaton* is a finite-state automaton equipped with a finite set of clocks which can hold nonnegative real-values. At any moment, the timed automaton can stay in only one *mode* (or *control location*). In its operation, one of the transitions can fire when the corresponding triggering condition is satisfied. Upon firing, the automaton instantaneously transits from one mode to another and resets some clocks to zero. In between transitions, all clocks increase their readings at a uniform rate.

In our input language, users can describe the timed automata as a *synchronized concurrent timed automata (SCTA)*. Such an automaton is in turn described as a set of *process automata (PA)*. Users can declare local (to each process) and global variables of type clock, integer, and pointer (to identifier of processes). Boolean conditions on variables can be tested and variable values can be assigned. Process automata can communicate with one another through binary synchronizations. Each transition (arc) in the process automata is called a *process transition*.

In figure 2, we have drawn two process automata, in a railroad crossing system. One process is for train-monitor and one for the gate-controller.

The monitor uses a local clock γ_1 while the controller uses γ_2. In each mode, we may label an invariance condition (e.g., $\gamma_1 \leq 300$). Along each process transition, we may label synchronization symbols (e.g. !TRAIN_NEAR), a triggering condition (e.g., $\gamma_1 \geq 100$), and assignment statements (e.g., $\gamma_1 := 0;$). When the monitor detects that a train is approaching the crossing, it sends out a !TRAIN_NEAR signal to the controller. On receiving the signal, the train will reach the crossing in 100 to 300 time units while the gate will be lowered down in 20 to 50 time units.

A process transition may not represent a *legitimate global transition (LG-transition)*. Only LG-transitions can be executed. Symbols TRAIN_NEAR and TRAIN_LEAVE, on the arcs, represent channels for synchronizations. Synchronization channels serve as glue to combine process transitions into LG-transitions. An exclamation (question) mark followed by a channel name means an *output (input)* event through the channel. For example, !TRAIN_NEAR means a sending event through channel TRAIN_NEAR while ?TRAIN_NEAR means a receiving event through the same channel. Any input event through a channel must match, at the same instant, with a unique output event through the same channel. Thus, a process transition with an output event must combine with another process transition (by another process) with a corresponding input event to become an LG-transition. For example, in figure 2, process transitions $T_1 \longrightarrow T_2$ and $C_1 \longrightarrow C_2$ can combine to be an LG-transition while $T_1 \longrightarrow T_2$ and $C_2 \longrightarrow C_3$ cannot. Also process transition $T_2 \longrightarrow T_3$ by itself can constitute an LG-transition since no synchronization is involved. The formal semantics of SCTA is left in appendix A.

4   TCTL (Timed CTL)

TCTL (Timed Computation-Tree Logic) [1] is a branching-time temporal logic for the specification of dense-time systems. An interval $\mathcal{I}$ specifies a continuous time segment and is denoted as the pair of (open) starting time and (open) stopping time like $(c, d), [c, d), [c, d], (c, d]$ such that $c \in \mathcal{N}, d \in \mathcal{N} \cup \{\infty\}$, and $c \leq d$. Open and closed intervals are denoted respectively with parentheses and square brackets.

Suppose we are given a set P of atomic propositions and a set X of clocks, a TCTL formulus ϕ has the following syntax rules.

$$\phi ::= p \mid x_1 - x_2 \sim c \mid \phi_1 \vee \phi_2 \mid \neg\phi_1 \mid \exists\phi_1\mathcal{U}_\mathcal{I}\phi_2 \mid \forall\phi_1\mathcal{U}_\mathcal{I}\phi_2$$

Here $p \in P$, $x_1, x_2 \in X$, $c \in \mathcal{N}$, ϕ_1 and ϕ_2 are TCTL formulae, and $\mathcal{I}$ is an interval.

$\exists$ means "there exists a computation." $\forall$ means "for all computations." $\phi_1\mathcal{U}_\mathcal{I}\phi_2$ means that along a computation, ϕ_1 is true until ϕ_2 becomes true and ϕ_2 happens at time in $\mathcal{I}$. For example, with a specification like

$$\forall \text{train\_status = ATCROSSING}$$
$$\mathcal{U}_{[0,10)} \text{train\_status = NOT\_ATCROSSING}$$

we require that for all computations, `train_status` becomes `NOT_ATCROSSING` in 10 time units.

Also we adopt the following standard shorthand : *true* for $\neg false$, $\phi_1 \wedge \phi_2$ for $\neg((\neg\phi_1) \vee (\neg\phi_2))$, $\phi_1 \rightarrow \phi_2$ for $(\neg\phi_1) \vee \phi_2$, $\exists\Diamond_\mathcal{I}\phi_1$ for $\exists true\,\mathcal{U}_\mathcal{I}\phi_1$, $\forall\Box_\mathcal{I}\phi_1$ for $\neg\exists\Diamond_\mathcal{I}\neg\phi_1$, $\forall\Diamond_\mathcal{I}\phi_1$ for $\forall true\,\mathcal{U}_\mathcal{I}\phi_1$, $\exists\Box_\mathcal{I}\phi_1$ for $\neg\forall\Diamond_\mathcal{I}\neg\phi_1$.

The formal semantics of TCTL formulae is left in appendix B.

5   Timed C

Engineers are trained to write programs in traditional programming languages, like C, C++, Verilog, ..., etc. Timed C (TC) is designed to bridge the gap between the engineering world and the verification research community. It supports most of the programming constructs in traditional C, like sequences, while-loops, and switch-statements. It also provides syntax constructs to abstract unimportant details for mechanical translation to SCTA. Moreover, we have added new constructs to make it easy to describe event-driven behaviors, like timeouts.

5.1   The Railroad Crossing Example

The TC program in table 1 models a simple railroad crossing system. The system consists of two processes: `monitor` and `gate_controller`, both executing infinite while-loops. In the beginning, we declare two variables of enumerate type, as in Pascal. The first value in the enumerated value set is the initial value of the declared variables.

After sending out a synchronization signal `!TRAIN_NEAR`, `train_status` will be assigned value `ATCROSSING` in 100 to 300 time units. If in between two statements there is no interval statements, it is equivalent to the writing of interval $[0, \infty)$. Lines beginning with $//$ are comments, in which we can write OVL assertions.

In this program, there are two OVL assertions which are explained in section 6.

5.2   Mechanical Translation to SCTA

The real-time system model-checkers nowadays are based on mathematical models, like SCTA, Petri net, hybrid automata, ... [8, 9, 14, 19, 34, 30, 31, 35, 36]. To make the model-checking technology more attractive, it will be nice if we can mechanically translate C-programs to SCTAs. The language of TC (Timed C) serves as a middle language from C-programs to SCTAs.

The SCTA (generated from RG) for the TC-program in table 1 is exactly the one in figure 2.

For convenience, given a TC program construct **B**, let $RG(\mathbf{B})$ be the subgraph in an SCTA representing the behavior of **B**. The SCTA subgraphs of $RG(y = 3;)$ (an atomic assignment), $RG(\mathbf{B_1B_2})$ (a sequence), $RG(\texttt{while } (x < 3)\ \mathbf{B})$, and $RG(\texttt{switch } (y)\ \{\ ...\ \})$, are shown in figures 3(a), (b), (c), and (f) respectively.

Table 1. TC program for the modeling of railroad crossing system

```
enum {NOT_ATCROSSING, ATCROSSING}   train_status;
enum {NOT_DOWN, DOWN}   gate_status;

process monitor() {
  while (1) {
//assert_change #([0,20], 1) A1(train_status == ATCROSSING,\
     train_status == NOT_ATCROSSING)
    <!TRAIN_NEAR>;
    (100,300);
    train_status = ATCROSSING;
//assert_always(gate_status == DOWN)
    [5,10];
    train_status = NOT_ATCROSSING;
    [0,0];
    <!TRAIN_LEAVE>;
    [100,oo];
  }
}

process gate_controller() {
  while (1) {
    <?TRAIN_NEAR>;
    [20,50);
    gate_status = DOWN;
    <?TRAIN_LEAVE>;
    [0,50];
    gate_status = NOT_DOWN;
  }
}
```

In construct switch$(y)\{\ldots\}$, y must be of type int. Constructs of if-else can be treated similarly as construct switch. Since we require the specification of the range of integer variable in their declaration in TC programs, constructs like if-else can be treated as special cases of constructs switch$(\ldots)\{\ldots\}$.

Note that in the subgraphs figure 3(c) and (f) for constructs while and switch, the test conditions for the cases are directly labeled on the incoming transitions as additional constraints. This means that the conditional statements in TC do not take time in our model. This assumption is important for efficient translation to SCTA, in which a transition with triggering condition testing and assignments is executed instantaneously. This assumption is suitable for embedded systems in which dedicated hardware is used for each process.

But the traditional program constructs in C-like languages do not capture all the elements in the modeling of real-time concurrent systems. One deficiency is that there is no way to tell at what time the next statement should be exe-

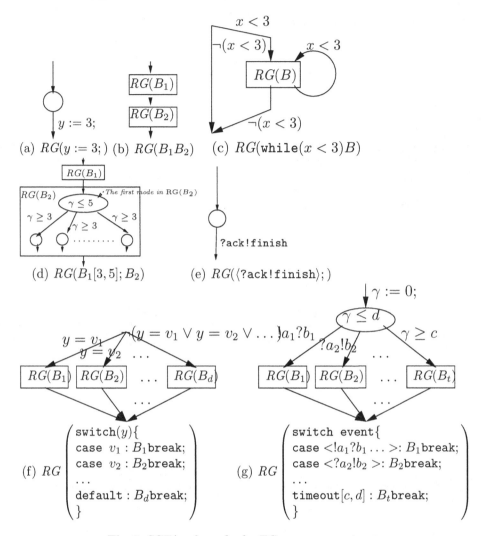

Fig. 3. SCTA subgraphs for TC-program constructs

cuted. In other words, users cannot describe the deadlines, earliest starting time of the next statement after the execution of the current statement. Here we propose a new type of statement, the *interval* statement, in the forms of "$[c, d]$;", "$[c, d)$;", "(c, d);", "$(c, d]$;", where $c \in \mathcal{N}$ and $d \in \mathcal{N} \cup \{\infty\}$ such that $c \leq d$ and $(c, \infty], [c, \infty]$ are not allowed. An interval statement, say $[c, d]$, is not executed but serves as a glue to bind the execution times of its predecessor and successor statements. For example, a statement sequence like $\mathbf{B}_1[3, 5]; \mathbf{B}_2$ means that the time lap from the execution of the last atomic statement in $\mathbf{B}_1$ to the execution of the first statement in $\mathbf{B}_2$ is within $[3, 5]$. The SCTA subgraph of $RG(\mathbf{B}_1[3, 5]; \mathbf{B}_2)$ is shown in figure 3(d). Note how we use an auxiliary system clock γ here to control the earliest starting time and deadline of the successor transition.

From real-world C-programs, interval statements can be obtained by abstracting out the execution time of blocks or sequences of program statements. Accurate execution time can be obtained with techniques of WCET [15] analysis. In many embedded systems, a processor exclusively executes one process and the execution time of a straight-line program segment can be obtained by accumulating the execution time (from CPU data-book) of the machine instructions in the segment.

Event-handling is an essential element in modeling languages for real-time systems. With different events observed, the systems may have to take different actions. We design the new construct of

```
switch event{
case⟨ss₁⟩ : B₁break;
case⟨ss₂⟩ : B₂break;
...
timeout[c, d] : Bₜbreak;
}
```

to capture this kind of system behaviors. $ss_1, ss_2, \ldots$ are sequences of synchronization labels, like ?receive, !send, ... The construct means that the system will wait for any of the event combinations of $\langle ss_1 \rangle, \langle ss_2 \rangle, \ldots$ to happen and take the corresponding actions $B_1, B_2, \ldots$ respectively. But the system will only wait for a period no longer than d time units because of the timeout event which will happen between c and d time units. The corresponding SCTA subgraph is drawn in figure 3(g). Note that the SCTA subgraph does have an auxiliary entry mode to enforce the timeout.

Finally e also allows programmers to use synchronizers in SCTA for the convenience of modeling of concurrent behaviors and construction of LG-transitions. For example, users can also write an atomic statement like "< ?ack !finish >;" and $RG(< ?ack !finish >;)$ is shown in figure 3(e).

5.3   Optimization of SCTA

The first phase of RG generates an SCTA, which is clumsy to verify. The SCTA will have a lot of null states connecting together the SCTA subgraphs generated for various TC program constructs. Also, many operations on local variables may create unnecessary partial-ordering and irrelevant intermediate states, which can only waste resources in the verification tasks for the given OVL assertions. We borrowed the code optimization techniques from compiler research [5] for the optimization of SCTAs. After the optimization, the reachable state-space representation of the SCTA can be reduced and verification performance can be enhanced.

A simple but effective technique for locally improving the target code is *peephole optimization*, a method to improve the performance of the target program by examining a short sequence of target instructions and replacing these instructions (called the peephole) by a shorter or faster sequence [5]. We followed this idea and developed our SCTA Optimizer. The optimization techniques, which we employed, include

- *bypass of null transitions*: For easy mechanical translation, sometimes we generate null modes and transitions. These modes and transitions can be eliminated without changing the system behaviors.

- *compaction of intermediate local transitions*: In SCTA, we can declare local variables of type integer and pointers. The exact execution time (within an interval) of assignments to such local variables may not affect the behavior of peer processes. This kind of situation can be analyzed and we can compact these local actions into one process transition.

- *elimination of unreachable modes*: After the bypassing of many transitions, some modes in the original SCTA may no longer be connected to the initial mode in the SCTA graph. We can simply ignore such modes.

- *elimination of intermediate temporary variables*: In the evaluation of complex expressions, sometimes we have to declare intermediate temporary state-variables to store the intermediate results, like the sum of an addition inside a multiplication. By properly analyzing the structure of the arithmetic expressions, we can avoid the usage of some intermediate temporary variables.

Because of the page-limit, we omit the details of our implementation here. But we have carried out experiment on the L2CAP used in section 9. The experiment reported in section 9 shows dramatic improvement in verification performance after the optimization.

6   OVL Assertions

We here demonstrate how to translate the following four types of OVL assertions to TCTL formulae for model-checking with RED.

$$//\texttt{assert\_always}(\phi)$$
$$//\texttt{assert\_never}(\phi)$$
$$//\texttt{assert\_change}\#(\mathcal{I}, f)ID(\phi_1, \phi_2)$$
$$//\texttt{assert\_time}\#(\mathcal{I}, f)ID(\phi_1, \phi_2)$$

Here ϕ, ϕ_1, ϕ_2 are Boolean predicates on variable values. $\mathcal{I}$ is an interval (as in section 4). f is a special flag. ID is the name of the assertion.

We choose these four assertion types from OVL as examples because many other assertion types can be treated with similar technique, which we use for these four types. In the four assertion types, $//\texttt{assert\_always}(\phi)$ and $//\texttt{assert\_never}(\phi)$ specify some properties at the current state. The first type

$$//\texttt{assert\_always}(\phi)$$

means that "now ϕ must be true." For example, in table 1, the second assertion in the while-loop of process monitor says that "now the gate must be down."

The second type

$$//\mathtt{assert\_never}(\phi)$$

means that "now ϕ must not be true."

The other two assertion types specify some properties along all computations from the current state. f is a flag specific to $\mathtt{assert\_change}$ and $\mathtt{assert\_time}$. When $f = 0$,

$$//\mathtt{assert\_change}\#(\mathcal{I}, f)ID(\phi_1, \phi_2) \qquad (1)$$

means that from now on, along all traces, THE FIRST TIME WHEN ϕ_1 is true, from that ϕ_1-state on, ϕ_2 must change value once within time in $\mathcal{I}$. That is, every time this assertion is encountered, it will only be used once, when ϕ_1 is true, and then discarded.

When $f = 1$, assertion (1) means that from now on, along all traces, WHENEVER ϕ_1 is true, ϕ_2 must change value once within time in $\mathcal{I}$. That is, this assertion will be assured once and for all. For example, in table 1, the first comment line in the while-loop of process monitor, is an $\mathtt{assert\_change}$, which says that when a train is at the crossing ($\mathtt{train\_status}$ == $\mathtt{ATCROSSING}$), then Boolean value of predicate $\mathtt{train\_status}$ == $\mathtt{NOT\_ATCROSSING}$ must change within 0 to 20 time units.

We have to make a choice about how to interpret "THE FIRST TIME" in a dense-time multiclock system. OVL assertions were originally defined to monitor *events* in VLSI circuits with the assumption of a discrete-time global clock [7]. In synchronous circuits, an atomic event can happen at a clock tick or sometimes can be conveniently interpreted as true in the whole period between two clock ticks. We believe the latter convenient interpretation is more suitable for this work because in concurrent systems, it is not true that all processes will change states at the tick of a "global clock." And this period between two ticks can be interpreted as a state in a state-transition system. According to this line of interpretation, we shall interpret assertion (1) as

"from now on, along all traces, in THE FIRST
INTERVAL WITHIN WHICH ϕ_1 is true,
from every state in that interval,
ϕ_2 must change value once within time in $\mathcal{I}$.

to better fit the need of dense-time concurrent systems. This choice of interpretation may later be changed to fit all domains of applications.

The last assertion

$$//\mathtt{assert\_time}\#(\mathcal{I}, f)ID(\phi_1, \phi_2) \qquad (2)$$

is kind of the opposite to $\mathtt{assert\_change}$. When $f = 0$, it means that from now on, along all traces, in THE FIRST INTERVAL WITHIN WHICH ϕ_1 is true, from every state in that interval, ϕ_2 must not change value at any time in $\mathcal{I}$. Similarly, when $f = 1$, assertion (2) means that from now on, along all traces, WHENEVER ϕ_1 is true, ϕ_2 must not change value at any time in $\mathcal{I}$.

In OVL, option $f = 0$ means that whenever this assertion is encountered, it will only be used once (when ϕ_1 is true) and then discarded. This is also the

default value. Option $f = 1$,oposite to option $f = 0$, means that this assertion
will be claimed once and for all. Option $f = 2$ is not addressed here since it's
used for handling the error message in OVL.

7 From Assertions to TCTL

Suppose we have n assertions $\alpha_1, \ldots, \alpha_n$. For each assertion α, we need a binary
flag b_α. Then we label the modes of the automata with $b_{\alpha_1}, \ldots, b_{\alpha_n}$ to denote
the scope within which the respective assertions are honored. For example, in
the TC-program in table 1, there are two assertions. Suppose the `assert_change`
assertion on the top is α_1 and the `assert_always` assertion in the middle is α_2.
The SCTA of this TC-program is shown in figure 2. Then b_{α_1} is only labeled at
mode T_1 while b_{α_2} is only labeled at mode T_3.

An assertion like $\alpha : //\texttt{assert\_always}(\phi)$ is translated to the TCTL formulus, denoted as $TCTL(\alpha)$,

$$\forall \square ((\bigvee_{(q \text{ labeled with } b_\alpha)} q) \to \phi).$$

Here "$\bigvee_{(q \text{ labeled with } b_\alpha)} q$" is a predicate, which we generate to signal when
assertion α must be satisfied.

For $\alpha : //\texttt{assert\_never}(\phi)$, $TCTL(\alpha)$ is

$$\forall \square ((\bigvee_{(q \text{ labeled with } b_\alpha)} q) \to \neg\phi).$$

For each `assert_time` or `assert_change` α with unique name ID, we need
to use auxiliary variables, auxiliary actions, and sometimes auxiliary processes
to monitor their satisfaction. We need an auxiliary Boolean state variable l_α to
monitor either

- when ϕ_1 has become true for the first time with option $f = 0$; or
- when ϕ_1 has become true with option $f = 1$.

For example, in figure 2, l_{α_1} is initially false and set to true at every process
transition to mode T_1. l_{α_1} is never reset to false with option $f = 1$. (Details are
discussed in the following.)

For $\alpha : //\texttt{assert\_change}\#(\mathcal{I}, f)ID(\phi_1, \phi_2)$, no matter whether $f = 0$ or
$f = 1$, $TCTL(\alpha)$ is

$$\forall \square \left(\begin{array}{l} (\bigvee_{(q \text{ labeled with } b_\alpha)} q) \\ \to \forall \square \left(\begin{array}{l} (l_\alpha \wedge \phi_1) \\ \to ((\forall \neg\phi_2 \mathcal{U}_\mathcal{I} \phi_2) \vee (\forall \phi_2 \mathcal{U}_\mathcal{I} \neg\phi_2)) \end{array} \right) \end{array} \right)$$

Formulus $\forall \neg\phi_2 \mathcal{U}_\mathcal{I} \phi_2$ captures the trace along which ϕ_2 changes from false to
true at time in $\mathcal{I}$ while $\forall \phi_2 \mathcal{U}_\mathcal{I} \neg\phi_2$ captures the trace along which ϕ_2 changes
from true to false at time in $\mathcal{I}$.

For $\alpha : //\texttt{assert\_time}\#(\mathcal{I}, f)ID(\phi_1, \phi_2)$, no matter whether $f = 0$ or $f = 1$,
$TCTL(\alpha)$ is the same

$$\forall \square \left(\begin{array}{l} (\bigvee_{(q \text{ labeled with } b_\alpha)} q) \\ \to \forall \square ((l_\alpha \wedge \phi_1) \to ((\forall \square_\mathcal{I} \neg\phi_2) \vee (\forall \square_\mathcal{I} \phi_2))) \end{array} \right)$$

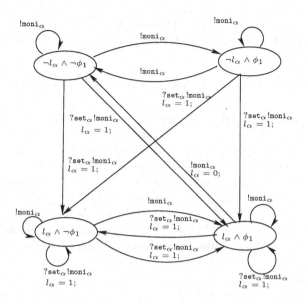

Fig. 4. Auxiliary monitor process with option $f = 0$

Formulus $\forall\Box_{\mathcal{I}}\neg\phi_2$ captures the trace along which ϕ_2 is maintained false within $\mathcal{I}$ while $\forall\Box_{\mathcal{I}}\phi_2$ is maintained true within $\mathcal{I}$.

When the assertions of type either `assert_change` or `assert_time` is written with option $f = 0$, we need one *auxiliary monitor process (AMP)* to report, with the auxiliary state-variable l_α, when ϕ_1 is true for the first interval. The AMP's behavior for α is shown in figure 4. There are four modes in AMP to reflect all combinations of truth values of l_α and ϕ_1. Every LG-transition in the original system will now have to synchronize with a transition in the AMP. This is done with synchronizer $\mathbf{moni}_\alpha$. We label the first process transition in each LG-transition with synchronization $?\mathbf{moni}_\alpha$. In this way, the AMP is tightly synchronized with the original system and the beginning and ending of the assertion scope are precisely monitored.

When the system transits into the scope of assertion α, the AMP will also receive a synchronizer $?\mathbf{set}_\alpha$, in addition to the sending out of synchronizer $!\mathbf{moni}_\alpha$. On receiving $?\mathbf{set}_\alpha$, the AMP will set the value l_α to report that the scope is entered. Then on every change value of ϕ_1 from true to false in a state with $l_\alpha = true$, l_α will be reset to false. When l_α changes from true to false, it means that the the system has left the first interval in which ϕ_1 is true in the scope of α.

When the assertions of type either `assert_change` or `assert_time` is written with option $f = 1$, we need the following minor modification to the process automata input to RED: *for every incoming transition to modes labeled with b_α, we need to label it with the auxiliary assignment $l_\alpha := 1$; to indicate that the* *scope of assertion* α *is entered.* This can be seen from label $l_{\alpha_1} := 1$; on the incoming transitions to mode T_1 in figure 2.

8   Localized Abstract Assertion-Checking

Verification problem is highly complex to solve with the state-space explosion problem. Thus it is very important to take advantage of whatever ideas, used in the designs, communicable from the design engineers to the verification engineers. The framework of OVL assertion-checking has advantage in this aspect because the assertions are given in between lines of process programs. Thus it is reasonable to assume that an assertion is either assured by the corresponding process or essential for the correctness of the process. Along this line of reasoning, we have developed three state-space abstraction technique, which we call *localized abstraction.* Unlike traditional abstraction techniques [35], our new technique adjust to the information coming with assertions.

Suppose we have an assertion α given in the program of process p. For α, a process p' is called *significant* if either $p = p'$ or some local variables of p' appear in α. All other processes are called *insignificant.* For an assertion, the three localized abstractions reduce the state-space representations by making abstractions on the state-variables of the insignificant processes. The three localized abstractions are described in the following. Suppose we have a state-space description η.

- $L^\alpha()$: *strictly local abstraction*
  $L^\alpha(\eta)$ is identical to η except all information about state-variables, except the operation modes, of insignificant processes are eliminated. The option can be activated with option -Ad of RED 4.0.
- $L_d^\alpha()$: *local and discrete abstraction*
  $L_d^\alpha(\eta)$ is identical to η except all information about local clocks of insignificant processes are eliminated. The option can be activated with option -At of RED 4.0.
- $L_m^\alpha()$: *local and magnitude abstraction*
  A clock inequality $x - x' \sim c$ is called a *magnitude constraint* iff either $x = 0$ or $x' = 0$. $L_m^\alpha(\eta)$ is identical to η except all non-magnitude clock difference constraints of the insignificant processes are eliminated. The option can be activated with option -Am of RED 4.0.

We report the performance of our three abstractions in section 9.

9   Verification Experiments

The wireless communication standard of Bluetooth has been widely discussed and adopted in many appliances since the specification [10] was published. To show the usefulness of our techniques for industry projects, in the following, we report our verification experiments with the *L2CAP (Logical Link Control and Adaptation Layer Protocol)* of Bluetooth specification [10].

9.1   Modelling L2CAP

L2CAP is layered over the Baseband Protocol and resides in the data link layer of Bluetooth. This protocol supports higher level message multiplexing, packet segmentation and reassembly, and the conveying of quality of service information. We model the behavior of L2CAP in TC and write specification in OVL assertions. The protocol regulates the behaviors between a master device and a slave device. We use eight processes: the *master upper* (user on the master side), the *master* (L2CAP layer), master L2CAP time-out process, master L2CAP extended time-out process, the *slave upper* (user on the slave side), the *slave* (L2CAP layer), slave L2CAP time-out process, and slave L2CAP extended time-out process to model the whole system.

The SCTA in figure 5 describes the behavior of a L2CAP device described in the Bluetooth specification [10]. A device may play the role of either master or slave depending on whether the device starts the connection. Both the master and the slave use the SCTA in figure 5. A master is a device issuing a request while a slave is the one responding to the master's request.

The original TC program has 303 lines of code. The optimized SCTA has 25 modes, 151 process transitions, 6 state variables, and 8 dense-time clocks in total.

The message sequence chart (MSC) in figure 6 may better illustrate a typical scenario of event sequence in L2CAP. The two outside vertical lines represent the L2CA interface from (slave's and master's) upper layers to the L2CAP layers (slave and master respectively). The scenario starts when the master's upper layer issues an L2CA_ConnectReq (Connection Request) through the L2CA interface. Upon receiving the request, the master communicates the request to the slave (with an L2CAP_ConnectReq), who will then convey the request to the slave's upper layer (with an L2CA_ConnectInd). The protocol goes on with messages bouncing back and forth until the master sends an L2CAP_ConfigRsp message to the slave. Then both sides exchange data. Finally the master upper layer issues message L2CA_DisconnectReq to close the connection and the slave confirms the disconnection.

We have made the following assumption in the model. When an upper layer process needs to send out an event in response to the receiving of an event, the time between the receiving and sending is in $[0, 5]$. Also, we assume that the timeout value of RTX timers and ERTX timers are all 60 time units. With one timeout, the L2CAP process aborts the session and changes to state CLOSED.

9.2   Performance Data

We have experimented with four OVL assertions. The first is

$$//assert\_always(M\_Con == 0) \qquad (a)$$

inserted at the beginning of the switch-case W4_L2CAP_CONNECT_RSP of the master TC process program. M_Con is a binary flag used to check if connection requests have been received from both master upper and

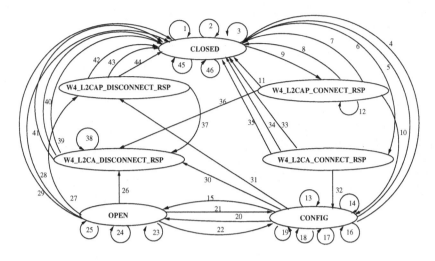

1. ?L2CAP_DisconnectReq!L2CAP_DisconnectRsp
2. ?L2CAP_ConfigReq!L2CAP_Reject
3. ?L2CA_ConfigReq!L2CA_ConfigCfmNeg
4. ?RTX_timeout!L2CA_TimeOutInd
5. ?ERTX_timeout!L2CA_TimeOutInd
6. ?L2CAP_ConnectReq!L2CA_ConnectInd
7. ?RTX_timeout!L2CA_TimeOutInd
8. ?ERTX_timeout!L2CA_TimeOutInd
9. ?L2CA_ConnectReq!L2CAP_ConnectReq
10. ?L2CAP_ConnectRsp!L2CA_ConnectCfm!disable_RTX
11. ?L2CAP_ConnectRspNeg!L2CA_ConnectCfmNeg!disable_RTX!disable_ERTX
12. ?L2CAP_ConnectRspPnd!L2CA_ConnectPnd!disable_RTX!start_ERTX
13. ?L2CA_ConfigRspNeg!L2CAP_ConfigRspNeg
14. ?L2CAP_ConfigRsp!L2CA_ConfigCfm, $con == 0$
15. ?L2CAP_ConfigRsp!L2CA_ConfigCfm, $con == 1$
16. ?L2CAP_ConfigReq!L2CA_ConfigInd
17. ?L2CAP_ConfigRspNeg!L2CA_ConfigCfmNeg!disable_RTX
18. ?L2CA_ConfigRsp!L2CAP_ConfigRsp, $con == 0$
19. ?L2CA_ConfigReq!L2CAP_ConfigReq; con=1;
20. ?L2CA_ConfigRsp!L2CAP_ConfigRsp, $con == 1$
21. ?L2CAP_ConfigReq!L2CAP_ConfigInd; buffer=2;
22. ?L2CA_ConfigReq!L2CAP_ConfigReq; buffer=2;
23. ?L2CA_DataWrite!L2CAP_Data
24. ?L2CA_DataRead; buffer=1;
25. ?L2CAP_Data!L2CA_DataRead; buffer=1;
26. ?L2CAP_DisconnectReq!L2CA_DisconnectInd
27. ?L2CA_DisconnectReq!L2CAP_DisconnectReq!start_RTX
28. ?ERTX_timeout!L2CA_TimeOutInd
29. ?RTX_timeout!L2CA_TimeOutInd
30. ?L2CAP_DisconnectReq!L2CA_DisconnectInd
31. ?L2CA_DisconnectReq!L2CAP_DisconnectReq!start_RTX
32. ?L2CA_ConnectRsp!L2CAP_ConnectRsp
33. ?ERTX_timeout!L2CA_TimeOutInd
34. ?RTX_timeout!L2CA_TimeOutInd
35. ?L2CA_ConnectRspNeg!L2CAP_ConnectRspNeg
36. ?L2CAP_DisconnectReq!L2CA_DisconnectInd
37. ?L2CAP_DisconnectReq!L2CA_DisconnectInd
38. ?L2CAP_DisconnectReq!L2CA_DisconnectInd
39. ?ERTX_timeout!L2CA_TimeOutInd
40. ?RTX_timeout!L2CA_TimeOutInd
41. ?L2CA_DisconnectRsp!L2CAP_DisconnectRsp
42. ?RTX_timeout!L2CA_TimeOutInd
43. ?ERTX_timeout!L2CA_TimeOutInd
44. ?L2CA_DisconnectRsp!L2CAP_DisconnectRsp
45. ?ERTX_timeout!L2CA_TimeOutInd
46. ?RTX_timeout!L2CA_TimeOutInd

Fig. 5. SCTA of a Bluetooth device

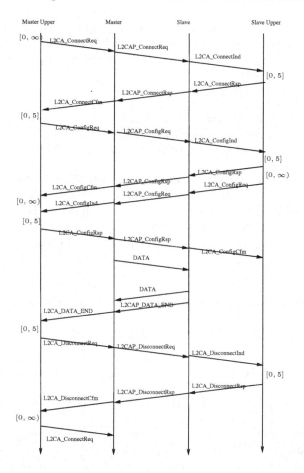

Fig. 6. A message sequence chart of L2CAP

slave. The TC program with assertion (a) are presented in appendices **??**. The assertion is satisfied because at the time process master enters state W4_L2CAP_CONNECT_RSP, the master reset M_Con to zero as initial value.

The second OVL assertion is

$$//\texttt{assert\_never(S\_Con==0)} \tag{b}$$

inserted at the beginning of the switch-case W4_L2CAP_CONNECT_RSP of k the slave TC process program. S_Con is the counterpart of M_Con. The assertion is thus not satisfied.

The third OVL assertion is

```
//assert_change #([0,60],1)
c(master_status==W4_L2CAP_CONNECT_RSP,            (c)
master_status==W4_L2CAP_CONNECT_RSP)
```

which says that if the master enters state `W4_L2CAP_CONNECT_RSP`, then it will eventually leave the state. The assertion is inserted at the beginning of the master TC process. This is satisfied because of the timeout issued from timer M_RTX.

The fourth OVL assertion is

```
//assert_time #([0,oo),0)
d(slave_status==W4_L2CAP_DISCONNECT_RSP,          (d)
  slave_status==W4_L2CAP_DISCONNECT_RSP)
```

which says that if the slave enters state `W4_L2CAP_DISCONNECT_RSP`, then it will never leave the state. "oo" is our notation for infinity ∞. The assertion is inserted at the beginning of the slave TC process. This is NOT satisfied because of the timeout issued from timer S_RTX.

The verification performance of RED 4.0 with and without localized abstraction technique against the four assertions is shown in table 2. The sizes of SCTAs

Table 2. Verification performance of assertions with various options

optimization?	abstraction?	size or performance?	assertion (a)	assertion (b)
optimized	no	#modes/#transitions	25/151	25/151
		time/memory	21.61s/845k	23.71s/845k
	$L^\alpha()$	time/memory	18.83s/845k	22.36s/845k
	$L_d^\alpha()$	time/memory	19.22s/845k	19.82s/845k
	$L_m^\alpha()$	time/memory	19.22s/845k	22.25s/845k
not	no	#modes/#transitions	258/360	258/360
optimzed		time	>20min	>20min

optimization?	abstraction?	size or performance?	assertion (c)	assertion (d)
optimized	no	#modes/#transitions	24/150	28/166
		time/memory	34.95s/858k	49.27s/1869k
	$L^\alpha()$	time/memory	32.63s/858k	48.81s/1869k
	$L_d^\alpha()$	time/memory	28.74s/858k	40.63s/1869k
	$L_m^\alpha()$	time/memory	31.46s/858k	47.57s/1869k
not	no	#modes/#transitions	258/360	262/376
optimzed		time	>20min	>20min

Data collected in cygwin environment on a Pentium 4 with 1.7GHz, 256MB, running MS Windows XP.

for the four assertions, before and after optimizaton, are also reported. In the following, we analyze the meaning of the performance data.

9.3   Performance Effect of Optimization

With our optimization techniques discussed in subsection 5.3, significant reduction in SCTA size is achieved for each of the assertions. In all four assertions, the numbers of modes in optimized SCTAs are reduced to around one tenth of those in unoptimized SCTAs. Also the numbers of transitions are reduced to less than half. In our experience, the time needed to model-check timed automata is exponential to the size of input. Thus we do expect that the unoptimized SCTA will be much harder to verify. This expectation is justified by comparing the verification performance for the optimized and unoptimized SCTAs. In all cases, the optimzed SCTAs allow efficient verification within less than 1 min while the corresponding SCTAs do not allow verification tasks to finish in 20 mins. The performance data in table 2 shows that our SCTA optimization techniques are indeed indispensible.

9.4   Performance Effect of Localized Abstractions

In table 2, for each assertion against their optimized SCTAs, we see that the verification performances with localized abstraction technique are all better than the one without. This is because that in the L2CAP process, there are local variables M_Con and S_Con and in the upper layer and timeout processes, there are local clocks metric. For the four assertions, only the process in whose program the assertion is written is significant. With the localized abstraction technique, state information on local variables of insiginificant processes can be eliminated to some extent and the state-space representations can be manipulated more efficiently. We believe that from the performance comparison, we find that our localized abstraction technique can indeed be of use in practice.

Among the three localized abstraction functions, we also observe difference in performance. Initially, since $L^\alpha()$ eliminate more state-information than $L^\alpha_m()$ and $L^\alpha_d()$ do, we expect $L^\alpha()$ will result in the most reduced state-space representations and the best verification performance. To our surprise, function $L^\alpha()$ performs the worst against three of the four assertions. We spent sometime to look into the intermediate data generated with $L^\alpha()$. We found that because information like M_Con==1 can be eliminated, state-space representations with both M_Con==0 and M_Con==1 will be generated. But the corresponding state-space with M_Con==0 may otherwise be unreachable without the abstraction of $L^\alpha()$. Such false reachable state-spaces can in turn trigger more transitions, which are otherwise not triggerable. Thus, with $L^\alpha()$, we actually may waste time/space in computing representations for unreachable state-spaces. This explains why there is the performance difference among the three localized abstraction functions.

10   Conclusion

This paper describes a new tool supporting formal OVL assertion-checking of dense-time concurrent systems. A formal state-transition graph model of the system and TCTL formulae of the properties are constructed from a description written in the TC language. We show how to mechanically translate TC-programs into optimized SCTAs. To take advantage of the information coming with OVL assertions for better verification performance, We demonstrate the power of new techniques by verifying the wireless communication L2CAP in Bluetooth.

Since our framework are based on RED, which supports high-performance full TCTL symbolic model checking, we feel hopeful that the techniques presented here can be applied to real world industry projects. The major motivation of this work is to provide a natural and friendly verification process to reduce the entry barrier to CAV technology, especially for engineers of real-time and embedded systems. And our experiment data on the real-world L2CAP indeed shows great promise of verification in the style of OVL assertion-checking for dense-time concurrent systems.

References

1. R. Alur, C. Courcoubetis, D.L. Dill. Model Checking for Real-Time Systems, IEEE LICS, 1990.
2. R. Alur, C.Courcoubetis, T.A. Henzinger, P.-H. Ho. Hybrid Automata: an Algorithmic Approach to the Specification and Verification of Hybrid Systems. in Proceedings of Workshop on Theory of Hybrid Systems, LNCS 736, Springer-Verlag, 1993.
3. R. Alur, D.L. Dill. Automata for modelling real-time systems. ICALP' 1990, LNCS 443, Springer-Verlag, pp.322-335.
4. R. Armoni, L. Fix, A. Flaisher, R. Gerth, B. Ginsburg, T. Kanza, A. Landver, S. Mador-Haim, E. Singerman, A. Tiemeyer, M.Y. Vardi, Y. Zbar The ForSpec Temporal Logic: A New Temporal Property-Specification Language (2001), TACAS'2002.
5. A.V. Aho, R. Sethi, J.D. Ullman. *Compliers - Principles, Techniques, and Tools*, pp.393-396, Addison-Wesley Publishing Company, 1986.
6. J. Bhasker. A VHDL Primer, third edition, ISBN 0-13-096575-8, Prentice Hall, 1999.
7. Bening, L. and Foster, H., i. Principles of Verifiable RTL Design, a Functional Coding Style Supporting Verification Processes in Verilog,li 2nd ed., Kluwer Academic Publishers, 2001. Symbolic Model Checking: 10^{20} States and Beyond, IEEE LICS, 1990.
8. M. Bozga, C. Daws. O. Maler. Kronos: A model-checking tool for real-time systems. 10th CAV, June/July 1998, LNCS 1427, Springer-Verlag.
9. J. Bengtsson, K. Larsen, F. Larsson, P. Pettersson, Wang Yi. UPPAAL - a Tool Suite for Automatic Verification of Real-Time Systems. Hybrid Control System Symposium, 1996, LNCS, Springer-Verlag.
10. Specification of the Bluetooth System Version 1.1, Feb, 2001. http://www.bluetooth.org
11. R.E. Bryant. Graph-based Algorithms for Boolean Function Manipulation, IEEE Trans. Comput., C-35(8), 1986. Verus: a tool for quantitative analysis of finite-state real-time systems. In: Workshop on Languages, Compilers and Tools for Real-Time Systems, 1995.
12. E.M. Clarke, S.M. German, Y. Lu, H. Veith, D. Wang. Executable protocol specificatoin in esl, FMCAD'2000, LNCS 1954, pp.197-216, Springer-Verlag.
13. D.L. Dill. Timing Assumptions and Verification of Finite-state Concurrent Systems. CAV'89, LNCS 407, Springer-Verlag.

14. C. Daws, A. Olivero, S. Tripakis, S. Yovine. The tool KRONOS. The 3rd Hybrid Systems, 1996, LNCS 1066, Springer-Verlag.
15. J. Engblom, A. Ermedahl, M. Sjoedin, J. Gubstafsson, H. Hansson. Worst-case execution-time analysis for embedded real-time systems. Journal of Software Tools for Technology Transfer, 2001. 14
16. F. Haque, K. Khan, J. Michelson. The Art of Verification with VERAR, 2001, Verification Central Com.
17. T.A. Henzinger, X. Nicollin, J. Sifakis, S. Yovine. Symbolic Model Checking for Real-Time Systems, IEEE LICS 1992.
18. C.A.R. Hoare. Communicating Sequential Processes, Prentice Hall, 1985.
19. P.-A. Hsiung, F. Wang. User-Friendly Verification. Proceedings of 1999 FORTE/PSTV, October, 1999, Beijing. Formal Methods for Protocol Engineering and Distributed Systems, editors: J. Wu, S.T. Chanson, Q. Gao; Kluwer Academic Publishers.
20. R.P. Kurshan. FormalCheck User's Manual, Cadence Design, Inc., 1998.
21. M.J. Morley. Semantics of temporal e. Banff'99 Higher Order Workshop (Formal Methods in Computation). University of Glasgow, Dept. of Computer Science Technical Report, 1999.
22. F. Nekoogar. Timing Verification of Application-Specific Integrated Circuits (ASICs), 2000, ISBN: 0-13-794348-2, Prentice-Hall.
23. http://www.verificationlib.com/
24. S. Palnitkar Verilog HDL: A Guide to Digital Design and Synthesis ISBN 0-13-451675-3, Sun Microsystems Press.
25. P.Rashinkar, P. Paterson, L. Singh. System-on-a-Chip Verification: Methodology and Techniques. Kluwer Academic Publishers, 2000; ISBN: 0792372794.
26. V. Sagdeo. The Complete VERILOG Book Kluwer Academic Publishers, 1998; ISBN: 0792381882.
27. Superlog, Co-Design Automation, Inc. 1998-2002; http://www.superlog.org/
28. F. Wang. Efficient Data-Structure for Fully Symbolic Verification of Real-Time Software Systems. TACAS'2000, March, Berlin, Germany. in LNCS 1785, Springer-Verlag.
29. F. Wang. Region Encoding Diagram for Fully Symbolic Verification of Real-Time Systems. the 24th COMPSAC, Oct. 2000, Taipei, Taiwan, ROC, IEEE press.
30. F. Wang. RED: Model-checker for Timed Automata with Clock-Restriction Diagram. Workshop on Real-Time Tools, Aug. 2001, Technical Report 2001-014, ISSN 1404-3203, Dept. of Information Technology, Uppsala University.
31. F. Wang. Symbolic Verification of Complex Real-Time Systems with Clock-Restriction Diagram, to appear in Proceedings of FORTE, August 2001, Cheju Island, Korea.
32. F. Wang. Symmetric Model-Checking of Concurrent Timed Automata with Clock-Restriction Diagram. RTCSA'2002.
33. F. Wang. Efficient Verification of Timed Automata with BDD-like Data-Structures. Technical Report, IIS, Academia Sinica, 2002. Automatic Verification on the Large. Proceedings of the 3rd IEEE HASE, November 1998.
34. F. Wang, P.-A. Hsiung. Efficient and User-Friendly Verification. IEEE Transactions on Computers, Jan. 2002.
35. H. Wong-Toi. Symbolic Approximations for Verifying Real-Time Systems. Ph.D. thesis, Stanford University, 1995.
36. S. Yovine. Kronos: A Verification Tool for Real-Time Systems. International Journal of Software Tools for Technology Transfer, Vol. 1, Nr. 1/2, October 1997.

APPENDICES

A   Definition of SCTA

A *SCTA (Synchronized Concurrent Timed Automaton* is a set of finite-state automata, called *process automata*, equipped with a finite set of clocks, which can hold nonnegative real-values, and synchronization channels. At any moment, each process automata can stay in only one *mode* (or *control location*). In its operation, one of the transitions can be triggered when the corresponding triggering condition is satisfied. Upon being triggered, the automaton instantaneously transits from one mode to another and resets some clocks to zero. In between transitions, all clocks increase their readings at a uniform rate.

For convenience, given a set Q of modes and a set X of clocks, we use $B(Q, X)$ as the set of all Boolean combinations of inequalities of the forms $\texttt{mode} = q$ and $x - x' \sim c$, where $\texttt{mode}$ is a special auxiliary variable, $q \in Q$, $x, x' \in X \cup \{0\}$, "$\sim$" is one of $\leq, <, =, >, \geq$, and c is an integer constant.

Definition 1. process automata A process automaton A is given as a tuple $\langle X, E, Q, I, \mu, T, \lambda, \tau, \pi \rangle$ with the following restrictions. X is the set of clocks. E is the set of synchronization channels. Q is the set of modes. $I \in B(Q, X)$ is the initial condition on clocks. $\mu : Q \mapsto B(\emptyset, X)$ defines the invariance condition of each mode. $T \subseteq Q \times Q$ is the set of transitions. $\lambda : (E \times T) \mapsto \mathcal{Z}$ defines the message sent and received at each process transition. When $\lambda(e, t) < 0$, it means that process transition t will receive $|\lambda(e, t)|$ events through channel e. When $\lambda(e, t) > 0$, it means that process transition t will send $\lambda(e, t)$ events through channel e. $\tau : T \mapsto B(\emptyset, X)$ and $\pi : T \mapsto 2^X$ respectively defines the triggering condition and the clock set to reset of each transition.   ∎

Definition 2. *SCTA (Synchronized Concurrent Timed Automata)* An SCTA of m processes is a tuple, $\langle E, A_1, A_2, \ldots, A_m \rangle$ where E is the set of synchronization channels and for each $1 \leq p \leq m$, $A_p = \langle X_p, E, Q_p, I_p, \mu_p, T_p, \lambda_p, \tau_p, \pi_p \rangle$ is a process automaton for process p.   ∎

A *valuation* of a set is a mapping from the set to another set. Given an $\eta \in B(Q, X)$ and a valuation ν of X, we say ν *satisfies* η, in symbols $\nu \models \eta$, iff it is the case that when the variables in η are interpreted according to ν, η will be evaluated *true*.

Definition 3. states Suppose we are given an SCTA $S = \langle E, A_1, A_2, \ldots, A_m \rangle$ such that for each $1 \leq p \leq m$, $A_p = \langle X_p, E, Q_p, I_p, \mu_p, T_p, \lambda_p, \tau_p, \pi_p \rangle$. A state ν of S is a valuation of $\bigcup_{1 \leq p \leq m}(X_p \cup \{\texttt{mode}_p\})$ such that

- $\nu(\texttt{mode}_p) \in Q_p$ is the mode of process i in ν; and
- for each $x \in \bigcup_{1 \leq 1p \leq m} X_p$, $\nu(x) \in \mathcal{R}^+$ such that $\mathcal{R}^+$ is the set of nonnegative real numbers and $\nu \models \bigwedge_{1 \leq p \leq m} \mu_p(\nu(\texttt{mode}_p))$.   ∎

For any $t \in \mathcal{R}^+$, $\nu + t$ is a state identical to ν except that for every clock $x \in X$, $\nu(x) + t = (\nu + t)(x)$. Given $\bar{X} \subseteq X$, $\nu \bar{X}$ is a new state identical to ν except that for every $x \in \bar{X}$, $\nu \bar{X}(x) = 0$.

Now we have to define what a legitimate synchronization combination is in order not to violate the widely accepted interleaving semantics. A *transition plan* is a mapping from process indices p, $1 \leq p \leq m$, to elements in $T_p \cup \{\bot\}$, where $\bot$ means no transition (i.e., a process does not participate in a synchronized transition). The concept of transition plan represents which process transitions are to be synchronized in the construction of an LG-transition.

A transition plan is *synchronized* iff each output event from a process is received by exactly one unique corresponding process with a matching input event. Formally speaking, in a synchronized transition plan Φ, for each channel e, the number of output events must match with that of input events. Or in arithmetic, $\sum_{1 \leq p \leq m; \Phi(p) \neq \bot} \lambda(e, \Phi(p)) = 0$.

Two synchronized transitions will not be allowed to occur at the same instant if we cannot build the synchronization between them. The restriction is formally given in the following. Given a transition plan Φ, a *synchronization plan* Ψ_Φ for Φ represents how the output events of each process are to be received by the corresponding input events of peer processes. Formally speaking, Ψ_Φ is a mapping from $\{1, \dots, m\}^2 \times E$ to $\mathcal{N}$ such that $\Psi_\Phi(p, p', e)$ represents the number of event e sent form process p to be received by process p'. A synchronization plan Ψ_Φ is *consistent* iff for all p and $e \in E$ such that $1 \leq p \leq m$ and $\Phi(p) \neq \bot$, the following two conditions must be true.

- $\sum_{1 \leq p' \leq m; \Phi(p') \neq \bot} \Psi_\Phi(p, p', e) = \lambda(\Phi(p))$;
- $\sum_{1 \leq p \leq m; \Phi(p) \neq \bot} \Psi_\Phi(p', p, e) = -\lambda(\Phi(p))$;

A synchronized and consistent transition plan Φ is *atomic* iff there exists a synchronization plan Ψ_Φ such that for each two processes p, p' such that $\Phi(p) \neq \bot$ and $\Phi(p') \neq \bot$, the following transitivity condition must be true: there exists a sequence of $p = p_1, p_2, \dots, p_k = p'$ such that for each $1 \leq i < k$, there is an $e_i \in E$ such that either $\Psi_\Phi(p_i, p_{i+1}, e_i) > 0$ or $\Psi_\Phi(p_{i+1}, p_i, e_i) > 0$. The atomicity condition requires that each pair of meaningful process transitions in the synchronization plan must be synchronized through a sequence of input-output event pairs. A transition plan is called an *IST-plan (Interleaving semantics Transition-plan)* iff it has an atomic synchronization plan.

Finally, a transition plan has a *race condition* iff two of its process transitions have assignment to the same variables.

Definition 4. <u>runs</u> Suppose we are given an SCTA $S = \langle E, A_1, A_2, \dots, A_m \rangle$ such that for each $1 \leq p \leq m$, $A_p = \langle X_p, E, Q_p, I_p, \mu_p, T_p, \lambda_p, \tau_p, \pi_p \rangle$. A *run* is an infinite sequence of state-time pair $(\nu_0, t_0)(\nu_1, t_1) \dots (\nu_k, t_k) \dots \dots$ such that $\nu_0 \models I$ and $t_0 t_1 \dots t_k \dots \dots$ is a monotonically increasing real-number (time) divergent sequence, and for all $k \geq 0$,

- for all $t \in [0, t_{k+1} - t_k]$, $\nu_k + t \models \bigwedge_{1 \leq p \leq m} \mu(\nu_k(\mathrm{mode}_p))$; and
- either
  - $\nu_k(\mathrm{mode}_p) = \nu_{k+1}(\mathrm{mode}_p)$ and $\nu_k + (t_{k+1} - t_k) = \nu_{k+1}$; or
  - there exists a race-free IST-plan Φ such that for all $1 \leq p \leq m$,
    * either $\nu_k(\mathrm{mode}_p) = \nu_{k+1}(\mathrm{mode}_p)$ or $(\nu_k(\mathrm{mode}_p), \nu_{k+1}(\mathrm{mode}_p)) \in T_p$ and
    * $\nu_k + (t_{k+1} - t_k) \models \bigwedge_{1 \leq p \leq m; \Phi(p) \neq \bot} \tau_p(\nu_k(\mathrm{mode}_p), \nu_{k+1}(\mathrm{mode}_p))$ and

∗ $(\nu_k + (t_{k+1} - t_k))\mathtt{concat}_{1 \le p \le m; \Phi(p) \ne \perp} \pi_p(\nu_k(\mathtt{mode}_p), \nu_{k+1}(\mathtt{mode}_p)) =$ ν_{k+1}. Here $\mathtt{concat}(\gamma_1, \ldots, \gamma_h)$ is the new sequence obtained by con-catenating sequences $\gamma_1, \ldots, \gamma_h$ in order.   ■

We can define the TCTL model-checking problem of timed automata as our verification framework. Due to page-limit, we here adopt the safety-analysis problem as our verification framework for simplicity. A safety analysis problem instance, $SA(A, \eta)$ in notations, consists of a timed automata A and a safety state-predicate $\eta \in B(Q, X)$. A is *safe* w.r.t. to η, in symbols $A \models \eta$, iff for all runs $(\nu_0, t_0)(\nu_1, t_1) \ldots (\nu_k, t_k) \ldots \ldots$, for all $k \ge 0$, and for all $t \in [0, t_{k+1} - t_k]$, $\nu_k + t \models \eta$, i.e., the safety requirement is guaranteed.

B   TCTL Semantics

Definition 5. (Satisfaction of TCTL formulae): We write in notations $\nu \models \phi$ to mean that ϕ is satisfied at state ν in S. The satisfaction relation is defined inductively as follows.

- The base case of $\phi \in B(P, X)$ was previously defined;
- $\nu \models \phi_1 \vee \phi_2$ iff either $\nu \models \phi_1$ or $\nu \models \phi_2$
- $\nu \models \neg\phi_1$ iff $\nu \not\models \phi_1$
- $\nu \models \exists\phi_1 \mathcal{U}_\mathcal{I} \phi_2$ iff there exist a ν-run $= ((\nu_1, t_1), (\nu_2, t_2), \ldots)$ in A, an $i \ge 1$, and a $\delta \in [0, t_{i+1} - t_i]$, s.t.
  - $t_i + \delta - t_1 \in \mathcal{I}$,
  - $\nu_i + \delta \models \phi_2$,
  - for all j, δ' s.t. either $(0 \le j < i) \wedge (\delta' \in [0, t_{j+1} - t_j])$ or $(j = i) \wedge (\delta' \in [0, \delta))$, $\nu_j + \delta' \models \phi_1$.
- $\nu \models \forall\phi_1 \mathcal{U}_\mathcal{I} \phi_2$ iff for every ν-run $= ((q_1, \nu_1, t_1), (q_2, \nu_2, t_2), \ldots)$ in A, for some $i \ge 1$ and $\delta \in [0, t_{i+1} - t_i]$,
  - $t_i + \delta - t_1 \in \mathcal{I}$,
  - $\nu_i + \delta \models \phi_2$,
  - for all j, δ' s.t. either $(0 \le j < i) \wedge (\delta' \in [0, t_{j+1} - t_j])$ or $(j = i) \wedge (\delta' \in [0, \delta))$, $\nu_j + \delta' \models \phi_1$.

Given a shared-variable concurrent timed automaton S and a TCTL formulus ϕ, we say S is a *model* of ϕ, written as $S \models \phi$, iff $\mathbf{0} \models \phi$ where $\mathbf{0}$ is the mapping that maps $\mathtt{mode}_p$ to $q_{p,0}$, all global variables and all clocks to zeros.   ■

System Support for Distributed Augmented Reality in Ubiquitous Computing Environments

Makoto Kurahashi, Andrej van der Zee, Eiji Tokunaga, Masahiro Nemoto, and Tatsuo Nakajima

Waseda University, 3-4-1 Okubo Shinjuku Tokyo 169-8555, JAPAN
{mik,andrej,eitoku,nemoto,tatsuo}@dcl.info.waseda.ac.jp

Abstract. Ubiquitous computing will dramatically change our lives due to the enhancement of our real world. Augmented reality (AR) is a promising technique for realizing the enhancement by superimposing computer generated images on video images. However, it is not easy to build applications using augmented reality techniques since the developer needs to deal with issues like distribution and context-awareness. It is desirable to provide a software infrastructure to hide the complexities from programmers.

In this paper, we propose a middleware called TEAR (Toolkit for Easy Augmented Reality) supporting augmented reality for ubiquitous computing environments. Our middleware provides several multimedia components that process video streams using AR techniques. New components to provide more complex functionality can be developed by composing these components.

1 Introduction

Ubiquitous computing [20] will change our lives dramatically by enhancing our real-world with smart objects. Smart objects are everyday objects that contain very small embedded processors in order to add functionality. Such objects are connected to a wireless network and can be accessed by the application programmer. The behavior of smart objects should be changed in a context-aware fashion.

In ubiquitous computing environments, a user needs technologies to access the enhanced real-world. Many HCI researchers have proposed various interaction devices to control everyday objects, or to retrieve information in our real-world.

Augmented reality [2] is a promising technology for realizing the enhancement of our real-world by superimposing computer generated digital images onto video frames. However, it is not easy to build augmented-reality applications in ubiquitous environments. Complex issues like distribution and context-awareness need to be addressed by the application programmer [15,19].

In this paper, we propose a middleware called *TEAR (Toolkit for Easy Augmented Reality)* for augmented reality support in ubiquitous computing environments. Our middleware provides several components that process video streams.

J. Chen and S. Hong (Eds.): RTCSA 2003, LNCS 2968, pp. 279–295, 2004.

We can create an augmented-reality application in a ubiquitous environment by composing several multimedia components. Complex issues like distribution and context-awareness are hidden by our middleware. In this way, the application programmer is not concerned with such complexities and can focus rather on the application logic. This paper describes the design and implementation of our middleware, and shows some of our experiences using our resulting system.

The remainder of this paper is structured as follows. In Section 2, we describe the design issues of our middleware. Section 3 explains the design and implementation of our middleware. In Section 4, we present two scenarios showing the effectiveness of our system. In Section 5, we describe related work, and Section 6 concludes the paper.

2   Design Issues

In this section, we describe the design issues involved for building our middleware. First, we present a brief overview of ubiquitous computing and augmented reality. Then, we show the requirements for building augmented-reality applications in ubiquitous computing.

2.1   Ubiquitous Computing and Augmented Reality

Augmented reality is a technology offering an augmented real-world to the user. More concretely, an augmented-reality application presents a view composed of the real-world and digital information managed by computers. Besides an augmented view of the real-world, it may provide a seamless human-computer interface as well.

Developing augmented-reality applications is not easy. Among other concerns, programmers must implement complex algorithms to detect visual markers. Some toolkits, like the ARToolkit [1], have been developed to equip the programmers with implementations of typical augmented reality problems.

In ubiquitous environments, computers and networks are accessed implicitly rather then directly. Most of the time, users are not even aware that they are connected to a network and accessing multiple computers at the same time. In the end, users want to deal with the real-world rather then with cyber-space. This requires a high level of transparency and makes ubiquitous environments even more complex.

2.2   Requirements

When developing ubiquitous augmented-reality applications, the developer is faced with the complexities inherent to ubiquitous environments. Existing AR toolkits are not designed for such environments and consequently do not address these complexities. We found it is necessary to meet the following three requirements when building augmented reality applications in ubiquitous computing environments.

High-Level Abstraction: Ubiquitous computing environments consist of various types of computers and networks. Networks may contain a mix of resource-constrained and specialized computers. Also, the existing augmented reality toolkits are platform-dependent. Consequently, application programmers must develop different software for each platform. A middleware to provide high-level abstraction to hide such differences from application programmers is necessary[14,16] in order to reduce the development costs.

Distribution: In ubiquitous computing environments, applications must be distributed over many processors. Since the environment usually consists of various types of computers, some may not be appropriate for heavy processing like video-data analysis. For example, cellular phones and PDAs are usually to weak for heavy processing, but they might want to utilize augmented-reality features. However, an application running on low CPU-resource could be distributed such that heavy processing is performed on strong computers. In ubiquitous computing, we think that such distribution needs to be hidden from the developer in order to keep development time and cost as low as possible.

Context-Awareness: In ubiquitous computing environments, applications must support context-awareness since users need to access computers and networks without knowing. It is required for an application to adapt itself to the users situation dynamically. However, implementing context-awareness in an application directly is very difficult. An application programmer does not want to be concerned with such complexities and we think that it is desirable to embed context-awareness in our framework and hide it from the developer.

3   Middleware Supporting Augmented Reality

In this section, we describe the design and implementation of TEAR, the middleware we developed to support augmented reality in ubiquitous computing.

3.1   Overview of Architecture

TEAR consists of two layers, as shown in Figure 1. The upper layer is the multimedia framework (see section 3.3) and the lower layer is a communication infrastructure based on CORBA (Common Object Request Broker Architecture). The support of context-awareness is handled by the communication infrastructure.

An augmented reality application using TEAR consists of an application composer and several multimedia components. An application composer is a user-side program that coordinates an entire application. It maintains references to objects contained by multimedia components, and configures them to build distributed context-aware applications. For example, as shown in Figure 1, a multimedia source component (a camera) and a multimedia sink component (a display) are connected. The setup is achieved by the application composer through the interface provided by the continuous media framework.

In TEAR, a proxy object in an application may hold several references to objects that provide identical functionality. In the example, there are two camera components and three display components. A proxy camera object in the application composer holds two object references to camera components, and a proxy display object holds three object references to display components. Which reference is used in an application is decided upon the context policies, specified in the application.

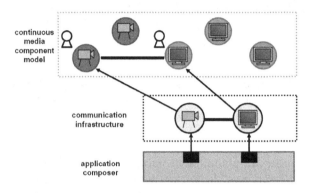

Fig. 1. Overview of TEAR Architecture

TEAR meets the requirements outlined in the previous section in the following way.

High-Level Abstraction: TEAR provides a multimedia framework for constructing augmented reality components in an easy way. Complex programs like detecting visual markers and drawing 3D objects are encapsulated in respective multimedia components. All the components offer an identical CORBA interface for standardized inter-component access. In our framework, a complex distributed and context-aware AR application can be developed with the application composer that configures existing multimedia components. We describe details about the multimedia framework in Section 3.3.

Distribution: For composing multimedia components in a distributed environment, we have adopted a CORBA-based communication infrastructure. Each multimedia component is designed as a CORBA object. Since CORBA hides differences among OS platforms and languages, the continuous media components run on any OS platforms, and can be implemented in various programming languages.

Context-Awareness: In the TEAR framework, the communication infrastructure is designed as a CORBA compatible system that supports context-awareness. The infrastructure supports user mobility by automatically reconfiguring media streams. Also, the infrastructure allows us to select a suitable component to process media streams according to the condition of each computer and the situation of a user by specifying policies.

We describe details about the communication infrastructure in Section 3.2.

3.2   CORBA-Based Communication Infrastructure

As described in Section 2, context-awareness is one of the most important features for implementing augmented reality applications in ubiquitous computing. Therefore, a middleware supporting augmented reality must support context abstraction which allows us to specify application preferences about context information such as user location. We have designed a context-aware communication infrastructure based on CORBA which provides dynamic adaptation according to the current context.

Dynamic Proxy Object. In our system, application programmers use a *dynamic proxy object* to access target objects, contained by multimedia components described in Section 3.3. The dynamic proxy object contains several object references to actual target objects, *context information*, and an *adaptation policy* for specifying how to adapt the invocation to a target object. A dynamic proxy object is a CORBA object like a multimedia component, and provides the same interface as actual objects. When a method in a dynamic proxy object is invoked, the request is forwarded to the most appropriate object according to the specified adaptation policy as shown in Figure 2.

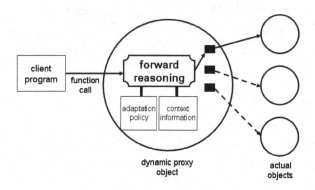

Fig. 2. Dynamic Proxy Object

In the current design, an adaptation policy is specified as a set of location and performance policies. Examples of location policies are "Choose an object in the same host with *", "Choose the nearest object from *" or "Any host". Performance policies might be "Light loaded host" or "Any host".

Context Trader Service. To create a dynamic proxy object described in the previous section, we we have developed a CORBA service called the *context trader service*. An application program can acquire a reference to the context trader by invoking the `resolve\_initial\_reference`-method provided by CORBA.

Figure 3 explains how a client program creates and uses a proxy object. (1) By invoking the `resolve` method on the context trader service a developer can acquire a reference to a proxy object. The method requires three parameters; a type specifying the proxy object, an adaption policy and the scope for selecting the target objects. (2) The context trader service creates a proxy object of the specified type and registers a target object within the specified scope. (3) A reference to the proxy object is returned to the client program. (4) Callback handlers may be registered through the reference. (5) Context changes are reported to the *context manager*. (6) The context manager notifies the proxy object upon context change and (7) the client program is notified by invoking the registered callback handlers.

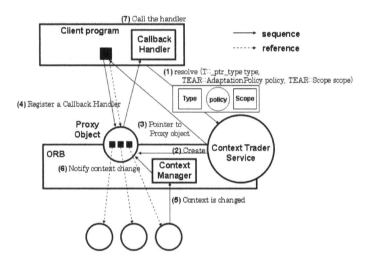

Fig. 3. Resolving Dynamic Proxy Object

3.3   Multimedia Framework

The main building blocks in our multimedia framework are software entities that externally and internally stream multimedia data in order to accomplish a certain task. We call them *components*. In the following subsections we describe components in more detail and provide source code to illustrate how a developer can configure a component.

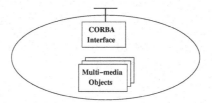

Fig. 4. General Component

Components. A continuous media component consists of a CORBA interface and a theoretically unlimited number of *subcomponents* or *objects* as shown in Figure 4. Video or audio data is streamed between objects, possibly contained by different components, running on remote machines. Through the CORBA interface virtual connections can be created in order to control the streaming direction of data items between objects. Components register themselves at the CORBA Naming Service under a user-specified name. Next, we will discuss the CORBA interface subcomponents, thread scheduling and virtual connections.

CORBA Interface. A component can be remotely accessed through one of three CORBA interfaces: `Component`, `Connector` and `Services`.

The `Component` interface is added to the component to provide a single object reference through which references can be obtained to other CORBA interfaces. The benefits of adding such an interface is to give clients access to all inter-component functionality through a single reference. Such a reference can be published in the Naming or Trading Service [8], provided by almost any OMG-compliant ORB vendor. In addition, the `Component` interface provides functions to query individual objects and the component as a whole. The `Component` interface is identical to all components.

The `Connector` interface provides methods to establish virtual connections between objects, possibly contained by different components, running on remote sites. More specific, the interface provides functions to access and update routing information of individual source objects (see subsection Routing and Virtual Connections). The `Connector` interface is identical to all components.

The `Services` interface provides methods for controlling specific objects within a component. Clients may find it useful to query and/or change the state of a multimedia object. For example, a client may want to query a display object for the resolutions it supports and may want to change the resolution to its needs. The `Services` interface varies from component to component, depending on the internal objects it contains.

The interfaces are part of the module IFACE and are written in CORBA IDL [8,11]. Here follows a snapshot of the `Connector` and `Component` interface[1]:

```
interface MConnIface
```

---

[1] The Services interface is not included since it varies for different component configurations.

```
{
   void
   addRoutingSeq(in ObjectId id,
                 in RoutingSeq seq)
   raises(InvalidObjectId);

   boolean
   removeRoutingSeq(in ObjectId id,
                    in RoutingSeq seq)
   raises(InvalidObjectId);
};

interface MCompIface
{
   MConnIface
   getConnIface();

   MServIface
   getServIface();

   boolean
   isInput(in ObjectId id)
   raises(InvalidObjectId);

   boolean
   isOutput(in ObjectId id)
   raises(InvalidObjectId);
};
```

Subcomponents or Objects. Typically, within a component, several objects run in separate threads and stream data in one direction. For example, a camera object may capture images from a video device, and stream the video data to a display object through a red-blue swapper that swaps the red and blue values of a video frame as shown in Figure 5.

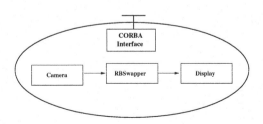

Fig. 5. Example Component

In our approach, the central focus is the stream of data from data producers to data consumers through zero or more data manipulators [10]. Data producers typically are interfaces to video or audio capture hardware or media storage hardware. In our framework we call them *sources*. Data manipulators perform operations on the media-data that runs through them. Data manipulators get their data from sources or other data manipulators and stream the modified data to a consumer or another manipulator. In our framework we call them *filters*. Data consumers are objects that eventually process the data. Data consumers typically interface to media playback devices or to media storage devices. In our framework we call them *sinks*. In our example from Figure 5, data is streamed from our camera source object, through the red-blue swapper filter object, into the display sink object.

Objects are categorized as *input* and/or *output* objects. For example, a filter object is both an input and an output object, meaning it is capable of respectively receiving and sending data. Clearly, a source object is of type output and a sink object of type input.

More concrete, our framework provides the abstract classes MSource, MFilter and MSink[2] written in C++. Developers extend the classes and override the appropriate hook-methods [7] to implement functionality. Multimedia objects need only to be developed once and can be reused in any component.

Components know two specialized objects for handling inter-component data streaming, namely *rtp-in* and *rtp-out*. An rtp-in object is a source object, consequently of type input, that receives data from remote components over a RTP connections. Semantically this is not strange at all, since from the components point of view, data is produced by means of receiving it from another component. Similarly, rtp-out is a sink object that is responsible for sending data to other components.

Thread Scheduling. Since all objects run in separate threads, priority values can be assigned as a criteria for preemption as multiple threads are competing for the CPU simultaneously. By assigning priority values, the underlying operating system decides which thread utilizes most CPU cycles during execution. For example, a developer of a component may assign higher priorities to objects that perform long calculations.

In our approach, data items are streamed between objects, possibly contained by different components. Individual objects, running in separate threads, are not scheduled for the CPU until they receive data for processing. In this way, the data items function as scheduling tokens for individual threads [10]. Also, idle objects do not waist any CPU cycles.

Routing and Virtual Connections. A typical augmented reality component might contain a filter object that adds digital images to a video frame at a

---

[2] The M preceding the class names indicate that they are part of the framework and stands for multimedia.

specified position within the frame. Different client components may want to use the service at the same time by sending video frames to the component and afterwards receiving it for playback.

This implies that the data streamed through filter objects within components might have different destinations. Solely setting up direct connections between objects does not satisfy the above described scenario. If each client would be connected to the filter object as a destination, how does the filter object know which data is to be send to which destination?

To solve the above issue we do not use direct connections between objects. Rather, source objects add a routing list to the produced data items, consisting of all its consecutive destination objects. In this approach, after a data item is processed by the filter object, the next destination is popped from the routing list and the data is forwarded to the indicated object. We say that the destination objects in a routing list are *virtually connected*.

In order to identify an object within a component a unique identifier is assigned to each object upon creation. Universally, we use a tuple containing a Component object reference (see subsection CORBA Interface) and an object identifier to denote one specific object. Such tuples are used as destinations in a routing list.

Component Configuration. In our framework, we use a component abstraction that hides much of the details that deal with CORBA and virtual connections. By extending the abstraction, a developer can configure a component. More specific, a developer specializes the C++ MComponent class provided by the framework. In its constructor it typically creates subcomponents, possibly creates virtual connections and finally adds the objects to the container component. Source code for the example component in Figure 5 might look something like this[3]:

```
// The variables starting with m_p
// are member variables declared in
// the derivation of MComponent.

m_pCamera = new Camera;
m_pSwapper = new RBSwapper;
m_pDisplay = new Display;

MRoutingList list = new MRoutingList;
list.add(0, m_pSwapper->getId());
list.add(0, m_pDisplay->getId());
m_pCamera->addRoutingList(list);

addObject(m_pCamera);
```

---

[3] Using a 0 for a component reference in the construction of a routing list denotes a local connection.

```
addObject(m_pSwapper);
addObject(m_pDisplay);
```

Under the hood, the component registers itself in the Naming Service under a specified name given on the command line. If successful, the component runs all its subcomponents and finally blocks control waiting for incoming CORBA requests.

The above example is an illustration of how to configure a simple component that streams data locally. Now assume a second component that contains a similar camera and display object and needs to be configured to swap red and blue values for the produced video frames. One possibility would be to connect the camera object to the first components red-blue swapper, and the red-blue swapper to the display object. Simplified source code for the component might look like this.

```
m_pCamera = new Camera;
m_pDisplay = new Display;

// Retrieve the object reference of
// the first component from the Naming
// Service and store it in pCompIface.

// Retrieve the object id of RBSwapper
// from the first component through its
// object reference and store it in
// nObjectId.

MRoutingList list = new MRoutingList;
list.add(pCompIface, nObjectId);
list.add(0, m_pDisplay->getId());
m_pCamera->addRoutingList(list);

addObject(m_pCamera);
addObject(m_pDisplay);
```

Alternatively, the virtual connections might be created by an external client. In this scheme, the external client retrieves the object references of both components from the Naming Service. Next, it constructs a routing list and invokes the appropriate function of the `Connector` interface to add the list to the routing information of the camera object.

Stream Reconfiguration. Supporting context-awareness by multimedia applications requires not only dynamic adaptation of object references, but also dynamic re-direction of continuous media streams. When the current object reference of a dynamic proxy object is changed, continuous media streams must be reconnected dynamically to change the current configuration of continuous media components according to the current context information. To achieve this, a callback handler described in Section 3.2.2 is used. It is registered to a dynamic proxy object by an application, and the handler is invoked when the current context is changed. Next, we discuss how our system reconfigures the connections among continuous media components by using the example described in the previous section.

Suppose a context change is reported to the context manager and a notification is triggered to the proxy object holding a reference to the red-blue swapper. In response, the proxy object might want to change its internal reference to the red-blue swapper in order to adapt to the new context. If so, its registered callback handlers are invoked. Typically, one of the callback handlers is concerned with updating routing information of affected source objects. Such handlers expect a parameter holding a reference to the new target object. In the example, the reference to the red-blue swapper is used to construct a new routing list, and the routing information of the camera source object is updated to reflect the new configuration.

By updating the routing information of source objects virtual connections are added and deleted. Subcomponents that do not appear in routing information of any source object are not presented any data and consequently reside in an idle state. By using virtual connections, no notification messages have to be sent to any filter or sink object to hold them from processing any data. Solely updating the routing information of source objects is sufficient.

Components for Augmented Reality. Among others, TEAR provides augmented reality components for the detection of visual markers in video frames and superimposing 3D objects at a specified location within a frame. Such components are implemented as objects contained by multimedia components as described in subsection 3.3. They use the ARToolkit to implement functionality.

A detection filter object expects a video frame as input and looks for visual markers. Information about visual markers, if any, is added to the original video frame and send as output. Since different types of visual markers will be available, the format of the marker information must be defined in a uniform way. Consequently, filter components detecting different types of visual markers can be used interchangeably .

A super-imposer object expects video frames with marker information as input, superimposes additional graphics at the specified location, and outputs the augmented video frame.

Figure 6 shows how the two components can be used in sequence to enhance a video stream with augmented reality. In this configuration, video frames are captured by an input device and sent to the output device through the detection filter and super-imposer. As a result, visual markers are replaced by digital images.

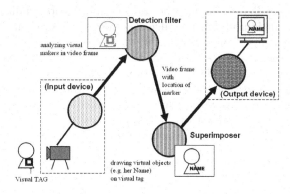

Fig. 6. Components for Augmented Reality

4   Sample Scenarios

This section describes two scenarios showing the effectiveness of TEAR. In the first scenario, we describe how *mobile augmented reality* can be used on low CPU-resource devices such as PDAs and cellular phones. In the second scenario, we describe a *follow-me* application that dynamically changes camera and display devices according to user location.

4.1   Mobile Augmented Reality

In a typical mobile augmented reality application, our real-world is augmented with virtual information. For example, a door of a classroom might have a visual tag attached to it. If a PDA or cellular phone, equipped with a camera and the application program, captures the tag, it replaces it by displaying the todays schedule for the classroom.

We assume that in the future our environment will deploy many augmented reality servers. In the example, a near server stores the information about todays schedule and provides a service for detecting the visual tag and replacing it by the information about the class room, as depicted in figure 7. Other augmented reality servers, located in a street, might contain information like what shops or restaurants can be found in the neighborhood and until how late they are open.

To build the application, an application composer uses components for capturing video data, detecting visual markers, superimposing video frames and displaying video data. In addition, the composer utilizes a sensor component. The application composer contacts a context trader service to retrieve a reference to a dynamic proxy object managing references to augmented reality server components. In this way, the most suitable server component is selected dynamically. The sensor component notifies sensing information to the context manager in a user side ORB, and the context manager might change the context of the proxy object. If the context is changed, the reference to the actual AR server component used by the current user is updated and the callback handler is called. In the callback handler, the routing information managed by the data source component is updated to reflect the new configuration. As a result, the new AR server components are utilized.

Users can utilize services and information provided by the most suitable server according to users context (location). If the user moves from one area to another, the actual server managed by its proxy object is updated dynamically without user intervention. Since the application composer uses the same proxy object, it is not concerned with the existence of multiple server objects. In this way, a developer can build context-aware application without to much additional effort.

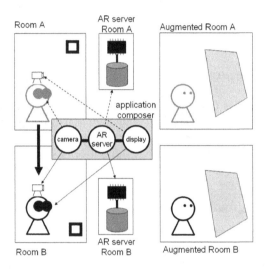

Fig. 7. Mobile Augmented Reality

4.2   A Follow-Me Application

In this section, we consider an application that receives a video stream from a camera and displays it on the nearest display to the user. As shown in Figure 8, there are two continuous media components. The first one is a camera component, and the second one is a display component. The two components are connected by an application composer. However, the actual display component is changed according to user location. An application composer holds a proxy object managing several display objects and constantly changes the target reference to a display nearest to the user. Also, the application composer has a context manager knowing which proxy object should be changed when it is notified of a context change (e.g. when a user moves).

When the user moves, a location sensor detects the movement of the user. As a result, the context manager is notified by the location sensor (1). In response, the context manager changes the context of the proxy object (2). Therefore, a method invocation is forwarded to the nearest display component (3). In this case, when a callback handler in the application composer is invoked, it updates the routing information held by the camera component (4).

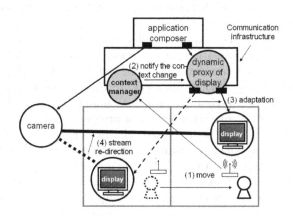

Fig. 8. Follow-me Application

5   Related Work

ARToolkit[1] is a software library that allows us to develop augmented reality applications easily. It provides several functions to detect square formed visual markers in a video frame. We have implemented continuous media components for augmented reality by reusing programs provided by the ARToolkit.

DWARF[3] is a component based framework for distributed augmented reality applications using CORBA. It aims to develop prototypes easily with extended XML or UIML. Our system is different from DWARF since our system offers context-awareness to develop augmented reality applications suitable for ubiquitous computing.

The VuSystem[10] is a framework for compute-intensive multimedia applications. It is divided into an in-band partition and an out-of-band partition. The out-of-band partition is written in Tcl and controls the in-band media processing modules written in C++. Compute-intensive means that computers perform analysis on multimedia data, and can take actions based on the findings. In our framework, we intend to use visual marker information contained within video frames more extensively. A visual marker might contain any kind of information. For example, a sensor device might use visual markers to estimate location or analyze what it is monitoring.

Infopipes[9] proposes an abstraction for building distributed multimedia streaming applications. Components such as sources, sinks, buffers, and filters are defined, and multimedia applications are built by connecting them.

In our framework, we explicitly specify the connection among components like Infopipes, but the connections are dynamically changed according to context information.

Fault Tolerant CORBA specification[17] allows us to create a replicated object to make a service highly reliable. In the specification, when we adopt the primary/backup scheme, one of the replicated objects actually receive a request. The primary replica is specified in an object reference that is passed to a client. When the object reference becomes invalid, the reference to the primary replica is returned by using the location forward mechanism in the IIOP protocol. The scheme is very similar to our context-aware support in CORBA.

A programmable network[5] allows us to change the functionalities of the network according to the characteristics of each applications. Each entity in a programmable network, like a router, has a programmable interface designed to change the functionalities. In our approach, an application can configure each continuous media component according to the characteristics of the application. The capability is similar to a programmable network.

The LocALE[13] framework provides a simple management interface for controlling the life cycle of CORBA distributed objects. It extends mobility support to the CORBA life cycle management mechanism. Objects can be moved to anywhere in a location domain by the explicit request from a client. In our framework, on the other hand, objects can be autonomously selected by the dynamic proxy object described in Section 3.2.1.

6   Conclusion

In this paper, we have described our middleware framework to support augmented reality for ubiquitous computing. We have described the design and the implementation of our system, and shown some experiences with our current prototype system. Our experiences show that our system is very useful to develop several augmented reality applications for ubiquitous computing.

In the future, we like to continue to improve our middleware framework, and to develop attractive augmented reality applications such as game, navigation, and enhanced communication applications. Currently, our system is running on Linux, and we like to exploit real-time capabilities provided by Linux to process video streams in a timely fashion. Also, we are interested to take into account to use a device proposed in [18] since the device can augment the real world without a display by projecting computer generated graphics on real objects directly.

References

1. ARToolkit, http://www.hitl.washington.edu/people/ grof/SharedSpace/Download/ARToolKitPC.htm.
2. R.T. Azuma, "A Survey of Augmented Reality", Presence: Teleoperators and Virtual Environments Vol.6, No.4, 1997.

3. Martin Bauer, Bernd Bruegge, et al.: *Design of a Component-Based Augmented Reality Framework*, The Second IEEE and ACM International Symposium on Augmented Reality, 2001.
4. G.S.Blair, et. al., "The Design and Implementation of Open ORB 2", IEEE Distributed Systems Online, Vol.2, No.6, 2001.
5. Andrew T. Campbell, Herman G. De Meer, Michael E. Kounavis, Kazuho Miki, John B. Vicente, Daniel Villela, "A Survey of Programmable Networks", ACM SIGCOMM Computer Communications Review, Vol.29, No.2, 1999.
6. A.K.Dey, G.D.Abowd, D.Salber, "A Conceptual Framework and a Toolkit for Supporting the Rapid Prototyping of Context-Aware Applications", Human-Computer Interaction, Vol.16, No.2-4, 2001.
7. Erich Gamma, Richard Helm, Ralph Johnson, John Flissides: *Design Patterns, Elements of Reusable Object-Orientated Software*, Addison-Wesley Publishing Company (1995), ISBN 0-201-63361-2.
8. Michi Henning, Steve Vinoski: *Advanced CORBA Programming with C++*, Addison-Wesley Publishing Company (1999), ISBN 0-201-37927-9.
9. R.Koster, A.P. Black, J.Huang, J.Walpole, and C.Pu, "Thread Transparency in Information Flow Middleware", In Proceedings of the IFIP/ACM International Conference on Distributed Systems Platforms, 2001.
10. Christopher J. Lindblad, David L. Tennenhouse: *The VuSystem: A Programming System for Compute-Intensive Multimedia*, In Proceedings of ACM International Conference on Multimedia 1994.
11. S Lo, S Pope, "The Implementation of a High Performance ORB over Multiple Network Transports", In Proceedings of Middleware 98, 1998.
12. D.Lopez de Ipina, "Visual Sensing and Middleware Support for Sentient Computing", PhD thesis, Cambridge University Engineering Department, January 2002
13. Diego Lopez de Ipina and Sai-Lai Lo, "LocALE: a Location-Aware Lifecycle Environment for Ubiquitous Computing", In Proceedings of the 15th IEEE International Conference on Information Networking (ICOIN-15), 2001.
14. T.Nakajima, "System Software for Audio and Visual Networked Home Appliances on Commodity Operating Systems", In Proceedings of the IFIP/ACM International Conference on Distributed Systems Platforms, 2001.
15. T.Nakajima, H.Ishikawa, E.Tokunaga, F. Stajano, "Technology Challenges for Building Internet-Scale Ubiquitous Computing", In Proceedings of the Seventh IEEE International Workshop on Object-oriented Real-time Dependable Systems, 2002.
16. T.Nakajima, "Experiences with Building Middleware for Audio and Visual Netwoked Home Appliances on Commodity Software", ACM Multimedia 2002.
17. OMG, "Final Adopted Specification for Fault Tolerant CORBA", OMG Technical Committee Document ptc/00-04-04, Object Management Group (March 2000).
18. C.Pinhanez, "The Everywhere Display Projector: A Device to Create Ubiquitous Graphical Interfaces", In Proceedings of Ubicomp'01, 2001.
19. K.Raatikainen, H.B.Christensen, T.Nakajima, "Applications Requirements for Middleware for Mobile and Pervasive Systems", Mobile Computing and Communications Review, Octorber, 2002.
20. M. Weiser, "The Computer for the 21st Century", Scientific American, Vol. 265, No.3, 1991.

Zero-Stop Authentication: Sensor-Based Real-Time Authentication System

Kenta Matsumiya[1], Soko Aoki[1], Masana Murase[1], and Hideyuki Tokuda[12]

[1] Graduate School of Media and Governance, Keio University
[2] Faculty of Environmental Information, Keio University {kenta,soko
masana,hxt}@ht.sfc.keio.ac.jp

Abstract. This paper proposes "Zero-stop Authentication" system, which requires no intentional interactions between users and authentication applications. Our Zero-stop Authentication model simplifies the current complicated authentication process by automating detection of users and objects. Our challenge is to eliminate the necessity for users to wait for a moment to be authenticated without reducing security level of authentication. To accomplish such real time user authentication in a physical environment, user mobility needs to be modelled. This paper models and formulates the user mobility and time constraints as "$1/N \times 1/M$ model", considering user speed, sensor coverage areas, communication time between the sensors and the server, and processing time consumed by an authentication process. We also prototyped a library application based on $1/N \times 1/M$ model, and installed it into Smart Furniture [1] which is an experimental platform to examine feasibility of our model.

1 Introduction

Environment surrounding us is becoming pervasive and ubiquitous [2], populated with mobile devices and various appliances. With the use of these devices, we can access computational resources with increased mobility. Moreover, sensor technologies make such an environment smart, and enable proactive behavior of applications. The applications proactively take the first action for the users by achieving both users' and objects' context. An example of the proactive behavior can be found in an automatic door. An IrDA sensor on top of the door detects a user coming, and opens the door without receiving any explicit commands from the user. Due to the proactive behavior, users can access and execute computer services such as check-out applications in supermarkets and libraries without the need of intentional interaction with systems. Despite the progress in above mentioned ubiquitous and mobile computing technologies, authentication system and its architecture are becoming more complicated. Existing authentication systems require users to input their names and passwords or show their identification cards to access computers and software. Let us assume, for example, that a user borrows books, and checks out of a library. In the library, the user needs to show an identification card to a librarian, and the librarian checks whether the user is valid. After authenticating the user, the librarian checks books to lend. In this process, both the user and the librarian need certain time for the authentication.

J. Chen and S. Hong (Eds.): RTCSA 2003, LNCS 2968, pp. 296–311, 2004.

The key challenge is to eliminate users' waiting time for authentication with security levels of authentication kept. This paper proposes a sensor-based automatic authentication: zero-stop authentication, which diminishes user-computer or user-software interaction mentioned above, providing "zero-stop" property. We define "zero-stop" property as a property of an authentication system not to make moving users pause during authentication process. To achieve this property, a system needs to meet the following four functionalities:

- Correctly detecting users and objects.
- Providing active authentication that requires no input from users.
- Providing real time response.
- Presenting feedback of authentication results.

To provide real time response, first user and object mobility need to be modeled. Modelling free mobility in which users and objects are assumed to move around through arbitrary physical point and in arbitrary direction can be difficult. Rather, we have modelled one specific class of mobility in which users and objects pass through a certain physical point in one direction. We can see such mobility pattern in real world, for example at gates in public buildings and infront of service counters. We expect that many applications can benefit if such a mobility class is formalized. Our model is called "Zero-stop Authentication". In this model, the aim is not so much as to provide guarantees for authenticaiton process to complete within certain time constraint. Our aim is to provide formulas to check if the entire authentication process can be completed within certain time, given the velocity of the user and system overhead, so necessary compensation can be provided. To keep the authentication safe, we adopt existing security technologies such as secure socket layer (SSL) [3] and IPSec [4]. Encryption technologies like DES [5] and RSA [6] also secure authentication process.

The rest of this paper is structured as follows. Section 2 details requirements to realize Zero-stop Authentication and our contribution. In Section 3, we compare related work with our system, and discuss whether current work can achieve the requirements of the Zero-stop Authentication. Section 4 introduces "Zero-stop Authentication model", and formalizes users' and objects' mobility in terms of soft real-time operations. Section 5 discusses the user-object binding problem that the system needs to distinguish which objects are whose, and then Section 6 designs system architecture of the sensor-based Zero-stop Authentication. In Section 7, we prototyped a library check-out application based on our Zero-stop Authentication model. Finally, we summarize this paper, and discuss future work in Section 8.

2   Challenges

Sensing and networking technologies are rapidly developing. Computing devices in general are also reducing their size, becoming more energy efficient and inexpensive. They are becoming pervasively available. These technological developments let us envision a computing environment where myriad devices actively sense and interact with us. For example, at the entrance gate in a subway station, users need to take their tickets out of their purses or their pockets, then put it into the ticket gate and receive it. In this context, exploiting an proactive ticket gate which detects the user's ticket automatically will decrease users' stress for handling the ticket.

Turning to our daily activities, situations in which we need to authenticate ourselves are increasing. For example, we log on to computers, show ID cards when entering authorized buildings and spaces, show credit cards to purchase merchandises (on-line as well as off-line), and so on. Making environments proactively authenticate users reduces stress on users greatly in aforementioned situations. In fact, such applications are starting to be even commercially available [7] [8]. However, these applications organize sensors, devices, and software functions on their own. A generic model is yet to be available.

The main challenge of this paper is achieving a sensor based real-time authentication which authenticates multiple users passing by an authentication gate carrying multiple objects. In realizing the authentication system, there are mainly two sub challenges: modeling user and object mobility and object binding.

To support the user's continuous mobility during the authentication process, the authentication system needs to finish its tasks within a certain time. The necessary time for authentication strongly depends on the hardware and software performance. Therefore we need to formalize the mobility of users and objects and utilize this formulation when designing and installing the zero-stop authentication system. In this formalization, we have made four models of mobility according to the number of users and objects. In the first model, there is one user carrying one object in the authentication area. In the second model, there is one user carrying multiple objects in the area. In the third model, there are multiple users and each of them brings one object. In the fourth model, there are multiple users and each of them brings multiple objects.

When multiple users carrying multiple objects go through the authentication area at the same time, the authentication system needs to distinguish which objects are whose. If the system fails, some objects might be wrongly assigned to other users. The binding of users and objects should be done either within the sensor or within the user's client device. In the former case, the sensor detects all the users and objects collectively and distinguish each object. In the latter case, the client device detects all the objects user choose and the client device informs the sensor collectively. As a result, the sensor can distinguish the objects by the data sent from the user's device.

In consideration of aforementioned model, we design and implement the sensor-based real-time authentication system. The architecture of the system includes sensors for detecting users and objects, authentication program, and result output devices. A generic model of authentication system needs to take several kinds of sensors and devices into consideration. An overall procedure of the new sensor-based authentication needs to be designed not only to reduce the users' burden on authentication but also to recognize, guide, and give feedback to the users. After implementing the zero-stop authentication system, the system needs to be applied to some contexts and be tested. In the experiment, multiple users with multiple objects go through the authentication area at a certain speed. In case the authentication system fails to detect or authenticate the users and objects, the users needs to be stopped and the system needs to run error recovery program.

3   Related Work

The ActiveBadge system [9] and BAT system [10] are sensor management systems for context-aware applications which tracks users and objects. In this tracking system, the users and various objects are tagged with the wireless transmitters, and their location is stored in a database. Therefore main goal of the BAT system is detection of users' and objects' accurate location. Since the objective of Zero-stop Authentication system is to build an authentication system on top of a sensor system, the ActiveBadge and the BAT can complement our system.

Intelligent Transport System (ITS) [11], especially, the electronic toll collection (ETC) system [12] allows cars to go through the toll gate without stopping. To realize non-stop payment at the toll gate, automotive vehicles are equipped with devices capable of wireless communication with the toll gate. When these vehicles enter the communication area that a toll gate covers, the toll gate begins to authenticate vehicles, and then withdraws money from banks. In this authentication process, it is necessary to identify automotive vehicles or IDs such as a credit card number or a unique number bound to a credit card number. [13] proposes the method to identify automotive vehicles by using a retroreflective optical scanner, whereas [14] identifies moving vehicles by smart cards with radio frequency (RF) or infrared (IR) transponders or RF smart tags. However, the ETC model does not address the binding problem since it assumes all the vehicles are serialized. Our model, on the other hand, deals with cases where multiple users bringing multiple objects need to be authenticated at a time.

Zero-Interaction Authentication (ZIA) [15] is an authentication system in which a user wears a small authentication token that communicates with a laptop computer over a short-range wireless link. Whenever the laptop needs decryption authority, the laptop acquires the decryption authority from the token and authority is retained only as long as it's necessary. ZIA is similar to our model in its goal of authenticating the user without stopping them. The main differences between these two models are that our model authenticate both users and objects, and formalizes their mobility by considering the real time aspect.

4   Models for Zero-Stop Authentication

We formulate Zero-stop Authentication in this section. To realize zero-stop operations of authentication, an authentication server embedded in a gate (gate server) detects users and objects by cooperating with sensors, and then authenticates users within real time. In our procedural assumption, the gate server can not process the authentication operations concurrently, because it runs according to the challenge-response manner. Moreover, we assume that a task deadline is a soft deadline. The gate server checks this deadline, and it processes authentication error operations, if a deadline miss occurs.

This paper discusses the following case: a user-detecting sensor observes N users, and an object-detecting sensor recognizes M_N objects, where M_i is the number of objects carried by user i. The reason why we use two types of sensors is to make the system practical. It is considered that inexpensive sensors can be used to detect objects, while richer sensors that can perform authentication protocols are needed for users.

In this section, we introduce four models of zero-stop authentication. These models can be applied to several applications such as library applications and supermarket check-out applications.

(a) $1/1 \times 1/1$ **model**
In this model, both the user-detecting sensor and the object-detecting sensor sense the only one entity at a time.

(b) $1/1 \times 1/M$ **model**
In this model, the user-detecting sensor detects only one user, while the object-detecting sensor recognizes multiple objects at a time.

(c) $1/N \times 1/1$ **model**
In this model, the user-detecting sensor detects N users, while the object-detecting sensor detects an object per user.

(d) $1/N \times 1/M$ **model**
In this model, a user-detecting sensor observes N users, and one object-detecting sensor recognizes M_N objects per user.

4.1   Models of Environment

Figure 1 illustrates the environment we assume. Although coverage-shapes of all sensors are not circular, many RF sensors with omni-directional antennas such as IEEE-802.11b standardized devices and RF-ID readers can detect objects appeared in a certain circular area. Thus, we model that the coverage areas of the user-detecting sensor and the object-detecting sensor are circles of radius R_{usr} and R_{obj}, respectively. If $R_{usr} \leq R_{obj}$ is satisfied, two sensors and a gate server are placed as Figure 1-(a) shows (each sensors are located at the gate). Figure 1-(b) depicts the contrary case i.e., in the case of $R_{usr} > R_{obj}$.

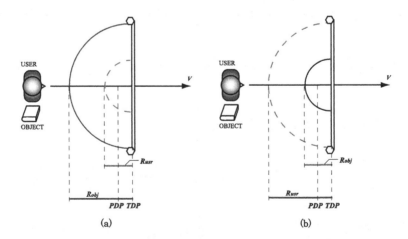

Fig. 1. Environment of The Zero-Stop Authentication System

As for user movement, we assume that a user walks straight along the collinear line of two sensors and the gate server at a constant velocity, V. By the time when a user reaches a processing deadline point (PDP), the gate server should finish both the authentication and the object processing. Then the server temporarily stores those results in its memory or storage. The gate server updates information about the user and objects by the time when the user passes through the gate (transaction deadline point: TDP). Users can obtain the feedback of authentication and object-binding by the gate server while they exist between PDP and TDP. The length between PDP and TDP depends on applications, since each application consumes different time required for feedback to users.

4.2   Time Constrained Operations

(a) $1/1 \times 1/1$ Model. In a single user case, we assume that the user enters the coverage area of the user-detecting sensor or the object-detecting sensor at time $t = 0$. In this condition, the gate server should authenticate the user within the following given time:

$$\frac{R_{usr} - l}{V} - \alpha - \beta - AT \geq 0 \tag{1}$$

where l stands for the distance between PDP and TDP, α is the processing time of the user-detecting sensor to discover users, β stands for the time to transfer a user-ID datum from the user-detecting sensor to the gate server, and AT is the authentication time.

The velocity of objects can be obtained by approximating user's velocity. This is because objects travel at the same velocity V, since the user carries objects. The gate server should process operations for the object within the time:

$$\frac{R_{obj} - l}{V} - \gamma - \delta - OT \geq 0 \tag{2}$$

where the parameter γ is the processing time of the object-detecting sensor, δ is the communication time to transfer an object-ID datum from the object-detecting sensor to the gate server, and OT stands for the time taken by the gate server to process the operation for the single object.

(b) $1/1 \times 1/M$ Model. The constraint of the authentication is the same inequality as formula 1, since the gate server also authenticate a single user in case (b). However, the gate server processes operations for M objects. Therefore, it should satisfy the following relationship to realize that the user does not need to stop at the gate:

$$\frac{R_{obj} - l}{V} - \sum_{j=1}^{M} \gamma_j - \sum_{j=1}^{M} \delta_j - \sum_{j=1}^{M} OT_j \geq 0 \tag{3}$$

for $1 \leq j \leq M$, where γ_j is the processing time consumed by the object-detecting sensor to discover object j, γ_j represents the communication time to send the ID of object j from the object-detecting sensor to the gate server, and OT_j is the processing time to modify the state of object j. Formula 3 assumes that the object-detecting sensor can not concurrently scan multiple objects. If it is possible, the new formula becomes simpler: $\sum_{j=1}^{M} \gamma_j$ is substituted with γ_{max} which is the greatest value of all γ_j. In addition, the communication time, $\sum_{j=1}^{M} \delta_j$, can be reduced, if object ID data can be transfered by less than M packets.

(c) $1/N \times 1/1$ **Model.** We consider a more complex case than case (a) and (b): N users pass through a gate carrying a single object for each. In the multiple users case, user i enters into the coverage area of a user-detecting sensor or an object-detecting sensor at time t_i. In this case, the time-constrained computation for authenticating user i is as follows:

$$t_i + \frac{R_{usr} - l}{V_i} - \alpha_i - \beta_i - AT_i \geq t_i \qquad (4)$$

for $1 \leq i \leq N$, where α_i represents the time to detect user i, β_i is the communication time between the user-detecting sensor and the gate server, and AT_i is the time taken by the gate server to authenticate user i.

If $\forall V_i = \forall V_j \ (i \neq j)$ is met, or operations for each users are serialized like ATM in a bank, the gate server just authenticates users, following the first-in-first-out (FIFO) discipline; otherwise the gate server should reschedule the order of authentication operations to minimize deadline misses. To address this issue, we have two approaches. One is using the earliest-deadline-first algorithm [16] which schedules the user with the closest deadline first. According to this scheduling policy, the gate server can determine the priority of each user by calculating D_i in the formula:

$$D_i = ET_i + \frac{R_{usr} - l}{V_i} - \alpha_i - \beta_i - AT_i \qquad (5)$$

where ET_i is the time when user i enters the coverage area of the user-detecting sensor.

The other one is building least-slack-time scheduling [17] into the gate server. In this case, the slack time for authenticating user i at time t is $D_i - p_i - t$, where p_i is the processing time to authenticate users.

(d) $1/N \times 1/M$ **Model.** A model for multiple users carrying multiple objects for each is discussed here. The order to authenticate all N users can be determined by user selection algorithms. To realize Zero-stop operations, the gate server should meet the following formula to modify the state of object j:

$$\frac{R_{obj} - l}{V_i} - \sum_{j=1}^{M_i} \gamma_j - \sum_{j=1}^{M_i} \delta_j - \sum_{j=1}^{M_i} OT_j \geq 0 \qquad (6)$$

for $1 \leq i \leq N$ and $1 \leq j \leq M_i$, where M_i is the number of objects that user i carries.

5   Object Binding

In both $1/N \times 1/1$ model and $1/N \times 1/M$ model, the authentication system needs to bind objects to users. Examples of objects are books in libraries, and merchandises in supermarkets. If these objects are appropriately bound to users, applications will be able to register, or charge them to the user. The main challenge is to correctly sense and distinguish objects belonging to a user. While mechanisms to sense an object is maturing, those to distinguish it, and to bind it to an appropriate user is not as thoroughly investigated.

We introduce three ideas in the following that can be used to effectively distinguish between objects belonging to a user from others'. In our assumption, objects are tagged with wireless identification devices, such as RF tags. We will classify these tags into two groups: Read-Only, and Read-Write.

guidance. The guidance approach is a technique to transform $1/N \times 1/1$ model or $1/N \times 1/M$ model to $1/1 \times 1/1$ model. In this approach, users are physically guided, so only one user is sensed by the system at a time. This method has analogies to traditional object binding methods, such as in supermarkets. However users often queue in supermarkets, so enough gates to realize the zero-stop property is required.

insulation. We use an insulator to obstruct radio wave to or from the tags attached to the objects. The insulator will likely take the form of specialized containers, such as shopping carts. In this approach, the authentication system detects a user who exists close to the gate, and authenticates him or her. After that, the authorized user opens the container so that the objects are exposed to, or freed to give off radio waves. The identification of the objects recognized at that point is bound to the target of the authentication. Other users must not open their container during this process, because object binding misses occur.

marking. Objects have writable tags attached, and users use devices to write their IDs to those tags. When objects are sensed, these IDs are also sensed, and reported to the system, allowing it to bind the objects to the user.

Table 1 classifies each binding method by types of tags and required devices.

Table 1. Binding methods

method	tag type	device
guidance	RO	gate
insulation	RO	insulation container
marking	RW	marking device

6   System Architecture

There are six modules as shown in Figure2 in our system. We assume that devices such as sensors, displays, and speakers can be controlled directly over a network, or from a computer that is connected to a network. The system itself runs on a designated computer.

Detection module manages sensors which detect users and objects, and throws events or data obtained from sensors. *Event process module* processes the raw events or data into a form that is recognizable to the rest of the system. It passes user identifiers to the authentication module, and object identifiers to the binding module. *Authentication module* manages authentication mechanisms and protocols, and conducts user authentication. If the authentication succeeds, *binding module* binds objects with the user. *Feedback process module* processes commands for output devices, from the feedback information passed from applications. *Output module* manages output devices, and dispatches commands to the correct output device based on users' context or requirements. Applications may choose to use the feedback functions of the system, or choose not to do so.

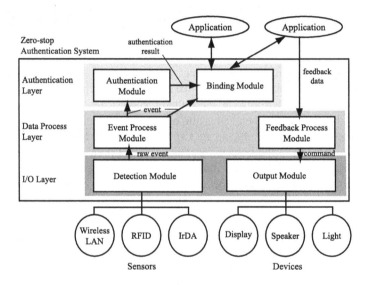

Fig. 2. Architecture

In the rest of this section, we describe in detail about four features which our authentication needs to acquire: Recognition and guidance of users and objects, binding objects to users, maintaining user and object state, and presentation of feedback and error correction.

6.1   Recognition and Guidance

The system needs to physically recognize and guide users and objects. Recognition may be done by existing sensor mechanisms. In order to achieve zero-stop property, users need to be successfully authenticated within a specific period of time. Thus, there are constraints on sensing overhead.

Guidance is an issue related to recognition. Existing examples of physical guidance include gates and doors at building entrances, cash counters in supermarkets, and various toll gates on roadways. Some sensing technologies have problems in sensing multiple objects within same physical area, or objects moving in exceedingly high speed. In order to accomplish the authentication task using such sensing technologies, objects must be physically guided to support the sensors. Objects are guided to pass a particular area, managed into sequential queues, and their speed may be reduced.

In case users carry objects that need to be bound to themselves such as merchandises in supermarkets, the sensors need to distinguish between multiple objects, or between objects belonging to an user from those that belong to others. If the sensors were not able to accomplish this task, objects may need to be bundled or separated accordingly.

6.2   User and Object State

The system need to keep track of user and object state. Their physical context should be mapped accordingly to the internal objects maintained by the system. Figure 3 illustrates the state graph of users and objects.

The system may loose or mix up users and objects due to sensing problems, and incorrect binding may occur. The system need to recover from these errors, and allow users to correct improper transactions.

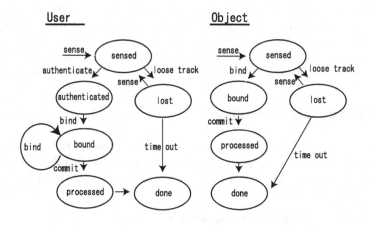

Fig. 3. State graph of users and objects

6.3   Feedback and Error Correction

The objective of the feedback is to allow users to acknowledge the result of the authentication, verify if objects were correctly bound to them, and browse other related information such as a due date of a book or credits withdrawn from their bank accounts.

The presentation of the feedback can be done visually, or through other methods such as audio synthesizing. Simple results that can be expressed in several patterns, may be presented using simple and intuitive presentation methods, such as color pattern of an LCD. We believe that this kind of presentation method will gain more popularity in the forthcoming ubiquitous computing environment as a way to output computational results.

Error correction is another important field for our system to address. Authentication and transaction might generate errors such as authentication failure, miss-binding of objects, and unreasonable withdrawal of credits. The system need to permit users to interact with the system, and correct these errors.

Traditional interaction devices such as keyboards and mice are not an ideal candidate for our interaction methods, since they are immobile and interaction intensive. One way to go around this problem is to construct a user interface which is accessible from voice operation or gesture operation. Their interaction method and physical form may vary between the different applications that adopt them. Another solution may be to construct a software agent that automatically corrects the errors on behalf of the users.

6.4 Development

Final point to consider when constructing a Zero-stop Authentication system, is development procedure. Usability of the system is limited mainly due to the overhead and ability of sensor devices and authentication methods. Current technologies may not be able to permit, for example, tens of automobiles each traveling over 100km/h to be authenticated at once. They are likely to be asked instead to slow down to under 50km/h, and pass a gate one by one. Development in the sensing and authentication technologies however, may enable the intended scenario. So, the development and deployment of the system should be done incrementally, gradually freeing users from physical constraints.

7   Prototype Implementation

We prototyped sensor-based authentication system based on the Zero-stop Authentication model proposed in this paper. Besides the prototype system of Zero-stop Authentication, a library check-out application is also implemented using JDK 1.3.1.

7.1 Authentication System and Application

Figure 4 depicts Smart Furniture which is an experimental platform of a gate server. Two types of sensors are equipped with the gate server, and they are RF-based sensor devices; a wireless LAN device to detect users and an RFID tag sensor to detect objects. Hardware composition is explained in Figure 5 with its specification in Table 2 and Table 3.

The prototype authentication system is composed of six modules mentioned in Section 6. In our current implementation, the detection module obtains sensor data from the wireless LAN device and the RFID tag sensor. Therefore, we developed their sensor driver programs for sending sensor data to the detection module. The wireless LAN sensor driver program detects users' portable devices using signal strength, and then provides the IP address of the user's terminal with the highest level of signal strength among others detected by the sensor. To measure signal strength, we utilize IBSS mode

(a)   (b)

Fig. 4. Smart Furniture: (a) a testbed for uqibuitous applications; (b) Zero-stop Authentication system with a library application

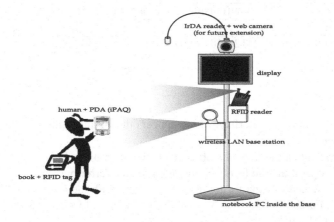

Fig. 5. Hardware Composition

of an IEEE 802.11b standardized device. After obtaining the IP address, the authentication module tries to communicate with the host to which the IP address is assigned, and then it starts an authentication process (simple challenge-response protocol). The authentication module authenticates users by searching within a PostgreSQL based data base server where student information (IDs, passwords, names etc.) is stored. In the authentication process, the communication link between users' terminals and the gate server is protected by SSL.

After authenticating the user successfully, the RFID tag sensor driver program detects books to which RFID tags are attached. At the same time, the binding module binds the user and books, and provides the authentication module with the binding information. Finally, the output module indicates authentication results on the LCD screen of Smart Furniture for users so as to confirm details. Figure 6-(b) illustrates the screen

Table 2. Computing Devices Used in Prototype Implementation

item	iPAQ	ThinkPAD
Type	User Terminal (PDA)	Gate Server (notebook PC)
CPU	StrongARM 206MHz	Intel PentiumIII 850MHz
Memory	64MB	256MB
OS	Familiar Linux v0.5.1	FreeBSD 5.0 CURRENT
Network Interface	802.11b	802.11b (IBSS-Mode)
Others	TFT Display	

Table 3. Sensor Devices Used in Prototype Implementation

item	Wireless LAN	RFID Sensor
Type	User Terminal (Wireless LAN)	Gate Server (RFID Reader)
Detection Range	160m(outside),50m(indoor)	15m(indoor)
Read Rate		75 tags / second
Operating Frequency	2412-2484 MHz	303.8 MHz
Others		

dump of graphical user interface which appears during the authentication process for the confirmation.

If the authentication fails, the object detection operation above is not processed. In stead of this operation, the feedback module produces error messages, and shows them on the LCD screen of Smart Furniture cooperating with the output module as Figure 6-(c) shows. Furthermore, it also blocks the path of a user by closing the library gate, or setting off an alarm.

(a)   (b)   (c)

Fig. 6. Screen dump of authentication results: (a) waiting for authentication; (b) authentication is successfully done; (c) authentication failure occurs

7.2   System Measurement

We have tested our system for 100 times under the condition of adjusting wireless LAN -40db to detect and -50db to lose the connection. This signal strength makes the authentication area as large as 2m in radius. The detection and authentication time necessary for our system was 599.33msec on average which is fast enough for the system to authenticate users before users passing through the authentication area. The standard deviation in our measurement result was 30.93.

7.3   Serialization Scheme

Since we have utilized RFIDs which are not data writable and read only, we have adopted the guidance method described in section 5 for the object binding.

Our library application and authentication system should deal with a concurrency access problem. When several users concurrently access the gate server at the same place, the gate server can not realize zero-stop property. Some tasks may fail and miss their deadline, because the gate server can not provide enough resources. To address this issue, the serialization scheme is introduced in our system as Figure 7 illustrates.

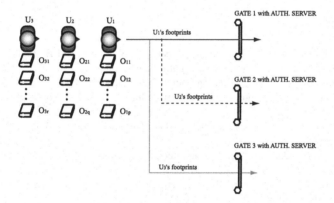

Fig. 7. Serialization Scheme

8   Conclusion

This paper presents Zero-stop Authentication, a sensor-based real-time authentication system in which no intentional interaction between users and authentication system is required. In our system, we have attached several sensors on the gate to detect users and objects and authenticate them. To realize Zero-stop authentication, the system needs to finish the authentication process within real time. Therefore we have formulated the mobility of users and objects. The prototype of Zero-stop Authentication is implemented in Java, and uses Wireless LAN and RFID reader to detect users and objects. We have applied our system to the library's authentication with Smart Furniture a test bed infrastructure. We are extending the current system to cope with several problems which are not overcome. Two examples of future work are object binding problem and terminal theft problem.

In our prototype implementation, we adopted the guidance method for object binding. Since it can transform complicated models into 1/1 x 1/1 model, we were able to keep the system simple. However, in order to provide higher usability by not making users queue up, the system needs to support 1/N x 1/1 model or 1/N x 1/M model. To realize these models, we need to implement a more complex system, and at the same time apply other binding methods such as insulation and marking.

We have tried to simplify the current complicated authentication process without diminishing security level by using several security and encryption technologies. However, there is still a threat that a client device or a tag which a user should have would be stolen. For these problems, authentication technology for the device such as biometrics is usable.

Acknowledgement. We thank Uchida Yoko Corporation for their collaborating work on "Smart Furniture".

References

1. K. Takashio, S. Aoki, M. Murase, K. Matsumiya, N. Nishio, and H. Tokuda, "Smart hotspot: Taking out ubiquitous smart computing environment anywhere", 2002, International Conference on Pervasive Computing (Demo Presentations).
2. M. Weiser, "The computer for the twenty-century", vol. 265, no. 3, pp. 94–104, 1991, Scientific American.
3. A. Freier, P. Kartiton, and P. Kocher, "The ssl protocol: version 3.0", 1996, Tech Rep., Internet-draft.
4. S. Kent and R. Atkinson, "Security architecture for the internet protocol", 1998, IETF RFC 2401.
5. W. Deffie and M. E. Hellman, "New directions in cryptography", 1976, pp. 644–654, IEEE Transactions on Information Theory IT-22.
6. R. Rivest, A. Shamir, and L. Adleman, "A method for obtaing digital signatures and public-key cryptosystems", in *Communications of the ACM*, 1978, vol. 21, pp. 120–126.
7. Ensure Technologies Inc., "Xyloc", 2001, http://www.ensuretech.com/.
8. Sony Corporation, "Felica: Contactless smart card system", 2002, http://www.sony.net/Products/felica/.
9. R. Want, A. Hopper, V. Falcao, and J. Gibbons, "The active badge location system", Tech. Rep. 92.1, ORL, 24a Trumpington Street, Cambridge CB2 1QA, 1992.
10. A. Harter, A. Hopper, P. Steggles, A. Ward, and P. Webster, "The anatomy of a context-aware application", in *International Conference on Mobile Computing and Networking*, 1999, pp. 59–68.
11. ITS America, "Intelligent transportation system", 2002, http://www.itsa.org/standards.
12. ETTM On The Web, "Electoronic toll collection system", 2002, http://www.ettm.com/.
13. H. Okabe, K. Takemura, S. Ogata, and T. Yamashita, "Compact vehicle sensor using a retroreflective optical scanner", in *IEEE Conference of Intelligent Transportation Systems*, 1997, pp. 201–205.

14. ETTM On The Web, "Automatic vehicle identification", 2002, http://www.ettm.com/avi.htm.
15. M. Corner and B. Noble, "Zero-interaction authentication", in *International Conference on Mobile Computing and Networking*, 2002.
16. M. L. Dertouzos, "Control robotics: The procedural control of physical processes", in *Proceedings of the IFIP Congress*, 1974, pp. 807–813.
17. R. W. Conway, M. L. Maxwell, and L. W. Miller, "Theory of scheduling", 1967, Addison-Wesley.

An Interface-Based Naming System for Ubiquitous Internet Applications

Masateru Minami[1], Hiroyuki Morikawa[2], and Tomonori Aoyama[1]

[1] Graduate School of Information Science and Technology, The University of Tokyo
[2] Graduate School of Frontier Sciences, The University of Tokyo
7-3-1 Hongo, Bunkyo-ku, Tokyo, Japan
`{minami,mori,aoyama}@mlab.t.u-tokyo.ac.jp`

Abstract. In the future, huge amounts of embedded and invisible devices, as well as software components, will be connected to the Internet, and these "functional objects" are expected to play an important role in providing convenience services to users. In such a "ubiquitous Internet," users will be able to utilize various applications through functional objects anytime and anywhere. Since the ubiquitous Internet will be a highly dynamic, heterogeneous, and context-dependent environment, applications should be able to change their functionality depending on dynamically changing user context. For example, when a user wishes to brows a PDF file on his small PDA display, a document-browsing application running on the PDA will need an additional transcoder function to reformat the PDF file. If the user wishes to use a voice-only device, such as a PDC (Personal Digital Cellular), to obtain information in the PDF document, the application will need to locate and use a PDF-to-text function as well as a text-to-voice function. Thus, to enable ubiquitous Internet applications to change their functionality on the fly, a mechanism capable of locating the appropriate functions transparently on the Internet is necessary. Generally, such locating mechanisms can be supported by a location-independent naming system. However, the name space of such a naming system tends to be flat; therefore, designing a scalable naming system is quite challenging. This paper describes the design of a new scalable location-independent naming system, called Interface-based Naming System (IFNS), which is capable of locating functional objects transparently in a ubiquitous Internet. In the design of IFNS, we utilize interface information to name functional objects. Interface information enables us to design scalable name management and name resolution algorithms in a fully distributed manner. In addition, interface information not only enables the transparent location of functional objects, but also enables the naming system to support automatic function synthesis. Simulation results show that the proposed IFNS has acceptable scalability and performance for utilizing functional objects in a ubiquitous Internet environment.

1 Introduction

The rapid deployment of broadband and wireless Internet technologies has not only brought a diffusion of network-enabled devices into our daily lives, but has also in

J. Chen and S. Hong (Eds.): RTCSA 2003, LNCS 2968, pp. 312–327, 2004.

creased the opportunities for end-users to use various applications. This trend will launch a future Internet environment where many users will employ many different kinds of "functional objects" seamlessly through network connections anytime and anywhere. This environment, which we call the "ubiquitous Internet," requires a new platform enabling users to utilize various applications seamlessly.

Consider the scenario where a user in an office environment uses various functional objects through a video-conferencing application. To start the application to contact a colleague, the user can either click an icon on his desktop computer or issue a command via voice recognition. Then, for seamless use of the video-conferencing application, the application needs to immediately locate the necessary functional objects (e.g., the nearest CCD (charge-coupled device) camera, nearest display, and so on). If the user moves around his office, the application must change devices to seamlessly continue the video conferencing according to the user's context. And, if there is a change of network or device (e.g., the user switches his device from a desktop PC with 100 Mbps LAN to a PDA with 802.11 wireless LAN), the application may need to find an additional transcoder function to adapt to the current network or device condition. Internet-scale services will require the same features described in this personal-area scenario,. For example, when a user wishes to obtain a document in a particular format or a video file at a specific resolution, some kind of conversion function is necessary. However, since the current Internet does not support such a mechanism, the user must manually download conversion software to convert the document or video file. For seamless use of applications, this manual configuration should not be necessary. In this case, it is desirable that an appropriate data conversion function is automatically assigned to the document, and the user obtains the document directly in the desired format with minimal effort.

Many readers may think that it is easy to construct the applications in the above scenario using existing technologies (e.g., Jini or other kinds of middleware). Of course, it is possible to implement the above scenario as a "scenario-specific application" based on existing technologies. However, once we try to build universal applications for the current Internet architecture, we may find that it is quite difficult and challenging. We believe that this is mainly due to the lack of a useful locating and adaptation mechanism for global scale networks:

Locating mechanism complementary to DNS: When we try to access a networked object, such as a functional object, we must first utilize a locating service (i.e., a naming system) to provide applications with the information needed to access these networked objects. Even if huge quantities of functional objects and multimedia contents are available to the Internet, the objects are worthless if we do not have a useful locating mechanism to access them. Of course, we can use the Domain Name System (DNS) to locate objects on the current Internet. Since DNS is a well-designed and extremely scalable locating system, we can handle all objects via DNS, even in a future ubiquitous Internet. However, because DNS inherently locates objects that are tightly coupled with an IP address (i.e., administrative domain), it would be inadequate for locating objects when building various ubiquitous computing applications.

For example, in the above video-conferencing scenario, applications need to immediately locate and utilize a transcoding function for adaptation. In such cases, the application is interested in the function of the transcoder, not the IP address or network location. Although it is possible to locate such a transcoder by resolving FQDN (Fully Qualified Domain Name), if the transcoder is unavailable—for example, due to system trouble or security policy—the application needs to locate another transcoder with another FQDN. This is because FQDN is location-dependent. It is better to avoid the continuous use of various applications in a ubiquitous computing environment.

Moreover, in the above scenario, the user would like to utilize the "nearest" devices for convenience. We believe that this kind of scenario will be popular in a ubiquitous Internet, because networking and computing will continue to be integrated into our daily lives. This means that networks and computers in the ubiquitous Internet must handle not only virtual objects such as web pages or multimedia files, but also physical objects existing in the real world. However, the current DNS cannot locate objects tightly coupled with a physical situation.

Adaptation mechanism for heterogeneity: Another important aspect of the above scenario is adaptation. Generally, when we wish to run an application seamlessly in a ubiquitous computing environment, the application must dynamically combine various devices and networks, depending on various contexts. However, we cannot assume that these devices and networks always utilize the same data format and protocol; in other words, the application must handle various types of data formats and protocols. Naturally, we also cannot assume that an application always supports all data formats and protocols. Thus, applications should dynamically locate the necessary data formats or protocol conversion functions to handle heterogeneity. This means that there needs to be some mechanism to detect and absorb differences of data format and/or protocol among objects.

The above discussions indicate that another naming system, which is complementary to the current DNS, could be one of the most essential components for realizing ubiquitous computing applications on the future Internet. Optimally, this naming system will need to handle multiple name spaces to support various kinds of situations, and to enable data formats and protocol adaptations in a heterogeneous environment. From this point of view, we have developed an application platform called Service Synthesizer on the Net (STONE), which is based on a naming system called Interface-based Naming System (IFNS). IFNS is designed to support the two stated requirements: locating and adaptation. In our platform, all objects are called functional objects. These objects can be named by multiple names, such as physical location, but should have at least one interface name. The interface name consists of both input and output interface information of the functional object, and the relationship between them. For example, a functional object for mpeg2-to-mpeg4 transcoding is named mpeg2/mpeg4. This naming scheme enables applications to directly specify necessary functions. In addition, since the interface name is independent of network location (e.g., IP address or administrative domain), we can transparently locate the functional objects.

One important and challenging problem in designing such a location-independent naming system is scalability. To overcome this problem, IFNS manages functional objects by aggregating multiple functional objects into one interface name.

In addition, the interface name must not only enable transparent and scalable access to functional objects, but also support an automatic function synthesis mechanism (AFS), which will be described later. This mechanism greatly improves the performance of IFNS, even if it cannot locate a desired functional object directly. For example, if IFNS cannot locate a mpeg2-to-mpeg4 transcoder, the automatic function synthesis mechanism decomposes mpeg2-to-mpeg4 into mpeg2-to-mpeg1 and mpeg1-to-mpeg4, then tries to locate these two functions.

This paper is organized as follows. In the next section, we introduce existing work related to naming and middleware for ubiquitous computing applications. In Section 3, we briefly summarize our STONE application platform for a ubiquitous Internet. Section 4 focuses on name-space definition, name management and the resolution algorithms used in IFNS. In Section 5, simulations are performed to show the scalability of the proposed naming system as well as the performance of the automatic function synthesis mechanism. Finally, we conclude this paper in Section 6.

2 Related Work

There has been a lot of research on naming systems and service adaptation mechanisms. The most primitive approach to locating objects is the use of a network address, such as an IP address and port number. However, since the IP address inherently represents a location in the network, it is difficult to identify the actual function of a functional object. And even more unfortunately, it is also difficult to enable applications to transparently access these functional objects. An alternate approach to locating functional objects with transparent access in the Internet is the use of the Domain Name System (DNS). DNS is a well-designed system for locating various services provided on the Internet [1][2][3]. By using DNS and FQDN, we can locate a host (or service) transparent to the IP address and port number. If we can describe the function of a functional object with FQDN, it is possible to transparently locate functional objects using DNS. However, since DNS has evolved as a mechanism to access services managed through specific organization, it is not suitable for locating functional objects. Moreover, using the DNS in a highly dynamic and distributed environment, such as the ubiquitous Internet, contradicts the design philosophy of the DNS [1]. This may cause other significant problems, such as cache consistency and load-balancing problems.

This implies that a new location-independent naming system for functional objects, which is complementary to conventional DNS, is required for future ubiquitous Internet applications. Designing such a naming system, however, is quite challenging, because the name space of a location-independent name usually tends to be flat and not scalable. In order to design a scalable location-independent naming system, scalable name space and efficient name management/resolution algorithms are desired.

The Grapevine [4] proposed by XEROX PARC is one of the earliest location-independent naming systems; it utilizes hierarchical name space, and enables users to locate persons or equipment in an office environment. The X.500 directory service [5], which works on the current Internet, enables users to locate various objects by utilizing a DNS-like hierarchical administrative domain. However, since these systems (or architectures) are designed as general-purpose naming systems, it is unclear whether they would work well in a highly dynamic and globally distributed environment.

The Intentional Naming System (INS) [6], which was recently proposed, is one attempt to use a naming system to achieve various transparencies. However, although INS has a great capability of transparently locating various objects, the name space of INS tends to be flat. Consequently, it would not be scalable in the ubiquitous Internet. The authors believe that, to make systems practical and scalable, the naming system should be designed as a special-purpose system, such as DNS. IETF URI/URN (Uniform Resource Identifiers, Uniform Resource Name) [7] is another approach for locating various objects in the Internet. It defines multiple name spaces, and also designs name resolution mechanisms for various objects. However, since the design of URI/URN is highly dependent on DNS architecture, it is unclear whether it would work well in the ubiquitous Internet.

Middleware platforms, such as Jini [8], UPnP (Universal Plug and Play) [9], or HAVi (Home Audio Video interoperability) [10], usually contain a directory service. However, these directory services are not designed for a global area network. Moreover, none of them clearly defines naming schemes.

3   Service Synthesizer on the Net

As described in Section 1, the authors believe that an application platform capable of dynamically combining functional objects will be very important in the future ubiquitous Internet. To this end, we have researched application platform technologies and developed a platform named Service Synthesizer on the Net (STONE). This section provides a brief overview of this platform.

Figure 1 shows the architecture of the STONE platform. The STONE platform is a distributed system overlaid on the Internet, and it creates a service by combining various functions. The STONE platform consists of two major components: a *functional object* (FO) and a *service resolver* (SR).

The FO is the most basic element of the platform. It may be a hardware device or software component, and it is capable of network connectivity. In the STONE platform, each functional object must have its own name (FO name) and an *access pointer* (AP). The FO name consists of multiple attribute-value pairs that indicate various properties of the FO. For example, a display FO capable of JPEG image viewing in Room 407 in building No. 3 can be described as [Location = room407 / building no.3], [Interface = JPEG / DISPLAY]. Although a functional object is allowed to have multiple names, it must have at least one interface name. As described later, the interface name plays a significant role in our platform.

The access pointer list is an identifier which globally and uniquely specifies the functional object on the Internet. Currently, we are using the IP address and port number as an access pointer.

The SR (service resolver) manages FOs, and composes various services. The SR consists of a *Service Synthesizer* (SS) and a *Multi-Name Service System* (MNSS). The service synthesizer is an API (Application Programming Interface) to client applications. It collects functional objects and combines them according to a *Service Graph* (SG). The SG is a functional diagram of a service in which functions are described by the FO name. Every client of the STONE platform will send the SG to the SS to request services. When the SS receives the SG, it extracts the FO names from the SG and tries to locate functions by querying the names to the MNSS.

The MNSS manages multiple *Name Service Components* (NSC) and resolves the FO name by querying the appropriate NSC. The NSC is in charge of specific name space. For example, the name [Location = room407 / building no.3] is stored and managed by a physical location NSC. The NSC is implemented as a plug-in module so that we can easily add a new NSC to the MNSS. The reason we design the MNSS as the manager of multiple name service components is that we believe the future ubiquitous Internet will require many kinds of naming systems. For example, if a user wishes to contact someone, a naming system capable of resolving the username will be necessary. If a user wishes to use a printer in a specific location, a naming system for resolving the name of a physical space will be required. And, more importantly, since the name space managed in each naming system will have a different information structure, it will require different name management/resolution algorithms. For example, because the name space of the physical address [7-3-1/Hongo / Bunkyo-ku / Tokyo / Japan] has a hierarchical information structure, it could be managed and resolved by a DNS-like name resolution/management scheme. On the other hand, a name space for multimedia contents will have a different information structure and require another algorithm. It is not known how many naming systems will be required in the ubiquitous Internet; however, it is important that any new naming system can be easily added to the STONE platform. For this reason, we designed MNSS as a composite system.

Although there will be many NSCs in the MNSS, the most important NSC in the STONE architecture is the *Interface-based Naming System* (IFNS) component. IFNS manages the name space of functions that are provided by functional objects. Using IFNS, the service synthesizer or any other MNSS client can transparently locate various functions. IFNS not only provides the capability of transparently locating a desired function, but it also provides an automatic function synthesis mechanism that automatically equalizes the function with multiple FOs. This mechanism greatly improves the performance of service synthesis when IFNS cannot directly locate the desired FO. IFNS is a key component in the synthesis of various services in the ubiquitous Internet, and its design is the scope of this paper. The following section describes IFNS.

4 Interface-Based Naming System

4.1 Overview

Figure 2 shows an overview of IFNS. IFNS is a distributed naming system which consists of many IFNS nodes, similar to the Gnutella system [11]. An IFNS node contains a local database and a wide-area database to store the interface name. Each IFNS node establishes logical connections to neighboring IFNS nodes, and manages the interface name by advertising information through logical links. A functional object registers its name to the IFNS node (usually, the node nearest the functional object). The IFNS client, such as the service synthesizer, locates the functional object by querying the interface name to the IFNS node. Since the interface name specifies the function of the functional object, it will be a location-independent name. Therefore, scalability is a significant issue in designing IFNS. To enable IFNS to scale well, we designed a defined name space as well as name management and name resolution algorithms, as described in the following section.

4.2 Name Space

Generally, in distributed systems like the Internet, the object- locating mechanism is provided by the naming system [12][13]. The essential feature in designing the naming system is how to assign a name to an object. This is because the semantics and syntax of the assigned name are directly related to the structure of the name space, and affect the scalability of the name management and resolution algorithms. Once the name space can be defined, we can design name management and name resolution algorithms suitable for the structure of the name space.

Name space is usually characterized by both naming semantics and naming syntax; generally, naming semantics is more important than naming syntax. For practical use of the naming system, defining naming syntax with sufficient expressiveness is necessary. However, due to the information structure in the name space, naming semantics is the dominant factor. For this reason, this paper focuses on naming semantics

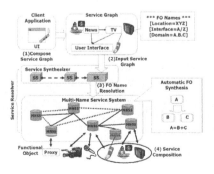

Fig. 1. Overview of STONE System

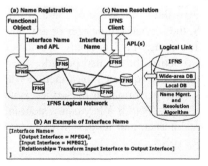

Fig. 2. Interface-based Naming System

and attempts to design name management and resolution algorithms reflecting the information structure of the name space.

In designing IFNS, we use the interface information of the functional object. Generally, the function of a functional object can be defined with its input/output interfaces and the relationship between these interfaces. For example, the function of a simple functional object mpeg2-to-mpeg4 transcoder can be defined as a function whose input interface, output interface and relationship between these interfaces are *mpeg2*, *mpeg4*, and *conversion*, respectively. The interface name we create in this paper utilizes these semantics. By naming a functional object with an interface and a relationship, we can transparently and definitely specify the desired function

Hereinafter, we denote the interface name as A/Z, where A and B indicate input and output, respectively, and $/$ denotes the relationship between A and Z. This function-centric naming is independent of a location-dependent identifier, such as network address, so we can transparently locate the desired functional object. Of course, there will be the problem of how to describe multiple I/O functional objects (e.g., audio data mixer). However, even if a functional object has multiple I/O, we believe that it is possible to describe the functional object by its I/O interface and relationship (e.g., $(A+B)/Z$). In other words, it is a problem of naming syntax, and is beyond the scope of this paper.

4.3 Name Management Algorithm

Name management and name resolution in the naming system should be designed by considering the data structure of the name space. For the case of interface name, the data structure of the name space can be aggregated: we can think of functional objects that have the same interface name as the same function. Since there will be many functional objects in the ubiquitous Internet, the possibility of the existence of functional objects that have the same function will be high. Therefore, we can effectively aggregate many functional objects scattered in the network into the interface name space. Even if multiple functional objects are aggregated into one interface name, this should not affect applications. This is because applications are interested in whether they can locate the desired function, not where the desired function is. By using the aggregate characteristic of the interface name space, efficient name management and resolution algorithms are described.

Figure 3 shows the name management algorithm of IFNS. When a functional object with the interface name A/Z is registered with IFNS node $N1$, the registered name and access pointer are stored in a local database (LDB) in node $N1$ (as shown in (1) of Figure 3). An example of the LDB table in node N1 is shown at the bottom left of Figure 3. The LDB table consists of an interface name section and an access pointer section. The registered access pointer corresponding to interface name A/Z is added to the appropriate cell in the access pointer section.

Meanwhile, a numerical value is assigned to the registered name and stored in a wide-area database (WDB) in node $N1$. This value, which we call the *evaluation value*, can be assigned based on the load of the functional object, or the network con-

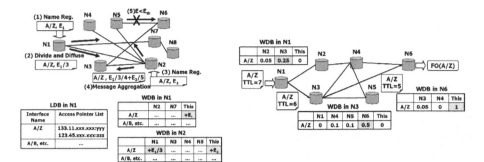

Fig. 3. Name Management Algorithm   **Fig. 4.** Name Resolution Algorithm

dition, or other similar parameters. This value is used to manage interface names on the IFNS logical network, as described later. An example of a WDB table is shown at the bottom right of Figure 3. Each row in the WDB table corresponds to an interface name, and each column corresponds to the logical connection established to a neighboring node. The column name *This* represents the IFNS node itself.

Here, we assume that the value E_i is assigned to the interface name *A/Z* at node *N1* (we denote this as $<A/Z, E_i>$). Initially, node *N1* adds the value E_i to the table element corresponding to the name *A/Z* in the column *This* (we denote this as *WDB[A/Z, this]*). Next, node *N1* advertises the name *A/Z* to all neighboring nodes that establish logical connections to node *N1*. The advertisement is triggered by a timer with a random initial value. When *N1* advertises the name *A/Z*, node *N1* divides the value E_i based on the number of neighboring nodes, and sends it to the neighboring node with the name *A/Z*. In this paper, we assume all nodes in IFNS divide the value E by $n+1$ (i.e., the value $E/(n+1)$ is advertised to each of the neighboring nodes), where n denotes the number of neighboring nodes. In this way, node *N1* advertises $<A/Z, E_i/3>$ to node *N2* and *N3*, respectively. Note that, in our name management algorithm, the total of advertised values must not exceed the original value. This constraint prevents divergence of the WDB table.

Now we focus on node *N2*. When node *N2* receives the advertisement from node *N1*, *N2* adds the advertised value $E_i/3$ to the element *WDB[A/Z, N1]* in *N2*'s WDB table. After that, node *N2* computes the new value $E_i/3/4$ for the name *A/Z*, based on the number of neighboring nodes (excluding node *N1*). Now we assume that a new functional object $<A/Z, E_2>$ is registered with *N2* before advertising $<A/Z E_i/3/4>$ (as shown in (3) of Figure 3). In this case, node *N2* initially updates the LDB with $<A/Z, E_2>$, then computes the value $E_2/5$ for advertisement. After that, node *N2* aggregates two advertisement messages, $<A/Z, E_i/3/4>$ and $<A/Z, E_2/5>$, into $<A/Z, E_i/3/4+E_2/5>$ (as shown in (4) of Figure 3). In this way, message advertisement and aggregation are repeated at each IFNS node, and the name *A/Z* propagates among the IFNS nodes. Each IFNS node has an advertisement threshold to limit propagation of the message. When the value E in the advertisement message $<A/Z, E>$ is less than the threshold E_{th} at a certain node, the node drops the message.

4.4 Name Resolution Algorithm

Name resolution is performed based on the WDB table constructed by the name management algorithm. Figure 4 shows the name resolution algorithm. Suppose that a client issues a query for interface name A/Z at IFNS node $N1$. Node $N1$ initially checks its WDB. Since the element $WDB[A/Z, this]$ in node $N1$ is zero, node $N1$ knows that it does not have a functional object named A/Z. Node $N1$ then forwards the query to the neighboring node which has the largest value in the WDB table. In this example, the query is forwarded to node $N3$. However, node $N3$ also does not have the functional object, and it simply forwards the query to $N6$. Because the element $WDB[A/Z, this]$ in $N6$ is not zero, $N6$ has functional objects corresponding to the query. $N6$ looks up the access pointer in the LDB and sends it back to the client. Note that, if all values corresponding to the name A/Z are zero or are the same, the IFNS node randomly forwards the query to neighboring nodes. Also, note that all queries in IFNS have a *TTL* (Time to Live), which decreases whenever the query is forwarded to neighbors. If TTL decrements to zero, IFNS terminates the query forwarding and sends an error message to the client application.

4.5 Automatic Function Synthesis

Using the above name resolution algorithm, we can locate a functional object by its interface name. However, even if there are many functional objects in the future ubiquitous Internet, we cannot assume a required functional object is always registered in IFNS. Moreover, since query propagation in IFNS is limited by TTL, we cannot guarantee that a query always arrives at the appropriate node. Consequently, these properties make it difficult for applications to change functionality seamlessly depending on the user's context. To avoid this problem, we designed the automatic function synthesis mechanism (AFS). The AFS composes one functional object with multiple functional objects by using composite characteristics of the interface name. For example, if IFNS cannot resolve the name mpeg2/mpeg4, the AFS decomposes the name into mpeg2/mpeg1 and mpeg1/mpeg4, and attempts to resolve the two names. Once the names are resolved to APLs, we can compose a mpeg2/mpeg4 function by combining the mpeg2/mpeg1 and mpeg1/mpeg4 functions.

Figure 5 shows the algorithm used for AFS. Now we assume a query for the name A/Z is forwarded to a specific node. The AFS works when there is no functional object for name A/Z in either the WDB or the LDB in this node. The name A/Z is initially decomposed into A/x and y/Z, where x and y are wildcards. If we can resolve the two names that satisfy $x=y=B$, we can compose the functional object A/Z of A/B and B/Z. Otherwise, if we can locate three functional objects, A/x, y/Z and x/y ($x=B$, $y=C$, for example), it is also possible to compose the functional object A/Z.

As the first step of AFS, the names A/x and y/Z are looked up in the LDB. If neither A/x nor y/Z are found in the LDB, the AFS cancels the function synthesis process, and the query for A/Z is randomly forwarded to a neighboring node. If both A/x and *y*/Z (*x*=*y*) are found in the LDB, the AFS process succeeds, and APLs for the two names are returned to the IFNS client.

Unfortunately, when neither A/*x* nor *y*/Z (*x*=*y*) are found in the LDB, the AFS attempts to look up A/*x*, *x*/*y*, and *y*/Z. If these three functional objects exist in the LDB, the AFS process succeeds and returns APLs. In the case where *x*/*y* does not exist in the LDB but exists in the WDB, the AFS translates the original query A/Z to *x*/*y*, which has the maximum total value in the WDB, where the maximum total value is defined as the sum of the values in a row of the WDB table. The translated query is then forwarded by a conventional name resolution algorithm.

When only A/*x* exists in the LDB, the AFS checks whether *x*/Z exists in the WDB. If *y*/Z does not exist in the WDB, the AFS process is canceled, and the original query is forwarded by a conventional name resolution algorithm. Otherwise, the original query is translated to *y*/Z, and the translated query is forwarded by a conventional name resolution algorithm.

In addition, we designed IFNS to iteratively use the AFS algorithm to maximize the chances of locating the functional object. To iteratively apply the AFS algorithm to name resolution, we defined an AFS field in a query. The AFS field indicates how many times the AFS process can be applied for the query. The AFS field is decremented each time the query is translated by the AFS algorithm.

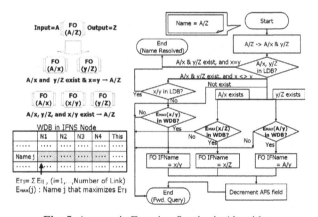

Fig. 5. Automatic Function Synthesis Algorithm

5 Simulations

In order to evaluate the scalability of IFNS and the performance of AFS, simulations were performed using the random spanning tree network, where various types of interface names were randomly registered with each IFNS node. In the simulations, name management and name resolution cost were computed and compared to a broadcast-based algorithm. In addition, by using the success ratio of name resolution, we evaluated how successfully the AFS could synthesize functional objects. Note that, since it is difficult to predict how many functional objects and how many kinds of functional objects are registered in IFNS, we did not evaluate our system quantitatively. Instead, we can only describe the behavior of the system in various situations. For this reason we limited the purpose of our simulation to evaluate only the qualitative performance of IFNS.

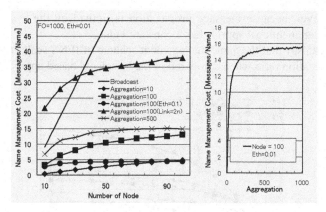

Fig. 7. Name Management Cost

5.1 Name Management Cost

In the simulation of the name management cost, 1000 interface names were registered with IFNS, and the evaluation value of each interface name was set to 1. Naturally, there would be more than 1000 objects in an actual ubiquitous Internet. However, these names are enough to evaluate the qualitative performance of IFNS.

Under this initial condition of 1000 objects, we computed the name management cost for one functional object. The name management cost is defined as the total number of messages among IFNS nodes that is required for managing one registered name. To investigate how the name management cost changes under various conditions, we set various values for the network size (i.e., the number of IFNS nodes), advertisement threshold and aggregation ratio. The aggregation ratio represents how many functional objects one interface name can aggregate. For example, when 1000 functional objects are aggregated by 100 interface names, the aggregation ratio is 0.1

Figure 6 shows the evaluation of the name management cost. In the left graph in Figure 6, name management cost increases as network size increases, because the name management message is replicated at each IFNS node. However, when compared to the broadcast-based algorithm, the IFNS name management algorithm considerably reduces name management cost. This is because, while the broadcast-based algorithm propagates a message to all nodes and does not aggregate any message, the IFNS name management algorithm limits message propagation by the evaluation value and aggregates messages that have the same interface name at certain nodes. Note that it is possible to use a very small evaluation value to reduce management cost. However, this degrades the performance of name resolution, as described later.

We also studied the relationship between name management cost and aggregation ratio. The right graph in Figure 6 shows the name management cost. In the simulation, the number of nodes and the advertisement threshold are set to 100 and 0.01, respectively. The name space of the interface name will be flat when the aggregation ratio is large, so the name management cost increases as the aggregation ratio increases. However, because message propagation is limited by the evaluation value, the name management cost approaches a constant value.

Thus, we can say that the name management scheme of IFNS scales to the network size and aggregation ratio when compared to the broadcast-based approach.

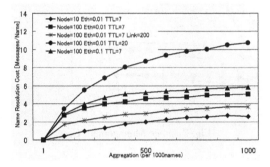

Fig. 7. Name Resolution Cost

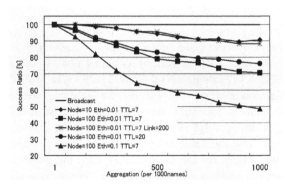

Fig. 8. Success Ratio

5.2 Name Resolution Cost

Name resolution cost in IFNS is defined as the mean value of the total number of messages generated in the name resolution process for one query. In the simulation, we registered 1000 interface names to IFNS, and measured the name resolution cost and success ratio by sending a query to a randomly selected IFNS node. Here, the success ratio is defined as the probability of IFNS successfully resolving a certain query.

Figures 7 and 8 represent the name resolution cost and success ratio. In the simulation, the number of IFNS nodes, advertisement threshold, and TTL are set to various values, as shown in the legends of Figures 7 and 8. Note that, since the name resolution cost of the Gnutella-like broadcast-based approach is quite high (around 100), it is not shown in Figure 7. As shown in Figures 7 and 8, although the name resolution cost of IFNS is quite low, the success ratio degrades as the aggregation ratio increases. The reason for this is that a query does not arrive when an IFNS node, which has a functional object for the query, is quite far from the node where the query was generated. To improve the success ratio, we set a large value for TTL (e.g., TTL=20). However, while this increases the name management cost, the success ratio was not significantly improved.

Next, we added some loops in the IFNS network by randomly adding links, where the total number of links was twice the number of nodes (see the plots for "Link=200" in Figures 6, 7 and 8). We found that adding loops greatly improves the success ratio in the name resolution process. This is because the link added to the original spanning tree functions as a shortcut, so that it can bring information from far nodes. However, as shown in Figure 6, adding loops in the IFNS when the node number is small results in an unnecessary increase of the name management cost. Therefore, we can say that the additional link works effectively when the network size is quite large. In other words, IFNS works well in the ubiquitous Internet.

Of course, there are complicated tradeoffs between name management cost and success ratio, depending on the aggregation ratio, advertisement threshold, number of loops, TTL, and other parameters. By controlling these parameters, we can adapt IFNS to various conditions with optimal performance. However, as described in the early part of this section, such adaptation is possible and meaningful only if we can predict the practical situation in which IFNS is used.

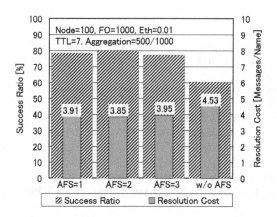

Fig. 9. Performance of AFS

5.3 Performance of AFS

Last of all, we investigated how the automatic function synthesis can improve the success ratio in name resolution. In this simulation, we set 100 as the number of IFNS nodes, 0.01 as the advertisement threshold, 7 as TTL, and 0.5 as the aggregation ratio. The network topology of IFNS was constructed as a random spanning tree. We computed the success ratio and resolution cost when the AFS field was set in the range 1–3. In Figure 9, we observe that the success ratio is improved by 1.2 to 1.3 times that of the normal name resolution process. Since AFS increases the number of successful name resolutions, this decreases the number of times a query is forwarded in IFNS. Consequently, the name resolution cost is also improved in our simulation. However, iterative use of the AFS process sometimes degrades the success ratio (e.g., AFS=3 in Figure 9). This is because a query permitting many ASF iterations with small TTL may not be resolved within a certain number of hops. Therefore, we should carefully determine the number of iterations for AFS by considering the TTL of the query.

6 Conclusion

This paper presented the IFNS as a location-independent naming system capable of locating functional objects in a ubiquitous Internet. The design philosophy of the IFNS has been described, and scalable name management and resolution algorithms have been designed. Simulations were performed, and it was shown that the name management and resolution algorithms have acceptable scalability, even when a large number of functional objects are registered in IFNS. In the future, it will be necessary to do more detailed analyses to clarify the characteristics of IFNS, and to proceed with our implementation of a STONE platform, as well as its applications.

References

1. P. Mockapetris, "Domain Names – Concepts and Facilities", IETF, RFC 1034, Nov. 1987.
2. P. Mockapetris, "Domain names – Implementation and Specification", IETF, RFC 1035, Nov. 1987.
3. P. Mockapetris and K. Dunlap, "Development of the Domain Name System", Proc. ACM SIGCOMM'88, Stanford, CA, USA, 1988.
4. A. Birrell, R. Levin, R. Needham, and M. Schroeder, "Grapevine: An Exercise in Distributed Computing", Communications of the ACM, Vol. 25, No. 4, Apr. 1982.
5. *X.500: The Directory - Overview of Concepts, Models, and Services*, CCITT Recommendation, 1987.
6. W. Adjie-Winoto, E. Schwartz, H. Balakrishnan, and J. Lilley, "The Design and Implementation of an Intentional Naming System", Proc. ACM SOSP, Charleston, SC, USA, 1999.

7. T. Berners-Lee, R. Fielding, and L. Masinter, "Uniform Resource Identifiers (URI): Generic Syntax", IETF, RFC 2396, Aug. 1998.
8. J. Waldo, "Jini Architecture Overview", Sun Microsystems Inc., 1998.
9. Universal Plug and Play Architecture, Microsoft Inc.
10. HAVi White Paper, http:// www. havi. org/
11. *Peer-to-Peer: Harnessing the Power of Disruptive Technologies*, A. Oram, ed., O'Reilly and Associates, 2001.
12. D. Oppen and Y. Dahl, "The Clearinghouse: A Decentralized Agent for Locating Named Objects in a Distributed Environment", Xerox Office Products Division Technical Report, OPD-T8103, 1981.
13. G. Coulouris, J. Dollimore, and T. Kindberg, Distributed Systems: Concepts and Design, Second Edition, Addison-Wesley, 1994.

Schedulability Analysis in EDF Scheduler with Cache Memories*

A. Martí Campoy, S. Sáez, A. Perles, and J.V. Busquets

Departamento de Informática de Sistemas y Computadores,
Universidad Politécnica de Valencia,
46022, Valencia (SPAIN)
{amarti,ssaez,aperles,vbusque}@disca.upv.es

Abstract. Cache memories can improve computer performance, but its unpredictable behaviour makes difficult to use them in hard real-time systems. Classical analysis techniques are not sufficient to accomplish schedulability analysis, and new hardware resources or complex analysis algorithms are needed. This work presents a comprehensive method to obtain predictability on the use of caches in real-time systems using an EDF scheduler. Reaching a predictable cache, schedulability analysis can be accomplished in a simple way through conventional algorithms.

At the moment, this is the first approach to consider cache in this kind of scheduler. The method is based in the use of locking caches and genetic algorithms. Locking caches allows to load and lock cache contents, ensuring its remains unchanged. Genetic algorithms help to select the cache content that offers the best performance. Experimental results indicate that this scheme is fully predictable, and this predictability is reached with no performance loss for around 60% of cases.

1 Introduction

Modern microprocessors include cache memories in its memory hierarchy to increase system performance. General-purpose systems can benefit from this architectural improvement, because it tries to make efficient the average case. But hard real-time systems require the worst case to be bounded, and therefore, to take advantage of cache memories, they need special hardware resources and/or speficic system analysis that guarantee the timeliness execution of the code.

Basically, two problems arise when cache memories are used in multitask, preemptive real-time systems: intra-task interference, in the domain of a single task; and inter-task interference, in the domain of multitask systems. The former one makes harder to calculate the Worst Case Execution Time (WCET), because a task can replace its own instructions in cache due to conflict and capacity problems. When previously replaced instructions are executed again, a cache miss increases the execution time of the task. This kind of interference has to be taken into account in the WCET of each task.

---

* This work was supported by the Spanish Government Research Office (CICYT) under grants TAP99-0443-C05-02 and TIC99-1043-C03-02

J. Chen and S. Hong (Eds.): RTCSA 2003, LNCS 2968, pp. 328–341, 2004.

The second problem is to calculate the cache-related preemption delay. This delay, also called inter-task or extrinsic interference, arises in preemptive multitasking systems when a task displaces from cache the working set of any other task of the system. When the preempted task resumes execution, a burst of cache misses increase its execution time over the precalculated WCET. This additional delay must be considered in the schedulability analysis.

The cache problems considered in this work deal with the resolution of cache interference in multitask, preemptive real-time systems. The paper only addresses the instruction cache problem and how it influences in the calculation of WCET of each task and in the schedulability analysis of the whole system, without regard to other architecture improvements.

Several solutions have been proposed to use cache memories in real-time systems. Some works analyse the cache behaviour to estimate the task execution time considering only the intra-task interference [1–4]. In [5, 6] the cache behaviour is analysed to estimate the task response time, but considering only the inter-task interference and using a precalculated cached WCET. These works deals only with fixed priority schedulers. Other works try to eliminate or reduce the inter-task interference by using hardware and software techniques [7–10], but they do not face the intrinsic interference problem. Additionally, in some cases, the extrinsic interference is only reduced, and therefore, the predictability problem of the cache-related preemption delay remains unresolved.

This work presents an integrated approach, based on a previous work [11], that offers *full predictability* for WCET estimation, and a bounded value of extrinsic interference under the Earliest Deadline First (EDF) scheduler.

First goal is achieved using instructions to manage cache, like selective preload (cache fill) and cache locking. These instructions are present on currently available processors. The way these characteristics are used offers the possibility to use a simple schedulability analysis joined with accurate estimations of cache performance.

The method here presented is based in the ability of several processors to disable or lock the cache, precluding the replacement of its contents but allowing references to the data or instruction already stored in cache. In this scenario, execution time of instructions is constant for each instance, and preemptions do not modify the cache contents. This way, intra-task and inter-task interference are eliminated since cache content remains unchanged during all system operation, and only a temporal cache buffer have to be taken into account in the schedulability analysis. Such a temporal buffer is introduced to improve temporal behaviour of the instructions not preloaded into the cache.

The rest of the paper is organised as follows: next section shows the hardware necessary to reach both predictability and the best possible performance. Section 3 is devoted to schedulability analysis, and the algorithms used to calculate the WCET and the schedulability analysis are presented when a locking cache is used. In section 4, the genetic algorithm to select the best set of instructions to load in cache is presented. Then, the experimental results are explained. And finally, conclusions and future work are described.

2   System Overview

Several processor offers the ability to lock cache memory contents, like Intel-960, some x86 family processors, Motorola MPC7400, Integrated Device Technology 79R4650 and 79RC64574, and others. Each of these processors implements cache locking in a different ways, allowing to lock the entire cache, only a part, or in a per-line basis. But in all cases, a portion of cache locked will be not selected later for refill by other data or instruction, remaining its contents unchanged.

The IDT-79R4650 cache schema offers an 8KB, two-set associative instruction cache. Also, the processor offers the instruction 'cache fill' instruction to selective load cache contents. However, this processor allows locking only one set of cache, leaving unlocked the other cache set. Since the main objective of this work is to reach a deterministic cache, locking the entire cache is needed. In the MPC7400 is possible to lock the entire cache, using a one-cache-line size buffer to temporally store instructions not loaded in cache, improving sequential access to these addresses. The problem with this processor is that not selective load of cache contents is available. This way, in this work, a merge of the two above processor is proposed, resulting in a cache system with the following characteristics:

- Cache can be totally locked or unlocked. When cache is locked, there are no new tag allocations.
- If the processor addresses an instruction that is in the locked cache, this instruction is served from cache.
- If the processor addresses an instruction that is in the temporal buffer, this instruction is served from this buffer in like-cache time.
- If the processor addresses an instruction that is not in the locked cache or temporal buffer, this instruction is served from main memory. Simultaneously, the temporal buffer is filled with that block regarding the address demanded by the processor.
- Cache can be loaded using a cache-fill instruction, selecting the memory block to load it.
- Cache can be locked using cache management instructions.
- Cache may be direct mapped or set associative. Increasing the associative-level may increase the performance of locking caches, but direct-mapped is enough to reach predictability.

Totally locking the cache allows obtaining the maximum possible performance, simultaneously making deterministic the cache. The temporal buffer reduce access time to memory blocks not loaded in cache, since only references to the first instruction in the block produce cache miss.

During system design step, a set of main memory blocks is selected to be loaded and locked in cache. When system start-up, a small routine will load selected blocks in cache, executing cache fill instructions. After last load, the cache is locked. In this way, when tasks begin full operation, the state of cache is known and remains unchanged during all system operation.

3   Schedulability Analysis

The main goal addressed in this paper is predictability. The designer of a real-time system have to be able to predict the timeliness execution of the critical workload before starting the system. This work can be accomplished using an schedulability test at design time.

In dynamic systems, the schedulability test can be performed by checking the system schedulability throughout a short interval named the Initial Critical Interval (ICI) [12]. In this section, this ICI schedulability test is presented and adapted to take into account the extrinsic interference in a dynamic scheduler, like Earliest Deadline First. As the entire instruccion cache is locked, the extrinsic interference is reduced to the refilling of the temporal buffer.

In a real-time system, the critical workload is typically composed by a set of periodic tasks $\mathcal{T}$. This task set is defined by $\mathcal{T} = \{T_i(C_i, D_i, P_i) : i = 1 \ldots n\}$ with $1 \leq C_i \leq D_i \leq P_i$, where C_i, D_i and P_i are the worst-case execution time (WCET), relative deadline and period of task T_i, respectively.

The ICI schedulability test is based on two analytical functions $G_{\mathcal{T}}(t)$ and $H_{\mathcal{T}}(t)$:

- **Function** $G_{\mathcal{T}}(t)$: Given a task set $\mathcal{T}$, function $G_{\mathcal{T}}(t)$ accumulates the amount of computing time requested by all activations of tasks in $\mathcal{T}$ from time zero until time t. Formally:

$$G_{\mathcal{T}}(t) = \sum_{i=1}^{n} C_i \left\lceil \frac{t}{P_i} \right\rceil . \tag{1}$$

- **Function** $H_{\mathcal{T}}(t)$: Given a task set $\mathcal{T}$, function $H_{\mathcal{T}}(t)$ is the amount of computing time requested by all activations of tasks in $\mathcal{T}$ whose deadline is less than or equal to t. Formally:

$$H_{\mathcal{T}}(t) = \sum_{i=1}^{n} C_i \left\lfloor \frac{t + P_i - D_i}{P_i} \right\rfloor . \tag{2}$$

In other words, $H_{\mathcal{T}}(t)$ represents the amount of computing time that the scheduler should have served until time t in order to meet all deadlines.

Using these functions, the initial critical interval, $\mathcal{R}$, can be calculated by using the recursive expression $R_{i+1} = G_{\mathcal{T}}(R_i)$ until $R_i = R_{i+1}$, where $R_0 = 0$. The last value of R_i indicates the ICI $\mathcal{R}$, that represents the first instant when all requests have already been served and no additional requests have been arrived yet.

Once $\mathcal{R}$ has been established, the system schedulability can be ensured if and only if the next expression is true:

$$H_{\mathcal{T}}(t) < t : \forall t, 1 \leq t \leq \mathcal{R} .$$

3.1 Extrinsic Interference

The schedulability test presented above does not consider any cache-related pre-emption delays. Though critical tasks have a portion of their code locked at instruction cache, every time a preemption is performed by the scheduler, the temporal buffer can be filled by the new task code. When the preempted task resumes its execution, it could undergo a penalty due to the possible refilling of the temporal buffer. Since the preemption point is not known a priori, the worst case scenario must be considered. In this case, a task can be preempted while executing a block of instructions from the temporal buffer. So, using the proposed structure of locking cache, the penalty suffered by the preempted task is T_{miss}, where T_{miss} is the time to transfer a block from main memory to the temporal buffer.

To determine the maximum number of preemptions a task can suffer in a dynamic system, and therefore, to calculate the WCET and the response time of a task taking into account these preemptions, is a very difficult problem. However, it is quite easier to determine the number of preemptions a task originates under a given scheduler. This information can be used in the schedulability test to incorporate the cache-related preemption delay into the task responsible for the preemption, instead of incorporating this delay in the task is preempted.

Earliest Deadline First scheduler is privileged scheduler among schedulers based on dynamic priorities: it generates a very low number of preemptions, and these preeemtions can only occur on task arrivals. Therefore, under EDF, a task generates a preemption when it arrives or does not generate any preemption at all. Taking this feature into account, the schedulability functions (1) and (2) remains as follows:

$$G_{\mathcal{T}}(t) = \sum_{i=1}^{n}(C_i + T_{miss})\left\lceil \frac{t}{P_i} \right\rceil, \tag{3}$$

$$H_{\mathcal{T}}(t) = \sum_{i=1}^{n}(C_i + T_{miss})\left\lfloor \frac{t + P_i - D_i}{P_i} \right\rfloor. \tag{4}$$

where C_i is the WCET of the task T_i considering the existence of cache and taking into account the blocks this task has locked in cache. Next subsection presents how this can be calculated.

Though the rest of the schedulability test remains unchanged, a very slight optimitation can be performed. It can be taken into account that the task with the largest relative deadline *never* can preempt any task when it activates, because it always has the slowest priority on arrival.

3.2 Worst Case Execution Time

The schedulability test needs the Worst Case Execution Time of each task T_i to accomplish the analysis. This WCET must be calculated considering the existence of cache. In conventional caches this is a hard problem, because two

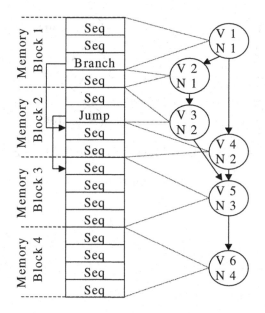

Cache line size: 4 instructions
V: Number of Vertex.
N: Number of Block.

Branch: Conditional Branch
Jump: Incondicional Branch
Seq: No Branch Instruction

Fig. 1. Example of c-cfg

execution of the same instruction must take different temporal cost. But in here presented cache scheme, an instruction will be in cache always, or never will be into, thus its execution time is always constant. To calculate the WCET of a task, the timing analysis presented in [13] is modified to taking account the presence of the locking cache. This analysis is based on the concept of Control Flow Graph of a task.

This work presents an extended Control Flow Graph, called Cached-Control Flow Graph (c-cfg), that takes into account cache line boundaries. In this c-cfg, a vertex is a sequence of instructions without flow break, and all instructions on a vertex map in the same cache line. This model differs from conventional CFG in the meaning of vertex, since the c-cfg models not only the flow control of the task but also how the task is affected from the point of view of cache structure. Figure 1 illustrates an example.

This c-cfg can be represented with a simple expression that can be evaluated to obtain the task WCET. Figure 2 shows the expression for three basic c-cfg, and Figure 3 shows an example. In these expressions, E_i represents the execution time of vertex V_i.

Task's WCET can be calculated evaluating the expression, considering the execution time of each vertex. The execution time of a vertex depends on the number of instructions into the vertex and the cache state when the vertex is executed. In a locked cache, the cache state remain unchanged, so the execution time of a vertex is constant for all executions: the vertex is always loaded into

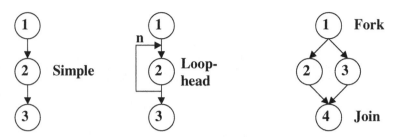

Fig. 2. Expressions for three basic structures

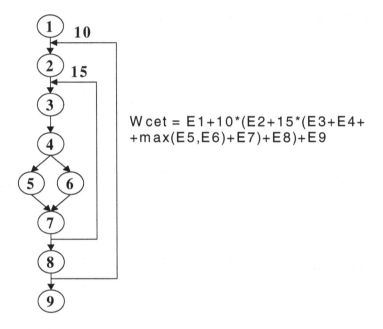

Fig. 3. Example of expression

the cache or it will never be. So, the execution time of a vertex can be calculate as follows:

- For a vertex V_i loaded and locked in cache, its execution time E_i is: $E_i = T_{hit} \cdot I_i$.
- For a vertex V_i not loaded nor locked in cache, its execution time E_i is: $E_i = T_{miss} + (T_{hit} \cdot I_i)$

where I_i is the number of instructions of vertex V_i, T_{hit} is the execution time of an instruction that is in cache, and T_{miss} is the time to transfer a block from main memory to the temporal buffer.

The execution time of vertexes can be directly used in the c-cfg expression to obtain the WCET of the task, giving an upper bound value, since execution time is now non cache-dependent. The existence of a temporal buffer may introduce, in some cases, a light error in the WCET estimation.

4 Selecting Blocks to Load and Lock in Cache

Performance improvements due to use of cache memories are very significant, and real-time systems should take advantage of it. Randomly loading and locking instructions in cache offers predictability but not guarantee good response time of the tasks. In order to reach both goals, a predictable cache and a cache performance close to the usual one, instructions to be loaded must be carefully selected, trying to find the best possible scenario. This scenario is a set of main memory blocks locked in cache that provides the minimum possible execution time, thus providing the minimum possible response time for a set of tasks.

Although there are several possibilities to select instructions to be locked, it is not easy to isolate an instruction and evaluate the impact of locking it in cache over the system behaviour, due to interacts between tasks. Response time of task is mainly related to the task's structure, but also how tasks are scheduled in the system concerns to the response time. Exhaustive search, including branch and bound, presents an intractable computational cost, since the number of possible solutions is very large. Genetic algorithms [14], performing a randomly-directed search, can be used in this problem, finding a sub-optimal solution within an acceptable computational time. The genetic algorithm used in this work is the evolution of a previous version presented in [11]. The main characteristics of the new algorithm are described next.

Each block of a task can be locked or not in cache. An individual represents the state of all blocks of all tasks in the system in one chromosome, where a chromosome is a set of genes. Each gene has a size of only one bit and represents the block state. The population is a set of individuals.

Fitness function must guide the genetic algorithm evolution, helping to find the best solution. The fitness function must have three main characteristic: low computational cost, find the best solution, and find this solution in fewer iterations. It is hard to find a fitness function that agree these characteristics, and usually it is a complex function. In this work, the used fitness function is the result of applying the schedulability test described in previous section to each individual, considering the state – locked or not – of the blocks. WCET for schedulability test is estimated using the WCET expressions described in previous section. From the fitness function four types of results are obtained:

- Schedulable system, with number of locked blocks minor or equal to the cache size. This is a valid individual.

– Schedulable system, with number of locked blocks greater than cache size. This is a non-valid individual.
– No schedulable system, with number of locked blocks minor or equal to the cache size. This is a very bad solution, but a valid individual.
– No schedulable system, with number of locked blocks greater than cache size. This is a non-valid individual.

Also, fitness function returns for schedulable individuals the system utilisation, and for not schedulable individuals it returns a factor indicating how bad is the individual (distance between failure time and the ICI). The existence of invalid and non-schedulable individuals precludes the use of direct probability setting as function of fitness value. This way, individuals are arranged in three segments: higher positions for schedulable-and-valid individuals, following valid-non-schedulable individuals, and lower positions for invalid individuals. Into first segment, schedulable-and-valid individuals are arranged as function of its utilisation (lower utilisation, higher position). Into second segment, valid-non-schedulable individuals are arranged as a function of its factor of failure (higher factor, higher position). Finally, invalid individuals are arranged as function of its number of locked blocks (lower number of blocks, higher position). Once all individuals are well arranged, selection probability for crossover is set as function of position. This allows including, with low probability, both non-schedulable and non-valid individuals that help to increase the variability of the algorithm.

Crossover is performed choosing randomly a gene that divides the individual into two parts, and exchanging the parts of two individuals, making two new individuals. This process is repeated until the number of new individuals make equal the population size.

Mutation is applied in a gene-basis to these new individuals in three ways:

– For individuals with number of locked blocks greater than cache size, mutation randomly eliminates blocks from the set of locked-blocks.
– For individuals with number of locked blocks smaller than cache size, mutation randomly adds blocks to the set of locked-blocks.
– For individuals with number of locked blocks equal than cache size, mutation randomly exchange blocks, leaving unchanged the number of locked blocks.

In order to guarantee the use of a direct-mapped locking cache, after the previous mutation, the algorithm looks if the set of locked blocks do not fit in a direct-mapped cache, randomly exchanging locked blocks, when needed, making them fit in a direct-mapped cache.

A new population is building with the individuals obtained from mutation, and process is repeated a prior-defined number of times. For the accomplished experiments presented further in this paper, the number of iterations is established in 2.000, with a population of 200 individuals.

The genetic algorithm solves, at the same time, the problem of selecting main memory blocks to load and lock in cache, and also, the schedulability analysis, since the result from the fitness function for a valid individual is the response of schedulability test.

5   Experimental Results

Above presented analysis allows to bound execution time interferences due to cache related issues. However, although the effects of using the proposed cache scheme can be bounded and incorparated to the schedulability analysis, the performance advantages obtained from using cache memories in a predictable way should be analysed.

Experimental results presented in this section show that preload and locking instructions in cache not only makes the system predictable: it also offers a performance close to the traditional caches (direct-mapped or set-associative) with LRU or Pseudo LRU replacement algorithm.

To make experiments, the SPIM tool [15], a MIPS R2000 simulator is used. The SPIM does not include neither cache nor multitask, so modifications to include an instruction cache, multitasking (simulated and controlled by the simulator and not by the O.S.) and to obtain execution times has been made to the original version of SPIM. Since this simulator does not include any architectural improvement, cache effects can be analysed without interference. The routine to load and lock in cache the selected instructions is incorporated in the simulator. Tasks used in experiments are artificially created to stress the proposed cache scheme. Main parameters of task are defined, like number of loops and nesting level, size of tasks, size of loops, number of if-then-else structures and its respective sizes. These parameters are fixed or randomly selected. A simple tool is used to create tasks. The workload of any task may be a single loop, if-then-else structures, nested loops, streamline code, or any mix of these. The size of task code range from near 64 Kb to around 1Kb.

Each experiment is composed of a set of tasks and a cache size, ranging from three to eight tasks and cache sizes from 1 Kbyte to 64 Kbytes. This way, the two extreme scenarios are presented: code size much greater than cache size (64:1) and code size lower than cache size. Each experiment is simulated using direct-mapped, two-set associative, four-set associative and full associative cache, calculating the system utilisation U_{cache}. For all cases, line size is 16 bytes (four instructions). Time to transfer a block from main memory to the temporal buffer is 10 cycles ($T_{miss} = 10$). Execution of any instruction from the cache is 1 cycle, and execution of any instruction from the temporal buffer is also 1 cycle. For each experiment, the system utilisation is estimated using the genetic algorithm $U_{estimated}$, and simulated in a locking cache using the blocks selected by the genetic algorithm $U_{locking}$.

Figure 4 presents the overestimation in the estimated utilisation by the genetic algorithm, respect the actual utilisation (simulated) of the system when locking cache is used. (($U_{estimated}/U_{locking}$) -1). Each bar represents the number of experiments with percentage of overestimation that lies in the interval of the x-axis (i.e., 36 experiments have an overestimation between 0,01% and 0,05%). This figure shows that the estimated utilisation is quite accurate: The overestimation is always below the 0,5%. So, pessimism introduced in WCET calculation and schedulability analysis is not significant.

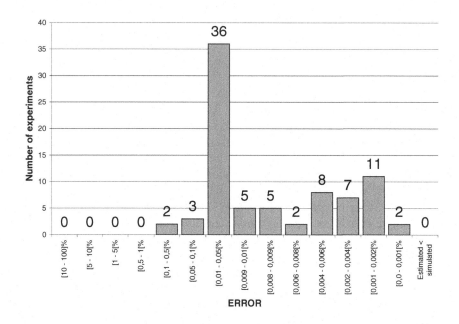

Fig. 4. Overestimation estimated by the genetic algorithm

Figure 5 shows the accumulated frequency. Accumulated number of experiments for the given overestimation between simulated and estimated system utilisation using locking cache. Axis-y value is the percentage of experiments with an overestimation lower than axis-x value. It can be observed that more than 90% of the experiments present an overestimation below 0,05%.

Regarding the performance of the locking cache, Figure 6 compares the system utilisation with or without locking cache. Conventional cache uses the mapping function that obtains the best performance for each case.

The figure depicts the performance ratio: simulation of actual system utilisation with the best conventional-cache arrangement, versus the estimated system utilisation obtained by the genetic algorithm with a locking cache ($U_{cache}/U_{estimated}$). Tasks are grouped regarding this ratio. Each bar represents the number of experiments with performance ratio ($U_{cache}/U_{estimated}$) that lies in the interval of the x-axis.

Figure 7 draws accumulative values of previous figure. Axis-y value is the percentage of experiments with performance ratio greater than axis-x value. For around 50% of the experiments, the system utilisation is equal or lower using locking cache, and in more than 60% of cases the performance loss is negligible. In these cases, the worst case response time (WCRT) is not only bounded, furthermore it makes the WCRT lower than execution time in a system with a normal cache.

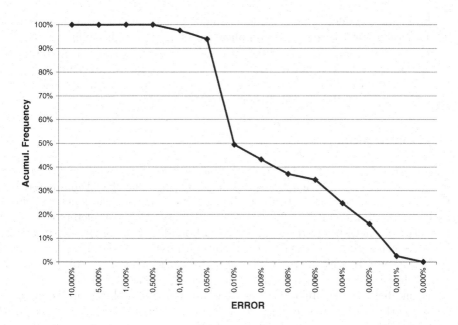

Fig. 5. Accumulated frequency of overestimation in estimated utilisation

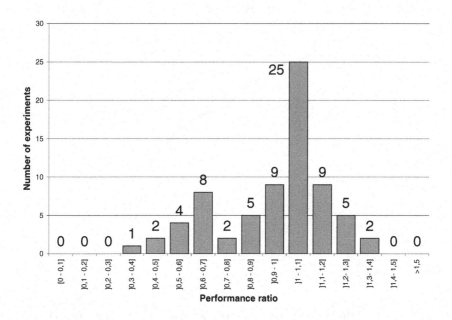

Fig. 6. Performance ratio obtained when using locking cache.

From the obtained results, we can conclude that the proposed cache scheme is predictable, and it allows the application of EDF schedulability analysis in systems with cache. The estimated utilisation is an upperbound of the actual utilisation using locking cache: ($U_{locking} < U_{estimated}$ for all experiments). With this technique, the predictability is obtained in many cases without performance loss ($U_{estimated} <= U_{cache}$) for around 60% of experiments).

6   Conclusions

This work presents a novel technique that uses locking caches in the context of real-time systems with EDF schedulers. In addition, algorithms to analyse the proposed system are described. Compared to known techniques to achieve cache predictability in Real-Time systems, this solution completely eliminates the intrinsic cache interference, and gives a bounded value of the extrinsic one.

This technique allows real-time systems with dynamic scheduling profit from the great performance increase produced by cache memories. And this is accomplished in a practical way, since the designer can easily analyse the system to accomplish the schedulability test. In addition, the architecture is compatible with other techniques to improve performance, like segmentation, precluding the consideration of the complex interrelations amongst these techniques and the cache.

This approach is very effective from the performance point of view. Simulations results show that for around 60% of experiments the performance achieved

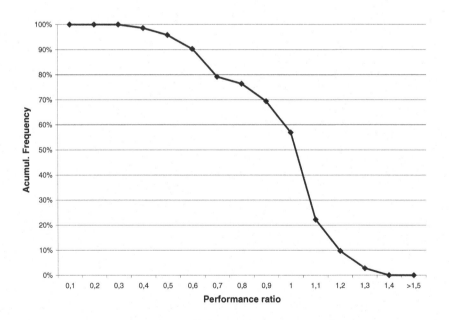

Fig. 7. Accumulative performance ratio when using locking cache.

by using locking caches is almost similar to the one obtained with conventional caches (without taking care of determinism).

The hardware resources required to implement this scheme are available in some contemporary processors. To obtain the best results, some minor changes have been proposed. These changes do not present difficulties in terms of technical complexity and production.

This work has also presented an algorithm to select the contents of the cache. This selection delivers the best performance. The algorithm also calculates the WCET and performs the schedulalibility analysis.

References

1. K. Takashio, S. Aoki, M. Murase, K. Matsumiya, N. Nishio, and H. Tokuda, "Smart hot-spot: Taking out ubiquitous smart computing environment anywhere", 2002, International Conference on Pervasive Computing (Demo Presentations).
2. M. Weiser, "The computer for the twenty-century", vol. 265, no. 3, pp. 94–104, 1991, Scientific American.
3. A. Freier, P. Kartiton, and P. Kocher, "The ssl protocol: version 3.0", 1996, Tech Rep., Internet-draft.
4. S. Kent and R. Atkinson, "Security architecture for the internet protocol", 1998, IETF RFC 2401.
5. W. Deffie and M. E. Hellman, "New directions in cryptography", 1976, pp. 644–654, IEEE Transactions on Information Theory IT-22.
6. R. Rivest, A. Shamir, and L. Adleman, "A method for obtaing digital signatures and public-key cryptosystems", in Communications of the ACM, 1978, vol. 21, pp. 120–126.
7. Ensure Technologies Inc., "Xyloc", 2001, http://www.ensuretech.com/.
8. Sony Corporation, "Felica: Contactless smart card system", 2002, http://www.sony.net/Products/felica/.
9. R. Want, A. Hopper, V. Falcao, and J. Gibbons, "The active badge location system", Tech. Rep. 92.1, ORL, 24a Trumpington Street, Cambridge CB2 1QA, 1992.
10. A. Harter, A. Hopper, P. Steggles, A. Ward, and P. Webster, "The anatomy of a context-aware application", in International Conference on Mobile Computing and Networking, 1999, pp. 59–68.
11. ITS America, "Intelligent transportation system", 2002, http://www.itsa.org/standards.
12. ETTM On The Web, "Electoronic toll collection system", 2002, http://www.ettm.com/.
13. H. Okabe, K.Takemura, S. Ogata, and T. Yamashita, "Compact vehicle sensor using a retroreflective optical scanner", in IEEE Conference of Intelligent Transportation Systems, 1997, pp. 201–205.
14. ETTM On The Web, "Automatic vehicle identification", 2002, http://www.ettm.com/avi.htm.
15. M. Corner and B. Noble, "Zero-interaction authentication", in International Conference on Mobile Computing and Networking, 2002.
16. M. L. Dertouzos, "Control robotics: The procedural control of physical processes", in Proceedings of the IFIP Congress, 1974, pp. 807–813.
17. R. W. Conway, M. L. Maxwell, and L. W. Miller, "Theory of scheduling", 1967, Addison-Wesley.

Impact of Operating System on Real-Time Main-Memory Database System's Performance

Jan Lindström, Tiina Niklander, and Kimmo Raatikainen

University of Helsinki, Department of Computer Science
P.O. Box 26 (Teollisuuskatu 23), FIN-00014 University of Helsinki,Finland
{jan.lindstrom,tiina.niklander,kimmo.raatikainen}@cs.Helsinki.FI

Abstract. As long as there have been databases there has been a large interest to measure their performance. However, operating system impact on database performance has not been widely studied. Therefore, this paper presents experimental results on operating system impact on database performance. Two different operating systems are studied: Linux and Chorus. Linux operating system is tested with different kernel versions and different network speeds. Chorus is used as reference point because it is a real-time operating system. Our results clearly indicate that Linux can be used as a platform for real-time main-memory databases, but the newest kernel version 2.4 should be used. Our simple experiment also confirms that the UDP gives better response time than TCP. The work done in the Linux community to reduce the long latency in the kernel has been successful and with sufficiently long request deadlines it can be used as a platform for real-time databases.

1 Introduction

Database performance is an important aspect of the database's usability. The performance of a database system depends not only on the database architecture and algorithms, but also on the platform the database is running on.

Real-time databases are needed when the database requests must be served within respecified time limits. The database is then designed to support the timely execution on all levels of the database architecture. It provides transaction scheduling, which supports priorities, deadlines, or criticality of the transactions. Alternatively they can be run on a general purpose operating system which supports real-time processes. Such functionality can be found, for example, in Solaris.

Telecommunication is an example of an application area, which has database requirements that require a real-time database or at least time-cognizant database. A telecommunication database, especially one designed for IN services [1], must support access times less than 50 milliseconds. Most database requests are simple reads, which access few items and return some value based on the content in the database.

Real-time databases have been designed for running mainly on real-time operating systems, which can provide real-time scheduling and guaranteed maximum latencies in the kernel. Previous work on real-time databases in general

J. Chen and S. Hong (Eds.): RTCSA 2003, LNCS 2968, pp. 342–350, 2004.
© Springer-Verlag Berlin Heidelberg 2004

has been based on simulation. However, several prototypes of general-purpose real-time databases has been introduced. StarBase [7] is constructed on top of RT-Mach. RTSORAC is implemented over a thread-based POSIX-compliant operating system and is based on an open OODB with real-time extensions [9]. Another object-oriented architecture is M^2RTSS-architecture, which is main-memory database system with real-time transaction scheduling [2].

Linux has gained popularity as a platform for web-servers and other network services. We wanted to find out if it would be suitable as a platform for a real-time database. The newest (February 2002) kernel version 2.4 supports priority-based scheduling and the latencies in kernel code have also been partially reduced.

This paper is organized as follows. Section 2 presents am overview of the main-memory databases and their requirements. Additionally, the prototype real-time database system used in experiments is shortly presented. Section 3 presents evaluation environment. Section 4 presents experimentation results. Finally, Section 5 concludes this paper.

2   Database System

In main memory database systems data resides permanently in the main physical memory. In some real-time applications, the data must be memory resident to meet the real-time constraints [3].

A network database system must offer real-time access to data [5,6]. This is due to the fact that most read requests are for logic programs that have exact time limits. If the database cannot give a response within a specific time limit, it is better not to waste resources and hence abort the request. As a result of this, the request management policy should favor predictable response times with the cost of less throughput. The best alternative is that the database can guarantee that all requests are replied to within a specific time interval. The average time limit for a read request is around 50ms. About 90% of all read requests must be served in that time. For updates, the time limits are not as strict. It is better to finish an update even at a later time than to abort the request.

Network database system services consist of two very different kinds of semantics: service provision services and service management services. *Service provision services* define possible extra services for customers [4]. Service provision transactions have quite strict deadlines and their arrival rate can be high (about 7000 transactions/second), but most service provision transactions have read-only semantics. In transaction scheduling, service provision transactions can be expressed as firm deadline transactions. *Service management services* defines possible management services for customer and network administration [4]. Service management transactions have opposite characteristics. They are long updates which write many objects. A strict consistency and atomicity is required for service management transactions. However, they do not have explicit deadline requirements. Thus, service management transactions can be expressed as soft real-time transactions.

The prototype system used is based on the *Real-Time Object-Oriented Database Architecture for Intelligent Networks* (RODAIN) [8] specification. RODAIN Database Nodes that form one RODAIN Database Cluster are real-time, highly-available, main-memory database servers. They support concurrently running real-time transactions using an optimistic concurrency control protocol with deferred write policy. They can also execute non-real-time transactions at the same time on the database. Real-time transactions are scheduled based on their type, priority, mission criticality, or time criticality. All data in the database is stored in the main-memory database. Data modification operations are logged to the disk for persistence.

In order to increase the availability of the database each Rodain Database Node consists of two identical co-operative units. One of the units acts as the Database Primary Unit and the other one, Database Mirror Unit , is mirroring the Primary Unit. Whenever necessary, that is when a failure occurs, the Primary and the Mirror Units can switch their roles.

The client requests arrive via TCP/IP over a network directly to the database process, which contains threads to serve the clients. Each client may use the same connection for multiple transaction requests. The precoded real-time transactions get all their parameters in the requests and give their answers in the replies. No communication during the transaction execution is allowed between the transaction and the calling client.

The client and RODAIN server are originally designed to communicate over TCP. It provides a handy way for the client to recognize the failure of the server assuming that the network does not fail in between. The client can trust in the reliable communication, that the server has received each request and that it can expect to receive a reply also.

3   Evaluation Environment

The database server was running on an Intel Pentium 450 MHz processor with 256 MB of main memory. A similar computer was used for the client. The computers were connected using a dedicated network, the speed of which was controlled by changing the hub connecting the computers. To avoid unnecessary collisions, there was no other network traffic while the measurements were performed.

Used database is based on a GSM model and transactions are simple one item reads to Home Location Register (HLR). Database size is 30000 items.

All time measurements were performed on the client computer using the gettimeofday function, which provides the time in microseconds. The client sends the requests following a given plan, which describes the request type and the time when the request is to be sent. When the request is about to be sent the current time is collected and when the reply arrives the time difference is calculated.

Linux provides static priorities for time-critical applications. These are always scheduled before the normal time-sharing applications. The scheduling policy chosen was Round-robin (SCHED_RR) using the scheduler function sched_setscheduler.

The database was also avoiding swapping by locking all the processes pages in the memory using mlockall function. The swap causes long unpredictable delays, because occasionally some pages are sent and retrieved from the disk. Because in our experiment environment our database system was the only application running no swapping occurred during the tests.

4   Experimentation Results

The measurements in the dedicated networks clearly show, that Linux can be used as platform for a real-time main-memory database, at least when the disk I/O is omitted and the request deadlines are suitably long (see Figure 1 for Linux and Figure 2 for Chorus).

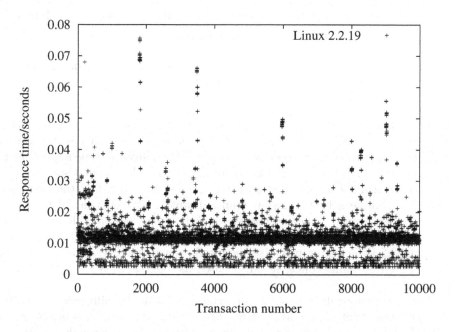

Fig. 1. The request responce times for each request using Linux kernel 2.2.19 with 10 Mb Ethernet. All the figures have as x the request sequence number over the test and as y the measured responce time in seconds.

Our initial tests with Linux-kernel 2.2.19 were not very encouraging (see Figure 1). The occasional delays were over 50 milliseconds. Also the long delays were grouped so, that when one went over the others were also more likely to go over the assumed deadline of 50 milliseconds. The database server itself (see

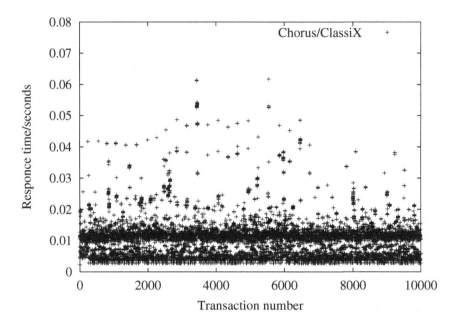

Fig. 2. The request responce times for each request using Linux kernel 2.2.19 as a client and Chorus as a server with 10 Mb Ethernet.

figure 3) used only a fraction of the observed time as seen on the client. This difference made us look more closely to the network behavior and the kernel itself. Our experience from other projects involving Linux and time requirements indicated that the change of the kernel to 2.4.x should be the first step.

Linux kernel 2.4 includes features that are designed to reduce the long time periods within kernel with the interrupts disabled. This change did the trick. The longest observed response time was slightly lower than 35 milliseconds, but most of the response times were still gathered around the 10 milliseconds line as in the 2.2 kernel experiment (see figure 4). Since 10 milliseconds is less than the required 50 milliseconds, it can be used as long as no swap to the disk is required.

However, there still is the same gathering around the 10 milliseconds. Adding the low latency patch (see http://www.zip.com.au/ akpm/linux/schedlat.html) did not remove that either, but it made the response times more deterministic. All the values are on some particular level meaning some particular time value (see figure 5). This is exactly what the patch is trying to do, it tries to reduce the kernel latencies within some time limits. The distribution of the response times clearly is no longer even over all time values.

The most surprising result came, when the speed of the network connection was increased (see Figure 6). We were hoping to see some reduction in the overall response times, since the network capacity was increased to almost 10 times. Some response times really dropped, but they reduced only to the nearest

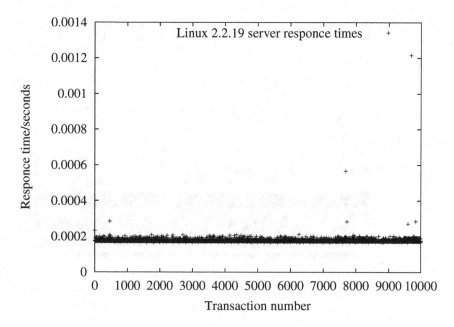

Fig. 3. The request responce times inside the database.

low 10 milliseconds. Because we used TCP as the communication mechanism between the client and the server the 20 milliseconds line is most probably due to retransmissions of messages. This gathering is mainly due to the 10 milliseconds scheduling delay usually visible on Linux.

We knew that the network communication was the dominating force, but the switch from using connectionless UDP communication instead of the connected TCP communication reduces all reply durations below 10 milliseconds (see Figure 7).

Of course, the number of messages drops to a third, since the TCP acks are not sent. This gives the most reduction, but it does not explain the concentration visible in the TCP measurement.

Finally, Table 1 shows minimun, maximum, median, and average responce times with different tests. Table shows also stardard deviation and variance of the responce times.

5   Conclusion

Linux can be used as a platform a for real-time main-memory database if the deadlines for the requests are feasible. The request must allow at least 10 milliseconds simply for the network and operating system overhead. Although the 10 milliseconds in this experimentation also covered the costs of our database,

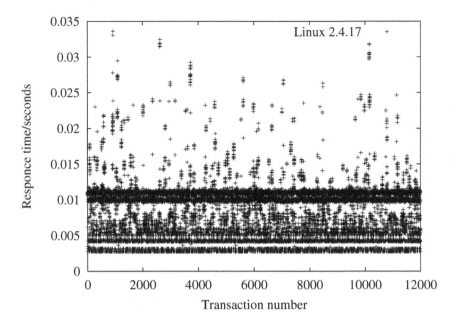

Fig. 4. The request performance time for each request using Linux kernel 2.4.17 with 10 Mb Ethernet

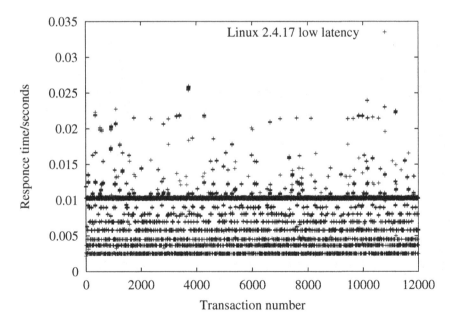

Fig. 5. The request performance time for each request using Linux kernel 2.4.17 low latency patch with 10 Mb Ethernet

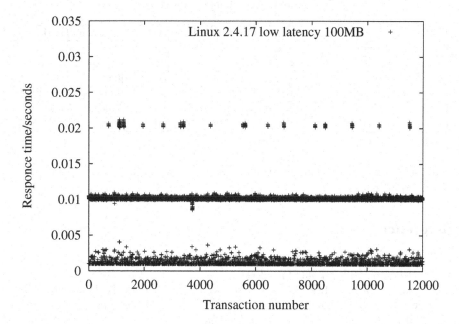

Fig. 6. The request performance time for each request using Linux kernel 2.4.17 low latency patch with 100 Mb Ethernet

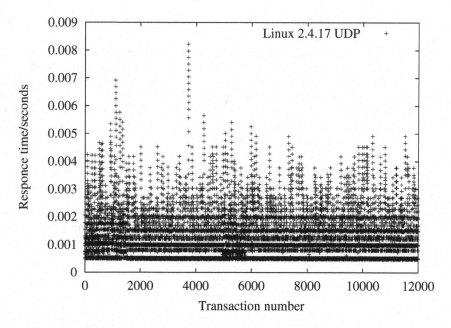

Fig. 7. The request performance time for each request using Linux kernel 2.4.17 with 100 Mb Ethernet, when the communication is connectionless

Table 1. Experimental statistics.

Test	Min	Max	Median	Average	Deviation	Variance
Linux 2.2.19 Figure 1	0.0027	0.0757	0.0116	0.0123	0.0065	4.2319-e-05
Chorus Figure 2	0.0023	0.0617	0.0109	0.0105	0.0063	3.9338e-05
Linux 2.4.17 Figure 4	0.0028	0.0336	0.0087	0.0081	0.0040	1.6035e-05
Linux 2.4.17 Figure 5	0.0022	0.0260	0.0092	0.0080	0.0034	1.1822e-05
Linux 2.4.17 Figure 6	0.000921	0.0212	0.0101	0.0086	0.0037	1.3739e-05
Linux 2.4.17 UDP Figure 7	0.00047	0.0082	0.000979	0.0012	0.00085	7.2258e-7

that was mainly due to the fact that there were no conflicts because all requests were simple reads.

References

1. I. Ahn. Database issues in telecommunications network management. *ACM SIG-MOD Record*, 23(2):37–43, June 1994.
2. S. Cha, B. Park, S. Lee, S. Song, J. Park, J. Lee, S. Park, D. Hur, and G. Kim. Object-oriented design of main-memory dbms for real-time applications. In *2nd Int. Workshop on Real-Time Computing Systems and Applications*, pages 109–115, Tokyo, Japan, October 1995.
3. H. Garcia-Molina and K. Salem. Main memory database systems: An overview. *IEEE Transactions on Knowledge and Data Engineering*, 4(6):509–516, December 1992.
4. ITU. *Introduction to Intelligent Network Capability Set 1. Recommendation Q.1211.* ITU, International Telecommunications Union, Geneva, Switzerland, 1993.
5. ITU. *Distributed Functional Plane for Intelligent Network CS-1. Recommendation Q.1214.* ITU, International Telecommunications Union, Geneva, Switzerland, 1994.
6. ITU. *Draft Q.1224 Recommendation IN CS-2 DFP Architecture.* ITU, International Telecommunications Union, Geneva, Switzerland, 1996.
7. Young-Kuk Kim and Sang H. Son. Developing a real-time database: The Star-Base experience. In A. Bestavros, K. Lin, and S. Son, editors, *Real-Time Database Systems: Issues and Applications*, pages 305–324, Boston, Mass., 1997. Kluwer.
8. J. Lindström, T. Niklander, P. Porkka, and K. Raatikainen. A distributed real-time main-memory database for telecommunication. In *Databases in Telecommunications*, Lecture Notes in Computer Science, vol 1819, pages 158–173, Edinburgh, UK, Co-located with VLDB-99, 1999.
9. V. Wolfe, L. DiPippo, J. Prichard, J. Peckham, and P. Fortier. The design of real-time extensions to the open object-oriented database system. Technical report TR-94-236, University of Rhode Island, Department of Computer Science and Statistics, February 1994.

The Design of a QoS-Aware MPEG-4 Video System*

Joseph Kee-Yin Ng ** and Calvin Kin-Cheung Hui

Department of Computer Science,
Hong Kong Baptist University,
Kowloon Tong, Hong Kong.
{jng,kchui}@comp.hkbu.edu.hk

Abstract. With the advance in computer and network technologies, the real-time interaction and the on-time delivery of multimedia data through the Internet by broadband network are becoming more popular. A variety of multimedia systems and Internet applications have been emerging, fulfilling the ever increasing demand on the Internet streaming applications. This paper outlines the design of a MPEG-4 video system. With the new features provided by the MPEG-4 standard, i.e. the object-based media with arbitrary- shaped coding, object-based QoS degradation is possible. It enables the system to discard the less important objects within the video stream when the network is congested. Our video system proposes a new transmission scheme for the system to transmit MPEG-4 video over an open network. Based on the nature of the video objects and their frames, transmission priorities among video objects are assigned. The transmission scheme then regulates the flow of the video data and their frames so that important data are delivered on time to the video client regardless the delay fluctuation of the open network.

Keywords: Quality of Service, QoS-Aware, MPEG-4 Video System, QoS Control

1   Introduction

With the advance in computer and network technologies, multimedia systems and Internet applications are becoming more popular. As broadband network is prevailing, more clients are able to watch streaming videos or to play multimedia data over the Internet in real-time. Therefore, there is an increasing demand in the Internet for streaming video systems. Since Internet streaming applications have a great demand on network bandwidth, video data should

---

* The work reported in this paper was supported in part by the RGC Earmarked Research Grant under HKBU2074/01E, and by the Faculty Research Grant under FRG/00-01/I-20.
** Dr. Joseph Kee-Yin Ng is a senior member of IEEE.

J. Chen and S. Hong (Eds.): RTCSA 2003, LNCS 2968, pp. 351–370, 2004.

be compressed before transmitted over the Internet. The Moving Pictures Experts Group (MPEG) intends to develop a digital media with high compression efficiency. The MPEG-1 and MPEG-2 standard are widely adopted for high quality video streaming and broadcasting system. Currently, MPEG keeps going to develop new media standards – MPEG-4 [1,2,3] and MPEG-7 [4,5,6]. The new MPEG standards focus not only on compression efficiency, but also on media description. MPEG-4 provides object-based representation and MPEG-7 provides semantic based representation. The MPEG-4 standard provides new features such as object-based media coding, scalability, and error-resilient techniques. With the object-based encoding system in MPEG-4, the coding of the scene can be classified into the coding of the foreground objects and the background objects. This is a good direction to take in attempting to reduce the transmission bit rate by object-based QoS degradation. For example, when the network is congested, the video stream can reduce the frame rate or the quality for the background scene in which human pays less attention to. Our video system proposes a transmission scheme to transmit MPEG-4 video over an open network. The transmission scheme assigns different video objects with different transmission priorities, which is based on the nature of the video content. The transmission scheme then regulates the flow of the video data and their frames so that important data are delivered on time to the video client regardless of the delay fluctuation of the open network. In this paper, we will outline the design of such a MPEG-4 video system.

2   Related Works

In a distributed MPEG video system, on time video delivery over an open network is our main focus of studies. Besides the fact that the current Internet can only provide best effort service, the major challenges of transmitting MPEG videos over the Internet are the variable bit rate (VBR) characteristic of the MPEG videos, insufficient bandwidth provided for video transmissions, and the uncontrollable and highly dynamic nature of the Internet environment. Among these facts, the special transmission characteristic from the variable bit rate (VBR) of the MPEG videos makes the system difficult to adopt any traditional scheduling algorithm for on-time video transmission.

To resolve these problems, many VBR transmission schemes have been developed and much effort have been put on the design of the transmission schemes for distributed video systems to handle network congestion when streaming videos over an open network [7,8,9,10,11]. For quality of service support, a number of QoS control mechanisms have been proposed. Bolot and Turletti [8] proposed a rate control mechanism for transmitting packet video over the Internet, Reibman et al [18,14] and Reininger et al [18] made use of an adaptive congestion control scheme to study the problem of transmitting VBR video over ATM networks. Hasegawa and Kato [13] have implemented and evaluated a video system with congestion control based on a two-level rate control.

To make the system adaptive to the change of network constraint and to prevent the network from further congestion, many systems use a software feedback mechanism [10,16] to monitor the system status. According to the video client's status, adjustment is made in order to maintain the quality of service for the video clients [12].

Players for streaming video systems like the Windows Media player from Microsoft [15], the QuickTime player from Apple [24], the WineCine Player from Philips [26], the RealSystem from RealNetwork [17] and the EnvivioTV from Envivio [25], are commercially available in the market. For these video systems, they adopted the MPEG-4 video compression technology. MPEG-4 enhances the encoded video quality and supports broad range of applications. The MPEG-4 encoding scheme is able to encode video ranging from narrow bandwidth network (mobile network) to broadband network (ADSL, cable modem). They can provide limited QoS guarantees on the video by stream switching. Based on the available bandwidth, the video systems will dynamically adjust the bit rate with high degree of overhead. The system encodes the media multi-bit-rates into a single streaming media. Then the system automatically determines the current available bandwidth and switches to the appropriate bit rate stream to serve the video client. According to the bandwidth demand, the stream switch allows the system to be adaptive to the environments. However, the drawback of the system is that it requires extra-storage for additional copies of the video tracks.

Much effort has been put on the design of distributed video systems. The OGI video system [12] is a preliminary design of a distributed video system with a rate control mechanism. The system is developed with a software feedback mechanism for adjusting the transmission rate for MPEG-1 video based on the fluctuation of the network environment. The video system is not only adaptable to the variations in the decoding frame rate, but also adaptable to the variations in network bandwidth, network delay and delay jitter. Furthermore, the OGI system uses the feedback mechanism with client/server synchronization, and supports dynamic QoS control.

Based on the OGI video system, we developed the QMPEG video system [19,20,23]. It enhances the software feedback mechanism that suits for multiple clients. With the Priority Feedback Mechanism (PFB), the bandwidth can be fairly shared among the video clients. QMPEG considers the transmission pattern of the MPEG videos based on human perspective. Referring to the current network status, the system dynamically adjusts the transmission patterns based on the pre-defined GOP mapping table such that the network will not get further congested and the video clients are better served. The QMPEGv2 video system [21,22,30] further considers the QoS control of the video by means of a video transmission scheduling scheme. It is a priority-driven transmission scheme that regulates the transmission sequence of the video stream. QMPEGv2 assigns transmission priority according to the urgency and the nature of the MPEG-1 video streams. The transmission scheme is responsible to regulate the flow of the video data. Once it detects that the bandwidth is insufficient or buffer is underflow through the feedback mechanism from the video client, the video quality would be gracefully degraded by video server. The transmission priorities scheme makes sure that important video data are delivered on time to the video client.

Since there are new features in the MPEG-4 standard which includes object-based media coding, arbitrary-shaped coding, and temporal/spatial scalability, we are trying to integrate most of these functions into the design of our proposed video system. However, there are relatively few studies in this front. Liang et al [31] outlines the design of a MPEG-4 client-server video system. It provides spatial scalability and temporal scalability to adapt different client side environments and network bandwidth. It also shows the idea of having a separate encoding for foreground figures and background scene. K. Asrar et al [32,33] implements the video system based on Delivery Multimedia Integration Framework (DMIF). The DMIF-based MPEG-4 streaming video system enables interactive media streaming over the internet.

Object-based coding is provided by the MPEG-4 standard, it provides not only temporal scalability, but also object scalability. With QMPEGv2's predefined priority driven transmission scheme for on-time video delivery, our video system can intelligently adjusts the bandwidth demand by means of skipping some less important or human undetectable frames and objects. This study shows the design of our proposed video system which is able to provide QoS guarantees control for on-time video delivery based on human perspective.

3   The Design of the MPEG-4 Video System

3.1   The Overview of MPEG-4 Video System

MPEG-4 is a new standard, which targets for streaming multimedia over the Internet. It was specified by the Moving Picture Experts Group (MPEG) committee, the working group within the International Organization for Standardization (ISO). This working group has defined the widely adopted standards, i.e. MPEG-1 and MPEG-2. The main concerns on MPEG-1 and MPEG-2 are about the improvements of the storage capacity and transmission efficiency by means of compressing the digital media. MPEG-1 tries to encode the digital storage media so that the bit-rate can reach 1.5 Mbps. This compression technique is widely applied to CD-ROM video application and MP3 audio systems. MPEG-2 is developed for handling a wider range of video applications and provides better video quality at a bit-rate of around 3 Mbps. For examples, DVD, Broadcast (Satellite) Services, Cable TV Distribution and Interactive Television Services. Consequently, the design of MPEG-4 not only achieves storage and transmission efficiency, but also supports a numerous of interactive multimedia applications. The encode bit rates for MPEG-4 ranged from 5 kbps for small, black-and-white security systems to 1 Gbps for large-screen, high-quality video systems and giant screen of electronic cinema.

The outstanding features of MPEG-4 are object-based media representation and scalability. Firstly, MPEG-4 represents the scene as composed of multiple audio-visual objects, which are co-related in space and time domains. Let us

Fig. 1. The original Akiyo scene

use a news broadcasting video clips as an example. The scene usually consists of a reporter, some background objects and the associated audio objects. With this object-based coding representation, MPEG-4 allows to encode individual video object with arbitrary-shape. It achieves not only higher compression ratios but also various quality metrics for QoS control. Next, scalability of the video provides the properties that enables the adaptation for transmission over heterogeneous networks and provides more flexibility to adjust the QoS for different environment and link bandwidth. Also, scalability allows a video decoder to decode a portion of the coded bitstreams so that the resulted video quality can be commensurate with the amount of data decoded. In fact, the temporal scalability enables adaptable frame rates, thus the portion of Video Object Plane (VOP) can be discarded. The object scalability allows the user to selectively display a subset of the video objects. Therefore, video objects like background scenes can be discarded based on the current environment.

3.2   Video Objects within a Video Scene

Video object is the basic element of a video scene. For a single video scene, it can be separated into foreground and background. In human perspective, those video objects in the foreground draw bigger attention than that in the background. For example, a composed news reporter scene (Akiyo) is shown in Figure 1. The news reporter is the main video foreground object of the scene. It is independent to video background, in which the separated background scene is shown in Figure 2. To encode by MPEG-4, each video object can be encoded

Background scene   Foreground scene

Fig. 2. Background and Foreground scenes of Akiyo

separately with different qualities based on its content or nature. Moreover, the visual object can be selectively displayed onto the screen. Let us consider the situation under network congestion. The video server can degrade the video streams by mean of discarding some less important video objects, such as objects in background. By doing so, the bandwidth demand by the resultant stream will be reduced so as to maintain the continuity and smoothness of the streaming of the video. Such QoS degradation on the video stream is possible because of the fact that human beings always focus mainly on foreground objects rather than background objects.

In our video system, the foreground video objects are sub-divided into Major-Video-Object (MajorVO) and Minor-Video-Object (MinorVO). The MajorVO refers to premier/key objects on the scene. It would be a person, a car or any object that the content creator intents to show. The MinorVO refers to the visual object in the foreground, but they may draw less attention from the users. On the other hand, the background object is any object in the backdrop scene. Compared to the foreground objects, the background is almost a still image. Note that the classification in these video objects is subjective to the content creator. While Figure 3 shows the original video scene for the container sequence, Figure 4 demonstrates the classification of the container scene decomposed into six video objects. The container is classified as a MajorVO, the small ship and the flag are classified as MinorVO, whilst the remaining object (the Sea, the Ground and the Sky) are classified as background video objects.

3.3   Data Size Ratios among Video Objects

In the previous section, we have discussed the video objects within a video scene. This section try to focus on the discussion of the data size ratios among the encoded video objects. We have set up an experiment for a container sequence which can be decomposed into six video objects as shown in Figure 4. We encode the whole video sequence with separated video objects by an MPEG-4 Video

Fig. 3. The original Container scene

encoder which uses the Microsoft MPEG-4 Visual CODEC. All video objects are encoded under the same environment including compression parameters and frame rate. Figure 5 and Table 1 shows the distribution and the average data size of the compressed bitstreams for each video object of the container sequence. We observe that background objects are taking up a majority share of the bitstreams from the video sequence and occupied over half of the bandwidth. Figure 5 also indicates that the MajorVO (34%) and background objects (53%) contribute a large proportion of the bitstream of the whole video sequence and the data size ratios among MinorVO, MajorVO and background object are 1: 2.89: 4.32.

By the object-based media representation of MPEG-4, this can greatly enhance the strategy of QoS control for the transmission of video streams. Our observation reveals that the majority of bitstreams is occupied by the background video objects, but the audience pay less attention to them. Therefore, we can use a higher compression ratio for the background bitstream so as to reduce its frame rate (temporal degradation) for this kind of video objects. An example is illustrated in Figure 6. We maintain the video quality for the MajorVO (i.e. container) and reduce the video quality for the other video objects in the scenes. Moreover, we also can enlarge the key frame interval for the background objects so that more bandwidth can be used by the foreground objects. In summary, results have shown that object-based video encoding can enrich the room for QoS control.

Sea (BG 1)   Ground (BG 2)

Sky (BG 3)   Ship (MinorVO 1)

Flag (MinorVO 2)   Container (MajorVO)

Fig. 4. Separate video objects of the Container scene

3.4   QoS Control within a Video Object

For video streaming system, the QoS control aims at maximizing the bandwidth
usage. It tries to maintain the video quality and keep the degradation of video

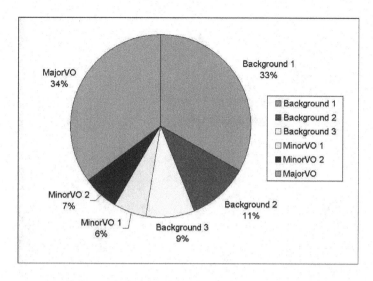

Fig. 5. Bandwidth distribution of the Container video

quality as small as possible. In our previous video streaming system [21,22], the mechanism for QoS control is based on temporal degradation of video quality. It discards video frame(s) according to the predefined frame skipping pattern when the current available bandwidth is not sufficiently enough to transmit all the frames within a GOP. For the design of our new system, the mechanism for QoS control employs the object-based coding characteristics. It is done by frame-based skipping and object-based coding. The detailed design of the QoS control mechanism for object-based MPEG-4 video streams is as follows.

A MPEG-4 video scene consists of a number of video objects(VOs). Each object composes of a sequence video object planes(VOPs), so-called Groups of VOPs (GOV) in MPEG-4. As mentioned in our studies [30], VOP dropping within a GOV is important to the video quality in terms of smoothness. For example, if a P-VOP within a GOV is discarded because of its late arrival, the subsequence P-VOPs and B-VOPs cannot be decoded. Hence, to maintain the minimum degradation of video quality, the VOPs would be dropped selectively

Table 1. Object size in the Container video

Object	Size(KB)
Background 1	76
Background 2	25
Background 3	20
MinorVO 1	13
MinorVO 2	15
MajorVO	81

Fig. 6. Reduce the video quality of the background scenes

Table 2. Different levels of QoS control

Level		VOPs								
B-VOP	2	B B	B B	B B	B B	B B
P-VOP	1		P		P		P		P
I-VOP	0	I

and evenly within a GOV. Since MPEG-4 support arbitrary GOV size, it is difficult to define a detail QoS level which is similar to the GOP mapping table as described in our previous studies [20,21]. Therefore, we simply quantize the QoS into three levels, as shown in Table 2. Every transmission starts from the lowest base level 0, which transmits the I-VOP only. If sufficient bandwidth is available, the next level, i.e. the transmission of the P-VOP, is triggered to improve the video quality. To further enhance the video quality, the last level, i.e. the transmission of the B-VOP, is activated. Besides that, if we quantize the QoS from three to six levels as shown in Table 4, we can see that the scalability can be further enlarged. The idea is to improve the smoothness of the video incrementally.

Noted that this design is different from the Fine Granular Scalability (FGS) as defined in MPEG-4. All levels are multiplexed into a single stream and the video client/ video encoder do not need any extra support for this feature. The video server dynamically transmits the video data from the base level to the enhancement level.

Table 3. Enhanced scheme for B-VOP in QoS control

Level		VOPs						
	5	B		B				B
	4		B			B		
	3	B			B			B
B-VOP	2		B			B		
P-VOP	1		P	P		P	P	
I-VOP	0	I						

Next, we want to show the inter-object degradation scheme for our video system. In previous sections, we classify video objects into three types. They are the background, the MinorVO and the MajorVO. Then, we prioritize these objects for QoS degradation/Improvement control. The background video object has the highest priority to be discarded, and the MajorVOs are the last to go. Let us use an example to illustrate our idea for the QoS Control. Assuming a scene with i background, j MinorVO and k MajorVO as shown in Figure 7. The QoS scheme discards the highest priority objects (i.e. background objects) first. The number of discarded objects is from 1 to i. If the resultant stream is still too much for the available bandwidth, the scheme will then drop the MinorVOs and lastly drop the MajorVOs. Figure 8 shows the aggregated bandwidth demand for the inter-object degradation for the container sequences. We observed that the bandwidth demand can be reduced by 33%, by discarding the first background objects. It can further reduce the bandwidth by not just discarding the background objects, but evenly discard all the other video objects except the MajorVO. In this case, it will save over 55% of the bandwidth. Figure 9 shows the sample scenes of object-based QoS degradation. In these examples, we assumed that the discarded VOP are replaced by the previous VOP of the corresponding objects. The left column shows the components for scene update, and the right column shows the resultant scene. The dark area shown in Figure 10 reflects the scene error (i.e. artifacts) when object is missed or discarded. However, the error becomes un-observerable if the scene is padding with the corresponding VOPs as shown in Figure 11.

With a frame-based and object-based QoS scheme, the demanded bandwidth can be progressive reduced whilst QoS degradation is kept to a minimum.

3.5   The Client-Server Video System

Overall Architecture. In the previous sections, we have discuss about the video objects within a video scene, the data size ratios among video objects, and the QoS control within a video object. These provide the bases on how to do QoS control, and by how much we can reduce the bandwidth demand. Having these information, we now have to put everything together to construct our MPEG-4 video system.

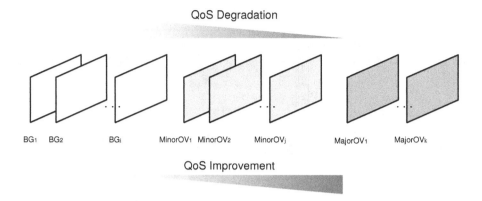

Fig. 7. Object-based QoS improvement/degradation control

The proposed system is a MPEG-4 video streaming system that aims at conveying MPEG-4 videos over an open network. That is, MPEG-4 videos are streamed to the video clients through the Internet. Video streaming is done by unicast transmission and Figure 12 shows an overall architecture of our video streaming system. In general speaking, the video server of the system transmits video streams to a number of video clients concurrently. Each video client, upon receiving video objects from the stream, will inform the video server about its

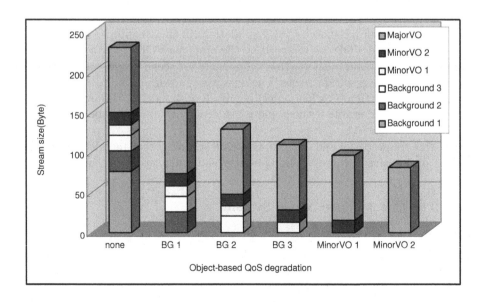

Fig. 8. Bandwidth demand on QoS degradation for the Container video

Full Video

Discard Background 1(Sea)

Discard Background 2(Sky)

Fig. 9. (a) An example to show Object-based QoS degradation

Discard Background 3(Ground)

Discard MinorVO 1(Flag)

Discard MinorVO 2(Ship)

Fig. 9. (b) An example to show Object-based QoS degradation

Fig. 10. The scene with discarded background objects

Fig. 11. The scene with artifacts fixed by previous container VOPs

current status by sending it feedback messages through the open network. The video server will then collect the feedback messages and react accordingly. That is, by improving or degrading the video stream through its QoS control so as to maintain the quality of the MPEG-4 video delivered for the video clients.

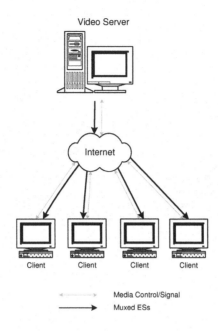

Fig. 12. System overview

The transmission scheduling scheme in the video system defines a transmission sequence based on our studies. The service discipline of the scheduling scheme divides the video transmission into rounds. Each round is a basic unit for the transmission management. Each round is divided into four sessions, namely SESSION 0 to SESSION 3, with SESSION 0 bearing the highest priority for transmission. Hence, each round starts from SESSION 0 and it switches to the next session when the current session is completed. A round must complete within the predefined round limit. At the end of a round, the current session is stopped and the next round starts from SESSION 0 again. For example, when the transmission cycle reaches the end of a round, which is still in SESSION 1, the unsent VOP are discarded. The first two sessions are designed for the

Table 4. A summary of the transmission scheme in the video server

Transmission	Real-time		Non real-time	
Session	SESSION 0	SESSION 1	SESSION 2	SESSION 3
Description	Convey I-VOP level and then P-VOP level (from MajorVOs to background objects)	Convey B-VOP level from low to high level.	Transmit for initial buffering.	Prefetch under transmission control.

real- time data. In fact, SESSION 0 is transmitting only the mandatory part and SESSION 1 is for the optional part of the real-time video data. The last two sessions, SESSION 2 and SESSION 3, are for non-real-time VOP. Table 4 summarized the functions of these sessions.

The video streaming system distinguishes itself from the others by its transmission scheduling scheme and the unique QoS control mechanism. These transmission scheduling schemes regulate the flow of the video data and ensures that important components are delivered on time at the client side if sufficient network bandwidth is available. At all time, video transmission is under the QoS control. This means VOPs may be discarded by the QoS control when the bandwidth demand exceeds the current bandwidth available.

Video Server. The main function of the server is to convey the stored MPEG-4 streams to the video clients. It monitors the overall streaming status among the streams and regulates the flow of the video stream so that the best QoS can be kept. The video server transmits video streams to a number of video clients concurrently. Each stream comprises of one or more Elementary Streams (ES). MPEG-4 organizes the ES in Access Unit (AU). Using this concept for the video ESs, the ES corresponds to a sequence of VOP and the AU comprises of the entire VOP. The ES are packetized to a stream of Sync Layer (SL) packet with timing information for synchronizing the Elementary Streams. The video server then convey the SL packet which is encapsulated by the Delivery Layer packet such as an IP packet. Figure 13 illustrates the streaming process of the video server. Each ES is assigned a transmission priorities based on the nature of the video objects. Video server transmits the VOP level by level and the video server primarily conveys the I-VOP for the MajorVOs, follows by MinorVOs and lastly the BackgroundVOs in each round.

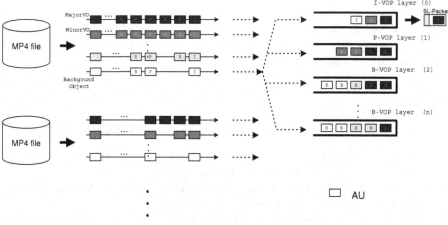

Fig. 13. Video server architecture

Video Client and QoS-Aware Middleware. Considering the complex construct of a MPEG-4 video client, it is complicate to design and to implement a fully functional MPEG-4 video client. The major difficulty is the complexity of the MPEG-4 decoder. It is because the decoder needs to handle and synchronize between different video objects from multi-leveled video streams. Moreover, it is also hard to support different MPEG-4 profiles. Therefore, instead of reinventing the wheel, a middleware is designed and placed in between the video server and video decoder. This middleware is used for handling the QoS control and communications to the third parity video decoders, like the EnvivoTV and the QuickTime Player.

The middleware is an interface between video server and MPEG-4 video players. It aims at monitoring the network status, the receiving buffer status, and the sending back of feedback messages from the client side to video server. Furthermore, the middleware is responsible for collecting and conveying the composed streams to video decoder. All VOPs missing their deadlines or incomplete VOP would be discarded by the middleware.

Based on the MPEG-4 standard and human behavior, we have explored the possibility and investigated the room for reducing the MPEG-4 video stream's bandwidth demand without degrading the video quality. Together with the transmission scheme in the server design, the feedback mechanism and the middleware design, we have started the actual implementation of our MPEG-4 video system.

4   Summary

We have outlined the design of the MPEG-4 video system. The system is designed to transmit MPEG-4 video over an open network. With the feedback mechanism from the video clients, the video server will react accordingly so as to maintain the video quality for each client. With the object shape coding method provided in MPEG-4, it enables object- based QoS improvement/degradation in our system. The QoS control is based on the transmission priorities for different video objects in human perspective. The transmission scheme regulates the flow of the video data, and at the same time the important data, which have the highest priority, are enforced to be delivered on time at the video client regardless of the delay fluctuation of the network.

References

1. Overview of the MPEG-4 Standard (http://mpeg.telecomitalialab.com/standards/mpeg-4/mpeg-4.htm).
2. Peiya Liu, "MPEG-4: A Multimedia Standard for the Third Millennium, Part 1", *IEEE multimedia*, pp.74-83, October-December 1999
3. Peiya Liu, "MPEG-4: A Multimedia Standard for the Third Millennium, Part 2", *IEEE multimedia*, pp.76-84, January-March 2000
4. MPEG-7 Overview (http://mpeg.telecomitalialab.com/standards/mpeg-7/mpeg-7.htm).

5. Peiya Liu, "MPEG-7: The Generic Multimedia Content Description Standard, Part 1", *IEEE multimedia*, pp.78-87, April-June 2002

6. Peiya Liu, "MPEG-7: Overview of MPEG-7 Description Tools, Part 2", *IEEE multimedia*, pp.83-93, July-September 2002

7. V. Baiceanu, C. Cowan, D. McNamme, C. Pu and J. Walpole, "Multiple Applications Require Adaptive CPU Scheduling", *Proc. of Workshop in Multimedia Resource Management*, December 1-2, 1996.

8. J. Bolot and T. Turletti, "A Rate Control Mechanism for Packet Video in the Internet", *Proc. of INFOCOM'94*, pp. 1216-1223, 1994.

9. W. Bolosky, J. Barrera III, R.Draves, R. fitzgerald, G. Gibson, M.Jones, S. Levi, N. Myhrvold, and R. Rashid, "The Tiger Video Fileserver", *Proc. The 6th International Workshop on Network and Operating System Support for Digital Audio and Video*, April 1996. Also available at http://www.research.microsoft.com/.

10. W. Bolosky, R. Fitzgerald, and J. Douceru, "Distributed Schedule Management in the Tiger Video Fileserver", *Proc. SOSP'97*, Also available at http://www.research.microsoft.com/research/os/bolosky/sosp/cdrom.html.

11. J. F. Koegel Buford, *Multimedia Systems*, Addison Wesley, 1994.

12. S. Cen, C. Pu and R. Staehli, " A Distributed Real-time MPEG video Audio Player", *Proc. of the 5th International Workshop on NOSSDAV'95*, April 1995.

13. T. Hasegawa, T. Hasegawa, T. Kato, "Implementation and Evaluation of Video Transfer System over Internet with Congestion Control based on Two Level Rate Control", *Proc of RTSCA'99*, pp.141-148, 1999.

14. H. Kanakia, P Mishra and A. Reibman, "An adaptive Congestion control Scheme for Real-Time Packet Video Transport" *Proc. of ACM SIGCOMM '93*, pp20-31, Sep. 1993.

15. Windows Media Technology from Microsoft (Available at http://www.microsoft.com)

16. C. Pu and R. Fuhere, "Feedback-Based Scheduling: a Toolbox Approach", *Proceeding of 4th Workshop on Workstation Operation Systems*, October 14-15, 1993.

17. RealPlayer and RealSystems G2 form RealNetworks (www.realaudio.com).

18. R. Reibman, and A. Berger, "On VBR video Teleconferencing over ATM Networks" *Proc. of IEEE GLOBECOM'92*, pp. 314-319, 1992.

19. H. K. Wai, and J. Ng, "The Design and Implementation of a Distributed MPEG Video System", *Proceedings of the First HK ACM Postgraduate Research Day*, pp. 101 — 107, October 1998.

20. H. K. Wai, "Priority Feed back Mechanism with Quality of Service Control for MPEG Video System" *MPhil Thesis*, Department of Computer Science, Hong Kong Baptist University, August 1999.

21. J. Ng, C. Hui, W. Wong, and K. Leung, "A Transmission Scheme for Providing Streaming Support and QoS Control in a Distributed MPEG Video System", *Technical Report*, Dept. of Computer Science, Hong Kong Baptist University, Sept. 2000. http://www.comp.hkbu.edu.hk/~jng/Tech-Rpt/JNG09-00.ps.

22. J. Ng, C. Hui, and W. Wong, "A Multi-server Design for a Distributed MPEG Video System with Streaming Support and QoS Control", *Proceedings of the 7th International Conference on Real-Time Computing Systems and Applications* (RTCSA 2000), pp. 160 — 165, December 2000.

23. K. Y. Lam, C. Ngan, and J. Ng, "Using Software Feedback Mechanism for Distributed MPEG Video Player Systems", *Journal of Computer Communication* , Vol. 21(15), pp. 1320 — 1327, 1998, Elsevier Science.

24. QuickTime from Apple (http://www.apple.com/quicktime).

25. EnvivioTv from Envivio (http://www.envivio.com).

26. WebCine from philips (http://www.digitalnetworks.philips.com/).

27. J. Ng, "A Reserved Bandwidth Video Smoothing algorithm for MPEG Transmission", *Journal of Systems and Software*, Volume 48, Issue 3, pp. 233 — 245, November 1999.

28. J. Ng, "Performance Analysis of Transmission schemes for VBR Traffic on a Real-Time Network", *International Journal of Parallel and Distributed Systems and Networks*", Volume 3, Issue 3, pp. 144 – 156.

29. J. Ng, K. Leung, and W. Wong, "Quality of Service for MPEG Video in Human Perspective", *Technical Report*, Department of Computer Science,Hong Kong Baptist University, July 2000.
(http://www.comp.hkbu.edu.hk/ jng/Tech-Rpt/JNG07-00.ps).

30. J. Ng, K. Leung, W. Wong, V. Lee, and C. Hui, "A Scheme on Measuring MPEG Video QoS with Human Perspective", *Proc. of the 8th International Conference on Real-Time Computing Systems and Applications* (RTCSA 2002), March 2002.

31. L. Cheung, M.E. Zarki, "The Analysis of MPEG-4 Core Profile and its system design" *Proceedings of Multimedia Technology and Applications conference* (MTAC 2001), November 2001.

32. L.A. Haghighi, Y. Pourmohammadi, H.M. Aluweiri, "Realizing MPEG-4 Streaming Over the Internet: A Client/Server Architecture using DMIF" , *Proceeding of International Conference on Information Technology - Coding and Computing* (ITCC 2001), April 2001.

33. Y. Pourmohammadi, L.A. Haghighi, A. Mohamed, H.M. Aluweiri, "Streaming MPEG-4 over IP and Broadcast Networks: DMIF Based Architectures", *Proceedings of The 11th International Packet Video Workshop*, April 2001

Constrained Energy Allocation for Mixed Hard and Soft Real-Time Tasks*

Yoonmee Doh[1], Daeyoung Kim[2], Yann-Hang Lee[3], and C.M. Krishna[4]

[1] CISE Department, University of Florida,
Gainesville, FL 32611-6120, USA
ydoh@cise.ufl.edu
[2] Information and Communications University, Munji-dong, Yusong-gu,
Daejon, 305-714, Korea
kimd@icu.ac.kr
[3] Dept. of Computer Science and Engineering, Arizona State University
Tempe, AZ 85287-5406, USA
yhlee@asu.edu
[4] Electrical & Computer Engineering Dept., University of Massachusetts
Amherst, MA 01003, USA
krishna@ecs.umass.edu

Abstract. Voltage-Clock Scaling (VCS) is an effective approach to reducing total energy consumption in low power microprocessor systems. To provide real-time guarantees, the delay penalty in VCS needs to be carefully considered in real-time scheduling. In addition to real-time requirements, the systems may contain non-real-time tasks whose response time should be minimized. Thus, a combination of optimization objectives should be addressed when we establish a scheduling policy under a power consumption constraint. In this paper, we propose a VCS approach which leads to proper allocations of energy budgets for mixed hard and soft real-time tasks. Based on the schedulability of VCS-EDF, we investigate the characteristics of energy demand of hard periodic and soft aperiodic tasks. Using simulation and subject to a given energy budget, proper voltage settings can be chosen to attain an improved performance for aperiodic tasks while meeting the deadline requirements of periodic tasks.

1 Introduction

Mobile computing and communication devices such as laptop computers, cellular phones, and personal digital assistants (PDA's) have become commonplace; the demands for embedded applications on those devices are increasing. However, processors are also becoming increasingly power-hungry. For this reason, the field of power-aware computing has gained increasing attention over the past decade.

---

* The work reported in this paper is supported in part by NSF under Grants EIA-0102539 and EIA-0102696.

J. Chen and S. Hong (Eds.): RTCSA 2003, LNCS 2968, pp. 371–388, 2004.

Simple techniques, such as turning off (or dimming) the screen while a system is idle and shutting down hard disks while it is not accessed is now commonly adopted in most portable device designs [1]. However, in many cases, re-activation of hardware can take some time, and affect response time. Also, deciding when and which device should be shut down and woken up are often far from trivial [3].

Another effective approach to power reduction is a technique called *Voltage-Clock Scaling* or *Dynamic-Voltage-Scaling* in CMOS circuit technology. The power consumed per every cycle in a digital circuit is given by $P_{cmos} = C_L N_{sw} V_{DD}^2 f$, where C_L is the output capacitance, N_{sw} the number of switches per clock, and f the clock frequency. Due to the quadratic relationship between the supply voltage (V_{DD}) and the clock frequency, a small reduction in voltage can produce a significant reduction in power consumption. However, lowering V_{DD} increases the circuit delay following the equation $t_d = kV_{DD}/(V_{DD} \Box V_T)^2$, where k is a constant depending on the output gate size and the output capacitance, and V_T is the threshold voltage. This implies that the clock frequency must be reduced and the execution time is extended [11]. Obviously, the longer execution time may lead to performance degradation in application response time and a failure to meet real-time deadlines.

Most of today's processor cores have been designed to operate at different voltage ranges to achieve different levels of energy efficiency, as shown in Table 1. For instance an ARM7D processor can run at 33MHz and 5V as well as at 20MHz and 3.3V. The energy-performance measures at these two modes of operation are 185 MIPS/WATT and 579 MIPS/WATT, and the MIPS measures are 30.6 and 19.1, respectively [7]. From these figures, if we switch from 33MHz and 5V to 20MHz and 3.3V, there will be around (579-185)/579=68% reduction in energy consumption at an expense of (30.6-19.1)/19.1=60% increase in processing time. Kuroda *et al.* use voltage scaling in the design of a processor core as shown in [4], in which they can adjust internal supply voltages to the minimum automatically according to its operating frequency.

Table 1. Microprocessors that allow the core operate at different voltages and frequencies

Processors	Voltage	Speed (MHz)	Power Consumption (Watt)	Features
StrongARM SA-2	1.30	600	0.45	12-fold energy reduction
[5]	0.75	150	0.04	
Pentium-III	1.60	650	22	SpeedStep Technology
[6]	1.35	500	9	- 2 modes
Crusoe (TM5400)	1.65	700	2	16 levels
[9][10]	1.10	200	1	in steps of 33MHz
ARM7D	5.0	33	0.165	185 MIPS/W
[7]	3.3	20	0.033	579 MIPS/W
PowerPC860	3.3	50	1.3	2 modes
[8]	2.4	25	0.241	

If low energy consumption is a desirable feature in real-time embedded systems, voltage-clock scaling must cooperate with the task scheduling algorithms since the power-delay tradeoff property in low power design affects meeting the strict time-constraints of real-time systems. The execution of a high-priority at a low voltage and slow clock rate may cause a low-priority task to miss the deadline due to the additional delay from the execution of the high priority task.

The concept of real-time scheduling has been applied to dynamic speed setting in [12] by Pering et al. Regarding the impact on energy of the number of available distinct voltage levels, Ishihara and Yasuura pointed out that at most two voltage levels are usually enough to minimize energy consumption [13]. A minimum-energy scheduler based on the EDF scheduling policy was proposed in [14], where an off-line algorithm assigned the optimal processor speed setting to a critical interval that requires maximum processing. Similar to the approach for EDF scheduling in [14], Hong et al. considered a low energy heuristic for non-preemptive scheduling in [15] and the optimal voltage setting for fixed-priority scheduling is studied in [16]. These approaches require that the task release times must be known *a priori*. Using two-mode voltage scaling under EDF scheduling, dynamic resource reclaiming was proposed in [17], which is useful when task arrival instances or phases are not known *a priori* and an extension of [18]. For the periodic task model and rate-monotonic scheduling, two on-line voltage-scaling methods [19] were proposed, which change voltage levels at the execution stage from the initially assigned levels as such changes become necessary.

While VCS has been a well-populated research area, power-aware system design has generally focused on minimizing total power consumption. For systems consisting of soft aperiodic tasks, the objective of minimizing power consumption will result in slow execution. On the other hand, in many cases, the battery capacity can be replenished or there is a finite mission lifetime. Minimizing power consumption that doesn't utilize all available energy may not lead to optimal system performance. A better power control strategy in such cases is to minimize the response times of soft real-time tasks, providing that the deadlines of hard real-time tasks are met and the average power consumption is bounded.

In this paper, we target battery-driven real-time systems, jointly scheduling hard periodic tasks and soft aperiodic tasks, whose battery capacity is bounded in the feasible range given by a set of tasks. The scheduling should guarantee meeting the task deadlines of hard real-time periodic tasks and achieve average response time of aperiodic tasks that are as low as possible. Under the constraints of a bounded energy budget, finding an optimal schedule for a task set should aim to satisfy both optimal power consumption and strict timing constraints simultaneously.

We first investigate the characteristics of energy demands of periodic and aperiodic tasks focusing an EDF scheduling exploiting the feature of VCS. Based on the energy requirement of mixed real-time tasks, we also propose a static scheduling for energy budget allocation, which determines the optimal two-level voltage settings of all tasks under bounded energy consumption, while guaranteeing that no deadline of any periodic task is missed and that the average response time of aperiodic tasks is minimized. The algorithm selects the voltage settings that have the minimum average response time among the schedulable ones within a given energy consumption. To schedule aperiodic tasks, we adopt the Total Bandwidth Server, which was proposed by Spuri and Buttazzo and handles aperiodic tasks like periodic tasks within the reserved bandwidth such that it outperforms other mechanisms in responsiveness [21].

The paper is organized as follows. In Section 2, we outline the preliminary system model having several assumptions. Then, we discuss the characteristics of energy demand and processor utilization under bounded energy budget in Section 3. Considering on the characteristics described in Section 3, energy allocation methods and an algorithm of voltage assignment are described in Section 4. To illustrate the effectiveness of the proposed algorithm, we evaluate its performance in Section 5 through simulation studies. In Section 6, a short conclusion is provided.

2   System Model

For the targeted real-time systems, tasks may arrive periodically and have individual deadlines that must be met. Or they can be aperiodic and can accrue computation values, which are inversely proportion to their response times. Under a given bound on energy consumption, we build a system model and make several assumptions as follows.

2.1   Schedule for Periodic Tasks

For Earliest Deadline First (EDF) scheduling, a periodic task τ_i is modeled as a cyclic computational activity characterized by two parameters, T_i and C_i, where T_i is the minimum inter-arrival time between two consecutive computation instances and C_i the worst-case execution time (WCET) of task τ_i. The EDF scheduling algorithm always serves a task that has the earliest deadline among all ready tasks. The following assumptions are analogous to assumptions made in real-time scheduling theory [20].

- Tasks are independent: no task depends on the output of any other task.
- The deadline for task τ_i is equal to D_i, which is less than T_i.
- The worst-case execution demand of each task τ_i, i.e. C_i, is known. The actual execution demand is not known a priori and may vary from one arrival instance to the other.
- The overhead of the scheduling algorithm is negligible when compared to the execution time of the application.

2.2   Schedule for Aperiodic Tasks

An infinite number of soft aperiodic tasks $\{J_i \mid i=0,1,2,...\}$ are modeled as aperiodic computation activities represented by two parameters, $\square$ and α, where $\square$ is the average inter-arrival time between two consecutive aperiodic instances and $\propto$ the average worst-case execution time of all aperiodic tasks.

Aperiodic tasks are scheduled by *Total Bandwidth Server* (TBS) algorithm that makes fictitious but feasible deadline assignment based on the available processor utilization guaranteed by the isolation of bandwidth between periodic and aperiodic tasks. In the TBS algorithm, the k-th aperiodic request arriving at time $t = r_k$, a task deadline

$$d_k = max(r_k, d_{k\square}) + \frac{C_k}{U_A} \tag{1}$$

is assigned, where C_k is the execution time of the request and U_A the allocated processor utilization for aperiodic tasks. By definition $d_0=0$. The request is then inserted into the ready queue of the system and scheduled by the EDF algorithm, as are any other periodic instances or aperiodic requests already present in the system.

Note that the assignment of deadlines is such that in each interval of time, the processor utilization of the aperiodic tasks is at most U_A. Hence, a set of periodic tasks with utilization factor $U_P = \sum_{i=1}^{n} C_i / T_i$ and a TBS with a bandwidth U_A is schedulable by EDF if and only if $U_A + U_P \square 1$. The definition and the formal analysis of this algorithm are proved in [21]. Comparing to other scheduling algorithms for aperiodic tasks, the TBS algorithm has a very simple implementation complexity and shows very good performance in average response time.

2.3 Voltage Clock Scaling

□ Voltage Switching

We assume voltage switching consumes a negligible overhead. This is also analogous to the assumption made in classical real-time scheduling theory that preemption costs are negligible [20]. Voltage switching typically takes a few microseconds. In fact, a bound of the total overhead can be calculated by simply counting the number of task arrivals and departures since voltage switches are only done at task –dispatching instances.

□ Two Voltage Levels

The system operates at two different voltage levels. Ideally, a variable voltage processor that has continuous voltage and clock setting in the operational range is available as explained in Table 1. We assume a simple setting arrangement that the processor in a real-time system can be dynamically configured in one of two modes: *low-voltage (L) -mode* and *high-voltage (H)-mode*. In *L-mode*, the processor is supplied with a low voltage (V_L) and runs at a slow clock rate. Thus, task execution may be prolonged but the processor consumes less energy. On the other hand, the processor can be set in *H-mode*, i.e. be supplied with a high voltage (V_H) and run at a fast clock rate, in order to complete tasks sooner at the expense of more energy consumption. The operating speeds at *L-mode* and *H-mode* are denoted as $\square_L$ and $\square_H$, respectively, in terms of some unit of computational work. Depending on the voltage setting for task T_i, the worst-case execution time is $C_i/\square_L$ or $C_i/\square_H$.

2.4 Bounded Energy Consumption

In battery-powered embedded systems, it is often equally important to control power consumption to extend the battery lifetime and to enhance system performance. Given that the battery can be replenished or the mission lifetime is limited, we may assume that the available capacity can safely be consumed during a predefined interval of operation. Thus, an average power consumption rate or energy budget can be set to the ratio of available capacity to the target operation interval. Also, it is possible to communicate with the battery such that the system and its scheduler can know the current status of the battery capacity. One of the mechanisms for doing this is the *Smart Battery System* (SBS), which has been now actively standardized and introduced to battery-driven systems [2]. In the paper, we assume the embedded system, whose processor is the major factor of the energy consumption

3 Energy Budget Allocation in Real-Time Embedded Systems

For all real-time tasks, the available energy consumption is confined to a given energy budget called E_C, which has to be shared among periodic and aperiodic tasks. Let E_P and E_A are the energy budget allocated to periodic tasks and aperiodic tasks, respectively. The voltage-clock scaling problem is to find voltage settings for both periodic and aperiodic tasks such that

- □ all periodic tasks are completed before their the deadlines and have an energy consumption less than E_P.
- □ all aperiodic tasks can attain the minimal response times while consuming an energy less that E_A.
- □ $E_P + E_A \square E_C$

3.1 Periodic Tasks

Assume that, for periodic task T_i, m_i is the voltage setting determined between the two possible modes, i.e. *L-mode* and *H-mode* and $\square_i(m_i)$ is the speed of task T_i at mode m_i. Given m_i for all of periodic task T_i, the energy demand for periodic task of E_p is

$$E_P(m_i) = \sum \frac{1}{\square_i(m_i)} \frac{\overline{C_i}}{T_i} p(m_i) \tag{2}$$

where $p(m_i)$ is the power consumption at mode m_i, $\overline{C_i}$ the average execution time of task T_i. In addition, the worst-case utilization is given by

$$U_P(m_i) = \sum \frac{1}{\Box_i(m_i)} \frac{C_i}{T_i} \tag{3}$$

If m_i is *H-mode* for all periodic tasks, the processor runs at a fast clock rate all the time, thereby minimizing the utilization. The maximum energy demand for the tasks is represented as

$$max\, E_P = \sum \frac{1}{\Box_H} \frac{\overline{C_i}}{T_i} p_H \tag{4}$$

and its utilization becomes

$$min\, U_P = \sum \frac{1}{\Box_H} \frac{C_i}{T_i} \tag{5}$$

On the contrary, if m_i is *L-mode* for every periodic task $\Box$, the processor runs at a slow clock rate all the time such that the utilization is maximized, but consumes the minimum possible energy. For the sake of schedulability, the tasks should be scheduled in such a way that the utilization is less than unity Therefore, we define *min* E_P as an energy demand when there exists a set of $\{m_i\}$ so that the worst-case utilization

$$U_P(m_i) = \sum \frac{1}{\Box(m_i)} \frac{C_i}{T_i} \Box 1 \text{ and } E_P(m_i) = \sum \frac{1}{\Box(m_i)} \frac{\overline{C_i}}{T_i} p(m_i) \text{ is minimized.} \tag{6}$$

In Fig. 1, we describe the relationship between energy consumption and utilization for a set of periodic tasks. The maxima and minima are denoted as *max* E_P and *min* E_P for the energy and *max* U_P and *min* U_P for the utilization, respectively. Again, *min* E_P follows equation (6). Regarding the feasibility of the energy constraint and the worst-case utilization, E_C must be greater than *min* E_P and *min* U_P should be no greater than 1. By its definition, if *min* U_P is greater than unity with all *H-mode* executions, it is impossible to find voltage settings to ensure that all tasks meet their deadlines. If *max* U_P is less than 1, the tasks are schedulable with all *L-mode* assignments and energy consumption can never be less than *min* E_P. In the case, *max* U_P becomes

$$U_P(L) = \sum \frac{1}{\Box_L} \frac{C_i}{T_i} \text{ and } min\, E_P \text{ does } E_P(L) = \sum \frac{1}{\Box_L} \frac{\overline{C_i}}{T_i} p_L.$$

If energy budget E_P is given in the range from *min* E_P to *max* E_P, $U_P^{available}$ is the available utilization corresponding to the allocated energy budget E_P. And, by searching a set of voltage settings meeting the given energy budget and schedulability, energy demand and utilization for periodic tasks are determined as $E_P(m_i) \Box E_P$ and $U_P(m_i) \Box U_P^{available}$, respectively.

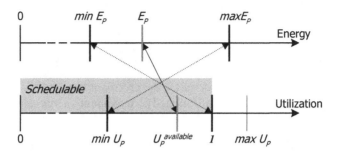

Fig. 1. The relationship between power consumption and utilization for a set of periodic tasks

3.2 Aperiodic Tasks

Denote by m_A the voltage setting determined between the two possible modes for aperiodic tasks, which have the average inter-arrival time of $\square$ and the average worst-case execution time of $\propto$ If all of them are assigned in mode m_A and the power consumption at mode m_A is $p\,(m_A)$, the energy consumption and utilization of them are

$$E_A(m_A) = \frac{1}{\square(m_A)}\frac{\propto}{\square}p(m_A) \tag{7}$$

$$U_A(m_A) = \frac{1}{\square(m_A)}\frac{\propto}{\square} \tag{8}$$

respectively.

Also, if all of them are assigned in *L-mode* or *H-mode*, they demand minimum energy *min E_A* or *max E_A* given by the following equations

$$min\,E_A = \frac{1}{\square_L}\frac{\propto}{\square}p_L \ \ \text{and} \ \ max\,E_A = \frac{1}{\square_H}\frac{\propto}{\square}p_H \tag{9}$$

having the utilization

$$min\,U_A = \frac{1}{\square_L}\frac{\propto}{\square} \ \ \text{and} \ \ max\,U_A = \frac{1}{\square_H}\frac{\propto}{\square} \tag{10}$$

3.3 Energy Budget Allocations and Utilization

While the constraint $E_P + E_A \ \square \ E_C$ must be satisfied, we can decide how processor utilization, task scheduling, and task response time are affected. From the viewpoint of utilization, the more utilization is available for aperiodic tasks, the shorter the deadlines that are assigned to them by the deadline assignment of equation (1). This assigns higher priorities to them in EDF scheduling such that they can get a faster response. To give more utilization to aperiodic tasks, the utilization of periodic tasks must be shrunk and it can be done by assigning more tasks to *H-mode*, but requires more energy consumption. Since the total energy budget is bounded, the energy budget left to aperiodic tasks will be reduced. As a result, the aperiodic tasks must be run in a low voltage mode and their response times will be extended.

Likewise, from the viewpoint of the energy budget, the portion assigned in *H-mode* for aperiodic tasks should be maximized within an assigned energy budget E_A to get faster responsiveness. But, as before, if the energy demand of aperiodic tasks is increased, the energy available for periodic tasks will be decreased. In consequence, the available utilization for aperiodic tasks will be decreased due to the increased execution time of periodic tasks, which may result in degradation in responsiveness.

Eventually, to get both schedulability and fast responsiveness under a bounded energy budget, an effective scheduling and energy allocation scheme is needed for jointly scheduling hard periodic and soft aperiodic tasks. The scheduling should address the concern of the trade-off between utilization and energy consumption as shown in Fig. 1.

4 Constrained Energy Allocation Using VCS-EDF Scheduling

In this section, we describe an energy allocation scheme, which allocates bounded energy budget to periodic and aperiodic tasks based on VCS-EDF scheduling, meeting the requirements of real-time tasks, i.e. to meet deadlines of periodic tasks and to get faster average response time for aperiodic tasks. Given an energy budget E_C, considering the feasible range of energy demand determined by tasks, it finds voltage settings for periodic tasks and the execution portion in *H-mode* and *L-mode* to the worst-case execution time for aperiodic tasks under a bounded energy budget.

4.1 Energy Allocation Factors

Suppose that E_P and E_A can be allocated in the range of *[min E_P, max E_P]* and *[min E_A, max E_A]*, respectively, $E_{max} = max\ E_P + max\ E_A$, and $E_{min} = min\ E_P + min\ E_A$. If the bounded energy consumption budget is given as E_C, E_C must fall into the range $E_{min} \square E_C \square E_{max}$ where *min E_P*, *min E_A*, *max E_P*, and *max E_A* are as defined in equations (4), (5), and (9) to a given set of tasks. Then, voltage settings must be determined such that the energy consumption satisfies the constraint of $E_P + E_A \square E_C$, while guaranteeing the schedulability of periodic tasks and minimizing average response time for aperiodic tasks. For ease of explanation, we define $E_{diff} = E_{max} \square E_{min}$.

Let $\square$ and $\square$ be energy allocation factors of aperiodic and periodic tasks, given by *0 $\square \square \square$ 1* and *0 $\square \square \square$ 1*, respectively. Then, the energy budgets E_P and E_A allocated to them are represented as

$$E_P = min\ E_P + \square(max\ E_P \square min\ E_P), \tag{11}$$

$$E_A = min\ E_A + \square(max\ E_A\ \square min\ E_A), \tag{12}$$

respectively.

Suppose $\square a = (max\ E_A\ \square min\ E_A)$, $\square p = (max\ E_P\ \square min\ E_P)$, and $\square c = E_C\ \square(min\ E_A + min\ E_P)$, respectively, then the inequality $(E_P + E_A\ \square E_C)$ becomes

$$\square\square a + \square\square p\ \square\ \square c.$$

Hence, $\square$ and $\square$ are determined by

$$0\ \square\ \square = \frac{\square c\ \square\ \square\square a}{\square p}\ \square\ 1 \quad \text{and} \quad \frac{\square c\ \square\ \square p}{\square a}\ \square\ \square\ \square\ \frac{\square c}{\square a} \tag{13}$$

respectively. The choice of $\square$ determines $\square$, and *vice versa*, and also determines E_A and E_P by equations (11) and (12).

If $\square = 0$ and $\square = 1$, energy *min* E_A and *max* E_A are assigned to aperiodic tasks, i.e. assigning all aperiodic tasks in *L-mode* and *H-mode*, respectively. If $\square$ is 0.6, energy assigned for aperiodic tasks becomes $(min\ E_A + 0.6\square a)$. Unlike voltage settings for periodic tasks, which are decided on the basis of a task, the running mode for aperiodic tasks are determined by the fraction in *H-mode* and *L-mode*. If the fraction assigned to *H-mode* is x_H, then that assigned to *L-mode* becomes $(1-x_H)$. The energy consumption needs to be bounded by the budget, and so

$$\frac{x_H}{\square_H}\ \frac{\propto}{\square}p_H + \frac{(1\ \square\ x_H)}{\square_L}\ \frac{\propto}{\square}p_L\ \square\ E_A \tag{14}$$

Similarly, the execution time of an aperiodic task is determined according to the voltage modes and the deadline assigned in Equation (1) is adjusted. As for responsiveness, the greater the fraction of the processor utilization that is given to aperiodic tasks, the better is the responsiveness expected under the TBS algorithm, because shorter deadlines are assigned to them. Under energy budgets of E_C and E_P, the utilization for aperiodic tasks will be increased if the voltage settings are determined to allocate more *H-mode* to periodic tasks within the energy budget such that it can minimize the utilization $U_P\ (m_i)$ and make an increase in $U_A^{available}$. We therefore have a constrained optimization problem to determine the optimal voltage settings, maximizing *H-mode* execution, within the constraint of budget E_P and guaranteeing that no deadline of any periodic task is missed.

The optimization problem to find voltage settings for periodic tasks can be stated as follows: Pick the task subsets H and L for voltage settings of *H-mode* and *L-mode* such that

$\square$ $H \square L = \{\square_1, \square_2, ..., \square_n\}$

$\square$ $H \square L = \square$

$\square$ $U_P(m_i) = \sum \frac{1}{\square(m_i)}\frac{C_i}{T_i}$ is minimized subject to the well-known sufficient condition[1] for the schedulability of periodic tasks under EDF, i.e.,

$$\frac{1}{\Box_H}\sum_{\Box H}\frac{C_i}{min(T_i,D_i)}+\frac{1}{\Box_L}\sum_{\Box L}\frac{C_i}{min(T_i,D_i)}\Box 1 \tag{15}$$

and the energy consumption constraint of

$$\frac{p_H}{\Box_H}\sum_{\Box H}\frac{\overline{C_i}}{min(T_i,D_i)}+\frac{p_L}{\Box_L}\sum_{\Box L}\frac{\overline{C_i}}{min(T_i,D_i)}\Box E_P$$

This optimization problem can be treated equivalently to the decision problem of the subset sum, which is *NP*-complete. Consequently, efficient search heuristics, e.g., branch-and-bound algorithms, should be employed to find a solution if *n* is large.

4.2 Algorithm for Energy Budget Allocation

We describe here the algorithm for the dynamic allocation explained in the previous section. The algorithm outputs the energy allocation factors,$\Box$ and $\Box$ voltage settings for periodic tasks, $\{m_i\}$, and the percentage of *H-mode* assignment for aperiodic tasks, x_H.

The Algorithm of VCS-EDF Scheduling Under Bounded Energy Consumption E_C

```
1. Compute min Eₚ, max Eₚ, min Eₐ, max Eₐ, Eₘₐₓ, and Eₘᵢₙ.

2. If E_C is less than Eₘᵢₙ = (min Eₚ + min Eₐ), there is
   not enough energy to execute the workload.

3. If E_C is in the range of Eₘᵢₙ ☐ E_C ☐ Eₘₐₓ, compute the
   range of ☐ and ☐, Eₐ and Eₚ, accordingly.

4. For each ☐ in the range of 0 ☐ ☐☐ 1, execute the
   following steps
```

(4a) Compute $\Box$, E_A and E_P,

(4b) Find $\{m_i\}$, which satisfies $\sum\frac{\overline{C_i}}{T_i}\Box\frac{1}{\Box(m_i)}\Box p(m_i)\Box E_P$ and

that $U_p(m_i)=\sum\frac{C_i}{T_i}\Box\frac{1}{\Box(m_i)}$ is minimized, where m_i is

voltage setting either in *H-mode* or *L-mode* for periodic task $\Box_i$, using simple search or branch-and-bound algorithms.

---

[1] The condition is also necessary if $D_i\Box T_i$ for all *i*.

(4c) Compute $U_A^{available} = 1 - U_P\ (m_i)$.

(4d) Given E_A, find x_H, the fraction of execution in H-mode for aperiodic tasks, and (1–x_H) the fraction in L-mode.

(4e) Applying the TBS algorithm for the deadline assignment $U_P\ (m_i)$ and $U_A^{available}$ computed in step (4b) and (4c), respectively, run VCS-EDF scheduling in voltage settings $\{m_i\}$ for periodic tasks and x_H and (1–x_H) for aperiodic tasks.

5. Find $\square$ having the minimum average response time from the result of the scheduling in step 4.

6. The value of $\square$ determined in step 5 is selected for energy allocation, which gives the best performance for aperiodic tasks, x_H for running the aperiodic tasks in H-mode and $\{m_i\}$ for voltage settings of the periodic tasks are determined accordingly.

---

5 Simulation Evaluation

We analyze here the properties of sharing the bounded energy budgets between periodic and aperiodic tasks based on VCS approach and evaluate the VCS-EDF scheme to schedule mixed real-time tasks. For the power consumption and speed settings, Motorola's PowerPC 860 processor is used for our simulation, which can be operated in a high-performance mode at 50MHz and with a supply voltage of 3.3V, or a low-power mode at 25MHz and with an internal voltage of 2.4V[8] such that V_H and V_L are fixed to $V_H=3.3$ and $V_L=2.4$. The power consumption in the high-performance mode is 1.3 Watts (p_H), as compared to 241mW (p_L) in the low-power mode. The clock rate at high voltage is 100% greater than at low voltage: $\square_H=2.0$ and $\square_L=1.0$.

A simulation study is performed to address the improvement of task execution time with extra available energy. In other word, the system is assumed to possess enough energy to complete the tasks and meet the deadline requirements. In addition, there is extra energy that can be allocated to improve the response time of aperiodic tasks. Our immediate objective of the simulation study is to see how the response time can be reduced through a proper voltage setting. Furthermore, this extra energy can be allocated to periodic tasks such that the processor utilization reserved for periodic tasks is reduced. This leads to a reduction of deadline assignment in the total-bandwidth scheduling scheme. On the other hand, the extra energy can be consumed by aperiodic tasks that can result in a first-order effect in the reduction of response time.

In our simulation, we first generate 10 random task periods in the range of 100 to 1000 and set the task deadlines equal to their respective periods. The worst-case execution demands of the tasks are randomly chosen such that, for each simulation case, no deadlines need be missed and the resultant utilization is set to $U_p(L)$=0.8, 1.0, or 1.2, respectively. For aperiodic tasks, we adopt the exponentially distributed execution time with an average ∞ equal to 45. Then we let the inter-arrival time be exponentially distributed with mean of between 450 (10% workload, i.e. $U_A(L)$=0.1) and 112.5 (40%, i.e. $U_A(L)$=0.4). The energy budget E_C is set at each of several energy levels in the range from $(E_{min}+0.6E_{diff})$ to $(E_{min}+E_{diff})$.

To get fast responsiveness, how much energy budget can be allowed to periodic and aperiodic tasks, respectively? Over various $\square$'s and constraint energy budgets, we obtain the average response times of aperiodic tasks from the simulation and plot them in Fig. 2. Regardless of increase in the energy budget, Fig. 2 reveals a trend of reduction in average response time of aperiodic tasks as $\square$increases. The average response time does not show always a monotonic decrease with an increase in $\square$ In some regions, it has an abrupt increase or is flat over increasing $\square$ This occurs especially when $E_C=(E_{min}+0.6E_{diff})$ or $E_C=(E_{min}+0.7E_{diff})$.

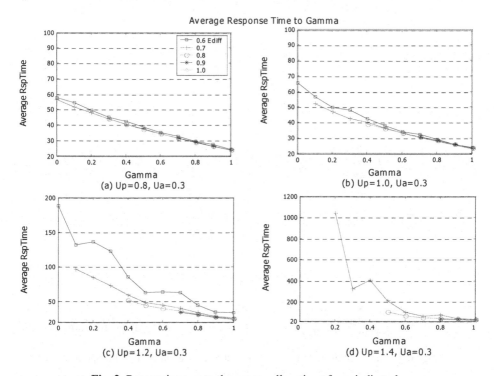

Fig. 2. Responsiveness to the energy allocation of aperiodic tasks

Note that when we increase $\square$ aperiodic tasks are invoked more in high-voltage high-speed execution. This results in a reduced CPU utilization, i.e. the utilization required by aperiodic tasks under the voltage setting. On the other hand, as $\square$is reduced, the energy allocated to the periodic tasks decreases which leads to an increase in $U_P(m_i)$ and a decrease in $U_A^{available}$. The two reductions, one on the demand to complete aperiodic tasks and the other one on the available utilization for aperiodic tasks, can have a profound impact on the response times. Let the CPU utilization required be denoted as U_A^{real} and we show the ratio of $U_A^{available}$ to U_A^{real} in Fig. 3. For instance, with $E_C = (E_{min} + 0.6E_{diff})$ and $\Box = 1.0$ in Fig. 3(a), there still exists extra energy to be assigned to periodic tasks ($\Box > 0$) and an optimal voltage setting is obtained which leads to $U_P(m_i) = 0.55$ and $U_A^{available} = 0.45$. On the other hand, U_A^{real} is reduced to 0.15 as we increase $\Box$ to 1.0. A ratio of 3 is then obtained and plotted in the Figure.

It is interesting to observe that, whenever the ratio is flat in Fig. 3, the average response times have uneven decreases in Fig. 3. In fact, as long as the ratio of $U_A^{available}$ to U_A^{real} continues to increase, the processor possesses greater capacity to complete aperiodic tasks and the response time drops. In contrast, there would be a monotonic decrease in response time if the ratio were flat as we increase $\Box$

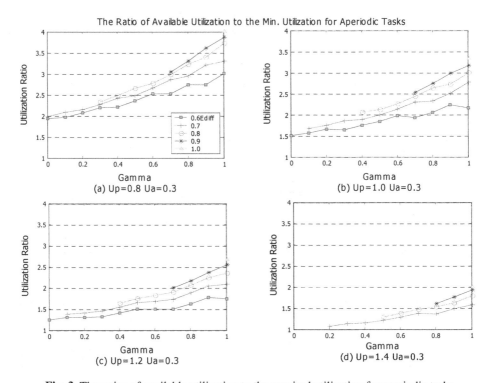

Fig. 3. The ratios of available utilization to the required utilization for aperiodic tasks

The other interesting observation in Fig. 3 is that utilization ratios are not available for all of $\Box$ values. It indicates that the possible choices of $\Box$ only exist in the range where the plots are shown. This is also evidenced in Equation (14) and is originated from the definition of $\Box$ in which the minimum value of $\Box$ means the percentage of energy available for aperiodic tasks after periodic tasks take energy budget as much as they can.

From these results, to get fast responsiveness of aperiodic tasks, the a greater portion of the energy budget should be allocated to aperiodic tasks, and then voltage settings of periodic tasks need to be determined within the energy budget remaining for them. Note that the way we formulate the minimal energy budget is based on the schedulability for periodic tasks and ensuring no CPU starvation for aperiodic tasks. If the energy budget is below this minimum, aperiodic tasks will incur much longer response times.

To reveal the causes that lead to the flat regions in Fig. 3, we now investigate how the energy budget is allocated to periodic and aperiodic tasks, respectively. In Fig. 4, we show the energy sharing as percentages of allocated energy E_P for periodic and E_A for aperiodic tasks to the maximum energy demand, E_{max}, that is the maximal energy consumption by a given task set. The plots in Fig. 4 (a)~(c) cover the case when E_C is bounded to $(E_{min}+0.6E_{diff})$. But in Fig. 4 (d), we plot the energy percentages under $E_C = (E_{min}+0.7E_{diff})$ unlike the ones for other periodic workloads. The reason is the energy budget $(E_{min}+0.6E_{diff})$ is too low to select proper voltage settings making the given set of tasks schedulable under the periodic workload of $U_P =1.4$.

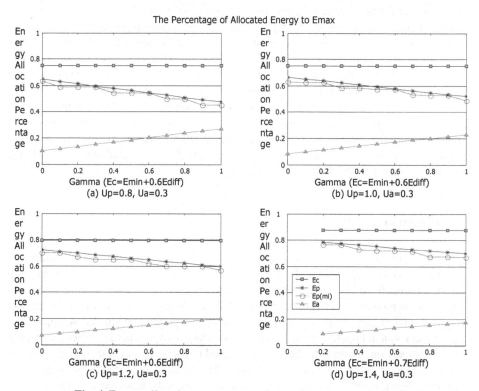

Fig. 4. Energy allocation percentage to the maximum energy demand

When a set of periodic tasks can make the most of the given energy budget E_P, i.e. E_P (m_i) $\Box E_P$, E_P (m_i) is determined by the chosen set of voltage settings, m_i, in the VCS-EDF algorithm subject to requirements imposed by the need to maintain schedulability. Thus, there is a small discrepancy in energy consumption between E_p and $E_p (m_i)$.

Over several regions of $\Box$, $E_p (m_i)$ is kept at the same level even if E_p is decreasing, while being less than E_p. In other words, the same voltage settings are selected for different E_p's. For all the possible combinations of voltage settings, if we sort them in descending/ascending order according to energy demands, a discontinuity in energy demands exists between any two sets of voltage settings adjacent in the sorted list. Let the discontinuity in energy demand be an energy gap. Then, even if there is a small amount of change in energy budget E_p, it cannot change voltage settings unless it jumps up/down any energy gap between adjacent energy levels. However, if the number of periodic tasks is getting bigger, the flatness in Fig. 4 will be reduced because of the fine energy gap between adjacent energy levels of discontinuous voltage settings.

It should be noticed the big drops in the response times of aperiodic tasks occur when the voltage settings of periodic tasks result in a energy allocation $E_p (m_i)$ that is very close to the available budget E_p. For instance, at $\Box=0.1$ and 0.5 of Fig. 4 (c), the settings lead to a little reduction of $U_A^{available}$ which, combining with the decrease of U_A^{real}, bring about a considerable decrease in the task response time of Fig. 2 (c).

We now consider how much improvement we can obtain from an increased energy budget. In Fig. 5, we show the evaluation results for the minimum average response time to the constraint energy ranging from 0.6 to E_{diff}. The responsiveness of aperiodic tasks for $U_A=0.1$ and 0.2 is not much affected by the periodic tasks' workload U_P and the constraint energy budget E_C. Since every aperiodic task is assigned to H-$mode$ (i.e. $\Box=1.0$ to ensure minimal response time) and is allocated with the maximal energy budget, the available energy budget for periodic tasks decreases as U_A increases. As a consequence, the increased workload in periodic tasks increases the average response time for the case of $U_A=0.3$ and 0.4 as $U_A^{available}$ is limited and the deadlines assigned to the aperiodic tasks are extended.

6 Conclusion

In this paper, we have presented an algorithm to carry out voltage clock scaling in workloads consisting of periodic hard and soft real-time tasks. The aim is to keep within a predefined energy budget. The objective of the scheduling scheme is to minimize the response time of aperiodic tasks while all deadlines of periodic tasks are met and the total energy consumption is bounded by the energy budget. As we apply total bandwidth scheduling for aperiodic tasks, we notice two conflicting factors in energy budget allocation. When extra budget is assigned to aperiodic tasks, their execution can be done in high-voltage and high-speed mode. This leads to a reduced response time. On the other hand, the extra energy budget allocated to periodic tasks can result in a lowering of the CPU utilization reserved for periodic tasks. This, in turn, leaves more available CPU utilization for aperiodic tasks and cause shorter deadlines as defined in the total bandwidth scheduling scheme.

Our simulation study assumes that there the energy budget is enough to meet the hard real-time periodic tasks and to complete the aperiodic tasks. In addition, here is extra energy that can be allocated to either periodic or aperiodic tasks. Our results demonstrate that the VCS-EDF scheduling gets the fastest responsiveness when the extra energy budget is allocated to aperiodic tasks at their maximum energy demand such that all of them can be run in *H-mode*. Given the requirement of responsiveness and any energy budget, the proposed scheduling method can decide the voltage settings for periodic tasks so that real-time tasks can share the bounded energy budget effectively. Therefore, the work provides the battery-driven embedded real-time system designer with a general view, which allows scheduling real-time tasks considering their general characteristics of energy demands and processor utilization, given a constraint of bounded energy availability.

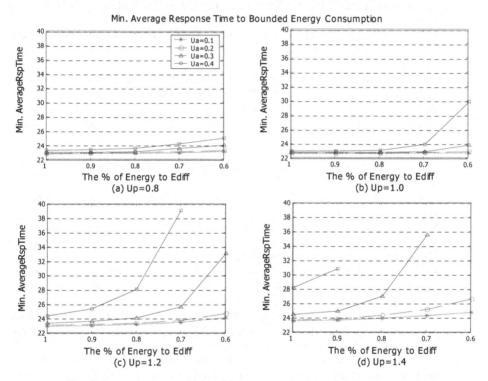

Fig. 5. Average response time with respect to the bounded energy budget

References

1. Compaq, Intel, Microsoft, Phoenix, and Toshiba, "Advanced Configuration and Power Interface specification," available at http://www.intel.com/ial/powermgm/specs.html (1996)
2. K.Lahiri, A.Raghunathan, S.Dey, D.Panigrahi, "Battery-Driven System Design: A New Frontier in Low Power Design", *International Conference on VLSI Design* /ASP-DAC, pp.261-267, Jan. 2002.

3. L. Benini, A. Bogliolo, and G. De Micheli, "A Survey of Design Techniques for System-Level Dynamic Power Management," *IEEE Trans. on Very Large Scale Integration Systems*, Vol.8, No.3, (2000) 299 –316

4. T. Kuroda et. al., "Variable supply-voltage scheme for low-power high-speed CMOS digital design," *IEEE Journal of Solid State Circuits*, Vol. 33, No. 3, (1998) 454-462

5. Jay Heeb, "The next generation of StrongArm," *Embedded Processor Forum*, MDR (1999)

6. Intel Corporation, "Mobile Pentium III Processor in BGA2 and micro-PGA2 packages," Datasheet Order #245302-00 (2000)

7. "Introduction to Thumb," ARM Documentation, Advanced RISC Machines Ltd.

8. *MPC860 PowerPC Hardware Specification*, MPC860EC/D, Motorola (1998)

9. Transmeta Corporation, "TN5400Processor Specification," available at http://www.transmeta.com (2000)

10. J. Pouwelse, K. Langendoen, H. Sips, "Dynamic Voltage Scaling on a Low-Power Microprocessor," *International Symposium on Mobile Multimedia Systems & Applications* (MMSA'2000) 157-164

11. A. P. Chandrakasan, S. Sheng, and R. W. Brodersen, "Low-power CMOS digital design," *IEEE Journal of Solid-State Circuits*, 27(4), (1992) 473-484

12. T. Pering and R. Brodersen, "Energy Efficient Voltage Scheduling for Real-Time Operating Systems," *The 4th IEEE Real-Time Technology and Applications Symposium*, Works In Progress Session (1998)

13. T. Ishihara and H. Yasuura, "Voltage scheduling problem for dynamically variable voltage processors," *Proceedings of International Symposium on Low power Electronics and Design* (ISLED'98) 197-202

14. F. Yao, A. Demers, and S. Shenker, "A Scheduling Model for Reduced CPU Energy," *IEEE Foundations of Computer Science* (1995) 374-382

15. I. Hong, D. Kirovski, G. Qu, M.P otkonjak and M. B. Srivastava, "Power Optimization of Variable Voltage Core-based Systems," *Proceedings of the 35th annual conference on Design Automation Conference* (DAC'98) 176-181

16. Gang Quan and Xiaobo (Sharon) Hu "Energy Efficient Fixed-Priority Scheduling for Real-Time Systems on Variable Voltage Processors," *Proceedings of 38th Design Automation Conference* (2001)

17. Y. H. Lee, Y. Doh, and C. M. Krishna, "EDF Scheduling Using Two-mode Voltage-Clock-Scaling for Hard Real-Time Systems," *Proceedings of Compilers, Architectures, and Synthesis for Embedded Systems* (CASES 2001)

18. C. M. Krishna and Y. H. Lee, "Voltage-Clock-Scaling Adaptive Scheduling Techniques for Low Power in Hard Real-Time Systems," *IEEE Proceedings of Real Time Technology and Applications Symposium* (RTAS 2000)

19. Y. H. Lee and C. M. Krishna, "Voltage-Clock Scaling for Low Energy Consumption in Real-Time Embedded Systems," *Real-Time Computing Systems and Applications* (RTCSA'99)

20. C.L.Liu and J. Layland, "Scheduling Algorithms for Multiprogramming in a Hard Real-time Environment," *Journal of the ACM*, Vol.20, (1973) 46-61

21. M. Spuri and G. Buttazzo, "Scheduling Aperiodic Tasks in Dynamic Priority Systems", *The Journal of Real-Time Systems*, Vol. 10, No. 2, (1996) 179-210

An Energy-Efficient Route Maintenance Scheme for Ad Hoc Networking Systems

DongXiu Ou[2], Kam-Yiu Lam[1], and DeCun Dong[2]

[1] Department of Computer Science City University of Hong Kong
83 Tat Chee Avenue, Kowloon Hong Kong
[2] Institute of Traffic Information Engineering, Tong Ji University Shanghai, China
dxou@sh163.net,cskylam@cityu.edu.hk

Abstract. Although in recent years many excellent works have been done on resolving the routing problem in ad hoc networking systems, the energy issue in route maintenance has been greatly ignored. Due to movement of mobile hosts, the energy consumption rate of a route may change with time. In this paper, we propose the *distance-based route maintenance* (DBRM) scheme in which a handoff mechanism is designed for switching the nodes in route maintenance to minimize the energy consumption rate. In addition, in DBRM, mobile hosts in a group may switch between different states of operations to conserve energy. In the simulation experiments, we have shown that the amount of energy conserved from using DBRM is significantly larger than both the IEEE standard 802.11 with fixed listen interval, and the power management scheme using GAF with random listen interval.

Keywords: Ad hoc networks, energy aware computing, route maintenance, data monitoring

1 Introduction

In recent years, the research in ad hoc networks has received growing interests. An ad hoc networking system consists of a collection of mobile hosts and the system does not have any fixed infrastructure, such as base stations in cellular networks. One of the most important issues in ad hoc networking systems is routing. Due to limitations in mobile communication, a mobile host may only communicate with the neighboring mobile hosts, which are within its communication range. If a mobile host, called *source node*, wants to communicate with another mobile host (node[1]), called *destination node*, it may initiate a *routing algorithm* to find the best route to connect to the destination node. If the destination node is far from the current position of the source node, the source node must depend on other mobile nodes, called *relay nodes*, to forward the messages to the destination node.

---

[1] Mobile hosts and nodes are used interchangeably in this paper.

J. Chen and S. Hong (Eds.): RTCSA 2003, LNCS 2968, pp. 389–397, 2004.
© Springer-Verlag Berlin Heidelberg 2004

In last decade, various efficient routing algorithms have been proposed. Some of them aim to minimize the communication overheads. Since most of the mobile hosts may only have limited energy supply, the issues on how to minimize energy consumption in route discovery and in data communication are attracting more and more interests in recent years. An important issue, which has been greatly ignored in the previous works in the area, is the energy consumption issue in route maintenance. Route maintenance is important to real-time monitoring in mobile ad hoc networking systems where a route has to be existed for a period of time until the end of the monitoring period. For example, in a battlefield management system, the mobile hosts may carry sensor devices to detect the existence of enemies. The commander, which is also a mobile host, may submit a continuous query to a mobile host to get enemy information. A continuous query has a begin time and end time. A route has to be existed between the two hosts during the monitoring period so that sensor data can be transmitted continuously to the commander.

The energy consumption rate of a route depends on the number of hops in the route as well as the length of each hop. In addition, as shown in [2], minimizing the number of the hops in a route may not be the most effective way in energy conservation. The biggest saving in energy is to switch a mobile host to doze mode of operation [5]. Thus, another important concern in route maintenance is to determine which mobile hosts in the system may be in doze mode and how long should they be in doze mode. If too long mobile hosts are in doze mode, the choice of routes for connecting the source and destination nodes will be affected.

In this paper, we propose a *distance-based route maintenance (DBRM)* scheme to minimize the energy consumption rate in route maintenance. DBRM consists of two parts. Firstly, it consists of a handoff mechanism for switching the nodes in forming the route to minimize the energy consumption rate of the route in data communication. Secondly, it includes a mechanism to determine how the mobile hosts in the system may switch between different states of operations with the objective to increase the number and the length of mobile hosts in doze state, and at the same time to minimize the impact on route maintenance. The remaining parts of the paper are organized as follows. Section 2 is the related works in the area. Section 3 presents the problems. In Section 4, we introduce the proposed route maintenance scheme to conserve energy. Section 5 reports the performance of the proposed methods. The conclusions of the paper are in Section 6.

2   Related Work

One of the most important areas in an ad hoc network is routing. In last few years, a lot of efficient routing algorithms have been proposed. These methods can be divided into two groups. The first group is called the on-demand protocols [1] in which a route to connect the source node to the destination node will be searched upon the receipt of the connection request. The second group is called the table-driven protocols [4] in which the topology of the whole network is maintained the system. When a connection is needed, the source node can select the route from its memory directly. As shown in the previous works, the on-demand protocols have lower overhead while the table-driven protocols have lower delay in route discovery. To reduce the delay in searching the route, a route maintenance scheme in the on-demand protocols is proposed [1]. But the energy issue in route maintenance has been greatly ignored.

Energy conservation is a very important issue in ad hoc network systems since the energy supply of most of mobile hosts is very limited. As explained in [3], a mobile host may have several modes of operations, i.e., idle, doze, receive and transmit. [3] shows that the ratios in energy consumption rate between *doze, idle, receive and transmit* states are: 0.08: 1: 1.15: 1.58. Doze state has lowest energy consumption rate and is much lower than the other states. Therefore, switching a mobile host to doze state can save a lot of energy and it is the most effective way to conserve energy.

GAF [2] is a routing algorithm in which some nodes may switch to doze state to conserve energy. The basic principle of GAF is to dividing the whole network area into grids. Each node in a grid may connect to the nodes in the adjacent grids directly. In GAF, only one node is needed to be active in a grid while the others may be in doze state. The problems of GAF are: (1) which node should be the active node for forming the route, and (2) how long the active node should be active. GAF propose that the period for a node in active and non-active state may be randomly distributed. It is obvious that if the random period is small, the nodes may change their states frequently resulting in higher energy consumption. If it is large, the procedure in route maintenance may be affected.

3   Problem Formulation

3.1   Operation Modes

The IEEE 802.11 standard [6] defines a power management scheme for ad hoc networking systems. A mobile host has two modes of operations: active mode and power-saving (PS) mode. Comparing with active mode, the energy consumption rate is lower if a mobile host is in PS mode. The mobile host in PS mode may either be in awake state or in doze state. The energy consumption rate in doze mode is much lower than that in awake state. To synchronize the operations of the mobile hosts in a system, one of the active mobile hosts periodically broadcasts beacons to other mobile hosts in the system. The time interval between the broadcast of successive beacons is called *beacon interval (BI)*. Each beacon contains an ATIM (ad hoc traffic indication message) window. A mobile host operating in doze state enters the *awake* state prior to each TBTT (Target Beacon Transmit Time). It listens to the ATIM from the beacon. It can easily see that the amount of energy conserved in a mobile host in doze state depends on the lengths of BI and ATIM window.

3.2   Route Maintenance Problem

The set of mobile hosts in the system are classified into groups based on their geographical locations. Given a network of N nodes and let $R = \{S, G_1, G_2, ..G_{ml}, D\}$ be a sequence of relay groups from source node S to destination node D. G_i is called a relay group. All the nodes in a relay group G_i are equivalent in forming the route such that each node in G_i can communicate with any nodes in G_{i+1} directly. The routing problem is to determine which member in a relay group should be chosen to form the route. Other than the node chosen to be a part of the route, all other nodes in a relay group may turn to doze mode to conserve energy.

It is assumed that initially the system adopts a route discovery algorithm to establish a route with minimum energy consumption rate for connecting node S to node D. Two important factors in determining the energy consumption rate of a route are: (1) the number of hop counts in the route; and (2) the energy consumption rate for communication between the nodes in each hop in the route.

It is assumed that the number of relay groups (hops) in a route is fixed. Therefore, the main concern in route maintenance is how to choose the next node in the groups to form the route with minimal energy consumption rate. Owing to mobility of mobile nodes, the energy consumption rate of a route may change with time. Thus the original route may not be the best, it should be replaced by a new route. This is called *handoff operation*. Therefore, the first problem in route maintenance is when and under which condition to perform handoff operation. The second problem is how each node determines when to go to doze state and its period for checking with ATIM in the beacons to determine whether it should stay in doze or switch to awake state.

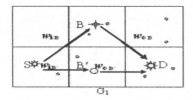

Fig. 1. Handoff operation

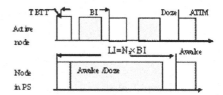

Fig. 2. Power Management in a Group

4   Distance-Based Route Maintenance (DBRM)

In this section, we introduce *DBRM* scheme which objective is to minimize the energy consumption rate in route maintenance. We will define a data model for the mobile hosts in a relay group, then discuss how to resolve the above two questions.

4.1   Mobile Host Modeling

The mobile hosts in a group are divided into two groups. One of the nodes, which is a part of the route, is called *active node* since it remains active for receiving data from the active node of its previous relay group and for transmitting data to the active node of the next relay group. The other nodes in the group are called *non-active nodes* since they stay in doze state. They periodically wake up to check with the beacons broadcasting from the active node. The active node in the relay group G_{i-1} is called the *up-hop node* of the active node in group G_i while the active node in the relay group G_{i+1}

is called the *down-hop node*. We define four attributes to model a node i in a relay group: $\{w_{ii}, w_{oi}, w_{di}, w_{ei}\}$.

- ☐ w_{ii} denotes the path loss between the up-hop node and node i;
- ☐ w_{oi} denotes the path loss between node i and the down-hop node;
- ☐ w_{di} is the distance attribute between the active node of its group and node i;
- ☐ w_{ei} is the remaining energy level of node i.

w_{ii} and w_{oi}, are for choosing the next node to form the route, i.e., handoff operation. The total path losses of two pairs of nodes (the up-hop node and node i, and node i and the down- hop node) is $w_{fdi} = w_{ii} + w_{oi}$. The objective in route maintenance is then to choose the node in a group with minimal energy consumption rate to be the relay nodes, i.e., $N_{Relay} = Min[w_{fdl} . w_{fdi}]$.

w_{di} and w_{ei} are for deciding the period that a non-active node may state in doze state before it wakes up to check with the beacons. w_{di} is defined as d_i/R_{max} where R_{max} is the maximum transmission range and d_i is the distance between the active node of its group and node i. w_{ei} is defined as E_r/E_m where E_m is the maximum amount of energy available at a node and E_r is the remaining energy at the node. We will explain in section 4.3 that how the doze time (T_s) is decided.

4.2   Handoff Operation and Energy Saving

The determination of when to perform handoff operation for a route is based on the energy consumption rate of the route. In this section, we will first explain how the handoff operation is performed. Then, we will show how to calculate the energy cost and the amount of energy conserved for the handoff operations.

The active node, which is a part of the route, broadcasts beacons to the members of its group and listens to the beacons from the up-hop and down-hop relay nodes periodically. When a non-active node wakes up, it listens to the beacons from the active node of its group. Based on the radio strength for broadcasting the beacons to the non-active nodes in its group, the active node can estimate the location of the just wake-up non-active nodes. At the same time, the active node can estimate the locations of the up-hop node and down-hop node from the strength of power required for receiving the beacons from the up-hop and down-hop nodes. According to the location information, the energy consumptions for transmitting a message through the non-active nodes and through the active node in a group can be estimated [7]. If the first one is significantly lower than the second one, the active node informs the non-active node in the ATIM of its beacons to remain in awake (active) state after wake-up and to become the next active node of the group. The currently active node then switches its radio off and goes into *doze* state. This is called *active node handoff*.

In communication between the nodes in a hop, the energy consumption rate P_T of the transmitter depends on the sensitivity ☐ of the receiver and the path loss L_{fd}. The path loss in free space L_{fd} [8]is a function of wavelength ☐ and distance d between the transmitter and receiver, such as:

$$L_{fd} = \frac{P_T}{P_R} = \left(\frac{4 \square d}{\square}\right)^2 \square \frac{1}{G_T \square G_R} \qquad (1)$$

where P_T and P_R are the powers of transmitter and the receiver in watt respectively . G_T and G_R are the gains of the transmitter and the receiver antennas respectively.

As it is assumed that the mobile hosts can adjust their transmission power P_T to satisfy the sensitivity $\Box$ of receiver according to the path loss. It can be seen that w_{ii} is L_{fd} between the up-hop node and node i. For example, in Fig. 1, B is the original active node and $B\Box$ is a node in doze state. For the mobility of nodes, it may be: w_{iB} + $w_{oB} > w_{iB\Box}$+ $w_{oB\Box}$ Define that $Diff_{B\Box B} = (w_{iB\Box}$+ $w_{oB\Box})$-$(w_{iB}$ +$w_{oB})$, if $Diff_{B\Box B} < \Box T_h$, B' will be assigned to take up the route and B will switch to doze state. T_h is the threshold for the handoff operation.

Assuming that the energy cost for performing a handoff operation is E_h. Then the amount of energy saved from the handoff operation is: E_{si} + E_h. If the number of handoff operations during the period T is N_h, the total amount of energy saved is:

$$ES = \Box(E_{si} + E_h), \; i = 1, ..N_h, \tag{2}$$

4.3 Doze Period Decision

In the IEEE 802.11 standard, non-active node may wake up frequently if BI is small. This is undesirable in conserving energy at a mobile node. We define the *active rate* to express the degree in energy saving. Active rate is the ratio of the period of time a node stay in awake state to the length of the period of time. To conserve more energy, it is important to achieve a smaller active rate by prolonging the *doze* period of a node such as in Fig. 2.

In DBRM, we aim to minimize the active rate of the nodes. Because the active node generates beacons periodically to the non-active nodes in the group. However, if the active node is not sending beacons, it may be in doze state for a moment in every BI in order to conserve energy. For example, as shown in Fig. 2, the active node can be in doze state during the leisure time $(BI \Box ATIM\_Win)$, such as $F \cdot (BI \Box ATIM\_Win)$, and $F\Box[0,1]$. Then, the active rate Ar_a of an active node is:

$$Ar_a = \big(BI \Box F \Box(BI \Box ATIM\_Win)\big)/BI . \tag{3}$$

To conserve more energy, in DBRM, the *doze* periods of the non-active nodes may not be fixed and are not all the same. Two factors are considered in determining the length of the *doze* period for a non-active node i. The first one is the distance attribute w_{di} of node i. If node i is far away from the active node (small value of w_{di}), its doze period T_{si} (T_{si} equals to LI_i minus $ATIM\_Win$ approximately) may be small. The listen interval of node i (LI_i) is set as $LI_i = k_i \Box BI$, $k_i = Min[(R_{max} \Box d_i)/(v_i \Box BI), k_{max}]$ = $Min[R_{max}/(v_i \Box BI)\Box(1 \Box w_{di}), k_{max}]$, where v_i is the velocity of the node i, d_i is the distance between node i and the active node, k_{max} is a preset parameter. The equation can make the node with a small w_{di} to have a large LI. $R_{max}/(v_i \Box BI)$ gives the maximum time that the node may move out of the transmission range of a node.

The second factor for determining the doze period of a node is the remaining energy level w_{ei} of the node. If w_{ei} is small, the node may have a low opportunity to become the active node. Because w_{ei} is same as w_{di}, if they are small, LI_i will be large. Thus w_{ei} can be combined with w_{di}, and the average weighted value of them is (w_{di} + w_{ei})/2. Thus, the listen interval and active rate of node i are:

$$LI_i = Min[\frac{R_{max}}{v_i \Box BI}(1 \Box \frac{w_{di} + w_{ei}}{2}), k_{max}] \cdot BI, \quad Ar_i = ATIM\_Win/LI_i. \quad (4)$$

The average active rate and the mean value of the active rates of the nodes in a group can be calculated by combining equations (3) and (4). Assuming that the number of nodes in a relay group is N_G. The average active rate of the nodes in a group (Avg_ar) is:

$$\text{Avg\_ar} = \frac{1}{N_G} \Box (Ar_a + \sum_{i=1}^{N_G \Box 1} Ar_i) = \frac{1}{N_G}(Ar_a + \sum_{i=1}^{N_G \Box 1} \frac{ATIM\_Win}{LI_i}). \quad (5)$$

5   Simulation Studies

In order to investigate the benefits of using DBRM, we have implemented a simulation program and performed simulation experiments to study the amount of energy saved using DBRM in route maintenance. In our simulation model, it is assumed that there are N mobile hosts moving in a service area of 1000m×1000m. The area is divided into grids and the size of a grid is 100m×100m. The maximum transmission range R_{max} of a mobile host is 224m. A conventional moving model, the random walk model, is adopted to model the mobility of the mobile hosts. The speed of a mobile host is uniformly distributed between $V_{min} = V_{max}/2$ and V_{max}. Its movement direction is distributed uniformly in [0, 2□]. At first the mobile hosts are uniformly distributed in the service area. To simplify the model, it is assumed that the mobile hosts cannot move out the service area.

In the simulation experiments, we compare DBRM with the power management scheme in the *IEEE 802.11 standard with fixed listen interval* (802.11-LI) and *GAF with random listen interval* (GAF-LI). We have performed two sets of experiments. The first set of experiments investigates the amount of energy saved in using DBRM when different values of handoff thresholds are used. In the second set of experiments, we compare the average active rate (Avg_ar) of DBRM with that in 802.11-LI and GAF-LI. In 802.11-LI, the active node, which broadcast beacons, is always active, and the nodes in PS mode listen to the beacons every beacon interval. In GAF-LI, the nodes in a relay group play the role as the active node in turn. When a node is active, other nodes are in doze state for a random period of time.

In this paper, the amount of energy saved is expressed as a negative value. When the absolute value is larger, the amount of energy saved is higher. Fig. 3 shows the amount of energy saved in DBRM when $V_{max} = 3$, 6 and 9m/s respectively. Different handoff thresholds are tested. When the velocity of the mobile hosts is higher, the amount of energy saved is larger. It is because when the mobile hosts move with a higher velocity, the active node will have a higher probability to move away from its current position and consequently the energy consumption rate of the route becomes higher. Therefore, performing a handoff operation may be beneficial in conserving energy. As shown in Fig. 3, the biggest saving in energy is achieved when a medium handoff threshold value is used. It is because if the threshold value is small, handoff operations are frequent and the total cost for handoff operation will be heavy. On the other hand, if the handoff threshold value is large, the number of handoff operations is small and the total amount of energy saved from the handoff operations will be low. Fig. 4 shows the results when handoff cost E_h is varied. Consistent with our intuition, when the handoff cost is smaller, the amount of energy saved is higher.

Fig. 5 shows the average active rate (Avg_ar) of the three schemes when the values of *ATIM_Win/BI* are changed. It can be seen that Avg_ar decreases with the value of *ATIM_Win/BI*. It is because if the value of *ATIM_Win/BI* is smaller, the period of time a node in active mode is shorter. Avg_ar of DBRM is smaller than that of 802.11-LI and GAF-LI. At the same time, if *ATIM_Win/BI* is large, GAF-LI is significantly better than 802.11-LI. However, if *ATIM_Win/BI* is very small, their Avg_ar are similar. It is because both of them require at least one node in active mode in the relay group at each time. Fig. 6 shows the results when the number of nodes is varied. It can be seen that if the number of nodes is larger, Avg_ar is smaller. The reason is when the number of nodes in the network increases, the node number in a relay group increases too. Thus there are more nodes can be in doze state for a longer duration. The consequence is a smaller Avg_ar. Consistent with the results in Fig. 5, even if the number of nodes is the same, Avg_ar of DBRM is still smaller than that of *802.11-LI* and *GAF-LI* if they have same value of *ATIM_Win/BI*.

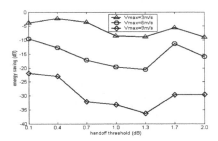

Fig. 3. Energy saved Vs. handoff threshold

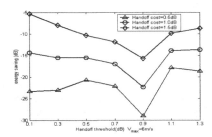

Fig. 4. Energy saved Vs. handoff threshold

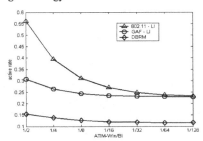

Fig. 5. Active rate Vs. ATIM_Win/BI

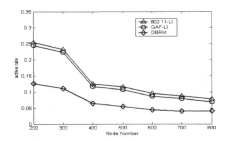

Fig. 6. Active rate Vs. number of nodes

6 Conclusions

Although routing is an important topic in mobile ad hoc networking systems, one of the important issues, which have been greatly ignored in the previous research works, is the energy issue in route maintenance. Route maintenance is an important issue for data monitoring in ad hoc networking systems. In this paper, we propose DBRM scheme for route maintenance. Handoff operations are designed for switching the nodes in route maintenance to minimize the energy consumption rate. In addition, in DBRM, only one node needs to be active in each relay group. Mobile hosts in a group may switch between different states of operations to conserve energy and at the same time to minimize the impact on handoff operations in route maintenance. In the simulation experiments, we have shown that the amount of energy conserved from using DBRM is significantly larger than both 802.11-LI and GAF-LI.

References

[1] David B. Johnson and David A. Maltz, "D ynamic Source Routing in Ad Hoc Wireless Networks (DSR)", in *Mobile Computing,* 1996.
[2] Xu Ya, Heidemann, J. and Estrin, D, "Geography-informed Energy Conservation for Ad Hoc Routing (GAF)", in *Proceedings of 2001 ACM Mobile Computing and Networking.*
[3] Laura Marie Feeney, "An Energy Consumption Model for Performance Analysis of Routing Protocols for Mobile Ad Hoc Networks", *Mobile Networks and Application,* vol. 6, 2001, pp. 239-249.
[4] Woo-Jin Choi, Sirin Tkinay, "An Efficient Table Driven Routing Algorithm for Wireless Ad hoc Networks", *VTC 2001*, pp. 2604-2608.
[5] Chavalit S. and C. C. Shen, "Coordinated Power Conservation for Ad hoc Networks", in *International Conference in Computer Communication,* 2002,pp. 3330-34.
[6] IEEE 802.11 standard, "Wireless LAN Medium Access Control (MAC) and Physical Layer (PHY) Specifications", *IEEE Press,* May 1997.
[7] Kyu_Tae Jin and D. Ho Cho, "Optimal Threshold Energy Level of Energy Efficient MAC for Energy-limited Ad-hoc Networks", in *2001 IEEE Global Telecommunications Conference*, pp. .2932-2936.
[8] Wei Ye, John Heidemann, DeBorah Estrin, "An Energy-Efficient MAC Protocol for Wireless Sensor Networks", in *IEEE InfoCom 2002,* pp. 1567-1576.

Resource Reservation and Enforcement for Framebuffer-Based Devices

Chung-You Wei[1], Jen-Wei Hsieh[1], Tei-Wei Kuo[1], I-Hsiang Lee[1],
Yian-Nien Wu[1], and Mei-Chin Tsai[2]

[1] Depatment of Computer Science and Information Engineering, National Taiwan
University, Taipei, Taitan 106, ROC
{r90023,d90002,ktw,b7506025,b7506027}@csie.ntu.edu.tw
[2] Microsoft, Bellevue, WA 98006, USA
a-meicht@microsoft.com

Abstract. A framebuffer device provides an abstraction for the graphics hardware. The way an application accesses a framebuffer device is to map the framebuffer to the user space for direct access. To guarantee real-time access to a framebuffer, the system should provide reservations; both a budget for the framebuffer usage as well as a budget for running on the CPU. In this paper, we propose an approach to reserve the usages of framebuffer devices through the inclusion of codes in application libraries. Without any modification of the original source code of framebuffer devices, we create a new "virtual" device which maintains internal data structures for framebuffer resource management. With the reservation mechanisms for both framebuffer devices and CPU, we can provide a much smoother display service under heavy system workloads ...

1 Introduction

The objective of an operating system is to provide a convenient and efficient environment for users. Commercial operating systems are now equipped with multimedia functionality and equipment, such as high-resolution monitors and 5.1-channel speakers. Although most commercial operating systems claim to provide real-time support, their support is mainly based on CPU scheduling and interrupt latency management. However, a multimedia presentation needs many kinds of resources allocated by the operating systems in the right amount and in an on-time fashion. For example, playing of video streams involves computation time for decoding, disk/CD-ROM access for stream retrieval, handling of audio and displaying devices, etc. With successful on-time resource allocations and coordination, it is possible to display the stream in a frame rate expected by the viewers.

The presentation of a multimedia session can require a substantial amount of system resources in many ways. Proper hardware support, e.g., DSP-based decoder chips or powerful display cards, is always a big help in meeting the response time or performance requirements of applications. A major technical issue is how to guarantee the allocation of the right resources, from hardware or

J. Chen and S. Hong (Eds.): RTCSA 2003, LNCS 2968, pp. 398–408, 2004.

even software aspects, to an application in an on-time fashion. The consideration of hardware and software resources together is now an even more important
issue because the advance of microprocessor technology has enabled the offload-
ing of many time-consuming services from CPU to hardware chips, such as those
for controllers and adaptor cards. The concept of special files in UNIX-like systems provides a good motivation for a uniform interface to the reservation of
hardware devices on UNIX-like systems. For example, I/O devices such as disks
and tape drives are special files, which could be manipulated by file and ioctl
operations. The goal of this paper is to explore a reservation methodology and
implementation methods for the reservation of I/O devices, especially that for
screen display.

Researchers in the area of real-time operating systems started exploring resource reservation and Quality-of-Service techniques over operating systems in
the last decade. Researchers proposed their work over various operating systems, such as Windows [7,8,9,10,11], Mach [13,14,15,16,17], Unix [1], Linux [2,3,
4,5,19,20] or other operating systems [12]. Sides [18] considered a real-time data
acquisition and display system in response to the requirements of the system-
wide adaptability to changes in the data stream. Mercer, et al. [13,14,15,16,17]
proposed the concept of time reservation and implemented the concept in the
Real-Time Mach at the Carnage Mellon University. The goal of this research
was to transform the Real-Time Mach into a multimedia operating system to
support various multimedia applications. They considered a microkernel-based
mechanism to let users reserve CPU cycles for threads. Kuo, et al. [8] proposed
to provide Windows NT soft QoS guarantee through the design of a Windows
NT middleware, called the Computing Power Regulator (CPR). Adelberg, et al
[1] presented a real-time emulation program to build soft real-time scheduling
on the top of UNIX. Childs and Ingram [5] chose to modify the Linux source
code by adding a new scheduling class called SCHED_QOS to let applications
to specify the amount of CPU time per period. QoS scheduling is supported for
CPU and IDE disks. Lin, et al. [19,20] directly modified the scheduling mechanism of Linux. The goal was to provide a "general-purpose" real-time scheduling
framework which can handle time-driven, priority-driven, share-driven, and even
new scheduling schedulers. RTAI proposed by Mantegazza at DIAPM and RT-
Linux proposed by Yodaiken, et al. at New Mexico Institute of Technology [2]
represent two of the most successful real-time Linux solutions so far, where RTAI
and RT-Linux share a very similar system architecture. Their objectives were to
guarantee the resource requirements of hard real-time applications and to favor
the executions of soft real-time processes simultaneously.

The purpose of this paper is to propose a reservation methodology and implementation methods for the resource reservation of framebuffers, which refer to
devices for screen display (and sometimes to the RAM buffer on display cards).
We propose not to modify the operating system or even any library functions
in libc/glibc for the portability of the implementation. We adopt a preload-
library approach, which loads specified library functions before any application
program executes so that the original library functions can be overridden. We

propose a Quality-of-Service reservation and enforcement mechanism to guarantee proper framebuffer usage for applications. The feasibility of the approach is demonstrated by the implementation of a system prototype over Linux.

The rest of this paper is organized as follows: Section 2 provides an overview of the entire problem. Section 3 describes the system architecture and our mechanism. Section 4 is the conclusion.

2   Problem Overview

There has been a lot of research done in resource reservation in real-time systems. Although much work has been done in the reservation of computation power, researchers have come to realize the need for multiple resources reservations. Consider a system which is playing a movie. We must consider resources for the processing unit and the display sub-system. The guarantee of the computation service for a real-time task may not fully ensure that the task will work as we expect. A display sub-system is an I/O device, similar to network or hard disks. If the I/O speed is far less than that of CPU, the CPU might be idle waiting for the completion of I/O requests for synchronous I/O. That may cause the utilization of the entire system to drop. When we consider a system which must have smooth display of video/data on the screen, we must not only consider the management of the computation time but also the resource usage of display devices.

Table 1. Performance of framebuffer-copying tasks and memory-copying tasks. *mem denotes the time for data copying to memory. ***fb denotes the time for data copying to framebuffer.

Machine	CPU	RAM	Video RAM	VGA card	*mem	**fb
Notebook (Sony PCG-SR7K)	Pentium3 600 MHz	128 MB	8 MB	NeoMagic MagicMedia256XL+	11.61s	18.35s
Desktop (Intel 440BX-82443BX/ZX host bridge)	Cerelon 400 MHz	32 MB	8 MB	Trident Microsystems Cyber 9525	16.29s	25.93s
Desktop (Intel 440BX-82443BX/ZX host bridge)	Pentium2 300 MHz	256 MB	8 MB	Nvidia/SGS Thomson Rival128	20.16s	33.01s

To motivate the research, two simple experiments were done: In the first experiment, we compared the efficiency levels between the task that copies data from memory to memory and the task that copies data from memory to a framebuffer device. In order to eliminate the interference of caching, each task was run 30000000 times copying 4 bytes at a time. During each run, the address of destination was chosen randomly in a 1024 * 768 integer array. The latter task is what is done for usual screen display. The experiment's result is shown in Table 1. The second experiment was to measure the impact of framebuffer-copying on the entire system. First, we ran two identical tasks that copy a huge amount of data from memory to memory. Then, we replaced one job of the two tasks with the copying of the same-size data from memory to the framebuffer. The evaluation process was run 15000000 times while another process was run 30000000 times to ensure the interference during the whole life time of the evaluation process. Besides, in order to eliminate the effect of caching, during each run, we chose the address of destination randomly for data copying in a 1024*768 integer array, where each copy was of 4 bytes. The result is shown in Table 2. Note that although the evaluation processes (data-copy from memory to memory) were the same, it took much time to complete while another framebuffer-copying task was running. That was because the data-copying to framebuffer had side effects for other processes on the system. It would deteriorate the performance of the whole system.

Table 2. Effect of a framebuffer-copying task on the entire system. *mem-to-mem denotes the time for data copying from memory to memory while another identical process running. ***mem-to-fb denotes the time for data copying from memory to memory while another process copies data from memory to framebuffer.

Machine	CPU	RAM	Video RAM	VGA card	*mem-to mem	**mem-to-fb
Notebook (Toshiba 3480)	Pentium3 600 MHz	128 MB	8 MB	S3 Savage IX	5.97s	6.20s
Notebook (Sony PCG-SR7K)	Pentium3 600 MHz	128 MB	8 MB	NeoMagic MagicMedia256XL+	5.6s	5.54s
Desktop (Intel 440BX-82443BX/ZX host bridge)	Pentium2 300 MHz	256 MB	8 MB	Nvidia/SGS Thomson Rival128	9.72s	9.94s

Two conclusion can be drawn: (1) Copying between memory and framebuffer/memory is very time consuming, especially for multimedia applications which display a large amount of data such as videos. (2) Data copying between memory and framebuffer is, in general, slightly slower than data copying between memory and memory for older or less powerful machines. By considering a general hardware architecture of a PC as shown in Figure 1, it is interesting to have an observation that the host bus is going to be a major hot spot in resource competition. All access to I/O devices must go through the north bridge (which is the next primary hot spot). This observation underlies the research motivation of this work.

The goal of this work is to manage the usages of displaying devices for applications. A process can reserve a budget for the usage of a displaying device for each specified amount of time. If the requests from an application is over the claimed budget reservation, the system can either skip the extra requests (saving host bus usage) or merely execute the requests on a backup memory for later retrieval for a batch display on the device (reducing competition on the north bridge).

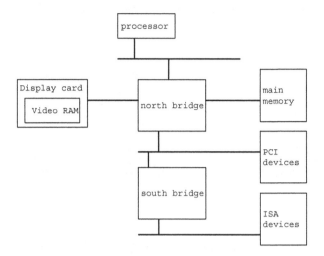

Fig. 1. The hardware architecture of various buses

3   Admission and Usage Control on Framebuffer Devices

3.1   System Architecture

Writing of data to a framebuffer device under Linux is like writing of data to a general I/O device. The speed of the I/O is dependent on several factors, such as the hardware architecture of the machine. Figure 2 illustrates a popular system diagram of the Intel 440BX AGPset system hardware architecture. The performance of the host bus is determined by the processor and the main memory. Usually the host bus is the fastest bus in the system. The AGP (Advanced Graphic Port) bus was introduced by Intel in 1997. It was designed for the heavy demands of 3-D graphics. The AGP bus, as shown in Figure 2, is connected to the host bus by the north bridge, and it could have the same performance as the host bus. Display cards are usually designed over AGP slots, instead of PCI slots or even ISA slots. Modern PCs are often used for entertainment, that require a lot of power in displaying 3-D graphics. That is why machines that are designed and delivered recently have less performance difference between memory-to-memory copy and memory-to-framebuffer copy. We must point out that although the research work in this paper targets framebuffer devices, the idea itself is very general. It can be applied to other memory-mapped I/O devices on slower buses.

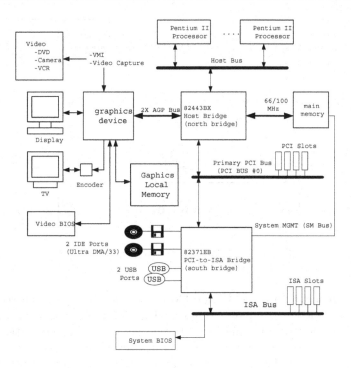

Fig. 2. Intel AGPset System Block Diagram

3.2   Reservation Algorithm and Mechanism

The Basic Mechanism. A framebuffer device in Linux is usually accessed by memory-mapped I/O. When a process wants to write data to the video RAM to show something on the screen, what it does is to first obtain the "memory address" of the video RAM and then just treat the video RAM as regular main memory. As a result, a graphic application uses the library function memcpy() to write graphic data to framebuffer devices. The common steps are as follows: (1) Open the framebuffer device by the system call "open" (2) Obtain the address of the video RAM and map the address to its user-program space by the "mmap" system call (3) Treat the mapped address of the video RAM as regular main memory. Write graphic data to the video RAM using the library function memcpy().

In this paper, we introduce a simple approach to insert an intermediate layer for resource management of framebuffer devices, as shown in Figure 3. We propose to modify the system in the following way: (1) We first create a new device which acts mostly like a framebuffer device with resource reservation and usage control functionality. (2) We modify the library function memcpy() to insert some usage control mechanism for the new device that we created in Step 1. The following section illustrates the algorithm for usage control.

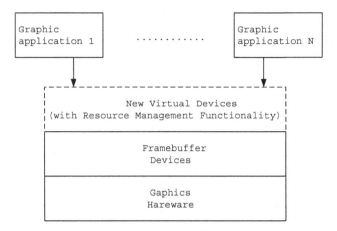

Fig. 3. Intel AGPset System Block Diagram

Resource reservation and Usage Control. The purpose of this section is to propose an algorithm for resource reservation and usage control of framebuffer devices. Suppose that an application A_i requests a resource reservation to write B_i bytes of data to a specified framebuffer devices within each W_i units of time. For most graphic applications, the data rate transferred to framebuffer devices is usually bounded. Thus, B_i and W_i can be determined reasonably by some evaluations in advance. After the resource reservation is granted, the mechanism proposed in the previous section should guarantee and ensure that A_i can write no more than B_i bytes of data to the specified framebuffer device within each W_i units of time. As shown in Figure 4, suppose that a request from A_i is made by memcpy() to write H byes of data to the framebuffer device at time t. If the total number of bytes being read and to be written to the framebuffer be $H + Y + Z$ within the W_i time frame is no more than B_i, then the request is granted, and the write is executed immediately. Otherwise, the request is denied.

When a request is denied, two alternatives could be considered, as pointed out in Section 2: (1) Throw away the request (saving bandwidth on the host bus), and pretend that the memcpy() invocation is done. (2) Copy the data of request to a backup memory for later retrieval for a batch display on the device (reducing competition on the north bridge with other process executions).

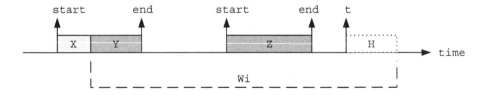

Fig. 4. Illustration of writing requests to a framebuffer device

Given a collection of admitted reservations $T = \{(B_1, W_1), (B_2, W_2), ..., (B_3, W_3)\}$ on a framebuffer device, suppose that a new reservation (B_0, W_0) is made on the device where (B_i, W_i) means that B_i bytes might need to be transferred within each W_i units of time. As long as the following formula is satisfied, the new reservation is granted; otherwise, it is rejected:

$$\sum \frac{C(B_i)}{W_i} \leq 1 . \tag{1}$$

Here $C(B_i)$ is the time needed to write B_i bytes to a framebuffer device. Note that we assume that enough CPU time is reserved for each application considered in this case because the focus of this research is on the reservation and usage control of framebuffer devices. The copying of data to framebuffer devices takes CPU time, and the copying time should be considered in the reservation of CPU time. We refer interested readers to work in CPU time reservation. As noticed by the readers, the formula above simply checks up whether the framebuffer devices is overloaded. The formula is obvious because each invocation of memcpy() is done synchronously, and we assume that no context switch happens. However, we must point out when memcpy() can be done asynchronously (as can be for writes to disks), the formula above must be revised to fit the scheduling algorithm that reorders requests of memcpy(). For example, if the rate monotonic algorithm is adopted, then the formula becomes as follows:

$$\sum \frac{C(B_i)}{W_i} \leq n(2^{\frac{1}{n}} - 1) . \tag{2}$$

When asynchronous writes to framebuffer devices are supported, the admission control for the reservations of CPU time will become slightly more complicated. A naive solution is to reserve a budget of system CPU time for memcpy() writes for the devices. It is similar to what is done for the reservations of CPU time for applications and the system in the open system architecture proposed by Liu, et al [6,10].

3.3 System Implementation

In system implementation, a "virtual" device could be created for resource reservation and usage control of each framebuffer device. Here, we use the word "virtual" to indicate that there does not really have a corresponding physical device. Instead, this virtual device needs to cooperate with an existing framebuffer device to achieve the task of drawing as shown in Figure 3. Instead of opening a framebuffer device, application programs must open its corresponding virtual device. Original requests to a framebuffer device are passed over to its corresponding virtual device. The granting and rejections of requests to a framebuffer device could be decided based on the algorithm presented in the previous section. An important issue here is to have compatibility with existing code when no resource reservation and usage control is needed. With renaming of devices, there should be absolutely no need to modify existing code. It is also highly important to minimize the efforts in code modifications for user and even system programs when resource reservation and usage control is needed. (Any modification to any hardware is simply out of the question.)

In this paper, we focus on framebuffer devices which use the library function memcpy() to write graphic data to the devices. Instead of modifying the operating systems, hardware, or even any library functions in libc/glibc (such as memcpy()), we propose to adopt the idea of *preload library*, which loads specified library functions before any application program (which needs resource reservation) executes so that the original library functions can be overridden. The procedure is simply done by setting the environment variable *PRELOAD_PATH* to the path where the overriding library functions exist. To replace the original memcpy(), an overriding library function memcpy() is implemented and saved at the specified path. The overriding function implements the resource reservation and usage control algorithm presented in the previous section and then calls the original memcpy() to make necessary data copying when any write request to a framebuffer device is granted. We refer the interested reader to [21,22] for the usage of preload library.

4   Conclusion

This paper explores a reservation methodology and implementation methods for the resource reservation of framebuffers. We propose a Quality-of-Service reservation and enforcement mechanism to guarantee proper framebuffer usage for applications. Based on the usages and reservations of framebuffer devices, our mechanism will determine when to drop the requests for displaying data. To keep the portability and compatibility of the original system, we create a new "virtual" device to maintain internal data structures for framebuffer resource management. We also adopt a preload-library approach, which loads specified library functions before any application program executes, to override the original library functions.

With the advance of software and hardware technologies, there is an increasing demand to study real-time resource reservation and Quality-of-Service support for various devices under heavy system workloads. For future research, we shall extend our methodology to input devices, such as TouchPad. We will also integrate various resource-reservation methodologies to have a general-purpose approach for real-time resource reservation systems.

References

1. B. Adelberg, H.Garcia-Molina, and B.Kao, "Emulating Soft Real-Time Scheduling Using Traditional Operating Systems Schedulers," IEEE 15th Real-Time Systems Symposium, December 1994, pp.292-298 .
2. M. Barabanov and V. Yodaiken, "Introducing Real-Time Unix," Linux Journal, No. 34, Feb 1997.

3. Li-Pin Chang, Tei-Wei Kuo, and Shi-Wu Lo, "A Dynamic-Voltage-Adjustment Mechanism in Reducing the Power Consumption of Flash Memory for Portable Devices," IEEE International Conference on Consumer Electronics, Los Angeles, USA, June 2001.

4. Hsu-Min Chen, Sheng-Yao Zhuo, Chih-Yuan Huang, Tei-Wei Kuo, "An USB-Based Surveillance System over Wireless Network, the 7th International Conference on Distributed Multimedia Systems, Taiwan, Sept 2001.

5. S. Childs and D. Ingram, "The Linux-SRT Integrated Multimedia Operating Systems: Bring QoS to the Desktop," IEEE 2001 Real-Time Technology and Applications Symposium, Taipei, Taiwan, ROC, pp. 135-140.

6. Z. Deng and J. W.-S. Liu, "Scheduling Real-Time Applications in an Open Environment," *IEEE 18th Real-Time Systems Symposium*, December 1997.

7. Mei-Ling Hsu, Wang-Ru Yang, Yuan-Ting Kao, Giun-Haur Huang, and Tei-Wei Kuo, 1997, "Providing Real-Time Access Control to Remote Resources," The Third Workshop on Real-Time and Media Systems (RAMS'97), Taipei, Taiwan, ROC, pp. 137-143

8. Giun-Haur Huang, Shie-Kai Ni, and Tei-Wei Kuo, 1996, "The Design and Implementation of the CPU Power Regulator for Multimedia Operating Systems," IEEE 17th Real-Time Systems Symposium (RTSS'96), Work-In-Progress Session Proceeding, Washington D.C., USA, pp. 27-30.

9. Tei-Wei Kuo, Sing-Ling Lee, Yi-Shan Lin, and Yu-Hua Liu, 1997, "Providing Video-On-Demand Services on Windows NT," 1997 International Symposium on Multimedia Information Processing (ISMIP'97), Taipei, Taiwan, ROC, pp. 226-231.

10. Tei-Wei Kuo and Ching-Hui Li, 1999,"A Fixed-Priority-Driven Open Environment for Real-Time Applications," the IEEE 20th Real-Time Systems Symposium, Phoenix, USA, December, 1999.

11. Tei-Wei Kuo and Mei-Ling Hsu, "A Software-Reuse Approach to Build Monitor Porgrams for Soft Real-Time Applications," Journal of Real-Time Systems (SCI), Vol 19, Number 2, September 2000, pp.123-148.

12. Tei-Wei Kuo, Ji-Shin Rao, Victor Lee, Jun Wu, 2001, "Real-Time Disk Scheduling for Block-Stripping I2O RAID," the 13th Euromicro Conference on Real-Time Systems, Delft, Netherlands, June 2001.

13. Clifford W. Mercer, S. Savage, and H. Tokuda, "Processor Capacity Reserves for Multimedia Operating Systems," Technical Report CMU-CS-93-157, School of Computer Science, Carneigie Mellon University, May 1993.

14. Clifford W. Mercer, S. Savage, and H. Tokuda, "Processor Capacity Reserves: An Abstraction of Managing Processor Usage," In Proceedings of the Fourth Workshop on Workstation Operating Systems (WWOS-IV), October 1993.

15. Clifford W. Mercer, S. Savage, and H. Tokuda, "Processor Capacity Reserves for Multimedia Applications," In Proceedings of the IEEE International Conference on Multimedia Computing and Systems (ICMCS), May 1994, pp. 90-99.

16. Clifford W. Mercer, Ragunathan Rajkumar and Jim Zelenka, "Temporal Protection in Real-Time Operating Systems," In Proceedings of the 11th IEEE WorkShop on Real-Time Operating Systems and Software, May 1994, pp. 79-83.

17. Clifford W. Mercer and Ragunathan Rajkumar, "An Interactive Interface and RT-Mach Support for Monitoring and Controlling Resource Management," IEEE Real-Time Technology and Applications Symposium, May 1995.

18. D.J. Sides, "A Dynamically Adaptive Real-Time Data Acquisition and Display System," IEEE Real-Time Technology and Applications Symposium, May 1995.

19. Y.C. Wang and K.J. Lin, "Enhancing the Real-Time Capability of the Linux Kernel," the 5th Real-Time Computing Systems and Applications Symposium, Hiroshima, Japan, 1998.
20. Y.-C. Wang and K.J. Lin, "Implementing a General Purpose Real-Time Scheduling Framework in the RED-Linux Real-Time Kernel," IEEE Real-Time Systems Symposium, Arizona, USA, 1999, pp. 246-255.
21. "Overriding Functions",
    http://sources.redhat.com/ml/libc-hacker/1998-12/msg00053.html
22. "overloading symbols in glibc-2.2.3" ,
    http://sources.redhat.com/ml/glibc-linux/2001-q3/msg00014.html

An Efficient B-Tree Layer for Flash-Memory Storage Systems

Chin-Hsien Wu, Li-Pin Chang, and Tei-Wei Kuo

Department of Computer Science and Information Engineering
National Taiwan University
Taipei, Taiwan, 106
Fax: +886-2-23628167
{d90003,d6526009,ktw}@csie.ntu.edu.tw

Abstract. With a significant growth of the markets for consumer electronics and various embedded systems, flash memory is now an economic solution for storage systems design. For index structures which require intensively fine-grained updates/modifications, block-oriented access over flash memory could introduce a significant number of redundant writes. It might not only severely degrade the overall performance but also damage the reliability of flash memory. In this paper, we propose a very different approach which could efficiently handle fine-grained updates/modifications caused by B-Tree index access over flash memory. The implementation is done directly over the flash translation layer (FTL) such that no modifications to existing application systems are needed. We demonstrate that the proposed methodology could significantly improve the system performance and, at the same time, reduce the overheads of flash-memory management and the energy dissipation, when index structures are adopted over flash memory.

Keywords: Flash Memory, B-Tree, Storage Systems, Embedded Systems, Database Systems.

1 Introduction

Flash memory is a popular alternative for the design of storage systems because of its shock-resistant, power-economic, and non-volatile nature. In recent years, flash-memory technology advances with the wave of consumer electronics and embedded systems. There are significant technology breakthroughs in both of its capacity and reliability features. The ratio of cost to capacity has being increased dramatically. Flash-memory storage devices of 1GB will soon be in the market. Flash memory could be considered as an alternative to replace hard disks in many applications. The implementation of index structures, which are very popular in the organization of data over disks, must be now considered over flash memory. However, with the very distinct characteristics of flash memory, traditional designs of index structures could result in a severe performance degradation to a flash-memory storage system and significantly reduce the reliability of flash memory.

J. Chen and S. Hong (Eds.): RTCSA 2003, LNCS 2968, pp. 409–430, 2004.

There are two major approaches in the implementations of flash-memory storage systems: The native file-system approach and the block-device emulation approach. For the native file-system approach, JFFS/JFFS2[5], LFM[12], and YAFFS [2] were proposed to directly manage raw flash memory. The file-systems under this approach are very similar to the log-structured file-systems (LFS) [17]. This approach is natural for the manipulation of flash memory because the characteristics of flash memory do not allow in-place updates (overwriting). One major advantage of the native file-system approach is robustness because all updates are appended, instead of overwriting existing data (similar to LFS). The block-device emulation approach is proposed for a quick deployment of flash-memory technology. Any well-supported and widely used (disk) file-systems could be built over a flash memory emulated block-device easily. For example, FTL/FTL-Lite [9], [10], [11], CompactFlash [4], and SmartMedia [22] are popular block device emulation, which provide a transparent block-device emulation. Regardless of which approach is adopted, they share the similar technical issues: How to properly manage garbage collection and wear-leveling activities.

With the increasing popularity of flash memory for storage systems (and the rapid growing of the capacity), the implementations of index structures could become a bottleneck on the performance of flash-memory storage systems. As astute readers could point out that why not using binary search tree as index structures. Binary search tree is applicable to be adopted in RAM, but flash memory is considered as a block device (such as a hard disk) which has a smallest unit (page) for reading or writing. If binary search tree is implemented in flash-memory storage systems, many nodes could be modified frequently when updates are needed. As a result, according to the characteristics of flash memory, many pages could be modified over flash memory for maintaining the binary search tree. Therefore, B-Tree index structures are considered in the paper instead of binary search tree. In particular, B-Tree is one of the most popular index structures because of its scalability and efficiency. B-Tree indices were first introduced by Bayer and McCreight [21]. Comer [6] later proposed its variation called B+-tree indices in 1979. B-Tree index structures are extended to many application domains: Kuo, et al. [23] demonstrated how to provide a predictable performance with B-Tree. Freeston [19] showed multi-dimensiona B-Trees which have good predictable and controllable worst-case characteristics. For the parallel environment, Yokota, et al. proposed Fat-Btrees [7] to improve high-speed access for parallel database systems. Becker, et al. [3] improved the availability of data by a multi-version index structure that supports insertions, deletions, range queries, and exact match queries for the current or some past versions.

There are two critical issues which could have a significant impacts on the efficiency of index structures over flash memory: (1) write-once with bulk-erase (2) the endurance issue. Flash memory could not be over-written (updated) unless it is erased. As a result, out-of-date (or invalid) versions and the latest copy of data might co-exist over flash memory simultaneously. Furthermore, an erasable unit of a typical flash memory is relatively large. Valid data might be involved in the erasing, because of the recycling of available space. Frequent erasing of some particular locations of flash memory could quickly deteriorate the overall lifetime of flash memory (the endurance issue), because each erasable unit has a limited cycle count on the erase operation.

In this paper, we focus on an efficient integration of B-Tree index structures and the block-device emulation mechanism provided by FTL (flash translation layer). We propose a module over a traditional FTL to handle intensive byte-wise operations due to B-tree access. The implementation is done directly over FTL such that no modifications to existing application systems are needed. The intensive byte-wise operations are caused by record inserting, record deleting, and B-tree reorganizing. For example, the insertion of a record in the system will result in the insertion of a data pointer at a leaf node and, possibly, the insertion of tree pointers in the B-tree. Such actions could result in a large number of data copyings (i.e., the copying of unchanged data and tree pointers in related nodes) because of out-place updates over flash memory. We demonstrate that the proposed methodology could significantly improve the system performance and, at the same time, reduce the overheads of flash-memory management and the energy dissipation, when index structures are adopted over flash memory. We must point that although only the block-device emulation approach is studied in this paper, however, the idea of this paper could be easily extended to a native flash-memory file system.

The rest of this paper is organized as follows: Section 2 provides an overview of flash memory and discussions of the implementation problems of B-Tree over flash memory. Section 3 introduces our approach and its implementation. Section 4 provides performance analysis of the approach. Section 5 shows experimental results. Section 6 is the conclusion and future work.

2   Motivation

In this section, we shall briefly introduce the characteristics of flash memory. By showing the very distinct properties of flash memory, the potential issues of building a B-Trees index structure over a NAND flash memory are addressed as the motivation of this work.

2.1   Flash Memory Characteristics

A NAND[1] flash memory is organized by many blocks, and each block is of a fixed number of pages. A block is the smallest unit of erase operation, while reads and writes are handled by pages. The typical block size and page size of a NAND flash memory is 16KB and 512B, respectively. Because flash memory is write-once, we do not overwrite data on update. Instead, data are written to free space, and the old versions of data are invalidated (or considered as dead). The update strategy is called "out-place update". In other words, any existing data on flash memory

---

[1] There are two major types of flash memory in the current market: NAND flash and NOR flash. The NAND flash memory is specially designed for data storage, and the NOR flash is for EEPROM replacement.

could not be over-written (updated) unless it is erased. The pages store live data and dead data are called "live pages" and "dead pages", respectively. Because out-place update is adopted, we need a dynamic address translation mechanism to map a given LBA (logical block address) to the physical address where the valid data reside. Note that a "logical block" usually denotes a disk sector. To accomplish this objective, a RAM-resident translation table is adopted. The translation table is indexed by LBA's, and each entry of the table contains the physical address of the corresponding LBA. If the system reboots, the translation table could be re-built by scanning the flash memory. Figure 1 illustrate how to retrieve data from flash memory by using the translation table.

After a certain number of page writes, free space on flash memory would be low. Activities consist of a series of read/write/erase with the intention to reclaim free spaces would then start. The activities are called "garbage collection", which is considered as overheads in flash-memory management. The objective of garbage collection is to recycle the dead pages scattered over the blocks so that they could become free pages after erasings. How to smartly choose which blocks should be erased is the responsibility of a *block-recycling policy*. The block-recycling policy should try to minimize the overhead of garbage collection (caused by live data copyings). Figure[2] 2 shows the procedure of garbage collection. Under current technology, a flash-memory block has a limitation on the erase cycle count. For example, a block of a typical NAND flash memory could be erased for 1 million (10^6) times. After that, a worn-out block could suffer from frequent write errors. A "wear-leveling" policy intends to erase all blocks on flash memory evenly, so that a longer overall lifetime could be achieved. Obviously, wear-leveling activities would impose significant overheads to the flash-memory storage system if the access patterns try to frequently update some specific data.

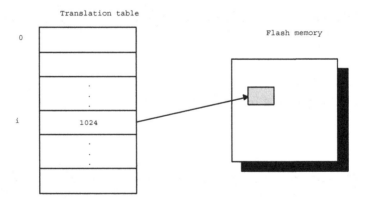

Fig. 1. The logical block address "i" is mapped to the physical page number "1024" by the translation table.

---

[2] A similar figure also appears in [18].

Table 1. Performance of a typical NAND Flash Memory

	Page Read 512 bytes	Page Write 512 bytes	Block Erase 16K bytes
Performance(μs)	348	909	1,881
Energy Consumption($\mu joule$)	99	237.6	422.4

There are many issues in the management of flash memory: As mentioned in the previous two paragraphes, the activities of garbage collection and wear-leveling could introduce an unpredictable blocking time to time-critical applications. In particular, Kawaguchi, et al. [1] proposed the cost-benefit policy which uses a value-driven heuristic function as a block-recycling policy. Kwoun, et al. [13] proposed to periodically move live data among blocks so that blocks have more an even life-time. Chang and Kuo [14] investigated how to properly manage the internal activities so that a deterministic performance could be provided. On the other hand, the performance and energy consumption of reads, writes, and erases are very different, as shown in Table 1. For portable devices, the endurance of batteries is a critical issue. Because flash memory could also contribute a significant portion of energy consumption, Chang and Kuo [15] introduced an energy-efficient request scheduling algorithm for flash-memory storage system to lengthen the operating time of battery-powered portable devices. Furthermore, the handling of writes could be the performance bottleneck: Writing to flash memory are relatively slow, and it could introduce garbage collection and wear-leveling activities. To improve the overall performance, Chang and Kuo [16] proposed an adaptive striping architecture which consists of several independent banks. A dynamic striping policy was adopted to smartly distribute writes among banks to improve the parallelism.

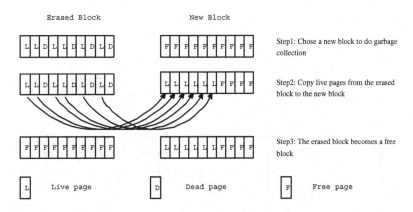

Fig. 2. Garbage collection

2.2   Problem Definition

A B-Tree consists of a hierarchical structure of data. It provides efficient operations to find, delete, insert, and traverse the data. There are two kinds of nodes
in a B-Tree: internal nodes and leaf nodes. A B-Tree internal node consists of a
ordered list of key values and linkage pointers, where data in a subtree have key
values between the ranges defined by the corresponding key values. A B-Tree
leaf node consists of pairs of a key value and its corresponding record pointer. In
most cases, B-Trees are used as external (outside of RAM) index structures to
maintain a very large set of data. Traditionally, the external storage are usually
block devices such as disks. In practice, we usually set the size of a B-Tree node
as the size which can be efficiently handled by the used block device. For example, many modern hard disks could have equivalent response times to access a
512B sector and a 64KB chunk (due to the seek penalty, the rotational delay,
the DMA granularity, and many other factors). Therefore, a B-Tree node could
be a 64K chunk on the hard disk. To insert, delete, and re-balance B-Trees, B-
Tree nodes are fetched from the hard disk and then written back to the original
location. Such operations are very efficient for hard disks.

Recently, the capacity and reliability of flash memory grew significantly.
Flash-memory storage systems become good mass storage solutions, especially
for those applications work under extreme environments. For example, those
systems operate under severe vibrations or limited energy sources might pre-
fer flash-memory storage systems. Since a large flash-memory storage system is
much more affordable than ever, the issue on the efficiency of data accessing
becomes critical. For the development of many information systems, B-Tree are
widely used because of its efficiency and scalability. However, a direct adoption
of B-Tree index structures over flash-memory storage systems could exaggerate
the overheads of flash-memory management. Let us first consider usual operations done over B-Tree index structures: Figure 3 shows an ordinary B-Tree.
Suppose that six different records are to be inserted. Let the primary keys of the

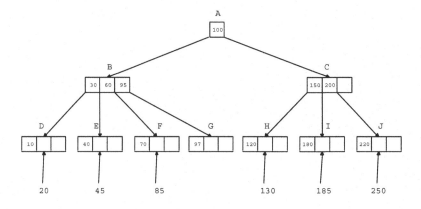

Fig. 3. A B-Tree (fanout is 4).

records be 20, 45, 85, 130, 185, and 250, respectively. As shown in Figure 3, the 1st, 2nd, 3rd, 4th, 5th, and 6th records should be inserted to nodes D, E, F, H, I, and J, respectively. Six B-Tree nodes are modified. Now let us focus on the files of index structures since we usually store index structures separately from the records. Suppose that each B-Tree node is stored in one page, then up to six page writes are needed to accomplish the updates. If rebalancing is needed, more updates of internal nodes will be needed.

Compared with operations on hard disks, updating (or writing) data over flash memory is a very complicated and expensive operation. Since out-place update is adopted, a whole page (512B) which contains the new version of data will be written to flash memory, and previous data must be invalidated. The page-based write operations could expectedly introduce a sequence of negative effects. Free space on flash memory could be consumed very quickly. As a result, garbage collection could happen frequently to reclaim free space. Furthermore, because flash memory is frequently erased, the lifetime of the flash memory would be reduced. Another problem is energy consumption. Out-place updates would result in garbage collection, which must read and write pages and erase blocks. Because writes and erases consume much more energy than reads, as shown in Table 1, out-place updates eventually cause much more energy consumption. For portable devices, because the amount of energy provided by batteries is limited, energy-saving could be a major concern. The motivation of this work is to reduce the amount of redundant data written to flash memory caused by index structures to improve the system performance and reduce energy consumption.

3   The Design and Implementation of BFTL

In this section, we present an efficient B-Tree layer for flash-memory storage systems (BFTL) with a major objective to reduce the redundant data written due to the hardware restriction of a NAND flash memory. We shall illustrate the architecture of a system which adopts BFTL and present the functionalities of the components inside BFTL in the following subsections.

3.1   Overview

In our approach, we propose to have an insertable module called BFTL (an efficient B-Tree layer for flash-memory storage systems, referred as BFTL for the rest of this paper.) over the original flash translation layer (FTL). BFTL sits between the application layer and the block-device emulated by FTL. The BFTL module is dedicated to those applications which use services provided by B-Tree indices. Figure 4 illustrates the architecture of a system which adopts BFTL. BFTL consists of a small *reservation buffer* and a *node translation table*. B-Tree index services requested by the upper-level applications are handled and translated by BFTL, and then block-device requests are sent from BFTL to FTL. When the applications insert, delete, or modify records, the newly generated records (referred as "dirty records" for the rest of this paper) would be

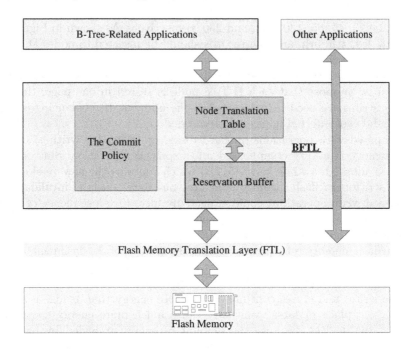

Fig. 4. Architecture of a System Which Adopts BFTL.

temporarily held by the reservation buffer of BFTL. Since the reservation buffer only holds an adequate amount of records, the dirty records should be timely flushed to flash memory. Note that record deletions are handled by adding "in-validation records" to the reservation buffer.

To flush out the dirty records in the reservation buffer, BFTL constructs corresponding "index units" for each dirty record. The usage of index units are to reflect primary-key insertions and deletions to the B-Tree index structure caused by the dirty records. The storing of the index units and the dirty records are handled in two different ways. The storing of the records is relatively simple: The records are written (or updated) to an allocated (or the original) locations. On the other hand, because an index unit is very small (compared with the size of a page), the storing of the index units is handled by a commit policy. Many index units could be smartly packed into few sectors to reduce the number of pages physically written. Note that the "sectors" are logical items which are provided by the block-device emulation of FTL. We would try to pack index units belonging to different B-Tree nodes in a small number of sectors. During this packing process, although the number of sectors to be updated is reduced, index units of one B-Tree node could now exist in different sectors. To help BFTL to identify index units of the same B-Tree node, a node translation table is adopted.

In the following sub-sections, we shall present the functionality of index units, the commit policy, and the node translation table. In Section 3.2 we illustrate how a B-Tree node is physically represented by a collection of index units. The commit policy which smartly flushes the dirty records is presented in Section 3.3. The design issues of the node translation table are discussed in Section 3.4.

3.2 The Physical Representation of a B-Tree Node: The Index Units

When applications insert, delete, or modify records, the dirty records could be temporarily held by the reservation buffer of BFTL. BFTL would construct a corresponding "index unit" to reflect the primary-key insertion/deletion to the B-Tree index structure caused by a dirty record. In other words, an index unit could be treated as a modification of the corresponding B-Tree node, and a B-Tree node could be logically constructed by collecting and parsing all relevant index units. Since the size of a index unit is relatively small (compared to the size of a page), the adopting of index units could prevent redundant data from frequently being written to flash memory. To save space needed by the storing of index units, many index units are packed into few sectors even though the packed index units might be belonging to different B-Tree nodes. As a result, the index units of one B-Tree node could exist in different sectors over flash memory, and the physical representation of the B-Tree node would be different from the original one.

To construct the logical view of a B-Tree node, relevant index units are collected and parsed for the layer above BFTL, i.e., users of BFTL. Figure 5 illustrates how the logical view of a B-Tree node is constructed: Index units (I1, I2, ... , Ik) of a B-Tree node are scattered over flash memory, and we could form the B-Tree node by collecting its relevant index units over flash memory. An index unit is of several components: data_ptr, parent_node, primary_key, left_ptr, right_ptr, an identifier, and an op_flag. Where data_ptr, parent_node, left_ptr, right_ptr, and primary_key are the elements of a original B-Tree node.

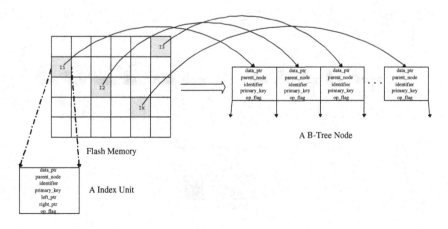

Fig. 5. The node consists of index units.

They represent a reference to the record body, a pointer to the parent B-Tree node, a pointer to the left B-Tree node, a pointer to the right B-Tree node, and and the primary key, respectively. Beside the components originally for a B-Tree node, an identifier is needed: The identifier of an index unit denotes to which B-Tree node the index unit is belonging. The op_flag denotes the operation done by the index unit, and the operations could be an insertion, a deletion, or an update. Additionally, time-stamps are added for each batch flushing of index units to prevent BFTL from using stale index units. Note that BFTL uses FTL to store index units. As shown in Figure 5, index units related to the desired B-Tree node are collected from flash memory. Index units could be scattered over flash memory. The logical view of the B-Tree node is constructed through the help of BFTL. As astute readers might point out, it is very inefficient to scan flash memory to collect the index units of the same B-Tree node. A node translation table is adopted to handle the collection of index units. It will be presented in Section 3.4.

3.3   The Commit Policy

Dirty records are temporarily held by the reservation buffer of BFTL. The buffer should be flushed out in a timely fashion. Index units are generated to reflect modifications to B-Tree index structures, and the index units are packed into few sectors and written to flash memory (by FTL). A technical issue is how

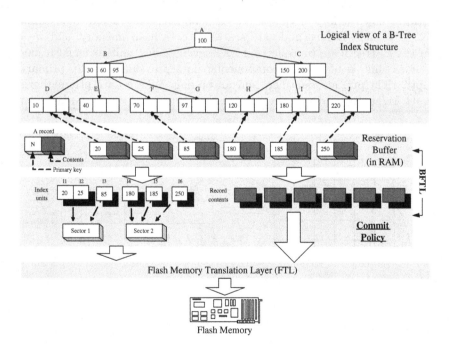

Fig. 6. The Commit Policy Packs and Flushes the Index Units.

to smartly pack index units into few sectors. In this section, we shall provide discussions on commit policies for index units.

The reservation buffer in BFTL is a buffer space for dirty records. The buffering of dirty records could prevent B-Tree index structures over flash memory from being intensively modified. However, the capacity of the reservation buffer is not unlimited. Once the reservation buffer is full, some dirty records in the buffer should be committed (written) to flash memory. We propose to flush out all dirty records in this paper because a better analysis of dirty records is possible to reduce updates of leaf nodes (We will demonstrate the approach later in the performance evaluation.) Beside the storing of records, BFTL would construct index units to reflect modifications to the B-Tree index structure. Since the size of an index unit is smaller than the sector size provided by FTL (or the page size of flash memory), many index units should be packed together in order to further reduce the number of sectors needed. On the other hand, we also hope that index units of the same B-Tree node will not be scattered over many sectors so that the collection of the index units could be more efficient. A commit policy is proposed to achieve both of the objectives. We shall illustrate the commit policy by an example:

The handling of a B-Tree index structure in Figure 6 is divided into three parts: the logical view of a B-Tree index structure, BFTL, and FTL. Suppose that the reservation buffer could hold six records whose primary keys are 20, 25, 85, 180, 185, and 250, respectively. When the buffer is full, the records should be written to flash memory. BFTL first generates six index units (I1 to I6) for the six records. Based on the primary keys of the records and the value ranges of the leaf nodes (D, E, F, G, H, I, and J in the figure), the index units could be partitioned into five disjoint sets: $\{I1, I2\} \in D$, $\{I3\} \in F$, $\{I4\} \in H$, $\{I5\} \in I$, $\{I6\} \in J$. The partitioning prevents index units of the same B-Tree node from being fragmented. Suppose that a sector provided by FTL could store three index units. Therefore, $\{I1, I2\}$ and $\{I3\}$ would be put in the first sector. $\{I4\}$, $\{I5\}$, and $\{I6\}$ would be put in the second sector since the first sector is full. Finally, two sectors are written to commit the index units. If the reservation buffer and the commit policy are not adopted, up to six sector writes might be needed to handle the modifications of the index structure.

As astute reader may notice, the packing problem of index units into sectors is inherently intractable. A problem instance is as follows: Given disjoint sets of index units, how to minimize the number of sectors in packing the sets into sectors?

Theorem 1. *The packing problem of index units into sectors is NP-Hard.*

Proof. The intractability of the problem could be shown by a reduction from the Bin-Packing [20] problem: Let an instance of the Bin-Packing problem be defined as follows: Suppose B and K denote the capacity of a bin and the number of items, where each item has a size. The problem is to put items into bins such that the number of bins is minimized.

The reduction can be done as follows: Let the capacity of a sector be the capacity of a bin B, and each item a disjoint set of index units. The number of disjoint sets is as the same as the number of items, i.e., K. The size of a disjoint set is the size of the corresponding item. (Note that although the sector size is determined by systems, the sector size could be normalized to B. The sizes of disjoint sets could be done in the same ratio accordingly.) If there exists a solution for the packing problem of index units, then the solution is also one for the Bin-Packing problem.

Note that there exists many excellent approximation algorithms for bin-packing. For example, the well-known FIRST-FIT approximation algorithm [24] could have an approximation bound no more than twice of the optimal solution.

3.4   The Node Translation Table

Since the index units of a B-Tree node might be scattered over flash memory due to the commit policy, a node translation table is adopted to maintain a collection of the index units of a B-Tree node so that the collecting of index units could be efficient. This section presents the design and related implementation issues of the node translation table.

Since the construction of the logical view of a B-Tree node requires all index units of the B-Tree node, it must be efficient to collect the needed index units when a B-Tree node is accessed. A node translation table is introduced as an auxiliary data structure to make the collecting of the index units efficient. A node translation table is very similar to the logical address translation table mentioned in Section 2.1, which maps an LBA (the address of a sector) to a physical page number. However, different from the logical address translation table, the node translation table maps a B-Tree node to a collection of LBA's where the related index units reside. In other words, all LBA's of the index units of a B-Tree node are chained after the corresponding entry of the node translation table. In order to form a correct logical view of a B-Tree node, BFTL would visit (read) all sectors where the related index units reside and then construct an up-to-date

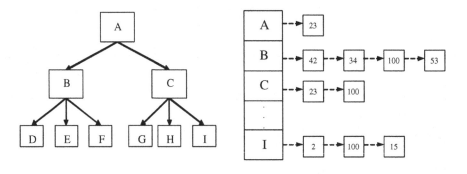

(a) The logical view of a B-tree   (b) The node translation table

Fig. 7. The Node Translation Table.

logical view of the B-Tree node for users of BFTL. The node translation table could be re-built by scanning the flash memory when system is powered-up.

Figure 7.(a) shows a B-Tree with nine nodes. Figure 7.(b) is a possible configuration of the node translation table. Figure 7.(b) shows that each B-Tree node consists of several index units which could come from different sectors. The LBA's of the sectors are chained as a list after the corresponding entry of the table. When a B-Tree node is visited, we collect all the index units belonging to the visited node by scanning the sectors whose LBA's are stored in the list. For example, to construct a logical view of B-Tree node C in Figure 7.(a), LBA 23 and LBA 100 are read by BFTL (through FTL) to collect the needed index units. Conversely, an LBA could have index units which are belonging to different B-Tree nodes. Figure 7.(b) shows that LBA 100 contains index units of B-Tree nodes B, C, and I. Therefore, when a sector is written, the LBA of the written sector might be appended to some entries of the node translation table accordingly .

The following example which illustrates how BFTL locates a record, as shown in Figure 8:

Step 1: An application issues a read command for accessing a record.

Step 2: If the record could be found in the reservation buffer, then return the record.

Step 3: Otherwise; traverse the whole B-Tree form the root node by the node translation table to search for the record.

Step 4: If the record is found, then return the record.

As astute readers may point out, the lists in the node translation table could grow unexpectedly. For example, if a list after a entry of the node translation table have 100 slots, the visiting of the corresponding B-Tree node might have to read 100 sectors. On the other hand, 100 slots are needed in the node translation table to store the LBA's. If the node translation table is handled in an uncontrolled manner, it will not only deteriorate the performance severely but also consume a lot of resources (such as RAM). To overcome the problem, we propose to compact the node translation table when necessary. A system parameter C is used to control the maximum length of the lists of the node translation table. When the length of a list grows beyond C, the list will be compacted. To compact a list, all related index units are collected into RAM and then written back to flash memory with a smallest number of sectors. As a result, the size of the table could be bounded by $O(N*C)$, where N denotes the number of B-Tree nodes. On the other hand, the number of sector reads needed to visit a B-Tree node can be bounded by C. Obviously, there is a trade-off between the overheads of compaction and the performance. The experimental results presented in Section 5 could provide more insights for system parameter configuring.

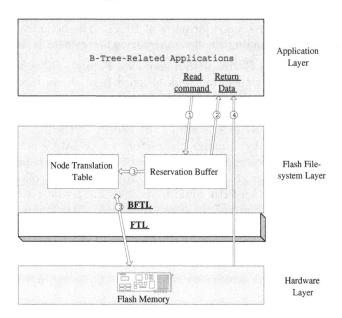

Fig. 8. The Procedures to Handle Searching in BFTL.

4   System Analysis

This section intends to provide the analysis of the behaviors of BFTL and FTL. We derived the numbers of sectors read and written by FTL and BFTL to handle the insertions of n records.

Suppose that we already have a B-Tree index structure residing on flash memory. Without losing the generality, let a B-Tree node fit in a sector (provided by FTL). Suppose that n records are to be inserted. That is, n primary keys will be inserted into the B-Tree index structure. Assume that the values of the primary keys are all distinct.

First, we shall investigate the behaviors of FTL. A B-Tree node under FTL is stored in exactly one sector. One sector write is needed for each primary key insertion when no node overflow (node splitting) occurs. If a node is overflowed, one primary key in the node will be promoted to its parent node, and the node is then split into two new nodes. The splitting could be handled by three sector writes under FTL. Let H denote the current height of the B-Tree, and N_{split} denote the number of nodes which are split during the handling of the insertions. The numbers of sectors read and written by FTL to handle the insertions could be represented as follows:

$$\begin{cases} R_{FTL} = O(n * H) \\ W_{FTL} = O(n + 2 * N_{split}) \end{cases} \tag{1}$$

Suppose that the sector size remains the same under BFTL (note that BFTL is above FTL), and the hight of the B-Tree is H. Let us consider the numbers of sectors read and written over flash memory when n records are inserted: Because BFTL adopts the node translation table to collect index units of a B-Tree node, the number of sectors that are read to construct a B-Tree node depends on the length of lists of the node translation table. Let the length of the lists be bounded by C (as mentioned in Section 3.4), the number of sectors that are read by BFTL to handle the insertions could be represented as follows: Note that C is a control parameter, as discussed in the previous section.

$$R_{BFTL} = O(n * H * C) \tag{2}$$

Equation 2 shows that the BFTL might read more sectors in handling the insertions. In fact, BFTL trades the number of reads for the number of writes. The number of sectors written by BFTL could be calculated as follows: Because BFTL adopts the reservation buffer to hold records in RAM and flushes them in a batch, modifications to B-Tree nodes (the index units) could be packed in few sectors. Let the capacity of the reservation buffer of a B-Tree be of b records. As a result, the reservation buffer would be flushed by the commit policy at least $\lceil n/b \rceil$ times during the handling of the insertion of n records. Let N^i_{split} denote the number of nodes which are split to handle the i-th flushing of the reservation buffer. Obviously, $\sum_{i=1}^{\lceil n/b \rceil} N^i_{split} = N_{split}$ because the B-Tree index structures under FTL and BFTL are logically identical. For each single step of the reservation buffer flushing, we have $b + N^i_{split} * (fanout - 1)$ dirty index units to commit because the additional $(fanout - 1)$ dirty index units are for the newly created nodes during the splitting, where $fanout$ is the maximum fanout of the B-Tree. Note that N^i_{split} times $(fanout - 1)$ in the formula because each splitting will result in 2 new nodes, and the number of records in the 2 new nodes is $(fanout - 1)$. Furthermore, the splitting will result in the update of the parent node of the new nodes (that contributes to b in the above formula). Similar to FTL, suppose that a B-Tree node could fit in a sector. That means a sector could hold (fanout-1) index units. Let $\Lambda = (fanout - 1)$. The number of sectors written by the i-th committing of the reservation buffer could be $(\frac{b}{\Lambda} + N^i_{split})$. To completely flush the reservation buffer, we have to write at least $\sum_{i=1}^{\lceil n/b \rceil} (\frac{b}{\Lambda} + N^i_{split}) = (\sum_{i=1}^{\lceil n/b \rceil} \frac{b}{\Lambda}) + N_{split}$ sectors. Since BFTL adopts the FIRST-FIT approximation algorithm (as mentioned in Section 3.3), the number of sectors written by BFTL could be bounded by the following formula:

$$W_{BFTL} = O(2 * (\sum_{i=1}^{\lceil n/b \rceil} \frac{b}{\Lambda}) + N_{split}) = O(\frac{2 * n}{\Lambda} + N_{split}) \tag{3}$$

By putting W_{FTL} with W_{BFTL} together, we have:

$$\begin{cases} W_{BFTL} = O(\frac{2*n}{\Lambda} + N_{split}) \\ W_{FTL} = O(n + 2 * N_{split}) \end{cases} \tag{4}$$

Equation 4 shows that W_{BFTL} is far less than W_{FTL}, since Λ (the number of index units a sector could store) is usually larger than 2. The deriving of equations could provide a low bound for W_{BFTL}. However, we should point out that the compaction of the node translation table (mentioned in Section 3.4) might introduce some run-time overheads. We shall later show that when $\Lambda = 20$, the number of sectors written by BFTL is between 1/3 and 1/13 of the number of sectors written by FTL.

5   Performance Evaluation

The idea of BFTL was implemented and evaluated to verify the effectiveness and to show the benefits of our approach. By eliminating redundant data written to flash memory, we surmise that the performance of B-Tree operations should be significantly improved.

5.1   Experiment Setup and Performance Metrics

A NAND-based system prototype was built to evaluate the performance of BFTL and FTL. The prototype was equipped with a 4MB NAND flash memory, where the performance of the NAND flash memory is included in Table 1. To evaluate the performance of FTL, a B-Tree was directly built over the block-device emulated by FTL. The *greedy* block-recycling policy [1,14] was adopted in FTL to handle garbage collection.

Because we focused on the behavior of B-Tree index structures in this paper, we did not consider the writing of data records over flash memory. Only the performance of index operations was considered and measured. The fan-out of the B-Tree used in the experiments was 21, and the size of a B-Tree node fits in a sector. To evaluate the performance of BFTL, BFTL was configured as follows: The reservation buffer in the experiments was configured to hold 60 records (unless we explicitly specified the capacity). As suggested by practical experiences in using B-Tree index structure, we assumed that a small amount of B-Tree nodes in the top levels were cached in RAM so that these "hot" nodes could be accessed efficiently. The bound of the lengths of lists in the node translation table was set as 3.

In the experiments, we measured the average response time of record insertions and deletions. A smaller response time denotes a better efficiency in handling requests. The average response time also implicitly reflected the overheads of garbage collection. If there was a significant number of live page copyings and block erasings, the response time would be increased accordingly. To further investigate the behaviors of BFTL and FTL, we also measured the numbers of pages read, pages written, and blocks erased in the experiments. Note that Sector reads/writes were issued by an original B-Tree index structure or BFTL when BFTL was not adopted or adopted, respectively. FTL translated the sector reads/writes into page reads/writes to physically access the NAND flash memory. Live data copyings and block erases were generated accordingly to recycle free space when needed. Readers could refer to Figure 4 for the system architecture. The energy consumption of BFTL and FTL was measured to evaluate their power-efficiency levels. Different simulation workloads were used to measure the performance of BFTL and FTL. The details will be illustrated in later sections.

5.2   Performance of B-Tree Index Structures Creation

In this part of the experiments, we measured the performance of FTL and BFTL in the creating of B-Tree index structures. B-Tree index structures were created by record insertions. In other words, the workloads consisted of insertions only. For each run of experiments, we inserted 24,000 records. We must point out that although a B-Tree constructed by the 24,000 record insertions under FTL occupied 868KB space on flash memory, however, the amount of total data written by FTL was 14MB. Because a 4MB NAND flash memory was used in the experiments, garbage collection activities would be started to recycle free space. In the experiments, a ratio rs was used to control the value distribution of the inserted keys: When rs equals to zero, that means all of the keys were randomly generated. If rs equals to 1, that means the value of the inserted keys were in an ascending order. Consequently, if the value of rs equals to 0.5, that means the values of one-half of the keys were in an ascending order, while the other keys were randomly generated. In Figure 11.(a) through Figure 11.(e), the X-axes denote the value of rs.

Figure 11.(a) shows the average response time of the insertions. We can see that BFTL greatly outperformed FTL: The response time of BFTL was even one-twentieth of FTL when the values of the keys were completely in an ascending order ($rs = 1$). BFTL still outperformed FTL even if the values of the keys were randomly generated ($rs = 0$). When the keys were sequentially generated ($rs = 1$), the number of sectors written could be decreased because index units of the same B-Tree node would not be scattered over sectors severely. Furthermore, the length of the lists of the node translation table would be relatively short and the compaction of the lists would not introduce significant overheads. As mentioned in the previous sections, writing to flash memory is relative expensive because writes would wear flash, consume more energy, and introduce garbage collection. Figure 11.(b) and Figure 11.(c) show the number of pages written and the number of pages read in the experiments, respectively. The numbers could reflect the usages of flash memory by FTL and BFTL in the experiments. If we further investigate the behaviors of BFTL and FTL by putting Figure 11.(b) with Figure 11.(c) together, we can see that BFTL smartly traded extra reads for the number of writes by the adoption of the commit policy. On the other hand, the extra reads come from the visiting of sectors to construct a logical view of a B-Tree node, as mentioned in Section 3.4.

For the garbage collection issue, in Figure 11.(d) we can see that BFTL certainly suppressed the garbage collection activities when compared with FTL. In some experiments of BFTL, garbage collection even did not start yet. As a result, a longer lifetime of flash memory could be faithfully promised by BFTL. Figure 11.(e) shows the overheads introduced by the compaction of the node translation table. In Figure 11.(e), we can see that the number of executions of compacting was reduced when the values of the inserted keys were in an ascending order. On the other hand, BFTL frequently compacted the node translation table if the values of the inserted keys were randomly generated since the index units of a B-Tree node were also randomly scattered over sectors. Therefore the length of the lists could grow rapidly and the lists would be compacted frequently.

5.3   Performance of B-Tree Index Structures Maintenance

In the section, the performance of BFTL and FTL to maintain B-Tree index structures was measured. Under the workloads adopted in this part of experiments, records are inserted, modified, or deleted. To reflect realistic usages of index services, we varied the ratio of the number of deletions to the number of insertions. For example, a 30/70 ratio denotes that the thirty percent of total operations are deletions and the other seventy percent of total operations are insertions. For each run the experiments, 24,000 operations were performed on the B-Tree index structures and the ratio of deletion/insertion was among 50/50, 40/60, 30/70, 20/80, and 10/90. Besides the deletion/insertion ratios, $rs = 1$ and $rs = 0$ (please see Section 5.2 for the definition of rs) were used as two representative experiment settings.

The X-axes of Figure 9.(a) and Figure 9.(b) denote the ratios of deletion/insertion. Figure 9.(a) shows the average response time under different ratios of deletions/insertions. The average response time shows that BFTL outperformed FTL when $rs = 0$ (the keys were randomly generated), and the performance advantage was more significant when $rs = 1$ (the values of the keys were in an ascending order). When $rs = 1$, the performance of BFTL greatly improved when the ratio of deletions/insertions changed from 50/50 to 10/90. For the experiment of BFTL under a 50/50 ratio, because records were frequently inserted and deleted, a lot of index units for insertions and deletions were generated. As a result, BFTL had to visit more sectors to collect the index units of a B-Tree node under a 50/50 ratio than under a 10/90 ratio. Different from those of $rs = 1$, the performance gradually degraded when the ratio changed from 50/50 to 10/90 when $rs = 0$ (random). Since the inserted keys were already randomly generated, a 10/90 ratio denoted more keys were generated and inserted than a 50/50 ratio. As a result, more index units could be chained in the node translation table so that the visiting of a B-Tree node was not very efficient. Figure 9.(b) shows the number of block erased in the experiments. The garbage collection activities were substantially reduced by BFTL, and they had even not started yet in the experiments of $rs = 1$ of BFTL.

5.4   The Size of the Reservation Buffer and the Energy Consumption Issues

In this part of experiments, we evaluated the performance of BFTL under different sizes of the reservation buffer so that we could have more insights in the configuring of the reservation buffer. We also evaluated the energy consumptions under BFTL and FTL. Because BFTL could have a reduced number of writes, energy dissipations under BFTL is surmised to be lower than under FTL.

There is a trade-off to configure the size of the reservation buffer: A large reservation buffer could have benefits from buffering/caching records, however, it

Table 2. Energy Dissipations of BFTL and FTL (*joule*)

Creation		
	BFTL	FTL
rs=0	11.65	12.94
rs=1	0.931	11.104

Maintainence		
	BFTL	FTL
50/50, rs=0	8.804	8.261
50/50, rs=1	6.136	9.826
10/90, rs=0	10.38	10.99
10/90, rs=1	1.593	9.515

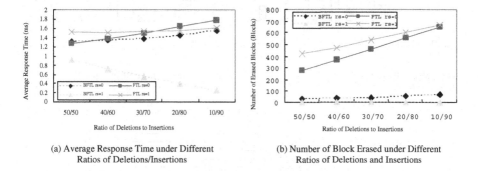

(a) Average Response Time under Different
Ratios of Deletions/Insertions

(b) Number of Block Erased under Different
Ratios of Deletions and Insertions

Fig. 9. Experimental Results of B-Tree Index Structures Maintenance.

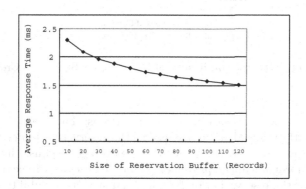

Fig. 10. Experimental Results of BFTL under Different Sizes of the Reservation Buffer

could damage the reliability of BFTL due to power-failures. Reservation buffers
with different size were evaluated to find a reasonably good setting. The experiment setups in Section 5.2 were used in this part of experiments, but the value
of *rs* was fixed at 0.5. The size of the reservation buffer was set between 10
records and 120 records, and the size was incremented by 10 records. Figure 10

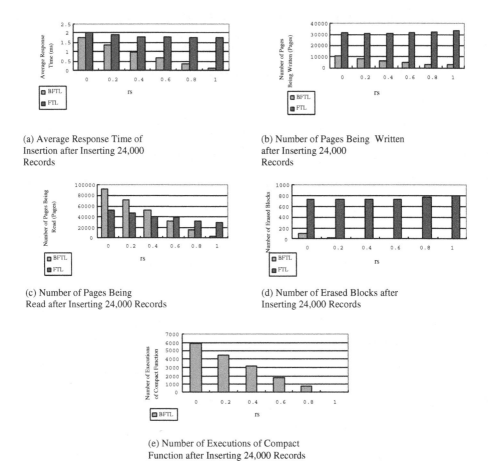

(a) Average Response Time of
Insertion after Inserting 24,000
Records

(b) Number of Pages Being Written
after Inserting 24,000
Records

(c) Number of Pages Being
Read after Inserting 24,000 Records

(d) Number of Erased Blocks after
Inserting 24,000 Records

(e) Number of Executions of Compact
Function after Inserting 24,000 Records

Fig. 11. Experimental Results of B-Tree Index Structures Creation.

shows the average response time of the insertions: The average response time
was significantly reduced when the size of the reservation buffer was increased
from 10 records to 60 records. After that, the average response time was linearly
reduced and no significant improvement could be observed. Since further increasing the size of the reservation buffer could damage the reliability of BFTL, the
recommended size of the reservation buffer for the experiments was 60 records.

Energy consumption is also a critical issue for portable devices. According to
the numbers of reads/ writes/ erases generated in the experiments, we calculated
the energy consumption contributed by BFTL and FTL. The energy consumptions of reads/ writes/ erases are included in Table 1. The calculated energy
consumption of the experiments are listed in Table 2: The energy consumed by
BFTL was clearly less than FTL. Since page writes and block erases consume relatively more energy than page reads, the energy consumption was reduced when

BFTL smartly traded extra reads for the number of writes. Furthermore, energy consumption contributed by garbage collection was also reduced by BFTL since BFTL consumed free space slower than FTL.

6   Conclusion

Flash-memory storage systems are very suitable for embedded systems such as portable devices and consumer electronics. Due to hardware restrictions, the performance of NAND flash memory could deteriorate significantly when files with index structures, such as B-Tree, are stored. In this paper, we propose a methodology and a layer design to support B-Tree index structures over flash memory. The objective is not only to improve the performance of flash-memory storage systems but also to reduce the energy consumption of the systems, where energy consumption is an important issue for the design of portable devices. BFTL is introduced as a layer over FTL to achieve the objectives. BFTL reduces the number of redundant data written to flash memory. We conducted a series of experiments over a system prototype, for which we have very encouraging results.

There are many promising research directions for the future work. With the advance of flash-memory technology, large-scaled flash-memory storage systems could become very much affordable in the near future. How to manage data records and their index structures, or even simply storage space, over huge flash memory might not have a simple solution. The overheads in flash-memory management could introduce a serious performance in system designs.

References

1. A. Kawaguchi, S. Nishioka, and H. Motoda, "A Flash-Memory Based File System," USENIX Technical Conference on Unix and Advanced Computing Systems, 1995.
2. Aleph One Company, "Yet Another Flash Filing System".
3. B. Becker, S. Gschwind, T. Ohler, B. Seeger, and P. Widmayer: "An Asymptotically Optimal Multiversion B-Tree," VLDB Journal 5(4): 264-275(1996)
4. Compact Flash Association, "$CompactFlash^{TM}$ 1.4 Specification," 1998.
5. D. Woodhouse, Red Hat, Inc. "JFFS: The Journalling Flash File System".
6. D. Comer, "The Ubiquitous B-Tree," ACM Computing Surveys 11(2): 121-137(1979).
7. H. Yokota, Y. Kanemasa, and J. Miyazaki: "Fat-Btree: An Update-Conscious Parallel Directory Structure," ICDE 1999: 448-457
8. Intel Corporation, "Flash File System Selection Guide".
9. Intel Corporation, "Understanding the Flash Translation Layer(FTL) Specification".
10. Intel Corporation, "Software Concerns of Implementing a Resident Flash Disk".
11. Intel Corporation, "FTL Logger Exchanging Data with FTL Systems".
12. Intel Corporation, "LFS File Manager Software: LFM".
13. K. Han-Joon, and L. Sang-goo, "A New Flash Memory Management for Flash Storage System", Proceedings of the Computer Software and Applications Conference, 1999.

14. L. P. Chang, T. W. Kuo, "A Real-time Garbage Collection Mechanism for Flash Memory Storage System in Embedded Systems," The 8th International Conference on Real-Time Computing Systems and Applications (RTCSA 2002), 2002.

15. L. P. Chang, and T. W. Kuo, "A Dynamic-Voltage-Adjustment Mechanism in Reducing the Power Consumption of Flash Memory for Portable Devices," IEEE Conference on Consumer Electronic (ICCE 2001), LA. USA, June 2001.

16. L. P. Chang, and T. W. Kuo, "An Adaptive Striping Architecture for Flash Memory Storage Systems of Embedded Systems," The 8th IEEE Real-Time and Embedded Technology and Applications Symposium (RTAS 2002) September 24 ¡V 27, 2002. San Jose, California.

17. M. Rosenblum, and J. K. Ousterhout, "The Design and Implementation of a Log-Structured File System," ACM Transactions on Computer Systems 10(1) (1992) pp.26-52.

18. M. Wu, and W. Zwaenepoel, "eNVy: A Non-Volatile, Main Memory Storage System," Proceedings of the 6th International Conference on Architectural Support for Programming Languages and Operating Systems (ASPLOS 1994), 1994.

19. M. Freeston, "A General Solution of the n-dimensional B-Tree Problem," SIGMOD Conference, San Jose, May 1995.

20. M. R. Garey, and D. S. Johnson, "Computers and intractability", 1979.

21. R. Bayer, and E. M. McCreight: "Organization and Maintenance of Large Ordered Indices," Acta Informatica 1: 173-189(1972).

22. SSFDC Forum, "$SmartMedia^{TM}$ Specification", 1999.

23. T. W. Kuo, J. H. Wey, and K. Y. Lam, "Real-Time Data Access Control on B-Tree Index Structures," the IEEE 15th International Conference on Data Engineering (ICDE 1999), Sydney, Australia, March 1999.

24. Vijay V. Vazirani, "Approximation Algorithm," Springer publisher, 2001.

Multi-disk Scheduling for High-Performance RAID-0 Devices

Hsi-Wu Lo[1], Tei-Wei Kuo[1], and Kam-Yiu Lam[2]

[1] Department of Computer Science and Information Engineering
National Taiwan University
Taipei, Taiwan, ROC
FAX: 886-23628167
{d89015,ktw}@csie.ntu.edu.tw
[2] Department of Computer Science
City University of Hong Kong
Kowloon, Hong Kong
Fax: 852-27888614
cskylam@cityu.edu.hk

Abstract. High-Performance I/O subsystems have become a must for multimedia systems, such as video servers [15,16,18]. The proposing of the Intelligent I/O (I2O) specifications [11] provides hardware vendors an operating-system-independent architecture in building their solutions for high-performance I/O subsystems. This paper targets one of the most important performance issues in building an I2O RAID-0 device, which is an important I2O implementation. We explore multi-disk scheduling for I2O requests, which are usually associated with soft deadlines to enforce quality-of-service requirements. The idea of Least-Remaining-Request-Size-First (LRSF) is proposed for the request-level multi-disk scheduling with the objective to improve the response-time requirements of I/O sub-systems. The proposed scheduling algorithm is then extended to resolve the starvation problem and for SCAN-like disk services. Finally, we exploit pre-fetching for I2O RAID-0 devices to further improve their performance. The proposed methodologies are verified by a series of experiments using realistic and randomly generated workloads.

Keywords: I/O subsystems, RAID-0 devices, intelligent I/O, multimedia storage systems, multi-disk scheduling, real-time disk scheduling

1 Introduction

High-Performance I/O subsystems have become a must for multimedia systems, such as video servers [15,16,18]. With the strong demanding of high-performance storage systems, more functionality is now pushed down to low-level drivers. Complicated and intelligent I/O devices are emerging. Traditionally, hardware vendors need to write drivers for each of their new products. The number of products must multiply with the different operating environments and markets. Significant overheads must also be paid for the testing and certification of the

J. Chen and S. Hong (Eds.): RTCSA 2003, LNCS 2968, pp. 431–453, 2004.
© Springer-Verlag Berlin Heidelberg 2004

OS and vendors' driver versions. As drivers are getting overloaded, more CPU time is consumed for low-level system (or I/O-related) operations. At the same time, computer systems may suffer from potential hazard or lengthy blocking time in system operations. It is often the price paid for better I/O performance.

The Intelligent I/O (I2O) specifications [11] are proposed by major players in the industry, such as Microsoft, Intel, Hewlett-Packard, 3COM, Compaq, etc, as a standard for the next-generation I/O subsystems. The goal is to provide intelligence at the hardware level and standardize platforms for all segments of the industry. The I2O specifications let hardware/software vendors build intelligent products that contain their own I/O controller for processing I/O transactions, such as RAID controllers for storage and even ATM controllers for networking. They specify an architecture that is operating-system-vendor-independent and also adapts to existing operating systems, such as Microsoft Windows NT and 2000. That is, the I2O specifications enable the OS vendors to produce a single driver for each class of devices and concentrate on optimizing the OS portion of the driver. With an embedded processor, I2O adaptors can offload the major I/O processing workload from the CPU and, at the same time, increase the I/O performance.

Traditional work on disk scheduling has been focused on single disk systems, such as SCAN, Shortest-Seek-Time-First (SSTF), Circular SCAN (C-SCAN), and FIFO [21], where SCAN services disk requests on the way from one side of the disk to the other side and then on the way back, etc. C-SCAN is a variation of SCAN, except that C-SCAN always services disk requests from one side to the other side, and as soon as the r/w head reaches the other side, it immediately returns to the beginning of the disk, without servicing any request on the return trip. SSTF always services the request closest to the current r/w head position. FIFO services requests according to their arrival order. In particular, Jacobson and Wilkes [12] proposed a highly efficient single-disk scheduling algorithm called *Shortest-Access-Time-First* (SATF) and a starvation-free variant, in which a request with the smallest access time is serviced first. They showed that SATF is superior than many traditional algorithms, such as SCAN, C-SCAN, SSTF, FIFO, etc, in terms of throughput. Methods are proposed to derive formula for the rotation delay and seek time for any disk. Andrews, et a., [1] showed that the optimization problem for single disk scheduling is an asymmetric traveling salesman problem and provided approximation algorithms.

Traditional disk scheduling algorithms aim at maximizing the disk throughput. They may not be suitable to multimedia applications where the requests have response-time constraints. Reddy and Wyllie [17] are few of the first researchers [2,3,5,7,10,17] who explored the tradeoff of seek-optimization techniques (such as C-SCAN) and deadline-driven scheduling techniques (such as the earliest-deadline-first algorithm [14]). They showed that a proper combination of the seek-optimization techniques and the deadline-driven scheduling algorithms, such as SCAN plus the earliest-deadline-first algorithm (EDF), did service a good number of video streams and have good response time. Abbott and Garcia-Molina [2] proposed a SCAN-like deadline-driven algorithm. The algorithm first picks up a request with the closest deadline and then services all requests residing at cylinders between the current cylinder and the cylinder of the request with the closest deadline. Chang, et al [5] proposed a deadline-monotonic SCAN algorithm which guarantee hard deadlines of disk access, where the workload distribution (such as deadlines, disk addresses, etc) of disk access is known. Chen and Little [8] explored storage allocation policies over single-disk storage multimedia systems. Media objects were interleaved within a block to maintain timing among the objects during data storage and retrieval. The goal is to minimize disk seek latency in playing back multiple multimedia sessions. Oyang, et al. [18] considered a group of multimedia storage servers over Ethernet to deliver video streams in an on-time fashion. A disk placement policy with a derived disk bandwidth was proposed. Escobar-Molano and Ghandeharizadeh [16] considers the display of structured video. A pre-reading technique was proposed to retrieve objects in a structured video when disk bandwidth was not enough. Stringent timing constraints were imposed on the system as hard deadlines.

Although researchers have proposed various excellent algorithms for single disk scheduling, little work has been done for real-time multiple-disk scheduling, especially for RAID storage systems. In particular, Weikum and Zabback [24] studied the impacts of stripping size on RAID concurrency and performance. Cheng, et al. [6] proposed to synchronize all disks for real-time RAID scheduling. Sequential access is favored, at the cost of random access. The goal of this research is to explore real-time disk scheduling for high-performance I2O RAID-0 storage systems, where RAID-0 stands for an array of independent disks with a block-stripping scheme. We shall focus on the design of high-performance I/O subsystems under disk scheduling and refer interesting readers to many excellent work on storage placement policies, e.g., [8,9,22]. We are interested in disk scheduling algorithm which must not only maximize the I/O performance, e.g., in terms of throughput or response time, but also minimize the number of requests which miss their deadlines. In particular, we consider a commercial product AC-ARD AEC 6850, which is a high-performance I2O RAID-0 adaptor released to the market in 2000 by the ACARD Corp, and it can manage up to 75 hard disks and contain 5 SCSI adaptors.

In this paper, we first illustrate the system architecture of I2O devices. We then propose a request-based multi-disk scheduling algorithm called *Least-Remaining-Request-Size-First* (LRSF), which can be integrated with any real-time/non-real-time single-disk scheduling algorithm, such as SSTF and SCAN. We extend LRSF by considering aging issues and SCAN-like disk scheduling schemes. In order to further boost the performance of I2O RAID-0 devices, we explore pre-fetching with and without enough caching memory. The proposed algorithms and methodologies are evaluated by a series of experiments using both randomly generated workloads and realistic workloads, for which we have obtained very encouraging results.

The major contributions are two-fold: (1) We consider real-time RAID-0 scheduling under the important I2O system architecture. The idea of *Least-Remaining-Request-Size-First* is proposed to improve the performance of I2O

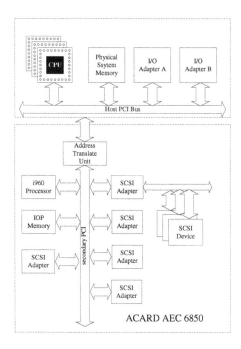

Fig. 1. An I2O hardware architecture

RAID-0 devices for systems which require high-performance storage systems, such as multimedia applications. (2) We extend LRSF-based scheduling to resolve aging issues and for SCAN-like disk service. We also explore pre-fetching under I2O RAID-0 devices, which are shown pretty effective in further improving the I/O system performance. We must emphasize that the disk scheduling problem and approaches considered in this paper are very practical, while not much real-time disk scheduling work has been done in the past, especially for RAID devices.

The rest of this paper is organized as follows: Section 2 illustrates the I2O system architecture and its RAID implementation. Section 3 first defines I2O RAID-0 requests and the performance goal. We then provide motivation for this research and propose our methodologies for multi-disk scheduling. The proposed methodologies are later extended to resolve aging issues and for SCAN-like disk service. We then address pre-fetching for I2O RAID-0 devices. Section 4 is for performance evaluation. Section 5 is the conclusion.

2   Intelligent Input/Output System Architecture

2.1   Intelligent Input/Output Architecture

An I/O interface provides a standard and uniform way for applications to access I/O devices. It defines I/O system calls and lets applications indirectly invoke vendor-supplied drivers to program the corresponding controllers/adaptors, and the controllers/adaptors control devices to accomplish I/O transfers. The Intelligent I/O (I2O) specifications [11] are proposed by major players in the industry as a standard for the next-generation I/O subsystems. We illustrate the architecture of the I2O specifications by an example product ACARD AEC 6850, which is to be released to the market in 2000 by the ACARD Corp. ACARD AEC 6850 is an I2O RAID adaptor, which can manage up to 75 hard disks, where RAID stands for the redundant array of independent disks. Its hardware architecture is as shown in Figure 1. There are two major components: Host and Target. A host can be any PC running a popular OS such as Microsoft Windows 2000. The host can have other I/O adaptors for other I/O devices. The target is an I2O adaptor, such as ACARD AEC 6850 in this example. The interface between the I2O adaptor and the host is currently defined as a PCI bus. ACARD AEC 6850 has an embedded processor, such as Intel i960, memory, and up to 5 SCSI adaptors. Each SCSI adaptor may be connected to 15 disks. (Note that IDE disks might be adopted in similar products.) The memory space of an I2O adaptor can be mapped to the memory address domain of the host so that the host and the target can communicate using DMA.

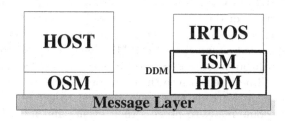

Fig. 2. I2O driver modules

The I2O architecture splits drivers into two parts: OS-Specific Module (OSM) and Device Driver Module (DDM), as shown in Figure 2. OSM is implemented at the host side, and DDM is at the target side. OSM provides an interface to the host operating system and is usually supplied by OS vendors. OSM communicates with DDM via messages (on the top of a PCI bus). An I2O real-time operating system (IRTOS) (and its related programs) runs on the I2O adaptor's processor to receive I/O requests from the host via OSM and schedules disk services. All disk operations are initiated by invoking the appropriate DDM handler functions. DDM may consist of two parts: Intermediate Service Module (ISM) and Hardware Device Module (HDM). HDM contains hardware-specific code to manage device controllers, and ISM lets hardware vendors add more functionality to plain devices (stacked over HDM), e.g., having real-time disk scheduling or resource management [11].

2.2   Intelligent Input/Output RAID

I2O devices are designed to fulfill the demand of high-performance I/O, and one of the most important applications is I2O RAID's. An I2O RAID device, such as ACARD AEC 6850, may need to manage a number of disks with data stripping technology. In particular, we are interested in RAID-0, in which data are stripped in units of blocks such that an I/O request may be serviced by several disks simultaneously. For the purpose of this section, an I/O request is tentatively defined as a collection of i jobs (for $i \geq 1$), which may be serviced by different disks (I/O requests will be formally defined in Section 3.2.1).

We shall illustrate the system operation in terms of an I2O RAID-0 device with four disks. According to the I2O specifications, there is an event queue for the entire RAID device and each of its disks, as shown in Figure 3. Each of the queues is a priority queue, where event priorities are determined by applications (via OSM). An IRTOS (and its related programs) is an event-triggered system. When the host issues an I/O request via OSM, the request is transformed into a message and inserted into the corresponding message queue, as shown in Figure 4. The message insertion will trigger the execution of the corresponding system thread to process the message and insert an event into the event queue for the entire RAID device, as shown in Figure 3. The event carries all of the necessary information for the I/O request received via OSM. In general, there is a thread associated with each event queue. The event insertion will trigger the execution of the thread assigned to the RAID device event queue. As a result, the I/O request will be decomposed into a collection of jobs, and an event for each of the jobs will be inserted into the event queue of the corresponding disk, as shown in Figure 3. Threads which are assigned to the event queues of the disks will then become ready to process their events and invoke DDM handler functions to initiate I/O operations.

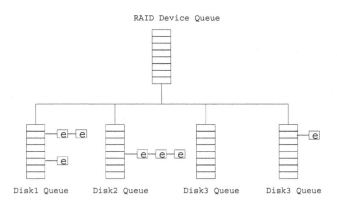

Fig. 3. The event flow in an I2O RAID-0 device

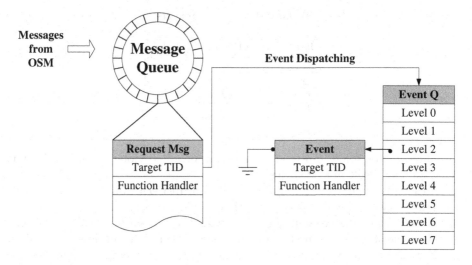

Fig. 4. Message dispatching in an I2O RAID-0 device

3 Real-Time I2O RAID-0 Scheduling

3.1 Motivation

An important objective of I2O RAID devices is to push down the I/O functionality to a lower level, i.e., the I2O controller level, such that high-performance storage devices can be obtained. In this paper, we are interested in I2O RAID devices, in which multiple disks are adopted to maximize the I/O bandwidth. Disks with/without internal scheduling, such as SCSI and IDE disks, are potential drives for our target I2O RAID devices. Our objective is to propose an effective scheduling framework for multiple-disk scheduling such that the deadlines of requests are satisfied, and their response times are minimized.

Data stripping is a popular technology to distribute data over multiple disks to utilize parallelism to maximize I/O bandwidth. Under the I2O specifications, each I/O request has a reasonable deadline, and an I/O request may be up to $4GB$ (the byte count is of 4 bytes in *BsaBlockRead request message*) [11]. In other words, a request may consist of a collection of jobs executing on several disks. The deadline setting of an I/O request depends on many factors, such as the type of the request, request slack (called TimeMultiplier in the I2O specifications), etc. For example, the deadline of a read (and write) request is defined as $TimeMultiplier \times (RWVTimeoutBase + (RWVTimeout \times size/64K))$, where $RWVTimeoutBase$ and $RWVTimeout$ are two constants set by OSM during system initialization, and $size$ and $TimeMultiplier$ are the byte count and the slack of the I/O request, respectively. The deadline of a cache flush request or a device reset request for a specified DDM is defined as $TimeMultiplier \times timeout\_Base$, where $timeout\_Base$ is another constant set by OSM during system initialization. The deadlines of I/O requests are, in general, soft deadlines

Table 1. I/O job parameters.

Jobs	Time to Process Each Job
$J_{1,1}$	$13ms$
$J_{2,1}$	$9ms$
$J_{3,1}$	$12ms$
$J_{3,2}$	$12ms$

although, under some implementations, any deadline violation of certain I/O requests may result in system reset.

Although various real-time and non-real-time disk scheduling algorithms have been proposed for single-disk systems, they may not be suitable to the scheduling of requests which involve multiple disks. Figure 5 shows a schedule of two disks based on the shortest job first algorithm (SJF), where SJF services the smallest job first. We ignore the seek time and rotation delay of jobs for the simplicity of idea presentation. Let $J_{i,j}$ denotes the j_{th} job of the i_{th} I/O request, and their job sizes are listed in Table 1. The average response time is $18.33ms$, where the response time of a request is the maximum response time of its jobs, e.g., $(25+9+21)/3$. As astute readers may point out, since $J_{3,2}$ already has a lengthy response time, it makes no sense to schedule $J_{3,1}$ before $J_{1,1}$. After switching the executions of $J_{1,1}$ and $J_{3,1}$, as shown in Figure 6, the average response time becomes $15.67ms$, e.g., $(13+9+25)/3$. This observation underlies the objective of this research.

We must point out that past work on real-time or non-real-time disk scheduling has been focused on pushing the performance of a single disk (in terms of throughput or response time). Although it is still highly important to maximize the performance of each disk in multi-disk scheduling, the consideration of each request as a logical unit is of paramount importance to maximize the performance of multi-disk devices, such as I2O RAID-0 devices. Nevertheless, we must emphasize that any disk scheduling algorithm which considers the (request) relationship among jobs over multiple disks should not sacrifice the performance of individual disk too much. A compromise between request-based multi-disk scheduling and single-disk scheduling must be achieved. In the following sections, we shall propose a framework to request-based multi-disk scheduling to improve soft real-time performance of the I/O sub-systems.

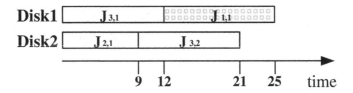

Fig. 5. A shortest-job-first schedule over two disks

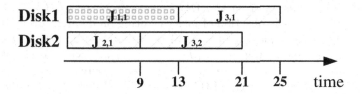

Fig. 6. A shortest-job-first schedule over three disks

3.2 Real-Time Multi-disk Scheduling

System Model for I2O RAID-0. Each I/O request on an I2O RAID-0 can be modeled by four parameters $r_i = (arr_i, LBA_i, s_i, d_i)$, where arr_i, LBA_i, s_i, and d_i are the arrival time, the starting logical block address (LBA), the size in bytes, and the deadline of the I/O request r_i, respectively. With block stripping, an I2O adaptor must re-number the logical block addresses of blocks over its disks, as shown in Figure 7, where the logical block address starts with 0. Suppose that there are N disks managed by the I2O adaptor, and the *block stripe size* (or *physical block size*) be B. A common approach is to assign the j_{th} LBA of the i_{th} disk as the $(N * B * \lfloor (j/B) \rfloor + (i-1) * B + (j\%B))_{th}$ LBA of the I2O device (for $0 \le j \le Max\_LBA\_Disk_i$ and $1 \le i \le N$), where an I2O device is defined as an I2O adaptor and its managed disks, and % is a mod operator. For example, under the LBA re-numbering scheme of the ACARD AEC 6850 I2O RAID-0 devices, the block stripe size is 32 sectors, and each sector on an ordinary PC disk is $512B$. The LBA number of a block for an I2O device is called a *I2O LBA number* or LBA number, when there is no ambiguity. The LBA number of a block for a disk (managed by the I2O adaptor) is called a *real LBA number*.

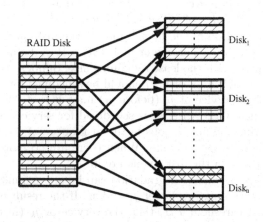

Fig. 7. The block stripping of a RAID-0 device

The four parameters of an I2O I/O request $r_i = (arr_i, LBA_i, s_i, d_i)$ can be further abstracted as a collection of jobs executing on different disks (or a single disk job if the I/O request is of a small size). That is, an I2O I/O request r_i can be re-defined as a tuple $(arr_i, \{J_{i,1}, \cdots, J_{i,n_i}\}, d_i)$, where each job $J_{i,j}$ has a disk number $dsk_{i,j}$ to execute the job, a size in bytes $s_{i,j}$, and a real LBA number $RLBA_{i,j}$ as its starting LBA on its assigned disk. The completion time of an I2O I/O request r_i is the maximum of the completion time of all of its jobs. Therefore, in order to meet the deadline of the I2O I/O request r_i, every job $J_{i,j}$ must complete the I/O access of $s_{i,j}$ bytes (starting from the real LBA address $RLBA_{i,j}$ on disk $dsk_{i,j}$) no later than the deadline d_i.

In this paper, we shall first propose the concept of request-based multi-disk scheduling and then present our methods for pre-fetching and aging issues.

Least-Remaining-Request-Size-First Scheduling - A Multi-Disk Scheduling Framework. The purpose of this section is to propose the idea of request-based multi-disk scheduling called *Least-Remaining-Request-Size-First scheduling* (LRSF). The objective is to speed up the service of the request with the least remaining jobs (or size) and, at the same time, to minimize the performance degradation of each individual disk. One major side-effect of LRSF is on the synchronization of jobs belonging to the same request. (We shall discuss the handling of large-size requests and the aging issue later.)

Let an I2O device manage N disks, and each disk be associated with a queue of pending jobs. Each individual disk is scheduled by a single-disk scheduling algorithm, such as SCAN, SSTF, EDF, etc, where the earliest deadline first (EDF) algorithm schedules jobs in the order of their deadlines. The queue of each disk is ordered according to its single-disk scheduling algorithm. Note that SCAN (/C-SCAN) mentioned in this paper is, in fact, LOOK (/C-LOOK), where LOOK (/C-LOOK) is a variation of SCAN (/C-SCAN), except that SCAN (/C-SCAN) always moves the read/write head from one end of a disk to the other end. LOOK (/C-LOOK) only moves the read/write head as far as the last request in each direction [21]. The idea of LRSF is as follows:

Let J_i be the collection of the first R jobs in the disk queue of the i_{th} disk, where R is called the *range* parameter of LRSF. Let j_k be a job in J_i and be belonging to a request with the least remaining size. Suppose that j_1 is the first job in the disk queue of the i_{th} disk. j_1 should be scheduled for service on the i_{th} disk if j_1 is j_k, or the service of j_k (before j_1) may degrade the performance of the i_{th} disk too much. Otherwise, j_k is scheduled for service. After the service, the next job following the first R jobs in the disk queue of the i_{th} disk joins J_i, and the job scheduling repeats again. When there are no more than R jobs in the disk queue, all jobs in the disk queue are in J_i.

The amount of performance degradation can be approximated by the evaluation of a value function $v(j_1, j_k)$ over j_1 and j_k. If the result of $v(j_1, j_k)$ is less than some specified threshold TH, then the service of j_k (in front of j_1) may degrade the performance of the i_{th} disk too much. For example, consider SSTF: The definition of $v(j_1, j_k)$ can be the ratio of the seek times of j_1 and j_k from the

Table 2. I/O job parameters.

Jobs	Byte Counts	Cylinder Number	Disk Number
$J_{1,1}$	512B	39	1
$J_{1,2}$	512B	39	3
$J_{2,1}$	512B	71	2
$J_{2,2}$	512B	71	3
$J_{3,1}$	512B	52	1
$J_{4,1}$	512B	62	1
$J_{4,2}$	512B	62	2
$J_{4,3}$	512B	62	3
$J_{5,1}$	512B	79	2

current r/w disk head's position. TH can be any reasonable big number (or a function of $v(j_1, j_k)$) as a threshold. In later sections, we shall address the issues in processing large-size requests.

We shall illustrate LRSF by an example:

Example 1. LRSF with SSTF:

Let an I2O RAID-0 consist of three HP97560 SCSI disks, where their rotation speed is $4,002rpm$. The seek time of the HP97560 SCSI disk can be modeled by the following formula [12,19]:

$$seek\_time(seek\_dist) = 3.24 + 0.4\sqrt{seek\_dist},$$

where $seek\_dist$ is the seek distance in terms of cylinder numbers. The transfer time of a sector, which is equal to $512B$, is approximated as $0.23ms$ (i.e., time to scan over a sector). Suppose that the disk r/w heads of the three disks are originally located at cylinder numbers 55, 75, and 65, respectively, and all of the disk arms are traveling towards smaller cylinder numbers initially.

Suppose that there are five requests with their byte counts, cylinder number, and disk assignments listed in Table 2. Figure 8.(a) shows the disk queues sorted according to SSTF. The response time of each job is listed in Table 3. The average response time of requests is $9.58ms$.

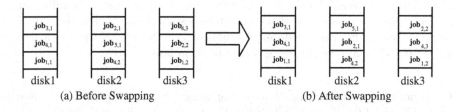

(a) Before Swapping   (b) After Swapping

Fig. 8. SSTF schedules with/without LRSF

Table 3. Response times of jobs under SSTF

Jobs in Disk1	Response Time	Jobs in Disk2	Response Time	Jobs in Disk3	Response Time
$J_{3,1}$	$3.933ms$	$J_{2,1}$	$4.04ms$	$J_{4,3}$	$3.933ms$
$J_{4,1}$	$9.091ms$	$J_{5,1}$	$8.411ms$	$J_{2,2}$	$8.373ms$
$J_{1,1}$	$13.596ms$	$J_{4,2}$	$13.301ms$	$J_{1,2}$	$13.876ms$

Table 4. Response times of jobs under LRSF-SSTF

Jobs in Disk1	Response Time	Jobs in Disk2	Response Time	Jobs in Disk3	Response Time
$J_{3,1}$	$3.933ms$	$J_{5,1}$	$4.04ms$	$J_{2,2}$	$4.220ms$
$J_{1,1}$	$8.615ms$	$J_{2,1}$	$8.411ms$	$J_{4,3}$	$8.660ms$
$J_{4,1}$	$13.773ms$	$J_{4,2}$	$12.851ms$	$J_{1,2}$	$13.818ms$

Suppose that LRSF is considered with SSTF, and that the range parameter R of LRSF is 3. Let the value function $v(j_1, j_k)$ be the ratio of the seek times of j_1 and j_k from the current r/w disk head's position, and TH be 0.75. Since $job_{3,1}$ is belonging to the request with the least remaining size on the first disk, and it is the first job in the first disk queue, $job_{3,1}$ is scheduled for service on the first disk. On the second disk, since $job_{5,1}$ is belonging to the request with the least remaining size on the second disk, and the value function $v(job_{2,1}, job_{5,1}) = \frac{4.04ms}{4.04ms} = 1$ is more than the threshold 0.75, $job_{5,1}$ is scheduled for service on the second disk, where $job_{2,1}$ is the first job in the second disk queue. On the third disk, $job_{2,2}$ and $job_{1,2}$ are both belonging to requests with the least remaining size on the third disk. Since $job_{2,2}$ is in front of $job_{1,2}$, $job_{2,2}$ is considered for servicing first. Because the value function $v(job_{4,3}, job_{2,2}) = \frac{3.93ms}{4.21ms} = 0.933$ is more than the threshold 0.75, $job_{2,2}$ is scheduled for service on the third disk, where $job_{4,3}$ is the first job in the third disk queue. The response time of each job under LRSF-SSTF is listed in Table 4, and the disk queues sorted according to LRSF-SSTF are shown in Figure 8.(b). The average response time of all requests is now 8.79ms, which is about 8% improvement in the average response time. □

3.3   Extensions: On-the-Way Scheduling and Aging Resolution

This section is meant to extend the proposed real-time disk scheduling algorithm by further considering disk characteristics and aging issues. We shall first integrate an on-the-way scheduling mechanism [12] (for SCAN-like service) with LRSF and then resolve the aging and starvation issues.

On-The-Way Scheduling. One major reason for the superior performance of SCAN and LOOK, especially when the workload is heavy, is because these algorithms always service jobs collectively on their trips without moving the disk head a lot. That is also the main reason why many real-time scheduling

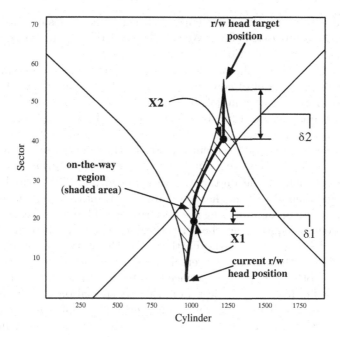

Fig. 9. The on-the-way region.

algorithms, such as EDF, do not perform well in general, when they are directly applied in disk scheduling.

The purpose of this section is to integrate the *Piggy-Back* concept, which was originally proposed to resolve the starvation problem in non-real-time single-disk scheduling, with LRSF to improve their performance and to resolve the starvation problems of large-size requests. We shall use the following example to illustrate the idea of "on-the-way" scheduling.

Let the current disk r/w head stay at the 975th cylinder and the 4th sector, as shown in Figure 9[1]. Because the disk r/w head needs acceleration in moving across cylinders, the two symmetric curves with the same ending point at the current cylinder in Figure 9 show the time needed to travel between the current cylinder and any target cylinder in terms of sectors. Suppose that the disk scheduler decides that the next job to service stays at the 1250th cylinder and the 55th sector. As shown in Figure 9, when the disk r/w head moves from the 975th cylinder to the 1250th cylinder, the disk r/w head would travel from the 4th sector to the 40th sector, because the disk keeps rotating. In order to go to the target position, the disk r/w head needs to wait until the disk rotates from the 40th sector to the 55th sector. Since the time to travel from the current position to the target position is the same as that from the latter to the former, the shaded area shown in Figure 9 denotes the collection of all blocks which can

---

[1] A similar figure appears in [12].

be serviced on the way from the current disk r/w head position to the target position without any extra effort. We call the shaded area the *on-the-way* region from the current head position to the target position.

Distinct from LRSF, the on-the-way concept (i.e., the *Piggy-Back* concept) provides a different level of consideration for disk scheduling. As the disk r/w head moves from the current job to the next job (i.e., from the current head position to the target position) based on LRSF and any single-disk scheduling algorithm such as EDF (abbreviated as EDF/LRSF), all the jobs which fall in the on-the-way region from the current job to the next job are serviced along the way, regardless of their remaining request size and job priorities.

The integration of the on-the-way mechanism and LRSF (and other single disk scheduling algorithm) has three major advantages: (1) The on-the-way mechanism may help in improving the performance of large-size requests because jobs of large-size requests may be serviced along the way when the disk is servicing jobs of small-size requests. Furthermore, the starvation problem may be minimized indirectly because the remaining sizes of the large-size requests may be reduced as other requests are serviced. Note that under LRSF, large-size requests may suffer from bad services and probably starvation. (2) The on-the-way mechanism can also help in improving the performance of real-time single-disk scheduling algorithms such as EDF. Note that with the on-the-way mechanism, EDF may service jobs collectively, similar to LOOK and C-LOOK, without moving the disk r/w head a lot. For example, on the way from the current job to the target job, EDF may service jobs X_1 and X_2 along the way, even though they may be belonging to large-numbered classes or have low priorities. (3) The on-the-way mechanism may even improve the performance of non-real-time requests without sacrificing real-time services, where non-real-time requests usually suffer from less attention in servicing.

Aging Effects. Although the on-the-way mechanism may help in resolving the starvation problem of large-size requests, there is still a chance that some large-size requests still suffer from starvation during a heavy disk workload if the jobs of some large-size requests may be located at cylinders which are always outside the on-the-way regions of small-size requests' jobs. The starvation problem is particularly serious when LRSF is used with some other single-disk scheduling algorithms which already suffer from the starvation problem, such as SSTF. Requests may starve from services when single-job requests or requests which have jobs located at cylinders close to the current head position keep coming, and the disk r/w head never has a chance to move towards the jobs of starved (larger-size) requests. Consequently, the large-size requests will have higher probability of missing their deadlines.

A simple but effective approach to resolve the starvation problem is to move jobs of those larger-size (or starved) requests forward (in starvation-oriented services, such as SSTF) such that their services can be delivered. We can upgrade the priorities/queue positions of (large-size) requests which have not been serviced for a specified amount of time. If a large-size (or starved) request is not serviced for a long time, it will be kept upgrading. Sooner or later, jobs of starved requests will be at the beginning of disk queues and receive immediate services.

3.4   Pre-fetching for I2O RAID-0 Devices

An I2O RAID-0 device may be equipped with a large amount of memory for pre-fetching or only a small amount of memory barely enough for its system operation. This section is meant to explore pre-fetching in both cases. We must emphasize that pre-fetching at the I2O RAID-0 level offers a different kind of performance improvement, compared to the pre-fetching at the OS and disk-drive levels. With the knowledge of the RAID configuration and workloads of different disks, different disks may be initiated in parallel to do pre-fetching. There are two ways for pre-fetching disk data into the memory. First, if the disk workload is not very heavy, a smart way of pre-fetching at the I2O level may utilize the disks, which may otherwise be idle, for pre-fetching. In this way, pre-fetching may be achieved almost "free" in many cases. Of course, the service of the disk cannot be interrupted while pre-fetching is performing. Therefore, if there is a new request entering into the system when the disk is servicing a prefetch command. The disk will not service the request until the prefetching is completed. In this situation, the performance of random access will be degraded. Second, we can use the on-the-way (OTW) region to service prefetch commands. This method needs more cost, because the prefetch commands, the large size requests and the non-real time requests will compete for the OTW service.

When an I2O RAID-0 device is equipped with a large amount of memory for pre-fetching, the pre-fetching can be done very intuitively: A segment of memory may be allocated as a buffering region. When a request r_i requests to access s_i bytes starting from the I2O LBA number lba_i, the I2O RAID-0 may soon issue another request r_i^{next} to access s_i bytes starting from the I2O LBA number $(lba_i + s_i)$. The deadline of r_i^{next} can be twice of the deadline of r_i. The buffering region can be managed under popular memory management schemes, such as the least-recently-used (LRU) or FIFO schemes, where the LRU scheme always selects the least recently used buffer for replacement.

When an I2O RAID-0 device is only equipped with a small amount of memory barely enough for its system operation, pre-fetching is still possible. Pre-fetching can be done by issuing SCSI commands, such as "PRE-FETCH" (the 0x34 SCSI command), so that disk drives are given hints to try to cache sectors (at disk drives' internal cache) which might be accessed later.

With a more powerful processor such as ARM, it is possible to run a more complicated pre-fetching algorithm inside an I2O RAID-0 device: For example, when a disk is idle, it is possible to pre-fetch some sectors whose I2O LBA numbers are close to the I2O LBA numbers of existing requests. As a result, in an ideal case, an application may never need to wait for disk operations to retrieve data. It might happen that, when an application sequentially reads data in the I2O LBA number order, disks always finish pre-fetching in time in obtaining data needed by the application.

Table 5. The value function of each algorithm.

Algorithm	Value Function $v(j_1, j_k)$	Threshold TH	Remark
EDF	$(deadline_1/deadline_k)$	0.6	ratio of request deadlines
SATF	$(access\_time_1/access\_time_k)$	0.8	ratio of access times
FIFO	$(arrival\_time_1/arrival\_time_k)$	0.0	ratio of arrival times
C-LOOK	$(seek\_time_1/seek\_time_k)$	0.1	ratio of seek times
SSTF	$(seek\_time_1/seek\_time_k)$	0.1	ratio of seek times

Table 6. Simulation Benchmarks: WinBench98, Simulation Time = 100 seconds.

Name	characteristics	Remark
Business	good locality, large request size	applications, such as graphic play back software such as Adobe PhotoShop and database applications
High End	good locality, small request size	applications, such as Visual C++

4 Performance Evaluation

4.1 Performance Metrics and Data Sets

The experiments described in this section are meant to assess the capability of the LRSF multi-disk scheduling framework, the on-the-way mechanism (OTW), and the pre-fetching mechanism in scheduling I2O RAID-0 requests. We have implemented a simulation model for an I2O RAID-0 device under realistic benchmarks and randomly generated workloads. We compare the performance of the earliest deadline first algorithm (EDF), Shortest Access Time First (SATF) [12], and some well-known disk scheduling algorithms, such as FIFO, C-LOOK, and SSTF, with or without the LRSF framework.

Table 5 shows the value function and the threshold of the LRSF framework for each simulated algorithm. The value function of each algorithm was defined based on its individual scheduling discipline. The threshold for an algorithm was defined based on a series of experiments to optimize LRSF for each algorithm. In general, a highly efficient single-disk scheduling algorithm, such as SATF, usually has a larger threshold to prevent LRSF from carelessly swapping jobs in queues.

Since we are interested in disk scheduling where the requests have soft real-time constraints, the primary performance metric used are the miss ratio and the average response time of the requests *AVG_Resp*. Note that in a soft real-time system, a request still has some value even after its deadline. Miss ratio is defined as the ratio of requests that their miss deadlines. Let num_i and $miss_i$ be the total number of requests and deadline violations during an experiment, respectively. *Miss Ratio* is calculated as $\frac{miss_i}{num_i}$.

There are two parts in the simulation experiments. The first one uses randomly generated workloads to evaluate the capability of LRSF and OTW in minimizing the miss ratio and the average response time of requests. The second part is based on real benchmarks, as shown in Table 6, to assess the performance improvement of pre-fetching. Note that disk-scheduling algorithms with

Table 7. Simulation Parameters.

Parameters	Value	Remark
Request Deadline Slack	$(1, 30)$	That is "TimeMultiplier"
RWVTimeoutBase	6.0	
RWVTimeout	0.1	
Arrival Pattern	Poisson Distribution	mean $= (3, 7)$
Block Stripe Size	32 sectors	1 sector $= 512B$
LBA Range	$(0, 100000)$	
Request Size	$(1, 512)$	unit: sector
Number of Disks	4	
Sustained Transfer Rate	$2MB/seconds$	
Time Granularity	$1ms$	
Simulation Time	$100 seconds$	

pre-fetching should only be evaluated under realistic workloads to have a meaningful performance comparison. Two major disk benchmarks were adopted: They are "Business" and "High-End" workloads under WinBench98 [4]. The "Business" workload stands for applications such as databases and graphic play back software such as Adobe PhotoShop, and the "High-End" workload stands for applications such as Visual C++. The randomly generated data sets were generated based on the parameters of real disks HP 97560 [12,19] and a commercial I2O product ACARD AEC 6850. The deadlines of requests were calculated based on the I2O specifications, where $TimeMultiplier$ ranged from 1 to 30. The deadline of a request was defined as $TimeMultiplier \times (RWVTimeoutBase + (RWVTimeout \times size/64K))$. The arrivals of requests followed the Poisson distribution with a mean ranging from $3ms$ to $7ms$. Each request may request data of a size ranging from 1 sector to 512 sectors. The block strip size (or physical block size) is 32 sectors. Four HP97560 SCSI disks were adopted, and their sustained transfer rate was $2MB/seconds$. The simulation time was $100,000ms$. The simulation parameters are summarized in Table 7.

4.2   Experimental Results

Randomly Generated Data. Figure 10.a and 10.b show the miss ratio and the average response time of requests under EDF with/without LRSF and OTW. EDF with LRSF and OTW (EDF/LRSF-OTW) and EDF with LRSF (EDF/LRSF) greatly out-performed EDF when the workload is heavy. For example, when the inter-arrival time of requests was $4ms$, EDF/LRSF-OTW improved EDF by 65% and 25% in terms of the average response time and the miss ratio, respectively. When the inter-arrival time of requests was large, e.g., $7ms$, LRSF and OTW still improved the performance of EDF significantly in terms of average response time although the miss ratios were similar.

Figure 11.a and 11.b show the miss ratio and the average response time of requests under SATF with/without LRSF and OTW. When the inter-arrival time of requests decreased from $7ms$ to $3ms$, the performance difference among SATF

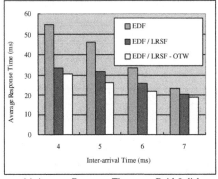 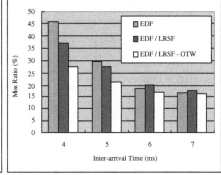

(a) Average Response Time over Raid-0 disks   (b) Miss Ratio over Raid-0 disks

Fig. 10. The miss ratio and the average response time of EDF with/without LRSF and OTW

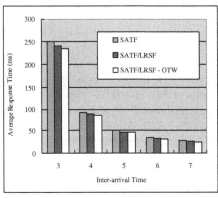 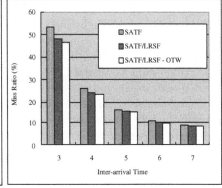

(a) Average Response Time over Raid-0 disks   (b) Miss Ratio over Raid-0 disks

Fig. 11. The miss ratio and the average response time of SATF with/without LRSF and OTW

with LRSF and OTW (SATF/LRSF-OTW), SATF with LRSF (SATF/LRSF), and SATF without LRSF (SATF) gradually increased. When the system workload was low, e.g., $7ms$, every SATF-based algorithm did equally well. We must point out that SATF is a very effective disk scheduling algorithm. That is why less improvement was achieved. Note that in [12], SATF was shown being superior than many traditional algorithms, such as SCAN, C-SCAN, SSTF, FIFO, etc. In general, SATF/LRSF improved SATF by around 5% in terms of average response time and by around 10% in terms of miss ratio when the workload is heavy. SATF/LRSF-OTW improved SATF/LRSF again by less than 5% in terms of average response time and by around 3% in terms of miss ratio. Totally, SATF/LRSF-OTW improved SATF by around 10% in terms of average response time and by around 13% in terms of miss ratio when the inter-arrival rate was

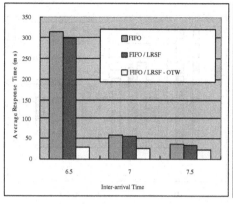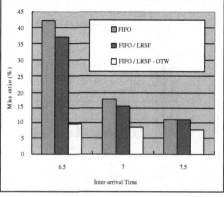

(a) Average Response Time over Raid-0 disks   (b) Miss Ratio over Raid-0 disks

Fig. 12. The miss ratio and the average response time of FIFO with/without LRSF and OTW

no more than $4ms$. The improvement of LRSF on SATF was not as large as that on EDF because SATF had better optimization on disk access time.

Figure 12.a and 12.b show the miss ratio and the average response time of requests under FIFO with/without LRSF and OTW. The inter-arrival time of requests ranged from $7.5ms$ to $6.5ms$, instead of from $7ms$ to $3ms$. It was because the performance of FIFO was very bad when the workload was heavy, e.g., $< 6ms$. From the figures, we can see that, in general, FIFO/LRSF improved FIFO by around 5% in terms of average response time and by around 12% in terms of miss ratio (when the inter-arrival time was no more than $7ms$). FIFO/LRSF-OTW improved FIFO/LRSF significantly (by around $1,100\%$) in terms of average response time and (by around 300%) in terms of miss ratio when the inter-arrival time was $6.5ms$. It was clear that LRSF slightly improved FIFO, and OTW improved the performance of FIFO significantly because of the SCAN-like service scheme under OTW.

Figure 13.a and 13.b show the miss ratio and the average response time of requests under C-LOOK with/without LRSF and OTW. The inter-arrival time of requests ranged from $7ms$ to $4ms$, instead of from $7ms$ to $3ms$, because the system was overloaded when the inter-arrival time was $3ms$. In general, LRSF improved the miss ratio of C-LOOK but at the cost of average response time. It was because LRSF might skip requests on the way from one side of the disk to the other side under C-LOOK. This affected the efficiency of the C-LOOK algorithm. Figure 13.a and 13.b show that OTW improved the performance of an I2O disk significantly because OTW also considered the optimization of rational delay, while C-LOOK only considered seek time. C-LOOK with LRSF and OTW had the best performance, compared to other combinations of C-LOOK, LRSF, and OTW. C-LOOK/LRSF-OTW improved the average response time and the miss ratio of C-LOOK by around 1100% and 40%, respectively.

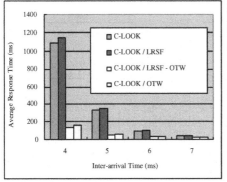 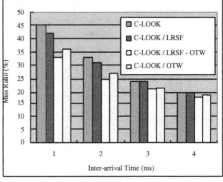

(a) Average Response Time over Raid-0 disks   (b) Miss Ratio over Raid-0 disks

Fig. 13. The miss ratio and the average response time of C-LOOK with/without LRSF and OTW

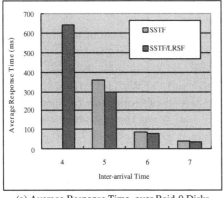 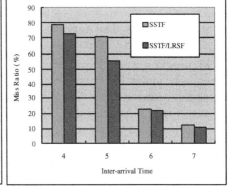

(a) Average Response Time over Raid-0 Disks   (b) Miss Ratio over Raid-0 Disks

Fig. 14. The miss ratio and the average response time of SSTF with/without LRSF and OTW

Figure 14.a and 14.b show the miss ratio and the average response time of requests under SSTF with/without LRSF. Since SSTF was not compatible with OTW (because there was virtually nothing in the on-the-way region between the current disk head and the shortest-seek-time job), SSTF was not simulated with OTW. The inter-arrival time of requests ranged from $7ms$ to $4ms$, instead of from $7ms$ to $3ms$, because the system was overloaded under SSTF when the request inter-arrival time was $3ms$. In general, LRSF improved the performance of SSTF significantly in both miss ratio and average response time. The average improvement on average response time and miss ratio was about 20% and 12%, respectively, when the request inter-arrival time was no more than $5ms$. The average response time under SSTF, when the request inter-arrival time was $4ms$,

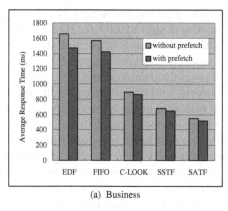
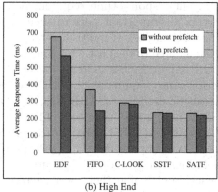

(a) Business   (b) High End

Fig. 15. The average response time of all scheduling algorithms under the WinBench98 "Business" and "High-End" workloads.

was not shown because the simulation disk queue was overflowed (where the queue has 512 entries).

WinBench98-Based Results for Pre-fetching. While the previous section explores the performance improvement of LRSF and OTW on multi-disk scheduling algorithms, the purpose of this section is to assess the performance improvement of the pre-fetching mechanism. We considered a commercial product AC-ARD AEC 6850 with four HP97560 SCSI disks. Let each disk drive have 1MB internal caching space for pre-fetching, and the I2O adaptor have no caching space. We must emphasize that if the I2O adaptor had non-zero caching space, the simulation results (to be described later) would be even better.

Figure 15.a and 15.b show the average response time of all scheduling algorithms with/without pre-fetching under the WinBench98 "Business" and "High-End" workloads, respectively. In general, SATF and SSTF out-performed other scheduling algorithms in terms of the average response time. Pre-fetching could improve the less-efficient single-disk scheduling algorithms such as EDF and FIFO significantly, e.g., about 10% improvement for EDF and FIFO under both WinBench98 "Business" and "High-End" workloads. Even for SATF and SSTF, pre-fetching improved their performance by around 4% under the "Business" workload and by around 3% under the "High-End" workload. As astute readers might point out, pre-fetching could be used with LRSF and OTW, as shown in the previous section. Similar improvement could be achieved.

5   Conclusion

There has been an increasing demand for high-performance I/O subsystems in the past decades. I2O devices are of the choices for application systems with

452 H.-W. Lo, T.-W. Kuo, and K.-Y. Lam

stringent response-time requirements, such as multimedia servers. This paper targets an important performance issue in the design of I2O RAID-0 devices, where scheduling of multi-disk requests with performance constraints has been often ignored in the past. Our goal is to improve the soft real-time performance of I2O RAID-0 devices to fit the needs of many application systems with stringent performance requirements, such as video servers, and to verify our results under a realistic product ACARD AEC 6850 and real workloads, where ACARD AEC 6850 is a high-performance I2O RAID-0 adaptor to be released to the market in 2000 by the ACARD Corp. We explore real-time multi-disk scheduling under I2O RAID-0 to improve the I/O performance in minimizing the number of deadline violations and mean response time. We illustrate the system architecture of I2O devices and define their performance goal. We propose a request-based real-time multi-disk scheduling algorithm called *Least-Remaining-Request-Size-First* (LRSF), which can be integrated with any real-time/non-real-time single-disk scheduling algorithm, such as SSTF and C-LOOK. We then explore aging issues and SCAN-like disk service. Pre-fetching is also explored under I2O RAID-0 to further improve the I/O system performance. The capability of our approach is evaluated using randomly generated and realistic workloads.

The emerging of I2O specifications provides a standard for the next-generation I/O subsystems. With major players in the industry actively involved, providing truly high-performance I2O devices is the only way to survive in the market. This work targets one of the most important issues in the design of I2O devices. For the future research, we shall explore various approximate algorithms for multi-disk and single-disk scheduling to fit different I2O RAID devices which might adopt embedded processors with different computing power. We shall also explore multi-disk scheduling for other types of I2O RAID devices, such as those for mirroring and parity-based stripping schemes.

References

1. M. Andrews, M.A. Bender, L. Zhang, "New Algorithms for the Disk Scheduling Problem," *Proceeding on the 37th Annual Symposium on Foundations of Computer Science*, 1996, pp. 550-559.
2. R.K. Abbott and H. Garcia-Molina, "Scheduling I/O Requests with Deadlines: a Performance Evaluation," *IEEE 11th Real-Time Systems Symposium,* Dec 1990, pp. 113-124.
3. J. Bruno, J. Brustoloni, E. Gabber, B. Ozden, and A. Silberschatz, "Disk Scheduling woth Quality of Service Guarantees," *IEEE International Conference on Multimedia Computing and Systems,* 1999, pp.400-405.
4. http://www.zdnet.com/etestinglabs/stories/benchmarks/0,8829,2326114,00.html
5. R.-I. Chang, W.-K. Shih, and R.-C. Chang, "Deadline-Modification-SCAN with Maximum-Scannable-Groups for Multimedia Real-Time Disk Scheduling," *IEEE 19th Real-Time Systems Symposium*, December 1998, pp. 40-49.
6. P. Chang, H. Jin, X. Zhou, Q. Chen, and J. Zhang, "HUST-RAID: High Performance RAID in Real-Time System," *IEEE Pacific Rim Conference on Communication, Computers, and signal Processing,,* 1999, pp. 59-62.

7. S. Chen, J.A. Stankovic, J.F. Kurose, and D.F. Towsley, "Performance Evaluation of Two New disk scheduling Algorithms for Real-Time Systems," *Journal of Real-Time Systems*, 3(3):307-336, 1991.

8. H.J. Chen, T.D.C. Little, " Storage Allocation Policies for Time-Dependent Multimedia Data," *IEEE Transactions on Knowledge and Data Engineering*, October 1996.

9. Ed Chang and A. Zakhor, "Cost Analyses for VBR Video Servers," *IEEE Multimedia*, Fall 1996.

10. K. Hwang and H. Shih, "Real-Time Disk Scheduling Based on Urgent Group and Shortest Seek Time First," *the 5th Euromicro Workshop on Real-Time Systems*, 1993, pp. 124-130.

11. Intelligent I/O (I²O) Architecture Specifications, Ver 2.0, I²O SIG^{TM}, March 1999.

12. D.M. Jacobson and J. Wilkes, "Disk Scheduling Algorithms Based on Rotational Position," *Technical Report HPL-CSP-91-7rev1*, Hewelett-Packard Company, 1991.

13. T.-W. Kuo, Y.-H. Liu, and K.J. Lin, "Efficient On-Line Schedulability Tests for Priority Driven Real-Time Systems," *IEEE 2000 Real-Time Technology and Applications Symposium*, Washington D.C., USA, June 2000.

14. C.L. Liu and J.W. Layland, "Scheduling Algorithms for Multiprogramming in a Hard Real-Time Environment," *JACM*, Vol. 20, No. 1, January 1973, pp. 46-61.

15. D. Meliksetian, F.F.K. Yu, C.Y.R Chen, "Methodologies for Designing Video Servers", *IEEE Transcations on Multimedia*, March 2000.

16. M.L.E- Molano, S. Ghandeharizadeh, "On Coordinated Display of Structured Video", *IEEE Multimedia*, July-September 1997.

17. A.L.N. Reddy, J.C. Wyllie, "I/O Issues in a Multimedia System", *IEEE Computer*, March 1994.

18. Y.J. Oyang, C.H. Wen, C.Y. Cheng, M.H. Lee and J.T. Li, "A Multimedia Storage System for On-Demand Playback", *IEEE Transactions on Consumer Electrontics*, February 1995.

19. C. Ruemmler and J. Wilkes, "An Introduction to Disk Drive Modeling," *IEEE Computer*, March 1994, 27(3):17-29.

20. A.L. N. Reddy and J.C. Wyllie, "I/O Issues in Multimedia System," *IEEE Transactions on Computers*, March 1994.

21. A. Silberschatz P.B. Glavin and G. Gagne"Operating System Concepts,", 6th Ed., Addison Wesley, 2001.

22. S. Tsao, "A Low Cost Optical Storage Server for Near Video-on-Demand Systems," IEEE Transcation on Broadcasting, March, 2001.

23. B.L. Worthington, G.R. Ganger, Y.N. Patt, and J. Wilkes, "On- Line Extraction of SCSI Disk Drive Parameters", *ACM SIGMETRICS*, May 1995, pp. 146-156.

24. G. Weikum and P. Zabback, "Tuning of Stripping Units in Disk-Array-Based File Systems," Interoperability in Multidatabase Systems, 1991. IMS '91. Proceedings., First International Workshop on , 1991 , Page(s): 280 -287.

Database Pointers: A Predictable Way of Manipulating Hot Data in Hard Real-Time Systems*

Dag Nyström[1], Aleksandra Tešanović[2],
Christer Norström[1], and Jörgen Hansson[2]

[1] Dept. of Computer Engineering, Mälardalen University
{dag.nystrom,christer.norstrom}@mdh.se
[2] Dept. of Computer Science, Linköping University
{alete,jorha}@ida.liu.se

Abstract. Traditionally, control systems use ad hoc techniques such as shared internal data structures, to store control data. However, due to the increasing data volume in control systems, these internal data structures become increasingly difficult to maintain. A real-time database management system can provide an efficient and uniform way to structure and access data. However the drawback with database management systems is the overhead added when accessing data. In this paper we introduce a new concept called database pointers, which provides fast and deterministic accesses to data in hard real-time database management systems compared to traditional database management systems. The concept is especially beneficial for hard real-time control systems where many control tasks each use few data elements at high frequencies. Database pointers can co-reside with a relational data model, and any updates made from the database pointer interface are immediately visible from the relational view. We show the efficiency with our approach by comparing it to tuple identifiers and relational processing.

1 Introduction

In recent years, the complexity of embedded real-time controlling systems has increased. This is especially true for the automotive industry [1]. Along with this increased complexity, the amount of data that needs to be handled has grown in a similar fashion. Since data in real-time systems traditionally is handled using ad hoc techniques and internal data structures, this increase of data is imposing problems when it comes to maintenance and development.

One possible solution to these problems is to integrate an embedded real-time database management system (RTDBMS) within the real-time system. A RTDBMS can provide the real-time system with a uniform view and access of data. This is especially useful for distributed real-time systems where data is

---

* This work is supported by ARTES, a network for real-time research and graduate education in Sweden.

J. Chen and S. Hong (Eds.): RTCSA 2003, LNCS 2968, pp. 454–465, 2004.

shared between nodes. Because of the uniform access of data, the same database request is issued regardless if the data is read at the local node or from a distributed node. Furthermore, RTDBMSs can ensure consistency, both logical and temporal [2]. Finally, RTDBMSs allow so called ad hoc queries, i.e., requests for a view of data performed during run-time. This is especially useful for management and system monitoring. For example, consider a large control system being monitored from a control room. Suddenly, a temperature warning is issued. An ad hoc query showing the temperatures and pressures of multiple sub-systems might help the engineers to determine the cause of the overheating.

Integrating a RTDBMS into a real-time system also has drawbacks. There will most certainly be an added overhead for retrieving data elements. This is partly because of the indexing system used by most database management systems (DBMS). The indexing system is used to locate where in the memory a certain data element is stored. Usually, indexing systems use some tree structure, such as the B-tree [3] and T-tree [4] structures, or a hashing table [5].

An increase of the retrieval times for data has, apart from longer task execution, one additional drawback. Since shared data in a concurrent system needs to be protected using semaphores or database locking systems, the blocking factor for hot data can be significant. Hot data are data elements used frequently by multiple tasks. Hot data is sensitive to congestion and therefore it is of utmost importance to lock hot data for as short time as possible. Furthermore, it is important to bound blocking times to allow response time analysis of the system. Examples of hot data are sensor readings for motor control of a vehicle, e.g., rpm and piston position. These readings are continuously stored by I/O tasks and continuously read by controlling tasks. A congestion involving these heavily accessed data elements might result in a malfunction. On the other hand, information regarding the level in the fuel tank is not as crucial and might be accessed less frequent, and can therefore be considered non-hot data.

In this paper we propose the concept of database pointers, which is an extension to the widely used tuple identifiers [6]. Tuple identifiers contain information about the location of a tuple, typically a block number and an offset. Database pointers have the efficiency of a shared variable combined with the advantages of using a RTDBMS. They allow a fast and predictable way of accessing data in a database without the need of consulting the DBMS indexing system. Furthermore database pointers provide an interface that uses a "pointer-like" syntax. This interface is suitable for control system applications using numerous small tasks running at high frequencies. Database pointers allow fast and predictable accesses of data without violating neither temporal or logical consistency nor transaction serialization. It can be used together with the relational data model without risking a violation of the database integrity.

The paper is outlined as follows. In section 2 we describe the type of systems we are focusing on. In addition, we give a short overview of tuple identifiers and other related work. Database pointers are explained in section 3, followed by an evaluation of the concept, which is presented in section 4. In section 5 we conclude the paper.

2   Background and Related Work

This paper focuses on real-time applications that are used to control a process, e.g., critical control functions in a vehicle such as motor control and brake control. The flow of execution in such a system is: (i) periodic scanning of sensors, (ii) execution of control algorithms such as a PID-regulators, and (iii) propagation of the result to the actuators.

The execution is divided into a number of tasks, e.g., I/O-tasks and control tasks. The functions of these tasks are fixed and often limited to a specific activity. For example, an I/O-task's only responsibility could be to read the sensor-value on an input-port and write it to a specific location in memory, e.g., a shared variable [7].

In addition to these, relatively fixed control tasks, a number of management tasks exists, which are generally more flexible than the control tasks, e.g., management tasks responsible for the user interface.

2.1   Relational Query Processing

Relational query processing is performed using a data manipulation language (DML), such as SQL. A relational DML provides a flexible way of viewing and manipulating data. The backside of this flexibility is performance loss.

Figure 1 shows a typical architecture of a DBMS. The DBMS provides access to data through the SQL interface. A query, requesting value x, passed to this interface will go through the following steps:

1. The query is passed from the application to the SQL interface.
2. The SQL interface requests that the query should be scheduled by the transaction scheduler.
3. The relational query processor parses the query and creates an execution plan.
4. The locks needed to process the query are obtained by the concurrency controller.
5. The tuple containing x is located by the index manager.
6. The tuple is then fetched from the database.
7. All locks are released by the concurrency controller.
8. The result is returned to the application.

Finally, since the result from a query issued to a relational DBMS is a relation in itself, a retrieval of the data element x from the resulting relation is necessary. This is done by the application.

In this example we assume a pessimistic concurrency control policy. However, the flow of execution will be roughly the same if a different policy is used.

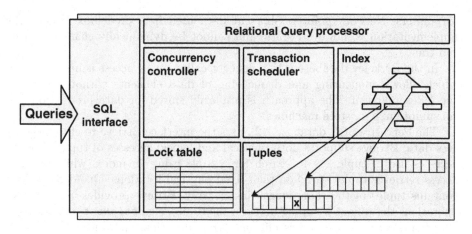

Fig. 1. Architecture of a typical Database Management System.

2.2   Tuple Identifiers

The concept of tuple identifiers was first proposed back in the 70's as internal
mechanisms for achieving fast accesses to data while performing relational operations, such as joins and unions. It was implemented by IBM in an experimental
prototype database called System R [6]. A tuple identifier is a data type containing a pointer to one tuple stored either on a hard drive or in main memory.
Usually, a tuple is a rather short array of bytes containing some data. For a
relational model, one tuple contains the data for one row of a relation.

A decade later, it was proposed in [8] that tuple identifiers could be used
directly from the application via the DBMS interface. This would enable applications to create shortcuts to hot data, in order to retrieve them faster. The
concept is also implemented in the Adabas relational DBMS [9] under the name
Adabas Direct Access Method. In Adabas, tuple identifiers are stored in a hash
table and can be retrieved by the user for direct data access. A disadvantage
of this concept is the inability to move or delete tuples at run-time. To be able
to perform deletions or movements of tuples in Adabas, a reorganization utility
must be run, during which the entire database is blocked.

Applications using tuple identifiers must be aware of the structure of the
data stored in the tuples, e.g., offsets to specific attributes in the tuple. This
makes it difficult to add or remove attributes from relations, since this changes
the structure of the tuples.

2.3   Related Work

Apart from tuple identifiers, the concept of bypassing the index system to achieve
faster data access has been recognized in other database systems. The RDM
database [10] uses a concept called network access, which consist of a network

of pointers. Network pointers shortcut data used in a predefined order. The implementation is, however, static and cannot be dynamically changed during run-time.

In the Berkeley database [11], a concept called queue access is implemented, which allows enqueueing and dequeueing of data elements without accessing the index manager. The approach is primarily suited for data production and consumption, e.g., state machines.

The Pervasive.SQL database [12], uses the interface Btrieve to efficiently access data. Btrieve supports both physical and logical accesses of tuples. Logical accesses uses a tuple key to search for a tuple using an index, while physical access retrieves tuples based on their fixed physical locations. One database file contains tuples of the same length in an array. Btrieve provides a number of operations that allows stepping between the tuples, e.g., stepNext or stepLast. The Btrieve access method is efficient for applications in which the order of accesses is predefined and the tuples are never moved during run-time. Furthermore, restructuring the data within the tuples is not possible.

Some database management systems use the concept of database cursors as a part of their embedded SQL interface [13]. Despite the syntactical similarities between database pointers and database cursors they represent fundamentally different concepts. While database cursors are used to access data elements from within query results, i.e., result-sets, database pointers are used to bypass the index system in order to make data accesses more efficient and deterministic.

3   Database Pointers

The concept of database pointers consists of four different components:

- The DBPointer data type, which is the actual pointer defined in the application.
- The database pointer table, which contains all information needed by the pointers.
- The database pointer interface, which provides a number of operations on the database pointer.
- The database pointer flag, which is used to ensure consistency in the database.

Using the concept of database pointers, the architecture of the DBMS given in figure 1, is modified to include database pointer components, as shown in figure 2. To illustrate the way database pointers work, and its benefits, we use the example presented in section 2.1, i.e., the request for retrieving the data x from the database.

Using the database pointer interface, the request could be made significantly faster and more predictable. First, a read operation together with the database pointer would be submitted to the database pointer interface. The database pointer, acting as an index to the database pointer table array would then be used to get the corresponding database pointer table entry. Each database pointer table entry consists of three fields: the physical address of data element x, information about the data type of x, and eventual locking information that shows which lock x belongs to. Next the lock would be obtained and x would be read. Finally, the lock would be released and the value of x would be returned to the calling application. The four components of the database pointer and its operations are described in detail in sections 3.1 to 3.4.

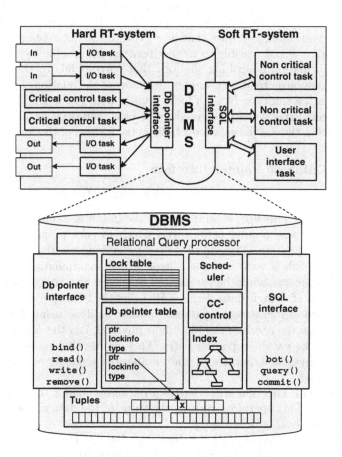

Fig. 2. Architecture of a controlling system that uses a DBMS with database pointers.

3.1   The DBPointer Data Type

The DBPointer data type is a pointer declared in the application task. When the pointer is initialized, it points to a database pointer table entry, which in its turn points to the actual data element. Hence the DBPointer could be viewed as a handle to a database pointer. However, due to the database pointer's syntactical similarities with a pointer variable, we have chosen to refer to it as a pointer.

3.2   The Database Pointer Table

The database pointer table contains all information needed for the database pointer, namely:

1. A pointer to the physical memory location of the data element inside the tuple. Typically, the information stored is the data block the tuple resides in, an offset to the tuple, and an offset to the data element within the tuple.
2. The data type of the data element pointed by the database pointer. This is necessary in order to ensure that any write to the data element matches its type, e.g., it is not feasible to write a floating point value to an integer.
3. Lock information describing the lock that corresponds to the tuple, i.e., if locking is done on relation granules, the name of the relation should be stored in as lock information. Note, if locks are not used in the DBMS, i.e., if optimistic concurrency control is used, some other serialization information can be stored in the database pointer table entry instead of the lock information.

3.3   The Database Pointer Interface

The database pointer interface consists of four operations:

1. `bind(ptr,q)` This operation initializes the database pointer *ptr* by binding it to a database pointer table entry, which in turn points to the physical address of the data. The physical binding is done via the execution of the query *q*, which is written using a logical data manipulation language, e.g., SQL. The query should be formulated in such a way that it always returns the address of a single data element. By using the bind operation, the binding of the data element to the database pointer is done using a logical query, even though the result of the binding is physical, i.e., the physical address is bound to the database pointer entry. This implies that no knowledge of the internal physical structures of the database is required by the application programmer.
2. `remove(ptr)` This operation deletes a database pointer table entry.
3. `read(ptr)` This operation returns the value of the data element pointed by *ptr*. It uses locking if necessary.
4. `write(ptr,v)` This operation writes the value *v* to the data element pointed by *ptr*. It also uses locking if necessary. Furthermore, the type information in the database pointer entry is compared with the type of *v* so that a correct type is written.

The pseudo codes for the **write** and **read** operations are shown in figure 3. The **write** operation first checks that the types of the new value matches the type of the data element (line 2), and then obtains a write lock for the corresponding lock (line 4), i.e., locks the relation that the data element resides in. The data element is then updated (line 5), and finally the lock is released (line 6). The **read** operation obtains the corresponding read lock (line 10), reads the data element (line 11), releases the lock (line 12), and then returns the value to the application (line 13).

```
1  write(DBPointer dbp, Data value){
2      if(DataTypeOf(value) != dbp->type)
3          return DATA_TYPE_MISMATCH;
4      DbGetWriteLock(dbp->lockInfo);
5      *(dbp->ptr) = value;
6      DbReleaseLock(dbp->lockInfo);
7      return TRUE;
   }

8  read(DBPointer dbp){
9      Data value;
10     DbGetReadLock(dbp->lockInfo);
11     value = *(dbp->ptr);
12     DbReleaseLock(dbp->lockInfo);
13     return value;
   }
```

Fig. 3. The pseudo codes for the **write** and **read** operations

3.4   The Database Pointer Flag

The database pointer flag solves the problem of inconsistencies between the index structure and the database pointer table, thus enabling tuples to be restructured and moved during run time.

For example, if an additional attribute is inserted into a relation, e.g., a column is added to a table, it would imply that all tuples belonging to the relation need to be restructured to contain the new data element (the new column). Hence, the size of the tuples changes, relocation of the tuples to new memory locations is most probable. Since a schema change is performed via the SQL interface, it will use and update the index in the index manager. If one of the affected tuples is also referenced from a database pointer entry, inconsistencies will occur, i.e., the database pointer entry will point to the old physical location of the tuple.

Each database pointer flag that is set in the index structure indicates that the tuple flagged is also referenced by a database pointer. This informs the index manager that if this tuple is altered, e.g., moved, deleted, or changed, the corresponding database table entry must be updated accordingly.

3.5   Application Example

To demonstrate how a real-time control system could use a RTDBMS with a database pointer interface, we provide an application example. Consider the system shown in figure 2 which is divided into two parts:

1. A hard real-time part that is performing time-critical controlling of the process. The tasks in this part use the database pointer interface.

2. A soft real-time part that handles user interaction and non-critical controlling. It uses the flexible SQL interface.

A hard real-time controlling task that reads a sensor connected to an I/O port is shown in figure 4. The task reads the current sensor value and updates the corresponding data element in the database. The task consists of two parts, an initialization part (line 2-4), which is run one time, and an infinite loop that is periodically polling the sensor and writing the value to the database (line 5-8).

The initialization of the database pointer is done by first declaring the database pointer (line 3) and then binding it to the data element containing the oil temperature in the engine (line 4). The actual binding is performed in the following four steps:

1. A new database pointer table entry is created.
2. The SQL query is executed and the address of the data element in the tuple is stored in the database pointer table entry.
3. The data type information is set to the appropriate type, e.g., **unsigned int**.
4. The locking information is set, e.g., if locking is done at relation granules, the locking information would be set to **engine**.

```
1 TASK OilTempReader(void){
2    int s;
3    DBPointer *ptr;
4    bind(&ptr, "SELECT temperature
              FROM engine WHERE
              subsystem=oil;");
5    while(1){
6      s=read_sensor();
7      write(ptr,s);
8      waitForNextPeriod();
     }
   }
```

engine

subsystem	temperature	pressure
hydraulics	42	27
oil	103	10
cooling water	82	3

Fig. 4. An I/O task that uses a database pointer and its corresponding relation.

After performing these four steps, the database pointer is initialized and ready to be used. The control loop is entered after the initialization (line 5). In the control loop a new sensor value is collected (line 6), the value is then written to the RTDBMS using the database pointer operation **write** (line 7). Finally, the task sleeps until the next period arrives (line 8).

4   Concept Evaluation

In table 1 we compare the different access methods: tuple identifiers (TiD's), database pointers (DbP's), and relational processing (Rel). Both tuple identifiers

Table 1. A comparison between tuple identifiers, database pointers, and relational processing.

Criteria		TiD's	DbP's	Rel
Interface	Pointer based	x	x	
	Relational			x
Data access	Physical	x	x	
	Logical		x	x
Characteristics	Can handle tuple movements		x	x
	Can handle attribute changes		x	x

and database pointers use a pointer based interface, which provides fast and predictable accesses to data inside a DBMS. However, it is not as flexible as most relational interfaces, e.g., SQL.

Furthermore, database pointer and tuple identifiers both access data based on direct physical references, in contrast to relational accesses that use logical indexing to locate data. However, database pointers bind the pointer to the data element using logical indexing, but access the data element using physical access.

Tuple identifiers have two drawbacks, firstly they are sensitive to schema changes, and secondly the physical structure of the database is propagated to the users. The former results in a system that can only add tuples instead of moving or deleting them, while the latter requires that the application programmer knows of the physical implementation of the database. Database pointers remove both of these drawbacks. Due to the flag in the index system, the database pointer table can be updated whenever the schema and/or index structure is changed, allowing attribute changes, tuple movements and deletions. Moreover, since the database pointer is bound directly to a data element inside the tuple instead of to the tuple itself, no internal structures are exposed.

The major advantage with accessing the data via pointers instead of going through the index system is the reduction of complexity. The complexity for the T-tree algorithm is $O(log_2n + \frac{1}{2}log_2\frac{n}{k})$, where n is the number of tuples in the system and k is the number of tuples per index node [14]. The complexity for database pointers and tuple identifier is $O(1)$. As can be seen, there is a constant execution time for accessing a data element using a database pointer or a tuple identifier, while a logarithmic relationship exists for the tree-based approach. There is however one additional cost for using the relational approach which we will illustrate with the following example.

We already showed how the oil temperature of an engine can be accessed using database pointers. Figure 5 shows the pseudo code for the same task, which now uses an SQL interface instead of the database pointer interface. In line 5, the **Begin of transaction** is issued and the actual update is performed in line 6, using a C-like syntax that resembles of the function **printf**. The actual **commit** is performed in line 7. In figure 5 all tuples in the relation **engine** have to be accessed to find all that fulfill the condition **subsystem = oil**. This requires accessing all three tuples.

```
1 TASK OilTempReader(void){
2   int s;
3   while(1){
4     s=read_sensor();
5     DB_BOT();
6     DB_Op("UPDATE engineSET temperature=%d
             WHERE subsystem = oil;",s);
7     DB_COMMIT();
8     waitForNextPeriod();
    }
  }
```

Fig. 5. An example of a I/O task that uses a Relational approach.

It can, of course, be argued that precompiled transactions would be used in a case like this. Precompiled transactions are transactions that have been evaluated and optimized pre-run time. Such transactions can be directly called upon during run-time, and is normally executed much more efficient than an ad-hoc query. However, this does not influence the number of tuples accessed, since no information of the values inside the tuples are stored there. Therefore, all three tuples have to be fetched anyway.

5   Conclusions and Future Work

In this paper we have introduced the concept of database pointers to bypass the indexing system in a real-time database. The functionality of a database pointer can be compared to the functionality of an ordinary pointer. Database pointers can dynamically be set to point at a specific data element in a tuple, which can then be read and written without violating the database consistency. For concurrent, pre-emptive applications, the database pointer mechanisms ensure proper locking on the data element.

We have also showed an example of a real-time control application using a database that supports both database pointers and a SQL interface. In this example the hard real-time control system uses database pointers, while the soft real-time management system utilizes the more flexible SQL interface.

The complexity of a database operation using a database pointer compared to a SQL query is significantly reduced. Furthermore, the response time of a database pointer operation is more predictable.

Currently we are implementing database pointers as a part of the COMET DBMS, our experimental database management system [15]. This implementation will be used to measure the performance improvement of database pointers for hard real-time controlling systems. Furthermore, different approaches for handling the interference between the hard real-time database pointer transactions and the soft real-time management transactions are investigated.

References

1. Casparsson, L., Rajnak, A., Tindell, K., Malmberg, P.: Volcano - a revolution in on-board communications. Technical report, Volvo Technology Report (1998)
2. Ramamritham, K.: Real-time databases. International Journal of distributed and Parallel Databases (1993) 199–226
3. Kuo, T.W., Wei, C.H., Lam, K.Y.: Real-Time Data Access Control on B-Tree Index Structures. In: Proceedings of the 15th International Conference on Data Engineering. (1999)
4. Lu, H., Ng, Y., Tian, Z.: T-tree or b-tree: Main memory database index structure revisited. 11th Australasian Database Conference (2000)
5. Litwin, W.: Linear hashing: A new tool for file and table addressing. In: Proceedings of the 6th International Conference on Very Large Databases. (1980)
6. Astrahan, M.M., et al.: System R: Relational Approach to Database Management. ACM Transactions on Database Systems 1 (1976) 97–137
7. Nyström, D., Tešanović, A., Norström, C., Hansson, J., Bånkestad, N.E.: Data Management Issues in Vehicle Control Systems: a Case Study. In: Proceedings of the 14th Euromicro Conference on Real-Time Systems. (2002)
8. de Riet, R.P.V., et al.: High-Level Programming Features for Improving the Efficiency of a Relational Database System. ACM Transactions on Database Systems 6 (1981) 464–485
9. Software AG / SAG Systemhaus GmbH: Adabas Database . http://www.softwareag.com (2003)
10. Birdstep Technology ASA: Rdm dbms. http://www.birdstep.com (2002)
11. Sleepycat Software Inc.: Berkeley db. http://www.sleepycat.com (2001)
12. Pervasive Software Inc.: Pervasive.sql. http://www.pervasive.com (2001)
13. Date, C.J.: An Introduction to Database Systems. Addison-Wesley (2000)
14. Lehman, T.J., Carey, M.J.: A Study of Index Structures for Main Memory Database Management Systems. In: Proceedings of the 12th Conference on Very Large Databases, Morgan Kaufmann pubs. (Los Altos CA), Kyoto. (1986)
15. Tešanović, A., Nyström, D., Hansson, J., Norström, C.: Towards Aspectual Component-Based Development of Real-Time Systems. In: Proceedings of the 9th International Conference on Real-Time and Embedded Computing Systems and Applications. (2003)

Extracting Temporal Properties from Real-Time Systems by Automatic Tracing Analysis

Andrés Terrasa[*1] and Guillem Bernat[2]

[1] Departamento de Sistemas Informáticos y Computación
Technical University of Valencia (SPAIN)
`aterrasa@dsic.upv.es`
[2] Real-Time Systems Research Group
Department of Computer Science
University of York (UK)
`bernat@cs.york.ac.uk`

Abstract. Statically analyzing real-time systems normally involves a high degree of pessimism, but it is necessary in systems requiring 100% guarantee. However, lots of less critical systems would significantly benefit from combining such static analysis with empirical tests. Empirical tests are based on observing the system at run time and extracting information about its temporal behavior. In this sense, this paper presents a generic and extensible framework that permits the extraction of temporal properties of real-time systems by analyzing their run-time traces. The analysis is based on event-recognition finite state machines that compute the temporal properties with a computational cost of $O(1)$ per observed event in most of the cases. The framework is instantiated in order to extract some typical temporal properties (such as computation time or response time of tasks), which can serve as a template to define new ones. Finally, the paper also shows how the framework can be implemented on a real system, exclusively using state-of-the-art technology; in particular, the Trace and Real-Time Extensions of the POSIX standard.

1 Introduction

One of the main problems of statically analyzing real-time systems is that it usually involves a high degree of pessimism. The typical a priori, *analytical* study of the system checks the worst-case scenario for each task against the task requirements. However, this worst-case scenario, which can make the analysis reject a task, may not actually happen at run time. For example, consider the highest priority task in a system where resources are shared by using some sort of Priority Ceiling Protocol. The worst-case blocking time of this task is the longest critical section of all the low priority tasks sharing a resource with the task. If this blocking time is too large for the task temporal requirements, then the

---

[*] This work was developed during a research stay of this author at the University of York, and partially funded by grant CTIDIB/2002/61 from the Valencian Government (Spain) and by EU funded project FIRST (IST-2001-34140).

J. Chen and S. Hong (Eds.): RTCSA 2003, LNCS 2968, pp. 466–485, 2004.
© Springer-Verlag Berlin Heidelberg 2004

task set will be rejected by the off-line analysis, even though the lower priority task may *never* happen to block the highest priority task (for example, if their periods are harmonic). In fact, the pessimism is likely to be higher, considering that techniques for calculating the critical section worst-case execution time have probably overestimated it.

Despite its inherent pessimism, this analytical study is required in systems needing 100% guarantee (such as mission-critical systems). However, lots of other less critical systems would significantly benefit from *combining* such static analysis with *empirical* tests. Empirical tests are based on *observing the system at run time and extracting information about its temporal behavior*. This benefit will be shown with three examples featuring different types of systems. In the first example, consider a hard system on which the off-line analysis has rejected a task because its worst-case response time slightly exceeds its deadline. If empirical tests show that the analytical test was very pessimistic, then the system designer may decide to run the system anyway, knowing that the probability of this worst-case scenario actually happening for the task is very low. The second example is a system with a mixed set of hard and soft tasks, scheduled by some sort of flexible scheduling algorithm in order to improve the overall response quality. Flexible scheduling techniques are speculative, in the sense that they try to guess which is the most effective way to schedule tasks in order to maximize the obtained value. If their speculations are based on pessimistic values, then part of their effectiveness is lost; conversely, more accurate, actually observed values can improve the overall scheduling process. The third and final example would be a soft real-time system, on which no schedulability analysis is normally performed. Again, this system would benefit from having a consistent mechanism of testing the system performance, allowing the designer to tune it appropriately. Please note that our aim is not to substitute the off-line analysis by empirical tests on systems requiring hard guarantees, but to *combine* the two approaches order to obtain the best of both.

Empirical tests involve two different activities: extracting run-time information and analyzing it. The extraction of system information at run-time can be done by several different *instrumentation* techniques, ranging from pure hardware to pure software mechanisms, with mixed hardware-software alternatives in the middle. In this range of solutions, there is a double (inverse) gradation of intrusiveness and price, with pure hardware instrumentation being at one end (least intrusive and most expensive) and pure software instrumentation being at the other end.

The analysis of the run-time information, which is usually called execution *trace*, can be performed by following a custom-made approach or by applying a general framework. In this paper, we introduce a general framework for extracting temporal properties from real-time systems by analyzing run-time traces. The characteristics of this framework are summarized as follows:

- The system needs to be instrumented, but the actual instrumentation technique is not imposed by the framework. The instrumentation typically places trace points at both the operating system and the application code.

- As the system runs, trace points generate events, which are sequentially stored to form a run-time trace.
- Traces are automatically analyzed in order to reconstruct the system evolution as state transitions.
- Temporal properties are defined as function over pre-defined sequences of state transitions. These sequences are detected by using finite state machines over the observed trace.
- The maximum computational cost of processing each observed event is $O(n)$, with n being the number of tasks, while the regular cost of many of the events is $O(1)$. This feature limits the properties that can be studied by the framework, but ensures the predictability and bounds the overhead related to the analysis. This, in turn, permits performing on-line analysis of events, if necessary.

The framework defined here is generic and extensible, meaning that it is intended to capture any interesting aspect of the system temporal behavior. However, since one of the main benefits of empirical tests is to compare their results with off-line analyses, the natural properties to be studied are those that are calculated by these analyses. These include system-related properties, such as utilization, and task-related properties such as response times, computation times, blocking times, jitter factors, etc. The paper presents how to instantiate the framework in order to deduce some of these properties, which can serve as a guideline on how to define new ones.

Finally, the paper also introduces a case study of the framework, entirely based on the POSIX suite of standards. In particular, the extraction of the properties described on the paper has been implemented on RT-Linux, a real-time kernel that follows a subset of the POSIX real-time extensions called the Minimal Realtime System Profile [1]. This kernel has been enhanced by a trace subsystem, conforming with the POSIX Trace standard [2], which has been used as the actual mechanism of extracting the traces [11]. The conclusion of the case study is that POSIX-conforming systems can successfully adopt the framework in real-life applications; and this, in turn, proves the framework's ability to be employed in systems using state-of-the-art, standard technology.

The paper outline is as follows: Section 2 presents the related work, including a brief survey of approaches using trace analysis and a summary of the POSIX Trace standard and the RT-Linux operating system. Section 3 introduces the general framework for automatically extracting temporal properties. Section 4 details how the framework can be used for study some of the most interesting temporal properties of a real-time system. This section is intended to be as a guide to any new temporal property that the designer is interested in. Section 5 presents the case study, on which the framework has been implemented in a POSIX-like real-time operating system. Implementation issues and results from the property extraction are also presented. Finally, Section 6 states the conclusions of the paper and proposes some future lines of work.

2   Related Work

2.1   Trace Analysis

The approach of studying the behavior of a system by observing its events is not novel, although it has been mainly applied to other, non-real-time domains. This section summarizes some contributions in this area.

Probably, one of the first approaches of expressing the behavior of a system in terms of traces, events, states (processes) and transitions is the theory of Communicating Sequential Processes (CSP) [7]. The purpose of such theory is to define a mathematical space of processes (along with its operators), by which it is possible to formally demonstrate communication properties of such processes.

Event Based Behavior Abstraction (EBBA) [6] is a general model intended to be used as a debugging formalism in distributed systems. It is based on a hierarchy of events, on which the lowest (primitive) event are directly observed from the distributed system under study, while higher level events are based on clustering of primitive or other higher level events. In short, EBBA provides an event recognition engine and an behavioral analysis model provided by the user (based on the EDL grammar). The comparison between the events detected by the engine and the models provided by the user permits to point out whether the system behavior is correct or not.

FORMAN (FORMal ANnotation) language [4] is a general framework for debugging programs. It is based on two concepts: an event grammar that permits an automatic instrumentation of the program source code (implemented in a high-level *target* language), and a language to express computations over the program trace (or *H-space*), after its execution. The language is used to write assertions over single events or event patterns (sequences) on the trace, allowing for the evaluation of debugging rules, queries of variable values, profile information, statistics, etc.

The trace assertion method for abstract specification of software [5,9] is a formal methodology for program specification on which programs are abstractly specified by means of its observable features or properties (outputs as a function of inputs), rather than by the algorithms that they implement. The specification method is founded on describing (1) which functions of the program can be called (events), (2) which are the legal sequences of these calls (traces) and (3) which is the observable output at the state reached by each legal sequence. The methodology was initially intended for demonstrating formal properties of the program specifications, such as consistency and completeness, but later work has used it for other purposes, such as specifying (and reproducing) program behaviors in terms of assertion about traces [12].

Our framework shares, or inherits, some of the key ideas of such pieces of work, such as deducting or validating behaviors by observing the system evolution, although with a complete different aim. The main purpose in our approach is not to specify, demonstrate or debug *functional* properties of a system, but to deduce *temporal* ones. The issue of temporal behavior of real-time systems has been actually addressed by some formalisms such as the timed automata [3];

however, these formalisms are normally focused on validating the intended behavior of a system, rather than extracting actual temporal properties.

Finally, another main difference between the framework proposed here and most of previous work, with maybe the exception of the work by Stewart et al. [10], is that the main source of event information is not the program to be run, but the operating system. Therefore, instrumentation is primarily done at the operating system code. Depending on the operating system support and on the properties that the user is interested on, it may be necessary to instrument the program source code too, but only as a complement to the information obtained from the operating system.

2.2   The POSIX Trace Standard

The POSIX Trace standard establishes a set of portable interfaces which allow applications to have access to trace management services, which are implemented at the operating system level. This standard has been recently integrated within the last approved version of the complete POSIX suite of standards [2]. The POSIX Trace standard is founded on two main data types (trace event and trace stream) and is also based on three different roles which are played during the tracing activity (the trace controller process, the traced process and the analyzer process). These concepts are now detailed.

A *trace event* is defined as a data object representing an action which is executed by either a running process (user trace event) or by the operating system (system trace event). User events are explicitly generated by the application, by calling a specific trace function, while system events are internally generated by the operating system. Each user or system event belongs to a particular *trace event type* (an internal identifier) and it is associated with a *trace event name* (a human-readable string), by which it can be later recognized. Each time an event is traced, the trace system is required to store some information about the event including, among others, the identifier of the process (and thread) that traced the event, the memory address at which the trace function was called and a timestamp (with a minimum precision of one microsecond). Optionally, arbitrary extra data can be associated with the event when the application or the operating system trace it. All this information, mandatory and optional, has to be reported when the event is retrieved for analysis.

A *trace stream* is defined as a non-persistent, internal (opaque) data object containing a sequence of trace events plus some internal information to interpret those trace events. That is, streams are where events are stored (when traced) and where events are read from (when retrieved). The standard defines that a trace stream is explicitly created to trace a particular process (or a set of related process). Trace events can be either retrieved directly from the stream (on-line analysis) or permanently stored in a file called a log. In the latter case, analysis can only be done after the tracing is over and all the events have been stored in the log file (off-line analysis).

The standard defines three different roles in each tracing activity: trace controller process (TCP), traced (or target) process (TP) and trace analyzer process

(TAP). In the most general case, each of these roles is executed by a separate process. However, nothing in the standard prevents from having two (or even the three) of these roles executed by the same process (possibly by different threads). The TCP is the process that sets the tracing system up, including the creation of the stream(s), in order to trace a (target) process. The TP is the process that is being traced. This process can only register new user event types and trace events belonging to these types. The TAP is the process in charge of retrieving the stored events from a trace stream, in order to analyze them. If the stream does not have a log, then both the target and the analyzer processes access the stream concurrently, the former for tracing events and the latter for retrieving these events.

2.3   RT-Linux and Its Implemented POSIX Standards

RT-Linux (Real-Time Linux) [13] is a small real-time operating system which is able to concurrently execute a set of real-time threads and a Linux *system*, which here refers to the Linux kernel plus all the user processes being executed by the kernel. The sharing of the processor between the real-time tasks and the Linux system is done in a complete unfair way, in the sense that real-time tasks are always given the processor in preference of the Linux system and without delays, independently of the actions taken by the Linux kernel. These bounded latencies are achieved by giving the Linux kernel a set of *virtual* interrupts instead of the real (hardware) ones, which are managed by RT-Linux only. Typical RT-Linux applications are decoupled in two parts: a real-time part, comprising a set of real-time tasks, and a non-real-time part, implemented as one or more Linux processes. Both parts can communicate via either shared memory or bidirectional channels called RT-fifos.

RT-Linux has lately adopted the external interface established by the POSIX Minimal Realtime System profile [1], which describes the requirements of the smallest POSIX-conforming real-time operating system. On the hardware side, these requirements include only one processor, no explicit memory protection, no mass storage devices and, in general, simple hardware devices operated synchronously. On the software side, the requirements establish a simple programming model in which the real-time system is executed by only one process (with complete POSIX thread support [2]), without the need of a file system or user interaction.

The POSIX Trace standard has been recently added to RT-Linux (see [11] for a detailed description). The implementation has restricted the subset of the standard to the case of having on-line analysis of events only, but with the possibility of dynamically filtering of event types. Following the RT-Linux model, the trace support has made available at both the RT-Linux and Linux levels. As a result, events can be traced and retrieved by real-time tasks and Linux processes *concurrently*.

3   Systems, Events, States, and Properties

This section introduces the framework to deduce temporal properties by observing the real-time system at run time. In short, the framework is based on four concepts: the *system* to be studied, the set of *events* that can be observed from the system, the set of *states* that can be derived from the events and the *properties* that can be calculated through the observation process. The framework's general structure is pictured in Figure 1, while each of these concepts is detailed below.

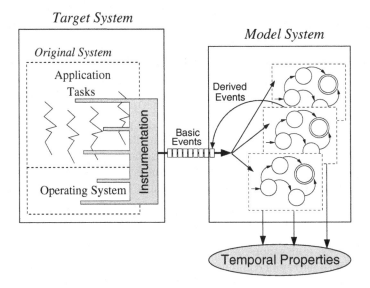

Fig. 1. An outline of the framework.

The framework distinguishes among three different systems: the original system, the target system and the model system. The *original system* (S) is the real system under study, before being instrumented. This system is formed by a set of runnable real-time tasks (potentially belonging to different real-time applications) plus an operating system or kernel in charge of scheduling and running these application tasks. The real system cannot be observed unless some instrumentation is performed over it. Since the framework does not impose a particular instrumentation mechanism, it cannot assume that the instrumentation does not affect the behavior of the original system. Therefore, the instrumented system is actually our *target system* (T), the system which properties are deduced from. The *model system* (M) is the view of the target system that can be deduced by means of the observation process, that is, it is the model of the target system. The model system is defined in terms of a set of properties of interest plus a set of finite state machines, which are used as recognition engines for events and as computation tools for properties. In general, if model system M successfully represents the behavior of the target system T, the properties than can be deduced in M also hold in T. These properties might also be extrapolated to S, probably with just some loss of precision. However, the exact influence of the instrumentation in the original system's behavior heavily depends on the actual instrumentation technique, and hence such extrapolations should be done carefully.

As the target system executes, its internal state changes. Some of these state changes are detected by the instrumentation and converted into basic events, which are the observation individuals. When observed, these basic events trigger state transitions in the model system. Some of these transitions can generate other (derived) events, and so on. The framework defines properties as functions over particular sequences of state transitions, with these transitions being detected by finite state machines (deterministic finite automata).

An *event* is a value that triggers an instantaneous state transition in the model system. In fact, since the system model is likely to be internally formed by several automata, a single event may produce transitions in more than one automaton (although this may still be seen as a single state change for the entire system model). For each automata, a transition is triggered if the last produced event matches the *transition condition*, which is formed by an event pattern and some logical expressions. There are two types of events: basic and derived. *Basic events* are directly observed from the target system, that is, they are produced by the instrumentation at either the operating system or the application code. These events usually represent significant state changes in the target system. *Derived events* are triggered inside the model system, when a particular sequence of events (basic or derived) is detected. The model system uses the same recognition engine, based on finite state machines, to trigger derived events and to calculate system properties. The process works like this: a basic event normally triggers a state transition in one or more automata; the result of these state transitions may result in a derived event being produced, which can in turn produce state transitions in the same or other automata. Note that, if the event recognition process is to be done on-line, then there must be an upper bound in the amount of events that can be successively derived by a single basic event being observed, in order to bound the computation time of the property extraction process. Each event is defined by means of an event type, a timestamp (which indicates the moment at which the event was either observed or derived) and, optionally, some extra data depending on the event type (as, for example, the task identifier in a task-related event type). The purpose of the timestamp is to partially order events[1].

At any particular point in time, the target system and the model system are each in a certain *state*. Strictly speaking, the state of the target system is the current hardware state, plus the internal state of the operating system, plus the internal state of each process (and each task inside the process). However, the

---

[1] Although this is not imposed by the framework, typical temporal properties of a real-time system will need the timestamp of basic events to be set by an absolute, monotonic real-time clock in the target system.

framework assumes that there is only a (normally small) subset of this state that can be detected by the instrumentation. This is called the set of *observable states* of the target system. State changes between observable states are notified by means of basic events. In the model system, the state of the system is the current state of all the automata used to derive events and properties plus the current value of all the properties. The calculation of some properties may need the use of auxiliary variables; if so, the current value of all the auxiliary variables also forms part of the model system state.

A *property* is some value about the system execution which is of particular interest. Each property is abstractly defined as a function of a sequence of states (or transitions). Conceptually, the model system defines a different finite state machine or automaton to calculate each property, although the implementation may join some of these automata in order to improve performance. The calculation of each property is actually carried out by means of *semantic rules*, which are pieces of code that can be attached to transitions and states of the automaton; these semantic rules are executed when the transition is triggered or when the state is reached. As a result, the evolution of the automaton naturally computes the property, whose final value is calculated when a terminal state of the automata is reached. Semantic rules may also use auxiliary variables in order to store partial results during the automata evolution. The framework defines three types of properties: single values throughout the execution (such as, for example, the total system utilization), sequences of values (such as the response times of a task) or a statistically accumulated figure over a value sequence (such as the worst-case computation time of a task).

Overall, the framework establishes a direct relationship between properties, events and states. This relationship can be looked at from two alternative viewpoints, depending on the instrumentation possibilities in the target system:

a) the properties to extract conditions the states that the model system has to keep track of, which in turn defines which basic events *need* to be observed from the target system; or
b) the events that *can* be observed in the target system restricts which states can be derived in the system model and thus which properties can be extracted.

4   Study of Basic Temporal Properties

This section explains how to apply the framework described above in order to extract some relevant temporal properties of a generic (but typical) real-time system. The study presented here is independent of a particular application, as long as it follows the computational model presented below. For space limitation reasons, this paper only shows how to extract four temporal properties; however, the study below can be seen as a template by which other properties can be defined.

The study begins with the presentation of the computational model, that is, the set of assumptions that the target system must follow. Then, it presents the automaton model, which establishes the characteristics and notation of the automata that will be used to deduce properties. The final subsection shows how to actually extract some interesting properties of the target system: a system-related property (utilization) and three task-related properties (computation time, blocking time and response time per task release). For each property, the computational cost of the automata processing is also included.

4.1 Computational Model of the Target System

The target system considered here is formed by a real-time application plus an operating system, both running on a single-processor computer. The following list summarizes the behavioral restrictions that must hold on the system:

- The application comprises a fixed set of N tasks.
- Each application task is either periodic or sporadic.
- Each task is statically assigned a priority.
- The operating system scheduler applies a fixed-priority preemptive dispatching policy.
- Tasks may share resources. If they do, resource access is exclusively arbitrated by using the Immediate Priority Ceiling Protocol.
- The *minimal* set of basic events that the instrumentation is required to report is the following: (1) for each context switch, an event denoted as CSW has to report the identifier of the new running task and the timestamp; (2) each time a task changes its runnable state, the new state has to be reported along with the task identifier and the timestamp. Significant states are: "ready" (RDY) and "finished" (FNS), respectively indicating that the task is runnable and finished (that is, suspended waiting for its next release); and (3) for each task, an event denoted as PRI has to report the initial (static) priority of each task, along with its identifier, when it is created.
- The process in charge of extracting the temporal properties is reported all the events without loss. The issue of building property automata which are robust under event loss conditions is currently being studied.

4.2 Event and Automaton Model

This section specifies a model for events and automata which is compatible with the framework. This model will be used below to define the properties under study.

Each event generated by the instrumentation is a tuple $(Y, t, i, \varkappa)$, where:

- $Y \in \{\text{CSW}, \text{RDY}, \text{FNS}, \text{PRI}\}$, that is, Y is the event type.
- t is the event timestamp.
- i is the task identifier (all the events here are to be task-related). Task identifiers are ordered inversely with task priorities, with task '0' being the highest and task 'N-1' the lowest. Task 'N' here denotes the 'idle task'.

- $\varkappa$ denotes additional, event-specific information. For example, in events of type PRI, this will stand for the task new priority.

According to the framework, each property is conceptually specified by an automaton, which can be defined by five related elements: (1) a set of states, (2) a set of transitions, (3) a list of semantic rules attached to the states and/or transitions, (4) variables to store the property values, and (5) an optional list of auxiliary variables. Among them, the set of transitions is probably the only issue that needs further explanation, particularly about how a transition can express the conditions on which it becomes triggered.

In this automaton model, each transition is labelled with a condition of the form: "[label]: *pattern* [, *expression* [,...]]". Inside this condition, the *label* simply identifies each transition. The *event pattern* is a tuple, equivalent to the event tuple, on which some of the elements are literal (constant) while some others can have a generic value. In the patterns of the automata below, the notation uses underline typeface for literals and italic typeface for generic values (i.e., values that can be instantiated). The optional *expressions* add more logical conditions to the transition to be triggered. In general, an event will trigger a particular transition if, first, the event matches the pattern (all the pattern literals occur in the event) and second, all the expressions is satisfied. Expressions are typically boolean conditions involving event data and/or some property values. The model also permits automata to have λ-transitions.

4.3   Some Property Examples

System Utilization. The system utilization can be easily calculated as 1 minus the utilization of the "idle" task. As a result, the only event needed to be observed for this property is the context switch (CSW). The utilization automaton, represented in Figure 2, needs two auxiliary variables, `itime` and `istart`, indicating the total accumulated idle time and the start of a idle period, respectively. The table in Figure 2 shows the semantic rules related to each transition. At any given time t, following formula can be used to calculate the system utilization: $U(t) = 1.0 - \frac{\text{itime}}{t}$. The computational cost of this automaton is $O(1)$ with each event of type CSW.

Response Time. The response time of a task is calculated as the time on which the task finishes its release minus the last time it was released. In terms of events, this is calculated as the time elapsed between the pair of events RDY and FNS for any particular task. The automaton for calculating the response time of task τ_i is shown in Figure 3. Note that, due to the λ-transition, the automaton successively calculates all the response times of task τ_i. The response-time automaton for each task τ_i needs two straightforward semantic rules. These rules operate with the property variable, called `rtime`, and an auxiliary variable to store the moment at which the release started, called `rstart`. The computational cost of this automaton is $O(1)$ for each RDY and FNS events corresponding to each task.

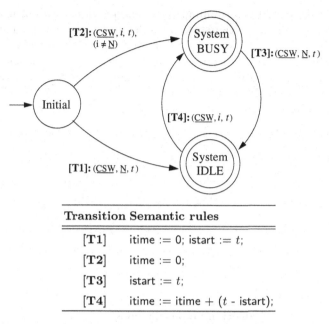

Transition Semantic rules

[T1]	itime := 0; istart := t;
[T2]	itime := 0;
[T3]	istart := t;
[T4]	itime := itime + (t - istart);

Fig. 2. System utilization automaton.

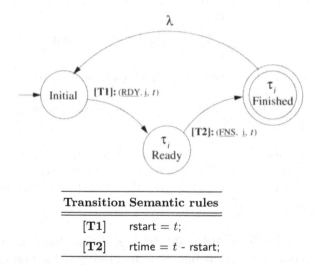

Transition Semantic rules

[T1]	rstart = t;
[T2]	rtime = t - rstart;

Fig. 3. Response-time automaton for task τ_i.

Computation Time. The computation time of a task is the sum of the intervals on which the task is running. Since the computation time is a typical per-release property, the automaton has to calculate the task computation time of a single release; that is, between a RDY and a FNS event of a given task τ_i. Apart from these two events, the automaton needs to get all CSW events that both put τ_i

to run and remove τ_i from running. As in the previous section, a λ-transition is used to return to the initial state, in order to repeat the calculation release over release. The computation time automaton for task τ_i is shown in Figure 4. Semantic rules in Figure 4 use `ctime` as the property variable to calculate the task computation time over a release and the auxiliary variable `cstart` to remember the start time of a running interval for task τ_i.

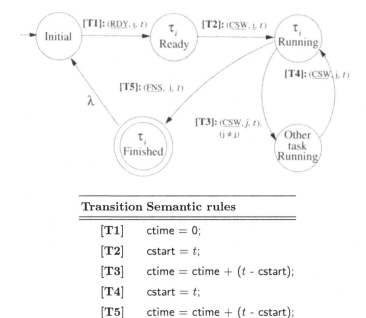

Transition	Semantic rules
[T1]	ctime = 0;
[T2]	cstart = t;
[T3]	ctime = ctime + (t - cstart);
[T4]	cstart = t;
[T5]	ctime = ctime + (t - cstart);

Fig. 4. Computation-time automaton for task τ_i.

The computational cost of this automaton is $O(1)$ for events RDY and FNS and $O(2)$ for each event CSW, since this event effectively removes a task from running and puts another task to run (thus, the event causes a transition in the automata of both tasks).

Blocking Time. In the IPCP algorithm [8], a task that wants to have exclusive access to a resource immediately raises its priority to the priority ceiling of that resource. In this protocol, a task τ_i may only be blocked when it is released, if a lower priority task τ_j has previously raised its priority to a ceiling which is higher than or equal to the priority of τ_i. Once τ_i is chosen to run, no more blocking can occur to the task in this release. An example of this behavior is shown in Figure 5, which depicts a time diagram of a real application execution, featuring tasks, A, B, and C (in decreasing priority order). The figure shows the blocking of medium-priority task B by lower-priority task C, due to the fact that the latter has locked semaphore m0 and raised its priority (at time 1) before the

former is released (at time 2). The blocking lasts until task C unlocks m0 and
retrieves its original priority (at time 3). During the blocking interval, higher
priority A preempts task C, but this execution interval is not to be considered
blocking time for task B.

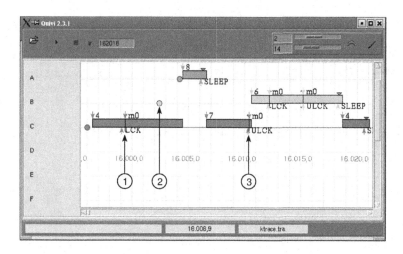

Fig. 5. Run-time scenario where task C blocks task B.

This behavior can be detected by an automaton that checks the priority of
the running task when a given task τ_i is released. If the running task has lower
priority, then blocking may happen, but only until τ_i gets to run. During this
interval, the task which is blocking τ_i may be preempted by tasks with priorities
higher than τ_i, with these intervals not forming part of τ_i's blocking time. As
explained for the computation-time automaton above, the blocking automaton
also needs a λ-transition in order to successively calculate the blocking factor of
each release of task τ_i. The automaton is presented in Figure 6. Some transitions
have logical tests in addition to event patterns, indicating that the transition
is only produced if the pattern is instantiated by the current event and the
condition is true at that moment. These conditions need two properties that
have to be calculated by auxiliary, simple automata: the property variable Run
stores the identifier of the currently running task; the property variable Prio[i]
stores the initial, static priority of task τ_i. The automata for these properties
are straightforward.

The semantic rules for this automaton effectively accumulate the blocking
time (btime) over a period of time between the task release and its first tick.
In order to do so, an auxiliary variable (bstart) is used to store the start of a
blocking interval. Note that this automaton could be simplified (for example, by
removing the "τ_i Finished" state and making the "τ_i Running" to be the final
state); however, we have chosen to present it in this form in order to illustrate

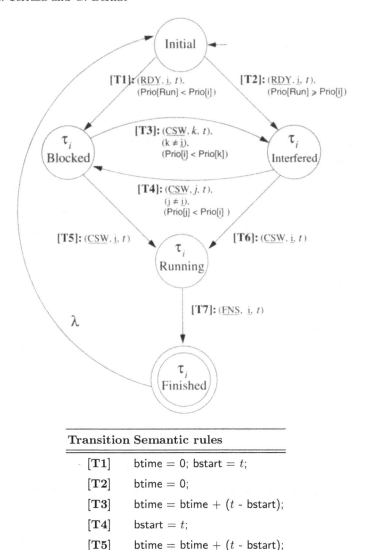

Fig. 6. Blocking-time automaton for task τ_i.

how release-like properties will typically use the FNS event type in order to mark the end of the property calculation.

The computational cost of this property is $O(1)$ for each RDY and FNS events and $O(N)$ for CSW events. A single context switch may affect the blocking state of many tasks at once. As a result, a CSW event may need to be given to the blocking-time automata of all tasks in the worst case.

5   Case Study

The previous section presented how to instantiate the framework to extract properties from a generic system. This section presents a case study in which the instantiation is followed a step further, presenting the low level, implementation issues that arise when these properties are extracted from a real system. In particular, the target system of the case study is a POSIX real-time application running on Open RT-Linux version 3.1, which has been enhanced by adding a POSIX Trace subsystem, as explained in Section 2.3. The section presents first the low-level system model, since it conditions the application behavior, and hence the event interpretation. Then, it explains how the target system has been instrumented in order to extract the required event types for analysis. And finally, it presents the *property extractor* process, which is the program that actually analyzes the trace and deduces the temporal properties.

The study presented in last section can directly be implemented in the case study because the target system follows the computational model presented above. In particular, sample applications have been implemented by using these restrictions:

- Each application consists of periodic and sporadic tasks with a static assignment of priorities. In particular, each task has been assigned a different priority.
- All tasks are scheduled according to the POSIX "SCHED FIFO" scheduling policy.
- Tasks sharing resources do so by means of using mutexes that follow the POSIX "PRIO PROTECT" protocol.
- Application tasks use a particular function to wait until its next release, with this function being *only* used for this purpose. In particular, periodic tasks use the absolute version of `clock_nanosleep` while sporadic tasks wait in a `pthread_cond_wait` call.

The mechanism used for extracting and retrieving events is the POSIX Trace system implemented in RT-Linux. According to the Trace standard, operating systems can introduce new *system* event types for their own needs. This possibility has been used here in order to extract as many of the required events as possible by instrumenting the RT-Linux kernel only. In fact, all the temporal properties studied so far (fully listed below) can be extracted by only analyzing a few system event types, which are compatible with the abstract event types defined in Section 4.1. The actual system event types that the RT-Linux kernel instrumentation produces are the following: (1) *context switch*, every time a new task is put to run, including the task identifier; (2) *task state change*, every time a task changes its runnable state, including both the task identifier and the new state; (3) *task priority change* when the task is created and each time that it explicitly changes its priority afterwards, including the task identifier and the new priority; and (4) *system call invocation*, every time a task invokes a system call of interest[2], including the invoked system call, the invoking task and any other relevant parameter in the call. According to the POSIX Trace standard, an automatic timestamp is registered for all the traced events, so this information does not have to be explicitly traced by the instrumentation.

At run time, a stream without log is created in RT-Linux before the application begins to execute. This stream is then set to filter out both all user event types and each non-interesting system event type. Thus, the stream only registers the event types which are relevant to the property extractor process, effectively minimizing the tracing overhead. Early experiments have shown that the overhead of tracing and retrieving a single event is usually less than 500 nanoseconds (each) in a typical Pentium III processor (see [11] for details).

The property extractor (PE) process (which corresponds to the framework's model system) has been implemented as a user Linux process. This program access the trace stream created in RT-Linux, retrieving all the events traced by the RT-Linux kernel as the real-time application runs. For each event retrieved, the PE process passes it to the appropriate automata, in order to calculate the temporal properties of interest. For each of these properties, a different automaton has been implemented as a as a table (of states versus events) containing pointers to the appropriate semantic rules. The PE main function contains the very simple and fast automata engine, which basically gets each new event, identifies which automata are "interested" in the event and then triggers the corresponding transitions in these automata. Our experiments show that the execution time of the PE typically takes less than $2\mu s$ per automaton transition on a 850 Mhz. Pentium III processor. This low overhead makes possible the on-line analysis of a reasonable amount of properties, specially given the fact that, from the RT-Linux application viewpoint, the property calculation is done in the background (that is, by a Linux process).

Currently, the set of properties that the PE is able to calculate are: the system utilization, the current running task, the base priority (and successive priorities) of each task, and eight properties per task invocation: computation time, response time, blocking time, interference, inter-arrival time, release jitter, input jitter (begin-to-begin) and output jitter (end-to-end). For each task, the PE stores all the release-dependent values for a maximum number of task invocations, but also keeps some statistical values of each of them, such as the minimum, maximum and average.

Finally, just to illustrate the utility of such property extraction, let us consider the following experiment involving a very simple, three-task application which use a single *mutex* to achieve mutual exclusion over a resource. From highest to lowest priority, tasks are labelled A, B and C and their periods are 5, 10 and 15 ms, respectively. The experiment show the effect of blocking in task B, in two cases: (1) task C is released slightly earlier than the other two (80 μs); and (2) all tasks are released at the same time. Figure 7 shows the results of these experiments.

---

[2] For example, the system call that is known to signal the finish of the task current release.

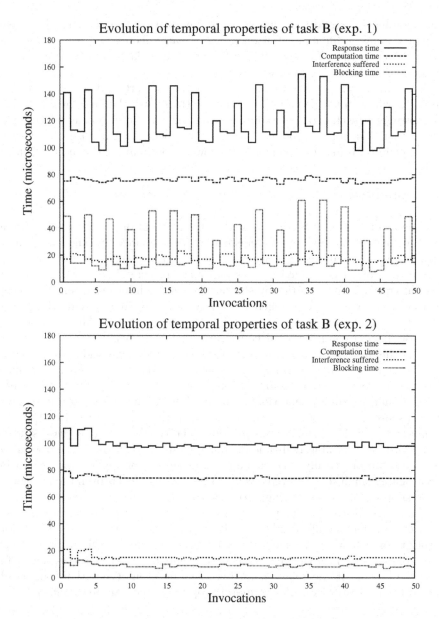

Fig. 7. Property extractor results for task B in experiments 1 (above) and 2. Experiment 1 had tasks A and B with a initial offset of 80 μs, while experiment 2 had all three tasks initially released at the same time.

The two graphics show the evolution of four temporal parameters of task B during its first 50 invocations, including the computation time, the blocking time, the interference and the response time. As it can be easily seen by comparing both graphics, the effect of the blocking time of task B practically disappears just by putting a different offset on task C, greatly decreasing task B's response time. However, the off-line analysis would have calculated the same worst-case response time for task B in either case.

This small example shows the utility of the property extractor has for the designer, who can use its results to compare them with the analytical test. Furthermore, just by changing the configuration and run the system again, the exact effects that this change produces in the system behavior can easily be checked, in real conditions and independently of how big or complex the application is.

6   Conclusions

The main conclusion of this paper is that the application of a consistent framework for observing real-time systems can greatly enhance our knowledge about their behavior, compared to the results of the off-line analysis, which can only obtain the worst-case behavior. This paper has presented such framework, and has illustrated its capabilities by showing how some interesting temporal properties can be deduced from a generic but typical real-time system. Many other properties can be extracted by applying the same scheme. The constant (or, at most, linear) computational complexity of the property extraction process permits this process to run as a part of the real-time application, if necessary.

The type of temporal properties which are naturally interesting to know about a real-time system (computation times, response times, etc.) influences the fact that the instrumentation is mainly done at the operating system level. In this sense, the paper's case study has shown the ability of the POSIX Trace standard to provide such instrumentation. The conclusion of the case study is that POSIX-conforming real-time operating systems with the Trace option can be used to automatically extract temporal properties of applications by tracing a reasonably small set of system events. This, in turn, has proven the framework to be adopted by systems using current technology.

Currently, research is being done towards using the temporal property extraction process to build flexible schedulers that work with actual observations rather than off-line estimations. Other research lines about this subject include fault-tolerant schemes that can deal with event loss in the process and a full characterization of the relationship between the event types that can be observed from a system and the temporal properties that can be extracted.

References

1. "1003.13-1998 IEEE Standard for Information Technology–Standardized Application Environment Profile (AEP)—POSIX® Realtime Application Support" [0-7381-0178-8].
2. "1003.1^{TM} Standard for Information Technology—Portable Operating System Interface (POSIX®)". IEEE Std. 1003.1-2001, Open Group Technical Standard Base Specifications, Issue 6.

3. Alur R., and Dill, D.L. (1994). "A Theory of Timed Automata". Theoretical Computer Science Vol. 126, No. 2, April 1994, pp. 183-236.
4. Auguston, M. (1995). "Program Behavior Model Based on Event Grammar and its Application for Debugging Automation", Proc. of the 2nd Intl. Workshop on Automated and Algorithmic Debugging, Saint-Malo, France, May 1995.
5. Bartussek, A.W., and Parnas, D.L. (1977). "Using traces to write abstract specifications for software modules". UNC Rep. TR 77-012, Univ. North Carolina, Chapel Hill.
6. Bates, P. (1995). "Debugging heterogeneous distributed systems using event-based models of behavior". ACM TransactIons on Computer Systems, Vol 13, No 1, Feb. 1995, pp. 1–31.
7. Brookes, S.D., Hoare, C.A.R., and Roscoe, A.W. (1984). "A Theory of Communicating Sequential Processes". Journal of the ACM, Vol. 31, No. 3, July 1984, pp. 560–599.
8. Klein, Mark H. and Ralya, T. (1990). "An analysis of input/output paradigms for real-time systems". Technical Report, Software Engineering Institute. CMU/SEI-90-TR-19, 1990.
9. McLean, J. (1984). "A formal method for the abstract specification of software". Journal of the ACM, Vol. 31, No. 3, July 1984, pp. 600–627.
10. Stewart, D.B., Schmitz, D.E., and Khosla, P.K. (1992). "The Chimera II real-time operating system for advanced sensor-based control applications". IEEE Transactions on Systems, Man, and Cybernetics, Vol. 22, No. 6, Nov./Dec. 1992, pp. 1282-1295.
11. Terrasa, A., Pachés, I., and Gacría-Fornes, A. (2001). "An Evaluation of the POSIX Trace standard implemented in RT-Linux". Proc. of the 2001 IEEE Intl. Symposium on Performance Analysis of Systems and Software, Tucson (AZ), pp. 30–37.
12. Wang, Y., and Parnas, D.L. (1993). "Simulating the behaviour of software modules by trace rewriting". Proc. of the 15th intl. conference on Software Engineering, Baltimore (MA), May 1993, pp. 14–23.
13. Yodaiken, V. (1999). "An RT-Linux Manifesto". Proc. of the 5th Linux Expo, Raleigh, North Carolina, May 1999.

Rigorous Modeling of Disk Performance
for Real-Time Applications

Sangsoo Park and Heonshik Shin

School of Computer Science and Engineering and Institute of Computer Technology,
Seoul National University, Seoul 151-744, Korea
sspark@cslab.snu.ac.kr,shinhs@snu.ac.kr

Abstract. Performance modeling of magnetic disks allows the prediction of the disk service time which is useful for on-line decision support for soft real-time applications. In this paper, we propose a new performance model of disk access time to estimate the bounded disk service time. Our proposed model focuses on modeling the head positioning time to fully utilize the disk I/O bandwidth by exploiting the geometric layout of the disk. The experimental results show that our proposed model can estimate the disk service time with less than 10% error on average.

1 Introduction

Magnetic disks play a key role in many modern applications, such as multimedia computing, internet services, and databases. Nowadays, demands for timely data services are rapidly increasing in soft real-time applications like on-demand media streaming and time-constraint query [3,10]. Performance modeling of disks is used to predict the disk service time for on-line decision support in these application areas. For example, the admission controller component of multimedia servers should decide whether a new request can be accepted or not by predicting available disk I/O bandwidth based on disk performance model. Also, the query optimizer of real-time databases makes use of the disk performance model to estimate the disk service time for each transaction to meet the query deadline [14].

Most of the disk performance models in the previous research are, however, oversimplified. Some of them are so pessimistic that disks are tend to be under-utilized while others only account for the average case so the timing constraints are not often satisfied. Though simulation-based models are able to predict the disk I/O performance very accurately, their high complexity makes on-line decision impossible.

The goal of this paper is to precisely model disk performance to estimate more accurate disk service time on-line for a given disk I/O workload. It attempts to bound the disk service time to help meet timing constraints for soft real-time applications.

The rest of this paper is organized as follows: An overview of characteristics of disks is provided for performance modeling in Section 2. Our proposed disk performance model is described in Section 3 and the experimental evaluation of its performance is presented in Section 4. Finally, this paper is concluded in Section 5.

J. Chen and S. Hong (Eds.): RTCSA 2003, LNCS 2968, pp. 486–498, 2004.

2   Characteristics of Disks and Disk Drives

2.1   Mechanical Components

A disk drive is composed of mechanical components and an embedded controller [11]. As depicted in Figure 1, mechanical components contain one or more platters with blocks and tracks on them. It should be noted that although there are several heads, the disk drive has only a single read/write channel that can be switched from a disk head to another. A block called a sector can be located by $< Cylinder\#, Head\#, Sector\# >$.

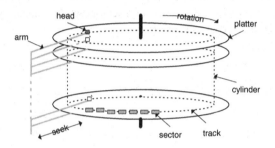

Fig. 1. Mechanical components of a disk drive

Traditional disks have the same number of sectors per track across the whole cylinders. Because the tracks are longer at the outside of a platter than at the inside, the storage density is not maximized in this configuration. Modern disks have adopted disk-zoning techniques to maximize the storage capacity [4]. A zone of disk is a group of contiguous cylinders with the same number of sectors per track. There are typically about a dozen of zones on a disk and the outer zones have more sectors per track than the inner ones. Also, as the platter rotates at a constant speed, disk has higher transfer rates from the outer zones than from the inner ones. Throughout the paper the terms tracks and cylinders are used interchangeably.

2.2   Embedded Controller

An embedded disk controller interfaces between the host and the mechanical components of the disk drive [7]. Figure 2 depicts the internal architecture of an embedded controller.

For each disk I/O session, the host issues a series of disk I/O requests to the disk with starting logical block address (LBA) and request size, or $< LBA, size >$. The details of the subsequent processes are hidden from the host. The embedded controller first queues the requests and decodes the LBAs according to the LBA to $< Cylinder\#, Head\#, Sector\# >$ mapping table.

While decoding an LBA, the controller performs sparing and track skewing operations. Because it is very expensive to manufacture platters without bad sectors, and bad

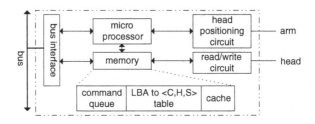

Fig. 2. Internal architecture of embedded controller

sectors may develop after manufacturing, it is necessary to maintain a list of bad sectors [11]. Remapping of bad sectors to good sectors while translating LBAs to physical sector numbers is referred to as sparing.

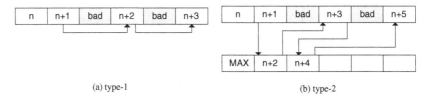

(a) type-1   (b) type-2

Fig. 3. Sparing

There are two types of bad sectors. The bad sectors found during low-level formatting are remapped as shown in Figure 3a. We denote this type of bad sectors as type-1. On the other hand, disks develop bad sectors as time elapses. We denote this type as type-2. There are several ways of remapping type-2 bad sectors that occur after the low-level formatting. For example, as depicted in Figure 3b, we can re-map the bad sectors to the spare sectors located beyond the last LBA sector.

The tracks have different starting positions. The distance of starting positions of two neighboring tracks is called a track skew as shown in Figure 4. Because the head switching requires a time delay, the head would pass the target sector LBA (n+1) during the head switching, if there were no track skew. In this case extra rotational delay may as well be required to access the target sector [11].

After decoding LBAs, the embedded controller schedules the requests in the queue so that it tries to minimize the service time. There have been well-known disk scheduling algorithms like SCAN, C-SCAN and SSTF [16]. The embedded controller also provides caches with read-ahead capability [2,12]. It utilizes the locality of the disk I/O requests in an attempt to minimize the service time [5,13].

3   Proposed Disk Performance Model

Traditional applications, which mainly deal with text-based data, have predictable disk access patterns. In general, their disk I/O requests are based on the sequential access

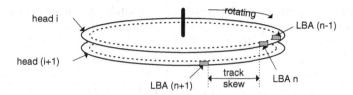

Fig. 4. Track skewing

pattern. But, in case of soft real-time applications with multimedia data, the disk access pattern is assumed to be random because the data is usually distributed over a disk and operations on them are often unpredictable [9]. This assumption obviates the need or the role of disk cache, for the cache reduces the overall disk service time only when the access patterns are suitable for the cache policies typically in the case of sequential access or repeated access on the same data.

To introduce a new disk performance model, we first illustrate the disk I/O requests and performance parameters. The notations used throughout are summarized in Table 1.

Table 1. Summary of notations

Symbol	Description
R_i	i-th disk I/O request (B_i, L_i)
B_i	Staring logical block address of R_i
L_i	Request size of R_i (Total number of sectors of R_i)
$L_{i,j}$	Number of sectors in Zone j of R_i
$E_{i,j}$	Number of bad sectors in Zone j of R_i
t_i	Service time of R_i (ms)
$t_{move(a,b)}$	Head positioning time from Sector a to Sector b (ms)
$t_{trans(i)}$	Data transfer time of R_i (ms)
B	Sector size (512 bytes)
t_{rev}	One revolution time of platter (ms), $\frac{60}{RPM} \times 1000$
$r_{disk(j)}$	Transfer rate in Zone j ($bytes/sec$), $\frac{D_j \times B}{R} \times 1000$
D_j	Number of sectors per track in Zone j
$t_{tskew(i)}$	Total track skewing time of R_i (ms)
$t_{zskew(j,h)}$	Maximum track skewing time in Zone j and Head h (ms)
t_{delay}	Maximum transfer delay (ms)
$t_{seek(a,b)}$	Seek time between two cylinders, which contain Sectors a and b respectively (ms)
$t_{\phi(a,b)}$	Angular difference between Sector a and b (ms)

For each disk I/O session, the host issues a series of disk I/O requests to the disk in the form of a tuple of starting LBA and request size. We denote a disk I/O request $i, < B_i, L_i >$, as R_i, and a set of sequential R_i's as R where B_i and L_i stand for starting logical block address and request size of the request R_i, respectively. In this paper our proposed disk performance model focuses on estimating the disk service time for any given R. The performance model thus developed will be used to bound the disk service time for soft real-time applications that have timing constraints.

Figure 5 describes a typical processing sequence when a host presents disk read requests R. The embedded controller receives the requests, adds them in the scheduling queue, schedules them by a predefined scheduling algorithm, and then accesses the target sectors by the head positioning circuits and read/write circuits. As a result of disk scheduling, R is re-ordered as $R' =< R_1, R_2, \cdots, R_n >$.

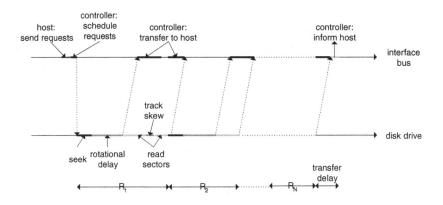

Fig. 5. The process of disk I/O requests

For any given ordered set of R', the total disk service time t is sum of the disk service time t_i of each disk I/O request R_i plus overheads incurred by the interface bus and command processing in the embedded controller. We assume these overheads are negligible compared with other performance parameters. Thus, for a disk I/O session the total disk service time for a set of requests R can be written as follows:

$$t = \sum_{i=1}^{n} t_i + t_{delay} \tag{1}$$

The disk service time of each disk I/O request R_i is the sum of the head positioning time from the last sector of the last disk I/O request R_{i-1} to the first sector of the current disk I/O request R_i and the data transfer time of R_i, i.e.,

$$t_i = t_{move(B_{(i-1)}+L_{(i-1)}-1, B_i)} + t_{trans(i)} \tag{2}$$

where B_0 is the LBA at which the previous disk I/O session terminates and L_0 is set to one to compensate the constant, -1.

3.1   Data Transfer Time

Data transfer time of disk I/O request R_i, $t_{trans(i)}$, is the sum of the read/write time of data as the head reads/writes the corresponding sectors and the track skewing time when the head moves from a track to its adjacent track (or cylinder). The read/write time of data is simply the number of corresponding sectors times the transfer rate in the zone that R_i deals with. In case the request addresses more than one zone, we must consider each zone separately for precise analysis. That is, the request size L_i is divided into smaller pieces for the zones under consideration, $L_{i,j}$.

Now we shall consider the effect of bad sectors encountered by R_i. Although a type-1 bad sector does not contain any data, it must pass by the disk head. For this reason, it is sufficient to add the number of corresponding sectors to L_i or $L_{i,j}$. For a type-2 bad sector, the remapped sparing sector is most probably located far from B_i; so it is reasonable to say that the type-2 bad sector requires additional head positioning time. Hence we suggest that a new disk I/O request R_{n+i} for each type-2 bad sector be added to R.

To calculate $t_{tskew(i)}$, the total track skewing time of R_i, we first count the number of occurrences of track skewing in R_i for each zone and for each head. Then we multiply it by corresponding maximum track skewing time, which can be found in $t_{zskew(j,h)}$ matrix as shown in Table 3. Therefore, the total data transfer time for R_i can be obtained as follows:

$$t_{trans(i)} = (\sum_j \frac{L_{i,j} + E_{i,j}}{r_{disk(j)}}) \times B \times 1000 + t_{tskew(i)} \tag{3}$$

where j is the zone number.

3.2   Head Positioning Time

The head positioning time consists of the seek time and the rotational delay. Most of the disk performance model in the previous research is oversimplified in modeling the head positioning time. Seek time is approximated for the average case as a function of the number of tracks s to be moved [11]. Eq. (4) summarizes this seek time model for the disk with voice coil mechanism.

$$t_{seek(s)} = \begin{cases} c_1 + c_2 \times \sqrt{s} & if \;\; s \leq threshold \\ c_3 + c_4 \times s & if \;\; s > threshold \end{cases} \tag{4}$$

where c_1 and c_3 are the head settle time, and c_2 and c_4 are proportional coefficients.

As for the second factor, some assume the rotational delay is one revolution time, i.e., the worst case delay [8,15]. Though it can estimate the bounded disk service time, obviously it under-utilizes a disk. The others assume rotational delay is half of the revolution time, i.e., the expected mean time when the requests are assumed to be randomly distributed over the sectors of the given cylinder [12]. Though this estimation better utilizes a disk, it cannot always satisfy the timing constraints of the real-time applications. Thus, the bounded disk service time t estimated based on the traditional disk performance model is as follows:

$$t = t_{seek(s)} + t_{rev} + t_{trans(b)} \tag{5}$$

where $t_{trans(b)}$ is the data transfer time of b sectors in the traditional model.

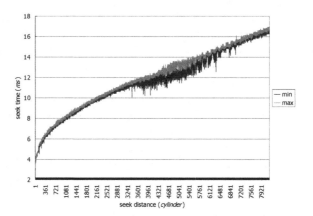

Fig. 6. DCAS-34330W seek time

In the sense of high precision, our proposed model focuses on accurate on-line estimation of head positioning time, rather than relying on approximate conceptual model. In order to grasp realistic behavior of a disk drive and its components, we have gone through extensive experiments to measure the seek time as a function of seek distance.

The experimental results are shown in Figure 6. In contrast to Eq. (4), microscopically speaking, the seek time is not a simple function of seek distance. Instead, it should be noted that there exist rather large differences between maximum and minimum values because of the thermal expansion, bearing conditions, and other factors. As seen from this experiment it is suggested to maintain the table by which a seek distance is mapped to a seek time. As to the variance in the seek time, we will return to this subject at the end of this section.

So far, in the analysis of disk service time, the seek time and rotational delay which are the two most important performance parameters have been considered separately; their obvious interplay has been neglected. Their interdependence will become clear if we utilize the geometrical layout information of a disk.

Let us now shed new light on the relationship between the seek time and the rotational delay. We now model the head positioning time from the previous sector of the last disk I/O request R_{i-1} to the first sector of the current disk I/O request R_i, i.e., $t_{move(B_{(i-1)}+L_{(i-1)}-1,B_i)}$, using the geometric location of two sectors: LBA at $(B_{(i-1)} + L_{(i-1)} - 1)$ and LBA at B_i. Figure 7 shows the three cases in calculating the head positioning time. Angular difference $t_{\phi(a,b)}$ is defined as the rotation time from Sector b to Sector a or the head movement line for a and b at $(B_{(i-1)} + L_{(i-1)} - 1)$ and B_i, respectively.

Case 1. $t_{seek(a,b)} \leq t_{\phi(a,b)}$ (Figure 7a)

Upon reading/writing Sector a, the disk head moves to the track which Sector b is located at. Meanwhile, the disk rotates at a given speed. What counts in these movements

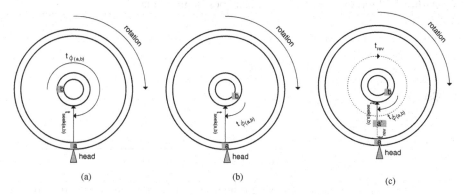

Fig. 7. Head positioning time from Sector a to Sector b

is whether the head can reach the target track before the target sector (Sector b) moves past the line of head movement. If the seek time is less than the angular difference as depicted in Figure 7a, upon reaching the target sector, the head must wait there until the target sector gets under the head. Thus, the total head positioning time is equal to the angular difference, i.e.,

$$t_{move(a,b)} = t_{\phi(a,b)} \tag{6}$$

Case 2. $t_{\phi(a,b)} < t_{seek(a,b)} \leq t_{rev}$ (Figure 7b)

In this case, the target Sector b passes by the line of head movement while the disk head moves towards the target track. This necessitates the disk to make one more full revolution before Sector b is placed under the head. Thus the total head positioning time amounts to the angular difference plus the full revolution time, i.e.,

$$t_{move(a,b)} = t_{\phi(a,b)} + t_{rev} \tag{7}$$

Case 3. $t_{seek(a,b)} > t_{rev}$ (Figure 7c)

In this case, after one revolution of disk, the head is still on the move towards the target track and the Sector b rotates past the same position as that given at the time when an initial seek started. If we take a snapshot at this moment, the disk behaves as if the head started a new seek one revolution time after the initial seek. Supposing that Sector a' is passing under the head at that instant of time, the total head positioning time (from Sector a to Sector b) is equivalent to the sum of t_{rev} and the head positioning time from Sector a' to Sector b, i.e.,

$$t_{move(a,b)} = t_{move(a',b)} + t_{rev} \tag{8}$$

It is noteworthy that the above procedure can be applied recursively so we can address the cases where the head requires more than one revolution of disk to reach the target sector. Algorithm 1 summarizes our approach to calculating the head positioning time.

Algorithm 1 Algorithm for calculating head positioning time

---

procedure $t_{move(a,b)}$
1: **if** $t_{seek(a,b)} \leq t_{\phi(a,b)}$ **then**
2:     Return $t_{\phi(a,b)}$
3: **else if** $t_{\phi(a,b)} < t_{seek(a,b)} \leq t_{rev}$ **then**
4:     Return $t_{\phi(a,b)} + t_{rev}$
5: **else**
6:     $a' = head\ position\ after\ t_{rev}$
7:     Return $t_{move(a',b)} + t_{rev}$
8: **end if**

As aforementioned, large variance in the seek time causes untoward effect on the prediction of disk performance. Depending on the degree of variation, the seek time may or may not be less than the angular difference, resulting in either Case 1 or Case 2. This uncertainty is illustrated in Figure 8 where $p_{min(b)}$ and $p_{max(b)}$ denote the geometric locations of Sector b after the minimum seek time and the maximum seek time, respectively. In the case of the minimum seek time, Case 1 is applied whereas in the case of the maximum seek time, Case 2 is applied when calculating the head positioning time. In other words, for the same head movement, the head positioning time may differ by as much as one revolution time. It is thus necessary to adopt the maximum seek time to estimate the bounded disk service time.

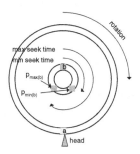

Fig. 8. Effect of the variance in seek time

4   Performance Evaluation

To verify our disk performance model, we have conducted a series of experiments on a Linux-based PC equipped with one IBM DCAS-34330W disk drive. We have obtained the values of parameters using its data sheet [6], SCSI commands in Table 2 and parameter extracting algorithms in [1,17]. As noted in Section 2.2, the embedded controller provides caches; however, we disable them to accurately evaluate the proposed model.

Table 2. Parameter extracting SCSI commands

SCSI command	Page	Disk drive parameters
MODE SELECT	0C	Cylinder range for each Zone
	03	Number of sectors per a track, maximum track skewing time
	08	Caching parameters
SEND DIAG	40	Request a translation from LBA to $< Cylinder\#, Head\#, Sector\# >$
RECV DIAG	40	Retrieve SEND DIAG result
READ DEFECT	N/A	List of bad sectors

The number of heads is 6 and the rotational speed is $5400RPM$. Figure 6 shows the seek time curve graph and Table 3 shows D_j, the number of sectors per track in Zone j, and $t_{zskew(j,h)}$, the maximum track skewing time in Zone j and Head h.

Table 3. Number of sectors per track, track skewing time (DCAS-34330W)

Zone	Cylinder range	Sectors per track	Maximum track skewing time for each head (ms)					
			0	1	2	3	4	5
0	0-857	211	1.89	2.00	1.84	2.05	2.31	2.68
1	858-2684	198	1.85	2.00	1.85	2.02	2.35	2.69
2	2685-3362	184	1.81	1.99	1.87	2.05	2.35	2.71
3	3363-4287	176	1.89	2.02	1.83	2.02	2.33	2.71
4	4288-5379	165	1.88	2.02	1.82	2.02	2.35	2.69
5	5380-6242	154	1.80	2.02	1.87	2.02	2.35	2.67
6	6243-6920	145	1.84	2.07	1.84	2.00	2.37	2.80
7	6921-8209	132	1.85	2.02	1.85	2.02	2.35	2.69

To minimize the effects of other processes, we activate only the process which is used to measure the disk service time. Figure 9 shows the disk service time with respect to disk I/O requests when the disk sequentially accesses the sectors which are allocated contiguously over Zone 0. In this experiment, $256KB$ is used for each disk I/O request. In this access pattern, the disk head moves to adjacent tracks only; so the transfer time and track skewing time are the only two factors that account for the disk service time. We first assess the disk performance with I/O requests through the file system, of which the results are shown in Figure 9b. Also, for the direct I/O technique, we disable the features which the file system provides such as read-ahead and buffer cache. The results of the direct I/O are shown in Figure 9a. It should be noted that using the file system produces much larger variance in disk service time. Judging from this comparison analysis, we suggest that the experiment should adopt direct disk I/O rather than disk I/O through file system.

In order to evaluate the proposed model, we have performed an experiment of reading randomly distributed sectors. The experiment employs $64KB$ per disk I/O request with 10 different workloads. We measure the actual disk service time for each disk I/O request

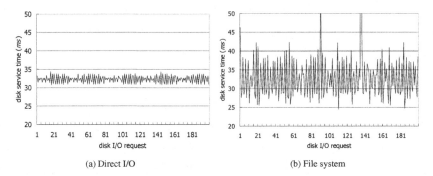

(a) Direct I/O   (b) File system

Fig. 9. Direct I/O vs File system

and compare the results with the estimated service time based on our proposed model. We also estimate the service time based on the traditional model shown in Eq. (5). Note that the traditional model assumes the worst case disk service time that includes the head positioning time equivalent to the seek time plus one revolution time. The estimation is performed using the randomly generated access patterns. These two models are compared experimentally as shown in Figure 10.

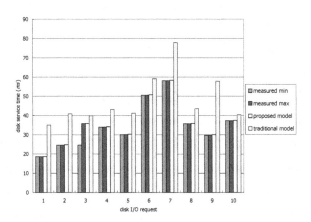

Fig. 10. Experimental result for $64KB \times 10$

Figure 10 shows that the estimated disk service time based on our model is very accurate and bound the actual measured disk service time. In the figure the third disk I/O request indicates that the seek time variance affects the head positioning time as illustrated in Figure 8. We may point out that in this case, the minimum and the maximum service time differ by one revolution time. The first two vertical bars in Figure 10 demonstrate this difference pictorially.

We have performed more extensive experiments by reading randomly distributed sectors for the performance evaluation of our model. We conduct experiments by reading randomly distributed sectors. The experiments use $100MB$ workloads with $512KB$, $1MB$, $1.5MB$, $2MB$ per disk I/O request. In Figure 11, we present the experimental results for $1MB$ request size only becase the requests of other sizes show the similar results. Table 4 summarizes the experimental results.

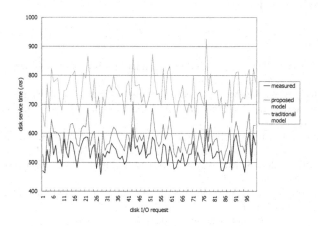

Fig. 11. Experimental result for $1MB$

From these results we can assert that our proposed model is plausible in the sense that it is able to estimate the bounded disk service time with less than 10% error on average. In contrast, the traditional model shows about 40% error on average as shown in Table 4

Table 4. Summary of experimental results

Disk I/O request size	Avg. measured service time (ms)	Avg. estimation error (ms)	
		Proposed model	Traditional model
512KB	285.26	28.00	113.02
1MB	530.87	51.03	214.62
1.5MB	774.19	71.74	312.43
2MB	1011.27	92.63	412.21

5   Summary

In this paper, we have proposed a new performance model of disks that is capable of estimating the bounded disk service time on-line precisely. In the traditional approach, the disk performance models deal with the seek time and the rotational delay separately on the basis of unrealistic conditions. For the rigorous analysis of disk service time, we exploit the geometric layout of disks to model the head positioning time more accurately in realistic conditions. We have verified our proposed model through extensive experiments on a Linux-based PC equipped with one SCSI disk drive. The experimental results show that our proposed model bounds the disk service time with less than 10% error, reducing the error bound by approximately 75% compared with the traditional disk performance model.

References

1. ANSI. Draft proposed american national standard for information systems - small computer system interface-2 (scsi-2), 1996.
2. Meng Chang Chen, Jan-Ming Ho, Ming-Tat Ko, and Shie-Yuan Wang. A SCSI disk model for multimedia storage systems. *International Journal of Computer Systems Science and Engineering*, 14(3):147–154, 1999.
3. Jim Gemmell, Harrick M. Vin, Dilip D. Kandlur, P. Venkat Rangan, and Lawrence A. Rowe. Multimedia storage servers: A tutorial. *IEEE Computer*, 28(5):40–49, 1995.
4. S. Ghandeharizadeh, S. Kim, C. Shahabi, and R. Zimmermann. Placement of continuous media in multi-zone disks, 1996.
5. A. Hospodor. Hit-ratio of caching disk buffer. In *Proceeding of the 97th IEEE Computer Society International Conferrence*, pages 427–432, 1992.
6. IBM. Hard disk drive specifications for dcas-34330w, 1996.
7. C. Y. Choi. K. Whang. Overlapped disk access for real-time disk I/O. In *Proceedings of the 6th International Conference on Real-Time Computing Systems and Applications*, pages 263–269, 1999.
8. C. Martin, P. Narayan, B. Ozden, R. Rastogi, and A. Silberschatz. The fellini multimedia storage system, 1998.
9. Banu Ozden, Rajeev Rastogi, and Abraham Silberschatz. Buffer replacement algorithms for multimedia storage systems. In *International Conference on Multimedia Computing and Systems*, pages 172–180, 1996.
10. Krithi Ramamritham. Real-time databases. *Distributed and Parallel Databases*, 1(2):199–226, 1993.
11. Chris Ruemmler and John Wilkes. An introduction to disk drive modeling. *IEEE Computer*, 27(3):17–28, 1994.
12. Elizabeth A. M. Shriver, Arif Merchant, and John Wilkes. An analytic behavior model for disk drives with readahead caches and request reordering. In *Measurement and Modeling of Computer Systems*, pages 182–191, 1998.
13. A. SilberSchatz, P. Galvin, , and G. Gagne. *Applied Operating System Concepts*. John Wiley & Sons, 2000.
14. Peter Triantafillou, Stavros Christodoulakis, and Costas Georgiadis. A comprehensive analytical performance model for disk devices under random workloads. *Knowledge and Data Engineering*, 14(1):140–155, 2002.
15. Harrick M. Vin, Pawan Goyal, and Alok Goyal. A statistical admission control algorithm for multimedia servers. In *ACM Multimedia*, pages 33–40, 1994.
16. B. L. Worthington, G. R. Ganger, and Y. N. Patt. Scheduling algorithms for modern disk drives. In *Proceedings of the 1994 ACM SIGMETRICS Conference on Measurement and Modeling of Computer Systems*, pages 241–251, Nashville, TN, USA, 16–20 1994.
17. Bruce L. Worthington, Gregory R. Ganger, Yale N. Patt, and John Wilkes. On-line extraction of SCSI disk drive parameters. Technical Report CSE-TR-323-96, 19 1996.

Bounding the Execution Times of DMA I/O Tasks on Hard-Real-Time Embedded Systems

Tai-Yi Huang, Chih-Chieh Chou, and Po-Yuan Chen

National Tsing Hua University, Hsinchu Taiwan 300, ROC
{tyhuang,ccchou,pychen}@cs.nthu.edu.tw http://eos.cs.nthu.edu.tw/

Abstract. A cycle-stealing DMA I/O task proceeds by stealing bus cycles from the CPU. The execution time of the DMA I/O task depends on the sequence of CPU instructions executing concurrently with it. This paper presents a method for bounding the worst-case execution time of a cycle-stealing DMA I/O task executing concurrently with a set of CPU tasks on a single-processor system. Our method uses the dynamic-programming technique to minimize the computational cost. We conducted exhaustive simulations on a widely-used embedded controller. The experimental results demonstrate our method safely and tightly bounds the worst-case execution times of cycle-stealing DMA I/O tasks.

1 Introduction

In a hard-real-time system, both CPU tasks and I/O tasks are required to complete executions by their deadlines. A task that executes longer than its allocated computation time may lead to missed deadlines and the failure of the whole system. In such a system, it is essential that the worst-case execution time (WCET) of each task be known in advance [10, 5, 13]. To tightly bound the WCET, the interference between concurrently executing CPU tasks and I/O tasks must be considered.

This paper presents a method for bounding the WCET of a cycle-stealing DMA I/O task. A DMAC may operate either in the burst mode or in the cycle-stealing mode. In the burst mode, a DMAC gains the control of the I/O bus once it is free and retains its ownership until all data transfers complete. Because a burst-mode DMA I/O task monopolizes the I/O bus, other tasks cannot interfere its execution time. In contrast, a DMAC that operates in the cycle-stealing mode transfers data by "stealing" bus cycles from an executing CPU task. We present here a method for bounding the WCET of a cycle-stealing DMA I/O task executing concurrently with a set of preemptable CPU tasks on a single-processor embedded system. We use the dynamic-programming technique in the development of this method to minimize the computational cost. Finally, we demonstrate the correctness of our method through exhaustive simulations.

Most of the previous studies focused on bounding the WCETs of CPU tasks [2, 9, 11, 6, 12, 14, 3, 8]. Muller *et al.* [11] developed a static cache simulation to bound the WCETs of CPU tasks executed on a contemporary machine with the

J. Chen and S. Hong (Eds.): RTCSA 2003, LNCS 2968, pp. 499–512, 2004.

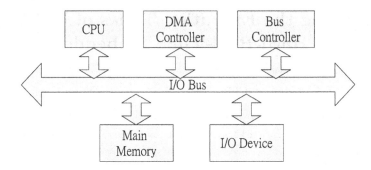

Fig. 1. The architecture of the machine model

instruction cache. Lim *et al.* [9] proposed a timing analysis technique for modern multiple-issue machines such as superscalar processors. Kim *et al.* [6] presented quantitative analysis results on the impacts various architecture features on the accuracy of WCET predictions. All of the above methods invariably assume that a CPU task to be analyzed executes without any interference of I/O tasks in the system. In a hard-real-time system, I/O tasks have been restricted to appear at the predefined areas such as the beginning and end of CPU tasks [15, 7]. To our knowledge, our work is the first one that attempts to bound the interference between CPU tasks and cycle-stealing DMA I/O tasks. For this reason, we cannot do any direct comparison between our work and any previous study.

The rest of the paper is structured as follows. Section 2 describes the machine model. Section 3 analyzes the properties of instruction sequences executing concurrently with cycle-stealing DMA I/O. Section 4 presents a recursive formula for bounding the WCET of the DMA I/O task. Section 5 implements the recursive formula with the dynamic-programming technique. We present our experimental results in Section 6. Finally, Section 7 concludes this paper.

2   The Machine Model

We adopt here the commonly-used single-processor machine model shown in Figure 1. In this model the DMAC operates in the cycle-stealing mode. Either the CPU or the DMAC, but not both, can hold the bus and transfer data at the same time. We assume that signal transmission in the bus is instantaneous. Our analytical method is applicable on a simple architecture where the instruction caching and pipelining is disabled.

An *instruction cycle* consists of a sequence of operations to fetch and execute an instruction. The sequence takes one or more machine cycles. A machine cycle requires one or more processor clock cycles to execute. We assume that the CPU is synchronous: the beginning of each machine cycle is triggered by the processor clock. We classify all machine cycles into two categories: B (bus-access) cycles and E (execution) cycles. A B-cycle is a machine cycle during which the CPU uses the I/O bus. In contrast, the CPU does not use the bus when it is in an E-cycle.

To access the bus, the DMAC first sends a bus request. If the bus is already used by the CPU, the DMAC waits. When the bus is free, there is a short delay, called the *bus master transfer time* (BMT), while the DMAC gains the control of the bus and start transferring data. At the end of each transfer of a unit of data, if there is no bus request from the CPU, the DMAC may continue to hold the bus and transfer data. Otherwise, the DMAC must release the bus, and after another BMT delay the CPU gains the control of the bus.

Let DT denote the time the DMAC takes to transfer a unit of data. Let m be the maximum units of data the DMAC can transfer during the sequence of machine cycles $B_i \to E_1 \to E_2 \to \cdots \to E_k \to B_{i+1}$. Let T be the total execution time of the k consecutive E-cycles when they execute alone. We can compute m by the equation

$$m = \left\lceil \frac{T - BMT}{DT} \right\rceil . \tag{1.1}$$

Let T_c be the period of a clock cycle. Because each machine cycle is triggered by the processor clock, the exact worst-case delay suffered by the sequence of E-cycles is equal to

$$d = \left\lceil \frac{m * DT + 2 * BMT - T}{T_c} \right\rceil * T_c. \tag{1.2}$$

The derivation for these two equations can be found in our previous work [4].

Because on a simple architecture each instruction cycle begins with a B-cycle to fetch the instruction, we can analyze the effect of cycle-stealing on each instruction independently, without considering the other instructions. Let $W(I)$ denote the WCET of an instruction I when it executes concurrently with DMA I/O and let $M(I)$ denote the maximum units of data the DMAC transfers during the execution of I. We obtain $W(I)$ by summing the execution time of the instruction when it executes without DMA I/O and the worst-case delays of all the E-cycle sequences, computed by Eq. (1.2), in the instruction. Similarly, we can use Eq. (1.1) to obtain $M(I)$.

The workload discussed in this paper consists of a DMA I/O task and K independent CPU tasks. The DMA I/O task, denoted by A_D, transfers Z units of data. Here we define the execution time of A_D as the interval from when the DMAC receives an interrupt indicating the start of the data transfer to when the CPU receives an interrupt notifying the completion of the data transfer. Based on the deterministic behaviors shown by most hard-real-time embedded software, we model a CPU task as a sequence of CPU instructions. Each of the K CPU tasks, denoted by $A_1, A_2, \ldots, A_K$, has an arbitrary release time and is preemptable. In contrast, the DMA I/O tasks A_D is nonpreemptable. We assume that A_D is initialized by a task other than the K CPU tasks. After A_D is initialized, this CPU task is blocked. Thus, A_D may execute concurrently with any of the K CPU tasks. The WCET prediction obtained by our method bounds

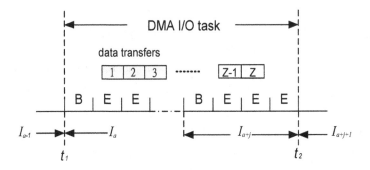

Fig. 2. The execution time of a DMA I/O task

the execution time of A_D whether the CPU tasks are scheduled by any fixed (such as Rate-Monotonic [10]) or dynamic (such as Earliest-Deadline-First [5]) priority algorithm.

To simplify the discussion, we assume that the CPU is never idle during the execution of A_D. We will remove this assumption later by modeling an idle period as an instruction of a special CPU task, and our method still bounds the WCET of A_D at the same time complexity.

3   The Properties of a Concurrent Instruction Sequence

Let S denote a sequence of instructions $I_a \to \cdots \to I_{a+j}$ executing concurrently with the DMA I/O task A_D. Because interrupts are processed between instruction cycles, A_D and I_a begin at the same time, and A_D and I_{a+j} end at the same time. Consequently, the WCET of the sequence S, denoted by $W(S)$, is bounded by the sum of the WCET of each instruction when it executes concurrently with DMA I/O. That is

$$W(S) = W(I_a) + \cdots + W(I_{a+j}).$$

Example 1: Let A_D execute concurrently with S as shown in Figure 2. The CPU signals the DMAC to start its data transfer at time t_1 and starts the execution of I_a at the same time. The DMAC signals the CPU the completion of the last unit of data during the execution of I_{a+j}. Because interrupt signals are processed between instruction cycles, the CPU is notified the completion of A_D at t_2, when the last instruction I_{a+j} completes its execution. The execution time of A_D is equal to $(t_2 - t_1)$, that is bounded by $W(I_a) + \cdots + W(I_{a+j})$.   □

Property 1: *The DMA I/O task A_D and the sequence S begin and end at the same time. The WCET of S is bounded by the sum of the WCET of each instruction when DMA I/O is present.*

The DMAC must transfer the last unit of data during the execution of I_{a+j}. Some of the E-cycles in I_{a+j} may not be utilized by the DMAC as shown by the example in Figure 2. In contrast, the DMAC must fully utilize all the E-cycles in the rest of the instructions to transfer data. The sequence of instructions $I_a \rightarrow \cdots \rightarrow I_{a+j}$ must satisfy

$$\sum_{i=a}^{a+j-1} M(I_i) < Z \leq \sum_{i=a}^{a+j} M(I_i).$$

Property 2: *The DMAC must fully utilize all the E-cycles in every instruction of S except I_{a+j}. In addition, the last unit of data must be transferred during the execution of I_{a+j}.*

The sequence S may contain instructions from any of the K CPU tasks. Among the instructions in S, let S_i denote the set of instructions from the CPU task A_i. S_i is either an empty set or a subsequence of contiguous instructions of the task A_i.

Example 2: Let S be the sequence of instructions $I_1 \rightarrow I_2 \rightarrow I_3 \rightarrow I_4 \rightarrow I_5$. Assume that $\{I_2, I_4, I_5\}$ are from the CPU task A_1, $\{I_1, I_3\}$ are from A_2. $I_2 \rightarrow I_4 \rightarrow I_5$ must be a subsequence of contiguous instructions of A_1. Similarly, $I_1 \rightarrow I_3$ must be a subsequence of A_2.   □

Property 3: *Among the instructions of S, the set of instructions from the same CPU task must be a subsequence of contiguous instructions of the CPU task.*

4   The Recursive Formula

Let Y denote the set of all possible sequences of instructions that may execute concurrently with the DMA I/O task A_D. We can obtain the WCET of A_D, denoted by $W(A_D)$, as the maximum $W(S)$ for every $S \in Y$; that is

$$W(A_D) = \max_{\forall S \in Y} W(S).$$

This brute-force method requires the availability of the set of all possible sequences. It is difficult, if not impossible, to find all possible sequences in a set of preemptable CPU tasks with arbitrary release times. In this section we describe a recursive formula for bounding $W(A_D)$ without enumerating all the possible sequences.

4.1   The Derivation

Let us divide Y into K disjoint subsets $Y_1, Y_2, \ldots, Y_K$ in such a way that the subset Y_α consists of all the sequences where the last instruction of each sequence is from the task A_α. Let $W_{(K,Z,\alpha)}$ denote the maximum $W(S)$ for every $S \in Y_\alpha$. We can redefine $W(A_D)$ as

$$W(A_D) = \max_{1 \leq \alpha \leq K} W_{(K,Z,\alpha)}. \tag{2}$$

Let us further divide Y_α into a number of disjoint subsets. Let $Y_\alpha^{(m_1,m_2,...,m_K)}$ denote a subset of sequences in Y_α such that each sequence S in this subset has the property: the DMAC transfers m_i units of data during the executions of the instructions from the task A_i. Let $W_\alpha^{(m_1,m_2,...,m_K)}$ denote the maximum $W(S)$ for every $S \in Y_\alpha^{(m_1,m_2,...,m_K)}$. We can define $W_{(K,Z,\alpha)}$ as

$$W_{(K,Z,\alpha)} = max\{W_\alpha^{(m_1,m_2,...,m_K)}\} \tag{3}$$

where

(1) $m_1 + m_2 + \cdots + m_K = Z$, and
(2) $0 < m_\alpha$, and $0 \leq m_i$ for $i \neq \alpha$.

To compute $W_\alpha^{(m_1,m_2,...,m_K)}$, we first define $f_i(m_i)$ and $p_i(m_i)$. Let $I_a \to \cdots \to I_{a+j}$ be a subsequence of contiguous instructions of the task A_i such that

$$m_i = \sum_{l=a}^{a+j} M(I_l). \tag{4}$$

Let $F_i^{m_i}$ denote the set of all possible subsequences of A_i that satisfy Eq. (4). We define $f_i(m_i)$ to be the maximum $W(S)$ for every $S \in F_i^{m_i}$. That is

$$f_i(m_i) = \max_{\forall S \in F_i^{m_i}} W(S). \tag{5}$$

Similarly, let $I_a \to \cdots \to I_{a+j}$ be a subsequence of contiguous instructions of the task A_i such that

$$\sum_{l=a}^{a+j-1} M(I_l) < m_i \leq \sum_{l=a}^{a+j} M(I_l). \tag{6}$$

Let $P_i^{m_i}$ denote the set of all possible subsequences of A_i that satisfy Eq. (6). We define $p_i(m_i)$ as

$$p_i(m_i) = \max_{\forall S \in P_i^{m_i}} W(S). \tag{7}$$

Let us get back to a sequence $S \in Y_\alpha^{(m_1,m_2,...,m_K)}$. According to Property 3, the sequence S is in fact the concatenation of the subsequence S_i of each task A_i such that the DMAC transfers m_i units of data during the execution of the subsequence S_i. Accordingly, $W(S)$ is equal to the sum of $W(S_i)$, $i = 1$ to K. We can use $f_i(m_i)$ and $p_i(m_i)$ to define $W_\alpha^{(m_1,m_2,...,m_K)}$ as

$$W_\alpha^{(m_1,m_2,...,m_K)} = e_1(m_1) + e_2(m_2) + \cdots + e_K(m_K) \tag{8}$$

where

$$e_i(m_i) = \begin{cases} p_i(m_i) \text{ if } i = \alpha, \\ f_i(m_i) \text{ if } i \neq \alpha. \end{cases} \tag{9}$$

In other words, $e_i(m_i)$ is equal to the maximum $W(S)$ for every $S \in F_i^{m_i}$, if $i \neq \alpha$, or equal to the maximum $W(S)$ for every $S \in P_i^{m_i}$, if $i = \alpha$.

Example 3: Let $K = 3$ and $Z = 3$. By Eq. (2), the WCET of the DMA I/O task A_D is equal to the maximum of $W_{(3,3,i)}$, $i = 1, 2, 3$. We use Eq. (3) to compute each $W_{(3,3,i)}$. For example,

$$W_{(3,3,1)} = \max\{W_1^{(1,2,0)}, W_1^{(1,1,1)}, W_1^{(1,0,2)}, W_1^{(2,1,0)}, W_1^{(2,0,1)}, W_1^{(3,0,0)}\}.$$

We then use Eqs. (8) and (9) to compute each term in the max function. For example,

$$W_1^{(1,2,0)} = p_1(1) + f_2(2) + f_3(0), \text{ and}$$
$$W_1^{(2,1,0)} = p_1(2) + f_2(1) + f_3(0).$$

□

The computation of $W_{(3,3,1)}$ in the example excludes the cases of $W_1^{(0,3,0)}$, $W_1^{(0,2,1)}$, $W_1^{(0,1,2)}$, and $W_1^{(0,0,3)}$ due to the requirement in Property 2. By implementing Property 2 with the settings of $p_i(0)$ to $-\infty$, $i = 1$ to K, we can generalize the definition of $W_{(K,Z,\alpha)}$ to the following form

$$W_{(K,Z,\alpha)} = \max\{e_1(m_1) + e_2(m_2) + \cdots + e_K(m_K)\}$$

where $e_i(m_i)$ is given by Eq. (9) and the max function is over all $m_1, m_2, \ldots, m_K$ such that

(1) $m_1 + m_2 + \cdots + m_K = Z$, and
(2) $0 \leq m_i \leq Z$, $i = 1, 2, \ldots, K$.

By considering m_K separately, we can further rewrite the above formula as

$$W_{(K,Z,\alpha)} = \max_{0 \leq g \leq Z}\{\max\{e_1(m_1) + e_2(m_2) + \cdots + e_{K-1}(m_{K-1})\} + e_K(g)\}$$

where the inner max function is over all $m_1, m_2, \ldots, m_{K-1}$ such that

(1) $m_1 + m_2 + \cdots + m_{K-1} = Z - g$, and
(2) $0 \leq m_i \leq Z - g$, $i = 1, 2, \ldots, K - 1$.

Since the inner term in the above formula is exactly $W_{(K-1,Z-g,\alpha)}$, we simplify it to

$$W_{(K,Z,\alpha)} = \max_{0 \leq g \leq Z}\{W_{(K-1,Z-g,\alpha)} + e_K(g)\}.$$

After considering the terminative condition of this recursive formula, we obtain

$$W_{(K,Z,\alpha)} = \begin{cases} e_1(Z) & \text{if } K = 1, \\ \max_{0 \leq g \leq Z}\{W_{(K-1,Z-g,\alpha)} + e_K(g)\} & \text{if } K > 1. \end{cases} \tag{10}$$

Again, $e_i(m_i)$ is given by Eq. (9). Finally, Eqs. (2) and (10) together give a recursive formula for computing the WCET of the DMA I/O task A_D.

Input: the CPU task A_α, a sequence of U_α instructions.
Output: the entries $f[\alpha, z]$ and $p[\alpha, z]$, $z = 0, 1, \ldots, Z$.

Procedure:
     for $z = 0$ to Z do
         for $j = 1$ to U_α do {
             1. find a longest subsequence that starts with the j-th instruction
                   and belongs to F_α^z;
             2. if ((such a subsequence exists) and
                   (its WCET is larger than $f[\alpha, z]$)) then
                   – set $f[\alpha, z]$ to the WCET of the subsequence;
             3. find a longest subsequence that starts with the j-th instruction
                   and belongs to P_α^z;
             4. if ((such a subsequence exists) and
                   (its WCET is larger than $p[\alpha, z]$)) then
                   – set $p[\alpha, z]$ to the WCET of the subsequence;
         }

Fig. 3. The procedure that computes $f[\alpha, z]$ and $p[\alpha, z]$ for the task A_α

4.2   Table Construction

The computation of Eq. (10) requires frequent accesses to both $f_i(m_i)$ and $p_i(m_i)$. To avoid computing the same $f_i(m_i)$ and $p_i(m_i)$ repeatedly, we pre-compute each $f_i(m_i)$ and $p_i(m_i)$, and store the results in the tables $f[i, m_i]$ and $p[i, m_i]$, respectively, for $i = 1$ to K and $m_i = 0$ to Z.

Figure 3 lists the procedure for constructing the tables $f[\alpha, z]$ and $p[\alpha, z]$ of a CPU task A_α, $z = 0, 1, \ldots, Z$. Here we let U_α denote the number of instructions in A_α. Initially, we set $f[\alpha, 0]$ to 0, $f[\alpha, z]$ to $-\infty$, $z = 1$ to Z. In addition, we set $p[\alpha, z]$ to $-\infty$, $z = 0$ to Z. We update the table $f[\alpha, z]$ each time we locate a subsequence in A_α that belongs to F_α^z and whose WCET is larger than the current value. Similarly, we update the table $p[\alpha, z]$ each time we locate a subsequence in A_α that belongs to P_α^z and has a larger WCET. If at the end of the procedure an entry $f[\alpha, z]$ (or $p[\alpha, z]$) still has the value of $-\infty$, this fact implies that it is impossible to find in the task A_α a subsequence of instructions that belongs to F_α^z (or P_α^z). The following examples illustrate how the procedure works.

Example 4: Table 1 gives the timing information of a CPU task A_α. This task consists of 5 instructions, I_1 to I_5. Column 2 and 3 lists the values of $W(I_i)$ and $M(I_i)$ for each instruction I_i. When $z = 3$ and $j = 3$, the procedure in Figure 3

Table 1. The timing information of a CPU task A_α

I_i	$W(I_i)$	$M(I_i)$
I_1	10	2
I_2	8	1
I_3	12	2
I_4	10	1
I_5	14	2

finds that the subsequence $I_3 \rightarrow I_4$ belongs to both F_α^3 and P_α^3 because

$$2 = \sum_{i=3}^{3} M(I_i) < z = 3 \leq \sum_{i=3}^{4} M(I_i) = 3.$$

The WCET of the subsequence is $22 = W(I_3) + W(I_4)$. We update $f[\alpha, 3]$ to 22 if 22 is larger than the current value of $f[\alpha, 3]$. Similarly, we update $p[\alpha, 3]$ if $22 > p[\alpha, 3]$. □

Example 5: When $z = 4$ and $j = 3$, the procedure finds the subsequence $I_3 \rightarrow I_4 \rightarrow I_5$ belongs to P_α^3 because

$$3 = \sum_{i=3}^{4} M(I_i) < z = 4 \leq \sum_{i=3}^{5} M(I_i) = 5.$$

The WCET of the subsequence $I_3 \rightarrow I_4 \rightarrow I_5$ is 36. We update $p[\alpha, 4]$ if 36 is larger than the current value of $p[\alpha, 4]$. On the other hand, because there is no subsequence that begins with I_3 and belongs to F_α^4, we leave $f[\alpha, 4]$ unchanged. □

4.3 Running-Time Complexity

Instead of searching through the sequence of instructions repeatedly, the steps 1 and 3 of the procedure shown in Figure 3 can be carried out in constant time by utilizing the information calculated in a previous iteration of the loop. Specifically, the subsequences that start with the $(j-1)$-th instruction can be used to locate the subsequences that start with the j-th instruction. Consequently, the running-time complexity of the procedure shown in Figure 3 can be optimized to $O(ZU_\alpha)$. To construct the whole tables of $f[k, z]$ and $p[k, z]$ for $k = 1$ to K and $z = 0$ to Z, we apply this procedure to each of the K CPU tasks. The time complexity is $\sum_{k=1}^{K} O(ZU_k) = O(ZU)$, where U is the sum of the number of instructions of these K CPU tasks.

The procedure shown in Figure 4 uses the tables $f[\alpha, z]$ and $p[\alpha, z]$ together with Eq. (10) to compute $W_{(K,Z,\alpha)}$. The time complexity for computing $W_{(K,Z,\alpha)}$ with this procedure is $O(Z^K)$. Finally, the time complexity of computing $W(A_D)$

Input: – the tables $f[\alpha, z]$ and $p[\alpha, z]$, $z = 0, 1, \ldots, Z$.
              – the definitions of $e_i(m_i)$ given in Eq. (9).
Output: the value of $W_{(k,z,\alpha)}$.

Procedure: $EQ10(k, z, \alpha)$
    1. if $(k == 1)$ then return $e_1(z)$;
    2. set R to 0;
    3. for $g = 0$ to z do {
        – set T to $(EQ10(k - 1, z - g, \alpha) + e_k(g))$;
        – if $(T > R)$ then set R to T;
    }
    4. return R;

Fig. 4. The procedure that implements Eq. (10)

with the recursive formula is $O(ZU) + O(KZ^K)$. In other words, the time complexity of the recursive formula grows exponentially as the number of CPU tasks grow.

5   A Dynamic-Programming Method

The problem with the procedure shown in Figure 4 is that it computes the same $W_{(k,z,\alpha)}$ repeatedly in the process of computing $W_{(K,Z,\alpha)}$. To avoid redundant computation, we implement Eq. (10) by the procedure shown in Figure 5. This procedure uses the dynamic-programming technique that first computes the solutions to all subproblems. It proceeds from the small subproblems to the larger subproblems, storing the answers in a table. Here we store the value of $W_{(k,z,\alpha)}$ in the entry $W[k, z, \alpha]$. The time complexity of computing $W_{(K,Z,\alpha)}$ by this dynamic-programming method is $O(KZ^2)$. Thus, the time complexity of computing $W(A_D)$ by this dynamic-programming method is $O(ZU)+O(K^2Z^2)$, where Z is the number of units of data to be transferred by A_D, K is the number of CPU tasks that may execute concurrently with A_D, and U is the sum of the number of instructions of these K CPU tasks.

Another advantage of the dynamic-programming method is that the table $W[k, z, \alpha]$ built for the purpose of bounding the WCET of A_D can be used to bound the WCET of other DMA I/O tasks which execute concurrently with the same K CPU tasks. For example, to compute the WCET of another DMA I/O task $A_{D'}$ which transfer Z' units of data, $Z' < Z$, by Eq. (10) we need to compute first $W[K, Z', \alpha]$. Because $W[K, Z', \alpha]$ had already been computed in the process of computing the WCET of A_D, we can obtain $W(A_{D'})$ directly, without another full evaluation of Eq. (10). Suppose that there are totally γ DMA I/O tasks in the system that can execute concurrently with these K CPU

Input: – the tables $f[k, z]$ and $p[k, z]$, $k = 1$ to K, $z = 0$ to Z.
    – the definitions of $e_i(m_i)$ given in Eq. (9).
Output: the table $W[k, z, \alpha]$, $k = 1$ to K, $z = 0$ to Z.

Procedure:
 1. set $W[1, z, \alpha]$ to $e_1(z)$, $z = 0$ to Z.
 2. for $k = 2$ to K do
   for $z = 0$ to Z do {
    set $W[k, z, \alpha]$ to $-\infty$;
    for $g = 0$ to z do {
     if $(W[k - 1, z - g, \alpha] + e_k(g) > W[k, z, \alpha])$ then {
      – set $W[k, z, \alpha]$ to $(W[k - 1, z - g, \alpha] + e_k(g))$;
     }
    }
   }
 }

Fig. 5. A dynamic-programming method for Eq. (10)

tasks, and each DMA I/O task transfers Z_i units of data, $i = 1, 2, \ldots, \gamma$. The time complexity of bounding the WCETs of these DMA I/O tasks is

$$O(Z_{\max}U) + O(K^2 Z_{\max}^2)$$

where $Z_{\max}$ is the maximum value of $Z_1, Z_2, \ldots, Z_\gamma$.

The discussion thus far assumes that the CPU is never idle during the execution of the DMA I/O task A_D. We now remove this assumption. Suppose that there is an idle period. Let m denote the number of units of data the DMAC transfers during this period. We model this idle period as an instruction I_l of a special CPU task A_{K+1}, called the *background* task. Because the DMAC takes at most $(2 * \mathrm{BMT} + \mathrm{DT})$ to transfer a unit of data, the execution time of this period is bounded by $m * (2 * \mathrm{BMT} + \mathrm{DT})$. That is

$$M(I_l) = m, \quad \text{and} \quad W(I_l) = m * (2 * \mathrm{BMT} + \mathrm{DT}).$$

Let S denote a mixed sequence of instructions and idle periods that executes concurrently with A_D. Let S' denote the new sequence of instructions after replacing each idle period in S with an instruction of the background task A_{K+1}. The new sequence S' holds the three properties discussed in Section 3. Consequently, by adding the background task A_{K+1} to the set of the K CPU tasks that can execute concurrently with A_D and setting

$$f[K + 1, z] = p[K + 1, z] = z * (2 * \mathrm{BMT} + \mathrm{DT}), \quad z = 0, 1, \ldots, Z,$$

the dynamic-programming method given in Figure 5 still bounds the WCET of A_D at the time complexity of $O(ZU) + O(K^2 Z^2)$ when CPU idle periods are allowed.

Table 2. The CPU task set

Program	Brief Description	Instructions
QuickSort	Recursive QuickSort	3,124
BubbleSort	Sequential BubbleSort	2,763
FFT	Fast Fourier Transform	3,662
Spline	Cubic Spline function	2,101
Gaussian	Gaussian Elimination	1,436
Mtxmul	Matrix Multiplication	1,170
Correlate	Track-Correlate function	814
Mtxmu12	Loop-unrolled version of **Mtxmul**	884

Table 3. The simulation results for DMA I/O tasks

	The length of the I/O task			
	250	500	750	1000
$W(A_D)/W_r(A_D)$	1.060	1.029	1.017	1.014
$W(A_D)/W_p(A_D)$	1.063	1.028	1.013	1.006

6   Experimental Results

We demonstrate the correctness of our method through exhaustive simulations. Given a set of CPU tasks and a DMA I/O task A_D, we first used our dynamic-programming method to compute $W(A_D)$. We next simulated the concurrent execution of the CPU task set and A_D under the round-robin scheduling algorithm and the fixed priority assignment algorithm, and recorded the execution time of A_D. Tasks were simulated for all possible combinations of release times, and in the case of fixed priority assignment, all possible combinations of priority assignments were simulated. To make exhaustive simulation feasible, we allowed scheduling points to occur only every 100 instructions. We use $W_r(A_D)$ and $W_p(A_D)$ to denote the maximum execution time of A_D found by the simulation when the CPU tasks are scheduled by the round-robin and fixed priority assignment scheduling algorithms, respectively.

Our tested workload consists of eight CPU tasks and a DMA I/O task. Table 2 lists the eight CPU tasks used in the simulation experiment. Each CPU task is an execution trace of a commonly-used program executed on the MC68030. We used the MC68030 in this experiment because it is a widely-used embedded processor for which instruction timing information is available. Column 3 of Table 2 lists the number of instructions in each CPU task. We obtained from the Motorola 68030 manual [1] the timing information of each instruction in the traces. The clock frequency of the microprocessor was 20 MHZ: the period of a clock cycle T_c was 50 ns. We assume a 0-wait memory was used in this experiment, and each DMA transfer of a unit of data took two clock cycles. Hence, we set DT to 100 ns. Finally, BMT was 5 ns.

Table 3 shows the experimental results for DMA I/O tasks that transfer different units of data. Rows 2 and 3 of Column 2 give the values of $W(A_D)/W_r(A_D)$ and $W(A_D)/W_p(A_D)$, respectively, when the DMA I/O task A_D transfers 250 units of data. We repeated the same experiment for DMA I/O tasks that transfer 500, 750, 1000 units of data, and the results are shown in Columns 3, 4, and 5. As explained in Section 5, our dynamic-programming method only computes the WCET of the DMA I/O task that transfers 1000 units of data. The WCETs of the other three DMA I/O tasks are obtained in a table-driven manner.

For every of the eight cases investigated in this experiment, our WCET prediction $W(A_D)$ is always larger than the maximum execution time of the DMA I/O task recorded in the exhaustive simulations, i.e., $1 \le W(A_D)/W_r(A_D)$ and $1 \le W(A_D)/W_p(A_D)$. This result verifies that our method safely bounds the WCET of the DMA I/O task. Our method overestimates the WCET for at most 6.3% when the CPU tasks are scheduled by the fixed priority assignment algorithm and the DMA I/O task transfers 250 units of data. The percentage of overestimation is smaller with a longer DMA I/O task. This behavior results from the overestimation on the last instruction of the sequence that executes concurrently with the DMA I/O task; our method assumes that every E-cycle sequence of the last instruction is fully utilized in the WCET computation. Obviously, the overestimation during the last instruction will have a smaller effect on the WCET prediction of a longer DMA I/O task. Finally, our method still produces 0.6% and 1.4% overestimation on the WCET of the DMA I/O task with the round-robin and the fixed priority assignment scheduling algorithms, respectively. This small amount of overestimation is caused by the 100-instruction scheduling distance allowed in the exhaustive simulation. This limit considerably trims down the set of possible instruction sequences that may execute concurrently with the DMA I/O task. We are confident that, by allowing scheduling points to occur on every instruction, the overestimation by our method will be practically negligible. In summary, the experimental results show that our method safely and tightly bounds the WCET of a cycle-stealing DMA I/O task.

7   Conclusions

In this paper we first analyzed the properties of an instruction sequence that executes concurrently with a cycle-stealing DMA I/O task. Based on these properties we next derived a recursive formula for bounding the WCET of a cycle-stealing DMA I/O task executing concurrently with a set of CPU tasks with arbitrary release times and priority assignments. We reduced the running-time complexity by a dynamic-programming technique. We demonstrated the correctness of the dynamic-programming method with an exhaustive simulation. The experimental results show that our method safely and tightly bounds the WCETs of cycle-stealing DMA I/O tasks. The success of our work encourages the inclusion of cycle-stealing DMA I/O to fully utilize the bandwidth of the I/O bus in a hard-real-time embedded system.

Acknowledgments. This research was supported in part by National Science Council, R.O.C., under Grant NSC 91-2213-E-007-034 and by Ministry of Education, R.O.C., under Grant MOE 89-E-FA04-1-4.

References

1. *MC68030 Enhanced 32-bit Microprocessor: User's Manual.* Motorola, 1987.
2. Jakob Engblom and Andreas Ermedah. Modeling complex flows for worst-case execution time analysis. In *Proceedings of the 21th Real-Time System Symposium*, pages 163–174, November 2000.
3. C. Healy, R. Arnold, F. Muller, D. Whalley, and M. Harmon. Bounding pipeline and instruction cache performance. *IEEE Transactions on Computers*, 48(1):53–70, January 1999.
4. Tai-Yi Huang and Jane W.-S. Liu. Predicting the worst-case execution time of the concurrent execution of instructions and cycle-stealing DMA I/O operations. *ACM SIGPLAN Notices*, 30(11), November 1995.
5. Kevin Jeffay, Donald F. Stanat, and Charles U. Martel. On non-preemptive scheduling of periodic and sporadic tasks. In *Proceedings of the 12th Real-Time System Symposium*, pages 129–139, 1991.
6. Sung-Kwan Kim, Rhan Ha, and Sang Lyul Min. Analysis of the impacts of overestimation sources on the accuracy of worst case timing analysis. In *Proceedings of the 20th Real-Time System Symposium*, pages 22–31, December 1999.
7. Mark H. Klein and Thomas Ralya. An anlysis of input/output paradigms for real-time systems. Technical Report CMU/SEI-90-TR-19, CMU Software Engineering Institute, July 1990.
8. Yan-Tsun Steve Li and Sharad Malik. Performance analysis of embedded software using implicit path enumeration. In *Proceedings of the 32nd ACM/IEEE Design Automation Conference*, pages 456–561, June 1995.
9. Sung-Soo Lim, Jung Hee Han, Jihong Kim, and Sang Lyul Min. A worst case timing analysis technique for multiple-issue machines. In *Proceedings of the 19th Real-Time System Symposium*, pages 334–345, December 1998.
10. C. L. Liu and J. Layland. Scheduling algorithms for multiprogramming in a hard real-time environment. *Journal of the ACM*, 10(1):46–61, 1973.
11. Frank Muller, David Whalley, and Marison Harmon. Predicting instruction cache behavior. In *ACM SIGPLAN Workshop on Languages, Compilers, and Tools for Real-Time Systems*, June 1994.
12. Chang-Yun Park and Alan C. Shaw. Experiments with a program timing tool based on source-level timing schema. *IEEE Computer*, pages 48–57, May 1991.
13. Lui Sha, Ragunathan Rajkumar, and John P. Lehoczky. Priority inheritance protocols: An approach to real-time synchronization. *IEEE Transactions on Computers*, 39(9):1175–1185, 1990.
14. Henrik Theiling and Christian Ferdinand. Combining abstract interpretation and ILP for microarchitecture modelling and program path analysis. In *Proceedings of the 19th Real-Time System Symposium*, pages 144–153, December 1998.
15. A. Vrchoticky and P. Puschner. On the feasibiity of response time predictions–an experimental evaluation. Technical Report 2/91, Institute fur Technische Informatik Technische Universitat Wien, March 1991.

Introducing Temporal Analyzability Late in the Lifecycle of Complex Real-Time Systems

Anders Wall[1], Johan Andersson[1], Jonas Neander[1], Christer Norström[2], and Martin Lembke[2]

[1] Department of Computer Engineering, Mälardalen University,
Box 883, Västerås, Sweden,
{anders.wall,jan98053,jonas.neander}@mdh.se
[2] ABB Robotics, Västerås, Sweden
{christer.e.norstrom,martin.lembke}@se.abb.com

Abstract. Many industrial real-time systems have evolved over a long period of time and were initially so simple that it was possible to predict consequences of adding new functionality by common sense. However, as the system evolves the possibility to predict the consequences of changes become more and more difficult unless models and analysis method can be used.

In this paper we describe our approach to re-introducing analyzability into a complex real-time control system at ABB Robotics. The system consists of about 2 500 000 lines of code. Traditional real-time models and analyses, e.g. fixed priority analysis, were not applicable on this large and complex real-time system since the models are too simple for describing the system's behavior accurately, and the analyses are too pessimistic.

The proposed method is based on analytical models and discrete-event based simulation of the system behavior based on these models. The models describe execution times as statistical distributions which are measured and calculated in the existing system. Simulation will not only enable models with statistical execution times, but also correctness criterion other than meeting deadlines, e.g. non-empty communication queues. Having accurate system models enable analysis of the impact on the temporal behavior of, e.g. customizing or maintaining the software. The case study presented in the paper shows the feasibility of the method. The method presented is applicable to a large class of complex real-time systems.

1   Introduction

Large and complex real-time computer systems usually evolve during a long period of time. The evolution includes maintenance and increasing the system's functionality by adding new features. Eventually, if ever existed, the temporal model of the system will become inconsistent with the current implementation. Thus, the possibilities to analyze the effect of adding new features with respect to the temporal behavior will be lost. For small systems this may not be that a big problem, but for large and complex systems the consequences of altering the

J. Chen and S. Hong (Eds.): RTCSA 2003, LNCS 2968, pp. 513–528, 2004.

implementation cannot be foreseen. Introduce, or re-introduce, analyzability is the task of re-engineer the system and construct an analytical temporal model of it. The work presented in this paper is the result from an activity where we tried to re-introduce temporal analyzability in a robot control system at ABB Robotics which consist of approximately 2 500 000 LOC. Initially, we tried to apply traditional real-time analyses. However, applying classical real-time models and analyses on large and complex system, e.g. as fixed priority analysis (FPA) [1] [2] [3], often results in a too pessimistic picture of the system due to large variations in execution times and semantic dependencies among tasks. FPA is based on the fact that if a set of tasks, possible periodical with worst case execution times (wcet) and deadlines less or equal to their periods, is schedulable under worst-case conditions, it will always be schedulable. The result from such an analysis is of a binary nature, i.e. it does not give any numbers on probability of failure, it just tell if the system is guaranteed to work or not. In this work, the result from an FPA would be negative, i.e. assuming worst-case scenarios, the system will not be temporal correct in terms of meeting all its deadlines. FPA assumes a task model where deadlines are assigned to every task. In the robot controller we have investigated is the temporal correctness defined in terms of other criteria. Some of the tasks can have their deadlines derived from these criteria, but not all tasks can easily be assigned a deadline. An example of another correctness criterion is a message queue that must never be empty.

Further, a task may execute sporadically and with great variations in execution times. To be safe in an FPA, the periodicity of sporadic tasks is modeled as having a frequency equal to the minimum inter-arrival time. Using the worst-case scenario in terms of both execution time (maximum) and periodicity (minimum), is not sufficient as the result would be to pessimistic.

Since traditional temporal models and analysis do not apply to the class of systems we have studied, we have used a simulation-based approach. In this paper we describe our approach to analysis of complex real-time system's temporal behavior. The simulations are based on analytical models of the system made in our modeling language ART-ML (Architecture and Real Time behavior Modeling Language). By using simulations, we can define other correctness criterion than satisfying deadlines as mentioned before. Instead of always assuming worst-case scenarios, we can use execution time distributions. ART-ML also permits the behavior of tasks to be modeled, i.e. on a lower level than the software architecture. This permits a more precise model to be created as semantic relations among tasks can be introduced. Moreover, we propose how to utilize our methodology by putting it into the scope of a development process. The tool suit, in which the simulator is a part, also includes tools for measuring an existing system implementation, as well as tools for processing measurements. For instance, we have developed a tool which given a set of different execution times of a task calculates the corresponding execution time distribution.

We have studied other simulators such as STRESS and DRTSS. The STRESS environment is a collection of CASE tools for analyzing and simulating behavior of hard real-time safety-critical applications [4]. STRESS is primarily intended as a tool for testing various scheduling and resource management algorithms. It can also be used to study the general behavior of applications, since it is a language-based simulator. STRESS has no support for modeling distributions of execution times or memory allocation.

Another simulation framework is DRTSS [5], which allows its users to construct discrete-event simulators of complex, multi-paradigm, distributed real-time systems. The DRTSS framework is quite different from STRESS, although they are closely related. DRTSS has no language where the behavior can be specified. A language that describes the behavior of components is necessary for achieving the goals of our work and excludes DRTSS as a possible solution.

In [6], an analytical method for temporal analysis of task models with stochastic execution times is presented. However, sporadic tasks cannot be handled. A solution for this could not easily be found. Without fixed inter-arrival times, i.e. in presence of sporadic tasks, a least common divider of the tasks inter-arrival times can not be found.

The outline of this paper is as follows: In Section 2, we put our method into the context of a developing process. Section 3 describes our approach to measure the existing system, build analytical models based on those measurements, and using the analytical models for simulating the system's temporal behavior. We also introduce the modeling language developed. In Section 4 we discuss the validation of our method which was done as a case study on a large and complex industrial real-time system. Finally Section 5 concludes the paper and gives indications of future work.

2   The Process

The introduction of a analyzable model of a system brings a continuous activity of maintaining the model. The model should always be consistent with the current implementation of the system, i.e. the implementation should be a true refinement of the model. Consequently, our method must be an integrated part of a company's development process. In this section we will briefly describe the activities associated with the analytical model. Figure 1 depicts the general activities required in our method. Note that the process described here only concerns the method we are proposing. Important activities such as verification and validation of the implementation are omitted.

The first activity in making an existing system analyzable with respect to its temporal behavior is re-engineering of the system. Typically, the re-engineering activity includes identifying the structure of the system, measuring the system, and populating the model. By comparing the result from analyzing the system using the analytical model with the temporal behavior of the real system confidence in the model can be established.This is exact the same procedure as used in developing models for any kind of systems.

As the system evolves, each new feature should be modeled and the impact of adding it to the existing system should be analyzed. This enables early analysis, i.e. before actually integrating the new feature into the system. Detecting flaws at

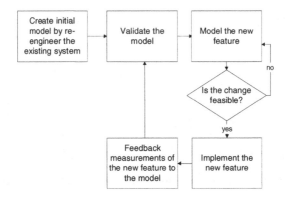

Fig. 1. The process of constructing and maintaining an analyzable system.

an early stage is often more cost effective than discovering the problem late in the testing phase of the development process. Note, that such an approach requires a modeling language that support models on different level of abstractions. ART-ML has this property which will be further described in Section 3. Modeling of new features should be part of the company's design phase.

Finally, when the new feature has been implemented and integrated into the system the model of that feature can be refined by feeding back information from the implementation into the model. Hence, a more précised model is implemented. This activity is typically performed in conjunction with the verification phase of a company's development process.

3   The Method

To create a model of the system data measured from the target system is needed. The accuracy of the model is dependent on the quality of the measured data. The measuring of the data should affect the system as little as possible. Too big probe effect on the system will result in an erroneous model and might cause wrong decisions regarding future developments.

A suitable notation is necessary for creating a system model. The language has to support both the architecture (i.e. nodes, tasks, semaphores, message queue) and the behavior of the tasks in different levels of abstractions. It should be possible to compare the beahvior of the created model with the target system in an easy way in order to iteratively improve the model to satisfactory level, illustrated in figure 2.

Our approach to analysis of the temporal behavior is simulation since our notation not only describes the architecture of the target system, but also the behavior of the included tasks. Simulation allows execution times expressed as distributions. We analyzing the output from the simulator by defining properties of interest. An example of such a property is the probability of missing a deadline

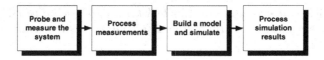

Fig. 2. The work flow of making an analytical model

requirement on a task. Moreover, the simulation approach allow us to define non-temporal related properties, e.g. non-empty message queues.

3.1   Measuring and Processing Data

Measuring data in a software system requires the introduction of software probes if no hardware probes are used [7]. The data of interest is resource utilization, e.g. task execution times, memory usage or sizes of messages queues. We used software probes in order to log task switches and message queues. The measured data is stored in static allocated memory at runtime, in binary format. All formatting of the output is done offline, writing to a file at runtime is too time consuming. This minimizes the probe effect, i.e. the part of the execution time that is caused by the probe.

The output from the system is a text-file containing task switches, time stamps, and the number of messages in different queues. The size of the output can be very big, several hundred kilobytes per monitored second of execution. To manually analyze that data for developing a model would be too time-consuming. We have therefore developed a tool that extracts data from a log and compute the statistical distribution of each task's execution time. In table 1 is the result of processing data from a task shown.

In order to calculate the statistical distribution for a set of execution times for a task, we divide all execution times into *instance equivalence classes* (IEC). Formally we define an IEC as:

Definition 1 *An instance equivalence class IEC is a subset of execution time instances of a task E, $IEC \subset E$, defined by its upper bound $\max(IEC) \in E$ and its lower bound $\min(IEC) \in E$ and a threshold that specifies the interval between $\max(IEC)$ and $\min(IEC)$.*   □

A task instance's execution time is a member of the IEC I_n iff it is larger or equal to $min(I_n)$ but less or equal than $max(I_n)$. In the model are all instances in a IEC represented as the average execution time of the IEC which have the probability of occurrence equal to the number of instances in the IEC divided by the total number of measured instances for a task. For example, consider the first entry in table 1 which express that, with the probability of 61.5 %, is the execution time for the task 360.097 time units. Consequently, the execution time of tasks in our method is represented as a set of pairs consisting of the average execution time of an IEC and its probability of occurrence.

Definition 2 *The execution time for task t, t.exe, is a set of pairs, $\langle iec, p \rangle$ where iec is the average execution time of an IEC and p is its probability of occurance.*

$\square$

An algorithm was developed to automatically identify the boundaries $\min(I)$ and $\max(I)$ for all IEC:s given a set of execution times for a task and a threshold. The algorithm is recursive. Initially all instances are sorted by their execution time using the quicksort algorithm. The sorted list constitutes the initial IEC, I_0 for the task. Next, the largest difference in execution time between two adjacent instances in the sorted list is located. If the largest difference is larger than a specified *threshold*, the list I_0 is split into two new IEC:s and recursive calls are conducted with each of the two new IEC:s. Consequently, the threshold specifies mathematically how big variations there can be in execution times belonging to the same IEC. From the system modeling point of view the threshold has two purposes. First, it can be used to filter small variations in execution times due to cache memories or branch prediction units, i.e. independent from the control-flow. Moreover, threshold can also specify the level of abstraction with which the temporal behavior is modeled. A large threshold results in a more coarse-grained distribution, i.e. less number of IEC:s for a task. Below the equation for finding distinct IEC:s, given a set of sorted execution times, is displayed.

$$\forall \langle x_i, x_{i+1} \rangle \exists \langle x_j, x_{j+1} \rangle \in I_0 :$$
$$abs(x_j - x_{j+1}) > abs(x_i - x_{i+1}) \land$$
$$abs(x_j - x_{j+1}) \geq threshold \land i \neq j$$

As a result from applying the equation above on a sorted set of execution time instances we may get two new potential IEC, I_k and I_{k+1} where $\min(I_k) = \min(I_{k-1})$, $\max(I_k) = x_j$, and $\min(I_{i+1}) = x_{j+1}, \max(I_{k+1}) = \max(I_{x-1})$. If no gap is found greater than the threshold, the final IEC is already found and the recursion is stopped. When the recursion is stopped, the largest and the smallest execution time in the list is considered to define the boundaries of an IEC.

The measured data can also be graphically visualized in a chronological order, see Figure 3. Studying such a graph may reveal executional dependencies among tasks. Introducing those dependencies will make the model more accurate with respect to the implemented system as they reduce pessimism.

3.2 The ART-ML Language

The notation developed, ART-ML, is composed of two parts, the *architecture model*, and the *behavior model*. The architecture model describe the temporal attributes of tasks, e.g. period times, deadlines, priorities. The architecture model also describes what resources there are in the system.

The behavior model describes the behavior of the tasks in the architecture model. Thus the behavior is encapsulated by the architecture model. The behavioral modeling language is an imperative, Turing-complete language close to Basic and C in its syntax.

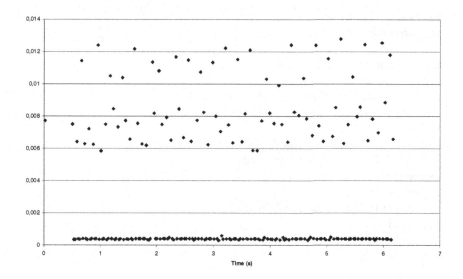

Fig. 3. An example of measured execution times

```
mainbox TASK_C_MAILBOX 4;
mainbox TASK_C_MAILBOX 6;

const msgcode_ref_request 1001;
const msgcode_ack 1002;

task APERIODIC_TASK_C
  trigger mailbox TASK_C_MAILBOX
  priority 2

behavior{
```

Table 1. An example of statistical distribution of a task. $N = \sum n$, were n is the number of instances in an IEC.

Min time	Max time	Average time	n	n/N
287.265	420.876	360.097	131	0.615
577.448	604.320	590.884	2	0.094
4176.659			1	0.047
4797.058	5024.122	4911.885	12	0.056
5177.941	6829.881	5829.924	65	0.305
11962.947			1	0.0047
12814.769			1	0.0047

```
variable incoming;
incomming = 0;

recv(incoming, TASK_C_MAILBOX)
  timeout 100;
if (incoming == msgcode_ref_request){
  recv(incoming, TASK_C_MAILBOX)
    timeout 10000;
  execute((60,6200),(40,6750));
  send(TASK_B_MAILBOX, msgcode_ack);
}else{
  chance(80){
    execute((63,400),(37,470));
  }else{
    execute((100,1000));
  }
}
}
```

Two constructs make ART-ML unique compared to other modeling languages that has been studied: the *execute-statement* and the *chance-statement*.

The execute statement describe the partial execution time of the code in the target system, i.e. the execution time for a complete task or part of a task. The execution time for a task is represented by a statistical distribution. A probability distribution is implemented as a list of pairs that corresponds to the calculated IEC:s described in Section 3.1. Every pair has a probability of occurrence and an execution time. When a task performs an "execute" it supplies a probability distribution as parameter. An execution time is picked according to the distribution and the task is put into "executing state". When a task has been allowed to execute for that amount of time, the next statement, if any, in that task's behavior description is executed. In the example below, the execute statement will execute 10 time units with the probability of 19 % and 56 time units with the probability of 81 %:

```
execute((19,10), (81, 56));
```

The chance statement implements a stochastic selection. Stochastic selection is a variant of an IF-statement, but instead of comparing an expression with zero, the expression is compared with a random number in the interval [1-100]. If the value of the expression is less than the random number, the next statement is executed. If not, the else-statement is executed if there is one. Stochastic selection is used for mimic tasks behavior observed as a black box. For instance, we can observe that a task sends a message to a particular queue with a certain probability by just logging the queue. This can be model with stochastic selection such that we send a message with the observed probability. For instance, it is possible to specify that there is a 19 % chance of sending a message:

```
chance(19)
  send(mbox1, msg)
```

The language has also support for message passing through the primitives *send* and *recv*. Both can be associated with timeouts. Moreover, binary semaphores can be specified in ART-ML through *semtake* and *semgive*. Semtake can be used in combination with a timeout as well.

3.3   Modeling on Different Level of Abstraction

When creating a model of the tasks in the target system, a level of abstraction has to be chosen. That level defines the accuracy of the model. The lower abstraction level, the more detailed and accurate model. There is no point in using the lowest possible level of abstraction, i.e. a perfect description. In that case, the actual code could be used instead. Using an extremely high level of abstraction results in a model that is not very accurate and is therefore of limited use. The best result is something in between these two extremes.

In the ART-ML language, very detailed models of task can be made, theoretically perfect ones. By describing blocks of code only by their execution time (i.e. an execute-statement in the model), the abstraction level is raised to a higher level. The more code that is described by an execute-statement, the higher level of abstraction. The highest abstraction-level possible is if all code of the task is described using a single execute statement.

It is possible to use any level of abstraction when describing a task using the ART-ML language. It is therefore possible to describe different tasks at different levels of abstraction. This property of the language enables the model to be improved (in terms of level of detail) task by task.

The execution time distributions used also has different levels of abstraction. The measured data from the target system is somewhat filtered when creating the distributions. The recorded instances are grouped into equivalence classes. This causes data to be lost. The level of abstraction is in this case the number of intervals used to describe the execution time of the task. This level of abstraction impacts the accuracy of the model.

If there are multiple tasks in the system that is of no interest and do not affect the behavior of other tasks, they can be modeled as a single task at maximum abstraction level, i.e. only by a single execution-time probability distribution. This reduces the complexity of the model without affecting the accuracy of the result regarding the tasks of interest. However, it is required that all tasks in a group has the same or adjacent priorities. Moreover, tasks can only be grouped in such a way that no other modeled task, i.e. not part of the group, has a priority within the range of a group. For instance, consider a composed task consisting of two task, a with high priority, and c having low priority. Moreover, consider task b which is also part of the system and runs at mid priority. Task a should be able to preempt task b, but task c should not. Thus, the composed task has to run on different priorities in order to reflect the control flow of the implemented system. We refer to such a group of tasks as a *composed task*.

Formally we can express the rules of grouping tasks into composed tasks, i.e. assigning execution time distribution, period time and priority, in a way that preserves the utilization of the CPU which the tasks in the group contributes with. First the set of tasks to compose, C, have to be normalized with respect to the period times. The composed task will run with the shortest period time among the participating tasks. Consequently, the period time of the composed task c is:

$$c.T = \min_{t \in C}(t.T)$$

Normilizing the tasks in such a way that the CPU utilization is preserved requires re-calculating the exection times for all IEC:s described in Section 3.1, for all tasks in C.

$$\forall t \in C \forall i \in t.exe : \frac{c.T}{t.T} i.iec$$

The resulting execution time distribution for the composed task is obtaind by calculating the cartesian product, V, of all $t.exe$ where $t \in C$, i.e. $t_1.exe \times t_2.exe \times ... \times t_n.exe$. Every n-pair which is part of the cartesian product corresponds to an executional scenario. For instance, $\langle x_1, x_2, ..., x_n \rangle$ corresponds to the scenario where task 1 executes for $x_1.iec$ time units, task 2 executes $x_2.iec$ time units, and so on.

$$c.exe = \{\langle iec, p \rangle | \forall v \in V : iec = \sum_{\forall j \in v} j.iec \wedge p = \prod_{\forall j \in v} j.p\}$$

The final c.exe is obtained by merging pairs in c.exe that have equal iec:s (cmp. the generation of IEC:s described in Section 3.1). For the set of pairs, $\{\langle iec, p_1 \rangle, ..., \langle iec, p_n \rangle\} \subseteq c.exe$, of all pairs having the same execution time, the merged pair remaining in c.exe is $\langle iec, \sum_{i=1}^{n} p_i \rangle$, where $\sum_{i=1}^{n} p_i$ is the probability that task c, executes iec time units.

Finally, the priority of the composed task c, $c.p$, is assigned the maximum priority of the tasks participating in the composition.

$$c.p = \max_{\forall t \in C}(t.p)$$

As an example consider the composition of two tasks: a and b. Task a executes with the distribution $a.exe=\{(1,0.75), (2,0.25)\}$, and $a.T=10$. Task b executes with the distribution $b.exe=\{(2,0.5), (3,0.5)\}$ and $a.T=5$. Normalizing the exe-cution of task a, i.e. $a.exe=\{(1\frac{5}{10},0.75), (2\frac{5}{10},0.25)\}$ gives the cartesian product, V, equal to $((0.5,0.75), (2,0.5)), ((0.5,0.75), (3,0.5)), ((1,0.25), (2,0.5)), ((1,0.25), (3,0.5))\}$. The cartesian product V results in a execution time distribution for the composed task, $c.exe$ equal to $\{(2.5,0.375), (3.5,0.375), (3,0.125),(4,0.125)\}$, $c.T = 5$.

The assignment of temporal attributes to composed tasks described above is a coarse approximation of the system behavior. Ideally, all tasks are modeled individually. However, in order to limit the modeling effort, and to prune the state space, such approximations can be practical. The result from the case study presented in Section 4 indicates that the use of composed tasks is quite adequate. The result of applying the proposed rules may lead to situations where execution times are longer than the period time. This corresponds to a system overload which are possible in the implementation.

3.4   Simulating the System Behavior

The simulation-based approach used in this work allows correctness criterion other than meeting deadlines. An example of other correctness criterion could be the non-emptiness of certain message-queues. The system studied in this work had such a criterion. If a certain message-queue got empty, it was considered a system failure.

Simulation also allows us to specify arbitrary system cycles. FPA assumes cycles equal to the Least Common Multiple of the period times in the task set (LCM). However, there exists systems such as the robot controller investigated as part of this work, where the cycle times are determined by other criterion. For instance, in the robot case, the system cycle is determined by the robot application, i.e. the cycle time of the repetitive task which it is programmed to do.

When designing the simulator, two different approaches were identified. The most intuitive was to let the simulator parse the model and execute it statement by statement. The other approach was to create a compiler that translated the high level ART-ML model into simple instructions and construct the simulator as a virtual machine that executes the instructions. A test was made to compare the performance of the two approaches based on two prototypes. The virtual machine solution performed significantly better which is crucial for an analysis tool.

The simulator engine is based on three parts, the *instruction decoder*, the *scheduler* and the *event-processing*. The instruction decoder executes the instructions generated by the compiler, i.e. it is the virtual machine. Some of the instructions generate events when executed, e.g. *execute, send, semtake*. The simulator engine acts upon the generated event, e.g. semtake, is only possible if the semaphore is free which only the simulator knows. An event contains a timestamp, type of event, and an id of the source task. The timestamp specifies when the event is to be fired. Consequently, new decisions about what task to execute are taken upon an event. The scheduler decides what task to execute according to the fixed priority strategy.

The execute kernel-call, the consumption of time, is what drives the simulation forwards. First, an execution time is selected according to the distribution that is provided as an argument to execute. The current time is increased with that amount of time, or until an event interferes with the execution. If an event occurs during the execution of a task, the execution is suspended, the event is taken care of and the scheduler makes a new decision. The next time the preempted task is allowed to execute, it will restart the execution of the execute-instruction, remembering how much time it has left for execution.

Since an "execute" kernel call is necessary for pushing the simulation forwards, there must always be a task that is ready to execute and contains such a statement. Due to this it is mandatory to have an idle-task in the simulation that consumes time if no other task is ready.

4   A Robotic Control Cystem

The method described in this paper was a result from studying the possibility of introducing analyzability in a large and complex real-time system. The system we have investigated is a robotic control system at ABB Robotics initially designed in the beginning of the nineties. In essence, the controller is object-oriented and consists of approximately 2 500 000 LOC divided on 400-500 classes organized in 15 subsystems. The system contains three nodes that are tightly connected, a main node that in essence generates the path to follow, the axis node, which controls each axis of the robot, and finally the I/O node, which interacts with external sensors and actuators. In this work we have studied a critical part in the main node with respect to control. The controller runs on the preemptive multitasking real-time operating system VxWorks. Maintaining such a complex system requires careful analyses to be carried prior to adding new functions or redesigning parts of the system to not introduce unnecessary complexity and thereby increasing both the development and maintenance cost.

4.1   The Model

We have modeled some critical tasks for the concrete robot system in the main node (see Figure 4). The main node generates the motor references and brake signals required by the axis computer. The axis node sends requests to the main node every 4'th millisecond and expects a reply in the form of motor references. This depends on three tasks: A, B, and C. B and C have high priority, are periodic, and runs frequently. A executes mostly in the beginning of each robot movement and has lower priority. The final processing of the motor references is performed by C. C sends the references to the axis node. Moreover, C is dependent on data produced by B. If the queue between them becomes empty, C cannot deliver any references to the axis node. This state is considered as a critical system state and the robot halts. A sends data to B when a movement of the robot is requested. If the queue between A and B gets empty, the robot movement stops. In this state, B sends default references to C. The complete model is presented in [8]. All comments have been removed and variable names have been changed for business secrecy reasons. The model is not complete with respect to all components in the system. All tasks, other than A, B and C, have been grouped into two composed tasks according to the rules described in Section 3.3. One of the two composed tasks has higher priority than A, and the other has lower priority than A. This is one way in which we can utilize different level of abstractions in our model.

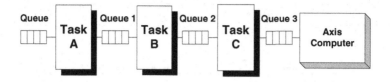

Fig. 4. The task structure of the critical control part of the system

4.2   The Results

The model we made is quite an abstraction of the existing system. There were approximately 60 tasks in the system which was reduced to six in the model. This level of abstraction was selected since there were three tasks of particular interest which was modeled in details. The rest of the tasks were modeled as two composed task. Finally, an extern subsystem was modeled as a task. The 2 500 000 LOC in the existing implementation was reduced to 200 LOC in the model.

A more detailed model would not only represent a more accurate view of the system, it will also prune the state-space which the simulator has to consider. For instance, removing impossible system states by introducing functional dependencies among tasks will reduce the states that the simulator must explore. Thus, the simulation time is reduced.

Despite our course-grained model, the result when comparing response times produced by the simulator and the response times measured on the system is quite good. In Figure 5 and Figure 6 are the response times from the simulation and the real system plotted. The resemblance is obvious. However, methods for formally analyzing the correctness of a model should be developed as a continuation of this work.

5   Conclusions

System complexity can be handled informally in early phases of large software system's life time. However, as the system evolves due to maintenance and the addition of new feature, the harder it gets to predict the temporal behavior. Even though a formal model of the temporal domain was initially constructed, it may become obsolete if it is not updated to reflect the changes in the implementation.

The method proposed in this paper is intended for the introduction, or re-introduction, of analyzability into complex system with respect to temporal behavior. A suitable modeling language, ART-ML, was developed, as well as tools for measuring execution times and the length of message queues in the existing system. Moreover, a tool for processing the measured data was developed. The data processing tool approximates the execution time distributions for the investigated tasks.

A discrete-event based simulator was used when analyzing the temporal behavior of systems described in ART-ML. The simulation approach was chosen

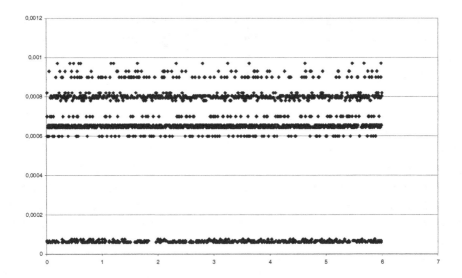

Fig. 5. The simulated response time distribution

since no existing analytical method for analyzing the temporal behavior of a
real-time system can express execution times as probabilistic distributions. Furthermore, the simulation approach enables us to define correctness criterion other
than meeting deadlines, e.g. non-empty message queues in the system.

The method has been successfully applied in a case study of a robot controller
at ABB Robotics where a model was constructed and the temporal behavior
was simulated. Even though the model was rather abstract in terms of both
functional dependencies and temporal behavior, the results were very promising.
Based on this result we claim that our method can be applied on a large class
of systems.

ART-ML is still a prototype, thus many improvements of the method and the
language are possible. Currently we are expanding ART-ML to also support the
modeling and analysis of multi-processor systems. Moreover, we are considering
constructions in ART-ML to describe complete product lines, i.e. a set of related
products that share software architecture and software components. If such constructions exist, the impact of altering the behavior of a software component can
be analyzed for all products that use it.

The scheduling strategy used by the simulator is fixed in the current implementation. To make our method more general in terms of the variety of systems
on which it can be applied we will consider the ability to specify different scheduling strategies in simulator.

The only output from the simulator is a trace of the execution. It contains
very much information. An ability to search that information would ease the
analysis of the result. Some sort of query language could be implemented where

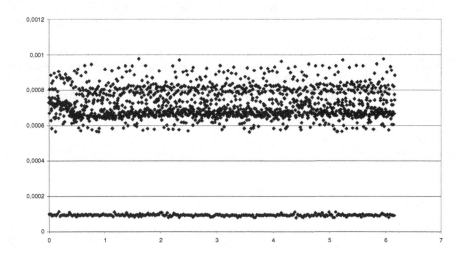

Fig. 6. The measured response time distribution

the user could specify *monitors* and *triggers*. A monitor specifies a property of the model that is to be recorded and what to record (min, max, average...). A trigger specifies a condition and an action, for example alert if a message-queue is empty.

Finally, we need methods for evaluating the validity of a model by considering the simulation results compared to the system behavior. Models are always abstractions of the real world, thus we must provide evidence that the implementation is indeed a refinement of the model.

References

1. Buttazzo, G.C.: Hard Real-Time Computing Systems: PredictableScheduling Algorithms and Applications. ISBN 0-7923-9994-3. Kluwer Academic Publisher (1997)
2. Audsley, N.C., Burns, A., Davis, R.I., Tindell, K.W., , Wellings, A.J.: Fixed priority pre-emptive scheduling: An historical perspective. Real-Time Systems Journal **8** (1995) 173–198
3. Liu, C.L., Layland, J.W.: Scheduling Algorithms for Multiprogramming in hard-real-time environment. Journal of the Association for Computing Machinery **20** (1973) 46–61
4. Audsley, N., Burns, A., Richardson, M., Wellings, A.: STRESS: A Simulator for Hard Real-Time Systems. Software-Practive and Experience **24** (1994) 534,564
5. Storch, M., Liu, J.S.: DRTSS: a simulation framework for complex real-time systems. In: Proceedings of the 2nd IEEE Real-Time Technology and Applications Symposium (RTAS '96), Dept. of Comput. Sci., Illinois Univ., Urbana, IL, USA (1996)

6. Manolache, S., Eles, P., Peng, Z.: Memory and Time-efficient Schedulability Analysis of Task Sets with Stochastic Execution Time. In: Proceedings of the 13nd Euromicro Conference on Real-Time Systems, Department of Computer and Information Science, Linköping University, Sweden (2001)
7. Shobaki, M.E.: On-chip monitoring of single- and multiprocessor hardware real-time operating systems. In: 8th International Conference on Real-Time Computing Systems and Applications, IEEE (2002)
8. Andersson, J., Neander, J.: Timing Analysis of a Robot Controller (2002)

RESS: Real-Time Embedded Software Synthesis and Prototyping Methodology[*]

Trong-Yen Lee[1], Pao-Ann Hsiung[2], I-Mu Wu[3], and Feng-Shi Su[2]

[1] Department of Electronic Engineering,
National Taipei University of Technology, Taipei, Taiwan, R.O.C.
tylee@ntut.edu.tw
http://www.ntut.edu.tw/~tylee
[2] Department of Computer Science and Information Engineering,
National Chung Cheng University, Chiayi, Taiwan, R.O.C.
pashiung@cs.ccu.edu.tw
[3] Department of Electrical Engineering,
Chung Cheng Institute of Technology, National Defense University, Taoyuan, Taiwan, R.O.C.
u9473@ms48.hinet.net

Abstract. In this work, we propose a complete methodology called RESS (*Real-Time Embedded Software Synthesis*) for the automatic design of real-time embedded software. Several issues are solved, including software synthesis, software verification, code generation, graphic user interface, and system emulation. To avoid design errors, a formal approach is adopted because glitches in real-time embedded software are intolerable and very expensive or even impossible to fix. *Time Complex-choice Petri Nets* are used to model real-time embedded software, which are then synthesized using a *time extended quasi static scheduling* algorithm. The final generated C code is prototyped on an emulation platform, which consists of an 89C51 microcontroller for executing the software, an FPGA chip for programming the hardware for different applications, and some input/output devices. Two application examples are used to illustrate the feasibility of the RESS methodology.

1 Introduction

Real-time embedded systems have made a man's life more convenient through easier controls and flexible configurations on many of our home amenities and office equipments. Due to the growing demand for more and more functionalities in real-time embedded systems, an all-hardware implementation is no longer feasible because it is not only costly, but also not easily maintainable or upgradeable. Thus, software has gradually taken over a large portion of a real-time embedded system's functionalities. But, along with this flexibility, real-time embedded software has also become highly complex. The past approach of starting everything from scratch is no longer viable.

---

[*] This work was partially supported by research project grant NSC-90-2218-E-014-009 from National Science Council, Taiwan, ROC.

J. Chen and S. Hong (Eds.): RTCSA 2003, LNCS 2968, pp. 529–544, 2004.

We need to use tools that automate several tedious tasks, but though there are some tools available for the design of embedded software, yet there is still a lack for a general design methodology. In this work, we are proposing a complete methodology, covering issues such as software synthesis, software verification, code generation, and system emulation.

An embedded system is one that is installed in a large system with a dedicated functionality. Some examples include avionics flight control, vehicle cruise control, and network-enabled devices in home appliances. In general, embedded systems have a microprocessor for executing software and some hardware in the form of ASICs, DSP, and I/O peripherals. The hardware and software work together to accomplish some given function for a larger system. Embedded software is often hardware-dependent, thus it must be co-developed along with the development of the hardware, or the interface must be clearly defined. To satisfy all user-given constraints, formal approaches are a well-accepted design paradigm for embedded software [1], [2], [3], [4], [5].

Software synthesis is a process in which a formally modeled system can be synthesized by a scheduling algorithm into a set of feasible schedules that satisfy all user-given constraints on system functions and memory space. Due to its high expressiveness, Petri nets are a widely-used model. We propose and use a high-level variant of the model called *Time Complex-Choice Petri Nets* (TCCPN). TCCPN extends the previously used models called *Free-Choice Petri Nets* [6]. Thus, our synthesis algorithm also extends a previously proposed quasi-static scheduling algorithm. Details on the model and the proposed *Time Extended Quasi-Static Scheduling* (TEQSS) algorithm along with code generation will be given in Section 3.2.

Software verification formally analyzes the behavior of synthesized software to check if it satisfies all user-given constraints on function and memory space. In this verification process, we use the well-known model checking procedure to automatically verify synthesized software schedules. Further, we also need to estimate the amount of memory used by a generated software schedule. Details of this procedure will be given in Section 3.3.

Finally, the generated real-time embedded software is placed into an emulation platform for prototyping and debugging. The software code is downloaded into a single chip microcontroller. The hardware for software code emulation is programmed on an FPGA chip. According to the real-time embedded software specifications, the settings of the input/output devices are configured. The embedded hardware and the I/O devices are then used for monitoring the functions of the real-time embedded software through a debugger.

The proposed RESS methodology will be illustrated using two examples: a *Vehicle Parking Management System* (VPMS) [7] and a motor speed control system. Details are given in Section 4.

This article is organized as follows. Section 2 gives a brief overview about previous work on embedded software synthesis, verification, and code generation. Section 3 describes the software synthesis method and our emulation platform architecture. Two real-time embedded system examples are given in Section 4. Section 5 concludes the article and gives directions for future research work.

2 Previous Work

Several techniques for software synthesis from a concurrent functional specification have been proposed [6], [8], [9], [10], [11], [12], [13], [14]. Buck and Lee [9] have introduced the *Boolean Data Flow* (BDF) networks model and proposed an algorithm to compute a *quasi-static schedule*. However, the problem of scheduling BDF with bounded memory is undecidable, *i.e.* any algorithm may fail to find a schedule even if the BDF is schedulable. Hence, the algorithm proposed by Buck can find a solution only in special cases. Thoen et al. [10] proposed a technique to exploit static information in the specification and extract from a constraint graph description of the system statically schedulable clusters of threads. The limit of this approach is that it does not rely on a formal model and does not address the problem of checking whether a given specification is schedulable. Lin [11] proposed an algorithm that generates a software program from a concurrent process specification through an intermediate Petri-Nets representation. This approach is based on the strong assumption that the Petri Net is safe, *i.e.* buffers can store at most one data unit. This on one hand guarantees termination of the algorithm, on the other hand it makes impossible to handle multirate specifications, like FFT computations and down-sampling. Safeness implies that the model is always schedulable and therefore also Lin's method does not address the problem of verifying schedulability of the specification. Moreover, safeness excludes the possibility to use Petri Nets where source and sink transitions model the interaction with the environment. This makes impossible to specify inputs with independent rate. Later, Zhu and Lin [12] proposed a compositional synthesis method that reduced the generated code size and thus was more efficient.

Software synthesis method was proposed for a more general Petri-Net framework by Sgroi et al. [6]. A quasi-static scheduling algorithm was proposed for *Free-Choice Petri Nets* (FCPN) [6]. A necessary and sufficient condition was given for a FCPN to be schedulable. Schedulability was first tested for a FCPN and then a valid schedule generated. Decomposing a FCPN into a set of *Conflict-Free* (CF) components which were then individually and statically scheduled. Code was finally generated from the valid schedule.

Balarin et al. [2] proposed a software synthesis produce for reactive embedded systems in the *Codesign Finite State Machine* (CFSM) [15] framework with the POLIS hardware-software codesign tool [15]. This work cannot be easily extended to other more general frameworks.

Recently, Su and Hsiung [13] proposed an *Extended Quasi-Static Scheduling* (EQSS) using *Complex-Choice Petri Nets* (CCPNs) as models to solve the issue of complex choice structures. Gau and Hsiung [14], [16] proposed a *Time-Memory Scheduling* (TMS) method for formally synthesizing and automatically generating code for real-time embedded software, using the *Colored Time Petri Nets* model. In our current work, we use a time extension of EQSS called TEQSS [17] to synthesize real-time embedded software and use the code generation procedure from [13] to generate the C code for 8051 microcontroller.

Several simulation or emulation boards for single chip micro-controller, such as Intel 8051 or ATMEL 89c51, have been developed. As we know, the platform for real-time embedded software synthesis is still lacking. Therefore, we develop a flexible emulation environment for real-time embedded software system. To the best of our knowledge, there are some emulation platforms available for embedded system design such as [18], [19]. In [18], a reconfigurable architecture platform for embedded control applications aimed at improving real time performance was proposed. In [19], the authors present the technology assessment of N2C platform of CoWare Inc., which proposes a solution to the co-design/co-simulation problem.

3   Embedded Software Synthesis and Prototyping Methodology

In the automatic design of real-time embedded software, there are several issues to be solved, including how software is to be synthesized and code generated, how software is to be verified, and how software code is to be emulated. Each of these issues was introduced in Section 1 and will be discussed at length in the rest of this Section.

The overall flow of real-time embedded software synthesis and the emulation of the generated software code on our prototype platform is as shown in Fig. 1. Given a real-time embedded software specification, we analyze it and then decide the requirements of the hardware within which the embedded software is to be executed. The hardware is then synthesized by an FPGA/CPLD development tool and programmed into the chip of ALTERA or XILINX on our platform.

On synthesis, if feasible software schedules cannot be generated then we rollback to the embedded software specification and ask the user to recheck or modify the specification. If feasible software schedules can be generated, then a C code for 8051 microcontroller will be generated by a code generation procedure. The machine executable code will be then generated using a 8051-specific C compiler. The target machine code is finally loaded into the 89C51 or 87C51 microcontroller chip on the platform.

3.1   Software Synthesis and Code Generation

Software synthesis is a scheduling process whereby feasible software schedules are generated, which satisfy all user-given functional requirements, timing constraints, and memory constraints. Here, we use a previously proposed *Time Extended Quasi-Static Scheduling* (TEQSS) method for the synthesis of real-time embedded software. TEQSS takes a set of TCCPN as input along with timing and memory constraints such as periods, deadlines, and an upper bound on system memory space. TCCPN is defined as follows.

Definition 1. Time Complex-Choice Petri Nets (TCCPN)
A Time Complex-Choice Petri Net is a 5-tuple (P, T, F, M_0, τ), where:

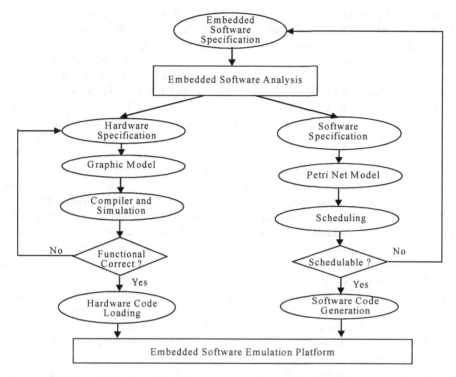

Fig. 1. Real-Time Embedded Software Synthesis and Prototyping Methodology

- *P is a finite set of places,*
- *T is a finite set of transitions, $P \cup T \neq \emptyset$, and $P \cap T = \emptyset$,*
- *F: $(P \cdot T) \cup (T \cdot P) \to N$ is a weighted flow relation between places and transitions, represented by arcs, where N is the set of nonnegative integers. The flow relation has the following characteristics.*
    - *Synchronization at a transition is allowed between a branch arc of a choice place and another independent concurrent arc.*
    - *Synchronization at a transition is not allowed between two or more branch arcs of the same choice place.*
    - *A self-loop from a place back to itself is allowed only if there is an initial token in one of the places in the loop.*
- *M_0: $P \to N$ is the initial marking (assignment of tokens to places). and*
- *τ: $T \to N \cdot (N \times N)$, i.e. $\tau(t) = (\alpha, \beta)$, where $t \in T$, α is the earliest firing time (EFT), and β is latest firing time (LFT). We will use the abbreviations $\tau_\alpha(t)$ and $\tau_\beta(t)$ to denote EFT and LFT, respectively.* □

Graphically, a TCCPN can be depicted as shown in Fig. 2, where circles represent places, vertical bars represent transitions, arrows represent arcs, black dots represent tokens, and integers labeled over arcs represent the weights as defined by F. Here, $F(x, y) > 0$ implies there is an arc from x to y with a weight of $F(x, y)$, where x and y can be a place or a transition. *Conflicts* are allowed in a TCCPN, where a conflict occurs when there is a token in a place with more than one outgoing arc such that only one enabled transition can fire, thus consuming the token and disabling all other transitions. The transitions are called *conflicting* and the place with the token is also called a *choice* place. For example, decelerate and accelerate are conflicting transitions in Fig. 2. Intuitions for the characteristics of the flow relation in a TCCPN, as given in Definition 1, are as follows. First, unlike FCPN, *confusions* are also allowed in TCCPN, where confusion is a result of synchronization between an arc of a choice place and another independently concurrent arc. For example, the accelerate transition in Fig. 2 is such a synchronization. Second, synchronization is not allowed between two or more arcs of the same choice place because arcs from a choice place represent (un)conditional branching, thus synchronizing them would amount to executing both branches, which conflicts with the original definition of a choice place (only one succeeding enabled transition is executed). Third, at least one place occurring in a loop of a TCCPN should have an initial token because our TEQSS scheduling method requires a TCCPN to return to its initial marking after a finite complete cycle of markings. This is basically not a restriction as can be seen from most real-world system models because a loop without an initial token would result in either of two unrealistic situations: (1) loop triggered externally resulting in accumulation of infinite number of tokens in the loop, or (2) loop is never triggered. Through an analysis of the choice structures in a TCCPN, TEQSS generates a set of conflict-free components and then schedules each of them, if possible. Once each component can be scheduled to satisfy all constraints, the system is declared schedulable and code is generated in the C programming language.

Semantically, the behavior of a TCCPN is given by a sequence of *markings*, where a marking is an assignment of tokens to places. Formally, a marking is a vector $M = \langle m_1, m_2, \ldots, m_{|P|} \rangle$, where m_i is the non-negative number of tokens in place $p_i \in P$.

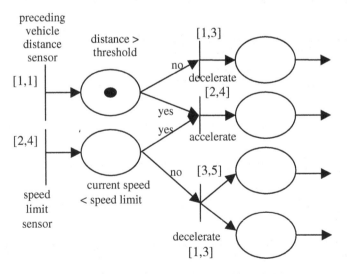

Fig. 2. Automatic Cruise Controller TCCPN Model

Starting from an initial marking M_0, a TCCPN may transit to another marking through the firing of an enabled transition and re-assignment of tokens. A transition is said to be *enabled* when all its input places have the required number of tokens, where the required number of tokens is the weight as defined by the flow relation F. An enabled transition not necessarily fire. But upon firing, the required number of tokens is removed from all the input places and the specified number of tokens is placed in the output places, where the specified number of tokens is that specified by the flow relation F on the connecting arcs.

Time Extended Quasi-Static Scheduling. The details of our proposed TEQSS algorithm are as shown in Table 1. Given a set of TCCPNs $S = \{ A_i \mid A_i = (P_i, T_i, F_i, M_{i0}, \mathcal{Q}), i = 1, 2, ..., n \}$ and a maximum bound on memory α, the algorithm finds and processes each set of complex choice transitions (Step (1)), which is simply called *Complex Choice Set* (CCS) and is defined as follows.

Definition 2. Complex Choice Set (CCS)

Given a TCCPN $A_i = (P_i, T_i, F_i, M_{i0}, \mathcal{Q})$, a subset of transitions $C \square T_i$ is called a complex choice set if they satisfy the following conditions.

- *There exists a sequence of the transitions in C such that any two adjacent transitions are always conflicting transitions from the same choice place.*
- *There is no other transition in $T_i \setminus C$ that conflicts with any transition in C, which means C is maximal.*   □

From Definition 2, we can see that a free-choice is a special case of CCS. Thus, QSS also becomes a part of TEQSS. For each CCS, TEQSS analyzes the mutual exclusiveness of the transitions in that CCS and then records their relations into an *Exclusion Table* (Steps (2)-(5)). Two complex-choice transitions are said to be *mutually exclusive* if the firing of any one of the two transitions disables the other transition. When the (i, j) element of an exclusion table is True, it means the ith and the jth transitions are mutually exclusive, otherwise it is False. Based on the exclusion table, a CCS is decomposed into two or more *conflict-free* (CF) subsets, which are sets of transitions that do not have any conflicts, neither free-choice nor complex-choice. The decomposition is done as follows (Steps 6-14). For each pair of mutually exclusive transitions t, t', do as follows.

- Make a copy H' of the CCS H (Step (11)),
- Delete t' from H (Step (12)), and
- Delete t from H' (Step (13)).

Based on the CF subsets, a TCCPN is decomposed into conflict-free components (subnets) (Steps (15)-(16)). The CF components are not distinct decompositions as a transition may occur in more than one component. Starting from an initial marking for each component, a *finite complete cycle* is constructed, where a finite complete cycle is a sequence of transition firings that returns the net to its initial marking. A CF component is said to be schedulable (Step (19)) if a finite complete cycle can be found for it and it is deadlock-free. Once all CF components of a TCCPN are scheduled, a valid schedule for the TCCPN can be generated as a set of the finite complete cycles. The reason why this set is a valid schedule is that since each component always returns to its initial marking, no tokens can get collected at any place. Satisfaction of memory

Table 1. Time Extended Quasi-Static Scheduling Algorithm

```
TEQSS_Schedule(S, ∝)
S = { A_i | A_i = (P_i, T_i, F_i, M_io, ⊡), i = 1, 2, …, n};
∝: integer; // Maximum memory
{
  while (C = Get_CCS(S) ⊡ NULL) {                          (1)
    // Construct Exclusion Table ExTable for CCS C
    Initialize_Table(ExTable);//Initialize table to
                                        False             (2)
    for each transition t in C                            (3)
      for each transition t' in C                         (4)
        if (M_Exclusive(t, t'))  ExTable[t, t'] = True;
                                                          (5)
    // Decompose CCS C into conflict-free subsets
    D = {C}; // D is a power-set of C                     (6)
    for each subset H in D                                (7)
      for each transition t in H                          (8)
        for each transition t' in H                       (9)
          if (ExTable[t, t'] = True) {                    (10)
            H' = Copy_Set(H);                             (11)
            Delete_Trans(H, t');                          (12)
            Delete_Trans(H', t);                          (13)
            D = D ⊡ H'; }                                 (14)
    // Decompose a TCCPN into subnets according to D
    for each subset H in D                                (15)
      Decompose_TCCPN(S, H);                              (16)
  }
  // Schedule all CF components
  for each TCCPN A_i in S                                 (17)
    for each conflict-free subnet X of A_i {              (18)
    X_s = Schedule(X, ∝);                                 (19)
    if (X_s=NULL) return ERROR;                           (20)
    else TEQSS_i=TEQSS_i ⊡ X_s; }                         (21)
  Check_Time(TEQSS_1, …, TEQSS_n);                        (22)
  Generate_Code(S, ∝, TEQSS_1, …, TEQSS_n);               (23)

}
```

bound is checked by observing if the memory space represented by the maximum number of tokens in any marking does not exceed the bound. Here, each token represents some amount of buffer space (i.e., memory) required after a computation (transition firing). Hence, the total amount of actual memory required is the memory space represented by the maximum number of tokens that can get collected at all the places in a marking during its transition from the initial marking back to its initial marking.

Finally, time is checked using a worst-case analysis (Step (22)) and the real-time embedded software code is generated (Step (23)), the details of which are given in the following paragraph.

Code Generation with Multiple Threads. In contrast to the conventional single-threaded embedded software, we propose to generate embedded software with multiple threads, which can be processed for dispatch by a real-time operating system. Our rationalizations are as follows:

With advances in technology, the computing power of microprocessors in an embedded system has increased to a stage where fairly complex software can be executed.

Due to the great variety of user needs such as interactive interfacing, networking, and others, embedded software needs some level of concurrency and low context-switching overhead.

Multithreaded software architecture preserves the user-perceivable concurrencies among tasks, such that future maintenance becomes easier.

The procedure for code generation with multiple threads (CGMT) is given in Table 2. Each source transition in a TCCPN represents an input event. Corresponding to each source transition, a P-thread is generated (Steps (1), (2)). Thus, the thread is activated whenever there is an incoming event represented by that source transition. There are two sub-procedures in the code generator, namely Visit_Trans() and Visit_Place(), which call each other in a recursive manner, thus visiting all transitions and places and generating the corresponding code segments. A TCCPN transition represents a piece of user-given code, and is simply generated as `call t_k;` as in Step (3). Code generation begins by visiting the source transition, once for each of its successor places (Steps (4), (5)).

In both the sub-procedures Visit_Trans() (Steps (1)-(3)) and Visit_Place() (Steps (6-8)), a semaphore `mutex` is used for exclusive access to the `token_num` variable associated with a place. This semaphore is required because two or more concurrent threads may try to update the variable at the same time by producing or consuming tokens, which might result in inconsistencies. Based on the firing semantics of a TCCPN, tokens are either consumed from an input place or produced into an output place, upon the firing of a transition. When visiting a choice place, a `switch()` construct is generated as in Step (3).

3.2 Embedded Software Verification

There are three issues to be handled in software verification, that is: "what to verify", "when to verify", and "how to verify"? Each of these issues is solved as follows.

In solution to the "what to verify" issue, TCCPN models are translated into timed automata models which are then input to a model checker. Timed automata models are easier to verify than TCCPN models because of its state space can be finitely represented. Since both TCCPN and timed automata are formal models, there is an exact mapping between the two. For example, a marking of a TCCPN is mapped to a state location of a timed automaton. Concurrency in TCCPN is mapped to two or more concurrent timed automaton. Source transitions in TCCPN are mapped to initial

Table 2. Code Generation Algorithm for TEQSS

```
Generate_Code(S, ∝, TEQSS₁, TEQSS₂, …, TEQSSₙ)
S = { Aᵢ | Aᵢ = (Pᵢ, Tᵢ, Fᵢ, Mᵢ₀, ▯), i = 1, 2, …, n};
∝: integer;    // Maximum memory
TEQSS₁, …, TEQSSₙ: sets of schedules of conflict-
free TCCPNs
{
  for each source transition tₖ ▯ ▯ᵢ Tᵢ do {      (1)
    Tₖ = Create_Thread(tₖ);                       (2)
    output(Tₖ, "call t_k;");                      (3)
    for each successor place p of tₖ             (4)
      Visit_Trans(TEQSSₖ, Tₖ, tₖ, p);            (5)
  }
  Create_Main();                                  (6)
}

Visit_Trans(TEQSSₖ, Tₖ, tₖ, p) {
  output(Tₖ, "mutexs_lock(&mutex);");            (1)
  output(Tₖ, "p.token_num += weight[t_k, p];"); (2)
  output(Tₖ, "mutexs_unlock(&mutex);");          (3)
  Visit_Place(TEQSSₖ, Tₖ, p);                    (4)
}

Visit_Place(TEQSSₖ, Tₖ, p) {
  if(Visited(p) = True) return;                   (1)
    if(Is_Choice_Place(p) = True)                 (2)
      output(Tₖ, "switch (p) {");                (3)
  for each successor transition t' of p           (4)
    if(Enabled(TEQSSₖ, t')) {                     (5)
      output(Tₖ, "mutexs_lock(&mutex);");        (6)
      output(Tₖ,"p.token_num-=weight[p,t'];");  (7)
      output(Tₖ, "mutexs_unlock(&mutex);");      (8)
      output(Tₖ, "call t';");                    (9)
      for each successor place p' of t'          (10)
        Visit_Trans(TEQSSₖ, Tₖ, t', p');        (11)
      output(Tₖ, "break;");   }                  (12)
    output(Tₖ, ")");                             (13)
}
```

states of timed automata. Non-deterministic choice places in TCCPN are mapped to
states with branching transitions in timed automata. Loops in TCCPN are mapped to
loops in timed automata.

In solution to the "when to verify" issue, we propose to verify software after scheduling (synthesis) and before code generation. Our rationalization is based on the fact that before scheduling or after code generation, the state-space is much larger than after scheduling and before code generation. A formal analysis proves this fact. Intuitively, before scheduling the state-space is much unconstrained than after scheduling, thus we have to explore a larger state-space if we verify before scheduling. Further, after code generation the state-space is also larger than that before code generation because upon code generation a lot of auxiliary and temporary variables are added, which add to the size of the state-space unnecessarily.

In solution to the "how to verify" issue, we adopt a compositional model checking approach, where two timed automata are merged in each iteration and reduced using some state-space reduction techniques such as read-write reduction, symmetry reduction, clock shielding, and internal transition bypassing. The reduction techniques have all been implemented in the State Graph Manipulators (SGM) tool, which is a high-level model checker for real-time systems modeled as timed automata with properties specified in timed computation tree logic (TCTL). After the globally reduced state-graph is obtained, it is model checked for satisfaction of some user-given TCTL property. Details can be found in [20].

3.3 Graphic User Interface and Platform Architecture

As shown in Fig. 3, we designed a graphical user interface for real-time embedded software specification input using Petri Net model. The designer draws the required behavior of embedded software as Petri Nets using the icons in the GUI. By clicking the "schedule" button, the tool generates the schedules. The designer can view the job scheduling states in the generation region and the scheduling bar of the GUI.

A platform supports a hardware-software environment for hardware emulation and software execution. In this work, we design a platform with an architecture as shown in

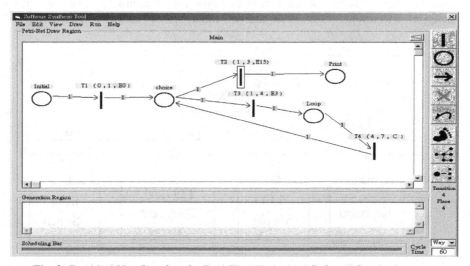

Fig. 3. Graphical User Interface for Real-Time Embedded Software Synthesis

Fig. 4. The FPGA/CPLD chip is programmed according to the hardware requirements of an embedded system. The embedded software is downloaded into the microcontroller. If microcontroller memory is not enough, then external memory can be used. The input/output devices, such as keyboard, LCD display, LED display, and input switch are connected to FPGA/CPLD chip and microcontroller using a bus. The procedure adopted for emulating embedded software in a platform is as follows. (1) The embedded software code is downloaded into the ROM or Flash memory, (2) The settings of the I/O devices are configured according to the embedded software specifications, (3) The emulation platform is booted, input conditions are changed, and the output functions are checked for satisfaction of the functional requirements of the embedded software.

4   Embedded System Examples

In this section, we use two embedded system examples to illustrate our proposed embedded software synthesis and prototyping methodology. The first example is display subsystem of Vehicle Parking Management System (VPMS) example, which includes three subsystems: entry management system, exit management system, and display system. The display system consists of a control system (counter and display interface) and a 7-segment display device. The counter value (count) indicates the number of available parking vacancies. Further details on the VPMS specification can be found in [7].

The display system in VPMS was modeled as a TCCPN as shown in Fig. 5 and the TCCPN transitions are given in Table 3. The embedded software code generated for the display system is shown in Fig. 6, which was emulated using our RESS platform. We use two input switches to simulate the Car in and Car out signals, respectively, and then use a 7-segment display to show the number of available parking vacancies.

Another example is a motor speed control system, whose TCCPN model is as shown in Fig. 7. The main function of this system is to adjust the speed of a motor based on its current speed. There are two timers T0, T1 and two interrupts INT0,

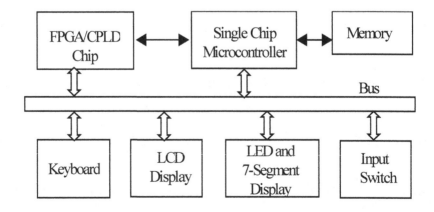

Fig. 4. Hardware-Software Prototype Platform Architecture

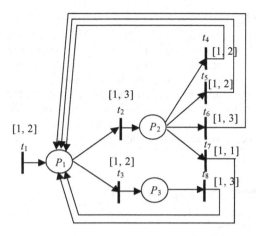

Fig. 5. Petri Net Model of Display System

Table 3. TCCPN Transitions in Display System

Place	Description
P_1	Counter value updated
P_2	Signal polling complete
P_3	Digit selected
Transition	**Description**
t_1	Initial counter
t_2	Poll signal
t_3	Select digit
t_4	Decrement counter
t_5	Increment counter
t_6	Check count
t_7	No operation
t_8	Display digit

```
Display C-code
{ (t1 t2 t4) (t1 t2 t5) (t1 t2 t6) (t1 t2 t7) (t1 t3
t8) }
t1;
while (true) {
if (p1) {
          t2;
          switch (p2) {
            Case Car in:      t4;
            Case Car out:     t5;
            Case Time stamp button pushed: t6;
            Case Default:     t7;
          }/* End of switch */
          }/* End of if */
          else {t3; t8;}
}/* End of while */
```

Fig. 6. Software Code for VPMS Display System

INT1 that drive the system. On software synthesis, that is, TEQSS, there are two feasible schedules for this system as given in Table 4, where an asterisk on a partial schedule indicates a loop of at least one iteration. The generated code is shown in Fig. 8, which was emulated on our RESS platform. We use two input switches to connect the trigger of INT0 and INT1, respectiv ely. Motor speed is displayed by an LCD display device.

5 Conclusion and Future Work

A complete methodology called RESS was proposed for emulating hardware and synthesizing and executing embedded software, which includes a time-extended quasi-static scheduling algorithm, a code generation procedure, and an emulation platform. The methodology will not only reduce development time for embedded software, but also aid in debugging and testing its functional correctness. This version of our real-time embedded software synthesis tool has a new graphical user interface to increase its user-friendliness. How to transfer the software code for applying to ARM-based systems will be our future work.

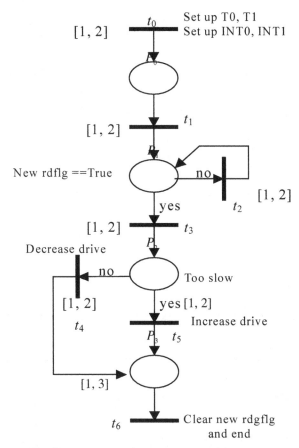

Fig. 7. Motor Speed Control System TCCPN Model

Table 4. Feasible Schedules for Motor System

TCCPN	#T	#P	#S	Schedules
MSCS	7	4	2	$<t_0, <t_1>*, t_2, t_3, t_5, t_6>$, $<t_0, <t_1>*, t_2, t_3, t_4, t_6>$

#T: #transitions, #P: #places, #S: #schedules

```
void *thread_run0(void *arg) {
 t0();  pthread_mutex_lock(&mutex);  opera-
tion(t0,p0,'+')
  switch(p0) { case 1 : do{ if(check_enable(t1)) {
                   mutex_operation(p0,t1,'-');
                   t1();mutex_operation(p0,t1,'+'); } }
                   while(pla0);
                   pthread_mutex_unlock(&mutex); break;
              case 2 : if(check_enable(t2))
                   { operation(p0,t2,'-'); t2();
                   pthread_mutex_unlock(&mutex);
                   pthread_mutex_lock(&mutex); opera-
tion(t2,p1,'+')
  switch(p1) { case 3 : if(check_enable(t3)) {
                   operation(p1,t3,'-'); t3();
                   pthread_mutex_unlock(&mutex);
                   pthread_mutex_lock(&mutex);
                   operation(t3,p2,'+') … }}}}
```

Fig. 8. Code for Motor Speed Control

References

1. K. Altisen, G. Gobler, A.Pneuli, J. Sifakis, S. Tripakis, and S. Yovine, "A framework for scheduler synthesis," In *Proceedings of the Real-Time System Symposium (RTSS'99)*, IEEE Computer Society Press, 1999.
2. F. Balarin and M. Chiodo. "Software synthesis for complex reactive embedded systems," In *Proceedings of International Conference on Computer Design (ICCD'99)*, IEEE CS Press, October 1999, 634 – 639.
3. L. A. Cortes, P. Eles, and Z. Peng, "Formal co-verification of embedded systems using model checking," In *Proceedings of EUROMICRO*, 2000, 106 – 113.
4. P.-A. Hsiung, "Formal synthesis and code generation of embedded real-time software," In *International Symposium on Hard-ware/Software Codesign* (CODES'01, Copenhagen, Denmark), ACM Press, New York, USA, April 2001, 208 – 213.
5. P.-A. Hsiung, W.-B. See, T.-Y. Lee, J.-M Fu, and S.-J. Chen, "Formal verification of embedded real-time software in component-based application frameworks," In *Proceedings of the 8th Asia-Pacific Software Engineering Conference* (APSEC 2001, Macau, China), IEEE CS Press, December 2001, 71 – 78.
6. M. Sgroi and L. Lavagno, "Synthesis of embedded software using free-choice Petri nets," *IEEE/ACM 36th Design Automation Conference* (DAC'99), June 1999, 805 – 810.
7. T.-Y. Lee, P.-A. Hsiung, and S.-J. Chen, "A case study in codesign of distributed systems — vehicle parking management system," In *Proceedings of the International Conference on Parallel and Distributed Processing Techniques and Applications* (PDPTA'99, Las Vegas, USA), CSREA Press, June 1999, 2982–2987.

8. P.-A. Hsiung, "Formal Synthesis and Control of Soft Embedded Real-Time Systems," In *Proceedings 21st IFIP WG 6.1 International Conference on Formal Techniques for Networked and Distributed Systems* (FORTE'01, Cheju Island, Korea), Kluwer Academic Publishers, August 2001, 35 – 50.

9. J. Buck, *Scheduling dynamic dataflow graphs with bounded memory using the token flow model*, Ph. D, dissertation, UC Berkeley, 1993.

10. F. Thoen et al, "Real-time multi-tasking in software synthesis for information processing systems," In *Proceeding of the International System Synthesis Symposium*, 1995, 48 – 53.

11. B. Lin, "Software synthesis of process-based concurrent programs," *IEEE/ACM 35th Design Automation Conference* (DAC'98), June 1998, 502 – 505.

12. X. Zhu and B. Lin, "Compositional software synthesis of communicating processes," *IEEE International Conference on Computer Design*, October 1999, 646 – 651.

13. F.-S. Su and P.-A. Hsiung, "Extended quasi-static scheduling for formal synthesis and code generation of embedded software," In *Proceedings of the 10th IEEE/ACM International Symposium on Hardware/Software Codesign*, (CODES'2002, Colorado, USA), IEEE CS Press, May 2002, 211 – 216.

14. C.-H. Gau and P. -A. Hsiung, "Time-memory scheduling and code generation of real-time embedded software," In *Proceedings of the 8th International Conference on Real-Time Computing Systems and Applications* (RTCSA'2002, Tokyo, Japan), March 2002, 19 – 27.

15. F. Balarin et al., *Hardware-software Co-design of Embedded Systems: the POLIS Approach*, Kluwer Academic Publishers, 1997.

16. P.-A. Hsiung and C.-H. Gau, "Formal Synthesis of Real-Time Embedded Software by Time-Memory Scheduling of Colored Time Petri Nets," In *Proceedings of the Workshop on Theory and Practice of Timed Systems* (TPTS'2002, Grenoble, France), *Electronic Notes in Theoretical Computer Science* (ENTCS), April 2002.

17. P.-A. Hsiung, T.-Y. Lee, and F.-S. Su, "Formal Synthesis and Code Generation of Real-Time Embedded Software using Time-Extended Quasi-Static Scheduling," In *Proceedings of the 9th Asia-Pacific Software Engineering Conference* (APSEC'2002, Queensland, Australia), IEEE CS Press, December 2002.

18. M. Baleani, F. Gennari, J. Yunjian, Y. Patel, R. K. Brayton, A. Sangiovanni-Vincentelli, "HW/SW partitioning and code generation of embedded control applications on a reconfigurable architecture platform," In *Proceedings of the Tenth International Symposium on Hardware/Software Codesign* (CODES'2002, Colorado, USA), IEEE CS Press, May 2002, 151 – 156.

19. S. Tsasakou, N. S. Voros, M. Koziotis, D. Verkest, A. Prayati, and A. Birbas, "Hardware-software co-design of embedded systems using CoWare's N2C methodology for application development," *In Proceedings of the 6th IEEE International Conference on Electronics, Circuits and Systems* (ICECS'1999, Pafos, Cyprus), IEEE CS Press, September 1999, Vol. 1, 59 – 62.

20. F. Wang and P.-A. Hsiung, "Efficient and User-Friendly Verification," *IEEE Transactions on Computers*, Vol. 51, No. 1, pp. 61-83, January 2002.

Software Platform for Embedded Software Development

Win-Bin See[1,4], Pao-Ann Hsiung[2], Trong-Yen Lee[3], and Sao-Jie Chen[4]

[1]Aerospace Industrial Development Company, Taichung, Taiwan, ROC
winbinsee@ms.aidc.com.tw
[2]National Chung Cheng University, Chiayi, Taiwan, ROC
[3]National Taipei University of Technology, Taipei, Taiwan, ROC
[4]National Taiwan University, Taipei, Taiwan, ROC

Abstract. The demands for new embedded system products that provide new functionality and adopting new hardware are booming. Parallel development in hardware and software is promising in reducing both the time and effort for the design of embedded system. Mostly, the development of embedded system application has been carried out on general purpose computing platform using cross target development tools, includes cross compiler and linker etc. Personal computers are used as cross development environment to host the embedded system software development tool set. We propose a software platform approach that promotes the role of PC based embedded software cross development platform to support the embedded software development even before the real hardware becomes available. Our approach is a *tunable embedded software development platform (TESDP)* that facilitates more extensive usage of the development platform. *TESDP* helps in decoupling the hardware and software development while maintaining very close semantic similarity for the function operates on both development and target platforms. We demonstrate the feasibility of the *TESDP* approach with the development of two embedded systems, a car-borne *modular mobile data terminal (MMDT)*, and an air-borne *navigation support display (NSD)* system. *MMDT* provides data communication and global positioning capability for applications in the domain of intelligent transportation system *(ITS)*. *NSD* is an important component in avionics systems that provides pilot with graphical flight instrument information to support aircraft navigation.

1 Introduction

Following the advances in the design and fabrication techniques for semiconductor devices, various micro-controllers and peripheral control chips are proliferating with decreasing price and increasing performance. These technology advancements have also enabled the development of inexpensive embedded systems that provide dedicated and integrated services. Mobile phones, digital camera and personal digital assistance (PDA) are examples of emerging embedded system applications. On the other hands, these kinds of embedded systems are suffered from having short life cycle time that have been caused by the changing appetite of customers and the

J. Chen and S. Hong (Eds.): RTCSA 2003, LNCS 2968, pp. 545–557, 2004.

introduction of new products from competitors. Hence, embedded system providers have to keep on developing new products based on new hardware components and new user demands in functionality and interface improvement, the embedded software will be the glue to all hardware components. To take advantage of cost reduction from mass production, programmable micro-controllers are used in embedded system design. Embedded system software drives the micro-controller and associated hardware components to provide the system functionality required. Embedded system software can program the same micro-controller and cooperate with proper peripheral configuration for various applications per requirement specified. To cope with the demanding requests for new embedded system products, the industry needs good design methods and tools for embedded system software development.

In order to reduce the development time for the embedded system software, various techniques could be taken, such as adopting software reuse technique, seeking for the advancement in software synthesis and verification [1, 3, 4, 6, 7].

Embedded system software is usually developed on a hardware platform that is different from the final target environment. Cross compilers are used in the software development station to generate target code, and then downloaded into the RAM or programmable ROM resides in embedded hardware platform for execution. Accordingly, development methods that could enable the parallelism in software and hardware development will also be helpful for embedded system development. Object-Oriented programming is a paradigm that has been pledged to enable better software re-use, object-oriented frameworks have been worked prominently in this aspect [7, 13, 14]. In this article, we propose a software platform approach that integrates the object-oriented paradigm to support the parallel development in embedded software and hardware. Our approach is a *tunable embedded software development platform (TESDP)* that facilitates extensive usage of the ordinary cross development platform. *TESDP* helps in decoupling the hardware and software development while maintaining very close semantic similarity for the function operates on both development and target platforms. It also provides framework for execution information collection to support the system verification and tuning.

This article is organized as follows. Section 2 gives a brief overview about previous work in object-oriented software framework and tools that support embedded software development. Section 3 describes the proposed embedded software development method that based on a *Tunable Embedded Software Development Platform (TESDP)*. Section 4 illustrates the feasibility of this development platform through the design and implementation of an embedded mobile data terminal for intelligent transportation system application. Section 5 gives an example in airborne embedded navigation display system application. Section 6 concludes the article and gives directions for future work.

2   Previous Work

Embedded system is a special purpose computer system that consists of controller and peripheral devices. Most embedded system needs to response to some external events with some timing constraints. To cope with proliferating demands in embedded system development, various methodologies and tools are developed for embedded real-time system development.

Object oriented frameworks [9] provide reusable domain specific software that can be applied with minor modification. Two recently proposed frameworks, *Object-Oriented Real-Time System Framework (OORTSF)* [13, 14] and *RTFrame* [5] are providing reusable real-time system frameworks. *VERTAF* [7] integrates verification capability into its framework.

Execution time information of functions in the embedded system provides base data for system design, analysis and verification. Classical scheduling policies [10, 11] use execution time information for schedulability check. Cortes *et al.* [4] introduce Petri Net based formal verification method that uses "transition delay" associated with transition to represent the execution time of the function. In the timed automata based formal verification method [7] for embedded system, mode predicates represent the information about execution time of function. It is desirable to have actual execution time collection mechanism as a baseline design for embedded system development. We introduce several objects into a kernel that is based on *OORTSF* to provide the actual execution time information collection.

Hardware development tool supports gate-level abstraction, this model would be too detailed to be suitable for the development of embedded system. Some embedded system development platform [16] provides higher level of abstractions include microprocessor, cache, memory, DMA, etc. Some embedded system development tools abstract the system into graph structure and use graph algorithm to explore the properties required by system specification [1, 3, 7, 15]. The abstractions used in the above tools are either too detailed or too high-level for the development of embedded system that need to address software and hardware at the same time.

It is suggesting in providing a development platform to support the abstractions of both the hardware and software that are manageable to the embedded system application designer. We propose a *Tunable Embedded Software Development Platform (TESDP)* that addresses this issue to support the parallel development of embedded software and hardware.

3 Tunable Embedded Software Development Platform

Typical embedded system consists of programmable micro-controller, memory, and peripherals. Embedded system reacts to its environment and needs to satisfy some kind of execution sequence and timing constraints. Accordingly, most embedded software is also real-time software. Embedded system exhibits its functionality through its input/output interconnections, and peripherals with respect to the environment. Software on micro-controller does the data computation and senses the environment data to generate the system output. Embedded system synchronizes and communicates with its environment via mechanisms such as hardware interrupts, port based input/output and memory-mapped input/output.

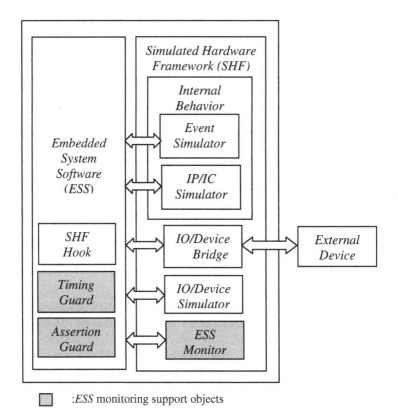

□ :*ESS* monitoring support objects

Fig. 1. Tunable Embedded Software Development Platform *(TESDP)*.

Since C/C++ programming language is a very popular programming language used by most of the micro-controllers and the systems running under a Windows or a Unix OS platform. Most of the micro-controller uses Windows and Unix OS platform as its cross development platform. From the C/C++ programming point of view, target platform and the cross development platform provide the same abstraction in using the same high-level language. From system behavior point of view, the major difference between target platform and the development platform will be the differences in hardware interrupts, input/output port, the peripherals that exhibit system functionality. After keen arrangement, we can make up an illusion of the target embedded system that can execute the C/C++ programs of the target systems, and exhibits the behavior of the peripherals of the target system on the development platform. We call this embedded software development system as *Tunable Embedded Software Development Platform (TESDP)*. Figure 1 shows the software architecture of *TESDP*, which consists of two major parts: *Embedded System Software (ESS)* and *Simulated Hardware Framework (SHF)*. The task scheduling and control of *ESS* is based on the design of *OORTSF* [13, 14] to integrate the required application functionality. *TESDP* further adapts an *ESS* from an original embedded system by compiling and linking it to the *SHF* for execution on the development platform.

We add three object classes into the *Embedded System Software (ESS)* to support verification data extraction and provide monitoring function of *TESDP*. We use *Timing Guard object* to collect the execution time information of function. The *Assertion Guard* object is used to provide run-time status information to the *ESS Monitor* in *SHF*.

- *SHF Hook:* This is an object-oriented class that supports the insertion and replacement of the operations in *ESS* operations for *SHF*. *SHF Hook* provides systematic and documented insertion of the mechanism to match *ESS* into the environment of our *TESDP* platform.

- *Timing Guard*: The execution time of a task depends on the speed of the processor used. We introduce a *timing guard object* to gauge the elapsed time of a function and to introduce the execution time offset as required for different platforms. Using *Timing Guard*, a user can mitigate the timing gap between *TESDP* and actual embedded system operation. *Timing Guard* supports the extraction of actual execution time information for a function. This information can be collected and refurbish to the system tuning process.

- *Assertion Guard*: System properties have to be formulated for formal verification[7]. Some programming paradigms focused on introducing pre-condition/post-conditions and invariants into the to-be-verified software in a structured manner[12]. System requirement compliance check can also be built into the software. For example, we can present condition of interest and its run-time verification using *Assert Guard* objects. Embedded system operation does not have rich user interface with outside world as general-purpose computer system does. Cooperating an *Assertion Guard* with the *ESS Monitor* in *SHF* can provide report to the system developer.

We choose C/C++ language to write programs executed in both the target micro-controller and development platform. To let the embedded software program executes on the *TESDP*, we need to find out a layer of separation that can derive an efficient *SHF* design. We categorized the hardware abstractions first and provide mechanisms to support the hardware abstraction using combinations of the software and hardware on the development platform and from the external devices connected to the *TESDP* software development platform. The layer of separation we choose for the micro-controller core and peripherals consists of three major abstractions described as follows.

- *Internal behavior*: It represents CPU interrupts, memory mapped I/O and special internal Integrated Circuit (IC) and/or Intellectual Proprietary (IP) components like programmable logic arrays. *Event Simulator* and *IC/IP*
- *Simulator* are used to simulate the *internal behavior* of components.
  IO/Device Bridge: It represents external communication interfaces like RS232 and parallel port. *IO/Device Bridge* simulates those IO

interconnections. *IO/Device Bridge* uses physical interface to connect the external devices.

- *IO/Device Simulator*: It represents IO devices, such as LCM display and keyboard/keypads. *IO/Device Simulator* simulates the IO/Device inside or externally connected to the embedded system. There are approaches that can simplify the design and implementation of *IO/Device Simulator*, such as: (a) choosing standard *application program interface* (*API*) that is supported both in cross development platform and target platform, and or (b) introducing a hypothetical interface and implement application over this abstraction. For example *OpenGL* API can be selected for graphical programming, if both platforms support the *OpenGL* library.

- *ESS Monitor:* It reads *ESS* execution status data from *ESS Assert Guard* Object. *ESS Monitor* provides a means for the report of system and application function execution status to the system developer. Execution status information is very useful for system verification and tuning.

Using these abstraction techniques, the *SHF* can be tuned to adapt to the changes in the target embedded configuration. *SHF* is an object-oriented software framework that provides an execution support environment for the *ESS*. We use the Windows-2000 platform on a Personal Computer for this *TESDP* design and implementation. Table 1 shows the *SHF* classes, *SHF* implementation and associated example embedded components. The object-oriented framework is a software reuse technique that provides half-done software to facilitate the reuse in both design and code. The *SHF* classes can be instantiated and composed to simulate the hardware configuration of an embedded system. During the evolution, if the embedded system is adapted to new hardware technology, the system developer can readjust the *SHF* according to the changes

Table 1. Major *SHF* object-oriented classes.

SHF Class	*SHF* Implementation	Example Embedded Component
Event Simulator	Thread	Scheduler Timer
IC/IP Simulator	Software API	Programmable Logic Device
IO/Device Bridge	Thread	RS232 connection
IO/Device Simulator	Thread	LCM Display
Timing Guard	Thread	LCM Display

The main advantage of this approach is to provide a simulated hardware environment associated with the stages of hardware architecture evolution in embedded system development. Some of the modular device control and/or inter-connections can be tested in the *TESDP* first, instead of building a total design to test the target system. In our experience, this saves a lot of time, because the *TESDP* is more stable and convenient in access. With confirmed protocol between controller and the device interactions, most of the code can be execute directly after re-compilation. Some of the devices are controlled via general interface, such as: RS232, the mismatch between the two platforms has been harmonized by the baud rate setting for the RS232 interface.

We are also aware of some mismatches between the embedded platform and the *TESDP* approach. These mismatches are timing mismatch, compiler mismatch and abstraction mismatch as follows. (1) *Timing mismatch*: Real-time system scheduling is done based on the clock of a platform. Running *TESDP* on a general purpose Personal Computer has the positive side of higher clock rate than on the target embedded system. Yet it also introduces additional system overhead posed by the underlying operating system. (2) *Compiler mismatch*: Specific compiler and linker might have specific flaws inside. However, *TESDP* could have more matured compiler than target micro-controller. Earlier *ESS* software development on *TESDP* turns out to be an efficient approach. (3) *Abstraction mismatch*: It depends on the availability of the hardware and software capability on the *TESDP* with respect to the embedded system. *TEDSP* user adjusts the configuration of *SHF* for target embedded system configuration, this also introduces deviation between them. However, the standard interface mechanism, like RS232, eases the abstraction deviation between *SHF* and the real target.

4   Application Example 1: Modular Mobile Data Terminal

Modular Mobile Data Terminal (*MMDT*), an embedded system to be installed in a commercial or private car, provides various remote management/support functionalities via the mobile data communication capability and global positioning system (*GPS*) built into the *MMDT*. *MMDT* also provides to the car driver a user interface that includes a large size LCM display module, a set of control buttons, and optional PS2 keyboard. *MMDT* handles two types of data communication protocols, MAP27 protocol stack software for trunking radio[8] and AT command interface software for Global System for Mobile communications (*GSM*) module[2]. Figure 2 shows the hardware architecture of *MMDT*.

In Figure 2, PLD is a filed programmable logic device that has been programmed with *VHDL* to handle the PS2 keyboard bit-level interrupts, pack the data bits into bytes of data, and send it to Micro-controller with another byte-level interrupts and associated memory-mapped data bytes for further processing. The keypad inputs are also encoded by this PLD, which interrupts the Micro-controller to notify the occurrences of the keypad depression with associated keypad code. The LCM module is a display panel with back light control that is capable to display large traditional Chinese font for easy reading by the car driver. However, the LCM module has relatively low duty cycle as compared to the speed of Micro-controller, and it needs polling based access to confirm the availability for updating further display data. The

LCM module display duty-cycle will also be a parameter that varies when the replacement of LCM in different design becomes necessary.

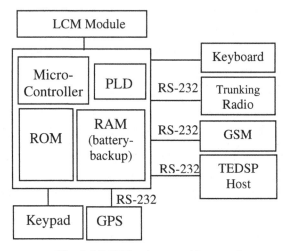

Fig. 2. *MMDT* hardware architecture.

In this system, RS232 interfaces are used to connect external devices that include *GPS*, Trunking Radio, *GSM* module and a remote host computer. *Simulated Hardware Framework (SHF)* on *TESDP* uses actual RS232 interface to control external hardware modules. We use Windows-2000 platform for this *TESDP* design and implementation. Table 2 shows the *SHF* classes and objects instantiated for the *MMDT* execution on our *TESDP* environment.

Table 2. *MMDT* components to *SHF* classes mapping.

Embedded components	*SHF* object	*SHF* class	*SHF* implement.
Scheduler Timer	Timer Thread	Event Simulator	Timer Thread
Keypad	Keypad Thread	*IP/IC Simulator*	Software API
PS2 Keyboard	Keyb Thread	*IP/IC Simulator*	Software API
GSM connection	GSM Bridge	*IO/Device Bridge*	RS232 Thread
Trunking Radio connection	Trunking Radio Bridge	*IO/Device Bridge*	RS232 Thread
GPS connection	GPS Bridge	*IO/Device Bridge*	RS232 Thread

LCM module	LCM display Simulator	*IO/Device Simulator*	Software API
TEDSP Host Connection	Host Computer Bridge	*IO/Device Bridge*	RS232 Thread

MMDT embedded software consists of a baseline *OORTSF* [13, 14] framework as its *Real-Time Kernel* to control application tasks. Figure 3 shows the embedded software architecture of *MMDT*. The *MAP27 Protocol Processing* consists data link layer processing *MAP27 DL Layer*, and network layer processing *MAP27 Net Layer*. An external radio set is connected to the *MMDT* for Trunking Radio communication. *NavCruRpt* does system navigation and cruise function based on the *GPS* data from *GPS Driver*, it reports the current vehicle position data to control center through mobile communication. *GPS* is a module built inside the *MMDT* box. *Display Page Control* manages the page displayed on the LCM module through *LCM Control*. *Keypad* selects the display menu page for user controls. *Keyboard* inputs data to the data field on LCM display page. *GSM Comm* controls the external *GSM* communication module using AT commands[2]. In Figure 3, the box with dashed-line delineates the implementation boundary between *ESS* and *SHF*.

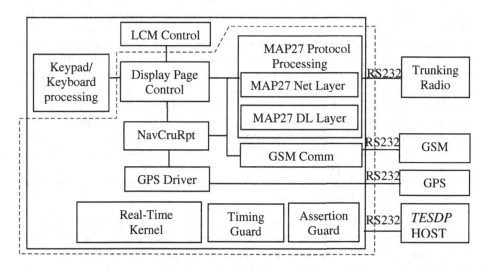

Fig. 3. *MMDT* software architecture.

During the development of *MMDT*, some hardware modules were added into the system follows the evolution of system requirements. The *GSM* communication module control has been integrated on the *TESDP* environment first and integrated into the real target platform after the control and operation scenario confirmed. Many of the devices are connected via *RS232* interface and the *SHF* uses actual *RS232* to drive the devices on *TESDP*. Therefore, there are little differences in the operational scenarios between actual embedded platform and *TESDP*, this further proves the feasibility of our *TESDP* approach.

5 Application Example 2: Airborne Navigation Support Display System

Aircraft pilot reads navigation support information from flight instrument indicators, such as attitude/direction indicator (*ADI*) and horizontal situation indicator (*HSI*). The *ADI* and *HSI* indicate aircraft attitude and flight direction indication etc, based on the data collected from various sensors onboard the aircraft. Traditionally, the *ADI* and *HSI* are mechanical indicators. Recently, aero-industry is taking advantage of electronic display devices like LCD display to provide a versatile and redundant cockpit display. Using LCD display, various sensor and mission data can be presented in forms of video, text, or graphical format to the pilot. Multiple LCD based display systems collocated in cockpit to present multiple number of information at the same time, and also enable the redundancy via pilot selectable information swapping among displays.

Airborne display systems are evolving with the technology of display and control hardware, starting from mono-display with proprietary hardware interface and migrating towards color-display with open standard graphics control interface, like *OpenGL*. In the development of a new airborne *navigation support display* (*NSD*) system to support *ADI, HSI* display and mission data access functionalities, we faced with the issue of parallel development in embedded display application software and hardware. Even worse, the exact display interface will be left undefined in the early stage of the project. The *TESDP* approach provides a good resolution to this situation. A hypothetical display layer of software interface, (*Hypo-Display*), provides an abstraction of display device to the application software. The *Hypo-Display* has been implemented on the cross platform to support the development of application software of upper layer. We chose the *OpenGL* library to developed the *Hypo-Display*. This enable the earlier development of display application software on cross platform, and reduce the possibility and the amount effort needed for the rework of software to adapt towards the final hardware interface.

Table 3 shows the *NDS* components to *SHF* class mapping. *Scheduler Timer* component is used to generate the task scheduling timer event. The *Bezel keys* components handles the bezel buttons input by the pilot through buttons located around the LCD display. The *Avionics Bus* component transports data coming from various flight status sensors onboard. The LCD display component displays the text, graphics and/or external video input, it has been implemented via *Hypo-Display* object as described previously. A commercial off the shelf (COTS) PowerPC board has been used for this *NDS* implementation, and TCP/IP network interconnection has been used for *TESDP* host connection.

Table 3. *NDS* components to *SHF* classes mapping.

Embedded components	*SHF* object	*SHF* class	*SHF* implement.
Scheduler Timer	Timer Thread	Event Simulator	Timer Thread
Bezel keys	Keypad Thread	*IP/IC Simulator*	Software API
Avionics Bus	Avionics Bus Thread	*IO/Device Bridge*	Av_Bus Thread
LCD display	Hypo-Display object	*IO/Device Simulator*	Software API
TEDSP Host Connection	Host Computer Bridge	*IO/Device Bridge*	TCP/IP Thread

Using *TESDP* platform with the *Hypo-Display* object provides a stable software development much earlier before the real embedded hardware become available. This approach enable the parallel development in embedded system software and hardware, and reduces the system time to market drastically.

6 Conclusion

The *TESDP* approach for embedded software development provides the possibility of parallel development in embedded hardware and software. Using the proposed development platform, the development of embedded system software can be de-coupled from the hardware platform while maintaining very close semantic similarity for the function operates on both platforms. This kind of development platform will be very desirable for electronic industry that is seeking for the grasp of booming embedded system market, such cell phone, digital camera, personal digital assistance (PDA), etc. We have used this approach in an evolutionary development of embedded *Modular Mobile Data Terminal* (*MMDT*) system for intelligent transportation system applications. With comprehensive communication and user interface, this *MMDT* can also be adapted to support other domain of application. With the support of *TESDP* approach, the cost of future adaptation of *MMDT* could be reduced. This also provides evidence for the value of *TESDP* approach in the development of other embedded systems. In this article, an example application of *TESDP* in the area of airborne embedded system, a *navigation display system* (*NDS*), has also been examined, and we found that the *TESDP* approach enables the parallel development in hardware and software. It drastically reduced the total system development cycle time of the *NDS* system development.

In the case of *MMDT*, the *TESDP* approach supports the development of software for embedded system that consists of micro-controller and peripheral integrated circuits (ICs). From hardware aspect, some hardware component providers provide their intellectual property (IP) cores of micro-controllers and peripherals in the form of electronic files. System designer integrates various IP cores as required and turn them into a System On a Chip (SOC). This SOC approach further provides embedded system hardware with even more cost competitiveness. However, SOC needs embedded software that executes on the micro-controller and elaborates the peripheral to fulfill the system functionality. We believe that our approach can also be applied to the SOC type of embedded system development.

We are working on the integration of more comprehensive software frameworks and code synthesis capability [1, 3, 4, 6, 15] to support the development of different types of embedded systems. We are also integrating software verification capability into this development platform [7] and make it both tunable and verifiable development environments for embedded system development environment.

References

[1] K. Altisen, G. Gobler, A. Pneuli, J. Sifakis, S. Tripakis, and S. Yovine, "A Framework for Scheduler Synthesis," In *Proceedings of the Real-Time System Symposium* (*RTSS'99*), IEEE Computer Society Press, 1999.

[2] AT command set for GSM Mobile Equipment (ME) (GSM 07.07 version 4.4.1), Digital cellular telecommunications system (Phase 2), European Telecommunications Standards Institute, France, March 1999.

[3] F. Balarin and M. Chiodo. Software synthesis for complex reactive embedded systems. In *Proceedings of International Conference on Computer Design (ICCD'99)*, pp. 634 – 639. IEEE CS Press, October 1999.

[4] L. A. Cortes, P. Eles, and Z.Peng, *"Formal Co-verification of Embedded Systems using Model Checking,"* In *Proceedings of EUROMICRO*, pp. 106-113, 2000.

[5] P. -A. Hsiung, "RTFrame: An object-oriented application framework for real-time applications," In *Proceedings of the 27th International Conference on Technology of Object-Oriented Languages and Systems (TOOLS'98)*, pp. 138-147, IEEE Computer Society Press, September 1998.

[6] P. -A. Hsiung, "Formal synthesis and code generation of embedded real-time software," In *International Symposium on Hard-ware/Software Codesign* (CODES'01, Copenhagen, Denmark), pp. 208   213. ACM Press, New York, USA, April 2001.

[7] P. -A. Hsiung, W.-B. See, T.-Y. Lee, J.-M Fu and S.-J. Chen, "Formal verification of Embedded Real-Time Software in Component-Based Application Frameworks," to appear in *The 8th Asia-Pacific Software Engineering Conference* (APSEC 2001).

[8] Introduction to MAP27 protocol, Web Site: "http://www.condor-cci.com/trunking.new/map27.htm".

[9] R. E. Johnson, "Frameworks = (Components + Patterns)," In *Communications of the ACM*, Vol. 40, No. 10, pp. 39-42, October 1997.

[10] C. L. Liu and J. W. Layland, "Scheduling Algorithms for Multiprogramming in a Hard Real-Time Environment," *Journal of ACM*, Vol. 20, No. 1, pp. 46-61,1973.

[11] J. -F. Lin, W. -B. See, and S.-J. Chen, "Performance Bounds on Scheduling Parallel Tasks with Communication Cost," *IEICE Trans. Information & Systems*, Vol. E78-D, No. 3, pp. 263-268, March 1995.

[12] M. Lippert and C. V. Lopes, "A Study on Exception Detection and Handling Using Aspect-Oriented Programming", In *Proceedings of ICSE'2000*, ACM Press.

[13] W. –B. See and S. -J. Chen, "High-level reuse in the design of an object-oriented real-time system framework." In *Proceedings of the International Computer Symposium,* pp. 363-370, December 1996.

[14] W. –B. See and S. –J. Chen, "Object-oriented real-time system framework." *Domain-Specific Application Frameworks,* pages 327-338, Ed. M.E. Fayad and R.E. Johnson, Wiley, 2000.

[15] M. Sgroi and L. Lavagno, "Synthesis of Embedded Software Using Free-Choice Petri Nets," In *Proceedings of IEEE/ACM Design Automation Conference (DAC'99)*, ACM Press, June 1999.

[16] F. Vahid and T. Givargis, "Platform Tuning for Embedded Systems Design," *IEEE Computer*, No. 34, Vol. 3, pp. 112-114, March 2001.

Towards Aspectual Component-Based Development of Real-Time Systems*

Aleksandra Tešanović[1], Dag Nyström[2], Jörgen Hansson[1], and Christer Norström[2]

[1] Linköping University, Department of Computer Science, Linköping, Sweden
{alete,jorha}@ida.liu.se
[2] Mälardalen University, Department of Computer Engineering, Västerås, Sweden
{dag.nystrom,christer.norstrom}@mdh.se

Abstract. Increasing complexity of real-time systems, and demands for enabling their configurability and tailorability are strong motivations for applying new software engineering principles, such as aspect-oriented and component-based development. In this paper we introduce a novel concept of aspectual component-based real-time system development. The concept is based on a design method that assumes decomposition of real-time systems into components and aspects, and provides a real-time component model that supports the notion of time and temporal constraints, space and resource management constraints, and composability. We anticipate that the successful applications of the proposed concept should have a positive impact on real-time system development in enabling efficient configuration of real-time systems, improved reusability and flexibility of real-time software, and modularization of crosscutting concerns. We provide arguments for this assumption by presenting an application of the proposed concept on the design and development of a configurable embedded real-time database, called COMET. Furthermore, using the COMET system as an example, we introduce a novel way of handling concurrency in a real-time database system, where concurrency is modeled as an aspect crosscutting the system.

1 Introduction

Real-time and embedded systems are being used widely in today's modern society. However, successful deployment of embedded and real-time systems depends on low development costs, high degree of tailorability and quickness to market [1]. Thus, the introduction of the component-based software development (CBSD) paradigm into real-time and embedded systems development offers significant benefits, namely: (i) configuration of embedded and real-time software for a specific application using components from the component library, thus reducing the system complexity as components can be chosen to provide exactly the functionality needed by the system; (ii) rapid development and deployment of real-time software as many software components, if properly designed and verified, can be reused in different embedded and real-time applications; and (iii) evolutionary design as components can be replaced or added to the system,

---

* This work is supported by ARTES, A network for Real-time and graduate education in Sweden, and CENIIT, Center for Industrial Information Technology, under contract 01.07.

J. Chen and S. Hong (Eds.): RTCSA 2003, LNCS 2968, pp. 558–577, 2004.

which is appropriate for complex embedded real-time systems that require continuous hardware and software upgrades.

However, there are aspects of real-time and embedded systems that cannot be encapsulated in a component with well-defined interfaces as they crosscut the structure of the overall system, e.g., synchronization, memory optimization, power consumption, and temporal attributes. Aspect-oriented software development (AOSD) has emerged as a new principle for software development that provides an efficient way of modularizing crosscutting concerns in software systems. AOSD allows encapsulating system's crosscutting concerns in "modules", called aspects. Applying AOSD in real-time and embedded system development would reduce the complexity of the system design and development, and provide means for a structured and efficient way of handling crosscutting concerns in a real-time software system.

Thus, the integration of the two disciplines, CBSD and AOSD, into real-time systems development would enable: (i) efficient system configuration from the components in the component library based on the system's requirements, (ii) easy tailoring of components and/or a system for a specific application by changing the behavior (code) of the component by applying aspects, and (iii) enhanced flexibility of the real-time and embedded software through the notion of system's configurability and components' tailorability.

However, to be able to successfully apply software engineering techniques such as AOSD and CBSD in real-time systems, the following questions need to be answered.

- What is the appropriate design method that will allow integration of the two software engineering techniques into real-time systems?
- What components and aspects are appropriate for the real-time and embedded environment?
- What component model can capture and adopt principles of the CBSD and AOSD in a real-time and embedded environment?

In this paper we address these research questions, by proposing a novel concept of aspectual component-based real-time system development (ACCORD). The concept is founded on a design method that decomposes real-time systems into components and aspects, and provides a real-time component model (RTCOM) that supports the notion of time and temporal constraints, space and resource management constraints, and composability. RTCOM is the component model addressing real-time software reusability and composability by combining aspects and components. It is our experience so far that applying the proposed concept has a positive impact on the real-time system development in enabling efficient configuration of real-time systems, improved reusability and flexibility of real-time software, and a structured way of handling crosscutting concerns. We show that the ACCORD can be successfully applied in practice by describing the way we have applied it in the design and development of a component-based embedded real-time database system (COMET). In the COMET example we present a novel approach to modeling and implementing real-time policies, e.g., concurrency control and scheduling, as aspects that crosscut the structure of a real-time system. Modularization of real-time policies into aspects allows customization of real-time systems without changing the code of the components.

The paper is organized as follows. In section 2 we present an outline of ACCORD and its design method. We present RTCOM in section 3. In section 4 we show an application of ACCORD to the development of COMET. In the COMET example we describe a new way of modeling real-time concurrency control policy as an aspect in a real-time database system. Related work is discussed in section 5. The paper finishes (section 6) with a summary containing the main conclusions and directions for our future research.

2   ACCORD Design Method

The growing need for enabling development of configurable real-time and embedded systems that can be tailored for a specific application [1], and managing the complexity of the requirements in the real-time system design, calls for an introduction of new concepts and new software engineering paradigms into real-time system development. Hence, we propose ACCORD. Through the notion of aspects and components, ACCORD enables efficient application of the divide-and-conquer approach to complex system development. To effectively apply ACCORD, we provide a design method with the following constituents.

- A decomposition process with two sequential phases: (i) decomposition of the real-time system into a set of components, and (ii) decomposition of the real-time system into a set of aspects.
- Components, as software artifacts that implement a number of well-defined functions, and where they have well-defined interfaces. Components use interfaces for communication with the environment, i.e., other components.
- Aspects, as properties of a system affecting its performance or semantics, and cross-cutting the system's functionality [2].
- A real-time component model (RTCOM) that describes how a real-time component, supporting aspects, should look like. RTCOM is specifically developed: (i) to enable an efficient decomposition process, (ii) to support the notion of time and temporal constraints, and (iii) to enable efficient analysis of components and the composed system.

The design of a real-time system using ACCORD method is performed in three phases. In the first phase, a real-time system is decomposed into a set of components. Decomposition is guided by the need to have functionally exchangeable units that are loosely coupled, but with strong cohesion. In the second phase, a real-time system is decomposed into a set of aspects. Aspects crosscut components and the overall system. This phase typically deals with non-functional requirements[1] and crosscutting concerns of a real-time system, e.g., resource management and temporal attributes. In the final phase, components and aspects are implemented based on RTCOM. As non-functional requirements are among the most important issues in real-time system development, we first focus on the aspectual decomposition, and then discuss RTCOM.

2.1   Aspects in Real-Time Systems

We classify aspects in a real-time system as follows: (i) application aspects, (ii) run-time aspects, and (iii) composition aspects.

---

[1] Non-functional requirements are sometimes referred to as extra-functional requirements [3].

Application aspects can change the internal behavior of components as they crosscut the code of the components in the system. The application in this context refers to the application towards which a real-time and embedded system should be configured, e.g., memory optimization aspect, synchronization aspect, security aspect, real-time property aspect, and real-time policy aspect. Since optimizing memory usage is one of the key issues in embedded systems and it crosscuts the real-time system's structure, we view memory optimization as an application aspect of a real-time system. Security is another application aspect that influences system's behavior and structure, e.g., the system must be able to distinguish users with different security clearance. Synchronization, entangled over the entire system, is encapsulated and represented by a synchronization aspect. Memory optimization, synchronization, and security are commonly mentioned aspects in AOSD [2]. Additionally, real-time properties and policies are viewed as application aspects as they influence the overall structure of the system. Depending on the system's requirements, real-time properties and policies could be further refined, which we show in the example of the COMET system (see section 4.3). Application aspects enable tailoring of the components for a specific application, as they change code of the components.

Run-time aspects are critical as they refer to aspects of the monolithic real-time system that need to be considered when integrating the system into the run-time environment. Run-time aspects give information needed by the run-time system to ensure that integrating a real-time system would not compromise timeliness, nor available memory consumption. Therefore, each component should have declared resource demands in its resource demand aspect, and should have information of its temporal behavior, contained in the temporal constraints aspect, e.g., worst-case execution time (WCET). The temporal aspect enables a component to be mapped to a task (or a group of tasks) with specific temporal requirements. Additionally, each component should contain information of the platform with which it is compatible, e.g., real-time operating system supported, and other hardware related information. This information is contained in the portability aspect. It is imperative that the information contained in the run-time aspect is provided to ensure predictability of the composed system, ease the integration into a run-time environment, and ensure portability to different hardware and/or software platforms.

Composition aspects describe with which components a component can be combined (compatibility aspect), the version of the component (version aspect), and possibilities of extending the component with additional aspects (flexibility aspect).

Having separation of aspects in different categories eases reasoning about different embedded and real-time related requirements, as well as the composition of the system and its integration into a run-time environment. For example, the run-time system could define what (run-time) aspects the real-time system should fulfill so that proper components and application aspects could be chosen from the library, when composing a monolithic system. This approach offers a significant flexibility, since additional aspect types can be added to components, and therefore, to the monolithic real-time system, further improving the integration with the run-time environment.

After aspects are identified, we recommend that a table is made with all the components and all identified application aspects, in which the crosscutting effects to different components are recorded (an example of one such table is given in section 4.3). As we show in the next section, this step is especially useful for the next phase of the design, where each component is modeled and designed to take into account identified application aspects.

3   Real-Time Component Model (RTCOM)

In this section we present RTCOM, which allows easy and predictable weaving of aspects, i.e., integrating aspects into components, thus reflecting decomposition of the system into components and aspects. RTCOM can be viewed as a component colored with aspects, both inside (application aspects), and outside (run-time and composition aspects). RTCOM is a language-independent component model, consisting of the following parts (see figure 1): (i) the functional part, (ii) the run-time system dependent part, and (iii) the composition part.

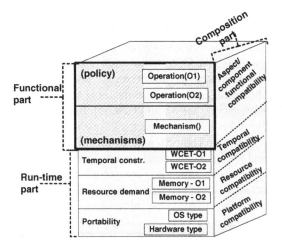

Fig. 1. A real-time component model (RTCOM)

The functional part represents the actual code that implements the component functionality. RTCOM assumes the following for the functional part of the component.

- Each component provides a set of mechanisms, which are basic and fixed parts of the component infrastructure. Mechanisms are fine granule methods or function calls.
- Each component provides a set of operations to other components and/or to the system. Implementation of the operations determines the behavior of the component, i.e., component policy. Operations are represented by coarse granule methods or function calls. Operations are flexible parts of the component as their implementation can change by applying different application aspects. Operations are implemented using the underlying mechanisms, which are fixed parts of the component.

In order to enable easy implementation of application aspects into a component, the design of the functional part of the component is performed in the following manner. First, the mechanisms, as basic blocks of the component, are implemented. Here, particular attention is given to identified application aspects, and the table reflecting the crosscutting effects of application aspects to different components is used to determine which application aspects are likely to use which component mechanisms. Next, the operations of the component are implemented using component mechanisms. Note, the implemented operations provide an initial component policy, i.e., basic and somewhat generic component functionality. This initial policy we call a *policy framework* of the component. The policy framework could be modified by applying different application aspects, and as such it provides a way of tailoring a component by changing its behavior, i.e., application aspects change the component policy. If all crosscutting application aspects are considered when implementing operations and mechanisms, then the framework is generic and highly flexible. However, if the system evolves such that new application aspects (not considered when developing the policy framework) need to be implemented into component code, then new mechanisms can be defined within the application aspect.

The development process of the functional part of a component results in the component that is colored with application aspects. Therefore, in the graphical view of RTCOM in figure 1, application aspects are represented as vertical layers in the functional part of the component, as they influence component behavior, i.e., change component policy.

The run-time system dependent part of RTCOM accounts for temporal behavior of the functional part of the component code, not only without aspects but also when aspects are weaved into the component. Hence, run-time aspects are part of the run-time dependent part of RTCOM, and are represented as horizontal parallel layers to the functional part of the component as they describe component behavior (see figure 1). In the run-time part of the component, run-time aspects are expressed as attributes of operations, mechanisms, and application aspects, as those are the elements of the component functional part, and thereby influence the temporal behavior of the component.

The composition part refers both to the functional part and the run-time part of a component, and is represented as the third dimension of the component model (see figure 1). Given that there are different application aspects that can be weaved into the component, composition aspects represented in the composition part of RTCOM should contain information about component compatibility with respect to different application aspects, as well as with respect to different components.

For each component implemented based on RTCOM, the functional part of the component is first implemented together with the application aspects, then the run-time system dependent part and run-time aspects are implemented, followed by the composition part and rules for composing different components and application aspects.

In the following sections we give a close-up of the application aspects and the run-time aspects within the RTCOM, followed by interfaces supported by RTCOM.

3.1   Application Aspects in RTCOM

Existing aspect languages can be used for implementation of application aspects, and their integration into components. The weaving is done by the aspect weaver corresponding to the aspect language [2]. All existing aspect languages, e.g., AspectJ [4], AspectC [5], AspectC++ [6], are conceptually very similar to AspectJ, developed for Java.

Each application aspect declaration consists of advices and pointcuts. A *pointcut* consists of one or more join points, and is described by a pointcut expression. A *join point* in an aspect language refers to a method, a type (struct or union), or any other point from which component code can be accessed. In RTCOM, the pointcut model is restricted to the mechanisms and the operations in the component, and a type (struct). This restriction is necessary for obtaining predictable aspect weaving, i.e., enabling the temporal analysis[2] of the resulting code. An *advice* is a declaration used to specify the code that should run when the join points, specified by a pointcut expression, are reached. Different kinds of advices can be declared, such as: (i) *before advice*, executed before the join point, (ii) *after advice*, executed immediately after the join point, and (iii) *around advice*, executed in place of the join point. In RTCOM, the advice model is also restricted for the reasons of enabling temporal analysis of the code. Hence, the advices are implemented using only the mechanisms of the components, and each advice can change the behavior of the component (policy framework) by changing one or more operations in the component.

3.2   Run-Time Aspects in RTCOM

We now illustrate how run-time aspects are represented and handled in RTCOM using one of the most important run-time aspects as an example, i.e., WCET. One way of enabling predictable aspect weaving is to ensure an efficient way of determining the WCET of the operations and/or real-time system that have been modified by weaving of aspects. WCET analysis of aspects, components, and the resulting aspect-oriented software (when aspects are weaved into components) is based on symbolic WCET analysis [7]. Applying symbolic WCET analysis to ACCORD implies the following: (i) WCETs of the mechanisms are obtained by symbolic WCET analysis, (ii) the WCET of every operation is determined based the WCETs of the mechanisms used for implementing the operation, and the internal WCET of the function or the method that implements the operation, i.e., manages the mechanisms, (iii) the WCET of every advice that changes the implementation of the operation is based on the WCETs of the mechanisms used for implementing the advice, and the internal WCET of the advice, i.e., code that manages the mechanisms. Figure 2 shows the WCET specification for mechanisms in the component, where for each mechanism the WCET is declared and assumed to be known. Similarly, figure 3 shows the WCET specification of the component policy framework. Each operation defining the policy of the component declares what mechanisms it uses, and how many times it uses a specific mechanism. This declaration is used for computing WCETs of the operations or the component (without aspects). Figure 4 shows the WCET

---

[2] Temporal analysis refers both to static WCET analysis of the code and dynamic schedulability analysis of the tasks.

```
mechanisms{
  mechanism{
      name      [nameOfMechanism];
      wcet        [value of wcet];
      }
            .........
  }
```

Fig. 2. Specification of the WCET aspect of component mechanisms

```
operations{
  operation{
    name      [nameOfOperation];
    uses{
        [Name of mechanism] [Number of times used];
    }
    intWcet [Value of internal operation wcet
                        (called mechanisms excluded)]
  }
  ......
}
```

Fig. 3. Specification of the WCET aspect of a component policy framework

```
aspect{
  advice{
    name [nameOfAdvice];
    type [typeOfAdvice:before, after, around];
    changes{
      name   [nameOfOperation];
      uses{
        [NameOfMechanism]   [Number of times used];
      }
      intWcet [Value of internal advice wcet
                (called mechanisms excluded)]
    }
  }
  ......
}
```

Fig. 4. Specification of the WCET aspect of an application aspect

specification of an application aspect. For each advice type (before, around, after) that modifies an operation, the operation it modifies is declared together with the mechanisms used for the implementation of the advice, and the number of times the advice uses these mechanisms. The resulting WCET of the component (or one operation within the component), colored with application aspects, is computed using the algorithm presented in [8]. The algorithm utilizes the knowledge of WCETs of all mechanisms involved, and

WCETs of all aspects that change a specific operation. The detailed explanation of the algorithm and the discussion on computing WCETs of components modified by aspects can be found in [8].

3.3 RTCOM Example

We now give a brief and simple example of one component and one application aspect. The purpose of this simple example is to provide guidance through the process of RTCOM implementation, and provide a clear understanding of RTCOM internals, introduced so far (a more complex and detailed example of RTCOM using COMET is discussed in section 4.4).

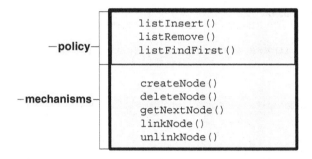

Fig. 5. The functional part of the linked list component

In this example, we consider a component implementing an ordinary linked list. The mechanisms needed are the ones for the manipulation of nodes in the list, i.e., `createNode, deleteNode, getNextNode, linkNode, unlinkNode` (see figure 5). Operations implementing the policy framework, e.g., `listInsert, listRemove, listFindFirst`, define the behavior of the component, and are implemented using the underlying mechanisms. In this example, `listInsert` uses the mechanisms `createNode` and `linkNode` to create and link a new node into the list in first-in-first-out (FIFO) order. Hence, the policy framework is FIFO.

Assume that we want to change the policy of the component from FIFO to priority-based ordering of the nodes. Then, this can be achieved by weaving an appropriate application aspect. Figure 6 shows the `listPriority` application aspect, which consists of one pointcut `listInsertCall`, identifying `listInsert` as a join point in the component code (lines 2-3). When this join point is reached, the `before` advice `listInsertCall` is executed. Hence, the application aspect `listPriority` intercepts the operation (a method or a function call to) `listInsert`, and before the code in `listInsert` is executed, the advice, using the component mechanisms (`getNextNode`), determines the position of the node based on its priority (lines 5-14). As a consequence of weaving an application aspect into the code of the component, the temporal behavior of the resulting component, colored with aspects, changes. Hence, run-time aspects need

```
aspect listPriority{
1:
2: pointcut listInsertCall(List_Operands * op)=
3:    call("void listInsert(List_Operands*)")&&args(op);
4:
5: advice listInsertCall(op):
6:    void before(List_Operands * op){
7:       while
8:          the node position is not determined
9:       do
10:         node = getNextNode(node);
11:         /* determine position of op->node based
12:         on its priority and the priority of the
13:         node in the list*/
14:    }
15: }
```

Fig. 6. The `listPriority` application aspect

```
operations(noOfElements){
  operation{
    name listInsert;
    uses{
       createNode 1;
       linkNode   1;
    }
    intWcet 1ms;
  }
  operation{
    name listRemove;
    uses{
       getNextNode noOfElements;
       unlinkNode  1;
       deleteNode  1;
    }
    intWcet 4ms;
  }
  ....
}
```

```
mechanisms{
  mechanism{
    name createNode;
    wcet  5ms;
  }
  mechanism{
    name deleteNode;
    wcet  4ms;
  }
  mechanism{
    name getNextNode;
    wcet  2ms;
  }
  ....
}
```

Fig. 7. The WCET specification of the policy framework

to be defined for the policy framework (the component without application aspects) and for the application aspects, so we can determine the run-time aspects of the component colored with different application aspects.

Figure 7 presents the specification of the WCET aspect for the policy framework of the liked list component. Each operation in the framework is named and its internal WCET (intWcet), and the number of times it uses a particular mechanism, are declared (see figure 7). The WCET specification for the application aspect listPriori-ty that changes the policy framework is shown in figure 8. Temporal information of the application aspect includes the internal WCET of an advice that modified the operation, and the information of the mechanisms used by the advice, as well as the number of times (upper bound) the advice has used a particular mechanism. Hence, the informa-

```
aspect listPriority(noOfElements){
  advice{
    name listInsertCall;
    type before;
    changes{
      name listInsert;
        uses{
          getNextNode noOfElements;
        }
      }
    intWcet 4ms+0.4*noOfElements;
  }
  ....
}
```

Fig. 8. The WCET specification of the `listPriority` application aspect

tion provided in the run-time part of the component enables temporal analysis of any combinations of the component policy frameworks and application aspects.

3.4   RTCOM Interfaces

RTCOM supports three different types of interfaces (see figure 9): (i) functional interface, (ii) configuration interface, and (iii) composition interface.

Functional interfaces of components are classified in two categories, namely provided functional interfaces, and required functional interfaces. Provided interfaces reflect a set of operations that a component provides to other components or to the system. Required interfaces reflect a set of operations that a component requires from other components. Having separation to provided and required interfaces eases component exchange and addition of new components into the system.

The *configuration interface* is intended for the integration of a real-time system with the run-time environment. This interface provides information of temporal behavior of each component, and reflects the run-time aspect of the component. Combining multiple components results in a system that also has the configuration interface, and enables the

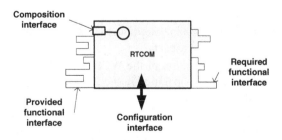

Fig. 9. Interfaces supported by the RTCOM

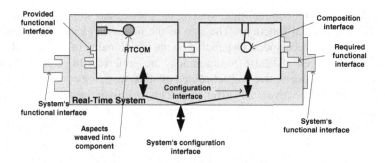

Fig. 10. Interfaces and their role in the composition process

designer to inspect the behavior of the system towards the run-time environment (see figure 10).

Composition interfaces, which correspond to join points, are embedded into the functional component part. The weaver identifies composition interfaces and uses them for aspect weaving. Composition interfaces are ignored at component/system compile-time if they are not needed, and are "activated" only when certain application aspects are weaved into the system. Thus, the composition interface allows integration of the component and aspectual part of the system. Aspect weaving can be performed either on the component level, weaving application aspects into component functionality, or on the system level, weaving application aspects into the monolithic system.

Explicit separation of software component interfaces into composition interfaces and functional interfaces is introduced in [9].

4   COMET: A COMponent-Based Embedded Real-Time Database

This section shows how to apply the introduced concept of aspectual component-based development on a design and development of a concrete real-time system by presenting the application of the design method to development of a configurable real-time embedded database system, called COMET.

4.1   Background

The goal of the COMET project is to enable development of a configurable real-time database for embedded systems, i.e., enable development of different database configurations for different embedded and real-time applications. The types of requirements we are dealing with can best be illustrated on the example of one of the COMET targeting application areas: control systems in the automotive industry. These systems are typically hard real-time safety-critical systems consisting of several distributed nodes implementing specific functionality. Although nodes depend on each other and collaborate to provide required behavior for the overall vehicle control system, each node can be viewed as a stand-alone real-time system, e.g., nodes can implement transmission, engine, or instrumental functions. The size of the nodes can vary significantly, from very small nodes to large nodes. Depending on the functionality of a node and the available memory, different database configurations are preferred. In safety-critical nodes tasks are often non-preemptive and scheduled off-line, avoiding concurrency by allowing only one task to be active at any given time. This, in turn, influences functionality of a database in a given node with respect to concurrency control. Less critical nodes, having preemptable tasks, would require concurrency control mechanisms. Furthermore, some nodes require critical data to be logged, e.g., warning and errors, and require backups on startup and shutdown, while other nodes only have RAM (main-memory), and do not require non-volatile backup facilities from the database. Hence, in the narrow sense of this application area, the goal was to enable development of different COMET configurations to suit the needs of each node with respect to memory consumption, concurrency control, recovery, different scheduling techniques, transaction and storage models.

In the following sections we show how we have reached our goal by applying AC-CORD to the design and development of the COMET system.

4.2   COMET Components

Following the ACCORD design method presented in section 2 we have first performed the decomposition of COMET into a set of components with well-defined functions and interfaces. COMET has seven basic components (see figure 11): user interface component, transaction scheduler component, locking component, indexing component, recovery and logging component, memory handling component, and transaction manager component.

The *user interface component* (UIC) enables users to access data in the database, and different applications often require different ways of accessing data in the system.

The *transaction scheduler component* (TSC) provides mechanisms for performing scheduling of transactions coming into the system, based on the scheduling policy chosen. COMET supports a variety of scheduling policies, e.g., EDF and RM [10]. Hard

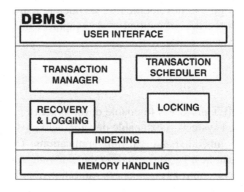

Fig. 11. COMET decomposition into a set of components

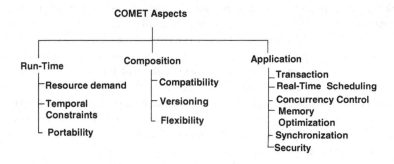

Fig. 12. Classification of aspects in an embedded real-time database system

real-time applications, such as real-time embedded systems controlling a vehicle, typically do not require sophisticated transaction scheduling and concurrency control, i.e., the system allows only one transaction to access the database at a time [11]. Therefore, the TSC should be a flexible and exchangeable part of the database architecture.

The *locking component* (LC) deals with locking of data, and it provides mechanisms for lock manipulation and maintains lock records in the database.

The *indexing component* (IC) deals with indexing of data. Indexing strategies could vary depending on the real-time application with which the database should be integrated, e.g., t-trees [12] and multi-versioning suitable for applications with a large number of read-only transactions [13]. Additionally, it is possible to customize indexing strategy depending on the number of transactions active in the system. For example, in vehicle control applications, where only one transaction is active at a time, non-thread safe indexing is used, while in more complex applications appropriate aspects could be weaved into the component to allow thread-safe processing of indexing strategy (this can be achieved by weaving the synchronization aspect).

The *recovery and logging component* (RLC) is in charge of recovery and logging of data in the database. As COMET stores data in main-memory, there is a need for different recovery and logging techniques, depending on the type of the storage, e.g., non-volatile EEPROM or Flash.

The *memory handling component* (MHC) manages access to data in the physical storage.

The *transaction manager component* (TMC) coordinates the activities of all components in the system with respect to transaction execution. For example, the TMC manages the execution of a transaction by requesting lock and unlock operations provided by the LC, followed by requests to the operations, which are provided by the IC, for inserting or updating data items.

4.3   COMET Aspects

Following ACCORD, after decomposing the system into a set of components with well-defined interfaces, we decompose the system into a set of aspects. The decomposition of

COMET into aspects is presented in figure 12, and it fully corresponds to the ACCORD decomposition (given in section 2.1) in three types of aspects: run-time, composition, and application aspects. However, as COMET is the real-time database system, refinement to the application aspects is made to reflect both real-time and database issues. Hence, in the COMET decomposition of application aspects, the real-time policy aspect is refined to include real-time scheduling and concurrency control policy aspects, while the real-time property aspect is replaced with the transaction model aspect, which is database-specific. The crosscutting effects of the application aspects to COMET components are shown in the table 1. As can be seen from the table, all identified application aspects crosscut more than one component.

The application aspects could vary depending on the particular application of the real-time system, thus particular attention should be made to identify the application aspects for each real-time system.

4.4   COMET RTCOM

Components and aspects in COMET are implemented based on RTCOM (discussed in section 3). Hence, the functional part of components is implemented first, together with application aspects. We illustrate this process, its benefits and drawbacks, by the example of one component (namely LC) and one application aspect (namely concurrency control).

The LC performs the following functionality: assigns locks to requesting transactions, and maintains a lock table, thus it records all locks obtained by transactions in the system. As can be seen from the table 1, the LC is crosscut with several application aspects. The application aspect that influences the policy, i.e., changes the behavior of the LC, is a concurrency control (CC) aspect, which defines the way lock conflicts should be handled in the system. To enable tailorability of the LC, and reuse of code in the largest possible extent, the LC is implemented with the policy framework in which lock conflicts are ignored and locks are granted to all transactions. The policy framework can

Table 1. Crosscutting effects of different application aspects on the COMET components

Application aspects \ Components	UIC	TSC	LC	IC	RLC	MHC	TMC
Transaction	X	X	X	X	X	X	X
Real-time scheduling		X					X
Concurrency control	X	X	X				X
Memory optimization	X	X	X	X	X		X
Synchronization		X	X	X	X		X
Security	X		X	X		X	X

be modified by weaving CC aspects that define other ways of handling lock conflicts. As different CC policies in real-time database systems exist, the mechanisms in the LC should be compatible with most of the existing CC algorithms.

The LC contains mechanisms such as (see left part of the figure 13): `insertLock-Record()`, `removeLockRecord()`, etc., for maintaining the table of all locks held by transactions in the system. The policy part consists of the operations performed on lock records and transactions holding and/or requesting locks, e.g., `getReadLock()`, `getWriteLock()`, `releaseLock()`. The operations in the LC are implemented using underlying LC mechanisms. The mechanisms provided by the LC are used by the CC aspects implementing the class of pessimistic (locking) protocols, e.g., HP-2PL [14] and RWPCP [15]. However, as a large class of optimistic protocols is implemented using locking mechanisms, the mechanisms provided by the LC can also be used by CC aspects implementing optimistic protocols, e.g., OCC-TI [16] and OCC-APR [17].

The right part of the figure 13 represents the specification for the real-time CC aspect (lines 1-30) that can be applied to a class of pessimistic locking CC protocols. We chose to give more specific details for the HP-2PL protocol, as it is both commonly used in main-memory database systems and a well-known pessimistic CC protocol.

The CC aspect has several pointcuts and advices that execute when the pointcut is reached. As defined by the RTCOM pointcut model, the pointcuts refer to the operations: `getReadLockCall()` and `getWriteLockCall()` (lines 10 and 12). The first pointcut intercepts the call to the function `getReadLock()`, which grants a read lock to the transaction and records it in the lock table. Similarly, the second pointcut intercepts

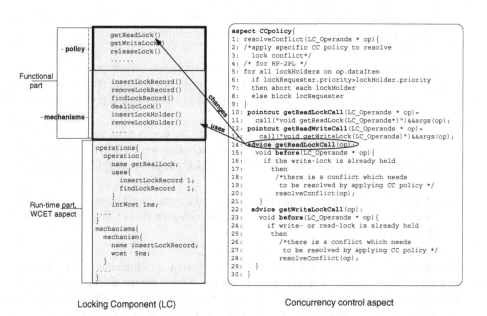

Locking Component (LC)   Concurrency control aspect

Fig. 13. The locking component and the concurrency control aspect

the call to the function that gives a write lock to the transaction and records it in the lock table. Before granting a read or write lock, the advices in lines 14-21 and 22-29 check if there is a lock conflict. If conflict exists, the advices deal with it by calling the local aspect function `resolveConflict()` (lines 1-9), where the resolution of the conflict should be done by implementing a specific CC policy. The advices that check for conflicts are implemented using the LC mechanisms to traverse the lock table and the list of transactions holding locks.

So far we have shown that the CC aspect affects the policy of the LC, but the CC aspect also crosscuts other components (see table 1). In the example of the CC aspect implementing pessimistic HP-2PL protocol (see figure 13), the aspect uses the information about transaction priority (lines 5-8), which is maintained by the TSC, thus crosscutting the TSC. Optimistic protocols, e.g., OCC-TI, would require additional pointcuts to be defined in the TMC, as the protocol (as compared to pessimistic protocols) assumes execution of transactions in three phases: read, validate and write.

Additionally, depending on the CC policy implemented, the number of pointcuts and advices varies. For example, some CC policies (like RWPCP, or optimistic policies) require additional data structures to be initialized. In such cases, an additional pointcut named `initPolicy()` could be added to the aspect that would intercept the call to initialize the LC. A before advice `initPolicy` would then initialize all necessary data structures in the CC aspect after data structures in the LC have been initialized.

The benefits of applying ACCORD to the development of COMET platform are the following (in the context of the given example).

- Enabling clean separation of concurrency control as an aspect that crosscuts the LC, which allows high code reusability as the same component mechanisms are used in almost all CC aspects.
- Weaving of a CC aspect into the LC changes the policy of the component by changing the component code, and provides an efficient way of tailoring the component and the system to fit a specific requirement (in this case specific CC policy), leaving the configuration of COMET unchanged.
- Having the LC functionality encapsulated into the component, and the CC encapsulated into an application aspect enables reconfiguring COMET to support non-locking transaction execution (excluding the LC), if other completely non-locking CC protocol is needed.
- Having a run-time part of the components and aspects enables analysis of the temporal behavior of the resulting code (see the run-time part of the LC in the left of the figure 13).

The drawback of applying ACCORD to real-time system development is an explosion in possible combinations of components and aspects. This is common for all software systems using aspect and components, and extensive research has being done in identifying and defining good composition rules for the components and aspects [18,19,9].

5   Related Work

In this section we address the research in the area of component-based real-time and database systems, and the real-time and database research projects that are using aspects to separate concerns.

The focus in existing component-based real-time systems is enforcement of real-time behavior. In these systems a component is usually mapped to a task, e.g., passive component [1], binary component [20], and port-based object component [21]. Therefore, analysis of real-time components in these solutions addresses the problem of temporal scopes at a component level as task attributes [20,1,21]: WCET, release time, deadline. ACCORD with its RTCOM model supports mapping of a component to a task, and takes a broader view of the composition process by allowing real-time systems to be composed out of tasks and components that are not necessarily mapped to a task. ACCORD, in contrast to other approaches building real-time component-based systems [20,1,21], enables support for multidimensional separation of concerns and allows integration of aspects into the component code. VEST [1] also uses aspect-oriented paradigm, but does not provide a component model that enables weaving of application aspects into the component code, rather it focuses on composition aspects.

In area of database systems, the Aspect-Oriented Databases (AOD) initiative aims at bringing the notion of separation of concerns to databases. The focus of this initiative is on providing a non-real-time database with limited configurability using only aspects (i.e., no components) [22]. To the best of our knowledge, KIDS [23] is the only research project focusing on construction of a configurable database composed out of components (database subsystems), e.g., object management and transaction management. Commercial component-based databases introduce limited customization of the database servers [24,25], by allowing components for managing non-standard data types, data cartridges and DataBlade modules, to be plugged into a fully functional database system. A somewhat different approach to componentization is Microsoft's Universal Data Access Architecture [26], where the components are data providers and they wrap data sources enabling the translation of all local data formats from different data stores to a common format. However, from a real-time point of view none of the component-based database approaches discussed enforce real-time behavior and use aspects to separate concerns in the system.

In contrast to traditional methods for design of real-time systems [27,28], which focus primarily on the ways of decomposing the system into tasks and handling temporal requirements, ACCORD design method focuses on the ways of decomposing a real-time system into components and aspects to achieve better reusability and flexibility of real-time software.

6   Summary

In recent years, one of the key research challenges in software engineering research community has been enabling configuration of systems and reuse of software by composing systems using components from a component library. Our research focuses on applying aspect-oriented and component-based software development to real-time system development by introducing a novel concept of aspectual component-based real-time system development (ACCORD). In this paper we presented ACCORD and its elements, which we have applied in the development of a real-time database system, called COMET. AC-CORD introduces the following into real-time system development: (i) a design method, which enables improved reuse and configurability of real-time and database systems by combining basic ideas from component-based and aspect-oriented communities with real-time concerns, thus bridging the gap between real-time systems, embedded systems, database systems, and software engineering, (ii) a real-time component model, called RTCOM, which enables efficient development of configurable real-time systems, and (iii) a new approach to modeling of real-time policies as aspects improving the flexibility of real-time systems. In the COMET example we have shown that applying ACCORD could have an impact on the real-time system development in providing efficient configuration of real-time systems, improved reusability and flexibility of real-time software, and modularization of crosscutting concerns.

Several research questions remain to be resolved, including:

- developing rules for checking compatibility of aspects and components,
- analyzing component and aspect behavior on different hardware and software platforms in real-time environments to identify trade-offs in applying aspects and components in a real-time setting,
- studying performance of the real-time system with different configurations of components and aspects, and
- providing automated tool support for the proposed development process.

Currently we are focusing on enabling predictable aspect weaving and component composition, and providing tools for automatized temporal analysis of aspects, components, and the resulting system.

References

1. Stankovic, J.: VEST: A toolset for constructing and analyzing component based operating systems for embedded and real-time systems. Technical Report CS-2000-19, Department of Computer Science, University of Virginia (2000)
2. Kiczales, G., Lamping, J., Mendhekar, A., Maeda, C., Lopes, C., Loingtier, J.M., Irwin, J.: Aspect-oriented programming. In: Proceedings of the ECOOP. Volume 1241 of Lecture Notes in Computer Science., Springer-Verlag (1997) 220–242
3. Crnkovic, I., Larsson, M., eds.: Building Reliable Component-Based Real-Time Systems. Artech House Publishers (2002) ISBN 1-58053-327-2.
4. Xerox: The AspectJ programming guide (2002)
5. Coady, Y., Kiczales, G., Feeley, M., Smolyn, G.: Using AspectC to improve the modularity of path-specific customization in operating system code. In: Proceedings of the Joint European Software Engineering Conference (ESEC) and 9th ACM SIGSOFT International Symposium on the Foundations of Software Engineering (FSE-9). (2002)
6. Spinczyk, O., Gal, A., Schröder-Preikschat, W.: AspectC++: An aspect-oriented extension to C++. In: Proceedings of the TOOLS Pacific 2002, Australian Computer Society (2002)
7. Bernat, G., Burns, A.: An approach to symbolic worst-case execution time analysis. In: Proceedings of the 25th IFAC Workshop on Real-Time Programming, Palma, Spain (2000)

8. Tešanović, A., Nyström, D., Hansson, J., Norström, C.: Integrating symbolic worst-case execution time analysis into aspect-oriented system development. OOPSLA 2002 Workshop on Tools for Aspect-Oriented Software Development (2002)
9. Aßmann, U.: Invasive Software Composition. Springer-Verlag, Universit t Karlsruhe (2002)
10. Liu, C.L., Layland, J.W.: Scheduling algorithms for multipprogramming in hard real-time traffic environment. Journal of the Association for Computing Machinery **20** (1973) 46–61
11. Nyström, D., Tešanović, A., Norström, C., Hansson, J.: Data management issues in vehicle control systems: a case study. In: Proceedings of the 14th EUROMICRO International Conference on Real-Time Systems, Vienna, Austria (2002) 249–256
12. Lu, H., Ng, Y., Tian, Z.: T-tree or b-tree: Main memory database index structure revisited. 11th Australasian Database Conference (2000)
13. Rastogi, R., Seshadri, S., Bohannon, P., Leinbaugh, D.W., Silberschatz, A., Sudarshan, S.: Improving predictability of transaction execution times in real-time databases. Real-time Systems **19** (2000) 283–302 Kluwer Academic Publishers.
14. Abbott, R.K., Garcia-Molina, H.: Scheduling real-time transactions: A performance evaluation. ACM Transactions on Database Systems **17** (1992) 513–560
15. Sha, L., Rajkumar, R., Son, S.H., Chang, C.H.: A real-time locking protocol. IEEE Transactions on Computers **40** (1991) 793–800
16. Lee, J., Son, S.H.: Using dynamic adjustment of serialization order for real-time database systems. In: Proceedings of the 14th IEEE Real-Time Systems Symposium. (1993)
17. Datta, A., Son, S.H.: Is a bird in the hand worth more than two birds in the bush? Limitations of priority cognizance in conflict resolution for firm real-time database systems. IEEE Transactions on Computers **49** (2000) 482–502
18. Bosch, J.: Design and Use of Software Architectures. Addison-Wesley (2000)
19. Bachmann, F., Bass, L., Buhman, C., Comella-Dorda, S., Long, F., Robert, J., Seacord, R., Wallnau, K.: Technical concepts of component-based software engineering. Technical Report CMU/SEI-2000-TR-008, Carnegie Mellon University (2000)
20. Isovic, D., Lindgren, M., Crnkovic, I.: System development with real-time components. In: Proceedings of ECOOP Workshop - Pervasive Component-Based Systems, France (2000)
21. Stewart, D.S.: Designing software components for real-time applications. In: Proceedings of Embedded System Conference, San Jose, CA (2000) Class 408, 428.
22. Rashid, A., Pulvermueller, E.: From object-oriented to aspect-oriented databases. In: Proceedings of the DEXA 2000. Volume 1873 of Lecture Notes in Computer Science., Springer-Verlag (2000) 125–134
23. Geppert, A., Scherrer, S., Dittrich, K.R.: KIDS: Construction of database management systems based on reuse. Technical Report ifi-97.01, Department of Computer Science, University of Zurich (1997)
24. Oracle: All your data: The Oracle extensibility architecture. Oracle Technical White Paper (1999)
25. Informix: Developing DataBlade modules for Informix-Universal Server. Informix DataBlade Technology (2001) Available at http://www.informix.com/datablades/.
26. (Papers, O.D.W.)
27. Gomaa, H.: Software development of real-time systems. Communications of the ACM **29** (1986) 657–668
28. Kopetz, H., Zainlinger, R., Fohler, G., Kantz, H., Puschner, P., Schütz, W.: The design of real-time systems: from specification to implementation and verification. Software Engineering Journal **6** (1991) 72–82

Testing of Multi-tasking Real-Time Systems with Critical Sections*

Anders Pettersson[1] and Henrik Thane[1]

[1] Mälardalen University, Mälardalen Real-Time Research Centre,
P.O. Box 883 SE-721 23 Västerås, Sweden
{anders.pettersson,henrik.thane}@mdh.se

Abstract. In this paper we address the problem of testing real-time software in the functional domain. In order to achieve reproducible and deterministic test results of an entire multitasking real-time system it is essential not to only consider inputs and outputs, but also the order in which tasks communicate and synchronize with each other. We present a deterministic white-box system-level control-flow testing method for deterministic integration testing of real-time system software. We specifically address fixed priority scheduled real-time systems where synchronization is resolved using the Priority Ceiling Emulation Protocol or offsets in time. The method includes a testing strategy where the coverage criterion is defined by the number of paths in the system control flow. The method also includes a reachability algorithm for deriving all possible paths in terms of orderings of task starts, preemptions and completions of tasks executing in a real-time system. The deterministic testing strategy allows test methods for sequential programs to be applied, since each identified ordering can be regarded as a sequential program.

1 Introduction

Testing software is challenging. A typical solitary program has a large state space and a discontinuous behavior. The latter due to containers with limited resolution, e.g., 32 bit integers, quantization errors, and program flow selections. The implication is that it is highly unreliable to make use of interpolation when testing programs. Consequently, a large part of the state space must be explored in order to verify that inputs produce correct outputs according to the specification. It is not surprising that a large part of software development budgets is spent on maintenance. Elevating to the level of real-time software testing, the challenge is even greater. Real-time software is usually built on an aggregate of multiple concurrently executing programs, i.e., it is multi-tasking. To begin with, this entails testing of multiple programs. What is worse however, is the state space explosion that occurs due to the interactions between the

---

* This work is funded by the national Swedish Real-Time Systems research initiative ARTES (www.artes.uu.se), supported by the Swedish Foundation for Strategic Research.

J. Chen and S. Hong (Eds.): RTCSA 2003, LNCS 2968, pp. 578–594, 2004.

tasks when they execute concurrently. These interactions are not limited to the functional domain but are also a function of the timing and the ordering of the tasks' execution in the system. The majority of current testing and debugging techniques have been developed for solitary (non real-time) programs. These techniques are not directly applicable to real-time systems, since they disregard issues of timing and concurrency. This means that existing techniques for reproducible testing cannot be used. Reproducibility is essential for regression testing and cyclic debugging, where the same test cases are run repeatedly with the intention of verifying modified program code or to track down errors. It is common that real-time software has a non-reproducible behavior. This is due to the fact that giving the same input and same internal state to a program is not sufficient. There are hidden variables that are ignored: Race conditions and ordering. An aspect of this is intrusive observations caused e.g., by temporary additions of program code, which incur a temporal probe-effect [6] by changing the race conditions in the system.

In theory it is possible to reproduce the behavior of a real-time system if we can reproduce the exact trajectories of the inputs to the system with an exact timing. For guaranteed determinism we would in addition need to control the frequency of the temperature dependent real-time clock that generates the periodic timer tick, which is the basis for all time driven scheduling decisions. The inputs, and state, of the tasks dictates their individual control flow paths taken, which in turn dictates the execution time of the tasks, which in the end dictates the preemption pattern for strictly periodic systems. Trying to perform exhaustive black-box testing of individual programs is in the general case infeasible, due to the large number of possible inputs. For example, two 32 bit inputs yields 2^{64} possible input combinations, not considering state, which for a test case every 10^{-12} seconds would take about half a year to execute. For a typical multitasking real-time system the number of possible input combinations is similarly bordering on the incomprehensible due to all possible temporal and functional interactions between the tasks. However, just as individual program's control flow structure can be derived and used for white-box testing (where the number of paths is usually significantly lower than the number of inputs), we can make use of the system level control flow for deterministic white-box testing of the multitasking real-time system software. We will elaborate on this issue in this paper.

Testing real-time systems controlling only the inputs have been attempted previously – mostly in the formal methods community were formal specifications models have been used for generating inputs to the system to test either the temporal [4][11][16] or the functional [10] behavior. In comparison to other sub-fields within the real-time systems research community the list of references dealing with testing of real-time software is quite meager, rather famished in fact. One reference that has inspired us is the work by Yang and Chung [23]. They define a system level control-flow testing method for testing of concurrent Ada programs (not real-time but concurrent). The system control flow is defined by all synchronization sequences (rendezvous) in the system. When testing a concurrent Ada program the executed synchronization sequence is defined as being part of the output. If a test case is applied twice, and the same synchronization sequence is observed, then the same behavior has been exercised – thus deterministic testing is achieved. However, it is not certain that the tests are reproducible, since there exist no explicit control over the synchronization sequences. The number of paths executed divided by the number of paths derived is used to define coverage. Similar work can be found in Hwang et al. [8] where they also attempt deterministic replay [21] in order to achieve reproducibility. Since Yang et al. and Hwang et al. only concentrate on the rendezvous sequences they do not handle more intricate real-time operating system issues like preemptions, interrupts or critical sections.

In this paper we extend the method for achieving deterministic testing of distributed real-time systems by Thane and Hansson [19][20]. They addressed task sets with recurring release patterns, executing in a distributed system, where the scheduling on each node was handled by a fixed priority driven preemptive scheduler supporting offsets. The method transforms the non-deterministic distributed real-time systems testing problem into a set of deterministic sequential program testing problems. Similarly to Yang's work, but with the inclusion of preemption, interrupts and communication delays, Thane and Hansson define the executed orderings between tasks (derived from task-switch monitoring) to be part of the system's output. Thus, achieving determinism is an issue of correlating inputs, with outputs and execution orderings (the system control-flow). Coverage is defined by the number of unique system control-flow paths tested, and by the number of test cases run per each path. The former criterion is derived from a system control-flow analysis and the latter criterion is defined by the testing technique applied, e.g., statistical confidence in black-box testing.

In their system control-flow analysis method they assumed that all synchronization was resolved offline, e.g., by an off-line scheduler, which assigns offsets and priorities to all tasks in the distributed system. That is, on-line synchronization mechanisms like semaphores are not allowed. All tasks in the system are also assumed to receive all input immediately at their start, and to produce all output at their termination. These limitations were quite severe, although the analysis proved that even off-line scheduled systems could yield enormous numbers of different scenarios, when subjected to preemption and jitter (execution time-, communication time-, and interrupt induced jitter), especially when the tested systems were of multi-rate character.

In this paper we elaborate on the approach presented by Thane and Hansson in [19][20] and expand the task model to also include critical sections, governed by the Priority Ceiling Emulation Protocol (*PCEP*) [2], a.k.a. the immediate inheritance protocol and immediate priority ceiling protocol. Since tasks may synchronize/communicate via critical sections, we will also relax Thane's and Hansson's input output assumption. Our extension is however only valid for the individual nodes in the distributed real-time system, unless we assume a global PCEP, which is quite complex to achieve [15]. The subsequent analysis in this paper is hence focused on a single node. The results by Thane and Hansson [19][20] on how to derive the *global* system control-flow can however successfully be applied if global scheduling is relying on offsets between tasks on different nodes, but this is outside the scope of this paper.

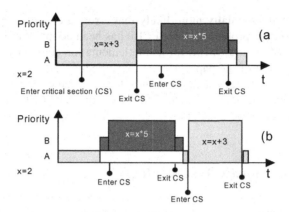

Fig. 1. Two different execution orderings with different results, caused by race conditions in accesses of a shared resource *x*.

The basic intuition behind deterministic testing can be illustrated as follows. Consider Fig. 1, which depicts two execution scenarios of two tasks *A*, *B*, who share a common resource *x*, which they do operations on. The resource, *x*, is protected by a semaphore governed by the priority ceiling emulation protocol which raises the priority of the task that is granted the resource to the priority ceiling of the tasks using the resource. In Fig. 1 scenario (a), task *A* enters the critical section before *B* and thus accesses *x* before *B* – with end result of scenario (a), $x=25$. In Fig. 1 scenario (b), task *B* enters the critical section before *A* and thus accesses *x* before *A* – with the end result of scenario (b), $x=13$.

As we can see in Fig. 1, even though the same input is provided, $x=2$, the end result of the execution is dependent of the task execution ordering, i.e., the system level control-flow path taken. However, if we run the same scenario with the same input, the result will always be the same on repeated executions. That is, the multitasking real-time system is deterministic if we consider both inputs and execution orderings.

1.1 Contribution

The contribution of this paper is a deterministic white-box system level integration testing method that includes:

☐ A testing strategy for achieving a required level of coverage, with respect to the number of paths in the system control-flow. The testing strategy also allows test methods for sequential programs to be applied, since each identified ordering can be regarded as a sequential program.

☐ A reachability technique for deriving the system level control-flow. The system control-flow is defined by all possible orderings of task starts, preemptions and completions for tasks executing in a system where synchronization is resolved using offsets or using PCEP.

The result in this paper substantially extends the applicability of the results by Thane and Hansson [19][20], since we now can handle systems with on-line synchronization, for which it is actually more likely that errors are caused by implementation and synchronization problems. Also, PCEP has been adopted in industry standards, like *POSIX*, *ADA95*, and *OSEK*, for its implementation simplicity [9][18].

The organization of the paper is as follows: Section 2 presents our deterministic integration testing strategy. Section 3 introduces a method for deriving the system control-flow when synchronization is resolved by the PCEP protocol or offsets. Finally, in Section 4, we conclude.

2 The Deterministic Test Strategy

In our test strategy we define an executed system level control-flow path (*SLCFP*) to be part of the system's output.

By correlating inputs with outputs and executed SLCFPs deterministic test results are achieved. Coverage is defined by the number of unique SLCFPs tested, and by the number of test-cases run per each path. The former criterion is based on a system control-flow analysis, which we present in section 3. The latter criterion is defined by the testing technique applied, e.g., statistical confidence in black-box testing [3].

For the testing strategy to work we need in addition to the inputs and outputs, means to extract the system control flow, usually in the form of task-switches and access to semaphores: activation of task, entering critical section, leaving critical section, preemption, and task completion. We thus expand on the work by Thane and Hansson [19][20] to also include races to critical sections. This SLCFPs extraction can be facilitated in a number of ways, ranging from intrusive software instrumentation, and hooks into the real-time kernel, to special non-intrusive hardware like *In Circuit Emulators*, with OS awareness. If the instrumentation is implemented in software, it is necessary to eliminate the probe effect, usually by leaving the instrumentation code in the deployed system. In our experience the execution time overhead for software instrumentation of the SLCFPs is minimal, typically below 0,1‰ of processor utilization.

Definition. The deterministic test procedure (as illustrated in Fig. 2) with no knowledge of the number of possible SLCFPs is defined as:
1. Test the system using any sequential technique of choice, and monitor the 3-tuple (*input*, *output*, SLCFP) for each test case. A test case includes all inputs to the participating tasks that are part of the SLCFP during the interval $[0, T^{MAX}]$, where T^{MAX} typically is equal to the Least Common Multiple (*LCM*) of the tasks period times.
2. Map the 3-tuple for the interval $[0, T^{MAX}]$ into a "bucket" for each unique SLCFP.
3. Repeat 1-2 until required coverage for the sequential testing technique applied is reached for every bucket.

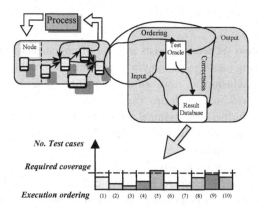

Fig. 2. A test rig with a set of system level control-flow buckets, and where the coverage for each bucket is illustrated.

With the above defined testing procedure we can achieve deterministic testing, with respect to failures that pertain to ordering, and its effect on the inputs and outputs via the systems legal interfaces. That is, the method is not deterministic with respect to failures like transient bit-flips, or arbitrary memory corruption from e.g., non-reentrant code, unless we regarded every assembly write operation as a critical section – which is unreasonable.

The above defined testing strategy is however not complete, since we do not know when to stop testing. We do not know how many SLCFPs there exist. In the next section we will present a technique for deriving all possible SLCFPs from which we can calculate the maximum number of SLCFPs and thus derive a stopping criterion. The stopping criterion can either be based on the system control flow for all tasks in the system or for just a sub set of the tasks. If we during testing after a while notice that certain paths have attained a low level of coverage (e.g., 0) then this can either be attributed to a pessimism in the system control flow analysis (e.g., two tasks may not execute their worst case execution time in the same execution scenario) such that too many paths are derived, or that certain paths are simply rare during execution. In any case deterministic replay technology [21] can be used for enforcing certain paths such that the required coverage for these paths is attained. The application of deterministic replay is however out of scope for this paper, and is something we will present in a later publication.

3 System Control-Flow Analysis

In order to derive a stop criterion for the deterministic testing strategy we now define the system level control-flow in terms of a System Level Control-Flow Graph (*SLCFG*) and present an algorithm that generates SLCFGs, from which we can derive all possible system level control-flow paths (*SLCFP*). We begin however, with a definition of the system task model.

3.1 Task Model

The real-time system software consists of a set of concurrent tasks. Tasks communicate by non-blocking message passing or shared memory. All synchronization, precedence or mutual exclusion, is resolved either offline by assigning different release-times/offsets and priorities, or during runtime by the use of semaphores which have PCEP semantics. Further, we assume a task model that includes both preemptive scheduling of off-line generated schedules [22] and fixed priority scheduling of strictly periodic tasks [1][13].

☐ The system contains a set of jobs J, i.e. invocations of tasks, which are released in a time interval $[t, t+T^{MAX}]$, where T^{MAX} is typically equal to the LCM of the involved tasks period times, and t is an idle point within the time interval $[0, T^{MAX}]$ where no job is executing. The existence of such an idle point, t, simplifies the model such that it prevents temporal interference between successive T^{MAX} intervals. To simplify the presentation we will henceforth assume an idle point at 0.

☐ Each job $j \square J$ has a release time r_j, worst case execution time ($WCET_j$), best case execution time ($BCET_j$), a deadline D_j, and a unique base priority bp_j. J represents one instance of a recurring pattern of job executions with period T^{MAX}, i.e., job j will be released at time r_j, $r_j+ T^{MAX}$, $r_j+ 2\ T^{MAX}$, etc. Jobs may have identical release times.

3.2 Synchronization Using PCEP

For PCEP we assume that:

☐ Each job $j \square J$ has a current priority p_i that may be different from the statically allocated base priority, bp_j, if the job is subject to priority promotion when granted a resource.

☐ Each resource R, used by a set of jobs S_R, has a statically computed priority ceiling defined by the highest base priority in S_R increased by one, i.e., $p_R= MAX (bp_i\ |\ I \square\ S_R) + 1$. We assume that all jobs have unique priorities so we need to increase p_R by one to achieve a unique priority for the priority ceiling; jobs that have higher priorities than p_r are also adjusted to have unique priorities.

☐ Each job, j, that enters a critical section protecting a resource R is immediately promoted to the statically allocated priority ceiling of the resource, if $p_R > pj$ then $p_j = p_R$.

☐ Each job, j, that is executing and releases a resource R is demoted immediately to the maximum of the base priority bp_j, and the ceilings of the remaining resources held by the job.

☐ Each critical section, k, has a worst case execution time ($WCET_k$) and a best case execution time ($BCET_k$) and a release time interval $[er_k, lr_k)$ ranging from the earliest release time to the latest release time.

□ All resources are claimed in the same order for all paths through the program in a job.

3.3 The System Level Control-Flow Graph

In essence, to derive the system level control-flow graph, we perform a reachability analysis by simulating the behavior of a real-time kernel conforming to our task model during one $[0,T^{MAX}]$ period for the job set J.

The System Level Control-Flow Graph (*SLCFG*) is a finite tree for which the set of possible paths from the root contains all possible execution scenarios.

We define a SLCFG as a pair <N, A>, where

□ N is a set of *nodes*, each node being labeled with a job, the job's current priority, and a continuous time interval, i.e., for a job set J: $N \Box J \Box$ {"_"} · P · $I(T^{MAX})$, where {"_"} is used to denote a node where no job is executing. P is the set of priorities, and $I(T^{MAX})$ is the set of continuous intervals in $[0,T^{MAX}]$.

□ A is the set of *edges* (directed arcs; transitions) from one node to another node, labeled with a continuous time interval, i.e., for a set of jobs J:$A \Box N$ · $I(T^{MAX})$ · N.

3.3.1 Basic Transitions

Intuitively, an edge corresponds to the transition (the task-switch) from one job to another, or when a job enters or leaves a critical section. The edge is annotated with a continuous interval of when the transition can take place, as illustrated in Fig. 3, showing SLCFGs for simple jobs without critical sections.

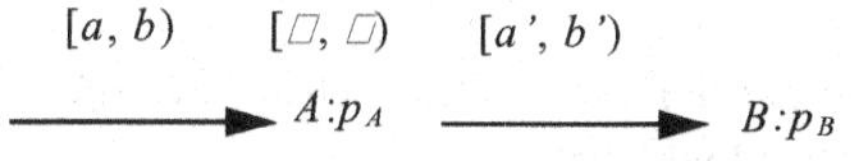

$$[a, b) \qquad [\Box, \Box) \qquad [a', b')$$
$$\xrightarrow{\hspace{2cm}} A{:}p_A \qquad \xrightarrow{\hspace{2cm}} B{:}p_B$$

Fig. 3. Two transitions, one to job A and one from job A to job B.

The interval of possible start times $[a\Box, b\Box)$ for job B, in Fig. 3, is defined by:

$$a\Box = \max(a, r_A) + BCET_A \tag{1}$$

$$b\Box = \max(b, r_A) + WCET_A$$

The max() functions are necessary because the calculated start times a and b can be earlier than the scheduled release of the job A. In the SLCFG a node represents a job annotated with a continuous interval of its possible execution time, $[\Box, \Box)$, as depicted in Fig. 4.

$$[a, b) \qquad\qquad [\alpha, \beta)$$

$$\xrightarrow{\hspace{5cm}} A : p_A$$

Fig. 4. A job annotated with its possible execution, start time and current priority.

We define the interval of execution, $[\alpha, \beta)$ as the interval in which job A can be preempted:

$$\alpha = \max(a, r_A) \tag{2}$$

$$\beta = \max(b, rA) + WCET_A$$

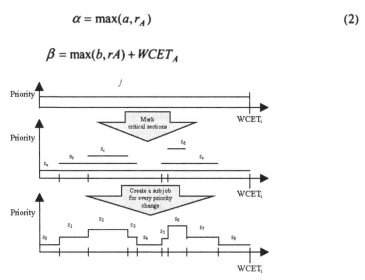

Fig. 5. A job split into a set of sub jobs, in order of changes in effective priority. The sub jobs s_0, s_4, and s_8 represent the base priority job.

3.3.2   Critical Section Transitions

Critical sections will be introduced by transforming the job set, such that a job with critical sections is split into a set of jobs corresponding to the different critical sections and executions in between. We assume that each job $i \in J$, which has a set of critical sections CS_i, is split into an ordered list of sub jobs, SJ_i, such that every time there is a change in the job's effective priority a new sub job is added (as illustrated in Fig. 5). Each sub job $s_i \in SJ_i$ of original job i have a release time interval $[er_s, lr_s)$ ranging from its earliest release time to its latest release time. The release time interval for a sub job s_i is given in terms of execution time run by the immediately preceding sub job, q_i, before it enters the critical section represented by sub job s_i, rather than in terms of the system clock tick. This means that all $BCET_s$ and $WCET_s$ for all sub jobs are calculated such that they represent execution time before entering the immediately succeeding critical section except the last sub job, which runs until termination.

$$[a, b) \xrightarrow[q_i:p_q]{[\alpha, \beta)} [a', b) \xrightarrow[s_i:p_s]{[\alpha', \beta')} [a'', b'] \xrightarrow[z_i:p_z]{[\alpha'', \beta'')}$$

Fig. 6. Three transitions, one to sub job q_i, one demoting transition from sub job q_i to sub job s_i and one promoting transition from sub job s_i to sub job z_i

The interval of possible start times $[a', b']$ for the sub job s_i, as illustrated in Fig. 6, is defined relative to its predecessor, q_i, by:

$$a' = \max(a, r_i) + BCET_q \tag{3}$$

$$b' = \max(b, r_i) + WCET_q$$

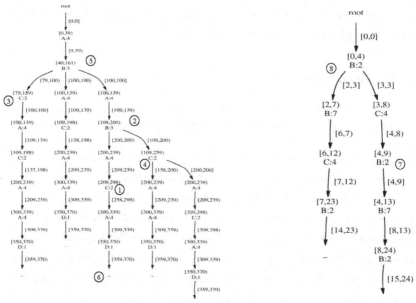

Fig. 7. The resulting execution order graphs for the job set in Table 1 and Table 2.

Table 1. A job set for a schedule with a LCM of 400 ms

Task	r	p	WCET	BCET
A	0	4	39	9
B	40	3	121	39
C	40	2	59	49
A	100	4	39	9
A	200	4	39	9
A	300	4	39	9
D	350	1	20	9

Table 2. A job set for a schedule where job B accesses a shared resource, and when entering the critical section boost its priority to 7. B is split into 3 sub jobs.

Task	r	p	WCET	BCET
B	0	2	4	2
-	-	7	4	4
-	-	2	9	7
C	3	4	5	1

The max() function in Equation 3 is needed since the sub job cannot be released earlier than scheduled release of the original job i. The transition interval can represent a promoted priority, denoted $[a,b]$, or demoted priority, denoted $[a,b)$.

A node represents a sub job in the same manner as a node represents a job, i.e., the node is annotated with a continuous interval of its possible execution and a priority, in this case the priority ceiling of the critical section.

We define the execution interval, $[\alpha',\beta')$ for the sub job s_i:

$$\alpha' = \max(a',r_i) \tag{4}$$

$$\beta = \max(b',r_i) + WCET_s$$

That is, the interval, $[a',b')$, specifies the interval in which sub job s_i with priority p_i can be preempted by a higher priority job.

3.3.3 Transition Rules

Below are rules for transitions to create a SLCFG, as exemplified and annotated in Fig. 7. The first six rules correspond to the basic transitions, and the remaining rules are rules for critical sections.

1. **If** the current job j_i completes without preemption, and there are no higher priority jobs that immediately succeeds j_i, **then** add a transition, $j_i \xrightarrow{[a'_i,b'_i)}$, where $[a'_i,b'_i)$ is the interval of possible finishing times of j_i.

2. **If** the current job j_i completes without preemption and a higher prioritized job j_k immediately succeeds j_i, **then** add a transition $j_i \xrightarrow{[r_k,r_k]} j_k$, where r_k is the release time of j_k and $[r_k,r_k]$ represents the preemption. In addition, **if** there is a lower prioritized job j_l ready, or made ready during the execution interval of j_i, **then** add a transition $j_i \xrightarrow{[a'_i,b'_i)} j_l$, where $[a'_i,b'_i)$ is the interval of possible finishing times of j_i.

3. **If** the current job j_i has a *BCET* such that it definitely is preempted by another job j_k **then** add a transition $j_i \xrightarrow{[r_k,r_k]} j_k$, where r_k is the release time of j_k and $[r_k,r_k]$ represents the preemption.

4. **If** the current job j_i has a *BCET* and *WCET* such that it may either complete or be preempted before any preempting job j_k is released **then** add a transition $j_i \xrightarrow{[r_k,r_k]} j_k$, where r_k is the release time of j_k and $[r_k,r_k]$ represents the preemption. In addition, **if** the set of ready jobs is empty **then** add a transition $j_i \xrightarrow{[a'_i,r_k)} j_k$, where $[a'_i,r_k)$ is the interval of completion times of j_i.

5. **If** the current job j_i has a *BCET* and *WCET* such that it may either complete or be preempted before any preempting job j_k is released **then** add a transition

$j_i \xrightarrow{[r_k, r_k]} j_k$, where r_k is the release time of j_k and $[r_k, r_k]$ represents the pre-emption. In addition, if there are lower prioritized jobs j_l ready and $\beta_i > \alpha_i$ holds then add a transition $j_i \xrightarrow{[a_i', b_i')} j_l$, where $[a_i', b_i')$ is the interval of start times of j_l and a transition $j_i \xrightarrow{[r_k, r_k]} j_k$, where r_k is the release time of j_k and $[r_k, r_k)$ represents the completion of j_i immediately before j_k.

6. **If** the current job j_i is the last job scheduled in this branch of the tree **then** add a transition $j_i \xrightarrow{[a_i', b_i')} \_$, where $[a_i', b_i')$ is the interval of finishing times of j_i.

7. **If** the current sub job s_i succeeded by a higher priority sub job s_j before the release of any higher priority job j_k. That is if $b_i' < r_k$, and $p_j > p_k > p_i$ **then** add a transition $s_i \xrightarrow{[a_i', b_i']} s_j$, where $[a_i', b_i']$ is the interval of start times of s_j.

8. **If** The current sub job s_i succeeded by a higher priority sub job s_j before the release of any higher priority job j_k or is preempted by j_k. That is, $a_i' < r_k < b_i'$, and $p_j > p_k > p_i$ **then** add a transition $s_i \xrightarrow{[a_i', r_k]} s_j$, where $[a_i', r_k]$ is the possible start interval of s_j. And a transition $s_i \xrightarrow{[r_k, r_k]} j_k$, where r_k is the release time of j_k and $[r_k, r_k]$ represents the preemption.

9. **If** the current sub job s_i is succeeded by a lower priority sub job s_j before the release of any higher priority job j_k, that is $a_j' < r_k$, **then** s_i is entered into the set of ready jobs and then governed by rule 4 or rule 5, above.

3.4 The Algorithm

We will now define an algorithm for generating a System Level Control-Flow Graph (*SLCFG*). Essentially, the algorithm simulates the behavior of a strictly periodic fixed priority preemptive real-time kernel, complying with the previously defined task model and SLCFG transition rules. The SLCFG for a set of jobs is generated by a call to the algorithm *SLCFG (NODE, RDYSET, $[a,b)$, $[Sl,Su)$)* given in appendix (List. 1), where NODE is a node that represents the root node of the SLCFG. RDYSET represents the set of tasks that is ready to run and is initially the empty set. The interval $[a,b)$ is the release interval and is initially $[0,0]$, and $[Sl,Su)$ the considered simulation interval, initialized to $[0, T^{MAX}]$. The algorithm is a recursive function to which the initial arguments are given, as defined above.

In the remainder of this section we will go through the details of the algorithm, the references to line numbers corresponds to the line numbers in List. 1, List. 2 and List. 3 in the appendix.

In the algorithm, line 1: we look ahead one job at a time, this is achieved by extracting the release time of the next job. To acquire the next release time that succeeds the currently running job the simulation interval is searched until the next job is found.

In lines 2-6 it is determined if the simulation has come to an end of a control-flow path. This is done by determining the state of the set of jobs ready to execute, if the ready queue is empty and there are no jobs in the simulation interval to put into the ready queue then we have reached the end of a path. Line 6: Draw the end node of the path that corresponds to rule 6.

If the simulation is in a state such that that it has not reached the end of a path, line 7-46, we consider if the current job may be preempted, line 13-29, or is definitely not preempted, line 30-46. Rule 1-2 will continue in the non-preemption case while rule 3, rule 4 and rule 5 will continue in the preemption case.

In the preemption case, for rule 4 and rule 5 it must be determined if the current job terminates before the release of a higher priority job, line 14. In those cases that the current job terminates before the release of any higher priority job, it must also be determined if there exists any succeeding lower priority job, line 20, or if any higher priority job immediately succeeds the current job, line 23. Line 27-29 will be visited for rule 3, rule 4 and rule 5 and represents the branch of the preemption of the current job.

Lines 33-34 corresponds to the case when a critical section is entered and the priority is promoted, rule 7. For rule 8, when the current job may enter the critical section before it is preempted there is two outgoing transitions from the current job and are govern by lines 16-17 for the sub job that is entering the critical section and lines 27-29 for the preemption before entering the critical section.

3.5 The Stop Criterion

By enumerating the possible and unique paths in the system control flow we get a measure of the number of system level control flow paths we need to test using the deterministic testing strategy for full coverage. The stopping criterion can be scaled such that it encompass a single task, multiple transactions or all tasks in the system. The above analysis is however pessimistic in the sense that it does not take into account the correlation between actual input and the execution time of a task, this introduces a pessimism such that in practice two tasks may never exhibit their worst case (or best case) execution time during the same system level control flow path. We thus run into the possibility of deriving too many paths that may never be executed in practice.

4 Conclusions

In this paper we have present a method for deterministic integration testing of strictly periodic fixed priority scheduled real-time systems where synchronization is either resolved using on-line synchronization, complying with the Priority Ceiling Emulation Protocol (PCEP) [2] (a.k.a., the immediate inheritance protocol), or offsets. The paper extends the results by Thane and Hansson [19][20] with handling of online synchronization. This substantially increases the applicability of the method, since it is more likely that errors are caused by synchronization and implementation problems.

Essentially the method is a structural white box testing method applied on the system level rather than on the individual tasks. The method includes a testing strategy where the coverage criterion is defined by the number of paths in the system control flow. The method also includes a reachability algorithm for deriving all possible paths in terms of orderings of task starts, preemptions and completions of tasks executing in a real-time system. The deterministic testing strategy allows test methods for sequential programs to be applied, since each identified ordering can be regarded as a sequential program.

In the presented analysis and testing strategy, we consider task sets with recurring release patterns, and accounted for the effects of variations in start and execution times of the involved tasks, as well as the variations of the arrival and duration of the critical sections.

For future work we plan to introduce deterministic replay technology [21] to testing in order to enforce certain system level control flow paths.

References

1. Audsley N. C., Burns A., Davis R. I., Tindell K. W.: Fixed Priority Pre-emptive Scheduling: A Historical Perspective. Real-Time Systems journal, Vol.8(2/3), March/May, Kluwer A.P., 1995.
2. Baker T.: Stack-based scheduling of real-time processes. Real-Time Systems Journal, 3(1):67-99, March, 1991.
3. Beizer B.: Software testing techniques. Van Nostrand Reinhold, 1990.
4. Cardell-Oliver R and Glover T.: A Practical and Complete Algorithm for Testing Real-Time Systems. In 5th International Symposium on Formal Techniques in Real-Time and Fault Tolerant Systems, pp. 251-261, September 1998.
5. El Shobaki M.: A Hardware and Software Monitor for High-Level System-on-Chip Verification. In Procc IEEE International Symposium on Quality Electronic Design. San Jose, USA, March 2001.
6. Gait J.: A Probe Effect in Concurrent Programs. Software – Practice and Experience, 16(3):225-233, Mars, 1986.
7. Hamlet R. G.: Probable Correctness Theory. Information processing letters 25, pp. 17-25, 1987.
8. Hwang G.H, Tai K.C and Huang T.L.: Reachability Testing: An Approach to Testing Concurrent Software. Int. Journal of Software Engineering and Knowledge Engineering, vol. 5, no. 4, pp. 493-510, 1995.
9. ISO/IEC. ISO/IEC 8652L 1995 (E),: Information Technology – Programming Languages – Ada, Febrary 1995.
10. Iversen T. K., Kristoffersen K. J.,.Larsen G. K., Laursen M., Madsen R. G., Mortensen S. K., Pettersson P. And Thomasen C. B.: Model-Checking of Real-Time Control Programs. In Proceedings of the 12th Euromicro Conference on Real-Time Systems (ECRTS'2000), pp. 147-255. Stockholm, Sweden, June 19-21, 2000.

11. Khoumsi A.: A new method for testing real time systems. In Proceedings. 7th International Conference on Real-Time Computing Systems and Applications, pp. 441-450, December 2000.

12. Laprie J.C.: Dependability: Basic Concepts and Associated Terminology. Dependable Computing and Fault-Tolerant Systems, vol. 5, Springer Verlag, 1992.

13. Lui C. L. and Layland J. W.: Scheduling Algorithms for multiprogramming in a hard real-time environment. Journal of the ACM 20(1), 1973.

14. McDowell C.E. and Hembold D.P.: Debugging concurrent programs. ACM Computing Surveys, 21(4), pp. 593-622, December 1989.

15. Mueller F.: Priority inheritance and ceilings for distributed mutual exclusion. Proc. 20th IEEE Real-Time Systems Symposium, pp. 340-349, Phoenix, Arizona, December 1999.

16. Nielsen B and Skou A.: Test Generation for Time Critical Systems: Tools and Case Study. In 13th Euromicro Conference on Real-Time Systems, 2001, pp. 155 – 162, June 2001.

17. Rushby J.: Formal Specification and Verification for Critical systems: Tools, Achievements, and prospects. Advances in Ultra-Dependable Distributed Systems. IEEE Computer Society Press. 1995. ISBN 0-8186-6287-5.

18. Technical Committee on Operating Systems and Application Environments of the IEEE. Portable Operating System Interface (POSIX) – Part 1: System Application Program Interface (API), 1996. ANSI/IEEE Std 1003.1, 1995 Edition, including 1003.1c:Amedment 2: Threads Extension C Language.

19. Thane H. and Hansson H.: Testing distributed real-time systems. Journal of Microprocessors and Microsystems (24):463-478, Elsevier, 2001.

20. Thane H. and Hansson H.: Towards Systematic Testing of Distributed Real-Time Systems. Proc. 20th IEEE Real-Time Systems Symposium, Phoenix, Arizona, December 1999.

21. Thane H. and Hansson H.: Using Deterministic Replay for Debugging of Distributed Real-Time Systems. In proceedings of the 12th Euromicro Conference on Real-Time Systems (ECRTS'00), Stockholm, June 2000.

22. Xu J. and Parnas D.: Scheduling processes with release times, deadlines, precedence, and exclusion, relations. IEEE Trans. on Software Eng. 16(3):360-369, 1990.

23. Yang R-D and Chung C-G.: Path analysis testing of concurrent programs. Information and software technology. vol. 34(1):425-432, Jan., 1992.

Appendix:

Listing of the System Control Flow algorithm.

```
Algorithm SL_CFG (NODE, RDYSET, [ a, b ), [ Sl, Su ) )
{
1   From the simulation interval [Sl, Su), get the next release time t
2   If the set of jobs ready to execute is empty do
3       Add the job at time t to the queue of jobs ready to execute
4       if the set of jobs ready to execute not is empty do
5           SL-CFG ( NODE, RDYSET, [ a, b ), [ Sl, Su ) );
        else
6           Draw the node that represents the end of a trajectory
    else
7       Extract the highest prioritized job j from the ready queue
8       Calculate the execution window for job j, [ α, β )
9       Calculate the start interval of the next job at time t, [ a', b' )
10      Draw the transition and the node of the current job, NODE->j
```

```
11      Add all jobs that have lower priority than the jobs at time t to
the ready queue
12      if the job j is preempted by a job at time t then do
13-29     SL_CFG_preemption ( j, RDYSET, [ a, b ), [ α, β ), [ a', b' ) ,
[ Sl, Su), t )
        else
30-46     SL_CFG__nopreemption ( j, RDYSET, [ a, b ), [ α, β ), [ a', b'
) , [ Sl, Su), t )
}
```

List. 1. The listing of the main loop of the System control Flow algorithm.

```
Algorithm SL_CFG_preemption (j, RDYSET, [ a, b ), [ α, β ), [ a', b' ) ,
[ Sl, Su), t )
{
13 Extract the next critical section sj from job j
14 If job j completes before the release of a job at time t then do
15    if job j enter a critical section and the priority is promoted
then do
16        Add sub job sj to the queue of jobs ready to execute
17        SL_CFG ( j , RDYSET, [ a', t ] , [ t, Su ] )
      else
18        Add sub job sj to the queue of jobs ready to execute
19        SL_CFG ( j , RDYSET, [ a', t ) , [ t, Su ] )
20        if the set of jobs ready to execute not is empty do
21            Add the job at time t to the queue of jobs ready to execute
22            SL_CFG ( j, RDYSET, [t, t), ( t, Su])
23        else if there are jobs that immediately succeeds job j then do
24            Add the job at time t to the queue of jobs ready to execute
25            Add sub job sj to the queue of jobs ready to execute
26            SL_CFG ( j, RDYSET, [ t, t), (t, Su] )
27 Add the job at time t to the queue of jobs ready to execute
28 Recalculate the execution time for job j
29 SL_CFG ( j, RDYSET, [ t, t], (t, Su])
}
```

List. 2. The listing of the System Control Flow algorithm, the part in which the job may or may not be preempted.

```
Algorithm SL_CFG_nopreemption (j, RDYSET, [a, b), [ α, β ), [a', b'),
[Sl, Su), t)
{
30 Extract the next critical section sj from job j
31 if this is the possible end of the simulation then do
32    Add sub job sj to the queue of jobs ready to execute
33    if job j enter a critical section and the priority is promoted
then do
34        SL_CFG ( j, RDYSET, [ a', b' ], [ b', Su ] )
      else
35        SL_CFG ( j, RDYSET, [ a', b' ), [ INF, INF ] )
   else
36    if job j enter a critical section and the priority is promoted
then do
37        Add sub job sj to the queue of jobs ready to execute
38        SL_CFG ( j, RDYSET, [a', b' ], [ b' , Su ] )
39    else if there exists a job that immediately succeeds job j then do
40        Add the job at time t to the queue of jobs ready to execute
41        Add sub job sj to the queue of jobs ready to execute
42        SL_CFG ( j, RDYSET, [t, t), ( t, Su] )
```

```
43        if the job at time t immediately succeeds job j the do
44           SL_CFG ( j, RDYSET, [ a', b' ), [ t, sr] );
      else
45        Add sub job sj to the queue of jobs ready to execute
46        SL_CFG ( j, RDYSET, [ a', b' ), [ t, sr ] );
}
```

List. 3. The listing of the System Control Flow algorithm, the part in which the job completes before the release of a higher prioritized job.

Symbolic Simulation of Real-Time Concurrent Systems*

Farn Wang[1], Geng-Dian Huang[2], and Fang Yu[2]

[1] Dept. of Electrical Engineering, National Taiwan University
farn@cc.ee.ntu.edu.tw
[2] Institute of Information Science, Academia Sinica, Taiwan
{view,yuf}@iis.sinica.edu.tw

Abstract. We introduce the symbolic simulation function implemented in our model-checker/simulator RED 4.0 for dense-time concurrent systems. By representing and manipulating state-spaces as logic predicates, the technique of symbolic simulation can lead to high performance by encompassing many, even densely many, traces in traditional simulation into one symbolic trace. We discuss how we generate traces with various policies, how we manipulate the state-predicate, and how we manage the trace trees. Finally, we report experiment with our simulator in the verification of the Bluetooth baseband protocol.

Keywords: Assertions, specification, state-based, event-driven, model-checking, verification

1 Introduction

Traditional simulation [8,14,18] uses memory to record the variable values in a state along a trace and makes it possible for engineers to visualize the behaviors of the system design even before the hardware prototypes are put into reality. For many decades, simulation has been the major tool for engineers to successfully guarantee the quality of system designs in early cycles of system development. But for the new system designs in the new century, e.g. System-on-a-Chip (SOC) with tens of millions of gates, there will not be enough time and manpower to run enough number of simulation traces of the system designs. The complexity incurred by the system designs in the next few years simply overwhelms the capability of traditional simulation technology.

On the other hand, model-checking technology [12,2] has promised to mathematically prove the correctness of system design. The development of model-checking with symbolic manipulation techniques [11,5] has made the full verification of many non-real-time industrial projects into reality. The symbolic manipulation techniques do not record the exact values of variables explicitly. Instead,

---

* The work is partially supported by NSC, Taiwan, ROC under grants NSC 90-2213-E-001-006, NSC 90-2213-E-001-035, and the by the Broadband network protocol verification project of Institute of Applied Science & Engineering Research, Academia Sinica, 2001.

J. Chen and S. Hong (Eds.): RTCSA 2003, LNCS 2968, pp. 595–617, 2004.

sets of states are succinctly represented and manipulated as logic constraints on variable values. For example, we have procedure to compute the state-predicate at the next-step from the current state-predicate. Such succinctness not only saves the memory space in representation but also allows us to construct a huge (or even dense) set of states in a few symbolic manipulation steps.

However, even with such powerful techniques of symbolic manipulation, the verification task of real-time concurrent system still demands tremendous resources beyond the reach of current technology. The reachable state-space representations in TCTL model-checking [2] tasks usually demand complexity exponential to the input system description sizes. Usually, verification tasks blow up the memory usage before finishing with answers.

In a sense, traditional simulation and model-checking represent two extremes in the spectrum. Traditional simulation is efficient (you may only have to record the current state) but the number of traces to cover full functionality of a system is usually forbiddingly high. On the other hand, model-checking can achieve functional completeness in verification but usually requires huge amount of system resources. Thus it will be helpful and attractive if a technique that makes a balance between the two extremes can be developed.

The technique of *symbolic simulation* represents such a balance [28]. The technique was originally introduced and proved valuable for the verification of integrated circuits. While traditional simulation runs along a trace of precise state recordings, symbolic simulation runs along a trace of symbolic constraints, representing a (convex or concave) space of "current states." In metaphor, traditional simulation is like a probe while the new symbolic simulation technique is like a searchlight into the space and can monitor a set of state-traces at the same time. With proper choice of the caliber of the searchlight, we have much better chance to discover the imminent risk and potential threats in the immense sky.

We have implemented a symbolic simulator, for dense-time concurrent systems, with GUI (Graphical User-Interface), convenient facilities to generate and manage the traces. The simulator is now part of RED 4.0, a model-checker/simulator for real-time systems. In the development of the symbolic simulation function, we encounter the following many challenges and opportunities.

What Is the Model We Adopt for Real-Time Concurrent Systems ?

In simulation, we construct a mathematical model for a system design (and the environment) with computer programs and observe how the model behaves in computer's virtual world. The semantics of the model will determine how efficiently we can approximate the system/environment interaction and how efficient we can compute the traces.

Symbolic simulation has gained much success in the verification of VLSI circuits, which are usually synchronous. We plan to extend the success in the area of real-time concurrent systems, like communication protocols, embedded softwares, ..., etc. For such systems, the assumption of the existence of a global clock is inappropriate and the synchronous discrete-time model can lead to imprecise simulation. In a real-world real-time concurrent system, each hardware module may have its own clock. Even the new SOC can have multi-clocks in the same chip. Based on all these consideration, we adopt the well-accepted timed automata [3], with multiple dense-time clocks, as our system model.

The input language of RED 4.0 allows the description of a timed automaton as a set of process automata communicating with each other through synchronizers (namely, input/output events through channels in [21]) and global variables. Users may use binary synchronizers to construct *legitimate global transitions* (to be explained in section 3) from *process transitions*. RED also allows users to control the "caliber of the searchlight" to better monitor a user-given goal (or risk) condition along traces.

How Do We Construct and Manage Traces ?

The traces can be constructed randomly or with a policy. *Random traces* are computed with random number generators without the bias of the designers and verification engineers. Many people do not feel confident with a design until it has been verified with random traces. On the other hand, directed traces are constructed with built-in or user-given policies. *Directed traces* can help in guiding the simulators to program lines which are suspicious of bugs or whose effects need to be closely monitored. With directed traces, the simulators can more efficiently construct the traces that are of interest to the verification engineers.

Symbolic simulation actually adds one more dimension to the issue of random vs. directed traces. Since we can use complex logic constraints to represent a space of states, from steps to steps, we are actually building traces of state-spaces, instead of a single precise state. So it is more like (even densely) many traces are constructed simultaneously. Symbolic simulation thus add the dimension of *"width"* to a trace of state-spaces. In section 5, we shall discuss how to control the width of traces with the many options supported by our simulator.

Organizations of the Paper

In the following sections, we first review some related work (section 2), describe our system models (section 3), and give a brief overview of what we have achieved in our implementations (section 4). Then we delve into more details of our achievements (sections 5, 6). Finally, we report our experiments with our implementations and the Bluetooth baseband protocol (section 7). We were able to verify that under some parameter-settings, the protocol guarantee that one device will eventually discover the frequency of its peer device. The experiment is also interesting since we have not heard of any similar result on the full model-checking of the protocol.

2   Previous Work

Symbolic Trajectory Evaluation(STE) [28], or *called symbolic simulation*, is the main alternative to symbolic model checking [5], in formal hardware verification. STE can be considered a hybrid approach based on symbolic simulation and model checking algorithms and can verify assertions, which express safety properties.

STATEMATE [19] is a tool set with a heavy graphical orientation and powerful simulation capability. Users specify systems from three points of view: structural, functional, and behavioral. Three graphical languages, includes modulecharts, activity-charts, and state-charts, are supported for the three views. The STATEMATE provides simulation control language(SCL) to enable user to program the simulation. Breakpoints can also be incorporate into the programs in SCL. It may cause the simulation to stop and take certain actions. Moreover, the simulation trace is recorded in trace database, and can be inspected later. The users may view a trace as a discrete animation of state-charts.

The MT-Sim [8] provides simulation platform for the Modechart toolset(MT) [14], which is a collection of integrated tools for specifying and analyzing realtime systems. MT-Sim is a flexible, extensible simulation environment. It supports user-defined viewers, full user participation via event injection, and assertion checking which can invoke user-defined handlers upon assertion violation.

UPPAAL [26] is an integrated tool environment for modeling, validation and verification of dense-time systems. It is composed of the system editor, the simulator, and the verifier. The behavior of simulated systems can be observed via the simulator, which can display the systems in many level of details. Besides, the simulator can load diagnostic trace generated by the verifier for further inspection. One technical difference between RED and UPPAAL is that RED uses a BDD-like data-structure, called CRD (Clock-Restriction Diagram) [31, 32, 33, 34], for the representation of dense-time state-space while UPPAAL uses the traditional DBM (Difference-Bounded Matrix) [15]. A CRD can represent disjunction and conjunction while a DBM can only represent a conjunction. With this advantage, CRD is more convenient and flexible in manipulating the "width" of simulation traces. Also in previous experiments [31, 32, 34], CRD has shown better performance than DBM w.r.t. several benchmarks of dense-time concurrent systems.

In [18], IOA language and IOA toolset, based on IO automaton, are proposed for designing and analyzing the distributed systems. The toolset can express designs at different levels of abstraction, generate source code automatically, simulate automata, and interface to existing theorem provers. The IOA simulator solves the nondeterminism in IOA language by user-defined determinator specification, random-number generator, and querying the user. IOA simulator provides paired simulation to check the simulation relationship between two automata. It simulates an automaton normally and executes another automaton according to user-defined step correspondence. It is useful in developing systems using levels of abstraction.

3   Synchronized Concurrent Timed Automata

A *timed automaton* [3] is a finite-state automaton equipped with a finite set of clocks that can hold nonnegative real-values. At any moment, the timed au-

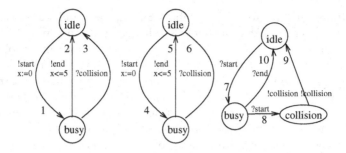

Fig. 1. The model of bus-contending systems

tomaton can stay in only one *mode* (or *control location*). In its operation, one of the global transitions can be triggered when the corresponding triggering condition is satisfied. Upon being triggered, the automaton instantaneously transits from one mode to another and resets some clocks to zero. In between global transitions, all clocks increase their readings at a uniform rate.

In our input language, users can describe the timed automaton as a *synchronized concurrent timed automaton (SCTA)* [31, 32, 33]. Such an automaton is in turn described as a set of *process automata (PA)*. Users can declare local (to each process) and global variables of type clock, integer, and pointer (to identifier of processes). Boolean conditions on variables can be tested and variable values can be assigned. Process automata can communicate with one another through binary synchronizations. One of the earliest devices of such synchronizations are the input-output symbol pairs through a channel, in process algebra [21]. Similar synchronization devices have been used in the input languages to HyTech [4], IO Automata [25], UPPAAL [9], Kronos [16], VERIFAST [37], SGM [22, 35, 36], and RED [29, 30, 31, 32, 33].

In figure 1, we have drawn three process automata, in a bus-contending systems. Two process automata are for senders and one for the bus. The circles represent modes while the arcs represent transitions, which may be labeled with synchronization symbols (e.g., !begin, ?end, !collision, ...), triggering conditions (e.g., $x \leq 5$), and assignments (e.g., $x := 0;$). Each transition (arc) in the process automata is called a *process transition*. For convenience, we have labeled the process transitions with numbers. In the system, a sender process may synchronize through channel **begin** with the bus to start sending signal on the bus. While one sender is using the bus, the second sender may also synchronize through channel **begin** to start placing message on the bus and corrupting the bus contents. When this happen, the bus then signals bus **collision** to both of the senders.

We adopt the standard interleaving semantics, i.e., at any instant, at most one *legitimate global transition (LG-transition)* can happen in the SCTA. For formal semantics of the systems, please check out appendix A. A process transition may not represent an LG-transition and may not be executed by itself. Only

LG-transition can be executed. Symbols **begin**, **end**, and **collision**, on the arcs, represent synchronization channels, which serve as glue to combine process transitions into LG-transitions. An exclamation (question) mark followed by a channel name means an *output (input)* event through the channel. For example, !begin means a sending event through channel **begin** while ?begin means a receiving event through the same channel. Any input event through a channel must match, at the same instant, with a unique output event through the same channel. Thus, a process transition with an output event must combine with another process transition (by another process) with a corresponding input event to become an LG-transition.

Thus the synchronizers in our input language are primarily used to help users in decomposing their programs into modules and to help the simulators to glue process transitions in constructing LG-transitions. For example, in figure 1, process transitions 1 and 7 can combine to be an LG-transition. Also process transitions 3, 6, and 9 can make an LG-transition since two output events matches two input events through channel **collision**.

In the following, we illustrate how to reason in one step of our simulator engine to construct the state-predicate of the next-step. Intuitively, in one step, the system will progress in time and then execute an LG-transition. For example, we may have a current state-predicate

$$(p = 1 \land q = 2) \lor (q = 4 \land 1 \leq x < 3) \tag{P}$$

and an LG-transition expressed as the following guarded command:

$$(p = 1 \land x > 5) \longrightarrow x := 0; p := 3; \tag{X}$$

which means

> "when $(p = 1 \land x > 5)$ is true with x as a clock,
> reset x to zero and assign 3 to p."

In a step of the simulation engine, we first calculate the new state-predicate obtained from states in (P) by letting time progress. This affects the constraint on clock x and yields

$$(p = 1 \land q = 2) \lor (q = 4 \land 1 \leq x) \tag{P'}$$

Then we apply the LG-transitions, selected by the users, to (P') to obtain the state-predicate representing states after the selected transitions. Suppose the only selected LG-transition is (X). Then the state-predicate at the next-step is

$$p = 3 \land x = 0 \land (q = 2 \lor q = 4)$$

Details can be found in [20].

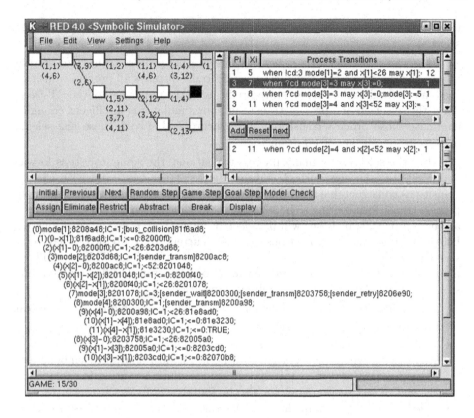

Fig. 2. The GUI of RED 4.0

4 Overview of Our Simulator

We have incorporated the idea in this report in our verification tool, RED 4.0, a TCTL model-checker/simulator [29, 30, 31, 32, 33]. The tool can be activated with the following command in Unix environment:

$ red [options] *InputFileName OutputFileName*

The options are
- -Sp: symmetry reduction for pointer data-structure systems [38]
- -Sg: Symmetry reduction for zones [17, 33],
- -c: Counter-example generation
- -s: Simulator mode with GUI

Without option -s, the tool serves as a high-performance TCTL model-checker in backward analysis. When the simulation mode GUI is activated, we will see the window like figure 2 popping up. The GUI window is partitioned into four frames respectively of trace trees (on the upper-left corner), current state-predicates (on the bottom), command buttons (in the middle), and candidate process transitions (PT-frame, on the upper-right corner) to be selected and already been selected.

Users can construct LG-transitions by selecting process transitions step-by-step in the PT-frame. At each step, the PT-frame displays all process transitions that can be fired at the current state-predicate in the upper-half of the PT-frame. After the selection of a process transition , our simulator is intelligent enough to eliminate those process transitions not synchronizable with those just-selected ones from the display of PT-frame.

After the selection of many process transitions, the simulator steps forward and computes the new current state-predicate at the next step with the LG-transitions constructable from the selected process transitions. If there are many process transitions waiting to be selected at the time the simulator steps forward, all those process transitions will be selected. Since these process transitions may belong to different LG-transitions, the new current state-predicate may represent the result of execution of more than one LG-transitions. This capability to manipulate a state-space represented in a complex state-predicate in symbolic steps is indeed the strength of symbolic simulation.

The architecture of our implementation is shown in figure 3. We explain briefly its components in the following:

- *RED symbolic simulation engine*: This is actually the timed-transition next-step state-predicate calculation routine in forward analysis. Symbolic algorithm for this next-step state-predicate calculation routine is explained at the end of last section and can also be found in [20].

- *assertion monitoring*: In the input language to the simulator, users can also specify a *goal predicate* for the traces. This goal predicate can be a risk condition, which the users want to make sure that it cannot happen. Or it can be a liveness condition, which the users want to see that it can happen. After each step of the simulation engine, our RED 4.0 will check if the intersection of the goal predicate and the next-step state-predicate is nonempty. If it is, the sequence of LG-transitions leading from the initial state to this goal predicate can be displayed. Such a capability is indispensable in helping the users debugging their system designs.

- *trace computation*: This component uses user-guidance, randomness, and various policies to select LG-transitions, in the generation of traces by repetitive invoking the RED symbolic simulation engine. More details is given in section 5.

- *state manipulation*: This includes facilities to inject faults, to either relax or restrict the current state-space, and to set symbolic breakpoints.

- *trace tree management*: (See the frame at the upper-left corner.) This component is for the maintenance of the trace tree structure and movement of current state nodes in the tree. The simulator can step forward and backtrack according to the plain interaction. After a few times of these forward-backward steps, a tree of traces is constructed and recorded in our simulator to represent the whole history of the session. The node for the current state-predicate is black while the others are white. Users can also click on nodes

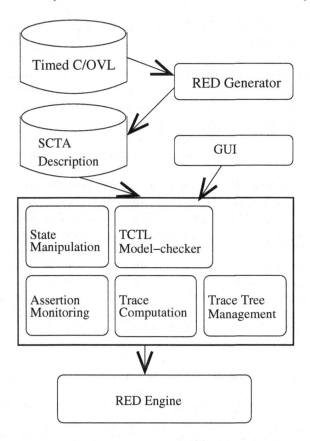

Fig. 3. The architecture of RED model-checker/simulator

in the trace tree and jump to a specific current state-predicate. On the arcs, we also label the set of pairs of processes and process transitions used in the generation of the next state-predicate.

- *GUI (graphical user-interface*: A user-friendly window for easy access to the power of formal verification.
- *RED symbolic TCTL model-checker*: The high performance backward analysis power of RED can be directedly activated to check if the system model satisfies the assertion.

5   Trace Computations

As mentioned in the introduction, symbolic simulation adds one new dimension of trace "width" , which reflecting the number of fired LG-transitions in each step in the construction of traces. With Red 4.0, users may choose from various options to construct traces with appropriate randomness, special search policy, and enough width. The options are:

- *plain interaction:* With selection of process transitions from the PT-frame and previous/next step commands, users have total control on how to select process transitions to make LG-transitions in the construction of the next-step state predicates along the current trace.
- *random steps:* The simulator could also randomly choose an LG-transition in each step. Users can command the autonomous execution of a given number of random steps.
- *game-based policy:* We use the term *"game"* here because we envision the concurrent system operation as a game. Those processes, which we want to verify, are treated as *players* while the other processes are treated as *opponents*. In the game, the players try to win (maintain the specification property) under the worst (i.e., minimal) assumption on their opponents.

  A process is a *player* iff its local variables appear in the goal state-predicate. Intuitively, the simulator constructs a trace segment with all possible reactions of the players in response to random behaviors of the opponents. With this option, we can observe the behavior of players' response to opponents' action. According to the well-observed discipline of modular programming [27], the behavioral correctness of a functional module should be based on minimal assumption on the environment. If we view the players as the functional module and the opponents as the environment, then this *game-based policy* makes a lot of sense.

  It can be useful when we try to verify the design of the player processes. In other words, at each step, the simulator is growing the trace with a width enough for one process transition from each opponent and all firable process transitions from players. Users can again command the autonomous execution of a few steps with this game-based policy.

- *goal-oriented policy:* This policy makes the simulator to generate fast traces leading to the goal states. This can be useful in debugging the system designs, when users have observed some abnormal states. The users can specify the abnormal states as the goal assertions.

  RED 4.0 achieves this by defining the *heuristic distance estimation (HD-estimation)* from one state to the other (to be explained in the following). Then process transitions which can the most significantly reduce the HD-estimation from any states in the current state-predicate to any states in the goal state-predicate will be selected in the hope of a short trace to the goal states can be constructed.

  The *HD-estimation* from one (global) state s to another s' is defined as follows. Suppose we have m processes and $s(p)$ is the mode in process p's automaton in state s. Then HD-estimation from s to s' is the sum, over all processes p, of the shortest path distance from $s(p)$ to $s'(p)$ in the graph (constructed with modes as nodes and process transitions as arcs) of process p's automaton. For each porcess p, the shortest path distance is gained from the backward breath-first algorithm.

For VLSI, usually people adopt the estimation of Hemming distance, which measures the number of bit-differences. But for dense-time concurrent systems, state-predicates are loaded with clock constraints and Hemming distance can be difficult to define in a meaningful way.

6   Manipulation of Current State-Predicate

Our simulator allows for the modification of the current state-predicate before proceeding to the next-step. The following methods can be used to manipulate the current state-predicate and affects the "width" of traces.

- **assign**: The simulator allows users to assign a new value to a state-variable. This can be used to change the behavior of the systems and insert faults.
- **eliminate**: By this method, users can eliminate all constraints w.r.t. a state-variable. This is equivalent to broadening the width of the trace on the dimension of the corresponding state-variable. We can observe the system behavior with less assumption on state-variables.
- **restrict**: In opposition to elimination, users can type in a new predicate and conjunct it with the current state-predicate. With this capability, we can narrow the width of the trace and focus on the interesting behaviors.
- **abstract**: As in the paragraph of game-based policy in section 5, we view the behavior of the target system as a game process and players, opponents can be identified. According to this, the simulator provides three abstract image functions to systematically abstract the current state-predicate. This is also equivalent to systematically broadening the width of the trace. The options for the abstract image functions are:
  - *Game-abstraction*: The game abstract image function will eliminate the state information of the opponents from its argument.
  - *Game-discrete-abstraction*: This abstract image function will eliminate all clock constraints for the opponents in the state-predicate.
  - *Game-magnitude-abstraction*: A clock constraint like $x - x' \sim c$ is called a *magnitude constraint* iff either x or x' is zero itself (i.e. the constraint is either $x \sim c$ or $-x' \sim c$). This abstract image function will erase all non-magnitude constraints of the opponents in the state-predicate.

Note that some of these methods can significantly simplify the representation of the current state-predicate. This also implies that the time and space needed to calculate the next-step state-predicates can be reduced. For example, we may have clocks x_1, x_2 as local clocks of processes 1 and 2 respectively. After applying the game-magnitude-abstraction image function to $x_1 \geq 4 \wedge x_2 \geq 3 \wedge (x_1 - x_2 \leq -2 \vee x_2 - x_1 \leq -1)$, we get $x_1 \geq 4 \wedge x_2 \geq 3$ and have changed a concave state-space down to a convex state-space. This kind of transformation usually can significantly reduce the time and space needed for the manipulations.

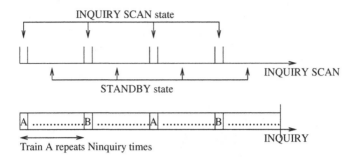

Fig. 4. Mode sequences of processes INQUIRY and INQUIRY SCAN in baseband protocol

7   Experiments on Bluetooth Baseband Protocol

In the following, we first give a brief introduction to the Bluetooth baseband protocol [23]. Then we present our model of baseband protocol in SCTA in subsection 7.2. The model will be used in two ways:bug-inserted and bug-free. We use two bug-inserted models in subsection 7.3 and 7.4 respectively, and show how to quickly find the bugs with symbolic traces of Red 4.0. In subsections 7.3, we also demonstrate how to generate traces to observe system behaviors step by step. Finally, in subsection 7.5, we use the bug-free model to report the performance in full verification of the Baseband protocol.

7.1   Bluetooth Baseband Protocol

Bluetooth is a specification for wireless communication protocols [23]. It operates in the unlicensed Industrial-Scientific-Medical (ISM) band at 2.4 GHz. Since ISM band is open to everyone, Bluetooth uses the frequency hopping spread spectrum (FHSS) and time-division duplex (TDD) scheme to cope with interferences. Bluetooth divides the band into 79 radio frequencies and hops between these frequencies. It is a critical issue for Bluetooth devices to discover the frequencies of other Bluetooth devices since FHSS and TDD scheme are used.

A Bluetooth unit that wants to discover other Bluetooth units enters an INQUIRY mode. A Bluetooth unit that allows itself to be discovered, regularly enters the INQUIRY SCAN mode to listen to inquiry messages. Figure 4 shows the INQUIRY and INQUIRY SCAN procedures. All Bluetooth units in INQUIRY and INQUIRY SCAN share the same hopping sequence, which is 32 hops in length. The Bluetooth unit in INQUIRY SCAN mode hops every 1.28 sec. Although a Bluetooth unit in INQUIRY mode also uses the same inquiry hopping sequence, it does not know which frequencies do receivers listen to. In order to solve this uncertainty, a Bluetooth unit in INQUIRY mode hops at rate of 1600 hop/sec, and transmits two packets on two different frequencies and then listens for response messages on corresponding frequency. Besides, the inquiry hopping sequence is divided into train A and B of 16 frequencies and a single train is repeated for Ninquiry (which is 256 in specification) times before a new train is used. In an error-free environment, at least three train switches must have taken place. Details can be found in [23];

7.2   The System Model

In this subsection, we will introduce our system model briefly. For more details, the timed automata are shown in Appendix B. For convenience, we have labeled the process transitions with numbers.

Every Bluetooth unit has a system clock. When the clock ticks, the Bluetooth unit updates its internal timer and frequency. So in our model, there are two clocks, tick_clk_scan and tick_clk_inq, for INQUIRY SCAN and INQUIRY processes, respectively. Every time unit, the processes loop through the modes to update the variables. For the INQUIRY SCAN procedure, there are two important variables, inqscanTimer_ and mode_scan. Variable inqscanTimer_, which is a timer updated in transitions 6 to 9, is used to determine when to enter INQUIRY SCAN mode. Variable mode_scan records the current mode of the process performing the INQUIRY SCAN procedure, and its value may be INQUIRY_SCAN or STANDBY.

For the INQUIRY procedure, when the value of variable clkmod, in transitions 13 to 16, is less than 2, the process transmits packets. Otherwise, it listens for response messages. The process sends packets via synchronization channel in transitions 19 and 20. If a packet is received successfully, it means that the frequency, through which the packet is received, is discovered and the process goes to SUCCESS mode. Otherwise, in transitions 21 to 24, variables id_sent, train_sent, and train_switch are changed. Variable id_sent records the packets sent in current train; variable train_sent records the number of repeat of a single train; variable train_switch represents how many train switches have taken place. After three train switches, the process goes to TIMEOUT mode via transition 25.

Our task is to verify whether two Bluetooth units in complementary modes will hop to the same frequency before timeout, so that the INQUIRY and INQUIRY SCAN procedures can go on. One can think of a printer equipped with Bluetooth in INQUIRY SCAN mode. When a notebook equipped with Bluetooth has data to print, it will inquiry nearby printers. We anticipate that the notebook can learn the existence of the printer with the Bluetooth protocols.

7.3   Using "Width" of Simulation Traces for Advantage

In this subsection, a bug is inserted in the INQUIRY SCAN process in the model. We demonstrate how to properly control the "width" of symbolic traces to quickly discover the bug, and manipulate the state-space predicate to pseudo-correct the bug. In the end of the simulation, we use game-based policy to automatically trace to our goal states.

Table 1. The step-by-step simulation

step	1	2	3	4	5	6	7	8
process transitions	(I,13)	(I,17)	(IS,5)	(IS,1)	(IS,6)	restrict	assign	game-based policy
			(I,20)	(IS,2)	(IS,7)			
				(IS,3)	(IS,8)			
					(IS, 9)			

I: process INQUIRY; IS: process INQUIRY_SCAN; (p,x): process p executing process transition x.

We use the step sequence shown in the second row of table 1 to experiment with RED and the Baseband protocol.

A pair like (p, x) in the row means that process p executes transition x. When several of these process transition execution pairs are stacked, it means that we select all these process transitions to broaden the trace width of simulation.

In our scenario with notebook and printer, the printer regularly enters the INQUIRY SCAN mode to listen to inquiry messages. The printer will periodically execute in mode INQUIRY SCAN and mode STANDBY in sequence (See the upper mode-sequence in figure 4). In the implementation of Baseband protocol, the alternation between these two modes is controlled with counter inqscanTimer_, which increments at every clock tick. When inqscanTimer_ < TwInqScan_c (TwInqScan_c is a macro constant defining the scan window size), the printer stays in mode INQUIRY_SCAN. At the time when inqscanTimer_ = TwInqScan_c, the printer changes to mode STANDBY. When counter inqscanTimer_ increases to macro constant TinqScan_c (the time span between two consecutive inquiry scans), it is reset to zero. We want to make sure that an INQUIRY SCAN process will periodically execute in the two modes of

$$\text{inqscanTimer\_} < \text{TwInqScan\_c}$$
$$\wedge \, \text{mode\_scan} = \text{INQUIRY\_SCAN}$$

and

$$\text{inqscanTimer\_} \geq \text{TwInqScan\_c}$$
$$\wedge \, \text{mode\_scan} = \text{STANDBY}$$

in sequence. Thus a risk condition saying that this sequence is violated is the following.

$$\left(\left\{ \begin{array}{l} \text{inqscanTimer\_} < \text{TwInqScan\_c} \\ \wedge \, \text{mode\_scan} \neq \text{INQUIRY\_SCAN} \\ \text{inqscanTimer\_} \geq \text{TwInqScan\_c} \\ \wedge \, \text{mode\_scan} \neq \text{STANDBY} \end{array} \right\} \right)$$

When the notebook starts to inquiry, the printer may be in mode INQUIRY_SCAN or mode STANDBY. With traditional simulation [8, 14, 18], a precise initial state, such as

$$\texttt{inqscanTimer\_} = 0 \wedge \texttt{mode\_scan} = \text{INQUIRY\_SCAN}$$

must be chosen to start the simulation. And the chosen initial state may either never reach the risk states or have a long way to do it. But in RED 4.0, we can start our simulation from the whole state-space represented by the following state-predicate.

$$\left(\left\{ \begin{array}{l} \left(\begin{array}{l} \texttt{inqscanTimer\_} < \texttt{TwInqScan\_c} \\ \wedge\, \texttt{mode\_scan} = \text{INQUIRY\_SCAN} \end{array} \right) \\ \vee \left(\begin{array}{l} \texttt{inqscanTimer\_} \geq \texttt{TwInqScan\_c} \\ \wedge\, \texttt{mode\_scan} = \text{STANDBY} \end{array} \right) \end{array} \right\} \right)$$

By starting simulation with this big state-space, we are actually using a great "width" of the symbolic trace and should have much better chance in detecting bugs.

By executing the first five steps in the sequence of table 1, we simulate the model step by step to observe if the system acts according to our expectation. At the fifth step, we have four executable process transitions, including transitions 6, 7, 8, and 9 (see the arc labels in figures in figure 5 in appendix B) of process INQUIRY SCAN. With RED 4.0, we can simulate all these possibilities in a single step.

Now we want to demonstrate what we can do with the discovery of bugs. After the fifth step, we reach a risk state. Inspecting the trace, we find a bug in transition 7 (see figure 5). According to Bluetooth specification [23], when counter $\texttt{inqscanTimer\_}$ increments from $\texttt{TwInqScan\_c}$-1 to $\texttt{TwInqScan\_c}$, process INQUIRY SCAN should change from mode INQUIRY SCAN to mode STANDBY. And transition 7 in figure 5 is supposed to model this mode change. The bug is inserted by changing the triggering condition of process transition 7 from $\texttt{inqscanTimer\_} = \texttt{TwInqScan\_c} - 1$ to $\texttt{inqscanTimer\_} = \texttt{TwInqScan\_c}$. It means that the printer enters mode STANDBY one tick too late and the system reaches the risk state of

$$\texttt{inqscanTimer\_} = \texttt{TwInqScan\_c} \wedge \texttt{mode\_scan} = \text{INQUIRY\_SCAN}$$

In order to pseudo-correct the bug, we want to test what will happen if the mode change does happen in time. To do this what-if analysis, we first restrict our attention to the state-predicate with $\texttt{inqscanTimer_} = $ equals $\texttt{TwInqScan\_c}$. We do this by keying state-predicate $\texttt{inqscanTimer_} = $ equals $\texttt{TwInqScan\_c}$ to restrict the current state-predicate.

Now the new current state-predicate satisfies

$$\texttt{inqscanTimer\_} < \texttt{TwInqScan\_c}$$
$$\wedge\, \texttt{mode\_scan} = \text{INQUIRY\_SCAN}$$

We want to see whether by correcting the bug of the late mode-change, we can indeed get the correct behavior (i.e. both parties hop to the same frequency). We change the value of $\texttt{mode\_scan}$ from INQUIRY_SCAN to STANDBY. Then we use generate traces automatically and see if we can see any faulty behaviors in the traces constructed with the game-based policy (i.e., all process transitions for players (process INQUIRY SCAN) and random transitions for opponents (process INQUIRY). In our experiment, RED 4.0 constructed a symbolic trace leading to SUCCESS mode. This give users confidence that the both parties indeed can hop to the same frequency.

7.4   Fast Debugging with Goal-Oriented Policy

Here we show how to find bugs in our Baseband model with our goal-oriented policy. The bug is inserted as follows. In transitions 19 and 20, variable id-sent is now incremented when a packet is sent. However, this increment is redundant because variable id_sent has already been incremented with variables train_sent and train_switch together in transitions 21 to 24. This bug would make id_sent to be incremented by 2 for each packet sent, and causes the INQUIRY process timeout quickly.

We generate directed traces with our goal-oriented policy. The simulator selects transitions that minimize the HD-estimation to the goal state. For example, transition 20 which leads to TIMEOUT mode would be taken rather than transition 19 that leads to SUCCESS mode, since our goal state is TIMEOUT mode which means the existence of a bug. In our first trial, we generate a trace that reaches the TIMEOUT mode, and fix the bug by observing the trace. It costs RED 4.0 8.21 seconds on an Pentium 1.7G MHz desktop with 256 MB memory to generate the directed trace. However, if we do full verification to generate a counter-example trace, it costs RED 4.0 137.78 seconds.

With random traces, the time needed to find a bug depends on how fast the random traces hit the bug. In our experiment, we generate a random traces, but it does not reach the TIMEOUT mode. Then we have to generate a new trace from the step that may lead to the TIMEOUT mode. Repeating this trial-and-error iterations for six times, we finally reaches the TIMEOUT mode. Our experiment shows that the goal-oriented policy is more efficient in debugging the model as compared with random steps and full verification.

7.5   Full Verification

Finally, we have finished simulating and debugging our model, and gained confidence in the correctness of our system. We can now proceed to the more expensive step of formal model-checking to see whether two Bluetooth units in complementary modes will hop to the same frequency before timeout. RED 4.0 uses 197 seconds on an Pentium 1.7G MHz desktop with 256 MB memory to check this model.

8   Conclusion

This paper has described RED 4.0, a symbolic simulator based on BDD-like data-structure with GUI for dense-time concurrent systems. RED 4.0 can generate symbolic traces with various policy, and manipulate the state-predicate.

By properly control the width of symbolic traces, we have much better chances in observing what we are interested. The usefulness of our techniques can be justified by our report on experiment with the Bluetooth baseband protocol.

Future work may proceed in several directions. Firstly, we hope to derive new HD-estimation functions used in the directed trace generation, and support customized automatic trace generation policy. These would help users finding bugs with fewer simulation traces. Secondly, the coverage estimation to gain confidence is also an important issue in our future work. Finally, we plan to make our GUI more friendly so that users can have easy access to the power of formal verification.

References

1. Asaraain, Bozga, Kerbrat, Maler, Pnueli, Rasse. Data-Structures for the Verification of Timed Automata. Proceedings, HART'97, LNCS 1201.
2. R. Alur, C. Courcoubetis, D.L. Dill. Model Checking for Real-Time Systems, IEEE LICS, 1990.
3. R. Alur, D.L. Dill. Automata for modelling real-time systems. ICALP' 1990, LNCS 443, Springer-Verlag, pp.322-335.
4. R. Alur, T.A. Henzinger, P.-H. Ho. Automatic Symbolic Verification of Embedded Systems. in Proceedings of 1993 IEEE Real-Time System Symposium.
5. J.R. Burch, E.M. Clarke, K.L. McMillan, D.L.Dill, L.J. Hwang. Symbolic Model Checking: 10^{20} States and Beyond, IEEE LICS, 1990.
6. M. Bozga, C. Daws. O. Maler. Kronos: A model-checking tool for real-time systems. 10th CAV, June/July 1998, LNCS 1427, Springer-Verlag.
7. Bening, L. and Foster, H., i. Principles of Verifiable RTL Design, a Functional Coding Style Supporting Verification Processes in Verilog,li 2nd ed., Kluwer Academic Publishers, 2001.
8. M. Brockmeyer, C. Heitmeyer, F. Jahanian, B. Labaw. A Flexible, Extensible Simulation Environment for Testing Real-Time, IEEE, 1997.
9. J. Bengtsson, K. Larsen, F. Larsson, P. Pettersson, Wang Yi. UPPAAL - a Tool Suite for Automatic Verification of Real-Time Systems. Hybrid Control System Symposium, 1996, LNCS, Springer-Verlag.
10. G. Behrmann, K.G. Larsen, J. Pearson, C. Weise, Wang Yi. Efficient Timed Reachability Analysis Using Clock Difference Diagrams. CAV'99, July, Trento, Italy, LNCS 1633, Springer-Verlag.
11. R.E. Bryant. Graph-based Algorithms for Boolean Function Manipulation, IEEE Trans. Comput., C-35(8), 1986.
12. E. Clarke, E.A. Emerson, Design and Synthesis of Synchronization Skeletons using Branching-Time Temporal Logic, in "Proceedings, Workshop on Logic of Programs," LNCS 131, Springer-Verlag.
13. E. Clarke, O. Grumberg, M. Minea, D. Peled. State-Space Reduction using Partial-Ordering Techniques, STTT 2(3), 1999, pp.279-287.
14. P. Clements, C. Heitmeyer, G. Labaw, and A. Rose. MT: a toolset for specifying and analyzing real-time systems. in IEEE Real-Time Systems Symposium, 1993.
15. D.L. Dill. Timing Assumptions and Verification of Finite-state Concurrent Systems. CAV'89, LNCS 407, Springer-Verlag.
16. C. Daws, A. Olivero, S. Tripakis, S. Yovine. The tool KRONOS. The 3rd Hybrid Systems, 1996, LNCS 1066, Springer-Verlag.

17. E.A. Emerson, A.P. Sistla. Utilizing Symmetry when Model-Checking under Fairness Assumptions: An Automata-Theoretic Approach. ACM TOPLAS, Vol. **19**, Nr. 4, July 1997, pp. 617-638.
18. S.J. Garland, N.A. Lynch. The IOA Language and Toolset: Support for Designing, Analyzing, and Building Distributed Systems. Technical Report MIT/LCS/TR.
19. D. Harel et al., STATEMATE: A Working Environment for the Development of Complex Reactive Systems. IEEE Trans. on Software Engineering, 16(4) (1990) 403-414.
20. T.A. Henzinger, X. Nicollin, J. Sifakis, S. Yovine. Symbolic Model Checking for Real-Time Systems, IEEE LICS 1992.
21. C.A.R. Hoare. Communicating Sequential Processes, Prentice Hall, 1985.
22. P.-A. Hsiung, F. Wang. User-Friendly Verification. Proceedings of 1999 FORTE/PSTV, October, 1999, Beijing. Formal Methods for Protocol Engineering and Distributed Systems, editors: J. Wu, S.T. Chanson, Q. Gao; Kluwer Academic Publishers.
23. J. Haartsen. Bluetooth Baseband Specification, version 1.0. http://www.bluetooth.com/
24. K.G. Larsen, F. Larsson, P. Pettersson, Y. Wang. Efficient Verification of Real-Time Systems: Compact Data-Structure and State-Space Reduction. IEEE RTSS, 1998.
25. N. Lynch, M.R. Tuttle. An introduction to Input/Output automata. CWI-Quarterly, 2(3):219-246, September 1989. Centrum voor Wiskunde en Informatica, Amsterdam, The Netherlands.
26. P. Pettersson, K.G. Larsen, UPPAAL2k. in Bulletin of the European Association for Theoretical Computer Science, volume 70, pages 40-44, 2000.
27. R.S. Pressman. Software Engineering, A Practitioner's Approach. McGraw-Hill, 1982.
28. C.-J.H. Seger, R.E. Brant Formal Verification by Symbolic Evaluation of Partially-Ordered Trajectories. Formal Methods in System Designs, Vol. 6, No. 2, pp. 147-189, Mar. 1995.
29. F. Wang. Efficient Data-Structure for Fully Symbolic Verification of Real-Time Software Systems. TACAS'2000, March, Berlin, Germany. in LNCS 1785, Springer-Verlag.
30. F. Wang. Region Encoding Diagram for Fully Symbolic Verification of Real-Time Systems. the 24th COMPSAC, Oct. 2000, Taipei, Taiwan, ROC, IEEE press.
31. F. Wang. RED: Model-checker for Timed Automata with Clock-Restriction Diagram. Workshop on Real-Time Tools, Aug. 2001, Technical Report 2001-014, ISSN 1404-3203, Dept. of Information Technology, Uppsala University.
32. F. Wang. Symbolic Verification of Complex Real-Time Systems with Clock-Restriction Diagram, to appear in Proceedings of FORTE, August 2001, Cheju Island, Korea.
33. F. Wang. Symmetric Model-Checking of Concurrent Timed Automata with Clock-Restriction Diagram. RTCSA'2002.
34. F. Wang. Efficient Verification of Timed Automata with BDD-like Data-Structures. Technical Report, IIS, Academia Sinica, 2002.
35. F. Wang, P.-A. Hsiung. Automatic Verification on the Large. Proceedings of the 3rd IEEE HASE, November 1998.
36. F. Wang, P.-A. Hsiung. Efficient and User-Friendly Verification. IEEE Transactions on Computers, Jan. 2002.
37. F. Wang, C.-T. Lo. Procedure-Level Verification of Real-Time Concurrent Systems. International Journal of Time-Critical Computing Systems **16**, 81-114 (1999).

38. F. Wang, K. Schmidt. Symmetric Symbolic Safety-Analysis of Concurrent Software with Pointer Data Structures. IIS Technical Report, 2002, IIS, Academia Sinica, Taipei, Taiwan, ROC.
39. S. Yovine. Kronos: A Verification Tool for Real-Time Systems. International Journal of Software Tools for Technology Transfer, Vol. 1, Nr. 1/2, October 1997.

A   Definition of SCTA

A *SCTA (Synchronized Concurrent Timed Automaton* is a set of finite-state automata, called *process automata*, equipped with a finite set of clocks, which can hold nonnegative real-values, and synchronization channels. At any moment, each process automata can stay in only one *mode* (or *control location*). In its operation, one of the transitions can be triggered when the corresponding triggering condition is satisfied. Upon being triggered, the automaton instantaneously transits from one mode to another and resets some clocks to zero. In between transitions, all clocks increase their readings at a uniform rate.

For convenience, given a set Q of modes and a set X of clocks, we use $B(Q, X)$ as the set of all Boolean combinations of inequalities of the forms $\texttt{mode} = q$ and $x - x' \sim c$, where $\texttt{mode}$ is a special auxiliary variable, $q \in Q$, $x, x' \in X \cup \{0\}$, "$\sim$" is one of $\leq, <, =, >, \geq$, and c is an integer constant.

Definition 1. process automata A process automaton A is given as a tuple $\langle X, E, Q, I, \mu, T, \lambda, \tau, \pi \rangle$ with the following restrictions. X is the set of clocks. E is the set of synchronization channels. Q is the set of modes. $I \in B(Q, X)$ is the initial condition on clocks. $\mu : Q \mapsto B(\emptyset, X)$ defines the invariance condition of each mode. $T \subseteq Q \times Q$ is the set of transitions. $\lambda : (E \times T) \mapsto \mathcal{Z}$ defines the message sent and received at each process transition. When $\lambda(e, t) < 0$, it means that process transition t will receive $|\lambda(e, t)|$ events through channel e. When $\lambda(e, t) > 0$, it means that process transition t will send $\lambda(e, t)$ events through channel e. $\tau : T \mapsto B(\emptyset, X)$ and $\pi : T \mapsto 2^X$ respectively defines the triggering condition and the clock set to reset of each transition.   ■

Definition 2. *SCTA (Synchronized Concurrent Timed Automata) An SCTA of m processes is a tuple, $\langle E, A_1, A_2, \ldots, A_m \rangle$ where E is the set of synchronization channels and for each $1 \leq p \leq m$, $A_p = \langle X_p, E, Q_p, I_p, \mu_p, T_p, \lambda_p, \tau_p, \pi_p \rangle$ is a process automaton for process p.*

A valuation of a set is a mapping from the set to another set. Given an $\eta \in B(Q, X)$ and a valuation ν of X, we say ν satisfies η, in symbols $\nu \models \eta$, iff it is the case that when the variables in η are interpreted according to ν, η will be evaluated true.

Definition 3. <u>states</u> *Suppose we are given an SCTA $S = \langle E, A_1, A_2, \ldots, A_m \rangle$ such that for each $1 \leq p \leq m$, $A_p = \langle X_p, E, Q_p, I_p, \mu_p, T_p, \lambda_p, \tau_p, \pi_p \rangle$. A state ν of S is a valuation of $\bigcup_{1 \leq p \leq m}(X_p \cup \{\texttt{mode}_p\})$ such that*

- $\nu(\texttt{mode}_p) \in Q_p$ *is the mode of process i in ν; and*
- *for each $x \in \bigcup_{1 \leq 1 p \leq m} X_p$, $\nu(x) \in \mathcal{R}^+$ such that $\mathcal{R}^+$ is the set of nonnegative real numbers and $\nu \models \bigwedge_{1 \leq p \leq m} \mu_p(\nu(\texttt{mode}_p))$.*   ■

For any $t \in \mathcal{R}^+$, $\nu + t$ is a state identical to ν except that for every clock $x \in X$, $\nu(x) + t = (\nu + t)(x)$. Given $\bar{X} \subseteq X$, $\nu\bar{X}$ is a new state identical to ν except that for every $x \in \bar{X}$, $\nu\bar{X}(x) = 0$.

Now we have to define what a legitimate synchronization combination is in order not to violate the widely accepted interleaving semantics. A transition plan is a mapping from process indices p, $1 \leq p \leq m$, to elements in $T_p \cup \{\perp\}$, where $\perp$ means no transition (i.e., a process does not participate in a synchronized transition). The concept of transition plan represents which process transitions are to be synchronized in the construction of an LG-transition.

A transition plan is synchronized iff each output event from a process is received by exactly one unique corresponding process with a matching input event. Formally speaking, in a synchronized transition plan Φ, for each channel e, the number of output events must match with that of input events. Or in arithmetic, $\sum_{1 \leq p \leq m; \Phi(p) \neq \perp} \lambda(e, \Phi(p)) = 0$.

Two synchronized transitions will not be allowed to occur at the same instant if we cannot build the synchronization between them. The restriction is formally given in the following. Given a transition plan Φ, a synchronization plan Ψ_Φ for Φ represents how the output events of each process are to be received by the corresponding input events of peer processes. Formally speaking, Ψ_Φ is a mapping from $\{1, \ldots, m\}^2 \times E$ to $\mathcal{N}$ such that $\Psi_\Phi(p, p', e)$ represents the number of event e sent form process p to be received by process p'. A synchronization plan Ψ_Φ is consistent iff for all p and $e \in E$ such that $1 \leq p \leq m$ and $\Phi(p) \neq \perp$, the following two conditions must be true.

- $\sum_{1 \leq p' \leq m; \Phi(p') \neq \perp} \Psi_\Phi(p, p', e) = \lambda(\Phi(p));$
- $\sum_{1 \leq p \leq m; \Phi(p) \neq \perp} \Psi_\Phi(p', p, e) = -\lambda(\Phi(p));$

A synchronized and consistent transition plan Φ is atomic iff there exists a synchronization plan Ψ_Φ such that for each two processes p, p' such that $\Phi(p) \neq \perp$ and $\Phi(p') \neq \perp$, the following transitivity condition must be true: there exists a sequence of $p = p_1, p_2, \ldots, p_k = p'$ such that for each $1 \leq i < k$, there is an $e_i \in E$ such that either $\Psi_\Phi(p_i, p_{i+1}, e_i) > 0$ or $\Psi_\Phi(p_{i+1}, p_i, e_i) > 0$. The atomicity condition requires that each pair of meaningful process transitions in the synchronization plan must be synchronized through a sequence of input-output event pairs. A transition plan is called an IST-plan (Interleaving semantics Transition-plan) iff it has an atomic synchronization plan.

Finally, a transition plan has a race condition iff two of its process transitions have assignment to the same variables.

Definition 4. <u>runs</u> *Suppose we are given an SCTA $S = \langle E, A_1, A_2, \ldots, A_m \rangle$ such that for each $1 \leq p \leq m$, $A_p = \langle X_p, E, Q_p, I_p, \mu_p, T_p, \lambda_p, \tau_p, \pi_p \rangle$. A run is an infinite sequence of state-time pair $(\nu_0, t_0)(\nu_1, t_1) \ldots (\nu_k, t_k) \ldots \ldots$ such that $\nu_0 \models I$ and $t_0 t_1 \ldots t_k \ldots \ldots$ is a monotonically increasing real-number (time) divergent sequence, and for all $k \geq 0$,*

- *for all $t \in [0, t_{k+1} - t_k]$, $\nu_k + t \models \bigwedge_{1 \leq p \leq m} \mu(\nu_k(\text{mode}_p))$; and*
- *either*
  - *$\nu_k(\text{mode}_p) = \nu_{k+1}(\text{mode}_p)$ and $\nu_k + (t_{k+1} - t_k) = \nu_{k+1}$; or*
  - *there exists a race-free IST-plan Φ such that for all $1 \leq p \leq m$,*

* *either* $\nu_k(\text{mode}_p) = \nu_{k+1}(\text{mode}_p)$ *or* $(\nu_k(\text{mode}_p), \nu_{k+1}(\text{mode}_p)) \in T_p$ *and*
* $\nu_k + (t_{k+1} - t_k) \models \bigwedge_{1 \le p \le m; \Phi(p) \ne \perp} \tau_p(\nu_k(\text{mode}_p), \nu_{k+1}(\text{mode}_p))$ *and*
* $(\nu_k + (t_{k+1} - t_k))\text{concat}_{1 \le p \le m; \Phi(p) \ne \perp} \pi_p(\nu_k(\text{mode}_p), \nu_{k+1}(\text{mode}_p)) = \nu_{k+1}$. *Here* $\text{concat}(\gamma_1, \ldots, \gamma_h)$ *is the new sequence obtained by concatenating sequences* $\gamma_1, \ldots, \gamma_h$ *in order.* ∎

We can define the TCTL model-checking problem of timed automata as our verification framework. Due to page-limit, we here adopt the safety-analysis problem as our verification framework for simplicity. A safety analysis problem instance, $SA(A, \eta)$ *in notations, consists of a timed automata A and a safety state-predicate* $\eta \in B(Q, X)$. *A is safe w.r.t. to* η, *in symbols $A \models \eta$, iff for all runs* $(\nu_0, t_0)(\nu_1, t_1) \ldots (\nu_k, t_k) \ldots \ldots$, *for all* $k \ge 0$, *and for all* $t \in [0, t_{k+1} - t_k]$, $\nu_k + t \models \eta$, *i.e., the safety requirement is guaranteed.*

B   Model of Bluetooth Baseband Protocol

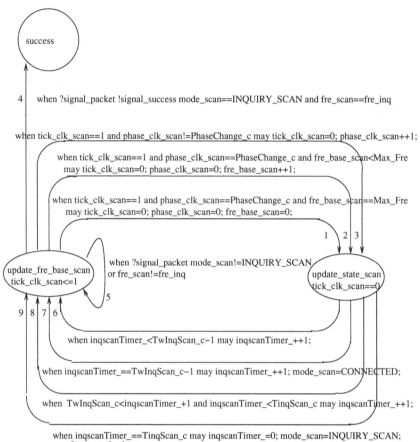

Fig. 5. INQUIRY SCAN

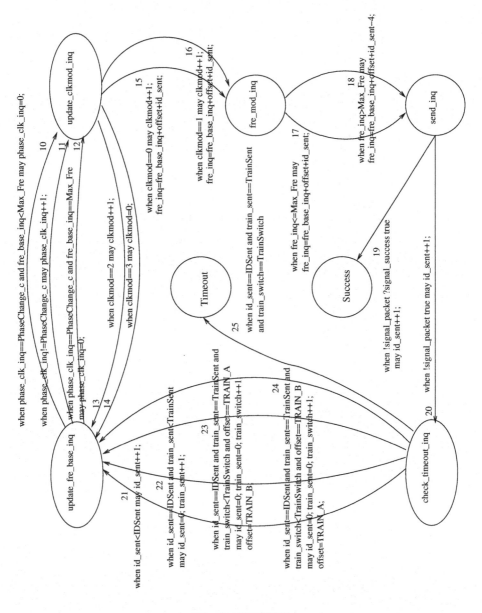

Fig. 6. INQUIRY

Author Index

Lecture Notes in Computer Science

For information about Vols. 1–2907

please contact your bookseller or Springer-Verlag

Vol. 2977: G. Di Marzo Serugendo, A. Karageorgos, O.F. Rana, F. Zambonelli (Eds.), Engineering Self-Organising Systems. X, 299 pages. 2004. (Subseries LNAI).

Vol. 2976: M. Farach-Colton (Ed.), LATIN 2004: Theoretical Informatics. XV, 626 pages. 2004.

Vol. 2973: Y. Lee, J. Li, K.-Y. Whang, D. Lee (Eds.), Database Systems for Advanced Applications. XXIV, 925 pages. 2004.

Vol. 2972: R. Monroy, G. Arroyo-Figueroa, L.E. Sucar, H. Sossa (Eds.), MICAI 2004: Advances in Artificial Intelligence. XVII, 923 pages. 2004. (Subseries LNAI).

Vol. 2971: J.I. Lim, D.H. Lee (Eds.), Information Security and Cryptology -ICISC 2003. XI, 458 pages. 2004.

Vol. 2970: F. Fernández Rivera, M. Bubak, A. Gómez Tato, R. Doallo (Eds.), Grid Computing. XI, 328 pages. 2004.

Vol. 2968: J. Chen, S. Hong (Eds.), Real-Time and Embedded Computing Systems and Applications. XIV, 620 pages. 2004.

Vol. 2966: F.B. Sachse, Computational Cardiology. XVIII, 322 pages. 2004.

Vol. 2965: M.C. Calzarossa, E. Gelenbe, Performance Tools and Applications to Networked Systems. VIII, 385 pages. 2004.

Vol. 2964: T. Okamoto (Ed.), Topics in Cryptology – CT-RSA 2004. XI, 387 pages. 2004.

Vol. 2963: R. Sharp, Higher Level Hardware Synthesis. XVI, 195 pages. 2004.

Vol. 2962: S. Bistarelli, Semirings for Soft Constraint Solving and Programming. XII, 279 pages. 2004.

Vol. 2961: P. Eklund (Ed.), Concept Lattices. IX, 411 pages. 2004. (Subseries LNAI).

Vol. 2960: P.D. Mosses (Ed.), CASL Reference Manual. XVII, 528 pages. 2004.

Vol. 2958: L. Rauchwerger (Ed.), Languages and Compilers for Parallel Computing. XI, 556 pages. 2004.

Vol. 2957: P. Langendoerfer, M. Liu, I. Matta, V. Tsaoussidis (Eds.), Wired/Wireless Internet Communications. XI, 307 pages. 2004.

Vol. 2956: A. Dengel, M. Junker, A. Weisbecker (Eds.), Reading and Learning. XII, 355 pages. 2004.

Vol. 2954: F. Crestani, M. Dunlop, S. Mizzaro (Eds.), Mobile and Ubiquitous Information Access. X, 299 pages. 2004.

Vol. 2953: K. Konrad, Model Generation for Natural Language Interpretation and Analysis. XIII, 166 pages. 2004. (Subseries LNAI).

Vol. 2952: N. Guelfi, E. Astesiano, G. Reggio (Eds.), Scientific Engineering of Distributed Java Applications. X, 157 pages. 2004.

Vol. 2951: M. Naor (Ed.), Theory of Cryptography. XI, 523 pages. 2004.

Vol. 2949: R. De Nicola, G. Ferrari, G. Meredith (Eds.), Coordination Models and Languages. X, 323 pages. 2004.

Vol. 2948: G.L. Mullen, A. Poli, H. Stichtenoth (Eds.), Finite Fields and Applications. VIII, 263 pages. 2004.

Vol. 2947: F. Bao, R. Deng, J. Zhou (Eds.), Public Key Cryptography – PKC 2004. XI, 455 pages. 2004.

Vol. 2946: R. Focardi, R. Gorrieri (Eds.), Foundations of Security Analysis and Design II. VII, 267 pages. 2004.

Vol. 2943: J. Chen, J. Reif (Eds.), DNA Computing. X, 225 pages. 2004.

Vol. 2941: M. Wirsing, A. Knapp, S. Balsamo (Eds.), Radical Innovations of Software and Systems Engineering in the Future. X, 359 pages. 2004.

Vol. 2940: C. Lucena, A. Garcia, A. Romanovsky, J. Castro, P.S. Alencar (Eds.), Software Engineering for Multi-Agent Systems II. XII, 279 pages. 2004.

Vol. 2939: T. Kalker, I.J. Cox, Y.M. Ro (Eds.), Digital Watermarking. XII, 602 pages. 2004.

Vol. 2937: B. Steffen, G. Levi (Eds.), Verification, Model Checking, and Abstract Interpretation. XI, 325 pages. 2004.

Vol. 2936: P. Liardet, P. Collet, C. Fonlupt, E. Lutton, M. Schoenauer (Eds.), Artificial Evolution. XIV, 410 pages. 2004.

Vol. 2934: G. Lindemann, D. Moldt, M. Paolucci (Eds.), Regulated Agent-Based Social Systems. X, 301 pages. 2004. (Subseries LNAI).

Vol. 2930: F. Winkler (Ed.), Automated Deduction in Geometry. VII, 231 pages. 2004. (Subseries LNAI).

Vol. 2929: H. de Swart, E. Orlowska, G. Schmidt, M. Roubens (Eds.), Theory and Applications of Relational Structures as Knowledge Instruments. VII, 273 pages. 2003.

Vol. 2926: L. van Elst, V. Dignum, A. Abecker (Eds.), Agent-Mediated Knowledge Management. XI, 428 pages. 2004. (Subseries LNAI).

Vol. 2923: V. Lifschitz, I. Niemelä (Eds.), Logic Programming and Nonmonotonic Reasoning. IX, 365 pages. 2004. (Subseries LNAI).

Vol. 2919: E. Giunchiglia, A. Tacchella (Eds.), Theory and Applications of Satisfiability Testing. XI, 530 pages. 2004.

Vol. 2917: E. Quintarelli, Model-Checking Based Data Retrieval. XVI, 134 pages. 2004.

Vol. 2916: C. Palamidessi (Ed.), Logic Programming. XII, 520 pages. 2003.

Vol. 2915: A. Camurri, G. Volpe (Eds.), Gesture-Based Communication in Human-Computer Interaction. XIII, 558 pages. 2004. (Subseries LNAI).

Vol. 2914: P.K. Pandya, J. Radhakrishnan (Eds.), FST TCS 2003: Foundations of Software Technology and Theoretical Computer Science. XIII, 446 pages. 2003.

Vol. 2913: T.M. Pinkston, V.K. Prasanna (Eds.), High Performance Computing - HiPC 2003. XX, 512 pages. 2003. (Subseries LNAI).

Vol. 2911: T.M.T. Sembok, H.B. Zaman, H. Chen, S.R. Urs, S.H. Myaeng (Eds.), Digital Libraries: Technology and Management of Indigenous Knowledge for Global Access. XX, 703 pages. 2003.

Vol. 2910: M.E. Orlowska, S. Weerawarana, M.M.P. Papazoglou, J. Yang (Eds.), Service-Oriented Computing - ICSOC 2003. XIV, 576 pages. 2003.

Vol. 2909: R. Solis-Oba, K. Jansen (Eds.), Approximation and Online Algorithms. VIII, 269 pages. 2004.

Vol. 2908: K. Chae, M. Yung (Eds.), Information Security Applications. XII, 506 pages. 2004.